Noelle Walsh was editor of *Good Ho...* ... and is the author of *The Good Deal Directory*. She is children's editor of the *Evening Standard* and has consumer columns in the *Daily Mail* and the *Daily Telegraph*.

Richard McBrien is the author of *The Global Shopper* and is a regular contributor to *New Woman* and *Cosmopolitan*.

the Virgin home shopping handbook

Noelle Walsh
&
Richard McBrien

Although every effort has been made to ensure the accuracy of the information contained in this book, neither the Authors nor Publisher can accept responsibility for any errors it may contain.

The Authors and Publisher do not assume and hereby disclaim any liability to any party for any loss or damage caused by errors or omissions in *The Virgin Home Shopping Handbook*, whether such errors or omissions result from negligence, accident, or any other cause.

The Publisher cannot give guarantees regarding goods or firms, nor deal with complaints. Inclusion in this book does not imply endorsement.

First published in Great Britain in 1994 by
Virgin Books
an imprint of Virgin Publishing Ltd
332 Ladbroke Grove
London W10 5AH

Copyright © Noelle Walsh and Richard McBrien 1994

The moral right of the authors has been asserted

This book is sold subject to the condition that it shall not, by way of trade or otherwise, be lent, resold, hired out or otherwise circulated without the publisher's prior written consent in any form of binding or cover other than that in which it is published and without a similar condition including this condition being imposed upon the subsequent purchaser.

A catalogue record for this book is available from the British Library

ISBN 0 86369   0 0

Typeset by Servis Filmsetting Ltd, Manchester

Printed and bound by Mackays of Chatham, plc, Lordswood, Chatham, Kent

Contents

Introduction 1

How Mail Order Works 3
  Methods of Payment 3

Your Rights 5
  Consumer Legislation 5
  Codes of Practice 6
  Guarantees 7
  Mail Order Preference Service 7

Complaining 9

Using the Handbook 11
  Mail Order Tips 11

Appendix 13
  Goods Prevented from Being Sent by Royal Mail 13
  Useful Addresses 14

Entries 15

Subject index 403

Introduction

The traditional image of mail order is of bulky catalogues selling rather tacky goods which take an age to arrive. But over the last few years all this has changed. Home shopping, as it is now called, is an efficient, convenient way to buy virtually anything. Literally hundreds of new companies have sprung up: small, one-person operations joining the giant multi-nationals. The result is a well-developed, sophisticated industry offering the consumer excellent choice and service.

However, many people remain wary of buying by mail. One of the main worries seems to be the delay – we have all read the dreaded 'Allow 28 days for delivery'. In fact this does not represent the average time to receive goods but is simply a legally required form of words. Many companies now guarantee delivery within 48 hours and even offer the option of next day delivery for a small extra fee.

Another concern, especially when ordering clothes or shoes, is that they will not fit or turn out to be different from as described in the catalogue. Again, things have improved over the years and most companies now offer a full money back guarantee, no questions asked – provided you return goods within a specified number of days. This level of service, combined with the convenience of shopping from your own armchair, has led to the current boom in mail order.

But while many more people are now shopping in this way there is no single guide to the market. Most consumers rely on advertisements they happen to see in newspapers or catalogues passed on by friends. It was to answer this need that we came up with the idea of *The Virgin Home Shopping Handbook*. This single volume is a comprehensive guide to the best of British mail order, listing hundreds of companies selling thousands of products. We hope you enjoy browsing through it and, more importantly, ordering some of the fascinating catalogues. Mail order has finally come of age in this country and now is the time to explore it.

How Mail Order Works

One of the reasons for the change in name from Mail Order to Home Shopping is that increasingly the process does not involve the mail at all. Although you can still send off for things by post, a great deal of business is now conducted over the phone, often using freephone numbers. Delivery may not even be by Royal Mail, companies preferring either to use their own vans or to subcontract courier services which will guarantee overnight carriage.

The vast majority of catalogues are free but some specialist companies do make a charge. This is to deter the 'catalogue collector'. Printing and distributing a catalogue is expensive and businesses cannot afford to hand them out free to people unlikely to order. In cases where a charge is made, the price of the catalogue is usually refundable against the first order.

When you order either a catalogue or goods your name will generally be kept on a computer database. This customer list is a valuable resource for the company. Not only can they mail you new catalogues and special offers but they can also sell your name to other, similar businesses. This selling of mailing lists is highly profitable and explains why you can find yourself receiving all sorts of literature which you never seemed to request.

Under current UK legislation it is quite legal to keep and sell customer details as long as a) the company is registered with the Data Protection Registrar and b) the customer has been given the opportunity to opt out. Very often this opportunity is hidden away in tiny print and requires the request to be put in writing. However, you can have your name removed from such lists by applying to an agency called the Mail Order Preference Scheme. Full details of this are given in the chapter 'Your Rights'.

When a company receives your order it may fulfil it on the same day or put it in a pile. It should only bank the cheque or process the credit card after the order is sent. So if you have been waiting some time for an item to arrive, check your bank account or credit card statement to make sure that your money has not already been deducted.

Most reputable companies will have some form of insurance for goods in transit. This will cover both the loss of items – and things do occasionally simply disappear – and breakages. It is nevertheless worth checking before you part with money just how comprehensive the cover is.

If the goods are not satisfactory you can usually return them but you may have to pay the return postage if this is just because you don't like the colour or style. It is best to keep and re-use the original packaging if you do have to send something back.

Methods of Payment

Most companies accept a number of ways of paying: cheque, postal order, credit card, Switch, Delta and sometimes stage payment. Credit card is by far the most flexible since it can be dictated over the phone, sent by fax or mailed.

How Mail Order Works

The two cards mostly widely accepted are Visa and Mastercard. Diners Club and American Express are less popular since they can be more complicated and expensive for the merchant to process.

Some people are reluctant to give their credit card details over the phone in case they get charged for items they never ordered. Certainly this is possible; after all, if someone has all your details they could ring up another supplier pretending to be you. However, it is most unlikely that a reputable supplier will misuse your card. They are carefully checked by the card issuing authorities and if there is any hint of fraud their merchant privileges are removed.

If there has been fraudulent use of a card, the supplier is responsible, not you. They will therefore have to reimburse the money in full and suffer the loss themselves. To minimise fraud always check your credit card bill as soon as it arrives and BEFORE paying it. If you find an item which you have not authorised, contact the credit card company immediately and ask for 'proof of purchase'. You might like to settle the remainder of the bill along with a letter explaining why you are withholding the disputed amount.

The credit card company will then contact the supplier and ask for further information. It is the supplier's responsibility to prove that it was indeed a genuine order. They will need to produce either the original, signed voucher or, in the case of a phone order, your full name and address as well as details of what you ordered and when. If they are unable to provide these you will not be charged.

Your Rights

Mail order transactions are protected in three ways: by general consumer legislation, standards of practice established by trade organisations and guarantees offered by the supplier or manufacturer.

Consumer Legislation

Most of the legislation is covered in the 'Sale of Goods Act, 1979'. All goods sold have to satisfy three requirements: they must be 'of merchantable quality', 'fit for the purpose for which they are intended' and be 'as described'. These purposely wide definitions are intended to prevent companies evading their responsibilities.

- Merchantable quality: products must be in good order. They shouldn't be damaged, scratched or broken.

- Fit for the purpose for which they are intended: this simply means the goods must do what they are supposed to do. The CD must play CDs, the iron must heat up, the fax must fax.

- As described: goods must be as described in promotional literature. This is true not just of basic features (for example a 'TV with teletext' must indeed have this facility) but also of properties. For example, if a tent or jacket is described as waterproof then it must indeed be so, and not simply showerproof. This clause refers both to written AND verbal descriptions. If, therefore, you are conducting a transaction entirely over the phone it is as well to record the conversation if possible. If not, insist on a written description.

These requirements are law – suppliers cannot avoid them simply by posting notices or including small print at the back of a catalogue disclaiming responsibility.

If goods are faulty in any way the consumer can legally insist on a replacement or a refund. You are not obliged to take a credit note, but if you do accept one you cannot change your mind later and ask for a refund.

A supplier can also offer to repair the product. This can be perfectly acceptable but make sure there is a written understanding that you retain the right to reject the goods if you feel the repair is not satisfactory. Without this you can end up with a botched repair and no further rights.

In some cases companies will offer compensation instead of a refund or replacement. For example, a pair of shoes might have a slight blemish on them and the company offers a small amount of money in compensation. This could be fine but you do not have to accept it – you have a legal right to insist on a replacement or full refund.

Your Rights

It is the responsibility of the supplier to make sure the goods arrive safely and in good condition. If they are faulty, do not try to repair them yourself but immediately contact the trader and ask for a replacement. It is also the supplier's responsibility to pay the return postage.

However, the consumer does not have the legal right to return an item simply because he or she does not like it. While many suppliers operate a 'no-questions-asked' policy, this is not enshrined in law.

Codes of Practice

The Mail Order Traders' Association

This association has drawn up a voluntary code of practice which aims to protect the consumer. Its main drawback is its lack of members, who number under a dozen. It may still be useful to know their guidelines.

MOTA Guidelines

- Consumers must know:
    the exact nature of the offer and its terms
    the features of goods and services
    the terms of delivery, exchange, return, reimbursement, after sales service, guarantees and any restrictions of rights.

- If goods cannot be dispatched then money must be returned as soon as possible and within a time limit of thirty days. If goods are returned then a refund must be made within seven working days.

- Consumers should be allowed 14 days in which to return unwanted goods.

- Consumers have a right to privacy (in other words their name must not be sold on to another company without permission).

The Advertising Standards Authority

The ASA oversees all advertisements, which must be 'legal, honest, decent, truthful and not misleading'. It can therefore be approached if you feel you have been misled by an advertisement (although they do not cover catalogues themselves).

The Mail Order Protection Scheme

MOPS is an organisation set up by the Fleet Street papers to vet companies advertising in the main national papers. If a registered company fails to deliver goods or defrauds you in some way you can request a refund directly from MOPS. They can also help with companies who have gone bust. The

Your Rights

Periodical Publishers Association is a similar organisation for magazines.
Full addresses of these organisations can be found under *Useful Addresses*.

Guarantees

Nearly all products come with a manufacturer's guarantee, but this will only be valid if it is stamped by the supplier and, in many cases, returned to the manufacturer. Do this as soon as you receive the goods and keep a record in a safe place.

Many mail order companies also offer their own guarantees, usually in the form of money-back offers. The inclusion of these in no way replaces or affects your statutory rights.

Mail Order Preference Service

This service is for consumers who wish to have their names removed (or added) to mailing lists. When you contact them your name is entered on a central registry which is then distributed to participating mailing list companies. Information can take around three months to filter through and can only offer protection from lists originating with companies registered with the service. You will still receive mailings from businesses you have dealt with directly, as they do not have to register their lists unless they sell them on. For their address see *Useful Addresses*.

Complaining

If you are in any way dissatisfied you should of course complain. The following are some strategies to adopt which will help win your case.

- Keep the receipt. It may seem obvious but the simple receipt is a powerful ally. It proves what you bought, when, from whom and for how much. But not all receipts are created equal. Do not accept one that simply reads: 'Goods, £32'. Insist on details. It should denote the date, the name and address of the supplier and a brief description of the goods.

- If the company won't send you such a receipt (which in itself should ring alarm bells) write the details in yourself at the time. And then keep the receipt for at least a year.

- If possible use a credit card. The 'Consumer Credit Act' states that for purchases over £100 made with a credit card the transaction is not between you and the supplier but between the credit card company and the supplier. This means that if there is a dispute you can claim the money back from the credit card company, leaving them to take it up with the supplier. This only refers to genuine credit cards and NOT to charge cards (e.g. American Express) or most gold cards.

- Keep copies of all correspondence, including faxes.

- Keep a record of phone calls. If you can't record conversations (most answering machines have this facility) then do write down what was said. Keep a note of the name of the person you spoke to and at what time.

- If complaining by phone or fax, send a hard copy to confirm and place the matter on record.

- When ordering write 'Time is of the essence' on the order form. This somewhat archaic phrase ensures that the delivery date you have agreed with the supplier (i.e. the one often written on the form itself) becomes legally binding. In its absence the delivery date has no legal standing.

- If returning a faulty item do so as quickly as possible. Delay may result in losing the right to a complete refund and only having recourse to compensation, which may mean a replacement or repair only.

- If you have a complaint, contact the retailer in person, preferably by phone, and let them know the nature of the problem. If that doesn't yield the proper response, write a letter to include:

Complaining

    the problem
    the date of purchase
    a copy of the receipt
    a copy of cancelled cheque, or itemised credit card bill
    what you would consider a fair and equitable settlement
    a date by which you would like a response.

If this still fails to elicit a satisfactory response, contact your local Office of Fair Trading and Citizens Advice Bureau.

Using the Guide

Mail Order Tips

Nearly all catalogues have simple-to-follow order forms but there are a number of tips worth noting.

- It is often better to call or fax your order since this gets a quicker response. It is also useful to speak to someone in case the price has changed, the item is no longer available and so on.

- If ordering over the phone, fill in the form first as if you were mailing it. You can then read off the information in the correct order for the sales assistant to take down and thereby save phone time and eliminate errors.

- If writing, make sure your address is clear and always write in capitals. Faxed handwriting can come out 'bitty' so be sure to write clearly in a bold, dark colour and never use pencil.

- When ordering by credit card make each number clear – it is easy to confuse 0 with 9 and 7 with 1. Write 1s as straight lines and do not put a slash through the middle of a 7 as this can get confused with a 3. Write zeros as 0 not Ø.

Split up the credit card number into a series of digits rather than one long number which can be misread. And of course do not forget to include the expiry date of the card, written as a number not as a full date, e.g. 5/95 rather than May 95.

Appendix

Goods Prohibited from being sent by Royal Mail

Pathological Specimens – e.g. blood, urine, semen etc; unless by an authorised person (doctor, vet, etc.)
Illegal Drugs
Poisons – any substance which could harm an employee
Living Creatures – with certain exceptions
Radioactive Materials
Compressed Gases
Oxidising Material
Corrosives
Asbestos
Flammable Liquids
Flammable Solids
Paints, Varnishes, Enamels, etc.
Matches
Obscene Materials
Counterfeit Currency & Stamps
Perishable Goods

Aerosols and lighters are allowed in certain circumstances. For a copy of the full regulations contact your local Customer Service Centre (see telephone book) or pick up a copy of 'Prohibited & Restricted Goods' from any Post Office.

Appendix

Useful Addresses

Advertising Standards Authority
Brook House
2-16 Torrington Place
London
WC1E 7HN

The British Direct Marketing
 Association
Grosvenor Gardens House
Grosvenor Gardens
London
SW1W 0BS

Consumers Association
2 Marylebone Road
London
NW1 4DF
Tel: 071 486 5544

Mail Order Protection Scheme
16 Tooks Court
London
EC4A 1LB

The Mail Order Traders'
 Association of Great Britain
100 Old Hall Street
Liverpool
L3 9TD
Tel: 051 236 7581
Fax: 051 227 2584

The Mailing Preference Service
Freepost 22
London
W1E 7EZ
Tel: 071 738 1625
Fax: 071 978 4918

The Office of Fair Trading
Room 310C
Field House
14-25 Breams Buildings
London
EC4A 1PS
Tel: 071 242 2858

Periodical Publishers Association
Imperial House
15-19 Kingsway
London
WC2B 6UN
Tel: 071 379 6268

Accessories/Jewellery

CAIRNCROSS OF PERTH
18 St John Street
Perth
Scotland
PH1 5SR

Telephone:
0738 24367
Fax:
0738 43913

JEWELLERY
Established in 1869 in Perth, this company produce a beautiful catalogue, displaying its range of Scottish riverpearl jewellery. Set in 9ct or 18ct gold, with semi-precious or precious stones, they are shown in a variety of designs, from floral brooches to more traditional drop earrings.

Prices range from a modest £63.00 for a simple pendant to £2,875.00 for a diamond and pearl cluster ring. Prices may also fluctuate according to the market value of precious stones and metals.

Catalogue: *A5, Catalogue, 10 pages, Colour, Free* Postal charges: *Varies with item* Delivery: *By arrangement* Methods of Payment: *Cheque*

INTERNATIONAL JEWELLERY CREATIONS
Prospect House
2 Queen Street
Henley-on-Thames
Oxon
RG9 1AP

Telephone:
0491 572666
Fax:
0491 578012

JEWELLERY
This catalogue displays a limited range of jewellery using gold, amethysts and diamonds.

An amethyst pendant with matching earrings is available in two carats, three and twelve. The actual size is shown by photograph and payment may be made in full or over ten months at no extra cost. The larger pendant costs £399.00.

The diamond collections are called 'Anniversary' and 'Eternity' and consist of earrings, pendant and ring. Diamonds can be 1/4 carat, 1/2 carat or 1 carat, the most expensive being the 1 carat ring at £990.00.

Catalogue: *Third A4, Leaflets, Colour, Free* Postal charges: *Free* Delivery: *Royal Mail* Methods of Payment: *Cheque, Postal Order, Visa, Access / Mastercard, Stage Payments, American Express, Diners Club*

MEGAGEM
P O Box 200
2 Church Road
Lymm
Cheshire
WA13 0JD

Telephone:
061 431 6431

COSTUME JEWELLERY
The jewellers who hand-craft the costume jewellery in this catalogue trace their pedigree back to 1760, though whether they were selling Megagems then is hard to know!

The gems in question are diamond-like cubic zircon stones, with 56 facets, set in solid silver or 22ct gold plated finish. Earrings have 9ct gold 'French' wire posts for pierced ears. Although it is difficult to determine the scale of the gems displayed they do look attractive. The selection includes earrings, necklaces, pendants and brooches.

A six stone drop pendant sells for £62.95 and small solid silver set studs £16.95.

Accessories/Jewellery

KERNOWCRAFT ROCKS & GEMS LTD
Bolingey, Perranporth,
Cornwall
TR6 0DH

Telephone:
0872 573888
Fax:
0872 573704

MAGIC MOMENTS
14 Rock Close
Hastings
Sussex
TN35 4JW

Telephone:
0424 853366

CCA GALLERIES
8 Dover Street
London
W1X 3PJ

Telephone:
071 499 6701
Fax:
071 409 3555

Catalogue: *A4, Leaflets, 3 pages plus inserts, Colour and B/W, Free* Postal charges: £2.95 Delivery: *Royal Mail* Methods of Payment: *Cheque, Postal Order, Visa, Access / Mastercard*

SUPPLIER OF SEMI-PRECIOUS STONE FOR JEWELLERY MAKING
Kernowcraft is one of the leading suppliers of semi-precious stones and mounts for jewellery making. The catalogue details tumble-polished stones, beads, cabochons and faceted stones in a wide range of natural materials from amethysts to zircons.

An extensive range of jewellery mounts in sterling silver, 9ct gold and plated metals is also available. The catalogue also features sterling silver and 9ct gold necklets, as well as a wide selection of tools and silver sheet and wires for jewellery making. A separate list is available for current stocks of crystals and minerals.

Catalogue: *56 pages, Catalogue, Colour, Free* Postal charges: *Varies with item* Delivery: *Royal Mail, Parcelforce* Methods of Payment: *Cheque, Postal Order, Visa, Access / Mastercard*

ADULT PRODUCTS
Over 250,000 adults have experienced the quality, service and value of a vast rage of adult products sold by Magic Moments from all over the world.

The 40 page sex toy catalogue contains probably the largest selection of vibrators, male and female pleasure products, revealing funwear and related items to be found anywhere. They also have five lingerie catalogues. They have asked readers to mention *The Virgin Home Shopping Handbook* when ordering.

Catalogue: *A4, Catalogue, 40 pages, Colour,* £5.00 Postal charges: *Varies with item* Delivery: *Royal Mail* Methods of Payment: *Cheque, Postal Order, Visa, Access / Mastercard*

LIMITED EDITION ORIGINAL PRINTS
CCA Galleries, formerly Christies' Contemporary Art, is one of the leading publishers of original limited edition prints in Europe. Their collection includes publications from a variety of contemporary artists, including prints from new young printmakers to respected names such as John Piper and Donald Hamilton Fraser.

Each print is numbered and signed by the artist. This exclusivity, thankfully, is not reflected in the cost. Prices start from around a modest £55.00 to £1,500. Their galleries in Mayfair, Cambridge,

Art & Art Materials

Oxford, Bath, Farnham and Selfridges house the complete range of prints. They also have an exciting exhibition programme which includes paintings and sculpture by their successful stable of artists.

Catalogue: *3 a year, A4, Catalogue, 6-12 pages, Colour, Free* Postal charges: *Varies with item* Delivery: *Parceline, Parcelforce, Royal Mail* Methods of Payment: *Cheque, Postal Order, COD, Visa, Access / Mastercard, American Express, Diners Club*

CHROMACOLOUR INTERNATIONAL LTD
11 Grange Mills
Weir Road
London
SW12 0NE

Telephone:
081 675 8422
Fax:
081 675 8499

CHROMA ARTISTS COLOURS AND MATERIALS
Chroma Artists Colour is an intermixable range of 80 water based, lightly pigmented colours which dry to a flat, matt finish. This is opaque, permanent, waterproof and lightfast. The paint is also extremely versatile. In its pure form, dry Chroma gives the appearance of gouache: flat, matt and highly opaque. When diluted with water, the paint can be used as a top quality water colour, giving pale and transparent washes.

Dilution with water also makes ink techniques possible as there is no granulation of the pigment upon drying. For acrylic techniques, Chroma can be used intermixed with its own range of gels and mediums. Other Chroma products available include brushes, watercolour papers and Sta-Wet palettes.

Catalogue: *Bi-annually, A4, Brochure, 4 pages, Colour, Free* Postal charges: *Varies with item* Delivery: *Royal Mail* Methods of Payment: *Cheque, COD, Postal Order, Visa, Access / Mastercard, American Express, Diners Club*

CONNAUGHT HERITAGE
Unit 6, Leaside
Business Centre
Millmarsh Lane
Brimsdown
Enfield
Middlesex
EN3 7BJ

Telephone:
081 805 8899

ART
The Connaught Heritage offers a set of six cameos of musical instruments handcrafted from an original design by artist Emma Daniels. The series is called Musical Moments and the cameos measure 7" × 6". Each comes inside a frame of solid antique gilded wood and has a picture hook so it can be hung immediately.

Each cameo contains a background of sheet music, which has also been faithfully reproduced in miniature, on a cream mount with a gold-edged border. Among the instruments in the collection are the violin and bow, classical guitar, trombone and slide and trumpet.

Catalogue: *A5, Brochure, 6 pages, Colour, Free* Postal charges: *£2.50* Delivery: *Royal Mail* Methods of Payment: *Cheque, Visa, Access / Mastercard*

Art & Art Materials

HOLLYWOOD SCRIPTS
Enterprise House
Cathles Road
London
SW12 9LD
Telephone:
081-673 3192
Fax:
081-675 1432

FILM SCRIPTS AND BOOKS
This is a unique catalogue which stocks genuine Hollywood film scripts. These come from both classics and new releases – indeed sometimes you can get the script before the film has even appeared in this country. Scripts are from £18.00 to £25.00.

They also sell TV scripts from £10.00 and books on screenwriting and cinema from between £9.00 and £13.00. An invaluable resource for film buffs and would-be William Goldmans.

Catalogue: *A4, Catalogue, 14, Colour, Free* Postal charges: *Varies with item* Delivery: *Royal Mail* Methods of Payment: *Cheque, Postal Order, Visa, Access / Mastercard, American Express, Diners Club*

NATIONAL GALLERY PUBLICATIONS
Freepost
Helston
Cornwall
TR13 0YY
Telephone:
0209 831888

CARDS, POSTERS, PRINTS
A must for art lovers, this is a beatifully produced catalogue. All sales help to support the nation's art collections in the National Gallery in London.

A stationery range is based on works by Impressionist and Renaissance artists, and there are also jigsaws, social journals, desk accessories, calendars, wrapping paper and greetings cards. All feature reproductions of one or more famous paintings from the Gallery. There is also a good selection of fine art books, including those based on special exhibitions held at the Gallery.

A pack of ten Christmas cards is £4.75 and an Impressionist address book £7.95.

Catalogue: *250 × 220 mm, Catalogue, Colour, Free* Postal charges: *Varies with item* Delivery: *Royal Mail* Methods of Payment: *Cheque, Postal Order, Visa, Access / Mastercard, American Express*

PAUL ROBERTS
21/23 High Street
Gillingham
Kent
ME7 1BE

AIRBRUSHING
Paul Roberts provide a full range of design and illustrative services. From typography and signwriting to technical illustration and mechanical engineering, Mr Roberts is able to offer total project control over projects of any scale.

You can also buy an airbrushed portrait – have those unsightly features smoothed over so you look like you've just stepped out of a 'Yes' album. Portraits are available from £200.00. For a lot less, you can have your portrait put on a T-shirt, for just £35.00.

Catalogue: *A5, Leaflets, 2, Colour, Free* Postal charges: *Varies with item* Delivery: *Royal Mail* Methods of Payment: *Cheque, Postal Order*

Automotive

POLAK
21 King Street
St James's
London
SW1Y 6QY

Telephone:
071 839 2871

FINE ART
Polak are not strictly speaking a mail order company but rather a high class art dealer in London's St James's. However, they will send out their catalogue of current exhibitions. These are lavishly produced with excellent colour reproductions of the paintings. There are, of course, no prices mentioned, but interested readers should contact the gallery direct.

Catalogue: *205 × 205 mm, Catalogue, 24 pages, Colour, Free* Postal charges: *Varies with item* Delivery: *By arrangement* Methods of Payment: *Cheque*

AMERICAN CAR IMPORTS
57 Coburg Road
Wood Green
London
N22 6UB

Telephone:
081 889 4545
Fax:
081 889 7500

AMERICAN CARS
American Car Imports will not exactly post you a car but they will do all the hard work of finding and delivering one to your doorstep. Recognised as the UK market leaders, they have been featured in the national press and on the BBC. They are regularly on-site in America and have permanent offices there.

As a result they have expert knowledge of the American car market and are able to supply any type of new or used vehicle at very competitive prices. They take care of everything for you, including registration and delivery. They can even offer an AA warranty. An ideal way to buy a car from the USA.

Catalogue: *Brochure & catalogue, Colour and B/W, Free* Postal charges: *Varies with item* Delivery: *ACI* Methods of Payment: *Cheque, Visa, Access / Mastercard, American Express, Diners Club, Stage Payments*

CC PRODUCTS
152 Markham Road
Charminster
Bournemouth
BH9 1JE

Telephone:
0202 522260

PORTABLE URINALS
The Hygienic Portable Loo (urinal only) is a great aid to motorists caught short on journeys. It is also invaluable for the disabled, the infirm who live alone and the whole family when conventional toilets are unavailable.

Two separate hand-held applicators in polythene, one male and one female, are connected by a short tube to a two-litre vacuum-packed reservoir with a built-in non-return valve which ensures no leaks or odours. The unit also includes a tap so it can be reused and it has been medically approved.

Each unit costs £17.00 and is sent under plain cover.

Catalogue: *Annually, 8" × 4", Brochure, 4 pages, Colour, Free* Postal charges: *Varies with item* Delivery: *Royal Mail* Methods of Payment: *Cheque, Postal Order*

Automotive

CORPORATE CARS UK
57 Coburg Road
Wood Green
London
N22 6UB

Telephone:
081 889 8889
Fax:
081 889 7500

ALL TYPES OF UK SPEC CARS
With over twenty years of commercial experience this company has established itself as the leading consultancy within the corporate sector in the procurement of executive vehicles.

Their aim is to be your Company Car Department without actually being 'in-house'. All cars come with a full manufacturer's warranty, which means servicing can be at the dealership of your choice. With their extensive dealer contacts and knowledge of the market, they can save you money as well as alleviate the burdens of car sourcing.

Catalogue: , *Brochure, Colour, Free* Postal charges: *Varies with item* Delivery: *In house delivery* Methods of Payment: *Cheque, Stage Payments, Visa, Access / Mastercard, American Express, Diners Club, Other*

SNOWCHAINS EUROPRODUCTS
Bourne Enterprise Centre
Borough Green
Sevenoaks
Kent
TN15 8DG

Telephone:
0732 884408
Fax:
0732 884564

SNOWCHAINS AND ROOF BOXES
Snowchains Europroducts stock a wide range of car roof boxes, roof bars and snow chains for passenger cars, light commercials and off-road vehicles.

The range of snow chains is produced by Weissenfels and will fit most cars and sizes of tyre. Roof boxes are made by Hapro, Autoform, Skandibox and Thule. Roofbars are available in different styles to take bicycles, sailboards, skis and luggage. Prices for roofbars start at around £50.00 and the Skandibox range of roof boxes at £299.00.

Snowchains also offer a roof box rental service for skiing holidays and breaks starting at £4.95 per day.

Catalogue: *A4, Catalogue, 20 pages, Colour, Free* Postal charges: *£4.50* Delivery: *Courier* Methods of Payment: *Cheque, Postal Order, Visa, Access / Mastercard, American Express, Diners Club*

THE AMERICAN STRETCH LIMOUSINE COMPANY
57 Coburg Road
Wood Green
London
N22 6UB

Telephone:
081 889 4848
Fax:
081 889 7500

LIMOUSINE SERVICE
The American Stretch Limousine Company is not strictly a mail order business, but they do send out a brochure detailing their interesting service. Their modern fleet of stretch limousines offers sumptuous upholstery, with seating for six in a cocoon of electronic sophistication. Absolute discretion is guaranteed with dual electric dividers and privacy glass.

Vehicles are fitted with television, video and stereo, as well as intercom and mood lighting. They also offer bar facilities incorporating crystal cut decanters and glasses and an ice chest. To keep in touch, a telephone and facsimile are also available. Sheer luxury!

Baby Products

Prices start from £35 per hour and include a selection of free drinks.

Catalogue: *Annually, D2, Brochure, 6 pages, B/W, Free* Methods of Payment: *Cheque, Postal Order, Visa, Access / Mastercard, American Express, Diners Club, Other*

CABOODLE BAGS
The White House
Newnham
Sittingbourne
Kent
ME9 0LW

Telephone:
0795 890511

BABY BAGS
The Caboodle Bag is a bag for mothers with young babies who have to carry a lot of equipment – nappies, food, clean clothes, wipes and lotions.

Designed by a mum who knows the problems, it will carry all necessary equipment and its many features have been carefully thought out. It has a separate changing mat, pockets for 'grubby stuff', a detachable shoulder strap, bottle pockets and see-through inside pockets.

This very useful bag costs £16.50, including postage.

Catalogue: *A4, Leaflets, 1 page, Colour, Free* Postal charges: *Varies with item* Delivery: *Royal Mail* Methods of Payment: *Cheque, Visa, Access / Mastercard*

COTTON MOON
Freepost
P O Box 280 (SE 8265)
London
SE3 8BR

Telephone:
081 319 8315
Fax:
081 319 8345

CHILDREN'S CLOTHES
Cotton Moon produces 100% cotton comfort clothing for children aged from twelve months to six years. Their philosophy is that children's clothing should be easy to wear, easy to care for, fun and good value.

They cut their clothes generously so they're very comfortable and add a great many pockets and just as many 'snaps' to make getting them on and off easier. Clothes include thick American T-shirts, hats, hairbands and socks from Tic Tac Toe. The range is fully colour-coordinated and includes everyday wear as well as items for special occasions.

Hooded tops are £14.95, drawstring twill trousers the same, dresses £22.95 and sun hats £5.95.

Catalogue: *Bi-annually, 14cms × 29.5cms, Catalogue, 8 pages, Colour, Free* Postal charges: *Varies with item* Delivery: *Royal Mail* Methods of Payment: *Cheque, Postal Order, Visa, Access / Mastercard*

Baby Products

ELIKO FOOD DISTRIBUTORS LTD
Unit 1
12–48 Northumberland Park
London
N17 0TX

Telephone:
081 801 9977

BABY FOOD
Beech-Nut Baby Foods, established since 1931, is the second largest producer of baby food products in the United States.

Their aim is to supply products of superior quality, taste and paediatric and nutritional value.

Beech-Nut Baby Foods come in a range of stages to match a baby's growing needs, beginning with single ingredient cereals, foods and juices as recommended by paediatricians in order to help determine any allergies.

Beech-Nut uses only the highest quality ingredients and all foods and juices are totally free of additives, preservatives, artificial colourings or flavourings. The foods do not contain salt, added sugar or chemically modified starches.

Stage 1 and 2: 4.5oz jars cost 55p each
Stage 3: 6oz jars cost 60p each
Stage 1: 8oz rice cereal cost £1.15 each
Small juice, 4.2oz, cost 47p each. Prices do not include VAT.

Catalogue: *None* Postal charges: *Varies with item* Delivery: *Courier* Methods of Payment: *Cheque*

THE NURSERY
103 Bishops Road
London
SW6 7AX

Telephone:
071 731 6637

BABY PRESENTS
The Nursery specialises in presents for the very young child and new-born baby. The mail order department of the shop in London has a wide range of presents for the new-born baby, including nightdresses and cardigans for 0–3 months.

For the older baby, among the more permanent presents are personalised Mason Pearson hair brushes and a personalised Bridgewater Spongeware Mug. There are also silver-plated rattles in three designs including one Peter Rabbit, which could form a set with a teething ring in a similar style. The silver-plated items come in boxes.

Catalogue: *A6, Brochure, 4 pages, Colour and B/W, Free* Postal charges: *£1.75* Delivery: *Royal Mail* Methods of Payment: *Cheque, Postal Order*

WILLEY WINKLE
Offa House
Offa Street
Hereford
HR1 2LH

PURE WOOL COT MATTRESSES
Willey Winkle make traditional cot, crib and Moses mattresses from pure wool, with a stain and water repellent finish. They also offer a full range of adult bedding, including mattresses, duvets and pillows.

Crib mattresses (80 × 42 × 5 cm or 70 × 34 × 5 cm) cost £47.00; cot mattresses cost from £79.99 to

Books

Telephone:
0432 268018
Fax:
0432 278585

£84.99; pure wool duvets range from £52.00 to £96.75; and pure wool pillows cost £11.00.

Catalogue: *A5, Brochure, 2 pages, Free* Postal charges: *Varies with item* Delivery: *GA & MM Express Parcels* Methods of Payment: *Cheque*

ADMIRALTY CHARTS
Hydrographic Office
Taunton
Somerset
TA1 2DN

Telephone:
0823 337900
Fax:
0823 323753

CHARTS AND PUBLICATIONS

Admiralty charts and publications, with their reputation for excellence, have been used by navigators worldwide for nearly 200 years. This particular leaflet advertises a range of products designed exclusively for the Small Craft user, whether in sail or power. The charts are selected Admiralty charts that have been modified to meet the needs of this kind of user.

The charts arrive folded to a convenient size (215 × 355 mm) for ease of storage and include a wealth of supplementary information derived from Admiralty nautical publications.

Products included are Tidal Stream Atlases at £5.20 each and Tide Tables for Yachtsmen at £4.00 each.

Catalogue: *A4, Catalogue, 16 pages, Colour and B/W, Free* Postal charges: *£1.00* Delivery: *Royal Mail* Methods of Payment: *Cheque, Visa, Access / Mastercard*

APPLAUSE BOOKS
406 Vale Road
Tonbridge
Kent
TN9 1XR

Telephone:
0732 357755
Fax:
0732 770219

THEATRICAL BOOKS

For anyone with a passion for the theatre this catalogue is a must. Packed with texts, critiques and books on acting, music and theatre history it is a wonderful reference source. Each book is given a brief but useful review which is clearly written by people who know what they are talking about.

Although the books are published by Applause, they are obtainable through high street bookshops as well as direct. Inspection copies may be requested without charge, if proof is given of a classroom order of ten or more copies. Trade terms are 35% discount. 'Chorus Line', the book of the musical is priced at £19.99.

Catalogue: *Bi-annually, 175mm × 250mm, Catalogue, 64 pages, B/W, Free* Postal charges: *Varies with item* Delivery: *Royal Mail* Methods of Payment: *Cheque, Postal Order, Visa, Access / Mastercard, American Express*

Books

BCA
Guild House
Farnsby Street
Swindon X
SN99 9XX

Telephone:
0793 512666
Fax:
071 323 5665

BOOK CLUB
BCA offers club services for several categories of books and music.

The leaflets included contain membership details for their children's club, which offers twelve Beatrix Potter books for £1.99 as a joining incentive; their music club, Music Direct, which offers 5 CDs for £2.50 each or five cassettes for £1.99 each, and the company's Ancient and Medieval history book club offering four books for 99p each.

Catalogue: *Monthly, 190mm × 210mm, Leaflets, 6 pages, Colour, Free* Postal charges: *Varies with item* Delivery: *Royal Mail* Methods of Payment: *Cheque, Postal Order*

BIBLIOPHILE BOOKS
21 Jacob Street
London
SE1 2BG

Telephone:
071 231 7918
Fax:
071 231 9296

BOOKS
This company offers a vast selection of hardback books at half publisher's price or less. You can find biography, history, travel, music and dance, literature, children's, war and militaria, health, entertainment and the arts, science, occult, Great Britain and much more. All titles are of course subject to availability and schools and libraries may be invoiced.

Bibliophile publish ten catalogues a year, each with over 700 titles. One of the great advantages is that there is no membership fee and no commitment to purchase. All the books are in mint condition, many out of print and likely to increase in value.

Prices are excellent, with a 1991 *Macmillan Encyclopaedia* of 1336 pages for £12.95 instead of £24.95; a *Dictionary of Genealogical Source*, £20.00 now £8.99; *Charles II Illustrated Biography*, £20.00 now £8.99 and something for the little man in your life, *The Penis: Performance and Enlargement*, £3.95.

Catalogue: *10 a year, Tabloid, Catalogue, 20 pages, B/W, Free* Postal charges: *Varies with item* Delivery: *Parcelforce* Methods of Payment: *Cheque, Postal Order, Visa, Access / Mastercard*

BIJOU CHILDREN'S MAGICAL THEATRE
Brook House
Dranllwyn Lane
Machen
nr Newport
Gwent
NP1 8QS

Telephone:
0633 440466

PERSONALISED CHILDREN'S BOOKS
Bijou was first established in 1959 and has brought the highest standards of magical entertainment to children both here and abroad. These same high standards are now being applied to the production of these lovely children's books.

In these books, your child becomes the STAR and appears on almost every full coloured page. A Personalised Baby Book costs only £8.50; *Dinosaur Adventure/Robin Hood/Tom and Jerry/Beauty and the*

Books

Beast/The Space Adventure/A Christmas Story, all at £6.50. There are more than twenty books available. Send for a leaflet and samples of these books which will make a gift to treasure.

Catalogue: *A4, Brochure, 4 pages, Colour, Free* Postal charges: *Varies with item* Delivery: *Royal Mail Parceline* Methods of Payment: *Postal Order, COD Cheque*

BLACKWELL'S
Broad Street
Oxford
Oxon
OX1 3BQ

Telephone:
0865 792792
Fax:
0865 794143

BOOKS
Blackwell's is of course something of an institution. Famed not only in Oxford but throughout the world as a supplier of books to libraries, universities and institutions. But it also has an extensive mail order arm for the private book buyer and will send books anywhere in the world.

Readers may join their mailing list and, by indicating what areas they are interested in, receive regular catalogues of relevant books. An excellent way of keeping up to date without having to commit to a book club.

Catalogue: *A4, Brochures, Colour, Free* Postal charges: *Varies with item* Delivery: *Royal Mail* Methods of Payment: *Cheque, Visa, Access / Mastercard, American Express*

BOOKS FOR CHILDREN
Membership Services Dept
PO Box 70
Cirencester
Glos
GL7 7AZ

Telephone:
081 606 3030

CHILDREN'S BOOK CLUB
The monthly magazine is divided into four sections: under fives; four to seven year old; seven to ten year old; and ten years and above. The first pages are devoted to the recommended selection for each of the four different age groups. Each of the other books on offer has a colour picture of the cover, name of author, short description, number of pages, size, whether colour or black and white, a reference number, name of publisher, and original price as well as discounted club price. There is usually an introductory offer such as 8 books for £1.99 plus p&p.

You pay within ten days of receipt of order, which arrives within eight weeks, but you can make an additional order in the meantime. Most of the books have to be bought in pairs or sets, and prices are usually over £5.00. You automatically receive the recommended title for the relevant age group unless you cross the box when you send back your invoice. Publishers include Dorling Kindersley, Hodder & Stoughton, Heinemann, Hamlyn and Oxford University Press. Prices range from £5.99 to £24.95 for a video.

Books

Catalogue: *Monthly, A5, Catalogue, Colour, Free* Postal charges: *Varies with item* Delivery: *Royal Mail* Methods of Payment: *Cheque, Postal Order, Visa, Access / Mastercard*

CALDER MAIL ORDER
Eddington Hook Ltd
PO Box 239
Tunbridge Wells
Kent
TN4 0YQ

Telephone:
0892 517439
Fax:
0892 517439

ART BOOKS
This is a specialist publisher for the Arts with some interesting and unusual titles. Literature and drama have a strong European flavour to them with most of the authors listed not being English. A good many of the titles are used on university courses and the company is in fact an educational trust.

As well as modern European fiction they distribute a range of catering and cookbooks from publisher Eddington Hook Ltd. These include many books for the professional caterer as well as the amateur cook.

Catalogue: *A5, Catalogue, 20 pages, B/W, Free* Postal charges: *Varies with item* Delivery: *Royal Mail* Methods of Payment: *Cheque, Visa, Access / Mastercard*

CHATER & SCOTT
8 South Street
Isleworth
Middx
TW7 7BG

Telephone:
081 568 9750
Fax:
081 569 8273

BOOKS AND VIDEOS ON MOTORING
Chaters claims to be 'Europe's No 1 Choice for Motoring Books and Videos' and certainly they have an impressive range. Their tightly printed catalogue is really more of a price list, with each entry given just a brief description and price.

There are sections on general interest as well as technical, motorsport, manufacturers, American cars and motorcycles. Clearly for the enthusiast who knows what he or she wants, this is about as comprehensive as you can get.

Catalogue: *A5, Catalogue, 32 pages, B/W, Free* Postal charges: *Varies with item* Delivery: *Courier* Methods of Payment: *Cheque, Postal Order, American Express, Visa, Access / Mastercard*

CHILDREN'S BOOK OF THE MONTH CLUB
Guild House
Farnsby St
Swindon X
SN99 9XX

Telephone:
0793 512666

CHILDREN'S BOOK CLUB
Potential members receive a leaflet offering them an introductory offer of, for example, twelve Beatrix Potter books for £1.99 plus p&p, a saving of £52.00. Having sent this off, you then receive the catalogue and membership details. There is a minimum order of six books in the first year, which are offered at discount of between £2.00-£6.00 each. The catalogue shows each book with a colour picture of the cover and some inside pages, a short description, size, number of pages, name of publisher, age recommendation, price and original price. As you pay for one set of books, so you order another.

Books

Monthly order form has an editor's choice which is sent automatically unless you cross a box and return within 10 days. If you pay by credit card, you still have to post your order. Publishers range from Dorling Kindersley to HarperCollins and Heinemann. Prices range from about £5.55 to £19.99.

Catalogue: *Monthly, A5, Catalogue, 24 pages, Colour, Free* Postal charges: *£1.95* Delivery: *Royal Mail* Methods of Payment: *Cheque, Postal Order, Visa, Access / Mastercard*

CLASSIC BINDINGS
PO Box 3222
LONDON
SW3 2RX

Telephone:
071-735 1872

Fax:
071-735 1872

ANTIQUARIAN BOOKS
What an extraordinary company! They sell antique leather-bound books by the foot! Apparently this is mainly for places like hotels which wish to have a 'study' look in a particular room. The footage is much cheaper if the books are in a foreign language – £150.00 per foot for English, a mere £64.00 for anything else.

They also sell complete sets which themselves take up quite a few feet of shelf space. For example there is a twelve volume set of *The Arabian Nights* for £480.00 or, if you think people are less likely to pick out a volume, you could go for *Narrative of the Exploring Expedition to the Rocky Mountains in the year 1842 and to Oregon and California in the years 1843–44* by Captain J.C.Fremont – the title alone must take up quite a few feet!

Catalogue: *Monthly, A4, Catalogue, B/W, Free* Postal charges: *Varies with item* Delivery: *Royal Mail* Methods of Payment: *Cheque*

COMICS BY POST
4 Springfield
Woodsetts
Worksop Notts
S81 8QD

Telephone:
0909 569428

COMICS
This interesting company specialises in comics, but not the sort that a modern child would buy – these are strictly for collectors. Their main stock consists of *Beano*s from 1940 onwards, some of which are very rare. Indeed they claim to have 'probably the broadest saleable stock in the world'.

As well as actual *Beano*s they have Annuals, Calendars, Dandy, Film Fun, Dennis the Menace and Cards. They also stock a considerable amount of material on Rupert Bear, including original artwork cells for which they are the sole suppliers.

Prices start at £5.00 and rise according to rarity.

Catalogue: *Quarterly, A5, Brochure, 12, B/W, Free* Postal charges: *Free* Delivery: *Royal Mail* Methods of Payment: *Cheque, Postal Order, Visa, Access / Mastercard*

Books

COMPUTER BOOKLIST
50 James Road
Birmingham
BA11 2BA

Telephone:
021 706 6000
Fax:
021 706 3301

COMPUTER BOOKS
Subscription to this catalogue is free and it is updated three times a year. With an enormous range of computer books from highly technical programming languages and techniques titles to the user-friendly 'Computers for Dummies' series, it has just about everything. They even promise to try and find anything for you that is not in the catalogue.

Some products are liable to VAT, such as software, and are marked accordingly. A 'Learning Wordperfect' manual, sells for £18.45 and an Apple Macintosh guide for £22.95.

Catalogue: *200mm × 270mm, Catalogue, 48 pages, Colour, Free* Postal charges: *Varies with item* Delivery: *Royal Mail* Methods of Payment: *Cheque, Postal Order, Visa, Access / Mastercard, American Express*

CURIOUS CATERPILLAR BY POST
Ravensden Farm
Bedford Road
Rushden
Northhamptonshire
NN10 0SQ

Telephone:
0993 410650
Fax:
0993 410108

CHILDREN'S BOOKS
Curious Caterpillar By Post offers a variety of different toys, games, stickers and books all based on different themes (sea animals, farm animals, dinosaurs, zoo animals and woodland animals). They are all aimed at children, helping them to read and learn as they play.

Each item specifies whether it is suitable for younger children or toddlers so that they are not put in any danger. The toys are educational as well as fun: for example, the 3-D Dinosaur kits (£1.65) or the Dinosaur stencils (£0.50 each).

Catalogue: *Annually, A5, Catalogue, 32 pages, Colour, Free* Postal charges: *Varies with item* Delivery: *Royal Mail* Methods of Payment: *Cheque, Postal Order, Access / Mastercard, Visa*

DILLONS
Dillons the Bookstore
82 Gower Street
London
WC1E 6EQ

Telephone:
071 636 1577
Fax:
071 580 7680

BOOKS
Dillons offers a bookstore by post with hundreds of different titles in categories as diverse as biographies, crime fiction, fiction, literature, craft, reference, and art . . . the list is endless. There is also a range of lower-priced books with up to 25% off.

Dillons bookstores are sited throughout Britain and therefore delivery is quick and easy. Books can be ordered at any time in any quantity with no limits on the numbers purchased.

Catalogue: *Quarterly, A5, Catalogue, 48 pages, Colour, Free* Postal charges: *Varies with item* Delivery: *Royal Mail* Methods of Payment: *Cheque, Postal Order, Visa, Access / Mastercard*

Books

DISNEY BOOK CLUB
Grolier
PO Box 75
Norwich
NR5 9QQ

Telephone:
0603 740400

CHILDREN'S BOOK CLUB
Disney Book Club operates by direct mail and has no catalogue. Members are offered two books every month, chosen by the club, and have ten days in which to accept or reject them. There is usually an introductory offer such as four free books and another non-book gift. The minimum order is six books a year, plus the introductory trial offer. Book characters are taken from the Disney video image, which means instant recognition from most children: Beauty and the Beast, Cinderella, 101 Dalmatians. All books cost £2.50 each.

Catalogue: *None* Postal charges: *£1.48* Delivery: *Royal Mail*
Methods of Payment: *Cheque, Postal Order*

DTS
20 Stafford Street
Market Drayton
Shropshire
TF9 1HY

Telephone:
0630 655875
Fax:
0630 655015

TATTOO EQUIPMENT AND SUPPLIES
For 85 years this family business has been supplying tattooists with all their needs: machines, materials, hygiene, designs and design resources. But they also stock an excellent range of books on the subject which will delight any tattoo enthusiast (see their entry in General Catalogues).

They also supply copyright-free designs which will be of interest not only to tattooists but also graphic artists and needleworkers. There is a good stock of overseas tattoo magazines, including many back issues which are sent post free.

Catalogue: *Annually, A4, Catalogue, 40 pages, B/W, Free* Postal charges: *Varies with item* Delivery: *Royal Mail, Parcelforce*
Methods of Payment: *Cheque, Postal Order, COD, Visa, Access / Mastercard*

EDWARD STANFORD
12–14 Long Acre
Covent Garden
London
WC2E 9LP

Telephone:
071 836 1321
Fax:
071 836 0189

MAPS & TRAVEL BOOKS
Established in 1852 Stanford's remains the first stop for adventurers and armchairs traveller alike. It is the world's largest map and travel bookseller, offering over 30,000 titles for travel or reference. Their unique selection includes touring or wall maps for every part of the world, including the complete range of Ordnance Survey maps of Britain.

Their travel guidebooks cover everywhere from Alaska to Zimbabwe and they also have an outstanding collection of travel literature. There are specialist sections on climbing, sailing, navigational charts, world atlases and even globes.

A *National Geographic* political wall map of the world is £9.95, the *Michelin Motoring Atlas of France*

Books

£11.95, *The Good Pub Guide* £12.99 and *India – A Travel Survival Kit* £14.95.

Catalogue: *Annually, A5, Catalogue, 32 pages, Colour, Free* Postal charges: *Varies with item* Delivery: *Parcelforce, Royal Mail* Methods of Payment: *Cheque, Visa, Access / Mastercard*

FREE ASSOCIATION BOOKS LIMITED
26 Freegrove Road
London
N7 9RQ

Telephone:
071 609 5646

Fax:
071 700 0330

BOOKS

A catalogue of books with such diverse titles as *Aids, Africa and Racism* to *The Provision of Primary Experience*. Mainly in-depth reading for those interested in a broad perspective on psychoanalytic and psychodynamic approaches to human nature, group culture, politics and society.

The books provide an international forum for critical thinking across the whole analytic tradition and include many different perspectives. Widely recognised as the leading English-speaking journal.

Catalogue: *A5, Catalogue, 48 pages, B/W, Free* Postal charges: *Varies with item* Delivery: *Royal Mail* Methods of Payment: *Cheque, Postal Order, Visa, Access / Mastercard, American Express*

G HEYWOOD HILL LTD
10 Curzon Street
London
W1Y 7FJ

Telephone:
071 493 3742

Fax:
071 408 0286

UNUSUAL BOOKS

Printed on quality paper with no commercial gimmicks, this catalogue is clearly aimed at serious literary collectors/investors. It specialises in presentation copies with authorial inscriptions. There is also a selection of copies from the publisher Hamish Hamilton's library – not the sort of books you will see on bestseller lists.

Descriptions of the book's condition are limited, a typical one being along the lines red buckram, nice. Obviously prices vary with author and rarity value. A 1926 copy of *Tess of the D'Urbervilles* signed by Hardy sells for £300.00.

Catalogue: *A5, Catalogue, 42 pages, B/W, Free* Postal charges: *Varies with item* Delivery: *Royal Mail* Methods of Payment: *Cheque, Postal Order*

GOOD BOOK GUIDE
24 Seward Street
London
EC1V 3PB

Telephone:
071 490 9900

Fax:
071 490 9908

BOOKS, CASSETTES AND ARTS, DOCUMENTARY AND CHILDREN'S VIDEOS

The Good Book Guide is ideal for bookworms who like to select their reading matter from the comfort of their home. It's an independent bi-monthly review magazine (not a book club) featuring the latest books, videos and cassettes from the UK. There are also special features, profiles and interviews with top writers, editors and critics.

Books

All books and cassettes are available through the Guide's award-winning international mail order service, at London bookshop prices.

For a free copy and £2.00 spending token contact *The Good Book Guide*, quoting *The Virgin Home Shopping Handbook*.

Catalogue: *Monthly, 25cm × 25cm, Catalogue, 40 pages, Colour, £18.50 refundable* Postal charges: *20%* Delivery: *Royal Mail* Methods of Payment: *Cheque*

HAWK BOOKS
Suite 309
Canalot Studios
222 Kensal Road
London
W10 5BN

Telephone:
081 969 8091
Fax:
081 968 9012

CHILDREN'S BOOKS AND T-SHIRTS

Dan Dare and Billy Bunter fans will be pleased to learn that Hawk Books have got this small space in the market sewn up. Dan Dare, the Mekon and Digby are featured on T-shirts (£12.00), as figurines (£45.00) or on the side of a Corgi Classic Dormobile (£30.00). Naturally, there are books, too, such as *Dan Dare Volume 5, The Man from Nowhere* which costs £12.99.

The spirit of Billy Bunter lives on in Hawk's new series of collectors' titles. The Fat Owl of the Remove is scared but his pleas for protection are ignored by the Famous Five – until he disappears – in *Billy Bunter's Bodyguard* (£14.95). A steamer excursion to Boulogne turns into hilarious chaos for the Removites in *Billy Bunter's Beanfeast* (£14.95). A must for enthusiasts.

Catalogue: *A4, Leaflets, 4 pages, Colour, Free* Postal charges: *Varies with item* Delivery: *Royal Mail* Methods of Payment: *Cheque, Postal Order, Visa, Access / Mastercard, American Express*

HEALTH SCIENCE
Addison-Wesley
Publishing Company
Finchampstead Road
Wokingham
Berkshire
RG11 2NZ

Telephone:
0734 794000
Fax:
0734 794035

BOOKS ABOUT HEALTH AND SCIENCE

The Health Science catalogue offers a wide variety of books all following the themes of health and science. These books are mainly suitable for teachers, lecturers and students on a scientific course and they cover a range of different subjects (ageing, child health, surgical nursing, nutrition, infant care, mental health etc). The books vary in price from £11.95–£53.95 and are written by a variety of different authors.

Catalogue: *Annually, 15 × 20.9 mm, Catalogue, 29 pages, B/W, Free* Postal charges: *Free* Delivery: *Royal Mail* Methods of Payment: *Cheque, Visa, Access / Mastercard, American Express, Diners Club*

Books

IAN ALLAN PUBLISHING LTD
Coombelands House
Coombelands Lane
Addlestone
Surrey
KT15 1HY

Telephone:
0932 820560
0932 820552
Fax:
0932 821258

BOOKS AND REGALIA

Ian Allan Regalia aim to satisfy the needs of all Freemasons. For those curious as to what Freemasons actually do, there are books, including *Masonic Ritual – a commentary on the Freemasonic Ritual* by Dr E. H. Cartwright and *Workman Unshamed*, an examination of the accusations often levelled against Freemasons.

The catalogue also features Masonic Regalia of every kind. There is a curious array of gloves for £6.25, finest lambskin aprons for £14.10, chain collars from £164.50 and other extravagant items which no doubt mean a great deal to the right people. To the wrong people, the illustration on page 16 of a portly gentleman in full Knights Templar regalia may raise more than an eyebrow.

Catalogue: *A5, Catalogue, 54 pages, Colour and B/W, Free* Postal charges: *Varies with item* Delivery: *Royal Mail* Methods of Payment: *Cheque, Postal Order, Visa, Access / Mastercard*

LEAF PUBLICATIONS
12 Summerdown Road
Eastbourne
BN20 8DT

CHILDREN'S BOOKS

Leaf Publications produce just one book, *The Xtra Pocket Handbook*. Written by an enterprising 14 year old, it tells children of a similar age how to supplement their pocket money by doing various odd jobs.

The book gives a full guide to the legal position, advice on how to best invest money and a large section on how get part-time jobs. An ideal birthday or Christmas present for a very reasonable £2.95.

Catalogue: *None* Postal charges: *Free* Delivery: *Royal Mail* Methods of Payment: *Cheque, Postal Order*

LETTERBOX LIBRARY
2nd Floor
Leroy House
436 Essex Road
London
N1 3QP

Telephone:
071 226 1633

CHILDREN'S BOOK CLUB

Run by a women's co-operative, Letterbox offers non-sexist, non-racist, multi-cultural books, as well as those about the environment and disability, for children up to the age of fourteen. Books are sold at discounts of between 10 and 25%. Not all the books are illustrated in the catalogue. Each has a number, short description, author, publisher, price and club price, age range and number of pages. This book club offers a genuinely different service.

Catalogue: *Quarterly, A5, Catalogue, 24 pages, Colour and B/W, Free* Postal charges: *Varies with item* Delivery: *Royal Mail* Methods of Payment: *Postal Order Cheque, Visa, Access / Mastercard*

Books

LIZ SEEBER
Antiquarian Cookery
Books
10 The Plantation
Blackheath
London
SE3 0AB

Telephone:
081 852 7807
Fax:
081 318 4675

ANTIQUARIAN COOKERY BOOKS

Liz Seeber stocks more than 400 antiquarian cookery books and also sells other items such as collectable menus, leaflets, cookery magazines and original manuscripts. Also stocked are antiquarian books on wine, beer, cocktails and other drinks.

Liz's stocklist provides very detailed descriptions of each book down to minute details of the condition of the pages and binding. The list contains books from the 17th century to the present day ranging in price from £2.00 to several hundred pounds and covers many aspects of cookery both English and foreign.

Liz Seeber herself is a cookery enthusiast with lots of practical experience and is both knowledgeable and willing to help others to find what they are looking for.

Catalogue: *Updated daily, A4, Stocklist, 32 pages, B/W, Free* Postal charges: *Varies with item. With valuable items also includes a charge for insurance in transit.* Delivery: *Royal Mail, Parcelforce* Methods of Payment: *Cheque, Visa, Access / Mastercard*

MAP MARKETING
92–104 Carnworth
Road
London
SW6 3HW

Telephone:
071 736 0297
Fax:
071 371 0473

MAPS

Map Marketing's range of laminated wall maps and charts incorporate over 400 different maps from around the world. If you need a permanent reminder of where you are or where you're going, you couldn't really ask for more. They also create composite maps, overprint and carry out framing.

The meticulous among us will no doubt be pleased to own the 'Planners' Postcode Area Map' (mounted/framed: £49.95) or a 'Geoplan District Map' (laminated: £25.00). Those who just want to see the world in all its glory will enjoy the 'Earth From Space' map (laminated: £34.99), created from images recorded by weather satellites. It is also available as a jigsaw (216 pieces: £9.99).

Catalogue: *A5, Leaflets, 20 pages, Colour, Free* Postal charges: *£3.95* Delivery: *Royal Mail* Methods of Payment: *Cheque, Postal Order, Visa, Access / Mastercard*

MUSIC SALES LIMITED
8–9 Frith Street
London
W1V 5TZ

SHEET MUSIC

Music Sales produce musical arrangements for a variety of instruments, including vocals, in all styles. The main part of their range is devoted to piano songbooks, including such titles as *An Old Fashioned Lovesong*, a collection of 35 love songs, and *The Folk Music Anthology*, which has songs by Gordon

Books

Lightfoot, Suzanne Vega and James Taylor. Among many other titles, there's the 'Musical Memories' series, ranging by decade from 1900 with *Beautiful Dreamer* and *Burlington Bertie* to 1980 and hits like *Bright Eyes*, *Thank You For the Music*, and *Three Times a Lady*.

Films, shows and TV series are equally well covered. You can buy the complete score with piano and vocals for *Cats* or the complete vocal score of *Cabaret*.

Catalogue: *Annually, A4, Catalogue, 64, Colour, Free* Postal charges: *Varies with item* Delivery: *Royal Mail* Methods of Payment: *Cheque*

MY ADVENTURE BOOKS
PO Box 569
Bristol
BS99 1QA

PERSONALISED CHILDREN'S BOOKS
My Adventure Books are personalised for your child so he or she becomes the star in every story. The name of your child and other personal details are printed on almost every page. Each book has 30 pages of full colour illustrations. The range of eight titles are *My Birthday Land Adventure, My Adventures in Nursery Rhyme Land, My Adventures in Fairytale Land, Me and the Great Zoo Mystery, My Dinosaur Adventure, My Underwater Adventure, My Topsy-Turvy Adventure and My Special Christmas Adventure*.

All books cost £7.90.

Catalogue: *A5, Brochure, 4 pages, Colour, Free* Postal charges: *95p* Delivery: *Royal Mail* Methods of Payment: *Cheque, Postal Order, Visa, Access / Mastercard*

NICK HERN BOOKS
14 Larden Road
London
W3 7ST

Telephone:
081 740 9539

THEATRICAL BOOKS
Nick Hern Books was founded as an imprint in 1988. It has now emerged as a fully fledged independent publisher of theatrical works.

A Year at the Court, written by arts journalist Christine Eccles, recalls the twelve months ending April 1992 that she spent as a 'fly on the wall' at the Royal Court theatre. During this time, Caryl Churchill's *Top Girls* was revived; Ariel Dorfman's *Death and the Maiden* was brought out of the studio and onto the main stage; and preparations were underway for Timberlake Wertenbaker's *Three Birds Alighting on a Field*. This fascinating account costs £17.99.

Catalogue: *Annually, Third A4, Catalogue, 24 pages, B/W, Free* Postal charges: *Varies with item* Delivery: *Royal Mail* Methods of Payment: *Cheque, Visa, Access / Mastercard, Postal Order*

Books

PILGRIM BY POST
48 Culver Street
Newent
Glos
GL18 1DA

Telephone:
0531 821075
Fax:
0452 386268

NEW AGE BOOKS
Pilgrim produce the kind of material that graces every New Ager's home. Tapes to inspire meditation and relaxation range from *Spirit of the Rainforest* by Terry Oldfield: Flute and Pan pipes. Authentic and deeply inspiring (£7.50); to *Celestial Harmony* by Chris Mitchell: Her Angelic Flute brings Albinoni, Bach, Vivaldi, Pachelbel, Ravel and Schubert to you (£8.00).

There are titles dealing with all the obvious subjects, from holistic health and healing to relaxation, meditation and astrology. Jessica Macbeth's *Moon Over Water* (£7.20) describes meditation techniques for beginners. *The Birth Chart Book* (£2.95) by Bill and Eileen Anderton shows you how to get the best from your birth chart.

Catalogue: *A5, Catalogue, 16 pages, B/W, Free* Postal charges: *Free* Delivery: *Royal Mail* Methods of Payment: *Cheque, Postal Order, Visa, Access / Mastercard*

POSTSCRIPT
22a Langroyd Road
London
SW17 7PL

Telephone:
081 767 7421
Fax:
081 682 0280

QUALITY BOOKS
Postscript is a family-run business specialising in high quality books at greatly reduced prices. They are not a book club, as there is no obligation to buy any books at any time. They cover a huge range of interests from art, gardening, cookery, biography, travel and reference to history, philosophy, psychology and literature – from classic works to the frankly esoteric, many of which cannot be found in bookshops and all priced at a fraction of publishers' latest prices.

Dictionary of Idioms and their Origins at £5.99, was originally £14.99; *Family Roots: How to Trace your Family History* at £7.95, was £15.99; *Cassell's Colloquial French* at £1.99, was £3.99; *County Guide to English Churches* at £4.99, was £9.95.

Catalogue: *Bi-monthly, A4, Catalogue, 48 pages, B/W, Free* Postal charges: *Varies with item* Delivery: *Parcelforce* Methods of Payment: *Cheque, Postal Order, Visa, Access / Mastercard*

PUFFIN BOOK CLUB
Freepost
27 Wright's Lane
London
W8 5BR

Telephone:
071 938 2200

CHILDREN'S BOOK CLUB
Aimed at schools, not individuals, nevertheless groups of parents or even NCT groups can join the club. Three magazines, each targeting a different age group, are mailed out seven times a year, based on school terms. Fledgling magazine is aimed at those under six; Flight is for six to nine year olds; and Post is for nine to thirteen year olds. The magazines

Books

contain puzzles, colouring pages, activity ideas and poems.

Each age group also receives a colour leaflet with book availability and there are teachers' notes with additional special book offers and ideas. There is no minimum order, but the introductory offer which allows you to keep 50% of the value of your first order encourages a big order.

The organiser orders the required number of leaflets for each of the three reading ages, collates the different orders and then chooses one free book for every ten paid for. The organiser can also order one each of all the new titles at a 25% discount so that the group can see before they order. These are non-returnable. The leaflets contain colour pictures of covers and some inside pages with price and a short description. Prices range from £1.99 to £4.99.

Catalogue: *A4, Brochure, 28 pages, Colour, Free* Postal charges: *Free* Delivery: *Royal Mail* Methods of Payment: *Cheque, Postal Order, Visa, Access / Mastercard*

REED BOOK SERVICES
PO Box 5
Rushden
Northamptonshire
NN10 6YX

Telephone:
0933 411292
Fax:
0933 410321

GENERAL, SPECIALIST, REFERENCE AND CHILDREN'S BOOKS

Reed Books are a major international company who publish famous names such as Hamlyn cookery and gardening books, Philips road and world atlases, Miller's antiques guides and Mitchell Beazley wine books. Their children's books include 'Postman Pat', 'Fireman Sam' and 'Winnie-the-Pooh' character books plus an extensive range of fiction and reference.

You can order books as frequently or infrequently as you like as there is no commitment to purchase as with book clubs. Full-colour catalogues containing hundreds of titles are available on request.

Miller's Antiques Price Guide '94 is £19.99, *Homes & Gardens Complete Curtain Book* £19.99, *Hamlyn All Colour Plant Directory* £15.99 and *Postman Pat Noisy Book* (with sound panel) £9.99.

Catalogue: *Annually, A4, 3 catalogues, 176, 56 & 48 pages, Colour, £3.00 refundable* Postal charges: *Varies with item* Delivery: *Parcelforce* Methods of Payment: *Cheque, Postal Order, Visa, Access / Mastercard, American Express, Diners Club*

Books

RUNNING HEADS INTERNATIONAL
82 East Dulwich Grove
London
SE22 8TW

Telephone:
071 738 4096

Fax:
071 738 4096

CONSUMER GUIDES
Running Heads are a small publisher who produce and distribute a range of consumer guides. One title, *The Deregulated Phone Book*, is an invaluable guide to getting cheap phone calls. Apparently it is now possible to use systems other than BT or Mercury and save a considerable amount in the process.

They also distribute a sister publication to *The Virgin Home Shopping Handbook*, called *The Global Shopper*. This comprehensive guide to international mail order means you can now shop with over 500 companies from 32 different countries. It just happens to be written by one of our own authors so must be worth the mere £9.99!

Catalogue: *None* Postal charges: *Free* Delivery: *Royal Mail* Methods of Payment: *Cheque, Postal Order, Visa, Access / Mastercard*

SCHOLASTIC BOOK CLUB
Westfield Road
Southam
Leamington Spa
Warks.
CV33 0JH

Telephone:
0926 813910

CHILDREN'S BOOK CLUB
Aimed at schools, the club follows the English and Scottish national curriculae. Packs will not be sent to private addresses, but local nursery, playgroups or NCT groups can band together and join. It comprises four clubs: See-Saw for pre-school to six year olds; Lucky for seven to nine year olds; Chip for nine to twelve year olds; and Scene for twelve year olds and above. Each group has its own newsletter with up to 30 books in each. This has colour pictures of each book cover with author, price, a short description and an order form which, when completed, is given to the organiser who orders for the group.

Each newsletter is accompanied by teachers' notes, which has extra offers. Books are sold at discount prices and are chosen from a range of publishers. Organisers receive a 10% discount or one free book for every ten purchased. There are sometimes also free gifts for each book ordered. Publishers range from World, Puffin, Angus & Robertson, Hippo and Red Fox to Hodder & Stoughton and Simon & Schuster. Prices range from 95p for a shot of a famous sportsman to £8.99 for a video. Credit cards are not accepted.

Catalogue: *A5, Leaflets, 50 pages, Colour and B/W, Free* Postal charges: *Free* Delivery: *Royal Mail* Methods of Payment: *Cheque, Postal Order*

Books

SCOPE INTERNATIONAL LTD
62 Murray Road
Waterlooville
Hants
PO8 9JL

Telephone:
0705 592255
Fax:
0705 591975

SELF-IMPROVEMENT BOOKS
In a series of fifteen books, Dr W. G. Hill promises the secret of life. The Reports, which can be purchased individually for £60.00 each or together at a substantial discount (£495.00 for fifteen), give the would-be-tax-exile vital information on how to escape the tax-man and where to escape to.

The first five reports offer advice on how to make your first million and avoid the burdens of life in today's Big Brother society, including how to get a second passport. There are eight more reports listing various tax havens to make the choice easier when becoming a tax exile becomes the only option left.

Catalogue: *A4, Brochure, 12 pages, Colour and B/W, Free* Postal charges: *Varies with item* Delivery: *Royal Mail* Methods of Payment: *Cheque, Postal Order, Visa, Access / Mastercard, Diners Club, American Express*

SWEET & MAXWELL LTD
South Quay Plaza
183 Marshwall
London
E14 9FT

LEGAL BOOKS
Sweet & Maxwell have published legal materials since 1799. They provide high quality law-based information for professionals, academics and students.

Key titles in their current catalogue include the Journal of Personal Injury Litigation (£120.00 bound), the International Maritime Law Journal (price details on application) and the Journal of Social Security Law (price details on application). There's also a wealth of information on every subject, from the 'Forfeiture of Leases' (£65.00) to 'Discrimination in Housing' (£48.00). If it weren't for the prices and, no doubt, the inevitable jargon, some of these could be recommended reading for most of us.

Catalogue: *Annually, A5, Catalogue, 304 pages, B/W, Free* Postal charges: *Free* Delivery: *Royal Mail* Methods of Payment: *Visa, Access / Mastercard, Diners Club, American Express Cheque, Postal Order*

THE BOOKWORM CLUB
Heffers Booksellers
20 Trinity St
Cambridge
CB2 3NG

Telephone:
0223 358351

CHILDREN'S BOOK CLUB
This club is aimed at schools, not individuals, though groups of parents or PTA members can get together and join. Children choose from two leaflets: The Bookworm Club for seven to thirteen year olds; and The Early Worm for under eights. Books are sold at the full published price, but 10% of the value of the total order is refunded to the organiser.

There is usually an introductory offer of, for example, ten free books. Leaflets, which usually feature about eighteen books each, include a colour

Books

picture of the book cover and inside pages, price, short description and number of pages. Posters, free gifts and other display material are also available.

There are separate order forms for each club, with additional teachers' notes giving extra details of each book. Prices range from £1.99 to £5.99 and publishers from Puffin, Usborne and Pan to Kingfisher and Ladybird. There is no charge for postage.

Catalogue: *A4, Leaflets, 4 pages, Colour, Free* Postal charges: *Free* Delivery: *Royal Mail* Methods of Payment: *Cheque, Postal Order*

THE GOOD DEAL DIRECTORY
PO Box 4
Lechlade
Glos
GL7 3YB

Telephone:
0367 860017
Fax:
0367 860013

NEWSLETTER AND BOOK ON BARGAINS
The Good Deal Directory is also known as the bargain hunter's bible. It comprises both a newsletter, which appears ten times a year, and a book. The book contains 1,500 outlets where you can buy brand names at well below retail prices. You can get almost anything, from designer outfits at amazing discounts, to fridges, freezers and top name nursery equipment cheaper than anywhere in the country.

The newsletter provides a monthly update of the book, with about 60 entries in each issue. It also offers a diary of the best showroom and designer sales taking place that month, and so is an invaluable guide to buying the best for less.

The book costs £9.99 (p+p free) from the address on the left and is also available from bookshops. The newsletter costs £25.00 a year.

Catalogue: *Monthly, A4, Newsletter, 4 pages, B/W, See right for details* Postal charges: *Free* Delivery: *Royal Mail* Methods of Payment: *Cheque, Postal Order, Visa, Access / Mastercard*

THE LITERARY GUILD
P O Box 199
Swindon
Wilts
SN3 4BR

Telephone:
0843 68841
Fax:
0843 64265

BOOK CLUB
The Literary Guild features many hundreds of different books, each of which is discounted by up to 50% and at least 25% on the publisher's price.

The range of titles is considerable, from the *Times Atlas of the World* (£5.00) to *Delia Smith's Christmas* (£1.00) or Dorling Kindersley's *Royal Horticultural Society Gardener's Encyclopaedia of Plants and Flowers* (£4.00). As with most book clubs, you have to guarantee to buy a certain number of books. Every two months, you will be sent a full colour review of all the books from which you must make a choice.

Catalogue: *A4, Leaflets, 2, Colour, Free* Postal charges: *Varies with item* Delivery: *Royal Mail* Methods of Payment: *Cheque*

Books

THE RED HOUSE
Range Road
Cotswold Business
Park
Witney
Oxon
OX8 5YF

Telephone:
0993 771144

CHILDREN'S BOOKS
An excellent catalogue of children's books, The Red House covers both educational matter, from learning to read to history, and practical activity books as well as fiction.

The aim is to encourage children to read and to make it fun. Some audio cassettes and videos are included and foreign language courses, particularly French, are available. Well laid out, with different sections for each age group and reading ability, it is easy to find one's way about.

The books are a mixture of hardback and paperback and good savings are to be made. A set of four pop-up dinosaur books for instance sells for £9.95 against a RRP of £15.96.

Catalogue: *A4, Catalogue, 20 pages, Colour, Free* Postal charges: *10% Delivery: Royal Mail* Methods of Payment: *Cheque, Postal Order, Visa, Access / Mastercard*

THE SOFTBACK PREVIEW
PO Box 415
Uxbridge
Middlesex
UB11 1DZ

Telephone:
081 606 3111

BOOK CLUB
The Softback Preview is different from other book clubs in that you are under no obligation to buy from them. Every four weeks you'll receive a copy of their magazine to see whether there's anything new you fancy. As an introductory offer, you're entitled to any three books from their leaflet for only £1.00 each.

The books are special softback editions of hardbacks. You can choose from between *1066 and All That*, originally £14.99; *The Dictionary of Quotations*, originally £17.99; and *Wild Swans* also originally £17.50. Fiction includes Iain Banks' *The Crow Road*, originally priced at £15.99.

Catalogue: *Monthly, A6, Brochure, 2, Colour, Free* Postal charges: *Varies with item* Delivery: *Royal Mail* Methods of Payment: *Cheque, Postal Order*

THE SOIL ASSOCIATION LTD
86 Colston Street
Bristol
BS1 5BB

Telephone:
0272 290661
Fax:
0272 252504

BOOKS
Founded in 1946, The Soil Association is a registered membership charity founded to promote organic food production as both safe and sustainable. It runs a mail order book service specialising in titles on organic growing, permacultures and health and nutrition as well as books on environmental and developing world issues. The catalogue is for anyone interested in healthy food and a better environment.

All profits go to supporting the work of the charity and titles include *The Soil Association Handbook* for

Books

£5.99, the *New Organic Grower* for £10.95, the *Good Health on a Polluted Planet* for £6.99 and *Permaculture in a Nutshell*, for £4.50.

Catalogue: *Quarterly, A4, Catalogue, 8 pages, B/W, Free* Postal charges: *Varies with item* Delivery: *Royal Mail, Parcelforce* Methods of Payment: *Cheque, Postal Order, Visa, Access / Mastercard*

THE TALKING BOOK CLUB
P.O. Box 993
London
SW6 4UW

Telephone:
071 731 6262
Fax:
071 736 0162

BOOKS ON CASSETTE
A comprehensive range of all types of books transferred on to tape. Ideal for blind people and for those who like to read but haven't the time! Maximum hire is two books of up to eight cassettes each. Annual subscription of £18.50 for adults and £12.50 for the Junior Talking Book Club. Gift membership also available.

Catalogue: *A4, Leaflets, B/W, Free* Postal charges: *Varies with item* Delivery: *Royal Mail* Methods of Payment: *Cheque, Postal Order, Visa, Access / Mastercard*

WATERSTONE'S
Mail Order Division
4 Milsom Street
Bath
Avon
BA1 1DA

Telephone:
0225 448595
Fax:
0225 444732

BOOKS
From the high street shops of the same name comes this catalogue selecting the 'best' of recently published books. It is split into various sections, such as travel, art and biography with each book receiving a mini-review. These are interspersed with interviews with some of the writers.

There is also an introduction to the Waterstone's 'Signed First Editions Club', which as its name implies enables you to buy signed books at normal retail prices but which in time could prove to be valuable investments. This club issues three catalogues a year, with up to 150 books to choose from.

Catalogue: *A4, Catalogue, 44 pages, Colour, Free* Postal charges: *Varies with item* Delivery: *Royal Mail* Methods of Payment: *Cheque, Postal Order, Visa, Access / Mastercard, American Express*

WILLEN LTD
Three Crowns Yard
High Street
Market Harborough
Leics
LE16 7AF

Telephone:
0858 410233
Fax:
0858 410233

HAIR AND BEAUTY BOOKS
Willen's catalogue provides a comprehensive listing of books on hair and beauty. It covers everything from massage and reflexology through colour, cosmetics and make-up to men's hair and sports science.

There are titles for the lay-reader as well as the expert. For example, *Aromatherapy for Everyone* is a useful introduction to the subject for £6.99, as is *Basic Hairdressing* for £8.99. For the more advanced there is *Science for the Beauty Therapist* for £11.99, a

Books

Manual of Structural Kinesiology for £15.95 and *Standard Textbook of Professional Barber Styling – Workbook* for £10.95.

Catalogue: *Annually, A5, Catalogue, 32 pages, B/W, Free* Postal charges: *Varies with item* Delivery: *Royal Mail* Methods of Payment: *Cheque, Visa, Access / Mastercard*

WORLD OF LEARNING
Springfield House
West Street
Bedminster
Bristol
BS3 3NX

Telephone:
0272 639159

LANGUAGE COURSES
Whether you want to learn a language for a holiday or a business trip then PILL – Programmed Instruction Language Learning – is for you. The complete PILL package comprises a set of easy-listening cassette tapes, programmed instruction books, fast word-finder and a letter-writing guide. The method claims to be faster than conventional lessons.

The languages covered are French, German, Spanish, Italian and Russian. You are taught from day one to speak with the correct accent, to understand and be able to speak at a normal conversational speed, and to build up a vocabulary of up to 800 words. World of Learning recommend spending just 45 minutes of your day for listening and learning. The whole package costs £123.50.

Catalogue: *Loose leaf, Catalogue, Colour, Free* Postal charges: *Varies with item* Delivery: *Royal Mail* Methods of Payment: *Cheque, Visa, Access / Mastercard, American Express, Diners Club, Postal Order*

ANIMAL HEALTH TRUST
PO Box 5
Newmarket
Suffolk
CB8 7DW

Telephone:
0638 661111
Fax:
0638 665789

CHRISTMAS CARDS AND GIFTS
The Animal Health Trust produces a one-sheet leaflet featuring on one side its range of Christmas cards. These come in just four designs – all with animals of course – and cost £4.00 for a pack of ten.

The other side has colour photographs of promotional clothes. These include T-shirts for £6.50, rugby sweatshirts at £24.50 and silk ties for £25.00. All are printed with the trust's logo and of course proceeds go towards their work. There are also some other items such as mugs, teddy bears, yo-yos and bottle stoppers.

Catalogue: *A4, Leaflet, 2 pages, Colour, Free* Postal charges: £2.00 Delivery: *Royal Mail* Methods of Payment: *Cheque, Postal Order, Access / Mastercard, Visa, American Express*

Charities

BARNARDO PUBLICATIONS LTD
PO box 20
Tanners Lane
Barkingside
Ilford
Essex
IG6 1QQ

Telephone:
0268 520224
Fax:
0268 520230

MISCELLANEOUS GIFTS
Barnardo's small colour catalogue features a wealth of gift ideas, for instance boxed stationery at £21.99, and useful practical knick-knacks. All profits made from catalogue sales go directly to Barnardo's.

The wide range of garden items includes pottery gnomes for £8.99 and a twin-bin compost maker for £42.99. For the kitchen there's re-usable baking foil at £4.45 and floral wooden trays for £7.99.

There's also a selection of furniture, including a folding bed with tubular steel legs and frame (£72.00); a telephone table, with a mahogany veneer tabletop finish (£19.99); and a sewing box, available in many different colours (£22.50).

Catalogue: *A5, Catalogue, 36 pages, Colour, Free* Postal charges: *Varies with item* Delivery: *Royal Mail* Methods of Payment: *Visa, Access / Mastercard Cheque, Postal Order*

BRITISH RED CROSS
Britcross Ltd.
PO box 28
Burton upon Trent
Staffs
DE14 3LQ

Telephone:
0283 510 111
071 235 5454
Fax:
071 245 6315

CARDS, STATIONERY, GENERAL GIFTS
The British Red Cross (registered charity no. 220949) uses its mail order catalogue to raise some of the vital income required to provide its wide-ranging services at home and abroad. The Christmas catalogue contains not only a range of unique cards and wrapping paper but also a wide variety of gifts for all the family.

There is also a collection of products designed to make life safe and easy, for example first aid kits, page magnifiers and bottle openers. A spring catalogue is also available. Christmas cards start from £2.15 for ten, first aid kits are £14.99, slim line calendars £1.85 and personalised address labels £5.99 for 100.

Catalogue: *Bi-annually, Catalogue, 36 pages, Colour, Free* Postal charges: *Varies with item* Delivery: *Parcelforce* Methods of Payment: *Cheque, Postal Order, Visa, Access / Mastercard*

CANCER RESEARCH CAMPAIGN
6–10 Cambridge Terrace
Regent's Park
London
NW1 4JL

Telephone:
0283 510 111
Fax:
071 487 4310

GIFTS AND CARDS
Each purchase from this catalogue makes a direct contribution to the Campaign's work. There is a diverse range of gifts including a 'Floating Whale Plug' at £2.99 and a 'Fish Design Waistcoat' at £15.99. Colourful bargains include a bright Noah's Ark rug from India – 38" by 24" – at £12.99 and an attractive Rose Chintz table cloth from £8.99. For the more practically minded, there's a sturdy 40-piece tool kit in its own carrying case for £22.99.

The easy tick-off order form makes sure you waste

Charities

no time choosing between those gift card sets or the wealth of personalised pens, pencils and even luggage straps.

Catalogue: *7 x 8, Catalogue, 36 pages, Colour, Free* Postal charges: *£3.35* Delivery: *Royal Mail* Methods of Payment: *Cheque, Visa, Access / Mastercard*

ENVIRONMENTAL INVESTIGATION AGENCY LTD
2 Pear Tree Court
London
EC1R ODS

Telephone:
071 4907040
Fax:
071 4900436

GIFTS

The Environmental Investigation Agency is a small organisation with limited resources, but they have made a very firm impression on the world of animal protection and conservation.

Their catalogue includes a great range of gifts, all of which have some loose or explicit connection with the animal world. You might want a useful duffel bag, in black canvas, for £9.99. There are also stunning picture postcards of wildlife, all printed on 100% recycled card, for £2.95. Less obviously animal is their Celtic trinket box, costing £13.95.

Catalogue: *Annually, A4, Brochure, 8, Colour, Free* Postal charges: *Varies with item* Delivery: *Royal Mail* Methods of Payment: *Cheque, Postal Order, Visa, Access / Mastercard*

HELP THE AGED
Helpage Ltd.
PO box 28
London
N18 3HG

Telephone:
081 803 6861
Fax:
071 895 1407

GIFTS AND CARDS

Help the Aged's catalogue is quite eclectic in its choice of goods and should appeal to most people. There are the usual cards and gifts but also useful devices specifically designed for older people. For example, the pill organiser is a neat box which ensures you take the right pill at the right time. There's an ingenious fold-away shopping bag which has wheels in the base and a thermal pad which can be put on any seat to take away the chill.

There is also a 'handyman corner' with a a selection of tools, devices to help one get in and out of the bath and a good range of gardening equipment. Overall, a nicely produced, interesting catalogue.

Catalogue: *A4, Catalogue, 40 pages, Colour, Free* Postal charges: *Varies with item* Delivery: *Royal Mail* Methods of Payment: *Cheque, Visa, Access / Mastercard*

Charities

NATIONAL CHILDBIRTH TRUST
Burnfield Avenue
Glasgow
G46 7TL

Telephone:
0416 335552
Fax:
0416 6335677

GIFTS
Proceeds from their catalogue help the National Childbirth Trust provide antenatal and postnatal support, help with breast feeding and education for the parents of tomorrow.

Winnie-the-Pooh would brighten up any bathroom or kitchen table and he appears on a range of hardy melanine items such as a training mug for £2.75 and a bowl at £2.95. There's also a toothmug with a special handle to hold a toothbrush, for £3.95.

Stationery, board books, nursery friezes and badges are for sale too, including a fun birth announcement card, either pink or blue, at £2.50 for ten.

Catalogue: *A5, Brochure, 8, Colour, Free* Postal charges: *Varies with item* Delivery: *Royal Mail* Methods of Payment: *Cheque, Postal Order, Visa, Access / Mastercard*

NATIONAL MARITIME MUSEUM
Greenwich
London
SE10 9NF

Telephone:
081 858 4422

MARITIME ITEMS
A vast array of maritime titles from the undoubted experts in the field – the National Maritime Museum. The range has something for everyone in love with the sea. There are books, music and models in this catalogue which can bring the sea to life for even the most committed land-lubber.

The collection contains books detailing the story of the *Titanic* from £2.50 to £30.00 and many explaining the technical wizardry involved in keeping today's Navy ship-shape, as well as a set of books telling you everything you could ever want to know about knots from £5.00 to £35.00.

Catalogue: *A5, Leaflets, 18 pages, Colour, Free* Postal charges: *Varies with item* Delivery: *Royal Mail* Methods of Payment: *Cheque, Postal Order, Visa, Access / Mastercard*

NAVS
261 Goldhawk Road
London
W12 9PE

GIFTS TO SUPPORT ANIMAL RIGHTS
The National Anti-Vivisection Catalogue provides a range of clothing and gifts for those who can't bear animal suffering.

There's a selection of gift cards featuring artistic images of animals such as badgers and turtles. Each card costs 85p. All cards and envelopes are, as you'd expect, printed on quality recycled paper.

T-shirts with a variety of slogans and rather more disturbing images are available from £5.00. There are also baseball caps (£3.00) and sports bags (£5.00). Jewellery, all of an ethnic flavour, starts at

45

Charities

NEW YEAR SHOPPER
Freepost, P.O. Box 38
Burton -on-Trent
Staffs.
DE14 1BR

Telephone:
0283 510111`

NOTTING HILL HOUSING TRUST
26 Paddenswick Road
London
W6 0UB

Telephone:
081 741 1570
Fax:
081 748 6258

OXFAM TRADING
Murdock Road
Bicester
Oxon
OX6 7RF

Telephone:
0869 245011
Fax:
0869 247987

£6.00 for a skeleton fish pendant and rises to a 'Female Thai Dancer Brooch' at £10.00.

Catalogue: *Bi-annually, A5, Brochure, 16, Colour, Free* Postal charges: *Varies with item* Delivery: *Royal Mail* Methods of Payment: *Cheque, Postal Order, Visa, Access / Mastercard*

GENERAL & HOUSEHOLD GOODS

A comprehensive range of household and general goods sold in aid of Marie Curie Cancer Care. All members of the family catered for. Items range from tableware sets to giftwrap. Prices from 1.99.

Catalogue: *A5, Catalogue, 36 pages, Colour, Free* Postal charges: *Varies with item* Delivery: *Royal Mail* Methods of Payment: *Cheque, Postal Order, Visa, Access / Mastercard*

GIFTS

The Notting Hill Housing Trust is fronted by no less a figure than the intrepid reporter Jon Snow. Designed to help the homeless, the trust's catalogue includes a fine range of gift ideas, quite a cut above the usual fare.

You can buy a Provençal-style print cotton bedspread (225 cm × 250 cm) for £29.99. Available in red tulip on navy, yellow tulip on red and yellow tulip on green, you should be able to find the right combination for your bedroom. There's also a floral appliqué quilted double bedspread for £99.99. A neo-Gothic three-flame iron candlestick is £9.99 and a linen and lace tablecloth £14.99.

Catalogue: *Bi-annually, A5, Catalogue, 16, Colour, Free* Postal charges: *£2.95* Delivery: *Royal Mail* Methods of Payment: *Cheque, Postal Order, Visa, Access / Mastercard*

GIFTS

The Oxfam catalogue offers gifts with an ethnic emphasis. This reflects links with Oxfam's overseas partners, who receive not only a fair price for their produce but help and advice to support skilled artisans of the type whose ware is displayed here.

Typical of the products is Ikat fabric, made by women working for the Swallows cooperative in Madras, India. The cloth takes a long time to prepare; before it's woven, each colour has to be dyed separately. You can buy an Ikat shirt from Oxfam for just £19.95. Suitable for both sexes, it fits up to 44" chest.

Catalogue: *Bi-annually, A5, Catalogue, 48, Colour, Free* Postal charges: *£3.25* Delivery: *Royal Mail* Methods of Payment: *Cheque, Postal Order, Visa, Access / Mastercard*

Charities

RSPB
The Lodge
Sandy
Beds
SG19 2DL

Telephone:
0767 680551
Fax:
0767 692365

GIFTS
The Royal Society for the Protection of Birds is the largest voluntary wildlife conservation organisation in Europe. One way in which they raise vital funds to further their work is to produce two catalogues a year. The autumn/winter catalogue includes Christmas cards, calendars and gifts, in addition to the product range found in the spring/summer catalogue: clothes, household items, personal stationery and of course, birdcare products. Many of the quality goods are exclusive to the RSPB.

Examples of prices include: woodcrete nesting box, £19.99; barn owl sweatshirt, £16.95; hanging feeder, £2.95; friends and neighbours calendar, £2.50; and personalised writing set, £14.99.

Catalogue: *Bi-annually, A4, Catalogue, 56 pages, Colour, Free* Postal charges: *Varies with item* Delivery: *Parcelforce* Methods of Payment: *Cheque, Postal Order, Visa, Access / Mastercard*

SAVE THE CHILDREN
S.C.F. Trading Dept.
P.O. Box 40
Burton upon Trent
Staffs.
DE14 3LQ

Telephone:
0283 510111

CHRISTMAS GIFTS, CARDS AND FAYRE
This catalogue has been released to help raise money for the Save The Children Fund. Any profit made goes towards helping all kinds of children in over fifty countries, who are either ill, homeless, orphaned or uneducated.

The catalogue offers a wide range of Christmas goods: for example, Christmas cards (£2.55 for ten), crackers (£19.99 for six), stationery kits, toys, kitchenware and jewellery (£2.99 for a pair of earrings). If you place an order costing £65.00 or over then postage and packaging is free.

Catalogue: *Annually, A4, Catalogue, 36 pages, Colour, Free* Postal charges: *Varies with item* Delivery: *Royal Mail* Methods of Payment: *Cheque, Postal Order, Visa, Access / Mastercard, American Express*

THE SPASTICS SOCIETY
12 Park Crescent
London
W1N 4EQ

Telephone:
071 636 5020
Fax:
071 436 2601

GIFTS
The Spastics Society catalogue contains a variety of gift suggestions, ranging from a 52-piece Staffordshire tableware set at only £29.99 to a 'Floribunda' T-Shirt.

The tableware set includes place settings for 4 people, all in 'Valencia' design – a floral pattern. All of the crockery is microwave, dishwasher and detergent safe. The stainless steel cutlery and accessories are designed in a complementary pattern.

The 'Floribunda' pattern T-shirt, in 100% combed

Charities

cotton, costs £7.99. You can also buy a 'Floribunda' house suit for £27.95.

Catalogue: *Bi-annually, A3, Catalogue, 36, Colour, Free* Postal charges: *Varies with item* Delivery: *Royal Mail* Methods of Payment: *Cheque, Postal Order, Visa, Access / Mastercard*

THE STROKE ASSOCIATION
CHSA Cards Ltd
20 Halcyon Court
St Margarets Way
Huntingdon
Cambs

Telephone:
0480 413280

GIFTS AND CARDS

The Stroke Association deals with research, advice, prevention, welfare and rehabilitation for stroke sufferers and their families. For over 21 years the charity has produced card and gift catalogues, and 100% of the profit is covenanted towards their work.

The catalogue is full to the brim with Christmas cards, both traditional and modern, complemented by novelty gifts, as well as good ideas for a healthier lifestyle and useful gadgets to use around the home.

Christmas cards start at £1.99 and go up to £2.75 for ten; wrapping paper at 99p; lap trays are £9.99; three ladies' handkerchiefs cost £2.99.

Catalogue: *Annually, A5, Catalogue, 16 pages, Colour, Free* Postal charges: *Varies with item* Delivery: *Parcelforce, Royal Mail* Methods of Payment: *Cheque, Postal Order, Visa, Access / Mastercard*

WILD THINGS
7 Upper Goat Lane
Norwich
NR20 SJQ

Telephone:
0603 765595
Fax:
0603 768212

CLOTHING AND GIFTS

Wild Things produces merchandise for the anti-fur organisation out of respect for animals, to whom all profits are donated. The range includes colourful T-shirts, jewellery and non-leather products.

Catalogue: *Annually, A5, Catalogue, 16 pages, Free* Postal charges: *Varies with item* Delivery: *Royal Mail* Methods of Payment: *Cheque, Postal Order, Visa, Access / Mastercard*

ACCUTEC AND CRAZY CLOCKS
Unit C3
Hays Bridge Bus Centre
S. Godstone
RH9 8JW

Telephone:
0342 842129

CLOCKS

Crazy Clocks have been manufacturing clocks in the UK for over fifteen years, alongside distribution of some of the best clocks from overseas. All clocks are manufactured to the highest standards and range from reproduction pine clocks to humorous pendulum and alarm clocks and commercial clocks. The 'Octagonal Drop Dial' clock costs £125.00; the 'Backward Clock': £19.95; 'Black Cat Washing Clock': £21.95; 'Football Clock' £17.95.

Catalogue: *A5, Catalogue, 8 pages, Colour and B/W, Free* Postal charges: *Varies with item* Delivery: *Royal Mail* Methods of Payment: *Cheque, Postal Order, Access / Mastercard, Visa*

Clothes

ABORIGINALIA
3 Cotswold Court
The Green
Broadway
Worcs
WR12 7AA

Telephone:
0386 853770
Fax:
0386 40202

ETHNIC CLOTHES AND ARTEFACTS
Aboriginalia's hand-crafted products enable you to 'experience the traditional myths of ancient Australia'. There's a good range of products, from the inevitable boomerangs, (£3.65 for a 6" model) up to larger pieces such as a 3'6" painted didgeridoo. This will set back aspiring Rolf Harrises some £115.00 and an extra £2.95 for a cassette on how to play it.

There are a variety of wooden carvings from £15.00 along with clay pottery emus, koalas and kangeroos, each at £22.25. More obscure is the woomera, a spear throwing aid or fighting stick costing £30.00 – though quite what one does with this is not clear.

Catalogue: *A4, Leaflets, 6 pages, B/W, Free* Postal charges: *Varies with item* Delivery: *Royal Mail* Methods of Payment: *Cheque, Postal Order*

ALEXANDRA WORKWEAR
Brittannia Road
Patchway
Bristol
BS12 5TP

Telephone:
0272 690808
Fax:
0272 799442

WORK CLOTHES
This company supplies workwear for industry, commerce and the public sector. Its comprehensive catalogue lists ranges for the medical profession, particularly nurses' uniforms and doctors' coats, industrial overalls, clothes for hotel cleaning, catering and waiting staff. They even have a range of clothing called 'careerwear', which consists of City type suits for men and women in 100% polyester fabric.

There are also clothes for severe weather conditions and outdoor work. Most items can be emblazoned with a name or logo by Alexandra's bespoke emblem service.

Catalogue: *A5, Catalogue, 148 pages, Colour, Free* Postal charges: *Free* Delivery: *Royal Mail* Methods of Payment: *Cheque, Postal Order*

ANN SUMMERS LTD
GSP Ltd
2 Godstone Road,
Whyteleafe
Surrey
CR3 OEA

Telephone:
081 763 0122

LINGERIE AND "ADULT" GOODS
Everything a woman needs to dress and undress in the sexiest way! This colourful catalogue of exotic underwear and swimwear embodies the essence of conventional romance and femininity.

But it isn't just restricted to those with model-like looks. The 'Twice as Sexy' range emphasises the appeal of the larger figure, while the 'Doing the Bump' collection of nightshirts caters for mums to be.

The erotica section is chock-full of rubber, PVC and leather-wear, along with numerous fun gadgets to add new dimensions to your love-life. The

Clothes

catalogue also includes a range of 'adult' gift ideas, from videos to board games that are guaranteed to give your sex life a lift – if it should need it.

Catalogue: *A4, Catalogue, 32 pages, Colour, Free* Postal charges: *Varies with item* Delivery: *Royal Mail* Methods of Payment: *Diners Club, American Express, Access / Mastercard, Visa Cheque, Postal Order*

ANNABEL LEE
P.O. Box 97
Banbury
OX16 7ER

Telephone:
0280 850052

BLOUSES AND SHIRTS

This small catalogue features an equally small range of women's clothes. However, they are all high quality, attractive designs which have clearly been chosen with some care. There are 8 different styles, which include floral blouses in long and short-sleeved versions.

All are made with care in pure 100% cotton and generously cut in three sizes: 10–12, 12–14, 14–16. Prices are between £33.00 and £40.00.

Catalogue: *Quarterly, A5, Brochure, 8, Colour, Free* Postal charges: *£1.50* Delivery: *Royal Mail* Methods of Payment: *Cheque, Visa, Access / Mastercard*

ANNE THOMAS FABRICS
Mainhill
Bridgend
Duns
Berwickshire
TD11 3ES

Telephone:
0361 83030
Fax:
0361 83030

DRESS FABRICS

Anne Thomas has been selling high-quality, classic natural fibre (wool, silk, cotton, linen) and couture fabrics since 1979. There are four catalogues per year showing actual samples (5 × 5cm) of coordinated fabrics.

There are at least 50 samples per catalogue, making some 200 plus per year. The fact that they export to 22 countries around the world is testament both to the quality of the products – which is excellent – and their highly competitive prices. A Swiss sea-island cotton costs £17.50 per metre, handkerchief cloth £14.95, silk/wool tweed £9.95 and wool flannel £18.50.

Catalogue: *Quarterly, A4, Catalogue, 5 pages, B/W, £16.00* Postal charges: *Varies with item* Delivery: *Royal Mail, Parcelforce Datapost* Methods of Payment: *Cheque, Postal Order, Access / Mastercard, Visa*

BEANS OF BRADFORD
203 Westgate
Bradford
BD1 3AD

Telephone:
0274 725177
Fax:
0274 390872

CLOTHES

New to mail-ordering, Beans is a Bradford store specialising in fashionable clothes, shoes and bed-linen. Their thin colour brochure offers a handful of classic garments, such as a ladies' luxury Scottish cashmere cardigan (£99.00), specially designed for Beans.

The emphasis is on beautiful tailoring and high-quality materials. Also on offer are a few luxury gift

Clothes

items, such as a lambswool scarf at £9.00–£23.00 for three – or a travelling rug, available in a variety of tartans for £49.00.

Catalogue: *A4, Catalogue, 8 pages, Colour, Free* Postal charges: *£2.50* Delivery: *Royal Mail* Methods of Payment: *Cheque, Postal Order, Visa, Access / Mastercard*

BIRKETT & PHILLIPS
1 Mill Buildings
Lea Bridge
Matlock
Derbyshire
DE4 5AG

Telephone:
0629 534331
Fax:
0629 534331

UNDERWEAR, OUTERWEAR AND NIGHT WEAR IN NATURAL FABRICS

Birkett & Phillips have been trading in natural fabrics by mail order since 1920. They carry many reputable lines including John Smedleys underwear and outerwear as featured on 'The Clothes Show', Brettles night wear, Chilprufe underwear plus their own brand of Interlock Cotton Cosijamas in eight beautiful colours (price £24.00).

Their knitwear and traditional underwear is suitable for customers from 15–70 plus. John Smedley Sea Island cotton underwear ranges from £13.00 to £30.00 and John Smedley woollen outerwear from £47.50 to £114.00. A John Smedley Sea Island cotton singlet costs £38.75 and a Brettles bed jacket £22.50.

Catalogue: *A5, Catalogue, 32 pages, Colour, Free* Postal charges: *Varies with item* Delivery: *Royal Mail, Parcelforce* Methods of Payment: *Cheque, Postal Order, COD, Visa, Access / Mastercard*

BLOOMING MARVELLOUS
PO Box 12F
Chessington
Surrey
KT9 2LS

Telephone:
081 391 4822
Fax:
081 397 0493

MATERNITY AND CHILDRENSWEAR

Blooming Marvellous is the largest specialist mail order maternity wear company in the UK. Judy and Vivienne started the business 11 years ago when they were frustrated at the lack of choice in the shops. Now they have over 250 exclusive styles including dresses (£32.99), leggings (£16.99), shirts (£24.99) and swimwear (£19.99).

Their mix and match range of childrenswear is designed to make your child stand out in a crowd. Exclusively designed in fun prints for ages 0-11 years, many of the fabrics co-ordinate with the maternity range. Dresses are £14.99, sweatshirts £12.99, trackpants £10.99 and leggings £8.99, all of which seem excellent prices for this quality of merchandise.

Catalogue: *Bi-annually, A4, Catalogue, 32 pages, Colour, Free* Postal charges: *Varies with item* Delivery: *Parcelforce* Methods of Payment: *Cheque, Access / Mastercard, Visa, Postal Order*

Clothes

BODY AWARE
Erskine House
Union Street
Trowbridge
Wilts
BA14 8RY

Telephone:
0225 774164
Fax:
0225 774452

MEN'S UNDERWEAR, SWIMWEAR
The Body Aware range of underwear for men is the most up-to-date catalogue of its type available in the UK. It features the sort of underwear and swimwear styles that you wish you could find in the shops but never can. The range includes silk briefs and thongs as well as items made from lycra, lace, velvet and PVC. All garments are exclusively designed and manufactured in the UK and suitable for use at home, in clubs or on the beach.

A pure silk thong retails at £10.95, a velvet brief for £8.50, a lace pouch at £4.95 and a swim thong £12.95.

Catalogue: Bi-monthly, A5, Catalogue, 24 pages, Colour, Free
Postal charges: Varies with item *Delivery:* Royal Mail *Methods of Payment:* Cheque, Postal Order, Visa, Access / Mastercard

BUBBLES CHILDREN'S CLOTHES
38 Holcombe Lane
Bathampton
Bath
BA2 6UL

Telephone:
0225 466835

CHILDREN'S CLOTHES
The leaflet illustrates Bubbles' summer collection of exclusive children's clothes for 0–8 year olds, featuring unique appliqué designs.

All Bubbles' clothes are made in England from 100% machine washable cotton to a high standard and are suitable for both girls and boys.

Prices for Navy Boat Dungarees start from £19.95, for a Tartan Duck Pinafore from £28.95 and for Clown Shorts from £13.95.

Catalogue: Quarterly, A5, Leaflets, 4 pages, Colour and B/W, Free
Postal charges: Varies with item *Delivery:* Royal Mail *Methods of Payment:* Cheque, Postal Order

BURBERRYS
MBNA International Bank Ltd
P.O. Box 1003
Chester Business Park
Wrexham Road
Chester
CH4 9YZ

Telephone:
071 930 7803
Fax:
071 839 2418

AN EXTENSIVE RANGE OF CLOTHES, ACCESSORIES, FOOD AND GIFTS
Burberry's of London provide a wide range of tailored clothes for both adults and children. All the merchandise in the catalogue is available from their stores in the United Kingdom or direct through mail order. Other goods on offer are toys (£25.00 for a teddy bear), knitwear, raincoats (£405.00), umbrellas, luggage, fragrances and watches (£325.00). There are also food hampers on offer containing jams, whisky, biscuits, chocolate etc.

If you order clothes, the Burberry's visiting tailor service will see that you have them made to measure and cut to your size and style. All gifts are gift wrapped on request with no extra charge and you can even have your raincoat monogrammed with your own initials.

Clothes

Catalogue: *A4, Catalogue, 20 pages, Colour and B/W, Free* Postal charges: *Varies with item* Delivery: *Royal Mail* Methods of Payment: *Cheque, Access / Mastercard, Visa*

CALIFORNIAN KIDS
36 Wadham Ave
London
E17 4HT

Telephone:
081 523 1944

CHILDREN'S CLOTHES

Californian Kids sell American designer label clothes for ages 0–6 years. Most of it is new, although they do stock a number of second hand items. In particular, they specialise in Oshkosh, with a basic line of dungarees from £18.50. Most of the stock is unavailable in the UK, and is sold at a heavy discount.

Weebok sweat-tops with a zip up hood cost £20.00; Weebok sweat-pants in 100% cotton cost £14.50 and a Weebok windsuit costs £32.00. They also stock items by Levi's, Esprit and Carter's.

Catalogue: *A4, Leaflets, 3, B/W, Free* Postal charges: *Varies with item* Delivery: *Royal Mail* Methods of Payment: *Cheque, Postal Order*

CARADOC
Mor Brook Barn
Morville
Near Bridgnorth
Shropshire
WV16 5NR

Telephone:
074 631 275

COUNTRY CLOTHES

Caradoc produces a range of all-year activity clothing and traditional country clothing for both men and women. Many of the garments have been developed to the company's own specifications and are not available elsewhere.

Caradoc's range of 'Field Classics' includes shooting jackets in Derby Tweed from £103.00 with matching waistcoats from £32.00. Also in this range are shirts, sweaters, breeches and trousers.

A selection of coats are supplied by traditional makers Grenfell, whose Grenotex range are completely weatherproof. Lighter wear is offered in the form of cotton casuals and a range of Fliweight separates. Polyester/cotton shorts start at £27.00 and shirts at £24.00.

Catalogue: *A1 folded, Catalogue, 42 pages, Colour, Free* Postal charges: *Varies with item* Delivery: *Royal Mail* Methods of Payment: *Cheque, Postal Order, Visa, Access / Mastercard*

Clothes

CASHMERE BY HERITAGE
8 Hirst Lane
Mirfield
West Yorkshire
WF14 8NS

Telephone:
0924 490044
Fax:
0924 492637

CASHMERE PRODUCTS
Cashmere by Heritage is a unique concept whereby the company purchases the finest Chinese raw material to produce a superb garment at the keenest price. All the knitwear and accessories are expertly manufactured in Scotland and renowned for their quality. At any one time there is over £250,000 worth of stock to choose from.

Ladies' two-ply 100% cashmere cardigan, DNA crew neck pullover at £99.00; men's two-ply 100% cashmere cardigans, crew and V-neck pullovers at £99.00. Any two of these for £175.00. Also, ladies' cashmere stole, 190 × 70 cms – £95.00; scarves, 140 × 30cms – £22.50.

Catalogue: *Annually, A5, Brochure, 10 pages, Colour, Free* Postal charges: *Varies with item* Delivery: *Royal Mail* Methods of Payment: *Cheque, Postal Order, Visa, Access / Mastercard*

CATALOG CONNECTION LTD
Nightingale House
7 Fulham High Street
London
SW6 3JH

Telephone:
071 371 7004
Fax:
071 371 0107

WE SELL CLOTHING CATALOGUES!
Catalog Connection is the 'one stop shop' for 35 different catalogues supplied by companies who produce and supply 'sexy' clothing. This ranges from basic lingerie through leather, rubber and PVC under and outerwear. Most of these catalogues are very stylish and include clothes to match. All feature clothing of a 'fantasy' nature but nothing shocking or adult.

Catalogues range in price from £1.00 to £16.00. All are reviewed by an independent critic to indicate each company's best expertise and most important features. If you like this kind of thing Catalog Connection is an ideal, independent source.

Catalogue: *Quarterly, A5, Brochure, 4-20 pages, B/W, Free* Postal charges: *Varies with item* Delivery: *Royal Mail* Methods of Payment: *Cheque, Postal Order, Visa, Access / Mastercard*

CAVENAGH SHIRTS
659 Fulham Road
London
SW6 5PY

Telephone:
071 610 2959
Fax:
071 610 2119

MEN'S AND LADIES' QUALITY SHIRTS, TIES, ACCESSORIES
Based in London, Cavenagh has been selling top quality, cotton Oxford classic shirts both through its retail outlet in Fulham and by mail order for the last two years. The shirts, for men and women, are constructed from two-fold poplin and made to top specifications in the UK. Men's shirts include removable collar bones, split yokes, French cuffs and a generous cut in body and length.

A range of accessories complements the shirts and

Clothes

includes pure silk ties, cotton boxer shorts, solid silver cuff-links and Italian leather belts.

Men's Oxford shirts are £25.00, poplin shirts start from the same price while women's versions are £25.00 and silk ties £12.50.

Catalogue: *Annually, A4, Brochure, 16 pages, Colour, Free* Postal charges: *Varies with item* Delivery: *Royal Mail* Methods of Payment: *Cheque, Postal Order, COD, Visa, Access / Mastercard, American Express*

CHARLES TYRWHITT SHIRTS
Freepost
Saddlers Court
Camberley
Surrey
GU17 7BR

Telephone:
0252 860940
Fax:
0252 861677

SHIRTS
This small company manufactures quality cotton poplin shirts for men and women. There are three collar styles to choose from – standard, cut-away and button-down. As well as shirts, there is also a selection of cufflinks, ties, boxer shorts, waistcoats and polo shirts. An interesting feature is that all are modelled by well-known people, for example Jilly Cooper, the writer, and Martin Bell, Olympic and World Cup downhill skier. It's a nice touch in what is a very classy catalogue.

Shirts sell for £37.50 and there is a sleeve alteration service for £5.00.

Catalogue: *A4, Catalogue, 32 pages, Colour, Free* Postal charges: £2.95 Delivery: *Royal Mail* Methods of Payment: *Cheque, Postal Order, Visa, Access / Mastercard, American Express, Diners Club*

CHARMIAN
PO Box 67
Bracknell
Berkshire
RG12 1GS

Telephone:
0344 55807
Fax:
0344 868537

CLOTHES
Collection of designer lingerie available by post. A family company making lingerie and nightwear in sizes 8–26 with prices from £45.00 to over £400.00 Items can be made to measure if required. Lingerie can be ordered in polysatin, or silk if preferred.

Catalogue: *A4, Brochure, Colour, Free* Postal charges: *Varies with item* Delivery: *Royal Mail* Methods of Payment: *Cheque, Postal Order, Visa, Access / Mastercard*

CORDINGS BY MAIL
FREEPOST
10 Fleming Road
Newbury
RG13 1BR

Telephone:
0635 31353
0635 580202
Fax:
0635 41678

CLASSIC ENGLISH COUNTRY CLOTHES
Cordings sell traditional English country clothes such as pure wool blazers, corduroy jackets and lambswool sweaters. The products are high quality with a county look to them. Models sport shooting suits and spaniels to give the right atmosphere.

The range includes shawls for women, a good selection of Tattersall check shirts and English silk ties. There is also a selection of luggage, umbrellas, travelling rugs and cufflinks along with belts and some hats.

Clothes

The wool blazer costs £265.00, a pair of cotton drill trousers £52.00, shirts from £49.00 and a Lincoln riding mackintosh £255.00.

Catalogue: *A4, Catalogue, 20 pages, Colour, Free* Postal charges: *£5.00* Delivery: *Royal Mail Courier* Methods of Payment: *American Express, Diners Club, Access / Mastercard, Visa, Cheque*

COTTON MOON
Freepost
P O Box 280 (SE 8265)
London
SE3 8R

Telephone:
081 319 8315
Fax:
081 319 8345

CHILDREN'S CLOTHES

Cotton Moon produces 100% cotton comfort clothing for children ages twelve months to six years. Their philosophy is that children's clothing should be easy to wear, easy to care for, fun and good value.

They cut their clothes generously so they're very comfortable and add a great many pockets and just as many 'snaps' to make getting them on and off easier. Clothes include thick American T-shirts, hats, hairbands and socks from Tic Tac Toe. The range is fully colour coordinated and includes everyday wear as well as items for special occasions.

Hooded tops are £14.95, drawstring twill trousers the same, dresses £22.95 and sun hats £5.95.

Catalogue: *Bi-annually, 14cms × 29.5cms, Catalogue, 8 pages, Colour, Free* Postal charges: *Varies with item* Delivery: *Royal Mail* Methods of Payment: *Cheque, Postal Order, Visa, Access / Mastercard*

COTTON TRADERS DIRECT
P.O. Box 42
Altrincham
Cheshire
WA14 1SD

Telephone:
061 926 8185

LEISUREWEAR

Managed by ex-England international Rugby star Fran Cotton, Cotton Traders has made its name by supplying the British public with top quality leisurewear at good value prices. Every item is designed to give you more for less – finer fabrics, better features and longer life all at a good price.

The company is the official supplier to the England and Wales Rugby Union teams and has exclusive shirt designs for them both.

Each item comes with the Cotton Traders Lifetime Guarantee and a free Cotton Traders T-shirt is included with any order over £50. Prices range from £9.99 for a long sleeve piqué shirt to £49.99 for an outdoor jacket.

Catalogue: *Bi-annually, 192mm × 265mm, Catalogue, 24 pages, Colour, Free* Postal charges: *Varies with item* Delivery: *Royal Mail* Methods of Payment: *Cheque, Postal Order, Visa, Access / Mastercard*

Clothes

COTTONTAIL
Unit 2
Tweedvale Mill West
Walkerburn
Peeblesshire
EH43 6AN

Telephone:
0896 870 482
Fax:
0896 870 483

CHILDREN'S CLOTHES
Cottontail sell clothes for children from six months to twelve years old. These include dresses, pinafores and skirts. There are also trews, shorts, cardigans, rompers and bloomers as well as baby wear, swimwear, nightdresses and gowns.

For older children there are cricket sweaters, fishing smocks, waterproofs and Norwegian jerseys. The style is miniature adult and on the formal side – the models look like tiny yuppies ready to off to boarding school, but the clothes are clearly well made and good value.

Pinafores are £20.50 to £27.50, trews £16.25 to £23.95 and smocked dresses £42 to £44.50.

Catalogue: *Quarterly, Catalogue, 11, Free* Postal charges: *Varies with item* Delivery: *Royal Mail* Methods of Payment: *Cheque, Visa, Access / Mastercard*

CROFT MILL
Lowther lane
Foulridge
Colne
Lancashire
BB8 7NE

Telephone:
0282 869625
Fax:
0282 870038

CLOTHING, BEDDING AND FURNISHING FABRICS
Home of the best in clothing and bedding/furnishing fabrics from the world's leading producers, Croft Mill is situated in a very pretty part of N.E. Lancashire and is open to visitors all year.

For those who can't visit they have a catalogue which details all offers and is issued seven or eight times per year.

Catalogue: *7 issues per year, A4, Catalogue, 16 pages, Colour, Free* Postal charges: *Varies with item* Delivery: *Parcelforce Datapost* Methods of Payment: *Cheque, Postal Order, Visa, Access / Mastercard*

DAMART
Bowling Green Mills
Bingley Cross
W. Yorks
BD97 1AD

Telephone:
0274 510000

LADIESWEAR AND MENSWEAR
An excellent range of outerwear, lingerie, shoes and much more that is practical, comfortable and reasonably priced. Damart gives you a wide choice of sizes, lengths and fittings.

There are two ranges specifically designed for people outside the normal size range. 'Richer Design' focuses on styles that have been carefully rescaled for persons of 5'2" or a little less. 'Jean Jerrard Design' blends comfort and design in fashions for the fuller figure.

Hand embroidered sweaters in a variety of colours £19.99. 100% cotton casual skirts £17.99 (sizes 10–22).

Catalogue: *A4, Catalogue, 126 pages, Colour, Free* Postal charges: *£1.50* Delivery: *Royal Mail* Methods of Payment: *Cheque, Visa, Access / Mastercard*

Clothes

DAVID NIEPER
Saulgrove House
Somercotes
Derby
DE55 9BR

Telephone:
0773 836000
Fax:
0773 520246

LINGERIE, LEISUREWARE, BLOUSES

Nieper specialise in romantic, traditional lingerie for women as well as a small selection of slippers, blouses, tops and dresses.

The collection includes lacy camiknickers, slips, nightdresses and wraps. There's a good choice of bras from Triumph, Lejaby bras and other well-known manufacturers. The catalogue itself is nicely laid out and attractive to look at. For a small extra fee goods can be sent in a gift box.

Catalogue: *8"x8", Catalogue, 32 pages, Colour, Free* Postal charges: £2.50 Delivery: *Royal Mail* Methods of Payment: *Cheque, Visa, Access / Mastercard, American Express, Diners Club*

DELIA MARKETING LTD
24 Craven Park Road
London
NW10 4AB

Telephone:
081 965 8707
Fax:
081 965 4261

BRAS AND LINGERIE

Nothing to do with the cookery Delia of television fame, this Delia deals in fashionable women's underwear. A well designed catalogue makes choosing easy. There is a comprehensive range of bras from Triumph, Gossard and Berlei amongst others along with other lingerie items, such as pants by Sloggi, basques, sports bras, swimwear, corsets, petticoats, night attire and thermal wear.

Delia also stocks nursing bras and bras for those who have had mastectomies. There is a useful measuring guide and prices are reasonable, ranging from £10.00 to £20.99. Discounts are also available on amounts over £60.00.

Catalogue: *200mm x 255mm, Catalogue, 32 pages, Colour, Free* Postal charges: £2.00 Delivery: *Royal Mail* Methods of Payment: *Cheque, Postal Order, Visa, Access / Mastercard, American Express, Diners Club*

DENNY ANDREWS
Clock House
Coleshill
Nr Swindon
Wilts
SN6 7PT

Telephone:
0793 762476

CLOTHES

Denny Andrews supply comfortable clothes in traditional styles from India, Ireland and Wales. Materials include pure cotton, silk or wool which is either hand embroidered, block printed or hand woven. Their range covers waistcoats, full swirly skirts, kaftans, kimonos, nightgowns, kurtas in silk or handloomed cotton and trousers in various Indian shapes. They also sell hardwearing flannelette or wool shirts, overalls, aprons and a great deal else – get the catalogue and see!

Quilted cotton waistcoats are £25.00, cotton nightgowns £26.00, kaftans £35.00 and really good, large cotton twill aprons £7.95 or £22.50 for three.

Clothes

Catalogue: *Bi-annually, 147 × 210 mm, Catalogue, 32 pages, Colour and B/W, Free* Postal charges: *Varies with item* Delivery: *Royal Mail, Parcelforce* Methods of Payment: *Cheque, Postal Order, Visa, Access / Mastercard*

FASHION WORLD
P O Box 123
China Lane
Manchester
M1 8BH

Telephone:
061 236 5511

WOMEN'S CLOTHES AND SHOES

Fashion World are a fashion mail order company specialising in women's wear with some children's wear as well.

Everything is available in sizes 12 to 26 and they give a guarantee of a full refund or replacement for any item if you are not happy with your purchase.

The full range of clothing is covered from separates, dresses and swimwear to lingerie, footwear and nightwear.

Catalogue: *Bi-annually, A4, Catalogue, 186 pages, Colour, Free* Postal charges: *Free* Delivery: *Royal Mail* Methods of Payment: *Cheque, Visa, Access / Mastercard*

FINE FIGURES
8 Nazeing Glassworks Estate
Nazeing New Road
Broxbourne Herts
EN10 6SF

Telephone:
0992 442974

WOMEN'S CLOTHES FOR LARGER FIGURES

Fine Figures produce a good range of clothes in larger sizes, i.e. from 16 through to 36. The selection includes skirts, dresses, shirts, trousers and some lingerie and nightwear. The catalogue comes with swatches of fabric to give you a proper idea of the material used.

They also sell a range of waterproof gear which includes capes and overtrousers and some sports bags.

Dresses are between £58.50 and £72.40, skirts £34.00 to £41.00 and long shirts £38.00 to £43.00. The high protection raincoat is £78.00 to £96.00.

Catalogue: *Bi-annually, A4, Brochure, 2, Free* Postal charges: *Varies with item* Delivery: *Royal Mail* Methods of Payment: *Cheque, Visa, Access / Mastercard*

FLAMBOROUGH MARINE LTD
The Manor House
Flamborough
Bridlington
East Yorkshire
YO15 1PD

Telephone:
0262 850943

TRADITIONAL KNITWEAR AND AUTHENTIC FISHERMAN'S GANSEYS

Flamborough Marine Ltd offers both a hand knitted and a machine knitted range, which are shown in photographs stuck down on the pages of the catalogue. The mainstay is the authentic gansey, knitted in one piece on five steel needles using the finest quality 5-ply weatherproof worsted wool.

Ideal for all outdoor activity for men, women and children, it also comes in kit form. There are several different designs: the Flamborough, which comprises

Clothes

a combination of diamonds (representing nets), cables (ropes) and moss stitch (sand and shingle); the Filey, which features two strips of herrringbone and a more pronounced cable as well as diamonds, moss stitch and ladders; and the riverine Humber Keel, which is unique in having a star as its main attraction.

The company also stocks a comprehensive range of quality knitwear including the traditional, classic Guernsey and the distinctive Easy Quay range, all in 100% pure new wool, as well as pure cotton French Breton shirts. Ganseys range from £42.00 for the smallest children's size (22") to £141.00 for the 48" adult size. The kits costs from £47.20. Le Tricoteur Guernseys cost from £49.95 and Breton shirts from £18.00.

Catalogue: *A4, Catalogue, 12 pages, Colour, Free* Postal charges: *£3.20* Delivery: *Royal Mail* Methods of Payment: *Cheque, Postal Order, Visa, Access / Mastercard*

FOLEY & FOLEY LTD
Unit 1
1A Philip Walk
London
SE15 3NH

Telephone:
071 639 4807
Fax:
071 277 5563

SHIRTS

Foley & Foley is a small family firm which has been making quality shirts for the last twenty years. Most are traditonal business shirts made out of cotton but there is a small range for women.

There are a number of styles to choose from, clearly illustrated with colour photographs. You can then choose the fabric from the pages of illustrated swatches. Collars can be either 'classic' or button-down, and cuffs either with buttons or for use with cuff links. All shirts are £36.50 with free delivery.

Catalogue: *A5, Catalogue, 12 pages, Colour, Free* Postal charges: *Free* Delivery: *Royal Mail* Methods of Payment: *Cheque, Visa, Access / Mastercard, American Express*

FRIENDS OF THE EARTH
Helston
Cornwall
TR13 0TE

Telephone:
0209 831999

GIFTS AND CLOTHES

Not surprisingly, everything in this catalogue is eco-friendly but also stylish and attractive. All cotton clothing items are 'green', in that no harmful sprays have been used on the plants or chemicals in the manufacturing process. In addition to its small range of clothes this catalogue offers soaps, stationery (recycled of course), unbleached towels, mugs, glasses, a birdfeeder and an umbrella with a rainforest design.

Mugs are £2.99 each, 100 envelope re-use labels £2.25 and a rugby shirt £18.00. Profits go to furthering the cause.

Catalogue: *A5, Catalogue, 8 pages, Colour, Free* Postal charges: *Varies with item* Delivery: *Royal Mail* Methods of Payment: *Cheque, Postal Order, Visa, Access / Mastercard*

Clothes

GALE CLASSIC CLOTHES
Dill House
69 Priory Street
Corsham
Wilts
SN13 0AS

Telephone:
0249 712241
Fax:
0249 712241

TRADITIONAL CHILDREN'S CLOTHES
Gales sell clothes which they claim are 'traditional, timeless and do not date'. These are said to appeal to parents 'who still believe children are children and not miniature adults'. What children themselves think is another matter as most of these clothes look pretty Victorian and may not appeal to kids who like to be kids.

The range includes infant gowns, matinée coats, day gowns, girls' smocked dresses, boys' rompers, separates, pull ups, breeches, dungarees and play-suits. There are also blouses, pinafores, skirts, sailor suits and christening gowns.

An infant gown costs £36.00 while a romper for an eighteen month old baby is £49.00. Deep smocked dresses for two year olds are £69.00 while a christening gown/coat is £105.50.

Catalogue: *A5, Catalogue, 18, B/W, Free* Postal charges: *Varies with item* Delivery: *Royal Mail* Methods of Payment: *Visa, Access / Mastercard Cheque, Postal Order*

GARSTANG & CO LTD
213 Preston New Road
Blackburn
Lancs
BB2 6BP

Telephone:
0254 59357

MADE TO MEASURE SHIRTS AND BLOUSES
High quality materials for made-to-measure shirts and ladies blouses in Viyella, pure spun silk and polyester and all prices are inclusive of VAT.

Colours are wide and varied. Minimum length per pattern – one metre. Trocas pearl buttons are also available, and collar linings are provided at £2.50 each.

Catalogue: *A4, Leaflets, 3 pages, Colour and B/W, Free* Postal charges: *Varies with item* Delivery: *Royal Mail* Methods of Payment: *Cheque, Access / Mastercard, Visa*

GLENEAGLES KNITWEAR
Abbey Road
Auchterarder
PH3 1DP

Telephone:
0764 662112

CASHMERE KNITWEAR
Gleneagles Knitwear is in its 145th year as a family firm of Cashmere Scottish Knitwear creators. The company stocks Aquascutum, Burberry's and Jaeger outerwear to accompany their own hand-knitted clothes. Although their speciality is knitwear they also make kilts in a number of tartans.

Gleneagles Knitwear is happy to supply overseas customers and will send any items by airmail. All the items are illustrated and described in detail, with information on the colours and sizes available. Throws, stoles, socks and sports coats can also be knitted. Some styles can be knitted with different neck styles, so it is worth remembering to specify this at the time of ordering.

Clothes

Catalogue: *Third A4, Brochure, 12 pages, Colour, Free* Postal charges: *Varies with item* Delivery: *Royal Mail* Methods of Payment: *Cheque, Postal Order, Visa, Access / Mastercard*

GOOD AS GOLD
The Doctor's House
Shipton under
Wychwood
Oxon
OX7 6BQ

Telephone:
0993 830144

CHILDREN'S CLOTHES

Good as Gold individually hand-make high quality children's clothes. There is no mass production and attention can be given to the measurements of each child. Customers also have the opportunity to telephone the company if their child is not a standard size and, provided the fabric is suitable, Good as Gold is happy to consider making up garments in the customer's own fabrics.

Clothes are made for both boys and girls and include shirts at £20.00, knickerbockers at £22.00 and fully smocked dresses with yokes from £68.00. Collars and cuffs for the clothing can be piped, stitched or lace-trimmed and can match or contrast.

Catalogue: *A5, Catalogue, 16 pages, B/W, Free* Postal charges: *Varies with item* Delivery: *Royal Mail* Methods of Payment: *Cheque*

HAMILTON CARHARTT WORKWEAR LTD
Angus Works
North Isla Street
Dundee
DD1 3LS

Telephone:
0382 819990
Fax:
0382 833844

WORKING CLOTHES

Hamilton Carhartt produce a variety of clothing for workers. They will embroider your monogram onto any article of clothing.

Work jeans in sizes 28" to 46" cost from £9.45 to £11.52. They have a zip fly, five pockets, gold stitching and rivets. Each pair is made from prime denim. Sweatshirts range from small to XXL sizes, and cost from £7.25 to £7.63. They have a round neck and long sleeves. Overalls start at £9.45 and go up to £14.45.

Catalogue: *A4, Brochure, 9, B/W, Free* Postal charges: *Varies with item* Delivery: *Royal Mail* Methods of Payment: *Cheque*

HARTSTRINGS
Merry-Hunt
Corporation Ltd.
Calico House
Plantation Wharf
York Road
London
SW11 3UE

Telephone:
071 924 3777
Fax:
071 924 3300

CLOTHES FOR YOUNG CHILDREN

Hartstrings offers a wide range of childrenswear for toddlers and young school children. The clothes are placed under named categories: for example, Tackle Box or Zany Zebra. The clothes are both for boys and girls with some matching outfits for the mothers to wear. They can be purchased through mail order only and postage and packaging is charged if the total is below £500.00. You can buy dresses (£13.50), dungarees (£16.00), leggings (£9.00), sweaters (£18.50) and much more. The choice is wide and the colours and designs are varied and bold.

Clothes

HAWKSHEAD COUNTRYWEAR
Rothay Road
Ambleside
Cumbria
LA22 0HQ

Telephone:
0539 434000

Catalogue: *Quarterly, A4, Catalogue, 23 pages, Colour, Free* Postal charges: *Varies with item* Delivery: *Royal Mail* Methods of Payment: *Cheque, Postal Order*

CLASSIC CASUALWEAR FOR MEN AND WOMEN
A well-established Lake District company, Hawkshead clothing is specially designed for a relaxed and comfortable fit. Choose from everyday knockarounds like jeans and jumpers to smarter skirts, blouses, trousers and jackets.

Country barn jackets in 100% cotton outer and lining, £49.99; the Moorland ladies' jacket, £39.99; men's Chambray shirt, £14.99; ladies' Wayfarer jacket, £29.99; fishermen's cardigans, £19.99; ladies' tailored jacket, £79.99; ladies' pumps, £24.99; loafers, £29.99; men's ferryman shoes, £39.99; ladies' Jacquard tunic, £24.99; and wax riding jacket, £79.99.

The clothes are shown on a variety of models and in still life format and each is well described. The order form is inside the catalogue and includes a self-addressed, though not stamped, envelope.

Catalogue: *Quarterly, A4, Catalogue, 48 pages, Colour, Free* Postal charges: *Varies with item* Delivery: *Royal Mail* Methods of Payment: *Cheque, Postal Order, Visa, Access / Mastercard*

HIGH AND MIGHTY
Old School House
High Street
Hungerford
Berkshire
RG17 ONF

Telephone:
0488 684666

MEN'S CLOTHES
High and Mighty sell clothes for big men. Once you've seen something you like in the catalogue you can order it by phone from one of their retail outlets.

The Knightsbridge collection offers exclusive menswear and designer names for anyone who'd normally find themselves choosing between the only two outsize garments most stores have to offer. A Freud double-breasted suit costs £599.00; a Stephens Bros shirt sells for £74.00. While the clothes certainly aren't cheap, they are very stylish.

Catalogue: *Bi-annually, A4, Catalogue, 8, Colour, Free* Postal charges: *Varies with item* Delivery: *Royal Mail* Methods of Payment: *Visa, Access / Mastercard Cheque, Postal Order*

Clothes

IAN ALLAN PUBLISHING LTD
Coombelands House
Coombelands Lane
Addlestone
Surrey
KT15 1HY

Telephone:
0932 820560
0932 820 552
Fax:
0932 821 258

BOOKS AND REGALIA

Ian Allan Regalia aim to satisfy the needs of all Freemasons. For those curious as to what Freemasons actually do, there are books, including *Masonic Ritual – a Commentary on the Freemasonic Ritual* by Dr E. H. Cartwright and *Workman Unshamed*, an examination of the accusations often levelled against Freemasons.

The catalogue also features Masonic Regalia of every kind. There is a curious array of gloves for £6.25, finest lambskin aprons for £14.10, chain collars from £164.50 and other extravagant items which no doubt mean a great deal to the right people. To the wrong people, the illustration on page 16 of a portly gentleman in full Knights Templar regalia may raise more than an eyebrow.

Catalogue: *A5, Catalogue, 54 pages, Colour and B/W, Free* Postal charges: *Varies with item* Delivery: *Royal Mail* Methods of Payment: *Cheque, Postal Order, Visa, Access / Mastercard*

IMMATERIAL
7 Gabriel's Wharf
56 Upper Ground
London
SE1 9PP

Telephone:
071 401 2323

T-SHIRTS

Frolly Shooter has been painting beautiful, original T-shirts and ties in her shop at Gabriel's Wharf for five years. Designs range from fine art echoing Miró and Klee to a witty line-up of cats and other animals.

Vivid colours (machine washable) and bold images are complemented by top quality American T-shirts and the finest silk ties. Oz Clarke wears Frolly's T-shirts on BBC 2's 'Food and Drink' programme.

Choose from hand painted designs at £20.00 or commission your own from £25.00. Startlingly original silk ties at £20.00. Printed T-shirts including the best-selling 'Just go away and let me sleep' design from £10.00.

Catalogue: *A5, Brochure, Colour, Free* Postal charges: *Varies with item* Delivery: *Royal Mail* Methods of Payment: *Cheque, Postal Order, Visa, Access / Mastercard, American Express*

ISABELLA BOURNE
PO Box 3
Stockbridge
Hants.
SO20 6JL

Telephone:
081 332 9755

CLASSIC CLOTHES IN BEAUTIFUL FABRICS

Timeless clothes in beautiful fabrics and soft, subtle, neutral shades. This small collection is elegant and simple with fluid shirts, easy-fitting jackets and sleeveless waistcoats available in navy, soft blue, lemon or stone in sizes 10, 12 and 14 only. Fabrics are silk, silk/linen, silk twill or ribbed silk. Prices are reasonable for the cut and quality, ranging from £49.00 for a silk/linen fully lined top; £49.00 for a pure fuji silk shirt; to £74.00 for silk/linen trousers,

Clothes

fully lined with two pockets and £96.00 for a pure silk twill jacket. The catalogue does not include a telephone number, so keep this book handy!

Catalogue: *Bi-annually, A4, Leaflets, 8 pages, Colour, Free* Postal charges: *£2.95* Delivery: *Royal Mail* Methods of Payment: *Cheque, Postal Order*

JAKE
176 Kennington Park Road
London
SE11 4BT

Telephone:
071 735 7577
Fax:
071 582 2876

LADIES' CLOTHES

Jake mail order is a well-known name to *Sunday* magazine readers, who will recognise the stylish ads offering up-to-the-minute, stylish clothes at reasonable prices. The outfits are not high fashion, but neither are they boring – Jake offers classic clothes in the latest fabrics and designs almost as soon as the catwalks have heralded a new way of dressing.

You will always look smart and well dressed in a Jake outfit and the catalogue offers a well-balanced selection from jeans (£27.00), dresses (£54.00) and shirts (£32.50) to jackets (£49.00), silk scarves (£25.00) and skirts (£42.00). They also have jewellery and belts for sale (£15.00 for an Italian leather belt.) Sizes range from 10-16 with a body measurement chart included to help you.

Catalogue: *Quarterly, A4, Catalogue, 22 pages, Colour, Free* Postal charges: *£1.50* Delivery: *Royal Mail* Methods of Payment: *Access / Mastercard, Visa Cheque*

JAMES MEADE LTD
48 Charlton Road
Andover
Herts
SP10 3JL

Telephone:
0264 333222
Fax:
0264 363200

CLOTHES

James Meade Ltd boast 'Jermyn Street quality at affordable prices'. The 32 page colour catalogue presents the Classic James Meade range of shirts for £39.50 alongside traditional and vaguely startling leisure shirts for roughly the same price. The company also offers a useful tailoring service, to re-cuff or collar those old favourites you can't bear to bin.

The collection of women's wear shares the same attention to detail, with formal and casual skirts and blouses selling at around the £40-£50 mark. Pyjamas and nighties are also available.

Catalogue: *A5, Catalogue, 32 pages, Colour, Free* Postal charges: *£1.95* Delivery: *Royal Mail* Methods of Payment: *Cheque, Visa, Access / Mastercard, Postal Order*

Clothes

JANET REGER
2 Beauchamp Place
London
SW3 1NG

Telephone:
071 584 9360
Fax:
071 581 7496

LINGERIE AND NIGHTWEAR
Janet Reger is famous for her luxurious and covetable lingerie and this black and white catalogue shows them off to their best advantage. Descriptions with sizes and colour availability are shown on the same page as the garments, which range from wired bras, mini slips, suspender belts, briefs and G-strings to pyjamas, nightdresses, robes and tights.

Prices range from £4.50 for the tights and £45.00 for briefs, £50.00 for French knickers to £145.00 for a Lou Lou nightdress and £298.00 for a Cindy short wrap. Janet Reger also has a shop in Beauchamp Place.

Catalogue: *A4, Catalogue, 24 pages, B/W, Free* Postal charges: *£5.00* Delivery: *Royal Mail* Methods of Payment: *Cheque, Postal Order, American Express, Visa, Access / Mastercard*

JEAN JERRARD
Designer House
Lime Street
Bingley X
BD97 1AD

Telephone:
0245 56 66 66

CLOTHES AND ACCESSORIES
The Jean Jerrard catalogue offers a wide range of practical, reasonably priced clothes, leisure wear, lingerie and accessories for men and women who are fuller figured or under 5'2" tall.

Sizes go from 12 up to 30 and the colours are bright and attractive (two-piece caramel suit, £44.99, floral tie-back dress, £19.99), but garments in the larger sizes (24 to 28) are more expensive.

Catalogue: *Quarterly, A4, Catalogue, 120 pages, Colour, Free* Postal charges: *£1.50* Delivery: *Royal Mail* Methods of Payment: *Cheque, Postal Order, Visa, Access / Mastercard*

JEM DESIGNS
Sydenham Farm
Cottage
Broadwell
Moreton-in-Marsh
Gloucestershire
GL56 0YE

Telephone:
0451 870624

ORIGINAL CLOTHING
The owners of Jem Designs, Jenny and Peter Moss, design and manufacture original jackets and waistcoats with skirts, hats and shoes to match, from their base in the Cotswolds.

The clothing is all hand made from a richly diverse range of brocades, linens and silks and ranges in price from Shoe Bows for £10.00 to Limited Edition designs, priced individually. Clients are welcome, by appointment, at their showroom.

The three collections – Classic, Current and Limited – are available in varying styles and fabrics and the company is happy to send swatches from the Classic and Current ranges on payment of £1.00.

Catalogue: *Third A4, Leaflets, 6 pages, Colour and B/W, Free* Postal charges: *Customer collects* Delivery: *Customer visits* Methods of Payment: *Cheque, Postal Order*

Clothes

JOHN BROCKLEHURST COMPANY
Bridge Street
Bakewell
Derbys
DE45 1DS

Telephone:
0629 812089
Fax:
0629 814777

MEN'S CLOTHES

John Brocklehurst specialise in high quality, traditional British clothing for men. The exclusive designs are on the conservative side and most are made in this country. The look is mostly gentleman farmer with plenty of checked shirts, cord trousers and sports jackets.

There is also a range of high class leather footwear, a few waistcoats and even some plus fours. Prices are good for this quality, with shirts around £22.00, twill trousers £21.00, corduroys £52.50 and a pair of waterproof leather boots £99.95.

Catalogue: *Bi-annually, A4, Catalogue, 16 pages, Colour, Free*
Postal charges: *£2.95* Delivery: *Royal Mail Courier* Methods of Payment: *Cheque, Access / Mastercard, Visa, American Express*

JOJO
134 Lots Road
London
SW10 0RJ

Telephone:
071 351 4112
Fax:
071 352 7089

MATERNITY AND BABYWEAR AND NURSERY EQUIPMENT

JoJo offers bright, fun beachwear, suits and dresses, comfortable separates and workwear for mothers-to-be. They also offer babywear essentials and party looks for babies 0–24 months and a limited range of nursery equipment including baby carriers, £17.99; changing bags, £15.99; table seats, £19.99; bouncy chairs, £18.99; and umbrella buggies, £54.99.

The maternity range includes smart office suits, denim dresses, £39.99; Mulberry print blouse and skirt, £29.99 and £22.99; pretty Empire-line short linen dresses, £32.99; swimsuits, £22.99; leggings and tops; dungarees, £34.99; jeans; nursing bras, £13.99; and nightshirts, £16.99.

Baby clothes range from zip sleepsuits, £6.99, and booties, £4.99, to print sundresses, £12.99, and nautical twill trousers, £8.99. All are featured on models and can be clearly seen. The maternity range includes some very wearable pieces.

Catalogue: *Bi-annually, A6, Catalogue, 24 pages, Colour, Free*
Postal charges: *Varies with item* Delivery: *Royal Mail* Methods of Payment: *Cheque, Postal Order, Visa, Access / Mastercard*

Clothes

JOLLIMAN LTD
18 Brighton Road
Worthing
Sussex
BN11 3EN

Telephone:
0903 202944
Fax:
0903 209926

TRADITIONAL CLOTHES
Jolliman could be called the Marks and Sparks of the catalogue business. Their clothes are conservative, well-made and perhaps best suited to the thirty pluses. Like M&S many of the items are made in Britain and these are indicated in the catalogue by Union Jacks.

There is a good range of trousers and shirts as well as sweaters, slippers and socks. There is the usual underwear plus dressing gowns, pyjamas and vests. For outside there are fleeces, waterproof jackets and hats. Nearly all the clothes are for men apart from a couple of 'slacks' for women.

Catalogue: *7.5" × 8", Catalogue, 36 pages, Colour, Free* Postal charges: *£2.49* Delivery: *Royal Mail* Methods of Payment: *Cheque, Visa, Access / Mastercard, COD, Postal Order*

JUDITH GLUE
25 Broad Street
Kirkwall
Orkney
KW15 1DH

Telephone:
0856 876263
Fax:
0856 874225

ORKNEY KNITWEAR AND HIGH QUALITY GIFTS, CRAFTS AND JEWELLERY AND ORKNEY FOOD
Now in its eighth year, Judith Glue's mail order brochure has customers from all over the world. Living and working in the remote Orkney islands in Scotland, Judith designs and manufactures a unique range of knitwear. The designs are based on Orkney's rich archaeological heritage and landscape.

To complement the knitwear collection there is an individual choice of clothing, gifts, silver jewellery and Orkney food and whisky produce.

A pure wool Donegal sloppy joe sweater is £39.50. The original Runic design V-neck cardigan £59.50 and an individually hand-knitted Pictish Bird design jacket £142.00. Finally a puffin minimal can be bought for as little as £1.40.

Catalogue: *Annually, A4, Catalogue, 28 pages, Colour, Free* Postal charges: *Varies with item* Delivery: *Royal Mail, Parcelforce* Methods of Payment: *Cheque, Postal Order, Visa, Access / Mastercard, American Express*

KALEIDOSCOPE
Desford Road
Enderby
Leicester
LE9 5XX

Telephone:
0533 751177
Fax:
0533 750108

GENERAL GOODS
The Kaleidoscope range extends from clothing and swimwear to barbecues and garden furniture. Their fashion section will appeal to career women unable to splash out in Covent Garden boutiques but wanting to steer clear of BHS. Pure cotton tops are available for £9.99; a Colour Block sweater sells for £29.99.

Moving to the bedroom, there's a romantic four-poster bed for £249.99. If you buy four pairs of

Clothes

curtains to go with it, you get four free valances. Pillows cost just £4.99 and a duvet set just £19.99.

Those with a taste for the great outdoors will enjoy the garden bench for £29.99, a barbecue for £19.99 or, if you're feeling particularly active, a two-man igloo tent for £49.99.

Catalogue: *Quarterly, A4, Catalogue, 174 pages, Colour, Free*
Postal charges: *Varies with item* Delivery: *Royal Mail* Methods of Payment: *Visa, Access / Mastercard, Diners Club, American Express, Postal Order Cheque*

KIDS' STUFF
10 Hensman's Hill
Clifton
Bristol
BS8 4PE

Telephone:
0272 734980

CHILDREN'S CLOTHES

Kids' Stuff has a great range of comfortable and good-value casual clothes. They have used only the best quality fabrics that keep their colour and shape through all those washes.

The co-ordinated collection ensures your child will mix-and-match with the best of them – a plain purple T-shirt (starting from £5.50 for a one-year-old), will go with fun purple sunburst leggings (starting at £4.50), or perhaps some stripey purple/mid-blue cycle shorts (starting at £4.90). Trendy young ones will also be able to sleep easy, and in the smartest of company – not only are colourful print cotton jersey pyjamas on offer (starting at £10.00) but teddy gets to wear a matching pair too (£3.20; with teddy bear – £9.20).

Catalogue: *Bi-annually, A5, Catalogue, 16 pages, Colour, Free*
Postal charges: *Free* Delivery: *Royal Mail* Methods of Payment: *Cheque, Postal Order, Visa, Access / Mastercard*

KINGS OF MAIDENHEAD
18 Ray Street
Maidenhead
Berks
SL6 8PW

Telephone:
0628 29283
Fax:
0628 29283

BARBOUR COUNTRY CLOTHING

J Barbour and Sons have been manufacturing the world's best outdoor clothing for nearly a century. Their now familiar range of clothing consists of 16 specially designed, waxed coats as well as trousers, jumpers, socks, boots and other accessories.

Whether you choose the rugged heavyweight thornproofs or the versatile lightweights there is certainly a style that will suit your needs. Whilst Barbour products are renowned for their durability, they still remain very smart and comfortable for everyday use.

Kings undercut high-street prices by some margin: the 'Border' RRP is £135.95 while the Kings price is £122.35, 'Gamefair' is £98.95 as opposed to £109.95, 'Beaufort' £113.35 against £125.95 and 'Bedale' £98.95 instead of £109.95.

Clothes

KINGSHILL
British Designer Collections
FREEPOST
Great Missenden
Bucks.
HP16 OBR

Telephone:
0498 890555
Fax:
0494 866003

Catalogue: *Annually, Catalogue, 67 pages, Colour, Free* Postal charges: *Varies with item* Delivery: *Parcelforce, Royal Mail Securicor Omega Express* Methods of Payment: *Cheque, Postal Order, Access / Mastercard, Visa, American Express*

BRITISH DESIGNER COLLECTIONS
Kingshill's line-up of designer names – Jean Muir Studio, Caroline Charles, Bellville Sassoon, Amanda Wakeley, Paul Costelloe, Betty Jackson, Roland Klein and Tomasz Starzewski – is very impressive indeed. As is their catalogue: a hardcover, Filofax-style brochure with stylish photographs showing covetable clothes. Each designer is pictured at the front of their section and items are often shown worn in more than one way.

There is also a fabulous array of accessories and jewellery from top labels such as Georgina Von Etzdorf, Anya Hindmarch, Shakira Caine, Mulberry, Farah Lister and Annabel Jones. Prices are in line with the profile of the famous designers' names. For example, Amanda Wakeley cashmere and cotton V-neck sweater with satin cuffs, £278.00; Jean Muir navy-blue wool crêpe unlined tapered trousers with elasticated waist, £196.00.

Kingshill have also recently produced a gift brochure with beautiful gifts selected by Jane Churchill.

Catalogue: *Bi-annually, 22.5x25mm, Catalogue, 125 pages, Colour,* £4.50 Postal charges: £5.00 Delivery: *Royal Mail* Methods of Payment: *Cheque, Postal Order, Visa, Access / Mastercard, American Express*

KINLOCH ANDERSON
Commercial Street/Dock Street
Leith
Edinburgh
EH6 6EY

Telephone:
031 555 1390
Fax:
031 555 1392

SCOTS CLOTHING
Experts in Highland dress since 1868, Kinloch Anderson produce a comprehensive range of traditional clothing that can be worn for just about any special occasion. They hold Royal appointments as tailors and kiltmakers to HM the Queen, HRH the Duke of Edinburgh and HRH the Prince of Wales. Each order takes about six to eight weeks to make up.

Evening wear includes a regulation doublet (made to measure for £326.00), a Montrose doublet in black Barathea (made to measure for £207.00) and a coatee and vest in black Barathea (made to measure, £270.00; ready to wear, £235.00).

Catalogue: *A5, Brochure, 12 pages, Colour and B/W, Free* Postal charges: *Varies with item* Delivery: *Royal Mail* Methods of Payment: *Cheque, Postal Order, Access / Mastercard, Visa, American Express, Diners Club*

Clothes

LAETITIA ALLEN LTD
26 Adam & Eve Mews
Kensington
London
W8 6UJ

Telephone:
071 937 3973
Fax:
071 221 0626

LINGERIE
Launched in 1993, this collection is available exclusively by mail order. Laetitia Allen commissions her design from British designers and sources easy-care fabrics both here and in Europe. All the designs are flattering, comfortable and made with meticulous attention to detail.

Items arrive beautifully packaged and a special gift wrap, together with a card, is available for a modest charge. Orders are usually dispatched on the day they are received, with next-day delivery offered as an option.

Among the highlights of the collection are new-look pyjamas with team stretch lace leggings with a pure cotton jersey top (£34.99); a stretch lace lingerie set which includes briefs at £8.00, and a matching bra at £12.99; and a figure-enhancing cotton Lycra body at £25.99.

Catalogue: *Bi-annually, Catalogue, 16 pages, Colour, Free* Postal charges: *Varies with item* Delivery: *Parcelforce, Royal Mail* Methods of Payment: *Cheque, Postal Order, Visa, Access / Mastercard, American Express*

LANDS' END DIRECT MERCHANTS UK LTD
Pillings Road
Oakham
Rutland
Leics
LE15 6NY

Telephone:
0800 220 106
Fax:
0572 722554

CLOTHES
Only introduced in the UK a couple of years ago, Lands' End is one of the most popular mail order clothing firms in the USA, much favoured by 'Preppies'. With no concessions made to English spelling, vernacular or sizing, the catalogue tirelessly promotes its American origins which can be wearing.

Predominantly featuring cotton leisurewear for men, women and children, the clothes are high quality and good value though increasingly similar products are available from British companies such as Racing Green. A man's sweater sells for £39.50 while a unisex polo shirt sells for £23.00. A swatch service is available and an essential size conversion chart is provided.

Catalogue: *A4, Catalogue, 72 pages, Colour, Free* Postal charges: £2.95 Delivery: *Royal Mail* Methods of Payment: *Cheque, Postal Order, Visa, Access / Mastercard, American Express*

Clothes

LIMETREE FASHIONS
Linetree Cottage
Selsted
Nr Dover
Kent
CT15 7HJ

Telephone:
0303 83274

LADIES TRENCHCOAT
Limetree Fashions only sell the one garment which they advertise in the press rather than describe in a catalogue. Their ladies nylon trenchcoat is an ingenious design which fits all sizes and can be folded up into a small holdall which comes with it. Available in either navy-blue or green, it costs just £27.50 which includes postage.

Catalogue: *By Advertising, Free* Postal charges: *Free* Delivery: *Royal Mail* Methods of Payment: *Cheque*

LITTLE TREASURES
10 Braemar Crescent
Leigh on Sea
Essex
SS9 3RL

Telephone:
0702 559005

CHILDREN'S CLOTHES
Little Treasures provide individually handmade traditional childrenswear. There's also a range of co-ordinating hand-framed soft cotton knitwear. The catalogue includes Oxford cottons in plains and stripes, classic gingham and tartan and pretty floral prints. A classic romper suit sells for between £30.00 and £38.00; a classic baby dress for between £31.00 and £40.00.

There are also Guernsey sweaters by Le Tricoteur (from £24.00 to £44.00), Husky jackets (from £19.50 to £24.50), Mark Regent Jackets (all £48.00) and Giesswein Austrian jackets (from £35.00 to £53.00).

Catalogue: *Bi-annually, A5, Brochure, 12 pages, Colour, Free* Postal charges: *Varies with item* Delivery: *Royal Mail* Methods of Payment: *Cheque, Postal Order, Visa, Access / Mastercard*

LONG TALL SALLY
75–77 Margaret Street
London
W1N 7HB

Telephone:
071 436 4114

CLOTHES FOR TALL WOMEN
Fashionable clothes for tall women are what Long Tall Sally are all about – as if the name wasn't enough of a clue. Their most popular styles are grouped under a separate catalogue: 'Essentials'.

There's a good selection of swimsuits, such as a cotton Lycra number in sizes 12 to 20, with a scooped back, for £23.95; and a Bubble swimsuit in 'bubble effect' fabric, in sizes 12 to 18, for £19.95. You'll also find jeans, including black denims in sizes 10 to 20 for £36.95, and extra-long tops, including long-sleeved T-shirts from £12.95.

Catalogue: *Quarterly, A5, Brochure, 26 pages, Colour, Free* Postal charges: *Varies with item* Delivery: *Royal Mail* Methods of Payment: *Cheque, Postal Order, Visa, Access / Mastercard, American Express, Diners Club*

Clothes

MACCULLOCH & WALLIS LIMITED
PO Box W1A 2DX
London
W1A 2DX

Telephone:
071-409 3506
Fax:
071-409 2481

BRIDAL WEAR

MacCulloch have been in business since 1902, selling fabrics and silks. They now offer a unique service by mail – complete kits for making silk wedding dresses. These come with everything you need: the pattern, the silk and the lining and haberdashery. They have been designed with the average dressmaker in mind so are not beyond most people.

There are five styles to choose from, all look splendid. And the prices are very reasonable at just £99.00 – where else would that buy you a fitted, silk wedding dress?

Catalogue: *A4, Brochure, 10 pages, Colour, Free* Postal charges: *Free* Delivery: *Royal Mail* Methods of Payment: *Cheque*

MACGILLIVRAYS
Benbecula
Outer Hebrides
Scotland
PA88 5LA

Telephone:
0870 602525

HAND-WOVEN TWEEDS

The MacGillivray company has been selling hand-woven Harris tweed along with hand-knitted sweaters all over the world since 1941. Harris tweed is made from pure new wool and comes in 28" (72cms) widths. The price is £10.50 per yard (£11.55 per metre). Hand-knitted sweaters are also made from pure new wool and contain a good deal of natural oil which renders them showerproof. Prices start from £44.00.

Catalogue: *Catalogue, 4 pages, B/W, 50p or 2 × first-class stamps* Postal charges: *Varies with item* Delivery: *Royal Mail* Methods of Payment: *Cheque, Postal Order, Visa, Access / Mastercard, American Express*

MIDNIGHT LADY
20–24 Cardigan Street
Luton
Beds
LU1 1RR

Telephone:
0582 391854

SEXY LINGERIE

Midnight Lady produce three brochures, each offering different varieties of exotic lingerie. As they say: 'No girl knows how daring she will be' – until she sees this collection of raunchy garments.

'Skin Fit' offers close-fitting ideas to help you fulfil your erotic fantasies. Admittedly, you may need an instruction manual to slip into some of these little numbers, but they're probably far easier to slip out of. If you've got the confidence, you could opt for a fishnet catsuit (£33.95) or a front-opening play suit with lace cups (£30.00) – careful with that two-way zip.

The 'Cameo' collection contains softer material see-through underwear of the more traditionally risqué type. A nightgown and thong will set you back £23.65.

Clothes

'Inspiration' include a range of 'Black Magic' outfits (a dress costs £71.80 or £90.00) that react to your body heat and change colour to red, green, blue or purple. If your lover doesn't mind you resembling a well-wrapped traffic light, you're onto a winner.

Catalogue: *A4, Catalogue, 16 pages, Colour, Free* Postal charges: *Free* Delivery: *Royal Mail* Methods of Payment: *Cheque, Postal Order, Visa, Access / Mastercard*

MILTON STAY DRY
Granby Court
Weymouth
DT4 9BR

Telephone:
0305 785108
Fax:
0305 785714

INCONTINENCE PRODUCTS

If you're unlucky enough to suffer from incontinence, Milton is a name to be thankful for. Their brochure comes with a handy guide to the subject, written by their consultant, Dr Alan Riley.

For men, the state-of-the-art product seems to be the 'Contenta Compleat for Men'. This looks like a normal fly-front pant but carries a built-in, highly absorbent pad. It's said to be ideal for 'dribbling and light incontinence'. A pair costs £10.45, with the price dropping to £28.75 for a pack of three.

Women can rely on the 'Contenta Female Compleat'. Designed to look and feel like ordinary women's underwear, it has a highly absorbent liner stitched into special 'stay-dry' fabric. These are £8.30 for a pair, dropping to £23.95 for a pack of three.

Catalogue: *A5, Catalogue, 16 pages, Colour, Free* Postal charges: *£2.55* Delivery: *Royal Mail* Methods of Payment: *Cheque, Postal Order*

MRS BEAR SMOCKS
Croft Cottage
36 Hammer Lane
Warborough
Wallingford Oxon
OX10 7DJ

Telephone:
0865 858212

SMOCKS

This company offers a personal, individual service to make smocked clothes for children. Styles and sizes are flexible and fabric can be chosen by the customer, or provided from stock.

Prices vary acccording to the material used and amount of work. A deposit of £20.00 needed with the balance on receipt of garment. They specialise is bridesmaids' outfits.

Catalogue: *A4, Leaflets, 5 pages, B/W, Free* Postal charges: *£2.50* Delivery: *Royal Mail* Methods of Payment: *Cheque, Postal Order*

Clothes

MURRAY BROTHERS
Freepost
Tower Mill
Hawick
Scotland
TD9 8BR

Telephone:
0450 73420
Fax:
0450 77656

WOOLLENS

Murray Brothers is part of the Scottish Woollen Millsgroup, which has retail outlets throughout the UK. They offer traditional, quality clothing at warehouse prices. The majority of the stock is woollen knitwear in classic styles with the odd tartan and Argyll motif to trade on its Scottish connection. Predominantly for women, there are some ranges for men along with Arran sweaters for children.

All the products seem well made and there are genuine bargains. A man's cable-knit sweater sells for just £32.50 and a woman's for £27.50.

Catalogue: *A1, Catalogue, 16 pages, Colour, Free* Postal charges: *Varies with item* Delivery: *Royal Mail* Methods of Payment: *Cheque, Postal Order, Visa, Access / Mastercard, American Express, Diners Club*

MYERSCOUGH-JONES OF LEIGH
8 Lonsdale Avenue
Leigh
Lancashire
WN7 3UE

Telephone:
0942 674836

LINGERIE

Myerscough-Jones are specialists in underwear by post. The underwear on show here is much less of the glamour type, and more practical if not entirely conservative. There's still room for a selection of 'Fantasie Lingerie'; the Renaissance collection includes an underwired bra (up to size 36E) to make the most of your credentials for just £15.50. There are also high-legged briefs for £8.25 and a full brief for the same price.

Vests cost from £17.95 and boxer panties from £14.25. There's also something called a 'Cosytop', with a V-neck and long sleeves which costs from £14.95.

Catalogue: *A5, Leaflets, 12 pages, B/W, Free* Postal charges: *Free* Delivery: *Royal Mail* Methods of Payment: *Cheque, Postal Order*

N PEAL OF BURLINGTON ARCADE
Customer Service Centre
Saddlers Court
Reading Road
Yateley
Camberley, Surrey
GU17 7RX

Telephone:
0800 220 222
Fax:
0252 876770

CASHMERE COLLECTION FOR MEN AND WOMEN

N Peal is a name famous for its cashmere and this catalogue brings together some of the popular items from the Burlington Arcade shop. The catalogue features cashmere cotton, cashmere silk and pure 100% Scottish cashmere, the world's finest. There are tunics, cardigans, waistcoats and fitted T-shirts for women, and for men, sweaters, cardigans, waistcoats and an updated version of the cricket sweater.

Prices are £185.00 for a long, classic cardigan with side slits, a dropped shoulder line and a single bold button; £255.00 for an easy-fitting tunic in a textured

Clothes

rib; £260.00 for a pair of lightweight palazzo trousers with an elasticated waistband and neat front pleats. The photographs are large and clear and have similarly clear descriptions and prices underneath.

Catalogue: *Bi-annually, A4, Catalogue, 20 pages, Colour, Free* Postal charges: *£5.00* Delivery: *Royal Mail* Methods of Payment: *Cheque, Postal Order, Visa, Access / Mastercard, American Express, Diners Club*

NEXT DIRECTORY
Enderby Road
Leicester
Leics
LE9 5AT

Telephone:
0345 100 500
Fax:
0533 738749

MEN'S, WOMEN'S AND CHILDREN'S CLOTHES

The Next Directory single-handedly changed the face of British mail order and remains one of the most stylish ways to order clothes through the post. The catalogue itself is a very well-designed hardback featuring the same ranges available in the high-street shops.

For women, a 'Houndstooth Check Jacket' or a hand-knitted chenille sweater both cost £69.99. A 'Dark Rose Beige Single Breasted Jacket' is £74.99, the trousers to match £39.99. Men's suits are more expensive: a navy gabardine jacket sells for £95.00, the matching trousers for £49.00.

There is also a selection of children's wear. Blue stonewashed denims for a six- to nine-month-old baby cost £9.99; a duffel coat costs £29.99. A must for any serious catalogue shopper.

Catalogue: *A4, Catalogue, 369 pages, Colour, £3.00* Postal charges: *£2.50* Delivery: *In house delivery* Methods of Payment: *Cheque, Postal Order, Visa, Access / Mastercard, Diners Club, American Express*

NIGHTINGALES LTD
Meadowcraft Mill
Bury Road
Rochdale
Lancashire
OL11 4AU

Telephone:
0706 620850
Fax:
0706 620838

WOMEN'S CLOTHES

Nightingales sell a collection of dresses, suits, skirts, blouses, evening dresses and pure cotton nightdresses combining exclusive British-made designs with quality, at excellent prices.

Catalogue: *Bi-monthly, A5, Brochure, 32–48 pages, Colour, Free* Postal charges: *Varies with item* Delivery: *Royal Mail* Methods of Payment: *Cheque, Postal Order, Visa, Access / Mastercard*

Clothes

NORTHAMPTON FOOTWEAR DISTRIBUTORS
Summerhouse Road
Moulton Park
Northampton
NN3 1WD

Telephone:
0604 790827

SHOES AND BOOTS

Northampton Footwear produce a comprehensive range of men's and women's budget footwear. There's everything here, from trainers and slippers to boots, brogues and high-heeled shoes.

Their men's 'Nubuck Suede Hiking Boot' has a strong ridged rubber sole, burgundy panels at the back and hook and eye lacing. Sizes range from 7 to 13 and costs £18.95. Men's slippers are available in dark brown plain bri-nylon or check cord material from £2.50.

Their lady's 'Navy Pigskin Moccasin' costs just £5.95. A black leather Chelsea boot retails for just £11.95.

Catalogue: *A4, Leaflets, 4 pages, Colour, Free* Postal charges: £6.00 Delivery: *Royal Mail* Methods of Payment: *Cheque, Postal Order*

OLIVIA
PO Box 232
Richmond
Surrey
TW9 2UJ

PURE SILK LADIES LINGERIE

The Olivia Pure Silk Lingerie catalogue offers a number of exquisitely styled pieces of luxury silk made from the finest quality satin and trimmed with matching lace. All articles are beautifully boxed.

The choice of lingerie ranges from camisole tops and knicker sets (£34.99), pyjamas (£85.00), and tangas (£9.99) to kimonos (£59.99), and chemises (£39.99). The colours available are white and cream and sizes range from 10-14. All items must be purchased through the order form enclosed with the catalogue.

Catalogue: *A4, Catalogue, 3 pages, Colour, Free* Postal charges: *Varies with item* Delivery: *Royal Mail* Methods of Payment: *Cheque, Postal Order*

ONE OF GILLIE'S
Llantrithyd
Cowbridge
S. Glamorgan
CF7 7UB

Telephone:
0446 781357

WOMEN'S CLOTHES FROM BEACH TO BALLROOM

Founded in 1980, One Of Gillie's specialise in hand-finished clothes in beautiful fabrics (mainly pure cotton, silk and wool) at prices reasonable for the quality. They make swimwear, shorts, trousers, skirts, dresses, soft jackets – in fact, almost anything except heavy items like coats.

Their beachware is notable in that they sell bikinis in separate sizes and styles, top and bottom, cup sizes A–DD (larger sometimes available). The service provided is very personal and customers are welcome to ring to discuss their individual requirements.

Clothes

Catalogue: *Bi-annually, A5, Catalogue, 18 pages, Colour and B/W, Free* Postal charges: *Varies with item* Delivery: *Royal Mail* Methods of Payment: *Cheque, Postal Order, Visa, Access / Mastercard*

ORKNEY ANGORA
Isle of Sanday
Orkney
KW 17 2AZ

Telephone:
08575-421
Fax:
08575-291

ANGORA THERMAL CLOTHING

Orkney Angora offers pure natural fibre thermal clothing produced from angora rabbits. All clothing has been tried and tested in Orkney, and is well known for its warming and therapeutic effects. A wide range of items are available from socks to sweaters and long johns. In summer months visitors can browse in the craft shop and see the enchanting angora rabbits. It is a family run croft-based business situated in one of Orkney's most northerly isles, and the high quality, locally produced goods are dispatched by mail order throughout the UK and abroad.

Catalogue: *A5, Catalogue, 23 pages, Colour, Free* Postal charges: *Varies with item* Delivery: *Royal Mail* Methods of Payment: *Cheque, Postal Order, Visa, Access / Mastercard*

OSBORNE'S BIG MAN'S SHOP
Fore Street
Beer
Devon
EX12 3JB

Telephone:
0297 20700/23481

OUTSIZE MENSWEAR AND OUTSIZE SHOES

Osborne's sell clothes for big and tall men, going up to 70" chest/waist, 40" inside leg and 23" collar. They can provide dinner and formal suits in mix-and-match fittings both at their shops and by mail order. They also stock sports coats, blazers, leisure jackets and trousers in terylene, cavalry twill, cord or denim.

They have an extensive range of formal and leisure shirts along with fancy waistcoats, workwear and underwear. A 54/56" suit is £126.85, 'Club Casual Extra Tall' trousers £25.95 and 'Double II King' shirts £19.95.

Catalogue: *Bi-annually, A4, Catalogue, 32 pages, Colour, £1.00 refundable* Postal charges: *Varies with item* Delivery: *Royal Mail, Parcelforce* Methods of Payment: *Cheque, Postal Order, COD, Visa, Access / Mastercard, Other*

OSH KOSH B'GOSH B'MAIL
Gothleney Hall
Charlynch
Bridgewater
Somerset
TA5 TPQ

Telephone:
0278 653800

CHILDREN'S CLOTHES

Osh Kosh provide children's dungarees, short dungarees, pinafores and jeans in 100% cotton by mail.

The clothes have been produced in Wisconsin in the USA since 1895 and were originally designed for the uniforms of the locomotive drivers. The children's dungarees supplied by Osh Kosh by Mail are a 'pint-size version' of the genuine article.

Clothes are suitable for both girls and boys ranging

Clothes

in age from three months to twelve years old. Striped dungarees start at £24.00, short dungarees from £22.00 and pinafore dresses are priced from £16.50.

Catalogue: *A5, Leaflets, 8 pages, Colour, Free* Postal charges: *£2.00* Delivery: *Royal Mail* Methods of Payment: *Cheque, Visa, Access / Mastercard*

PAKEMAN, CATTO AND CARTER
No 5 the Market Place
Cirencester
Gloucestershire
GL7 2NX

Telephone:
0285 641113
Fax:
0285 641114

MENSWEAR

Six generations of Pakemans have been tailors since the late 18th century, making them one of the oldest tailoring firms in the land. Today they have a thriving shop in Cirencester but also operate a mail order service for those of us who do not live locally.

Their attractive catalogue features trousers, belts, shirts, woollens and even some rather nice shaving accessories. Everything here is very English, very good quality, although the prices are reasonable.

Corduroy trousers are £49.50, while cotton drills, moleskins and grey flannels are £59.50. Woollens and shirts are £38.00, ties £24.50, dress shirts £45.00 and shaving brushes, £25.00.

Catalogue: *A5, Brochure, 14 pages, Colour, Free* Postal charges: *£3.00* Delivery: *Royal Mail* Methods of Payment: *Cheque, Postal Order, Visa, Access / Mastercard*

PALOMA
28 Liston road
London
SW4 0DF

Telephone:
071 720 4283

OUTDOOR CLOTHING

Detachable sleeved jackets and reversible bodywarmers from Paloma are water-resistant, breathable, lightweight and windproof, and are designed to give warmth without weight. State-of-the-art fibres are used to give high performance against wind, rain and low temperatures. They can be machine-washed and tumble-dried with no danger of shrinkage or loss of colour.

Bodywarmers start at £28.00 for children and £43.00 for adults. Jackets start at £46.00 for children and £70.00 for adults.

Catalogue: *Third A4, Leaflets, Colour, Free* Postal charges: *Varies with item* Delivery: *Royal Mail* Methods of Payment: *Cheque, Postal Order*

Clothes

PATRA SELECTIONS LIMITED
1–5 Nant Road
London
NW2 2AL

Telephone:
081 209 1112
Fax:
081 458 3207

HANDMADE SILK CLOTHES

Patra specialise in handmade silk clothing. They make not just clothing but also duvet covers, pillow cases and cushion covers. Although mainly for women, Patra does offer a range of shirts and underwear for men. Strangely for a company which specialises in silk, the cover shows one of the very few items which is made entirely of cotton.

The catalogue conveniently lists the range of sizes and colours available for each item, as well as a useful guide on the care of the relevant piece. There is also a half-page of general hints on how to care for silk.

Catalogue: *A5, Catalogue, 16 pages, Colour, Free* Postal charges: *Free* Delivery: *Royal Mail* Methods of Payment: *Access / Mastercard, Visa, Postal Order Cheque*

PENNY PLAIN LIMITED
10 Marlborough Crescent
Newcastle Upon Tyne
NE1 4EE

Telephone:
091 232 1124
Fax:
091 222 0316

DESIGNER CLOTHES IN COTTON, LINEN, SILK AND WOOL

Penny Plain make exclusive and unusual clothes that will last longer and look good always.

Founded in 1981 by Gillian Banyard and Christine Kerr, theirs is a largely natural-fibres catalogue – cottons, linens, silks and wool (including Liberty), etc.

They never skimp on fabric or cut, and use only top-quality materials which are usually woven and dyed exclusively for them. Their range of ladies separates, leisure wear and knitwear comes in sizes 10–22. Prices range from £17.95 for their cotton polo shirt to £299.00 for suede coats. Their ever-popular, classic wool pleated skirt is £89.95 and silk shirts are £59.95.

Catalogue: *Bi-annually, A4, Catalogue, 32 pages, Colour, Free* Postal charges: *Varies with item* Delivery: *Parcelforce, Royal Mail* Methods of Payment: *Cheque, Postal Order, Visa, Access / Mastercard*

PRINGLE OF SCOTLAND
Victoria Mill
Hawick
Roxburghshire
TD9 7AL

GOLF CLOTHING

Pringle's are of course famous for their golfing sweaters which include a 'Nick Faldo' range. Many of the clothes just bear the Pringle logo, the Trophy round-neck sweaters (£49.95), for instance. These, like the Trophy V-neck (£49.95) and waistcoat (£56.95), are available in 10 colours. Other items, like the Trophy Burnview sweaters carry an explicitly golfing motif on the chest.

Pringle's 'Ladies Golf' collection includes many

Clothes

different ideas for the woman golfer. Of course, the majority of these items, like the men's, will no doubt be seen in the bar as much as on the course. 'Sports Yasmin' pullovers cost £58.95.

Catalogue: *Quarterly, A4, Catalogue, 26 pages, Colour, Free* Postal charges: *Varies with item* Delivery: *Royal Mail* Methods of Payment: *Cheque, Postal Order, Visa, Access / Mastercard*

PURPLE FISH
St Mary's Mill
Chalford
Glos
GL6 9PX

Telephone:
0453 882820

CHILDREN'S SHOES
Purple Fish primary footwear make fashionable, comfortable and durable shoes, trainers and boots for young children. Contoured soles, extra padding and double stitching at all key points make their trainers, starting at £20.00, a shrewd investment.

Clogs voted 'the most fashionable shoes around' by *She* magazine, are available in an assortment of colours, from £19.00. The cork sole of the sandal is contoured to the natural shape of the foot, and the inside is lined with leather.

Catalogue: *A4, Catalogue, 22 pages, Colour, Free* Postal charges: *£2.50* Delivery: *Royal Mail* Methods of Payment: *Visa, Access / Mastercard, Cheque, Postal Order*

RACHEL GRIMMER LIMITED
21 Devonshire Place
Harrogate
Yorkshire
HG1 4AA

Telephone:
0423 524236

DESIGNER KNITWEAR
Using bold colours and original designs, this is a glorious catalogue of inspiring knitwear for women and men. Although measurements are given in standard lengths and sizes, adaptations to suit the customer's needs can be made. Clearly laid out, with diagrams to illustrate the basic styles and availability, the only foreseeable difficulty could be in choosing from so many attractive possibilities.

Expensive perhaps but classic and designed to last a lifetime, a Fair Isle jumper of wool, silk and cotton sells for £178.00. Plain jumpers are also available in cashmere. Delivery time is between 28 and 56 days, depending on the complexity of the pattern.

Catalogue: *A4, Catalogue, 20 pages, Colour, Free* Postal charges: *Varies with item* Delivery: *Royal Mail* Methods of Payment: *Cheque, Postal Order, Visa, Access / Mastercard*

Clothes

RACING GREEN
PO Box 100
Morley
Leeds
LS27 0BX

Telephone:
0532 382444
Fax:
0532 382465

CASUAL CLOTHES

Stylish UK rival to American-based mail order firm, Lands' End, Racing Green has only been operating since 1992, yet has already carved out a successful niche for itself. Most of its clothes are in unisex sizes, a large range of colours and in natural fabrics, particularly cotton. The style is relaxed, American influenced and geared to the baby-boomer market.

Typical products are the short-sleeve piqué polo shirts, retailing at £19.00, rollneck sweaters at £18.00 and button-down poplin shirts at £27.00. There is also a small range of accessories, including belts, shoes, hats and scarves.

Catalogue: *A4, Catalogue, 76 pages, Colour, Free* Postal charges: *£3.00* Delivery: *Royal Mail* Methods of Payment: *Cheque, Postal Order, Visa, Access / Mastercard, American Express*

RAPPORE
Spring Gardens
Off Bolton Road
Darwen
Lancashire
BB3 1BZ

Telephone:
0254 704040
Fax:
0254 701989

BATHROBES AND TOWELS

Rappore produce personalised, embroidered bathrobes and towels. Mostly they do this for large companies, such as Forte and Holiday Inn, however, they do claim that 'no order too small'. Good news for those who fancy wrapping themselves in something unique when stepping out of the bath. Prices start at £13.95 for the Kimono Robe rising to £21.95 for a hooded version.

Rappore also produce unisex slippers, at £1.99 a pair (but this is based on quantities of 50), and sarongs in one adjustable size at £5.50. Towels come in a variety of sizes – a face cloth is 55p; a jumbo towel £9.95.

Catalogue: *A4, Brochure, 2 pages, Colour, Free* Postal charges: *Varies with item* Delivery: *Royal Mail* Methods of Payment: *Cheque*

REDISCOVERED ORIGINALS
Springfield Mills
Town End
Bramley
Leeds
LS13 3LY

Telephone:
0532 564416
Fax:
0532 361790

FASHION ITEMS AND UNUSUAL GIFTS

A collection of unusual fashion items and gifts from around the world. They are authentic products, some of which were popular in past times, but are worn today. For example, Drizabone stockman's coat, £119.00, Australian leather hat, £39.98, LAPD leather jacket, £125.00, juggling kit, £14.98, Harley Davidson key ring, £4.98.

Catalogue: *Bi-annually, Catalogue, 24 pages, Colour, Free* Postal charges: *Varies with item* Delivery: *Parcelforce* Methods of Payment: *Cheque, Postal Order, Visa, Access / Mastercard*

Clothes

RICHER
Royal Mills
Station Road
Steeton
Keighley
West Yorkshire
BD20 6RA

Telephone:
0274 564747

CLOTHES FOR 5' 2" AND UNDER
A variety of outerwear, lingerie and shoes for men and women 5' 2" and under, and for sizes 8 to 34 for women and sizes 32 to 56 for men. Order phoneline available between 8.30 a.m. and 4.30 p.m. Monday to Friday. Recommend a friend and save £5.00 on first order. Good quality clothing and clear illustrated catalogue.

Catalogue: *A4, Catalogue, 126 pages, Colour, Free* Postal charges: *Varies with item* Delivery: *In house delivery* Methods of Payment: *Cheque, Postal Order, Visa, Access / Mastercard*

ROBERT NORFOLK
Dualfold Ltd
67 Gatwick Road
Crawley
West Sussex
RH10 2RD

Telephone:
0293 616775
Fax:
0293 533832

CASUAL CLOTHES
Robert Norfolk produce a range of elegant, co-ordinated separates, which are lavishly illustrated in this glossy catalogue. Specialising in sweatshirts with various motifs from sporting to animals, it caters principally for women, although there are small sections for men and children.

One of the nice things about this catalogue is the refreshing use of models who are clearly older than 17. Most of the products are made from 100% cotton and come in small, medium and large. Sweatshirts start at £29.95 and polo shirts at £27.95.

Catalogue: *A4, Catalogue, 32 pages, Colour, Free* Postal charges: *Varies with item* Delivery: *Royal Mail* Methods of Payment: *Cheque, Postal Order, Visa, Access / Mastercard*

ROHAN DESIGNS
30 Maryland Road
Tongwell
Milton Keynes
MK15 8HN

Telephone:
0908 618888
Fax:
0909 211209

OUTDOOR CLOTHING
Rohan outdoor clothing have, for some time, been one of the market leaders in this area. Their lightweight, durable clothing is easy to care for and ingeniously designed by people who actually use them.

The Summit jacket is made from two layers of Goretex with a polyester lining. The principle is that two thin linings are more comfortable and more flexible than a single heavy one. Available in all sizes, it costs £269.00.

Summit overtrousers (£179.00), also made from Goretex, are ideal for alpine skiing or mountaineering. They feature two-way full-length zips with storm flaps and hinged knees to stop them riding up.

Catalogue: *Quarterly, A4, Catalogue, 20 pages, Colour, Free* Postal charges: *£3.00* Delivery: *Royal Mail* Methods of Payment: *Cheque, Postal Order, Visa, Access / Mastercard, American Express*

Clothes

ROSIE NIEPER
12 Munster Road
Teddington
Middlesex
TW11 9LL

Telephone:
081 977 2863

DESIGNER T-SHIRTS AND GIFTS
An idiosyncratic collection of young designers, whose artwork is printed onto T-shirts, is brought together in this interesting and lively catalogue. Styles range from the primitive, almost childlike designs of animals in 'Bang On The Door's Ark' collection, to cartoon pictures with humorous captions or pictures of famous but dead personalities such as Oscar Wilde.

Most T-shirts are one size and only the Ark range offers children's sizes. There are also three designs for jokey, handmade felt slippers, including a fabulous pair of 'Jolly Jester' slippers. Prices for T-shirts are between £9.99 and £19.99.

Catalogue: *A4, Leaflets, 20 pages, Colour, Free* Postal charges: *Free* Delivery: *Royal Mail* Methods of Payment: *Cheque, Postal Order, Visa, Access / Mastercard*

ROSIE POCKETT
Trenowan
49 Pendarnes Road
Camborne
Cornwall
TR14 7QJ

Telephone:
0209 713065

CHILDREN'S CLOTHES AND RELATED ACCESSORIES
Rosie Pockett is a small family business specialising in traditional clothes for little girls, with a small range for boys. Made to a high standard, using 100% cotton and striking fabrics, Rosie Pockett dresses have their own petticoat. Look for the secret pocket in the petticoat to make sure it is a Rosie Pockett dress!

Reversible trousers, reversible shorts, attractive sweatshirts: best dresses from £24.50; sleeveless cotton dresses, £12.99; baby dresses from £15.00; brocade waistcoat, £14.99.

Catalogue: *Bi-annually, A5, Brochure, 4 pages, Colour, Free* Postal charges: *Varies with item* Delivery: *Royal Mail* Methods of Payment: *Cheque, Postal Order, Visa, Access / Mastercard*

SARTOR LTD
Glen View Road
Eldwick
Bingley
W Yorks
BD16 3EF

Telephone:
0274 565136
Fax:
0274 565139

CLOTHES
Sartor cater for the cost-conscious and those with special needs. Three small pamphlets are included within the main catalogue. 'Personal Choice' contains useful items like the 'Bean Bag Lap Tray' (£14.99) and a commode chair (£99.99). 'Home-Comforts' covers bedding, kitchen and garden equipment – everything from a traditional quilt (single: £20.99; double: £25.99) and a hearth rug (£33.99) to gutter-mesh (£5.99).

'The Country Selection' features a conservative range of men's wear, ranging from the 'Clevedon' lightweight grey or stone casual jacket (from £27.99)

Clothes

to the anticipated lovat polyester trousers (£12.99).

The main colour catalogue presents ladies' wear at affordable prices. These are not high fashion items but prices are low and the clothes practical.

Catalogue: *A5, Catalogue, 48 pages, Colour, Free* Postal charges: *95p* Delivery: *Royal Mail* Methods of Payment: *Cheque, Postal Order, Visa, Access / Mastercard, COD*

SECRET LOOKS
9 Swan Lane
Norwich
Norfolk
NR2 1HZ

Telephone:
0603 616322

LACE UNDERWEAR

This range contains lingerie from some of the country's top designers, including Charnos, Gossard and Triumph, as well as four of Secret Looks' own collections.

An underwear set, including bra, brief, suspenders and stockings costs from £19.99, and bodies from £27.99.

Catalogue: *A4, Catalogue, 8 pages, Colour, Free* Postal charges: *Varies with item* Delivery: *Royal Mail* Methods of Payment: *Cheque, Postal Order, Visa, Access / Mastercard, American Express*

SELECTIVE MARKETPLACE LIMITED
Belton Road West
Loughborough
LE11 0XL

Telephone:
0509 235 235

WOMEN'S CLOTHES

With a range of exclusive styles in sizes from 12–24 this catalogue provides an excellent choice of women's clothes at competitive prices.

The clothes come in a range of natural fabrics and are generously cut to ensure they are comfortable as well as smart. Many styles are carefully tailored to be particularly flattering to the fuller figure, something which all too few catalogues bother to do.

Among the items are a linen-mix suit for only £59.95 and a cotton jersey shirt in a range of colours for £16.95.

Catalogue: *Quarterly, A4, Catalogue, 24 pages, Colour, Free* Postal charges: *Varies with item* Delivery: *Royal Mail* Methods of Payment: *Cheque, Postal Order, Visa, Access / Mastercard*

SELFRIDGES LTD
400 Oxford Street
London
W1A 1AB

Telephone:
0800 101 101

LADIES CLOTHES

The Selfridges Selection offers immediate service to every customer. Every item has been carefully chosen to meet high standards, giving the customer a wide choice of colourful and stylish clothes. The clothes are a range of casual wear (jacket £169), formal wear (dress £145) and underwear (bra & briefs £16.95). There are styles to suit all ages with varying tastes.

Catalogue: *Quarterly, A4, Catalogue, 52 pages, Colour, Free* Postal charges: *Free* Delivery: *Royal Mail* Methods of Payment: *Cheque, Visa, Access / Mastercard, American Express, Diners Club*

Clothes

S SEYMOUR AND CO (SHIRTS) LTD
Seymour's Shirts
136 Sunbridge Road
Bradford
West Yorkshire
BD1 2QG

Telephone:
0274 726520
Fax:
0274 735911

SHIRTS
Seymour's Shirts have specialised in traditionally producing made-to-measure shirts, blouses and pyjamas for 65 years. Each garment is exclusively hand cut and individually sewn by Seymour's own seamstresses according to each customer's measurements, and choice of style and cloth.

Free sample swatches showing over 400 superb designs taken from the world's finest fabrics are available to choose from. Any size can be made. Shirts and blouses start at £39.95 for polyester/cotton fabrics. Garments in 100% cotton commence at £43.35; wool/cotton blends at £57.15, and pure silk at £79.50.

Catalogue: *Annually, Third A4, Brochure, 8 pages, Colour, Free* Postal charges: *Varies with item* Delivery: *Royal Mail, Parcelforce* Methods of Payment: *Cheque, Postal Order, Visa, Access / Mastercard*

SHANKARA LIMITED
Alton House Office Park
Aylesbury
Bucks
HP19 3DB

Telephone:
0296 393989

SWIMWEAR
Shankara's glossy, well-produced catalogue features up-market women's swimwear from Paris. A St Tropez swimsuit, available from sizes 10 to 16, costs £95.00. More daring, the Yacht Club bikini costs £66.00. Many of these swimsuits and bikinis are quite stunning and unavailable elsewhere.

There is also a selection of summer shoes for £17.50 and some wraps and skirts as well as blouses and tops for warm weather. A thoroughly attractive catalogue.

Catalogue: *Bi-annually, A4, Catalogue, 50 pages, Colour, Free* Postal charges: *£1.90* Delivery: *Royal Mail* Methods of Payment: *Cheque, Postal Order, Visa, Access / Mastercard*

SHETLAND KNITWEAR ASSOCIATES
31 King Harald Street
Lerwick
Shetland
ZE1 0EQ

Telephone:
0595 2746
Fax:
0595 2746

HAND AND HAND-FRAME KNITTED REAL SHETLAND KNITWEAR
This company only sells the real thing – genuine Shetland knitwear made in the islands themselves by the world-renowned knitters. The range includes traditional Fair Isle and lace as well as more contemporary designs. All the items are either hand or hand-frame knitted.

Sweaters are around £155, hand-framed cardigans £98.75, shawls from £60 and hand-knitted gloves £15.25. This may seem on the expensive side but the products are beautifully made and will last for years.

Catalogue: *Annually, A5, Brochure, 8 pages, Colour, Free* Postal charges: *Varies with item* Delivery: *Royal Mail* Methods of Payment: *Postal Order Cheque, Visa, Access / Mastercard*

Clothes

SIMPLICITY AT HOME
Freepost GW2588
Glasgow
G72 9BR

Telephone:
0968 826900

PATTERNS
Simplicity offers a range of clothing patterns, craft products and sewing accessories. Patterns cost between £2.99 and £3.99 and include waistcoats, dresses, jackets and skirts. For children there are badge-making kits (£2.99), colour-in T-shirts and books. The range of sewing aids includes a point presser/banger reduced from £39.95 to £14.95 and an ultraglide iron at £19.95.

Catalogue: *A4, Catalogue, 12 pages, Colour, £1.50* Postal charges: *£2.50* Delivery: *Royal Mail* Methods of Payment: *Cheque, Postal Order, Visa, Access / Mastercard*

ST ANDREWS WOOLLEN MILL
The Golf Links
St Andrews
Fife
KY16 9JH

Telephone:
0334 72366

MEN'S AND WOMEN'S WOOLLEN CLOTHING
The St Andrews Woollen Mill, located at the famous golf links in Scotland, create cashmere clothing in a variety of classic styles. They are quite happy to discuss producing any item of clothing that doesn't feature in their catalogue.

Their ladies V-neck pullovers, made from 100% pure lambswool and available in yellow, pale blue, grey, navy, red, pink, white, black, natural, dark green and camel comes in all sizes from 36" to 44" and costs £53.00. A men's lambswool pullover is slightly cheaper, at £49.50.

Catalogue: *A4, Leaflets, 2 pages, Colour, Free* Postal charges: *£4.00* Delivery: *Royal Mail* Methods of Payment: *American Express, Visa, Access / Mastercard, Postal Order Cheque*

STAMFORD CLOTHIERS
30 York Road
Leeds
W Yorks
LS9 8RH

Telephone:
0532 488160
Fax:
0532 481137

MADE TO MEASURE AND READY-MADE CLOTHES
This catalogue ofers a range of clothes for the office and for the outdoors.

Shirts come in almost twenty fabrics and there is a Double Two range for those who prefer extra width and more comfort in their clothes. Trousers, breeches and plus-twos for men and women come ready-made or can be made to measure in fabrics ranging in price from £49.95 to £84.95. To compliment the trousers and shirts are blazers and wool sweaters which will complete the country look.

Catalogue: *A5, Leaflets, 13 pages, Colour, Free* Postal charges: *Varies with item* Delivery: *Royal Mail* Methods of Payment: *Cheque, Postal Order, Visa, Access / Mastercard*

Clothes

START SMART
Woodgate Manor Farm
Woodgate
Bromsgrove
Worcs
B60 4HG

Telephone:
0527 821766

CHILDREN'S CLOTHES
Start Smart offers a wide range of children's clothes, aimed at the younger child up to age ten. The range of designs is extensive and modern, including Bermuda shorts and culottes, as well as classical dresses and romper suits.

Not only is the selection of styles very broad, but the choice of colours is also wide. Swimwear for girls is available, both in one-piece and bikinis, and sun-hats too. The hand-framed knitwear in machine-washable cotton is also available as machine-washable anti-tickle wool knitwear. As with other items, the selection of these jumpers is also wide.

Catalogue: *A5, Catalogue, 10 pages, Colour and B/W, Free* Postal charges: *Varies with item* Delivery: *Royal Mail* Methods of Payment: *Cheque*

SULIS
Hinton
Charterhouse
Bath
BA3 6BJ

Telephone:
0225 722770
Fax:
0225 722993

SILK CLOTHING FOR WOMEN
Sulis is a small, independent company which specialises in pure silk clothing for women. The range includes nightwear, lingerie, casual tops and thermal wear. Extensive use is made of silk jersey, a machine-washable fabric with natural stretch, softness and resilience. The garments are designed for everyday wear, the accent being on simple yet elegant styling, comfort and practicality.

Prices start at £5.00 for a silk underskirt, around £6.00 for briefs, a silk jersey body is £15.00, a long-sleeved ribbed top £25.00, a silk satin robe £36.00 and a silk satin embroidered nightdress £45.00.

Catalogue: *Bi-annually, A5, Catalogue, 12–16 pages, Colour, Free* Postal charges: *£1.00* Delivery: *Royal Mail* Methods of Payment: *Cheque, Postal Order, Visa, Access / Mastercard*

SWALEDALE WOOLLENS LTD
Muker
Richmond
N Yorkshire
DL11 6QG

Telephone:
0748 86251
Fax:
0748 886251

WOOLLEN CLOTHING
Established in 1974, Swaledale Woollens consciously make use of Swaledale wool and try to encourage local knitting and similar skills in the Swaledale area. The Swaledale is a horned sheep able to forage and fend for itself in remote areas where other breeds would find it hard to survive. For those who like to do their own hand or machine knitting, Swaledale can provide several natural yarns on cone and in packs.

Woollen wear from Swaledale includes 'Fisherman Rib' sweaters (£34.95–£36.95) with suede patches, 'Bobby' cardigans (5 buttons: £47.95; 7 buttons: £48.95) and the 'Kisdon' sweater

Clothes

(£36.95) or cardigan (£44.50). There are also Swaledale ties and tweeds in attractive colours.

Catalogue: *A4, Brochure, 8 pages, Colour, Free* Postal charges: *Varies with item* Delivery: *Royal Mail* Methods of Payment: *Cheque, Postal Order, Visa, Access / Mastercard*

T.M. LEWIN & SONS LTD
106 Jermyn Street
London
SW1Y 6EQ

Telephone:
071 839 1664
Fax:
071 839 7791

QUALITY SHIRTS AND TIES FOR MEN AND WOMEN

Lewin & Sons began making fine-quality shirts and ties in 1898 and are still leading specialists in corporate, club and regimental ties.

Shirts are made from the finest quality two-fold Poplin or pinpoint Oxford cotton, giving a luxurious feel and comfortable fit. All are generously cut and available in a range of sleeve lengths. There are also two collar styles to choose from and a choice of double or button cuffs.

The quality silk ties are designed and produced in Lewin's own workshops. Dress accessories, such as cuff-links, braces, handkerchiefs and collar stiffeners are also available, along with a selection of cotton blouses, jewellery and capes for women.

Shirts start at around £40.00, ties at £25.00, blouses at £45.00, and capes at about £100.00.

Catalogue: *A5, Catalogue, 20 pages, Colour, Free* Postal charges: *Varies with item* Delivery: *Royal Mail* Methods of Payment: *American Express, Access / Mastercard, Visa Cheque*

TARTAN FLING
19 Gayfield Square
Edinburgh
Scotland
EH1 3NX

Telephone:
031 557 6399

SCOTTISH CLOTHES

If you like tartan, you'll want the Tartan Fling catalogue. Steeping their sales blurb in the noble history of Scotland, they state that all the items have some connection with Scotland although quite what this is with something like the hand-painted terracotta plant pot and saucer is not clear.

But the tartan clothing offers excellent value and would make the perfect gift for any Scotofile. A tartan dressing gown in 100% new wool is £80.00, a tartan tie £9.00, while a pair of lady's tartan trews are £75.00.

Catalogue: *A4, Catalogue, 8 pages, Colour, Free* Postal charges: *Varies with item* Delivery: *Royal Mail* Methods of Payment: *Cheque, Postal Order, Visa, Access / Mastercard*

Clothes

TARTAN LANDSCAPES
20 St Cuthbert Street
Kirkcudbright
DG6 4HZ

Telephone:
0557 330371
Fax:
0557 331572

TARTAN WAISTCOATS, TIES, WRAPS, SCARVES, RUGS

Based in Kirkcudbright, south-west Scotland, this company specialises in top-quality tartan waistcoats using 100% pure wool cloth produced in Scotland. Their products are sent not only throughout Britain but also worldwide, with customers in the USA, Australia, Canada, Germany, Belgium, Portugal, Indonesia and Hong Kong.

All the waistcoats are individually tailored and come in ten of the most popular tartans. However, they also carry a range of some 320 tartans which can be supplied at short notice. In addition they make waistcoats in Paisley pattern and lightweight tartan taffetta.

Ladies and gents waistcoats are £41.50, with scarves at £14.50, ties £14.00 and wraps £42.50.

Catalogue: *Annually, Brochure, 6 pages, Colour, Free* Postal charges: *Varies with item* Delivery: *Royal Mail* Methods of Payment: *Cheque, Postal Order, Visa, Access / Mastercard*

THE ALPACA COLLECTION
Peel Place
50 Carver Street
Birmingham
B1 3AS

Telephone:
021 212 2550
Fax:
021 212 1948

BOLIVIAN KNITWEAR

A range of knitwear new to Britain, 'The Alpaca Collection' consists of a selection of unisex garments made from high-quality yarn from the alpaca, cousin to the llama. The sweaters on offer are designed and produced in Bolivia, with many of them being hand-knitted and all hand-finished. Fully environmentally friendly, all sweaters are either made from natural or vegetable dyed wool.

The 'Trio-Alpaca' design has, as its name suggests, three of the company's namesakes on the front. This comes in two styles; both a round-neck sweater and a V-neck cardigan – £32.95 and £42.95 respectively. For a more intricate design choose 'Classic Morena', again both a V-neck sweater for £69.95 and cardigan for £74.95. Also on offer are a scarf at £11.95 and beret at £9.49.

Catalogue: *A5, Catalogue, 8 pages, Colour, Free* Postal charges: *£3.00* Delivery: *Royal Mail* Methods of Payment: *Cheque, Postal Order, Visa, Access / Mastercard*

Clothes

THE BRETON SHIRT COMPANY
PO Box 15
Brampton Cumbria
CA8 1RB

Telephone:
06977 41936
Fax:
06977 41937

BRETON SHIRTS
With a name like that, they couldn't really sell much else! In fact their colourful catalogue features a number of variations on the basic idea – the traditional French jersey. There is a Seafarer's sweatshirt, a polo shirt and a Regatta shirt with a collar as well as the original style. All are made out of 100% unbleached cotton.

They also sell a Breton cap and beret as well as shorts, and sweatshirts. The Original Breton costs £14.95, with a children's version at £7.95. The Breton Cap is £12.95, an Arran Sweater £39.95 and a Fisherman's Smock £17.50.

Catalogue: *A5, Brochure, 8 pages, Colour, Free* Postal charges: *Varies with item* Delivery: *Royal Mail* Methods of Payment: *Cheque, Postal Order*

THE CASHMERE STORE
2 St Giles Street
Edinburgh
EH1 1PT

Telephone:
031 556 9882
Fax:
031 225 6503

CASHMERE CLOTHING
The Cashmere Store stocks an assortment of pullover designs. They also sell silk shirts and ties to complement cashmere clothing. Separate designs are available for men and women.

A diamond cable sweater with a round neck, comes in navy-blue, light grey and cream, in sizes small, medium and large for £129.00. Plainer designs include their cabled polo sweater (£139.00), with an intricate cable pattern on the front, and their traditional fisher rib cashmere sweater at £140.00. Cardigans are catered for by the Speyside cardigan at £139.00 and the round-neck cardigan at £139.00.

Catalogue: *A5, Catalogue, 40 pages, Colour, Free* Postal charges: *Varies with item* Delivery: *Royal Mail* Methods of Payment: *Cheque, Postal Order, Visa, Access / Mastercard*

THE COACH STORE
8 Sloane Street
London
SW1X 9LE

Telephone:
071 235 1507
Fax:
071 235 3556

LEATHER ACCESSORIES
The Coach Store offers an exclusive range of luxury leather goods for men and women. The prices of these items reflect the quality of the materials and the workmanship. There are thirteen sections containing examples of bags, belts, wallets and other accessories, along with their classic Manhattan and Sheridan collections.

The business collection has briefcases from £430.00 and accessories from £175.00. The Eliot bag, a lightweight, pebble-textured leather bag with bridle leather trim and signature brass hardware, is available in a range of colours for £250.00.

Clothes

Catalogue: *Quarterly, A5, Catalogue, 66 pages, Colour, Free* Postal charges: *Varies with item* Delivery: *Royal Mail* Methods of Payment: *Cheque, Postal Order, Visa, Access / Mastercard, American Express*

THE COLLAR COMPANY
Hall Farm,
Silchester
Berkshire
RG7 2NH

Telephone:
0256 881680

LADIES WEAR

The Collar Company offers a selection of colourful, fashionable and individual styles. They come in four different sizes (small, medium, large and extra large) with styles for those who wish to look fashionable but smart for little expense. They also offer casual wear for the younger woman which can also be mixed and matched with other outfits from the catalogue.

Each outfit has a name to describe its style; for example, Augusta (£34.00 for a casual shirt), or St Andrews (£36.50 for a smart shirt). Cardigans are also on offer in a variety of vibrant colours (£91.50 for a raspberry cardigan).

Catalogue: *Bi-annually, A4, Catalogue, 7 pages, Colour, Free* Postal charges: *£1.50* Delivery: *Royal Mail* Methods of Payment: *Cheque, Visa, Access / Mastercard*

THE DUFFLE COAT COMPANY
140 Battersea Park
Road
London
SW11 4NB

Telephone:
071 498 8191
Fax:
071 498 0990

WINTER OVERCOATS

The Duffle Coat Company operates entirely by mail order. All its duffle coats are manufactured in England by Gloverall and made from a luxurious soft double-faced cloth with horn-style toggles and leather fastenings. Coats in the classic colours navy-blue and camel are available for both men and women at £124.50. Especially for women are a range of different colours including juniper green, cranberry red, grey and black at £129.50.

Duffle jackets for both sexes cost £119.50, smarter reefer jackets again for both sexes are £124.50, while children's duffle coats available only in navy-blue cost between £54.50 and £69.00 depending on size.

Catalogue: *Annually, A5, Brochure, 11 pages, Colour, Free* Postal charges: *Free* Delivery: *Royal Mail* Methods of Payment: *Cheque, Visa, Access / Mastercard*

THE GRANDFATHER SHIRT COMPANY
10 Willan Drive
Portrush
Co. Antrim
BT56 8PU

Telephone:
0265 823697

SHIRTS

The Grandfather Shirt Company specialise in Gleneske Original Irish Grandfather shirts. For generations, the Gleneske shirt has been a traditional part of everyday life in rural Ireland. 100% cotton, fully shrunk with fast colours, the Gleneske offers warmth, comfort and durability. It is probably as fashionable as it is practical. A small to extra large

Clothes

sizes cost £19.99; XXL to XXXL costs slightly more, at £21.99.

The shirts are also available for children, ranging in price between £10.99 and £14.99. There are also Gleneske Grandfather Nightshirts from £24.99 to £26.99.

Catalogue: *A4, Leaflets, Colour, Free* Postal charges: *Free* Delivery: *Royal Mail* Methods of Payment: *Cheque, Postal Order, Visa, Access / Mastercard*

THE SCOTCH HOUSE
2 Brompton Road
Knightsbridge
London
SW1X 7PB

Telephone:
071 581 2151
Fax:
071 589 1583

CLOTHES

The Scotch House offers a wide range of beautifully made clothes, mainly woollen, with a Scottish feel. Cashmere and lambswool are the main fabrics, but there are Fair Isle and Merino too. The Scottish theme is clearly shown by the range of tartans on offer. As well as clothes, the company has diversified into pens, china and accessories, all of which also have a distinctive Scottish look.

The Scotch House has half a dozen branches, three in London, one on Brompton Road and two on Regent Street, one in Glasgow, one in Edinburgh and one at Terminal 4, Heathrow Airport.

Catalogue: *A4, Catalogue, 24 pages, Colour, £1.00* Postal charges: *Varies with item* Delivery: *Royal Mail* Methods of Payment: *Postal Order Cheque, Visa, Access / Mastercard, American Express, Diners Club*

THIMBELINA
17 Oxford Street
Woodstock
Oxon
OX20 1TH

Telephone:
0993 812686

CHRISTENING GOWNS

Hand-made, traditional style christening outfits are the speciality of this catalogue. Everything is well presented with clear pen and ink diagrams and helpful fabric swatches. The garments themselves are beautifully made and evidently designed as future family heirlooms.

Christening gowns sell for between £115.00 and £235.00 and come fully lined with matching bonnets. They are packed in Edwardian-style lined boxes. The range also includes rompers, short frocks and a sailor suit. The company will also make them in fabrics other than those suitable for christenings if requested.

Catalogue: *A4, Leaflets, 12 pages, B/W, Free* Postal charges: *Varies with item* Delivery: *Royal Mail* Methods of Payment: *Cheque, Postal Order, Visa, Access / Mastercard*

Clothes

THOMAS PINK
85 Jermyn Street
London
SW1

Telephone:
071 498 3882
Fax:
071 498 3325

EXCLUSIVE SHIRTS FOR MEN

If there is an occasion on which you need to dress to impress then contact Thomas Pink. *The Times* said they were *the* place to buy shirts in London today and one look at their catalogue will show you why.

They maintain a stock of classic shirts in a range of the most popular fabrics and also have a limited range of exclusive designs which change month by month. Every shirt shows the painstaking attention to detail which has won the company such a good reputation.

Their best-selling shirts are £42.50, while silk ties are £24.00 and cufflinks from between £5.00 and £44.00.

Catalogue: *A5, Catalogue, Colour, Free* Postal charges: *Varies with item* Delivery: *Royal Mail* Methods of Payment: *Cheque, Postal Order, Visa, Access / Mastercard, American Express*

TOLLYBANDS
PO Box 5
Twyford
Reading
Berkshire
RG10 100YZ

Telephone:
0800 350 350

WRIST BANDS

Tollybands are designed for those times when gloves are impractical. By using one of nature's most warming materials – pure lambswool – a band worn around the wrist will apparently be as effective as wearing gloves. The proximity of the specially prepared sheepskin and its high lanolin content improves blood heat and circulation in the extremities. Tollybands are also beneficial to arthritis sufferers.

Available in 3 sizes, large, medium or small, they cost £14.99 per pair. Bands for ankles are £16.50. They are available in black, brown or green.

Catalogue: *A4, Leaflet, 1 page, B/W, Free* Postal charges: *Free* Delivery: *Royal Mail* Methods of Payment: *Cheque, Postal Order, Visa, Access / Mastercard*

TOTZ
PO Box 123
St Albans
Herts
AL2 1EL

Telephone:
0727 821697

CONTINENTAL CHILDREN'S CLOTHING

Hand-picked range of stylish clothes for children from France, Germany, Britain, Portugal and beyond. Jazzy jackets, cool dungarees and dungarettes, ethnic outfits, new-look denim, boisterous basics and plenty of accessories. Delivery is guaranteed within 28 days.

Catalogue: *Bi-annually, A4, Catalogue, 12 pages, Colour, Free* Postal charges: *Varies with item* Delivery: *Royal Mail* Methods of Payment: *Cheque, Postal Order, Visa, Access / Mastercard*

Clothes

TRAIDCRAFT
Traidcraft plc
Kingsway
Gateshead
Tyne & Wear
NE11 0NE

Telephone:
091 491 0591

LADIES CLOTHES
Traidcraft has joined with Third World producers to offer clothes with continental and ethnic style. The styles are from India (embroidered waistcoat £29.95), South America (blockprint dress £29.95), and Traidcraft's own female range (drawstring top £24.95). They also offer accessories and jewellery all based on the South American theme (Shan star brooch £3.95, Eastern jumbo bag £18.95). Sizes range from 10 to 18 and from small and medium to large.

Catalogue: *Bi-annually, A4, Catalogue, 27 pages, Colour, 85p*
Postal charges: *Varies with item* Delivery: *Royal Mail* Methods of Payment: *Cheque, Visa, Access / Mastercard*

TRAVELLING LIGHT
Morland House
Morland
Penrith
Cumbria
CA10 3AZ

Telephone:
0931 714488
Fax:
0931 714555

HOT WEATHER CLOTHING FOR MEN AND WOMEN
Travelling Light is the only company in the UK to specialise in hot weather clothing which it produces for both men and women. The clothes are ideal for travel, safaris, cruises and for on the beach. Each item is made in the UK from top-quality fabrics. They also offer a made-to-measure service and stock a range of useful travel accessories.

A man's safari jacket costs a reasonable £59.95, a ladies Swiss cotton shirt £36.95, a sunhat with chin cord £15.95 and a Cordura elephant flight bag £34.95.

Catalogue: *Bi-annually, A4, Catalogue, 40 pages, Colour, Free*
Postal charges: *Varies with item* Delivery: *Royal Mail* Methods of Payment: *Cheque, Postal Order, Visa, Access / Mastercard*

TREFRIW WOOLLEN MILLS

Trefriw
Gwynedd
LL27 0NQ

Telephone:
0492 640462

WOOLLEN ARTICLES
The Trefriw Woollen Mills produce a range of traditional woollen clothing, tableware and bedspreads. As one might expect there's a strong Welsh flavour to everything here.

Tapestry bedspreads range from the single-bed version (70" × 100") at £69.85, to a king-size spread (116" × 100") costing £111.95. There's also a throw of 50" × 70" for £37.55.

Mohair rugs and stoles are actually composed of 70% mohair, 25% wool and 5% nylon. The rugs (70" × 50") cost £35.10 and the stoles (70" × 17") cost just £13.80.

Catalogue: *A4, Leaflets, 1 page, B/W, Free* Postal charges: *Varies with item* Delivery: *Royal Mail* Methods of Payment: *Cheque, Visa, Access / Mastercard*

Clothes

TUFF CLOTHING
Blackworth Industrial Park
Highworth
Swindon
Wiltshire
SN6 7NA

Telephone:
0793 765292
Fax:
0793 766017

WORK CLOTHES
The Tuff Stuff brochure contains a small range of Osh Kosh clothing for kids. All the clothes are made from 100% cotton, are machine-washable and can be tumble-dried.

Based on the uniforms for American locomotive drivers, the Osh Kosh pint-sized versions start at £24.00 for dungarees and £22.00 for shortalls and pinafores. The colours available are sky-blue and white, navy and white, red and white, pink and white and denim. Denim jeans start at £24.00, sweatshirts at £25.00 and to complete the look there are engineering caps at £6.95.

Catalogue: *Annually, A4, Catalogue, 20 pages, Colour, Free* Postal charges: *£3.75* Delivery: *Parcelforce* Methods of Payment: *Cheque, Postal Order, Visa, Access / Mastercard*

WATKINS & COLE
39 Highfield Road
Felixstowe
Suffolk
IP11 7YZ

MEN'S AND WOMEN'S CLOTHES
Watkins & Cole produce a range of conservative clothing for men and women. The men's 'Country Collection' includes a 'Countryman jacket' in slate grey or lovat, starting at £31.99; 'The Buckingham' overcoat in finest gaberdine from £42.99; and a number of casual shirts priced from £14.99. Women's fashion is reflected in standard summer dresses like the 'Lavender', from £24.99, in linen-look polyester fabric and 'Felicity', from £23.99, with a pleasant floral print. There are also the usual skirts and blouses.

An additional 'Personal Choice' booklet offers a variety of products for the elderly or infirm, such as 'The Original McKenzie Super Roll Lumbar Support' for £16.99.

Catalogue: *Bi-annually, A5, Catalogue, 48 pages, Colour, Free* Postal charges: *95p* Delivery: *Royal Mail* Methods of Payment: *Cheque, Visa, Access / Mastercard, Postal Order, COD*

WEALTH OF NATIONS
Unit 28
The Talina Centre
Bagleys Lane
London
SW6 2BW

Telephone:
071 371 5333
Fax:
071 371 5398

THE BEST OF TRADITIONAL CLOTHES FROM AROUND THE WORLD
The two Wealth of Nations catalogues, plus other specials at Christmas, gather together traditional, elegant clothes that have been worn in their countries of origin for thousands of years, but still look superb today.

Having travelled to Guatemala, Mexico, Hungary, the Czech Republic, India, Bangladesh, China, Brittany, Ireland, as well as searching the archives of

Clothes

old English country tradition (shepherd's smocks, child's dress), the owner, Julia Woodham-Smith, brought back the best examples of shirts, waistcoats, skirts and shawls. She arranges for these to be adapted by skilled pattern cutters, correctly sized and then manufactured in the countries of origin.

Examples include: Cheongsam silk dress, £125.00; Fu trousers, £65.00; Mandarin Ma Kwa jacket, £95.00 from the China Silk Collection catalogue. From the main Wealth of Nations catalogue there are items for men, women and children ranging from Indian poplin shirts, £35.00, to Pashmina shawls, £85.00, children's Hungarian shirts, £18.00 to Gansey knits, £75.00. A pretty and covetable range of clothes.

Catalogue: *A6, Catalogues, 12 pages/52 pages, Colour, Free* Postal charges: *£2.95* Delivery: *Royal Mail* Methods of Payment: *Cheque, Postal Order, Visa, Access / Mastercard, American Express*

WEARITE
Park View Works
257 West Green Road
London
N15 5EG

Telephone:
081-802 3399
Fax:
081-809 2912

OUTDOOR CLOTHING FOR COUNTRY PURSUITS

Wearite manufacture the L'avenir range of outdoor clothing. This is along Barbour lines, with waxed jackets, as well as the sort of quilted jackets much beloved by the horsey fraternity. Suitable for hunting, shooting, fishing, riding and posing in the King's Road, they are well-made, practical clothes.

An executive dry waxed cotton jacket costs £39.50, a quilted casual jacket £23.50, a hunter jacket £60.00.

Catalogue: *A5, Catalogue, 16 pages, Colour, Free* Postal charges: *Varies with item* Delivery: *Royal Mail* Methods of Payment: *Cheque*

WELLERWEAR (R.G.H. LTD)
Flaska house
Troutbeck
Penrith
Cumbria
CA11 0ST

Telephone:
07687 79012
Fax:
07687 79014

COUNTRY WEAR

Wellerwear, a Cumbrian company, offers a wide range of clothes suitable for wear in the wettest part of England. If it keeps the local people dry and comfortable in this region, then it will do the same everywhere else. Although now in fashion, the clothes are essentially functional for those who work or relax in the country.

With the stress on comfort, the range of sizes is exceptional, with a style of wax-proofed jacket, the Lakelander, starting from a child's 24", going up to a large adult's 60". Cotton shirts are also available in sizes up to 18" collars with generous full cuts.

Clothes

WEST CLOTHING
36–38 Station Street
West
Coventry
W Midlands
CV6 5NB

Telephone:
0203 638121

Catalogue: *Third A4, Catalogue, 12 pages, Colour, Free* Postal charges: *Varies with item* Delivery: *Royal Mail* Methods of Payment: *Cheque, Visa, Access / Mastercard*

CLOTHES FOR LARGER MEN
Everything for the bigger man in one publication. Clothes and accessories to ensure that you are well dressed for the office, party or weekend. There's even a wide (sic) range of bedclothes for the end of the day!

With suits up to 60" chest and trousers, including chinos, to 60" waists, the range is both fashionable and practical. The choice of colours is generous and despite the leading brand names many of the goods are very reasonably priced with chinos from £33.95, sports jackets from £75.95 and pinstripe suits from £125.95.

Catalogue: *Bi-annually, A5, Catalogue, 28 pages, Colour, Free* Postal charges: *Varies with item* Delivery: *Royal Mail* Methods of Payment: *Cheque, Postal Order, Visa, Access / Mastercard*

WESTWARD BOUND
27 Old Gloucester
Street
London
WC1N 3XX

SEXUAL GOODS
Westward Bound's 'Kinky Catalogues' include the 'Connoisseur Collection' (£8.00). The fact that anyone could become a connoisseur of photos showing a man, naked but for some thigh-length boots, pulling a cart in which a leather-clad blonde brandishes a whip, hopefully says more for their sense of humour than the bizarre nature of their sexual fantasies. Included within the collection, photographed on location at Westward Bound's dungeon, are 'outrageous' articles in leather, rubber and PVC. Good for a laugh, at least.

More understandable is the range of dildos, vibrators, stimulators and blow-up dolls featured in their 'Sextasy' catalogue (£2.50).

Catalogue: *A5, Leaflets, 1 page, B/W, Free* Postal charges: *Varies with item* Delivery: *Royal Mail* Methods of Payment: *Cheque, Postal Order*

Clothes

WETHERALL LTD
Diamond Buildings
Love Lane
Denbigh
Clwyd
LL16 3LE

Telephone:
0745 815592
Fax:
0745 815147

WOMEN'S CLOTHES

This company produces up-market, sophisticated co-ordinates for women. The idea is that by carefully choosing a limited number of items you can combine them in a huge number of ways – up to 4,500!

The clothes themselves are conservative in style, with plenty of skirts, jackets, trousers and tops. Skirts are between £45.00 and £55.00 depending on the materials used. The choice is pure wool, pure wool crêpe, silk and viscose, tweed and worsted brown check.

Catalogue: *A5, Catalogue, 8 pages, Colour, Free* Postal charges: *£3.50* Delivery: *Royal Mail* Methods of Payment: *Cheque, Visa, Access / Mastercard*

WIGGLETS
50 Stockwell Park
Crescent
London
SW9 0DG

Telephone:
071 738 5124

CLASSICAL NIGHT CLOTHES FOR CHILDREN

The Wigglets range offers children's classic nightclothes from newborn to twelve years to cater for every season. They are made from the finest natural fabrics by a team of expert shirtmakers working to Jermyn Street standards.

For winter, there is a range of pyjamas and dressing gowns in brushed cotton. To stay extra cool in summer they have a selection of short-sleeved cotton pyjamas in Bermuda length and full length, all with co-ordinating bath robes.

The company has a London showroom and prices for items start at £12.00 for Australian slippers to £64.00 for fine wool and cotton-mix dressing gowns.

Catalogue: *Annually, A5, Brochure, 12 pages, Colour, Free* Postal charges: *Varies with item* Delivery: *Royal Mail* Methods of Payment: *Cheque, Postal Order, Visa, Access / Mastercard*

WILD DESIGNS
1 Chestnut Road
London
SE27 9EZ

Telephone:
081 766 7550
Fax:
081 766 6896

CLOTHING (CLUBWEAR, GLAMOURWEAR, LINGERIE)

Wild Designs produce an exciting range of clubwear, glamourwear and lingerie. Their clothes will appeal to people of all ages who like to get the most out of life. The range includes fishnet bodystockings and catsuits, a selection made from stretch PVC (skirts, dresses, bodystockings, jeans, T-shirts etc) and romantic lingerie.

They offer a wide range of women's sizes, from 8 to 22 (though not in all styles) and S–XL for men. A fishnet catsuit is £26.00, a satin and lace teddy £21.99, a stretch PVC mini-skirt £23.00 and stretch PVC jeans £50.00.

Clothes

WINEBERGS LIMITED
Shannon Street
Leeds
West Yorkshire
LS9 8SS

Telephone:
0532 488131

MADE-TO-MEASURE CLOTHES
Winebergs have been in business since 1900, making custom-made clothes by mail order. They do not publish a catalogue but send an envelope bulging with samples of cloth. You can then choose a design from their simple order form, giving your own specific measurements on the useful line drawings.

They will also copy any clothes you send – an invaluable service for your favourite suit. They have a separate form for women's clothes and offer a 10% discount on the first order. Prices seem very reasonable, with a pair of tailor-made moleskin trousers for £59.95, a Harris Tweed jacket £149.95 and twill trousers £49.95. At these prices it seems silly NOT to have tailor-made outfits!

Catalogue: *Annually, A4, Catalogue, 24 pages, Colour, £2.50*
Postal charges: *Varies with item* Delivery: *Royal Mail* Methods of Payment: *Cheque, Postal Order, Visa, Access / Mastercard*

Catalogue: *A4, Brochure, 4 pages, B/W, Free* Postal charges: *Free* Delivery: *Royal Mail* Methods of Payment: *Cheque, Postal Order, Visa, Access / Mastercard*

WOODS OF MORECAMBE LTD
42 Queen Street
Morecambe
LA4 5EL

Telephone:
0524 412101
Fax:
0524 832947

WOMEN'S UNDERWEAR
Underwear and nightwear are Woods' speciality. With an emphasis on modesty, there's nothing here to give your grandmother a heart-attack or for that matter to make your lover break out in a heavy sweat. But if you're looking for something comfortable and feminine, Woods are ideal.

Their range comprises woollen and cotton tops and bottoms of various types, from decidedly practical Thermal Long Johns (£7.50), to a more casual poly/cotton built-up shoulder slip (£14.00). There's a vaguely slinky slip at £12.95, with a 100% Acetate Celenese Kite Gusset. If you know what that involves, the Fancy Knit Panties with 'gently elasticated legs' won't hold any terrors!

Catalogue: *Bi-annually, 215 × 215 mm, Catalogue, 24 pages, Colour, Free* Postal charges: *Varies with item* Delivery: *Royal Mail* Methods of Payment: *Cheque, Postal Order, Visa, Access / Mastercard*

Collectables

XTEND
Admail 375
Leicester
LE1 9AD

Telephone:
0354 556644
Fax:
0539 433993

CLOTHES

Xtend is in the mould of the Next catalogue, in other words stylish, sophisticated clothes for people who a few years ago would never have dreamt of ordering from a catalogue. There are ranges for both men and women, with an emphasis on the 20 to 35-year-old market. Their poplin women's shirt is £19.00 while a denim shirt is £22.00.

Other items include a woman's linen-mix jacket for £69.00 and matching trousers at £35.00. A leather jacket is £149.00, a canvas one £39.00 and men's chinos are £27.00. There is also a selection of boots and brogues at around £35.00.

Catalogue: *Bi-annually, A4, Catalogue, 48 pages, Colour, Free* Postal charges: *£2.95* Delivery: *Royal Mail* Methods of Payment: *Cheque, Postal Order, Visa, Access / Mastercard*

ZIG ZAG DESIGNER KNITWEAR LTD
Riverford Mill
Stewarton
Ayrshire
KA3 5DH

Telephone:
0560 485187
Fax:
0560 485195

DESIGNER KNITWEAR

Zig Zag Design offer an exciting range of knitwear for ladies, gents and children. Their unique styles are in various colours from soft gentle shades through to brilliant brights. Sweaters and cardigans are available in 100% wool and pure cotton.

Children's sweaters are £18.95, ladies and gents' patterned sweaters £36.95, lambswool cardigans £39.95 and gents' chunky rib sweaters £24.95.

Catalogue: *Bi-annually, A5, Catalogue, 20 pages, Colour, Free* Postal charges: *Varies with item* Delivery: *Royal Mail* Methods of Payment: *Cheque, Postal Order, Visa, Access / Mastercard*

ANDREW BOTTOMLEY
The Coach House
Huddersfield Road
Thongsbridge
Holmfirth
West Yorkshire
HD7 2TT

Telephone:
0484 685234
Fax:
0484 681551

ANTIQUE ARMS AND ARMOUR

The catalogue contains over 500 antique weapons from all over the world, each fully described and often accompanied by photographs. All items are guaranteed original and are available without a licence.

The main areas covered are pistols and revolvers, long guns, imperial German and Third Reich swords and daggers, cavalry swords, naval swords, dirks and cutlasses, Scottish weapons, Japanese swords, African and Oriental weapons and armour and helmets.

Prices range from around £40.00 to just under £10,000.00. Examples include a 17mm French model 1816 flintlock cavalry pistol at £230.00 and a fine Argyll & Sutherland Highlander Officer's full dress dirk c. 1900 at £1000.00.

Catalogue: *A4, Catalogue, 56 pages, B/W, Free* Postal charges: *Free* Delivery: *Royal Mail* Methods of Payment: *Cheque, Postal Order, Visa, Access / Mastercard, American Express*

Collectibles

BUTTERFLIES GALORE
21 Westall Centre
Holberrow Green
Nr Redditch
Worcestershire
B96 6JY

Telephone:
0386 793240
Fax:
0386 793253

DECORATIVE BUTTERFLIES

This is an unusual catalogue, specialising in ornamental butterflies. They come in two sizes – 15" and 7½" across the wingspan. Photographs illustrate how you can display them on walls, fences or even plants. Special fixings are supplied and presentation gift boxes of three butterflies are available.

The six most popular British butterflies are represented here, and cost £12.80 each for the small version and £23.50 for the large. If you order six large butterflies there is a reduction in price, effectively giving you one free.

Catalogue: *A4, Leaflet, 2 pages, Colour, Free* Postal charges: *£2.40* Delivery: *Royal Mail* Methods of Payment: *Cheque, Postal Order*

CELEBRATION CRYSTAL CO LTD
Freepost
Montford Bridge
Shrewsbury
Shropshire
SY4 1BR

Telephone:
0743 850851
Fax:
0743 850146

CUT-GLASS CRYSTAL

A family-run business, Celebration Crystal has been established for over fifteen years producing decorated glassware. There are three ranges, one of which is machine-made the other two hand-cut from lead crystal. The products can be etched, giving a frosted effect, coloured, with up to three enamel colours or silvered (or a combination of all three).

Examples in the catalogue reflect commissions as diverse as Ruddles Brewery and Ford's Amateur Golf Tournament. A full range of glassware is available from tankards to decanters, jugs, glasses, trophy cups, rose bowls and plaques. Prices are individually determined according to requirements.

Catalogue: *A4, Leaflets, 4 pages plus inserts, Colour, Free* Postal charges: *Varies with item* Delivery: *Royal Mail* Methods of Payment: *Cheque, Postal Order*

COINCRAFT
45 Great Russell Street
London
WC1B 3LU

Telephone:
071 636 1188
Fax:
071 323 2860

COINS, BANKNOTES, ANCIENT COINS, ANTIQUITIES

Founded in 1955, Coincraft is a family firm which deals in coins, banknotes, ancient coins and antiquities. Their shop is just across the street from the British Museum but they also issue a catalogue and monthly newspaper, *The Phoenix* for customers who cannot come in person.

They pride themselves in helping collectors and tell us they just might have the most interesting shop/catalogue in the country – and they may well be right! Certainly the range is impressive. Charles II Silver Crowns issued in the 1600s sell from £150, Ancient Roman Oil Lamps, 3rd–4th Century AD are from

Collectibles

£25.00 while 100 different uncirculated world banknotes are only £28.00. They also stock all the supplies and books you need to start or advance a collection. A fascinating company.

Catalogue: *A3, Catalogue, 24 pages, B/W, Free* Postal charges: *Varies with item* Delivery: *UPS, Fed Ex, TNT Courier, Royal Mail, Parcelforce* Methods of Payment: *Cheque, Postal Order, Visa, Access / Mastercard, American Express, Diners Club*

COLLECTORS' TOYS
Fisher's Mill,
Bridge Hill,
Topsham,
Exeter
Devon
EX3 OQQ

Telephone:
0392 877600
Fax:
0392 877600

WOODEN DOLLS

Since 1976 Eric Horne has been making modern collectors' versions of the classic 'Dutch' (peg) dolls so popular at the turn of the century. Produced both in 'Contemporary' and 'Traditional' styles, these beechwood dolls are turned by hand and painted with high-gloss enamel.

The dolls range in height from a minuscule ¼" up to 18". Most are jointed at the elbows, knees, shoulders and hips, the joints held together by wooden pins. Male and female versions are available, with a choice of hair and shoe colour. Doll prices start at £10.20 and climb to £83.25.

A range of 1/12 scale miniature furniture is also available. Spring 1994 sees the launch of a new range of hand-painted 6" dolls, and a limited edition of Eric Horne's Pedlar Man.

Catalogue: *A5, Brochure, 8 pages, B/W, Free* Postal charges: *Varies with item* Delivery: *Royal Mail* Methods of Payment: *Visa, Access / Mastercard Cheque, American Express*

COMICS BY POST
4 Springfield
Woodsetts
Worksop Notts
S81 8QD

Telephone:
0909 569428

COMICS

This interesting company specialises in comics, but not the sort that a modern child would buy – these are strictly for collectors. Their main stock consists of *Beano*s from 1940 onwards, some of which are very rare. Indeed they claim to have 'probably the broadest saleable stock in the world'.

As well as actual *Beano*s they have annuals, calendars, *Dandy, Film Fun, Dennis the Menace* and cards. They also stock a considerable amount of material on Rupert Bear, including original artwork cells for which they are the sole suppliers.

Prices start at £5.00 and rise according to rarity.

Catalogue: *Quarterly, A5, Brochure, 12 pages, B/W, Free* Postal charges: *Free* Delivery: *Royal Mail* Methods of Payment: *Cheque, Postal Order, Visa, Access / Mastercard*

Collectibles

LAWLEYS BY POST
Minton House
London Road
Stoke on Trent
Staffs
ST4 7QD

Telephone:
0782 744787
Fax:
0782 416962

COLLECTIBLE PORCELAIN

Lawleys offer a range of collectible porcelain figurines, commemorative tankards, plates, floral boxes and prints by renowned makers such as Minton, Royal Albert, Royal Crown Derby and Royal Doulton.

All limited editions, the collection includes Royal Doulton's 'Henry VIII and his Six Wives' modelled by sculptress Pauline Parsons, which range in price from £195.00 for Catherine of Aragon to £595.00 for Henry himself. Royal Doulton also produce 'Defenders of the Realm', a fine-art print commemorating the Battle of Britain by artist Geoff Hunt priced at £99.00.

Most items can be bought either in a one-off payment or over 10 instalments.

Catalogue: *A5, Catalogue, 24 pages, Colour, Free* Postal charges: *Free* Delivery: *Royal Mail* Methods of Payment: *Cheque, Postal Order, Visa, Access / Mastercard*

PADDINGTON & FRIENDS
1 Abbey Street
Bath
BA1 1NN

PADDINGTON BEAR PRODUCTS

If you're a devotee of the small brown bear, Paddington, who turned up from Peru with a label and no fixed address, this is the catalogue for you. Dolls start at £38.00 for a 'Junior Paddington', standing 14" high with a choice of colours for his hat, coat and boots, and rise to £99.50 for a special limited edition 14" model with jointed legs, made of quality mohair. He comes with a real leather suitcase containing 'Peruvian' coins.

There are numerous other products, including books at £4.99 each; stationery from £2.40 for an A4 document wallet; and jigsaws at £3.99. Towelling bibs (from £3.50); unbreakable tableware from £3.99; and rattles from £2.50 are available for babies and toddlers.

Catalogue: *A5, Catalogue, 16 pages, B/W, Free* Postal charges: *£3.00* Delivery: *Royal Mail* Methods of Payment: *Cheque, Postal Order, Access / Mastercard, Visa, American Express*

PETER JONES CHINA
PO Box 10
22 Little Westgate
Wakefield
West Yorkshire
WF1 1LB

PORCELAIN AND GLASS

This is a well-illustrated, glossy catalogue of commemorative china. There are plenty of household names such as Wedgwood and Royal Doulton. Glancing through the pages is a bit like being put in the shop window itself. There are dozens of figurines, mugs, vases, plates, plant pots, clocks and crystal.

Collectibles

Telephone:
0924 362510
Fax:
0924 290284

There is even a whole section of Royal commemorative ware exclusive to Peter Jones.

A royal plate with a picture of the Queen surrounded by her royal residences sells for £29.95.

Catalogue: *A4, Catalogue, 8 pages plus inserts, Colour, Free* Postal charges: *Varies with item* Delivery: *Royal Mail* Methods of Payment: *Cheque, Postal Order, Visa, Access / Mastercard*

RIDINGS CRAFT LTD
Grey St
Leeds Rd
Newton Hill
Wakefield
West Yorks
WF1 3HQ

Telephone:
0924 822666
Fax:
0924 822766

PORCELAIN AND VINYL DOLLS WITH ACCESSORIES

Ridings Craft is the largest mail order supplier of porcelain doll kits to the public in the UK. They offer a selection of doll kits in a range of prices from £18.75 upwards. Also ready-made dolls to dress.

All are complemented by a superb range of dress patterns including their own exclusive costume range. Also in the catalogue are to be found accessories such as stands, hats, parasols, jewellery etc.

There is also a wide range of vinyl dolls to dress, including some very convincing 'porcelain look' vinyls from £4.50.

Catalogue: *Bi-annually, A4, Catalogue, 16 pages, Colour, 80p* Postal charges: *£2.25* Delivery: *Royal Mail, Parcelforce* Methods of Payment: *Cheque, Postal Order, American Express, Visa, Access / Mastercard*

ROBIN AND NELL DALE
Bank House Farm
Holme Mills
Holme, Carnforth
Lancashire
LA6 1RE

Telephone:
0524 781646

HANDMADE STUMP DOLLS AND CHESS FIGURES

Having worked together for twenty years, Robin and Nell Dale have had plenty of time to develop their range of limited-edition chess sets. They started off making stump dolls, which became collector's items. Some of their chess sets are now in national collections.

Chess sets cost from £380.00 to £5000.00. The 'Battle of Waterloo' set costs £470.00. Individual pieces cost from pawns for £38.00 to knights for £50.00.

A stump doll nativity set contains pieces from £25.00 to £40.00. Among the other alternatives are model sportsmen: a cricketer (£25.00), a huntsman (£20.50) or mad golfers (£26.50).

Catalogue: *A5, Leaflets, 2 pages, Colour and B/W, Free* Postal charges: *Varies with item* Delivery: *Royal Mail* Methods of Payment: *Cheque, Postal Order*

Collectibles

SCROLL NAMES LTD
The Towers
Village Way
Bispham
Nr Blackpool
FY2 0AB

Telephone:
0253 595454

HERALDIC SCROLLS AND SHIELDS

The Hall of Names has over 70,000 authentic surname histories which are kept on record in their computer database. Each history outlines the profile of the family name, often from around 1100 AD, starting in early tribal time and tracing the family as it grew, branched, feuded and dispersed throughout the world. These histories cost only £5.99 or £15.98 fully framed.

The House of Heraldry library contains more than 500,000 Coats of Arms that have been recorded over the centuries. Nearly all names of British and European origin are included. Coats of arms are hand-painted on an embossed copper and hardwood shield or as an elegant armorial with your surname emblazoned above the crest and the motto beneath the arms. All items are equipped for wall hanging. Shields start at £39.99 and go up to £79.99.

Catalogue: *A4, Leaflet, 1 page, B/W, Free* Postal charges: *Free* Delivery: *Royal Mail* Methods of Payment: *Cheque, Postal Order*

SOTHEBY'S
Catalogue Subscription Department
34–35 New Bond Street
London
W1A 2AA

Telephone:
0234 841041
Fax:
0234 841043

FINE ART AND FURNITURE

This splendid publication by the famous auction house is really a catalogue of catalogues. Those listed are by subscription only and last for one year. Split into subjects such as Old Master Paintings and Drawings, they give brief descriptions of what is covered along with the locations of sales.

For American Furniture and Decorative Arts , for example, there are three sales in New York and the subscription is £70.00. For English Furniture and Decorations, there are twelve sales, eight in London and four in New York. A discount is offered if a subscription is taken out for both centres.

Catalogue: *A4, Catalogue, 24 pages, Colour, Free* Postal charges: *Varies with item* Delivery: *Royal Mail* Methods of Payment: *Cheque, Visa, Access / Mastercard, American Express*

TÉMÉRAIRE
20 Church Street
Brixham
Devon
TQ5 8HG

Telephone:
0803 851523
Fax:
0803 858494

PHILOSOPHICAL AND SCIENTIFIC INSTRUMENTS

Téméraire recreate unique precision instruments from the past, wherever possible using original blueprints and dies and often the original manufacturing companies.

One of their finest models is the 'Edinburgh Display Barograph', a superb weather forecasting and recording instrument. The mechanism is English-made in solid brass, set on a dark mahogany base

Collectibles

French-polished in the traditional manner. A drawer in the base keeps a year's supply of recording papers. It costs £499.50 and has the option of a personalised engraving at £9.75.

Also available are World War II Marching Compasses, recommissioned from the original makers, a Pocket Barometer and Desk-top Weather Forecaster.

Catalogue: *A5, Leaflets, Many inserts, Colour, Free* Postal charges: *Varies with item* Delivery: *Royal Mail* Methods of Payment: *Cheque, Postal Order, Visa, Access / Mastercard*

TRIDENT
PO Box 335
Maldon
Essex
CM9 8UP

Telephone:
0621 891858
Fax:
0621856819

COINS

Trident specialise in coins, banknotes, toy cars, glass and lamps, medals and other small collectibles. The catalogue contains a large range of coins from every period including the Roman Empire. Other examples include: George V Rare Half-crowns of 1925 and 1930 for £18.95; Proof Olympic Half-Dollar 1992 issued by the US mint £14.95; Napoleon Crowns in silver £59.95; Edward VI Shilling in silver £135.00.

Apart from coins there are three different Victorian Match Labels for £22.50, an unbroken piece of Roman glassware over 1600 years old for £95.00 and old copies of *The Beano* from the 60s and 70s at £3.95.

Catalogue: *Annually, A5, Catalogue, 36 pages, B/W, Free* Postal charges: *Varies with item* Delivery: *Royal Mail* Methods of Payment: *Cheque, Postal Order, Visa, Access / Mastercard, American Express*

WESTMINSTER COLLECTION
Freepost
Watford
Herts
WD2 8FP

Telephone:
0923 254022

COINS AND STAMPS

This is a collector's catalogue full of objects such as coins, stamps and porcelain plates. The coins are specifically minted to commemorate certain events, such as a US half-dollar for the World Cup 1994, or the D-Day silver dollar to celebrate the 50th Anniversary of the Allied landing in Europe.

Stamps also commemorate events or people, including the Queen Mother, and come from all over the world. For example, there is a special edition of stamps issued by Norway to celebrate the Winter Olympics. Both coins and stamps are available in presentation packs.

The World Cup coin costs £5.95 and the Olympic stamps £14.95.

Catalogue: *A4, Leaflets, Colour, Free* Postal charges: *Varies with item* Delivery: *Royal Mail* Methods of Payment: *Cheque, Postal Order, Visa, Access / Mastercard*

Computers

ACTION COMPUTER SUPPLIES
12 Windmill Lane
Southall
Middlesex
UB2 4QD

Telephone:
0800 333 333
0500 333 333
Fax:
0800 10 20 30
0500 10 20 30

COMPUTERS – HARDWARE & SOFTWARE
Action Computers produce a fat A5 catalogue crammed with everything for the computer buff. They sell a good range of computers themselves, including models from Toshiba, Compaq, Canon, AST, IBM, NEC and Hewlett-Packard. Then there is a huge range of accessories and hardware, including cards, modems, carrying cases, VDU filters and so on.

The software section covers DOS, Windows and Mac applications on floppies and CD-ROMS. Finally there are printer supplies, discs, cartridges and cassettes. In short a one-stop catalogue for everything to do with computers.

Catalogue: *A5, Catalogue, 598 pages, Colour, Free* Postal charges: *Varies with item* Delivery: *Courier* Methods of Payment: *Cheque, American Express, Visa, Access / Mastercard, Diners Club*

AJP BUSINESS COMPUTERS LTD
Units 6 & 7
The Edge Business Centre
Humber Road
London
NW2 6EN

Telephone:
081 452 9090
Fax:
081 450 6360

NOTEBOOK COMPUTERS
AJP have received many accolades in the computer press and they use these write-ups to show their products to best advantage. A favourite among the experts, they provide portable computers which are versatile and powerful at prices that won't break the bank.

AJP provide a range of notebooks designed with the user in mind. The sleek looks and built-in features of models such as the 6510M make them the mobile executive's dream machine. Prices start at £1295.00 and include a full twelve-month warranty.

Catalogue: *A4, Leaflets, 12 pages, Colour, Free* Postal charges: *Varies with item* Delivery: *Royal Mail* Methods of Payment: *Cheque, Visa, Access / Mastercard*

BKPW LTD
82 Chaplin Road
London
NW2 5PR

Telephone:
081 830 1958
Fax:
081 830 1959

NOTEBOOK COMPUTERS
This company is a direct vendor of notebook computers under the name NotePro. The range is fully upgradable from a 486 SX-25 to a 486 DX2-66 Intel processor. They also have easily replaceable CPUs, screens and hard disks up to 340Mb. In March 1994, *Windows Magazine* gave NotePro its Recommended award.

A NotePro 486 SX-25 with a colour screen sells for £2465.00 and a 16MB Ram upgrade for £895.00. Also listed are accessories like car adaptors, batteries and battery chargers.

Catalogue: *A4, Leaflets, 9 pages, B/W, Free* Postal charges: *Varies with item* Delivery: *Courier* Methods of Payment: *Cheque, Visa, Access / Mastercard*

Computers

BLUE MOUNTAIN IMPORTS (UK) LTD
Block 3
Burkes Close
Burkes Road
Beaconsfield
Bucks
HP9 1BR

Telephone:
0494 678181
Fax:
0494 674482

COMMUNICATIONS HARDWARE
Blue Mountain communications equipment help you stay in touch with your business wherever you are in the world. Their Andest VPA (Virtual Personal Assistant) combines the functions of an answerphone and a fax, receiving and sending electronic mail, automatically forwarding messages and it can be accessed by remote control from anywhere in the world. It connects to a single phone line. All this for £499.95 – one of the new generation of communications devices that, if nothing else, make impressive gadgets.

Similarly, they can provide you with a lightweight 'Roadrunner Rocket', which allows you to send or receive faxes or data files while on the move.

Catalogue: *A4, Leaflets, Colour, Free* Postal charges: *Varies with item* Delivery: *Royal Mail* Methods of Payment: *Visa, Access / Mastercard Cheque, Postal Order*

BRANDS DIRECT LTD
1 Roundwood Avenue
Stockley Park
Uxbridge
Middx
UB11 1AF

Telephone:
081 561 4588
Fax:
081 561 3329

COMPUTER HARDWARE
Brands Direct offer a complete IBM compatible PC system for under £300.00. The printer is extra but at only £89.00 seems a bargain. Software is in the form of Locoscript PC Easy, one of the simpler word processing packages which started life on the Amstrad PCW range (as did many computer users!). With a 14" monitor (mono or colour) you won't be squinting to see what's on your screen.

Also from Brands come the Virgin SD-Series 486 PCs. Fast and durable with free software worth £300.00, there's enough here to set you up for some time. Prices range from £799.00 to £1249.00.

Catalogue: *A4, Catalogue, 4 pages, Colour, Free* Postal charges: *£15.00* Delivery: *Royal Mail* Methods of Payment: *Access / Mastercard, Visa Cheque*

CLP COMPUTER SUPPLIES
Unit 7/8
Holland Way
Blandford
Dorset
DT11 7TA

Telephone:
0258 459544
Fax:
0258 459565

COMPUTER SUPPLIES
One of the advantages of this computer supply catalogue is that delivery is free in the UK however small your order. In fact, if it weighs over 2 kg it even comes overnight at no extra cost.

The selection of items is comprehensive and includes stationery such as paper and labels, ribbons and toners, cables and connectors, screen filters, desk accessories and even some computer furniture. They also have a competitive line in disks and an interesting section on gadgets and accessories.

Computers

COLVIN LIMITED
Hammond House
Croydon Road
Caterham
Surrey
CR3 6PB

Telephone:
0883 340 511
Fax:
0883 340 327

COMPUTER SUPPLIES
Everything you need to ensure that your computer network (or your computer) is running as smoothly as possible. The Colvin catalogue has a vast selection of materials from footrests to workstations, available singly or in bulk.

By providing clear information on the advantages of their products and how they can fit into your office environment, the catalogue can help new businesses plan their needs effectively and show existing managers how their systems can be improved.

With complete workstations from £164.00, this range provides value for money.

Catalogue: *A4, Catalogue, 48 pages, Colour, Free* Postal charges: *Free* Delivery: *Royal Mail Courier* Methods of Payment: *Cheque, Visa, Access / Mastercard, American Express*

COMPUSYS LTD
58 Edison Road
Rabans Lane Ind Estate
Aylesbury
Bucks
HP19 3TE

Telephone:
0296 395531
Fax:
0296 24165

COMPUTERS AND COMPUTER SYSTEMS
Compusys manufacture everything from PC systems to laptops and supply them to large corporate bodies such as the Littlewoods Organisation, the Eastern Electricity Board, health authorities and many Government departments, including the British Army on the Rhine. This flexibility makes them an ideal partner when you are looking for someone to help you build the system you need with their hardware, software and peripherals.

They are very proud of their reputation and include testimonials from customers and reviews from the computer press in their catalogue.

Catalogue: *Annually, A4, Catalogue, 33 pages, Colour, Free* Postal charges: *Varies with item* Delivery: *Royal Mail* Methods of Payment: *Cheque, Postal Order, Visa, Access / Mastercard*

COMPUTER BOOKLIST
50 James Road
Birmingham
BA11 2BA

Telephone:
021 706 6000
Fax:
021 706 3301

COMPUTER BOOKS
Subscription to this catalogue is free and it is updated three times a year. With an enormous range of computer books from highly technical programming languages and techniques titles to the user-friendly 'Computers for Dummies' series, it has just about everything. They even promise to try and find anything for you that is not in the catalogue.

Some products are liable to VAT, such as software,

Catalogue: *A4, Leaflets, 64 pages, Colour and B/W, Free* Postal charges: *Varies with item* Delivery: *Royal Mail* Methods of Payment: *Cheque, Visa, Access / Mastercard*

Computers

and are marked accordingly. A 'Learning Wordperfect' manual sells for £18.45 and an Apple Macintosh guide for £22.95.

Catalogue: *200 × 270mm, Catalogue, 48 pages, Colour, Free* Postal charges: *Varies with item* Delivery: *Royal Mail* Methods of Payment: *Cheque, Postal Order, Visa, Access / Mastercard, American Express*

COMPUTERS BY POST
5th floor
Alperton House
Wembley
Middx
HA0 1EH

Telephone:
081 760 0014
Fax:
081 760 9861

COMPUTERS
Computers by Post offer a full range of software and hardware. They are currently the UK's largest 'Direct Channel' reseller of PCs and related products.

Of the portable machines on offer, the most striking seem to be in the Toshiba T1950 series, starting at £2515. At 3.3 kg they won't break your back. A wide range of modems, from £85.00, and networking paraphernalia should enhance your communicative abilities. The Hewlett-Packard range of LaserJet printers look well-priced from £472.00. All in all, a good source.

Catalogue: *A4, Leaflets, 16 pages, Colour, Free* Postal charges: *Varies with item* Delivery: *Courier* Methods of Payment: *Cheque, Visa, Access / Mastercard, American Express*

CROWN COMPUTER PRODUCTS
Crown House
Plantation Road
Burscough Industrial Estate
Burscough
Lancashire
L40 8JT

Telephone:
0704 895815
Fax:
0704 895854

COMPUTERS AND ACCESSORIES
From the UK's largest mail order dealer of computers and accessories comes a catalogue offering variety and savings. The largest computer manufacturers are featured, with the latest Toshiba colour portables from £2546.00. The range of Apple systems is made more attractive by Crown's offer of free accessories with every purchase of Apple's Powerbook Duo (priced at £699.00).

Other resources ideal for those setting up in business include telephones incorporating fax machines from £235.00 and colour scanners from £545.00. The range of printers from Canon, Hyundai, Panasonic and Hewlett-Packard is extensive enough to suit most business needs and provides good value.

Catalogue: *Monthly, A4, Catalogue, 32 pages, Colour, Free* Postal charges: *Varies with item* Delivery: *Royal Mail* Methods of Payment: *Cheque, Postal Order, Visa, Access / Mastercard*

Computers

DELL COMPUTER CORP
Millbanke House
Western Road
Bracknell
Berks
RG12 1RW

Telephone:
0344 720220
Fax:
0344 723699

COMPUTERS AND ACCESSORIES
Affordable and reliable personal computers with a range of capacities that leaves room for expansion in the future. The Dell Dimension range of eight computers provides state-of-the-art power and performance for users' needs, whether as individuals or as part of a networked system.

All systems are pre-loaded with Microsoft software, including Word for Windows, and come with the security of a full one-year warranty. Prices range from £969.00 to £2649.00 depending on your needs, and compatible Hewlett-Packard printers can be provided from £209.00.

Catalogue: *A5, Brochure, 16 pages, Colour, Free* Postal charges: *Varies with item* Delivery: *In house delivery* Methods of Payment: *Cheque, Postal Order, Visa, Access / Mastercard, American Express*

DNCS
Truedata House
Green Lane
Heywood
Manchester
OL10 2DY

Telephone:
0706 367567
Fax:
0800 367567

COMPUTERS, ACCESORIES AND SOFTWARE
DNCS have given their catalogue the subtitle 'We're all your computer needs' which conjures up an image of computers having needs and therefore probably therapists. But they do seem to live up to their claim and this publication covers virtually everything you can buy for a computer.

Hardware includes IBM, AST, Compaq, Canon and Toshiba computers as well as laptops from a number of other suppliers such as Hewlett-Packard. They also sell data communications equipment, printer supplies, faxes, answering machines, discs and even computer furniture. Delivery is overnight and you can also arrange to lease equipment at very competitive rates.

Catalogue: *7.5 × 10.5in, Catalogue, 196 pages, Colour, Free* Postal charges: *Varies with item* Delivery: *Courier, Royal Mail* Methods of Payment: *Cheque, Visa, Access / Mastercard, American Express*

DUAL GROUP (UK) LTD
Unit D4, Button End
Harston
Cambridge
CB2 5NX

Telephone:
0223 872622
Fax:
0223 872859

PORTABLE COMPUTERS
Winner of the *Byte* Magazine Best Notebook Computer Award, the Professional K series by Dual is a step forward in portable computers, by providing desktop and notebook resources in one machine.

There are accessories compatible with the Professional K series such as scanners (the mono version is £99.00), modems and mains adaptors at £399.00. The Professional K series itself is available from £1199.00 to £2549.00.

Computers

The company has more than twelve years experience of manufacturing, and the computer is upgradable.

Catalogue: *A4, Brochure, 4 pages, Colour, Free* Postal charges: *Varies with item* Delivery: *Royal Mail* Methods of Payment: *Cheque, Postal Order, Visa, Access / Mastercard*

EAGLE PRINT COMPUTERS
Abbot's Hill Chambers
Gower Street
Derby
DE1 1SD

Telephone:
0332 292840
Fax:
0332 205603

COMPUTERS AND UPGRADES
This is a catalogue from a direct vendor computer supplier, often the source of the best bargains in computers. Offering a range of basic systems, Eagle Print will supply upgradable parts and virtually build a system to your requirements. They also offer a repair service, software, printers and other computer accessories, such as mouse mats, heavy-base keyboards and so on.

A standard 386SX-40 AMD CPU system costs £609.00 excluding VAT and a 486SX-25 ISA/VESA Motherboard upgrade £215.00.

Catalogue: *A5, Catalogue, 8 pages, B/W, Free* Postal charges: *Varies with item* Delivery: *Courier* Methods of Payment: *Cheque*

ENSIGN SYSTEMS
Freepost
London
SE26 5BR

Telephone:
081 778 2871
Fax:
081 776 8477

SHAREWARE
Ensign's catalogue comes on a 3.5" IBM disk and is, as far as we can ascertain, full of details of shareware for the PCs. However, since we are devoted Mac users we were unable to get inside the disk to see the contents! For those with PCs, you simply slip in the disk and type 'Go', press 'Enter' and you're in – or so they say! You can choose ten disks of shareware for just £18.95 which does seem a bargain.

Catalogue: *Bi-annually, 3.5" IBM disk, Free* Postal charges: *Varies with item* Delivery: *Royal Mail* Methods of Payment: *Cheque*

EUROPEAN COMPUTER USER
A2/A3 Edison Road
St Ives
Huntingdon
Cambs
PE17 4LF

Telephone:
0480 498889
Fax:
0480 496379

COMPUTER GAMES AND SOFTWARE
European Computer User do not produce a catalogue but several tightly printed price lists which they call Complete Buyers Guide. These just give the name of the game, the publisher, the Recommended Retail Price and their own price.

This simple approach is presumably why they can offer such good discounts, undercutting conventional shops by quite some margin. There are sections on Amiga, Atari and PC, with software both on floppy 3.5 and CD-ROMs. They have daily special offers which are available by phone only. If you know what

Computers

you want and like a no-frills, best-price operation this seems a good bet.

Catalogue: *A4, Leaflets, 14 pages, B/W, Free* Postal charges: *Varies with item* Delivery: *Royal Mail Courier* Methods of Payment: *Cheque, Visa, Access / Mastercard*

EUROTECHNIX LTD
24 Kingfisher Court
Hambridge Road
Newbury
Berks
RG14 5SJ

Telephone:
0635 550777
Fax:
0635 524302

COMPUTERS AND ACCESSORIES
Eurotechnix is a one-stop solution for all your computer requirements. There is a range of computers, printers and software for personal or business use, and more specialised extras for those looking to expand and upgrade.

MITAC desktop PCs start at £799.00 and the portable range at £699.00. The new range of Hewlett-Packard printers and scanners is available, with the Scanjet IICX at £738.00. The software range includes all the usual business software, and in addition has some of the most impressive new leisure programmes available including Mortal Combat by SEGA at £49.99.

Catalogue: *A4, Leaflets, 13 pages, B/W, Free* Postal charges: *Varies with item* Delivery: *In house delivery* Methods of Payment: *Cheque, Visa, Access / Mastercard*

EXPRESS TECHNOLOGY LTD
Ashford Road
Ashford
Middx
TW15 1XE

Telephone:
0784 421123
Fax:
0784 421910

MODEMS
Express Technology sell the Zoom range of modems through their subsidiary, Zoom Direct. These BABT-approved modems come highly recommended by the computer press and are sold either as stand-alone devices or as internal cards.

They can be used in conjunction with WINFAX software to send and receive faxes direct from the screen and a complete package is available. However, they do not offer similar software for Macs. An internal card cost £179.00, a desktop version £199.00. WINFAX software is £35.00.

Catalogue: *A4, Brochure, 6 pages, B/W, Free* Postal charges: *Varies with item* Delivery: *Royal Mail* Methods of Payment: *Cheque*

Computers

HIGHMEAD OFFICE DIRECT LIMITED
Jupiter House
Travellers Lane
Welham Green
Hatfield
Herts AL9 7DA

Telephone:
0707 272627
Fax:
0707 267400

COMPUTER SYSTEMS
Voted 'Best Value for Money' by *What PC*, Fountain Highmead provides computer systems for educational authorities, government departments and large corporations as well as small businesses and individuals. With everything from stand-alone PCs to advanced Multimedia systems, Fountain Highmead are able to supply CD-ROM systems at competitive prices. For £1099.00 (plus VAT) the 25MHZ i486SX-based system provides enough power for most multimedia and office uses. An after-sales service is available and is free for the first twelve months.

Catalogue: *Bi-monthly, A4, Brochure, 48 pages, Colour, Free* Postal charges: *Varies with item* Delivery: *By arrangement* Methods of Payment: *Cheque, Postal Order, Visa, Access / Mastercard*

HOBBYKIT LTD
Unit 19 Capitol Ind Park
Capitol Way
London
NW9 0EQ

Telephone:
081 205 7485
Fax:
081 205 0603

COMPUTERS AND COMPUTER PARTS
Hobbykit can supply computer parts from individual boards up to a complete computer system. Their stock includes fax modems, CD-ROMs, Multimedia products, motherboards, memory, computer cases, controller cards, operating systems, tape streamers, hard and floppy disk drives, monitors, graphics cards and input devices.

They will also give advice and provide a complete computer system tailored to your exact requirements from the parts required at no additional cost.

Catalogue: *None, Free* Postal charges: *Varies with item* Delivery: *Royal Mail, Parcelforce* Methods of Payment: *Cheque, Postal Order, Visa, Access / Mastercard, Other*

IANSYST LTD
United House
North Road
London
N7 9DP

Telephone:
071 607 5844
Fax:
071 607 0187

COMPUTER TRAINING
This no-nonsense catalogue is revised frequently and often only printed on demand, the idea being that information is kept as up to date as possible. Iansyst provides a comprehensive list of video, disk and audio-based training products for computers and software.

Subjects covered include word processing, DTP/Graphics, spreadsheets, databases, networks and communications. They also provide help with project management, typing training and accounting. There is even a range of products for those with special educational needs, such as dyslexia, to enable them to use PCs.

Catalogue: *A5, Catalogue, 14 pages plus inserts, Colour and B/W, Free* Postal charges: *Varies with item* Delivery: *Royal Mail* Methods of Payment: *Cheque, Postal Order, Visa, Access / Mastercard*

Computers

KINGSWAY COMPUTER SERVICES
72 Glencoe Road
Sheffield
S2 2SR

COMPUTER SHAREWARE

Kingsway's shareware catalogue includes public domain and shareware software for the Macintosh. Public domain software has been donated for general use by the author; shareware authors sometimes request some form of donation or a registration fee. You send for disks containing the programs you require at a flat fee of £4.99.

There are programs on most subjects, from education to health. There's also a generous selection of clip art ideas and customised fonts.

Catalogue: *A5, Catalogue, 32 pages, B/W, Free* Postal charges: *Free* Delivery: *Royal Mail* Methods of Payment: *Access / Mastercard, Visa Cheque, Postal Order*

LAPLAND UK LIMITED
3 Faraday Court
Rankine Road
Basingstoke
Hampshire
RG24 0PF

Telephone:
0256 812720
Fax:
0256 812719

COMPUTERS

Lapland sells a wide range of notebook computers, desktop PCs, printers and software.

On offer are AST's Bravo and Powerexec ranges all of which come with DOS 6.0, Windows 3.1 and a mouse, starting at £1165.00 for the Bravo NB M80. Compaq ranges include Contura, LTE Elite, Portable and Concerto all of which come with DOS 6.0 and Windows 3.1.

Other manufacturers represented are DEC, Hewlett-Packard, IBM, NEC, Panasonic, Sanyo, Sharp, Toshiba and Texas Instruments.

Catalogue: *Annually, A4, Brochure, 5 pages, B/W, Free* Postal charges: *£15.00 per system* Delivery: *Courier* Methods of Payment: *Cheque, Visa, Access / Mastercard*

MACPOW!
96 John Street
Brierley Hill
West Midlands
DY5 1HF

Telephone:
0384 481728
Fax:
0384 481728

SHAREWARE

MacPow! send out their Mac shareware catalogue on a disc. This contains three stuffed catalogues which can be read on screen or printed out. There are thousands of titles including over 6000 colour images and many different fonts.

The shareware itself can be ordered by phone, mail or fax and costs £2.75 if on a DD disk and £3.75 on a HD disk. There is also a 'swapshop' service, where you can swap your own shareware with MacPow's if they do not already have it. They also sell blank disks at very reasonable prices: 38p for DSDD and 56p for DSHD (in boxes of 50).

Catalogue: *Disc, Catalogue, Colour, Free* Postal charges: *Varies with item* Delivery: *Parcelforce* Methods of Payment: *Cheque, Postal Order*

Computers

MACWAREHOUSE
Teledirect House
Queens Road
Barnet
Herts
EN5 4DL

Telephone:
081-447-1142
Fax:
081 447 1696

APPLE COMPUTERS AND ACCESSORIES
MacWarehouse is a long-established American company which sells everything for Apple computers. They now have an operation over here, although the catalogue is identical to the US version except for the prices.

A thoroughly professional publication, it has a huge range of products each of which is given a helpful description. They have recently started to sell actual Macs themselves and this has rounded out what is an invaluable catalogue for any Apple user.

Apple CD-ROM players are currently £159.00, PowerBook 145Bs £849.00 and Microsoft Office £219.95.

Catalogue: *Catalogue, 90 pages, Colour, Free* Postal charges: *Varies with item* Delivery: *Courier* Methods of Payment: *Visa, Access / Mastercard Cheque*

MESH COMPUTERS
Apsley Court
Apsley Way
London
NW2 7HF

Telephone:
081 452 1111
Fax:
081 208 4493

COMPUTERS
The complete range of MESH computer systems covers all types of machines, from notebooks to extremely powerful professional models. One of the industry's more established names, they have been supplying to government, corporate and educational users since 1987, so you can be sure they'll be around to offer you support this time next year.

A 60 mhz PCI Plus P60 with 8Mb of RAM, capable of displaying 16.7 million colours, costs from £2935.00 with a 250Mb hard disk to £4179.00 with a 2.0Gb hard disk. You can expand your machine from the range of Upgrades and Add Ons, and choose your software from over 5,000 titles.

Catalogue: *A4, Catalogue, 24 pages, Colour, Free* Postal charges: *£18.00* Delivery: *Courier* Methods of Payment: *Cheque, Visa, Access / Mastercard*

MISCO
Misco Computer
Supplies Ltd.
Freepost
Wellingborough
Northhants
NN8 6BR

Telephone:
0993 400400
Fax:
0993 401520

COMPUTER SUPPLIES AND ACCESSORIES
Misco offers an extensive range of supplies for the modern office. They deliver goods such as computers (£899), filing cabinets (£799), printers (£189), and floppy disks (£12.80 each), (the four-minute desk, which can be self assembled at £209.00 for two). Prices are reasonable with some reductions offered for customers buying two or more products. Misco promises free delivery if an order is over £500.00.

Catalogue: *Monthly, A4, Catalogue, 120 pages, Colour, Free* Postal charges: *Varies with item* Delivery: *Royal Mail* Methods of Payment: *Cheque, Visa, Access / Mastercard*

Computers

NIGHTHAWK ELECTRONICS
P O Box 44
Saffron Walden
Essex
CB11 3ND

Telephone:
0799 540881
Fax:
0799 541713

COMPUTER ACCESSORIES

Nighthawk goods – a range of easy-to-install PC accessories which can save money and power on customer's machines – are produced in the UK. The accessories include a Modem Mate to provide remote access to PCs for £199.00 and the Ecomonitor, a screen saver that will help prevent screen burn and cut down on radiation emissions, for £49.00.

There is an impressive range of printer switches and buffers. The APS and Jellybean range can increase the performance of your printers and increase the number of PCs that can use the same machine, a significant improvement in the efficiency of any business.

Catalogue: *A4, Leaflets, 38 pages, Colour and B/W, Free* Postal charges: *Varies with item* Delivery: *In house delivery* Methods of Payment: *Cheque, Visa, Access / Mastercard*

PANRIX ELECTRONIX
56B Roseville Road
Leeds
Yorks
LS8 5DR

Telephone:
0532 444958
Fax:
0532 444962

COMPUTERS

Panrix Electronix produce a range of motherboards for computers. The PCI 4000 was voted Editors' Choice by *PC Magazine* in December '93. They said that 'with a large 128Mb maximum memory capacity and PCI Local bus, the Panrix PCI 4000 not only gives outstanding performance now, but provides an excellent platform on which to base future upgrades'. This board is priced at £480.00.

Also available are a range of Vesa and other PCI local buses ranging in price from £999.00 to £1849.00 plus a range of options and upgrades.

Catalogue: *A4, Leaflets, 10 pages, Colour and B/W, Free* Postal charges: *£20.00 per system* Delivery: *Courier* Methods of Payment: *Cheque, Visa, Access / Mastercard*

PERSONA PLC
Unit 1
Silverglade Business Park
Leatherhead Road
Chessington
Surrey
KT9 2NQ

Telephone:
0372 729611
Fax:
0372 743535

COMPUTER SYTEMS

Persona offer everything you need to get your office hooked up on a sound footing for the future. A broad range of networking solutions is designed to meet the test of time, being multi-vendor and 'future proofed'.

Fibre-optic cables, very much part of the future, start at £170.00 for 3' suitable for Linkbuilder 3GH. Data tapes start at £6.08 for a 256Mb tape.

Their Cheyenne software is designed to protect an enhance tour network, transforming traditional fileservers into a platform for data and network management.

Computers

Catalogue: *Quarterly, A4, Catalogue, 96, B/W, Free* Postal charges: *Varies with item* Delivery: *Parcelforce* Methods of Payment: *Visa Cheque, Postal Order, Access / Mastercard*

PORTABLE COMPUTERS LTD
Arden Court
Arden Road
Alcester
Warks
B49 6HN

Telephone:
0789 490606
Fax:
0789 765493

LAPTOP COMPUTERS

Portable Computers provide top name laptops for government, educational and business establishments around the country from among brand names such as Toshiba, NEC and AST.

This selection of computers provides something for everyone's needs, many with features such as handwriting recognition. In order to provide a complete service, there is a comprehensive range of printers and software which are compatible with all the laptops.

Catalogue: *Annually, A4, Catalogue, 14 pages, Colour, Free* Postal charges: *Varies with item* Delivery: *Royal Mail* Methods of Payment: *Cheque, Visa, Access / Mastercard, American Express*

PUBLIC DOMAIN SOFTWARE
Winscombe House
Beacon Road
Crowborough
Sussex
TN6 1UL

COMPUTER SOFTWARE

Public Domain's PC shareware reference guide covers every aspect of shareware from business to astronomy. As the name implies, shareware can be used for a limited period on your PC without the threat of something dire when Big Brother finds out you've got unlicensed software up and running. Occasionally, the product comes completely free; more often, you get an incomplete version of the full program.

Public Domain also provide a disk format translation service, costing £10.50 per disk (charges vary for very large disks). You should remember, though, that no program can be run under a different operating system from the one it was designed for.

Catalogue: *A5, Catalogue, 128 pages, B/W, £2.50* Postal charges: *Free* Delivery: *Royal Mail* Methods of Payment: *Visa, Access / Mastercard Cheque, Postal Order*

SELECT DIRECT
Freepost (NG5132)
Nottingham
NG7 1BR

Telephone:
0800 889944

APPLE COMPUTER SOFTWARE AND HARDWARE

Select Direct is a trading name of KRCS Ltd., the UK's largest Apple Centre group. You can choose any number of extras for your Macintosh, including printers, hard disk drives and the most popular desktop publishing software.

QuarkXpress costs £579.00. Many publishing houses use Quark's powerful qualities to piece together their books and magazines. You can also buy

Computers

the complete Microsoft Office package, comprising four separate programs, for £269.00.

Complete computer systems, on the other hand, cost from £799.00 for the low-cost Macintosh LC 475 4/80. This comes complete with a 14" colour monitor.

Catalogue: *Monthly, A3, Leaflets, 2 pages, Colour, Free* Postal charges: *£4.95* Delivery: *Royal Mail* Methods of Payment: *Cheque, Postal Order, Visa, Access / Mastercard, American Express*

SHAREWARE PUBLISHING
3A Queen Street
Seaton
Devon
EX12 2NY

Telephone:
0297 24088
Fax:
0297 24091

SHAREWARE
Shareware's 'Software Source Reference Guide' takes you through the options for low-cost, high-quality software for the IBM PC and compatibles. The bulk of the catalogue consists of shareware disks, but there's also fully licensed shareware and non shareware.

Shareware allows you to 'try before you buy'. The author receives nothing until you've decided whether you want to keep the program. All shareware disks in the catalogue incur a £3.00 handling charge.

Catalogue: *A4, Catalogue, 104 pages, Colour, £3.99* Postal charges: *£4.00* Delivery: *Royal Mail Courier* Methods of Payment: *Cheque, Postal Order, Visa, Access / Mastercard*

SOFTCODE (UK) LTD
Winter Hill House
Marlowe Reach
Station Approach
Marlow
Bucks
SL7 1NT

Telephone:
0628 488866
Fax:
0628 488855

COMPUTER SOFTWARE
Softcode's 'Tracker for Windows' allows you to log any call or enquiry as part of a database. The search function of each database instantly gives you the history of a business contact and allows you to build up a huge cross-referenced system.

Each record is effectively a four-sided record card consisting of up to 75 different information fields. You can tag each of these fields with a keyword, or link them to information available in the notepad function. The program costs £395.00.

Catalogue: *A5, Leaflets, 3 pages, Colour, Free* Postal charges: *Varies with item* Delivery: *Royal Mail* Methods of Payment: *Cheque*

TANDY BY MAIL
Bilston Road
Wednesbury
West Midlands
WS10 7JN

Telephone:
021 556 6429

ELECTRONICS, HI-FI, COMPUTERS, PARTS
The high-street chain Tandy stocks a huge range of most types of electrical goods and accessories including televisions, stereo equipment, computers, satellite systems, telephone equipment, video games and a host of electrical accessories. In-car stereo radio cassette players start at £39.99, while flush mount speakers start at £9.99.

Computers

Tandy stocks computer games from SEGA, Amiga, Nintendo and Commodore and offers a selection of business and entertainment software for personal computers. 'Wordstar Windows' retails at £79.99 while 'Indiana Jones and the Last Crusade' costs £15.99. Tandy also has a good selection of Karaoke equipment with complete systems starting at £79.95.

They also have a giant stock of adaptors, cables, leads and so on.

Catalogue: *A4, Catalogue, 132 pages, Colour, Free* Postal charges: *£3.00* Delivery: *Royal Mail Courier* Methods of Payment: *Cheque, Postal Order, Visa, Access / Mastercard*

THE JUMPING BEAN CO.
Leon Gate
Lenton
Nottingham
Notts
NG7 2LX

Telephone:
0602 792838
Fax:
0602 780963

COMPUTER GAMES
'Noddy's Playtime' is a graded creativity and entertainment package for home computers based on solid entertainment principles for three- to seven-year-olds. 'Noddy's Big Adventure' is the sequel. There is a choice of three carefully defined learning levels which have been designed in consultation with teachers.

In 'Noddy's Playtime' children can drive with Noddy and explore the magic world of Toytown where there are 8 special learning locations including Market Place (a game of letter recognition), Post Office (counting) and Chimney House (musical fun). Also included is a junior Art Package which develops your child's creative ability.

'Playtime' is available on PC, Amiga, ST and Acorn Archimedes and 'Big Adventure' on Acorn Archimedes, Amiga, PC and PC Windows. Prices range from £24.99–£34.99.

Catalogue: *A4, Leaflets, 4 pages, Colour, Free* Postal charges: *£1.95* Delivery: *Royal Mail* Methods of Payment: *Cheque, Postal Order*

THE MAC ZONE
PO Box 34
Ripley
Woking
Surrey
GU23 6YR

Telephone:
0483 211456
Fax:
0483 211567

COMPUTERS, ACCESSORIES AND SOFTWARE
The world's second largest mail order company in its class, The Mac Zone is another American company now over here. As the name suggests, they sell exclusively Apple Macintosh products. An alphabetical list features brief product details, system requirements, restrictions and drawbacks. If you register with The Mac Zone, you receive a certain number of Air Miles every time you buy a product.

Their illustrated display section gives a much fuller account of what's on offer. All the most popular soft-

Computers

ware seems competitively priced: Illustrator for £319.95; Photoshop for £459.95; and PageMaker for £449.50. A good range of hardware is also listed: 2082 Triniton monitor for £1499.95; Magneto optical drive for £699.95.

Catalogue: *A4, Catalogue, 48 pages, Colour, Free* Postal charges: *Varies with item* Delivery: *Royal Mail Courier* Methods of Payment: *Cheque, Visa, Access / Mastercard*

TINY COMPUTERS LIMITED
53 Ormside Way
Holmethorpe Industrial Estate
Redhill
Surrey
RH1 2LW

Telephone:
0737 779511
Fax:
0737 779541

COMPUTERS
Tiny Computers' Building Block range of IBM compatible PCs are well priced. Among the many recommendations plastered on their catalogue, *IBM System User* magazine states that their 80486 desktop system is vastly cheaper than any other 33Mhz 80846 machine available. Sadly, their catalogue doesn't seem to give this price.

A BB386SX 33Mhz system starts from £349.00 with a mono VGA monitor and 40 MB of VGA RAM. Further up the range, a BB Pentium 60Mhz system starts at £1499.00 with a mono VGA and 40Mb VGA RAM.

Catalogue: *A4, Brochure, Colour and B/W, Free* Postal charges: *Varies with item* Delivery: *In house delivery* Methods of Payment: *Cheque, Visa, Access / Mastercard, Postal Order*

TRANSEND SHAREWARE
Keighley Business Centre
Knowle Mills
South Street
Keighley
Yorks
BD21 1AG

Telephone:
0274 622228

COMPUTER SHAREWARE
Transend Shareware supply all their software on recycled disks that have been virus checked. A full catalogue lists the extraordinary range of shareware now available for computer users. They are also able to field technical queries.

Also advertised is the 'Practical PC Group', one of the largest user groups in the UK. The group offer a high level of technical support not only for shareware you may have purchased, but also for commercial packages. A variety of goods are available at a discount for members, including 1.44 meg branded 3.5" disks for £12.99 a box.

Catalogue: *A5, Leaflets, 6 pages, B/W, Free* Postal charges: *Free* Delivery: *Royal Mail* Methods of Payment: *Visa, Access / Mastercard Cheque, Postal Order*

Computers

UK HOME COMPUTERS
Unit 22
Cheney Manor
Industrial Estate
Swindon
Wilts
SN2 2PJ

Telephone:
0793 695034

COMPUTERS
UK Home Computers sell PCs and peripherals at discounted prices. UK Star, their manufacturing division, build PC systems to suit your requirements. They even let you choose the CPU casing.

The range includes mini towers, desktop or slimline desktop machines all with digital displays. A 486 desktop machine costs £69.95; extra monitors are available from £69.99 for a 14" VGA to £133.00 for a 14" colour VGA. Extra hard disks start at £49.95 for 20Mb.

Components are sold as part of a system or individually, which is sometimes a little more expensive. A 210Mb Maxtor hard disk, for instance, costs £179.00 bought individually but only £170.24 when purchased as part of a system.

Catalogue: *no info, A4, Leaflets, Colour and B/W, Free* Postal charges: *Varies with item* Delivery: *In house delivery* Methods of Payment: *Visa, Access / Mastercard Cheque, Postal Order*

VIGLEN LIMITED
Viglen House
Alperton Lane
Alperton
Middx
HA0 1DX

Telephone:
081 758 7000
Fax:
081 991 5115

PERSONAL COMPUTERS
Viglen is a UK PC maker with a track record as suppliers of multi-user systems, providing all PC needs for, among others, the Royal College of Nursing.

The Genie Executive 4SX25 PC has a reputation as a well-integrated PC with all-round performance and room for expansion, and is available for £1099.00. In addition to their range of computers, Viglen provide technical support and a twelve-month warranty for all materials.

Catalogue: *A4, Leaflets, 96 pages, Colour, Free* Postal charges: *Varies with item* Delivery: *Royal Mail* Methods of Payment: *Cheque, Postal Order, Visa, Access / Mastercard, American Express*

WHITE KNIGHT TECHNOLOGY
PO Box 2395
Waltham Cross
Hertfordshire
EN8 7HT

Telephone:
0992 714539
Fax:
0992 714539

COMPUTER ACCESSORIES
White Knight supply a wide range of 'serious' or professional computer hardware and software, audio products and broadcast equipment. On offer are a range of A4000 accelerators including RCS Excalibur 25MHz 68040 + 32-Bit RAM for £649.00 and GVP G-Force 40MHz 68040 + 4MB 32-Bit RAM for £1275.00. Amiga 1200 Hard Drives range from 80Mb at £439.00 to 340Mb at £689.00.

Audio ranges include the Sunrize AD1012/Studio 16 which features 4 Track Mono, 12-Bit, Direct to Disk Recording, Editing & Playback for £499.00.

DIY Supplies

Catalogue: *A4, Leaflet, 1 page, B/W, Free* Postal charges: *Varies with item* Delivery: *Royal Mail* Methods of Payment: *Cheque, Postal Order, Visa, Access / Mastercard*

C & A SUPPLIES
Bidder Street
London
E16 4ST

Telephone:
071 474 0474
Fax:
071 474 5055

BUILDING SUPPLIES
C & A Supplies are offering numerous discounts on bulk orders over a certain price. This is because they are celebrating their 25th anniversary this year. This well-established business offers every accessory and item for the building trade (tarpaulins £2.79–£14.58 or mastics £2.90). Orders are usually delivered by the next day by C & A Supplies home-delivery lorries. This company is based in London with a warehouse containing everthing that is advertised in the brochure.

Catalogue: *Annually, A4, Brochure, 22 pages, Colour, Free* Postal charges: *Varies with item* Delivery: *In house delivery* Methods of Payment: *Cheque, Access / Mastercard, Visa*

DAVIES & CLIFFORD LTD
Beta Works
Oxford Road
Tatling End
Gerrards Cross
Bucks
SL9 7BB

Telephone:
0753 886254
Fax:
0753 887319

PORTABLE WOODEN BUILDINGS FOR GARDEN AND HOME
Portable wooden buildings made with utmost care and attention to detail by qualified craftsmen. The catalogue features a large range of buildings with their different sizes and specifications.

Range includes garden sheds, garages, workshops, chalets, dens, pavilions and greenhouses. A 2.1m × 1.8m garden shed in deal cladding will cost £351.90, a 3m × 2.4m shed is £458.43. Erection by the company is a further 15%. The company will also quote for the construction of individual designs to the customer's own specification. Black and white illustrated catalogue provided along with detailed price list.

Catalogue: *A5, Brochure, 24 pages, B/W, Free* Postal charges: *Varies with item* Delivery: *In house delivery* Methods of Payment: *Cheque*

DORSET RESTORATION
Cow Drove
Bere Regis
Dorset
BH20 7JZ

Telephone:
0929 472200
Fax:
0929 472292

TRADITIONAL BUILDING MATERIALS AND ANTIQUES
The most fashionable of homes now boast a range of original features. However, if your home no longer has them, you can re-create the golden age with original items from Dorset Restoration.

The comprehensive service includes advice on the best materials to use in your home, an index for more unusual items, and craftsmen who will ensure that any product will blend perfectly with your property.

DIY Supplies

Whether you are looking to improve the outside of the house, with period chimney pots, guttering or sundials or to create stunning internal features such as dressers and fireplaces, there is an enormous and varied range to choose from.

Catalogue: *A4, Leaflets, 2 pages, B/W, Free* Postal charges: *Varies with item* Delivery: *Royal Mail* Methods of Payment: *Cheque, Visa, Access / Mastercard*

HOMEBREW MAIL ORDER
Freepost
67/69 Park Lane
Hornchurch
Essex
RM11 1BR

Telephone:
0708 745943
Fax:
0708 743699

BEER AND WINE KITS

For those who prefer to make their own wine or beer, Homebrew is just the catalogue. It offers a good range of kits, ingredients and equipment for beginners and experts alike.

The catalogue is straightforward and easy to use, each section and individual prices being clearly marked. For beginners there is an inclusive beginners' kit and the company will also happily offer advice over the phone.

A gallon Muscadet kit sells for £5.99 and a 40-pint John Bull bitter kit for £5.15. There are even kits for spirits and liqueurs.

Catalogue: *A5, Catalogue, 12 pages, B/W, Free* Postal charges: *£3.50* Delivery: *Royal Mail* Methods of Payment: *Cheque, Postal Order, Visa, Access / Mastercard*

IMPACT POWER TOOLS (SURREY) LTD
Unit 10
Trowers Way
Holmthorpe Industrial Estate
Redhill
Surrey
RH1 2LH

Telephone:
0737 772436
Fax:
0737 765944

TOOLS

IPT produce their own small catalogue of special offers plus the large *Good Tool Guide*, which is an independent guide to the best tools. This features just about every tool available from the world's best manufacturers.

It is by no means restricted to the professional builder either (although there are large, industrial items available). You can buy individual pliers, hammers and saws and there is also a good range of gardening tools. Prices far too many to mention but seem competitive.

Catalogue: *Annually, A4, Catalogue, 186 pages, Colour, £1.95* Postal charges: *Varies with item* Delivery: *Royal Mail Courier* Methods of Payment: *Cheque, Visa, Access / Mastercard*

DIY Supplies

J SIMBLE & SONS
76 Queens Road
The Broadway
Watford
Herts
WD1 2LD

Telephone:
0923 26052
Fax:
0923 817526

TOOLS

Simble produce two catalogues, a major, 250-page one which costs £2.50, and a shorter 60-page supplement which is free. Unfortunately the former was not ready as we went to press but if the supplement is anything to go by it should be worth the money.

There is a terrific range of tools, from large power drills and saws down to individual wrenches and chisels. Each one is illustrated with a line drawing and given a brief description. Prices seem good, with cordless screwdrivers at £28.00, a hot air paint stripper £35.50 and battery chargers from just £7.50.

Catalogue: *Annually, A5, Catalogue, 60 pages, B/W, Free* Postal charges: *Varies with item* Delivery: *Courier* Methods of Payment: *Cheque, Visa, Access / Mastercard*

M & B ELECTRICAL SUPPLIES LTD
Pilgrim Works
Stairbridge Lane
Bolney
Sussex
RH17 5PA

Telephone:
0444 881965

ELECTRICAL DIY SUPPLIES

With everything from plugs to field telephones, this catalogue is the ideal place to start if you are tackling any job in your home or on your land.

The range which M & B supply is constantly changing and prices are kept low by selling stocks the moment they come into stock. It's therefore advisable to buy when you see, as M & B cannot guarantee that they will be able to buy in more items at a later date – or at the same price.

Ultrasonic burglar alarms, ideal for both home and car, for only £10.00, a 15-metre extension lead is £2.00 and over 100 DIY essentials in 'bargain packs' are available.

Catalogue: *Monthly, A4, Leaflets, 18 pages, B/W, Free* Postal charges: *Varies with item* Delivery: *Royal Mail* Methods of Payment: *Cheque, Postal Order, Visa, Access / Mastercard*

PAINT MAGIC
116 Sheen Road
Richmond
Surrey
TW9 1UR

Telephone:
081 940 5503
Fax:
081 332 7503

PAINTS, WASHES AND STENCIL PAINTS FOR THE HOME

The Paint Magic brochure is full of new products and ideas designed to put more excitement into your decorating projects.

Jocasta Innes, who founded Paint Magic, believes that the right paint finish can transform quite ordinary rooms without exceptional furniture or expensive fabrics or accessories.

Paint Magic sell new colours, old-fashioned as well as high-tech paints, a comprehensive range of pigments, varnishes, brushes, stencils, books and videos.

DIY Supplies

1 litre of Mulberry (or any other) colourwash is £23.00. Stencil paints are £3.35 for 45ml and 500ml of crackle glaze is £12.00.

Catalogue: *A4, Catalogue, 10 pages, Colour, Free* Postal charges: *Varies with item* Delivery: *Royal Mail* Methods of Payment: *Cheque, Visa, Access / Mastercard*

PEELS OF LONDON LTD
P O Box 160
Richmond
TW10 7XL

Telephone:
081 948 0689

ARTIFICIAL STAINED GLASS
Peels enable you to obtain a stained-glass effect with a minimum of effort. You can transform your doors and windows in minutes. The idea is to take pre-made transfers which peel off and can then be pressed into place.

A variety of designs are available, including door-numbers. You can choose from designs like 'Art Deco' and 'Fanlight' (both £23.99 for a 19" × 26½" section).

Catalogue: *A4, Leaflets, 2 pages, Colour, Free* Postal charges: *£3.00* Delivery: *Royal Mail* Methods of Payment: *Cheque, Postal Order*

POLYVINE
Vine House
Rockhampton
Berkeley
Glos
GL13 9DT

Telephone:
0454 261276
Fax:
0454 261286

PAINTS AND ACRYLIC FINISHES
Increasing public awareness of industrial pollution and concern about handling hazardous chemicals has made Polyvine's water-based alternatives an increasingly popular option. To help you make the most of these acrylics, Polyvine provides videos showing you how to master modern painting techniques such as marbling, dragging and stippling.

The wall colours, varnish and floor coatings come in a wide variety of finishes. As well as matt, silk and gloss in both vivid and muted colours there are various woodgrains.

Catalogue: *Third A4, Brochure, 8 pages, B/W, Free* Postal charges: *Varies with item* Delivery: *Royal Mail* Methods of Payment: *Cheque, Postal Order, Visa, Access / Mastercard*

SLINGSBY TRADING POST
Preston Street
Bradford
West Yorkshire
BD7 1JF

Telephone:
0274 721591
Fax:
0274 723044

COMMERCIAL AND INDUSTRIAL EQUIPMENT
Slingsby produce a diverse range of commercial and industrial equipment. Originally known for materials handling, they still maintain a large stock of handtrucks, hoists, stackers and so on. A folding handtruck (975 mm × 380 mm) costs £80.00; heavy duty handtrucks cost from £99.00 (1257 mm high) to £121.00 (1000 mm high). Among their safety and security stock you'll find road signs from £4.79 ('road narrows on left ahead'); automatic parking barriers at

DIY Supplies

£2263.00; traffic mirrors at £51.00 and galvanised bins from £72.00.

Catalogue: *Annually, A4, Catalogue, 656 pages, Colour, Free* Postal charges: *Varies with item* Delivery: *Royal Mail* Methods of Payment: *Cheque, Visa, Access / Mastercard*

STENCIL ESSENTIALS
Ash Farm House
Poole Keynes
Cirencester
Glos
GL7 6EG

Telephone:
0285 770535

STENCIL EQUIPMENT

This company produce a stencil pen that is supposed to take the effort out of stencil cutting. It comes with a standard or fine tip suitable for use on thick acetates or very fine designs. You need to specify which you prefer. It costs £19.95 or £21.95 with both tips.

There are also a number of different stencil designs. 'Galleons' cost £10.00 cut or £5.00 uncut; 'Fleur de Lys' is the same. Other items include five acetate sheets 16" × 12" for £4.75 and five acetate sheets 24" × 18" for £8.50.

Catalogue: *A4, Leaflets, Colour, Free* Postal charges: *Free* Delivery: *Royal Mail* Methods of Payment: *Cheque, Postal Order*

STOPSHOP BY MAIL
2a Ealing Road
Aintree
Liverpool
L9 0LR

Telephone:
051 5238440
Fax:
051 5238121

SECURITY PRODUCTS

With the current crime figures escalating there is now an increasing demand for high quality and low cost security systems. StopShop claim to provide everything necessary to protect the home and the office.

The Logic 4 DIY system starts at £89.00, is ideal for homes, and can be tailored to your individual needs. The Phillips Observation Kit is a complete closed-circuit TV system for £385.00, which can also be extended to provide you with the security you need.

There is also reasonably priced security lighting and a collection of dummy security boxes and cameras to deter intruders.

Catalogue: *Monthly, A4, Catalogue, 16 pages, Colour, Free* Postal charges: *Varies with item* Delivery: *Royal Mail* Methods of Payment: *Cheque, Postal Order, Visa, Access / Mastercard*

THE MEMORIAL FIRMS
Masonry Works
Priors Haw Road
Weldon
Corby
NN17 1JG

Telephone:
0536 260781
Fax:
0563 204265

FUNERALS

The Memorial Firms carry out a comprehensive headstone service. Included in the price of your headstone (inscription set out at the discretion of their letter cutters unless you state otherwise) are delivery and installation to any mainland English or Welsh cemetary; execution of any formalities with the church authorities; and the erection of any kerbing or additional plinth, where necessary.

There's a broad range of memorial stones to

DIY Supplies

choose from. A headstone shaped as a heart, with finely carved sprays of roses will set you back £395.00 in Italian White Marble, £369.00 in Fossil or hard limestone, or £425.00 in Nabresina. Something more solemn, a classic headstone carved to appear like a record of remembrance, with a garland of roses, costs £410.00 for polished black or red granite, £367.00 part-polished; £401.00 in light or dark grey polished marble, or £348.00 part-polished.

Catalogue: *Annually, A4 landscape, Catalogue, 20 pages, B/W, Free* Postal charges: *Varies with item* Delivery: *In house delivery* Methods of Payment: *Visa, Access / Mastercard Cheque*

THE MERCHANT TILER
Twyford Mill
Oxford Road
Adderbury
Oxfordshire
OX17 3HP

Telephone:
0295 812179
Fax:
0295 812189

WALL AND FLOOR TILES

The Merchant Tiler offers the most comprehensive range of distinctly individual tiles in one catalogue. All of the tiles are carefully chosen to give you a wide choice at a low price. The Fired Earth Collection of tiles are all handmade. After selecting your tiles from many samples, The Merchant Tiler will install them for free.

The tiles come in a wide range of colours and designs for nearly every room in your house. For example, if you are an animal lover you can purchase tiles with hand-painted mice, badgers, squirrels, rabbits or hedgehogs (£0.33 each) and anyone with exotic taste can choose from the old Mexico range (£1.67 each).

Catalogue: *A4, Catalogue, 28 pages, Colour, Free* Postal charges: *Varies with item* Delivery: *Royal Mail* Methods of Payment: *Visa, Access / Mastercard Cheque*

WOOD FLOOR SALES
Unit 4 Tything Park
Arden Forest Trading
Estate
Alcester
Warwickshire
B49 6ES

Telephone:
0789 400050
Fax:
0789 400049

WOOD FLOORING

Free samples provided of any flooring shown in brochure, which usually arrive within 24 hours. Samples of trims and underlays are also available. Free delivery to all mainland areas. Telephone budgeting service available for fitting service to individual requirements. Discounts on larger orders. For DIY supply, payment required before dispatch. Wide range of wood flooring on offer.

Catalogue: *A4, Brochure, 31 pages, Colour, Free* Postal charges: *Varies with item* Delivery: *Royal Mail* Methods of Payment: *Cheque, Postal Order*

Electrical Appliances

BT BUSINESS CATALOGUE
FREE POST (BS7632)
Bristol
BS1 2QX

Telephone:
0800 700 999
Fax:
0800 222 444

TELEPHONES AND ACCESSORIES
No expense seems to have been spared with this glossy publication, but when you make £70.00 profit a second why skimp? Much of this beautifully produced catalogue is aimed at the business user, with specific sections devoted to 'Data Services', 'Business Publications' and 'Business Support'. You can order fax machines, phone systems, answering machines, video conferencing equipment and pagers.

For those leading simpler lives there is a good range of telephones which can be either bought or rented. One of the best features of the catalogue is the jargon busting, with full translations of all those strange terms associated with the telecoms world, such as ISDN, fax polling and ERB numbers.

Catalogue: *A4, Catalogue, 148 pages, Colour, Free* Postal charges: *£2.54* Delivery: *Courier* Methods of Payment: *Access / Mastercard, Visa Cheque, Postal Order*

BUYERS & SELLERS LTD
120/122 Ladbroke Grove
North Kensington
London
NW10 2AL

Telephone:
071 229 8468
Fax:
071 221 4113

APPLIANCES, INCLUDING COOKERS, MICROWAVES AND FRIDGES
Buyers & Sellers stock an enormous number of household appliances: fridges, microwaves, vacuum cleaners, washing machines, tumble-driers, hobs, freezers and so on. They also supply almost every brand of cooker currently available in the UK. They have an advice line for telephone shoppers as well as a large showroom for personal callers. Although they do not have a catalogue as such, they will send out a selection of makers' brochures to assist choice.

They often have 'special purchases' on display or end-of-line models and are well known for their excellent prices. Indeed the company is often cited in bargain-hunting guides and articles.

Catalogue: *Annually, 170 × 100 mm, Brochure, 2 pages, Colour, Free* Postal charges: *Varies with item* Delivery: *Courier* Methods of Payment: *Cheque, COD, Visa, Access / Mastercard, American Express, Diners Club*

Electrical Appliances

MEDIVAC PLC
Freepost
Wilmslow
Cheshire
SK9 5YE

Telephone:
0625 539401
Fax:
0625 539507

VACUUM CLEANERS
Medivac produce a range of products which provide immediate, risk-free relief from asthma, rhinitis, eczema and dust allergy.

The Medivac vacuum cleaner incorporates a unique 4-stage dust microfiltration system not found in any conventional cleaner and comes with a range of accessories such as extension hoses, animal grooming brushes and an electronic dust monitor. It costs £399.00 without VAT (as an acknowledged medical aid it is VAT free when supplied to eligible persons).

'Banamite' anti-allergy spray is for use on mattresses, furniture and carpets throughout the home. A single-room treatment costs £12.95 and a one-year treatment £79.95.

The 'Banamite' bedding range includes mattress covers, duvets and pillows. Prices start at £24.25 for one pillow.

Catalogue: *A4, Catalogue, 8 pages plus inserts, Colour, Free*
Postal charges: *£2.85* Delivery: *Royal Mail Courier*
Methods of Payment: *Cheque, Postal Order, Visa, Access / Mastercard, American Express*

TANDY BY MAIL
Bilston Road
Wednesbury
West Midlands
WS10 7JN

Telephone:
021 556 6429

ELECTRONICS, HI-FI, COMPUTERS, PARTS
The high-street chain Tandy stocks a huge range of most types of electrical goods and accessories including televisions, stereo equipment, computers, satellite systems, telephone equipment, video games and a host of electrical accessories. In-car stereo radio cassette players start at £39.99, while flush mount speakers start at £9.99.

Tandy stocks computer games from SEGA, Amiga, Nintendo and Commodore and offers a selection of business and entertainment software for personal computers. 'Wordstar Windows' retails at £79.99 while 'Indiana Jones and the Last Crusade' costs £15.99. Tandy also has a good selection of Karaoke equipment with complete systems starting at £79.95.

They also have a giant stock of adaptors, cables, leads and so on.

Catalogue: *A4, Catalogue, 132 pages, Colour, Free* Postal charges: *£3.00* Delivery: *Royal Mail Courier* Methods of Payment: *Cheque, Postal Order, Visa, Access / Mastercard*

Electrical Appliances

THE HIFI ATTIC
58 New George St
City Centre
Plymouth
Devon
PL1 1RR

Telephone:
0752 669511

WIDE RANGE OF HI-FI AND AUDIO VISUAL EQUIPMENT

Hifi Attic is a well-established retail/mail order business that has been trading for over 30 years. They stock a wide range of hi-fi separates, selected because they represent excellent reliability and value for money.

Many customers are bewildered by the choice of separates and midi-systems, and to help Hifi Attic have put together a buying guide to make the customer's decision as informed and painless as possible. They can also provide a laserdisc film catalogue free of charge for home entertainment enthusiasts. If you require expert advice and value for money then contact the Hifi Attic.

Catalogue: *A4, Catalogue, Colour, Free* Postal charges: *Varies with item* Delivery: *TNT* Methods of Payment: *Cheque, Visa, Access / Mastercard, American Express*

HOBBYKIT LTD
Unit 19 Capitol Ind Park
Capitol Way
London
NW9 0EQ

Telephone:
081 205 7485
Fax:
081 205 0603

COMPUTERS AND COMPUTER PARTS

Hobbykit can supply computer parts from individual boards up to a complete computer system. Their stock includes fax modems, CD-ROMs, Multimedia products, motherboards, memory, computer cases, controller cards, operating systems, tape streamers, hard and floppy disk drives, monitors, graphics cards and input devices.

They will also give advice and provide a complete computer system tailored to your exact requirements from the parts required at no additional cost.

Catalogue: *None* Postal charges: *Varies with item* Delivery: *Royal Mail, Parcelforce* Methods of Payment: *Cheque, Postal Order, Visa, Access / Mastercard*

LORRAINE ELECTRONICS
716 Lea Bridge Road
Leyton
London
E10 6AW

Telephone:
081 558 4226

SURVEILLANCE EQUIPMENT

Lorraine Electronics manufacture an extensive range of professional audio surveillance equipment. This allows the monitoring of room or telephone conversations, recorded either in situ or transmitted to a receiver elsewhere. Room conversations can be monitored by either portable or static systems e.g. 'The Recording Briefcase' or 'Calculator Transmitter'. Telephone conversations can be monitored by a 'wire-tap' or telephone transmitter.

The basic 'Room Transmitter' costs £70.00, receiver/recorders start at £1600.00 and a 'Pen Transmitter' costs £700.00.

Electronics

These products are supplied for export only. Transmitting radio signals without a licence and connecting unapproved equipment to the public telephone network is an offence in the UK.

Catalogue: *A4, Catalogue, 16 pages plus inserts, Colour, Free* Postal charges: *Varies with item* Delivery: *Royal Mail* Methods of Payment: *Cheque*

TANDY BY MAIL
Bilston Road
Wednesbury
West Midlands
WS10 7JN

Telephone:
021 556 6429

ELECTRONICS, HI-FI, COMPUTERS, PARTS
The high-street chain Tandy stocks a huge range of most types of electrical goods and accessories including televisions, stereo equipment, computers, satellite systems, telephone equipment, video games and a host of electrical accessories. In-car stereo radio cassette players start at £39.99, while flush mount speakers start at £9.99.

Tandy stocks computer games from SEGA, Amiga, Nintendo and Commodore and offers a selection of business and entertainment software for personal computers. 'Wordstar Windows' retails at £79.99 while 'Indiana Jones and the Last Crusade' costs £15.99. Tandy also has a good selection of Karaoke equipment with complete systems starting at £79.95.

They also have a giant stock of adaptors, cables, leads and so on.

Catalogue: *A4, Catalogue, 132 pages, Colour, Free* Postal charges: £3.00 Delivery: *Royal Mail Courier* Methods of Payment: *Cheque, Postal Order, Visa, Access / Mastercard*

TIDMAN MAIL ORDER
236 Sandycombe Road
Kew
Middx
TW9 2EQ

Telephone:
081 948 3702

VIDEO PARTS
Tidman Mail Order supply an extremely wide range of video parts, spares and accessories. Their general spares catalogue covers everything from Wickman fuses priced between £1.10 and £1.38, and line output transformers by major firms, including Bang and Olufson (from £17.95) and Bush (from £14.43).

They also specialise in replacement remote controls. Judging by their extensive catalogue, which features all possible cross-references, there can't be too many videos for which they'd be stuck to find a replacement.

Catalogue: *A4, Catalogue, 50 pages, B/W, Free* Postal charges: *Varies with item* Delivery: *Royal Mail* Methods of Payment: *Cheque*

Flowers and Chocolates

WORLDWIDE FLOWERS LTD
PO Box 299
Haywards Heath
West Sussex
RH16 3FZ

Telephone:
0444 483555
Fax:
0444 483777

FLOWERS AND CHOCOLATES
Worldwide Flowers will send flowers from all round the world, beautifully presented in their special gift boxes. But they don't just stop with flowers, you can also include such delights as luxury Belgian chocolates or English handmade truffles. Chocolates can be sent on their own too.

A 'Rio Floral Gift Box' starts at £13.50, while a 'Fresh Floral Basket Arrangement' is £21.95 and a 'Baby Cradle Arrangement' £19.95. The 'English Rose Box' starts at £25.00. Belgian chocolates or English handmade truffles can be included for an extra £5.50 or sent separately in boxes starting at £9.95.

Catalogue: *Bi-annually, A4, Brochure, 4 pages, Colour, Free* Postal charges: *Varies with item* Delivery: *Royal Mail Courier* Methods of Payment: *Cheque, Postal Order, Visa, Access / Mastercard, American Express*

ABERGAVENNY FINE FOODS
Unit 4 Castle Meadows Park
Abergavenny
Gwent
NP7 7RZ

Telephone:
0873 850001
Fax:
0873 850002

WELSH FOOD
Abergavenny specialise in fine Welsh foods. They have an interesting selection of cheeses from their own dairy including Pantysgawn Farm, a soft goat's cheese; St Illtyd, a mature cheddar; Y-Fenni, a mature cheese with wholegrain mustard and brown ale; and St David's Welsh, a washed rind cheese.

They also sell Glamorgan sausages, chicken, pheasant, vegan and lamb pâté and even Welsh spring water. Strangely they have a line of Mexican foods made by Aztec, which has apparently set up in Wales!

Prices are around £3.50 for 500g of cheese, £1.00 for 150g sausages and £10.00 for 2lb of pâté.

Catalogue: *A4, Catalogue, 12 pages, B/W, Free* Postal charges: *Varies with item* Delivery: *Royal Mail* Methods of Payment: *Cheque*

ADNAMS
The Crown
High Street
Southwold
Suffolk
IP18 6DP

Telephone:
0502 724222
Fax:
0502 724805

FINE WINES
Twice listed Joint Wine Merchant of the Year, this Suffolk-based company has been selling wine through mail order for the past twelve years. It also has two retail outlets in Norwich and Southwold which are well worth a visit if you are in the area.

The catalogue is splendidly laid out with excellent and witty reviews of both regions and wines. There is a best-buy section for bottles under £5.00 along with ranges of fortified wines and spirits. Other products include olive oil, vinegar, and for the enthusiast,

Food & Drink

Adnams ties at £19.50 and silk waistcoats at £65.00. A thoroughly enjoyable, beautifully produced catalogue.

Catalogue: *Annually, A4, Catalogue, 98 pages, B/W, £2.50* Postal charges: *Varies with item* Delivery: *Courier* Methods of Payment: *Cheque, Postal Order, Visa, Access / Mastercard*

ALGERIAN COFFEE STORES
52 Old Compton Street
London
W1V 6PB

Telephone:
071 437 2480

COFFEE

If you enjoy coffee, you'll welcome the opportunity to sample something from the Algerian Coffee Stores. Anyone who's bored with the standard pre-packed article, and who expects their coffee and tea to actually taste of something should either drop by their shop in Old Compton Street, London or at least take a good look at their price list.

Original coffees include Pure Blue Mountain at £9.90 for a ½ lb and Nicaragua at £2.56 for the same amount. If you want something a little different, there are flavoured coffees from £3.92 for ½ lb of Banana Hazelnut to £5.36 for Swiss Water P. Daff.

Catalogue: *A6, Brochure, 2 pages, B/W, Free* Postal charges: *Varies with item* Delivery: *Royal Mail* Methods of Payment: *Cheque, Visa, Access / Mastercard, American Express, Diners Club*

BEER PARADISE LIMITED
Unit 11 Riverside PLace
South Accomodation Road
Leeds
LS9 0RQ

Telephone:
0532 359082
Fax:
0532 359217

BEERS

This membership-only club offers more than 300 beers at cash-and-carry prices direct to your door. Beer Paradise has German, French and Belgian beers along with the choicest British and Irish brews, which can be delivered or collected, depending on your needs.

The prices are all low enough to help you to work up a thirst and there is a deposit on each returnable bottle – an incentive to drink even more.

Catalogue: *Monthly, A4, Leaflets, 11 pages, B/W, Membership £4.00 annually* Postal charges: *Varies with item* Delivery: *Royal Mail* Methods of Payment: *Cheque, Postal Order*

BERKMANNS WINE CELLARS LTD
12 Brewery Road
London
N7 9NH

Telephone:
071 609 4711
Fax:
071 607 0018

WINES

Berkmanns have built up a reputation for supplying restaurant wines, with an accent on prompt and useful service extras like the possibility of reserving wine to ensure a continuous stock. Their minimum order for free delivery is three cases, but they're quite happy to supply mixed cases and single cases for a small extra charge.

Their house wines start at £26.64 for a dozen bottles of Cuvée de l'Amitié Blanc or Rouge.

Food & Drink

Sauvignon de Sauvion costs £29.40 for twelve bottles. Moving up-market, Berkmanns have a fine stock of Australian wines, including Coldstream Hills Chardonnay and Pinot Noir at £80.04 for twelve bottles.

Catalogue: *Quarterly, A4, Catalogue, 32 pages, B/W, Free* Postal charges: *Varies with item* Delivery: *In house delivery* Methods of Payment: *Cheque, Visa, Access / Mastercard*

BERRY BROS & RUDD LTD
3 St James's Street
London
SW1A 1EG

Telephone:
071 396 9600
Fax:
071 396 9611

WINES

Connoisseurs of wines, spirits, liqueurs and cigars will no doubt be familiar with Berry Bros. Among the vast amount of literature which makes up their catalogue is a well-designed booklet describing and pricing their large range of wines and spirits. Organised by country and region, it gives useful background on each wine. South Africa, for instance, is represented by five varieties of red wine, ranging from 1991 Doorberg Cabernet Sauvignon (£4.45 per bottle) to 1990 Beyerkloof Cabernet/Merlot (£15.95 a bottle).

Another leaflet explains their 'like Clockwork' service, a handy way of sampling a variety of wines. Each quarter you receive a case of twelve bottles with at least six different wines. At £75.00 per case, this is quite a bargain – especially if you opt for the easy monthly payment scheme.

Catalogue: *6 x 12, Catalogue, 8 pages, Colour, Free* Postal charges: *Free* Delivery: *In house delivery* Methods of Payment: *Cheque, Visa, Access / Mastercard*

BERRYDALES
Berrydale House
5 Lawn Road
London
NW3 2XS

Telephone:
071 722 2866
Fax:
071 722 7685

NOVELTY CHOCOLATES/CONSERVES

Berrydales produce a mouth-watering selection of edible gifts, including chocolate bears, dinosaurs and spring flowers. All are made from quality, dairy-free, plain Belgian chocolate. They also come as gift packs with children's books suitable for the 3–6-year age group.

In addition there is a range of farmhouse quality jams and spreads. These include sugar-free jams sweetened with apple juice, real lemon curd and Berrydale Bear chocolate spread packed in glass 'bear' jars. These chocolate-spread bears also come with books.

The chocolate bears and dinosaurs are £1.49 with chocolate and book gift packs £2.99. Sugar-free whole strawberry jam sells for £1.69, real lemon curd

Food & Drink

for £1.49 and chocolate spread and book gift packs for £3.49.

Catalogue: *Quarterly, A4, Brochure, 2 pages, Colour and B/W, Free* Postal charges: *Varies with item* Delivery: *Royal Mail Courier* Methods of Payment: *Cheque, Postal Order*

BETTYS & TAYLORS OF HARROGATE BY POST
1 Parliament Street
Harrogate
HG1 2QU

Telephone:
0423 531211
Fax:
0423 565191

TEA, COFFEE AND GIFT SUPPLIERS
Bettys supplies specialist teas and coffees along with presentation gifts.

Traditional Easter specialities range from a luxury Easter Hamper at £137.12, including wine, simnel cake and chocolate goodies, to Milk Chocolate Eggs with Primroses, for £12.50. The eggs are made from the finest quality Belgian chocolate and the company's team of Swiss-trained confectioners fill the moulds twice to give an extra luxurious coating of chocolate.

Catalogue: *Third A4, Catalogue, 20 pages, Colour, Free* Postal charges: *£5.60* Delivery: *Royal Mail* Methods of Payment: *Cheque, Visa, Access / Mastercard*

BEVERLEY HILLS BAKERY
3 Egerton Terrace
London
SW3 2BX

Telephone:
071 584 4401
Fax:
071 584 1106

CAKES
Deep in the heart of Knightsbridge, the Beverley Hills Bakery produce unusual handmade mini-muffins, cookies and brownies. Made to order each day, the goods are baked on the premises using only the finest ingredients: Belgian chocolate, Georgia pecans, fresh lemon juice and buttermilk.

Each order is carefully packaged to make an ideal gift. An 18-piece gift basket costs £16.00, prices rise to £75.00 for a 118-piece basket, just in case you're throwing a banquet. Gift tins are slightly more expensive, at £25.00 for 24 pieces and £35.00 for 38 pieces.

Catalogue: *A3, Leaflets, 2 pages, Colour, Free* Postal charges: *Free* Delivery: *In house delivery* Methods of Payment: *Cheque, Visa, Access / Mastercard*

BIBENDUM WINE
113 Regent's Park Road
London
NW1 1YR

Telephone:
071 916 7706
Fax:
071 916 7705

WINES
Bibendum buy their wines direct from growers in order to keep costs as low as possible and to stay abreast of the latest developments and opportunities in the wine business. Regular tastings are held at Regent's Park Road in London and they also produce a large, helpful catalogue.

From their range of house wines, a case of La Serre Sauvignon Blanc, Vin de Pays d'Oc 1993 costs

Food & Drink

£51.00. If you choose to buy by the bottle, the same wine costs £4.25. Better quality wines look well-priced. You can choose from a range of Burgundy varying in price from Macon Aze Rouge, Domain de Rochebin 1992/3 at £59.76 a case (£4.98 a bottle) to François Jobard Meursault Blagny at £351.00 a case (£29.25 a bottle).

Catalogue: *Quarterly, A4, Catalogue, 36 pages, B/W, Free* Postal charges: *Varies with item* Delivery: *By arrangement* Methods of Payment: *Cheque, Postal Order, Visa, Access / Mastercard, American Express*

BORDEAUX DIRECT
New Aquitaine House
Paddock Road
Reading
Berkshire
RG4 7BR

Telephone:
0734 481718
Fax:
0734 461953

WINE

Bordeaux Direct is the UK's leading home-delivery wine company. With over 50,000 customers and 24 years of experience, the company has earned a reputation for pioneering superb wines from quality vineyards throughout the world. And by always going straight to the winemaker in his vineyard and shipping direct to the customer, Bordeaux Direct can ensure value for money.

In addition to the wine service, the company offers regular newsletters. The leaflet offers a saving of over £20.00 on the special introductory case of twelve bottles of red and white wines, which is available for £44.74 including postage.

Catalogue: *A5, Leaflets, 4 pages, Colour, Free* Postal charges: *Varies with item* Delivery: *Royal Mail* Methods of Payment: *Cheque, Access / Mastercard, Visa, American Express, Diners Club*

CAREW OYSTER FARM
West Williamstone
Kilgetty
Pembrokeshire
SA68 0TN

Telephone:
0646 651452

OYSTERS

Carew Oysters are named after the Carew river, where they are grown about two miles downstream from Carew Castle, in the upper reaches of Milford Haven within the Pembrokeshire coast National Park. Some 25,000 a year are sold to farm visitors, another 30 tonnes to UK traders and 30 tonnes to Europe.

Mail order prices range from 27p each for 20 × 1 dozen or 83p for gift packs. The commonest purchase is a group buy of twelve dozen at 30p each (£45.00). All prices include 24-hour delivery. Oyster knives and rubber holding blocks are available at £2.50 each or £5.00 for both.

Catalogue: *Annually, A4, Brochure, 2 pages, Colour, Free* Postal charges: *Varies with item* Delivery: *Interlink Express Parcels* Methods of Payment: *Cheque, Postal Order, Visa, Access / Mastercard*

Food & Drink

CHARBONNEL ET WALKER
One The Royal Arcade
28 Old Bond Street
London
W1X 4BT

Telephone:
071 491 0939
Fax:
071 495 6279

CHOCOLATES

Quality chocolatiers under royal appointment, Charbonnel et Walker offer a series of leaflets to take you through their delicious range of high-quality fare. Original cooking chocolate costs £7.95 for just over 1lb, traditional classics Crèmes Parisiennes are available at £5.00 for an 8oz box and Marron glacé costs £16.50 for an 8.4oz box.

They also offer more down-to-earth chocolates for after dinner, or exclusive foil-covered chocolate letters for your personal messages (£33.00 for 15 letters, rising to £185.00 for 50!). But perhaps the most tempting is their own drinking chocolate which makes it impossible to go back to anything else.

Catalogue: *A5, Leaflets, 10 pages, Colour, Free* Postal charges: *Varies with item* Delivery: *Royal Mail Courier* Methods of Payment: *Visa, Access / Mastercard, American Express Cheque*

CHATSWORTH
31 Norwich Road
Strumpshaw
Norwich
NR13 4AG

Telephone:
0603 716815
Fax:
0603 715440

HIGH-QUALITY CATERING SUPPLIES

Chatsworth are 'purveyors of high-quality catering supplies' and their simple brochure lists quite some range. There are all sorts of bags, kitchen foil, bin-liners and cleaning supplies as well as garden accessories. Their selection of clingfilms is quite an eye-opener if you thought there was only one type.

They also sell a few luxury foods such as chocolate Charbonnel and a particularly attractive-sounding simnel cake made specially for Easter. This sells for £15.95 while the chocolate is £7.90 for 500g and 140g of white-chocolate mints are £1.99.

Catalogue: *Brochure, 8 pages, B/W, Free* Postal charges: *£2.95* Delivery: *Royal Mail* Methods of Payment: *Cheque, Postal Order, Visa, Access / Mastercard, American Express*

CHATSWORTH FARM SHOP
Stud Farm
Pilsley
Bakewell
Derbyshire
DE4 1UH

Telephone:
0246 583392
Fax:
0246 583464

FINE FOODS

The Chatsworth Farm Shop produces olde English rustic fayre from one of Derbyshire's most famous stately homes. Hampers crammed with delicious, traditional farm produce range from £19.95 to £95.00, or you can choose your own Farm Shop goodies from the butcher, baker or even the gift-maker.

Best buys include a free-range haunch of venison, fresh from wandering the Chatsworth parklands at £52.50; a 3lb game pie complete with lead-shot warning at £14.00; Granny's favourite, the clootie dumpling at £3.75; and the Chatsworth regular sheepskin at £29.00.

Food & Drink

CHOCEXPRESS LTD
PO Box 45
Royston
Hertfordshire
SG8 5DZ

Telephone:
0763 241444
Fax:
0763 244666

CHOCOLATES

The ideal gift by post, Thorntons offer a selection of their most popular products in this express catalogue. Delivery is guaranteed within 24–48 hours of ordering – it can be even quicker in urgent cases. All orders are packed in protective boxes, complete with a greetings card bearing a message of up to 20 words.

On offer are various sizes of the Continental range available with or without gift wrapping, ranging in price from £10.95 to £33.00, a Continental Casket at £14.00 and boxes of toffee at £6.45. Gift wrapping costs £1.50.

A new introduction are ChocoGrams available either with 18 (£12.95) or 32 (£19.95) assorted chocolates. These fit through most letterboxes so are guaranteed to be delivered. The ultimate gift, however, is the Luxury Hamper which contains every possible chocolate confection for an all-in price of £35.95.

Catalogue: *A5, Brochure, 6 pages, Colour, Free* Postal charges: *Free* Delivery: *Royal Mail Courier* Methods of Payment: *Cheque, Postal Order, Visa, Access / Mastercard*

CLARKSONS
1–7 Allansway
Ottery St Mary
Devon
EX11 1NR

Telephone:
0404 813581
Fax:
0404 815973

MEAT AND FISH

Variety packs of meat and fish are dispatched by Clarksons in approximately eight different combinations. Top of the range is the 'Spring Holiday Fresh Hamper' (£42.00) containing fresh farm chicken; leg of pork; gammon joint; 'our own make of tasty pork sausages'; back bacon; lean streaky bacon; and farmhouse English cheddar cheese. Gift packs of sliced smoked salmon (£15.90) and a 'Special Fish Pack' (£35.90), including kippers and trout, are also available.

Clarksons guarantee next-day delivery from the date of dispatch and all food is specially packed.

Catalogue: *A5, Leaflets, 4 pages, Colour, Free* Postal charges: *Free* Delivery: *Royal Mail* Methods of Payment: *Cheque, Postal Order, Visa, Access / Mastercard*

Food & Drink

COOKIE CRAFT
Michaelmas
Common Platt
Purton, Wiltshire
SN5 9LB

Telephone:
0793 770250

CAKES AND COOKIES
This is a real cottage industry, with all the cakes being made in the home. They can be packed up in tins and sent anywhere, along with a card if you wish. There are twelve different varieties, which can be ordered in small or large sizes.

There is an English wine cake, honey and mead cake, spiced apple cake and organic cider cake. Prices are £9.50 or £11.50 depending on size. They also sell truffles and marzipan fruits at £5.00 and Christmas puddings from between £3.75 and £9.50.

Catalogue: *A5, Leaflets, 3 pages, B/W, Free* Postal charges: *Free* Delivery: *Royal Mail* Methods of Payment: *Cheque, Postal Order*

CORNEY & BARROW
12 Helmet Row
London
EC1V 3QJ

Telephone:
071 251 4051
Fax:
071 608 1373

WINE
Corney started his wine merchants in 1780 and the company has since earned three Royal Warrants. Their aim is to supply high-class wines which are not only chosen with extreme care but are exclusive to them.

Their marvellous catalogue is packed with useful information on the wines and is like having an expert on hand as you choose. Full-page descriptions of the wines and regions make just browsing a pleasure. The company offers free delivery if you order over a couple of cases and will even refund your money if you don't like a wine – after you've tasted it! A terrific publication.

Catalogue: *9"× 5", Catalogue, 128 pages, Colour and B/W, Free* Postal charges: *Varies with item* Delivery: *Courier* Methods of Payment: *Cheque, Visa, Access / Mastercard*

CRAIGROSSIE SMOKE HOUSE
Hall Farm
Auchterarder,
Perthshire
PH3 1HD

Telephone:
0764 662596
Fax:
0764 63172

SMOKED FOODS
The Craigrossie Smoke House sells all manner of smoked foods which are then dispatched in special containers to keep it fresh. Everything comes with a 'use by' date and they suggest that fish be eaten within three weeks. Alternatively it can be frozen for up to three months.

Their range includes the usual smoked salmon as well as trout, duck and chicken breast, wild venison and Scottish beef. A 2lb pack of smoked salmon is £30.00, with 1lb £16.30. 8oz venison thin slices are £11.00 and a Christmas special pack £48.00.

Catalogue: *Quarterly, A5, Brochure, 6 pages, B/W, Free* Postal charges: *Free* Delivery: *Royal Mail* Methods of Payment: *Cheque*

Food & Drink

DAVENPORT & SON LTD
The Courtyard
52 Market Street
Ashby-de-la-Zouch
Leicestershire
LE6 5AN

Telephone:
0530 412827
Fax:
0530 412551

WINES

Davenport is the oldest wine merchants in Leicestershire, dating back to the 17th century. Its catalogue of fine wines, spirits, sherry and port is clearly laid out, with a brief description of each region and its wines. There is also a useful vintage chart.

Their speciality, however, is personalised presentation gifts, which are largely aimed at the corporate market. There are gift boxes and wooden cases along with rattan and wicker baskets. In addition everything can be personalised with the company name. They also stock some sumptuous looking hampers. A four-bottle gift box of French wine sells for £35.31.

Catalogue: *A4, Catalogue, 23 pages, Colour and B/W, Free* Postal charges: *Varies with item* Delivery: *Royal Mail* Methods of Payment: *Cheque*

DEERCARE VENISON
Horridge
Ashreigney
Chumleigh
Devon
EX18 7NE

Telephone:
07693 283

VENISON

Deercare Venison is a small family-run business supplying venison from deer farmed by the proprietors.

Venison is a lean tasty red meat which is lower in cholesterol and fat than poultry. The red and fallow deer, from which Deercare Venison produce their meat, are raised on the farm and are fed only natural forage so there are no growth promoters or hormones in their feed.

The meat is hung to mature, then cut into boneless, oven-ready portions and vacuum-packed to retain its freshness. Cookery cards, which are supplied with the meat, give basic do's and don'ts along with interesting recipes.

Catalogue: *Loose leaf, Leaflets, 4 pages, B/W, Free* Postal charges: *Varies with item* Delivery: *Courier* Methods of Payment: *Cheque*

DENHAY FARMS
Broadoak
Bridport
Dorset
DT6 5NP

Telephone:
0308 422770
Fax:
0308 424846

CHEESES AND HAMS

Established in 1952, Denhay Farms makes premium farmhouse cheddar from its own cows' milk produced in Dorset's beautiful Marshwood Vale. Developed with the mail order market in mind, the Dorset Drum is a traditionally made 2kg cloth-bound mature cheddar cheese. Denhay Air Dried Ham is a unique cured meat, produced from the farm's own whey-fed pigs. Delicious with melon, pear or avocado, the 'English prosciutto' also enhances chicken or pasta dishes and is superb in sandwiches. The Dorset Drum is £16.75 while Denhay hams come in 4oz or 8oz vacuum packs at £4.70 and

Food & Drink

£8.70. Discounts and current prices available on application.

Catalogue: *Annually, A5, Brochure, Colour and B/W, Free* Postal charges: *Varies with item* Delivery: *Parcelforce, Royal Mail* Methods of Payment: *Cheque, Postal Order, Visa, Access / Mastercard*

DUKESHILL HAM COMPANY
Deuxhill
Bridgnorth
Shropshire
WV16 6AF

Telephone:
074 635 519
Fax:
074 635 533

HAMS

Dukeshill, based in Shropshire, sell ham on the bone and deliver overnight. You can order either Wiltshire or traditional York ham. The former is cured over a period of two weeks in brine and then allowed to mature. It comes either smoked or unsmoked.

Traditional York ham, often called the smoked salmon of the meat world, is the traditional farmhouse ham. Dry-cured with salt and saltpetre it is left to condition for at least ten weeks to give it a unique flavour.

Half hams start at £26.00 and rise to £60 for a complete dry-cured York ham. There is also a range of sliced ham from £6.00 for an 8oz pack.

Catalogue: *A5, Leaflets, 6 pages, Colour, Free* Postal charges: *£2.00* Delivery: *Courier* Methods of Payment: *American Express, Visa, Access / Mastercard Cheque*

EASTBROOK FARM
Bishopstone
Swindon
Wilts
SN6 8PW

Telephone:
0793 790460
Fax:
0793 791239

ORGANIC MEATS

Eastbrook supplies a full range of fresh, organically produced meats all of which come up to Soil Association Standards. You can choose from pork, beef, lamb and poultry plus 15 different varieties of delicious meaty sausages. They also sell home-cured and oak-smoked hams, bacon and gammon and a range of beautifully presented oven-ready meat dishes.

A cushion of lamb filled with apricot and almond stuffing is £2.85 a lb and beef cordon bleu £6.55 a lb. A leg of lamb is £3.15 a lb, beef topside £4.32 and sausages £2.37. Gammon on the bone is £2.51 a lb (prices may fluctuate).

Catalogue: *A3, Brochure, Colour, Free* Postal charges: *Varies with item* Delivery: *Courier* Methods of Payment: *Cheque, Postal Order, Visa, Access / Mastercard*

Food & Drink

EL VINO CO LIMITED
47 Fleet Street
London
EC4Y 1BJ

Telephone:
071 936 4948
Fax:
071 936 2367

WINES

This famous wine bar of Fleet Street, dating back to 1879, offers a workmanlike list of its wines, spirits and cigars, with minimal descriptions. A good vintage Burgundy for example, described as 'superb, dry, elegant with depth' will set you back £504.00 for a case, whereas a recent Bordeaux – 'elegant, light, fruity' – only £57.00.

Delivery charges are only made on orders of less than two cases and a special lower rate applies in central London areas. Women will be glad to know that their sexist practice of not serving females at the bar is not carried over into the mail order side.

Catalogue: *120 × 210mm, Catalogue, 8 pages, B/W, Free* Postal charges: *Varies with item* Delivery: *Courier* Methods of Payment: *Cheque, Visa, Access / Mastercard, Postal Order*

FERRY FISH SMOKEHOUSE
131 Dalrymple Street
Girvan
Ayrshire

Telephone:
0671 820630
0465 5283

FRESH AND SMOKED FISH

Ferry Fish Smokehouse is one of the last remaining smokehouses to operate in south-west Scotland using the traditional smoking process. Oak-smoked salmon is available sliced in sizes from a 4oz sliced pack through to a 2lb whole side trimmed but unsliced. Loch Fyne kippers are also available, oak-smoked and free from all artificial colourings.

Ferry Fish Smokehouse promise to dispatch an order on the day payment is received. There is no charge for postage and packing for orders in Britain, but a 25% surcharge on orders to be sent overseas.

Catalogue: *A4, Leaflets, 2 pages, B/W, Free* Postal charges: *Free* Delivery: *Royal Mail* Methods of Payment: *Cheque*

FINDLATER MACKIE TODD & CO
Deer Park Rd
Merton Abbey
London
SW19 3TU

Telephone:
081 543 0966
Fax:
081 543 2415

WINES, SPIRITS AND LIQUEURS FROM AROUND THE WORLD

Findlater Mackie Todd & Co, wine merchants to HM The Queen, can supply by mail order a wide range of fine wines from all over the world. Wines are available from France, Spain, Italy, Portugal, Germany and the Eastern Mediterranean and from as far away as Chile and Australia. You can buy cases of one wine and also mixed cases selected by yourself.

As well as supplying wines from their extensive list (Nobilo Hawkes Bay Chardonnay, £47.88 per case, Bourgogne Pinot Noir AC 1990, £63.00 per case) they also provide a range of other services.

They sell spirits, cigars and liqueurs, offer a gift-pack service, and will create their own label for clubs,

Food & Drink

societies and companies. They also run a wedding advisory service to help you choose the wines for your reception with confidence and will advise on the building and maintaining of a wine collection.

Catalogue: *A4, Catalogue, 29 pages, Colour, Free* Postal charges: *Varies with item* Delivery: *Royal Mail* Methods of Payment: *Visa, Access / Mastercard Cheque*

FITZBILLIES
52 Trumpington Street
Cambridge
CB2 1RG

Telephone:
0223 352500

CAKES AND BUNS
Fitzbillies has been in the centre of Cambridge since the 1920s and has maintained a loyal clientele for its unique bakery products. Indeed the demand has grown so much that they now operate a mail order service which extends all over the world.

Their speciality is Chelsea buns but they also sell Dundee, Genoa and rich fruit cakes as well as hampers, which can be bespoke or seasonal.

Four Chelsea buns are £6.95, a small Dundee cake £9.75 and a Cambridge Eight cake £20.50. A decorated rich fruit cake £42.50.

Catalogue: *A5, Leaflets, 4 pages, Colour, Free* Postal charges: *Free* Delivery: *Royal Mail* Methods of Payment: *Cheque, Visa, Access / Mastercard*

FJORDLING SMOKEHOUSES
West Winterslow
Salisbury
Wilts
SP5 1SA

Telephone:
0980 862689
Fax:
0980 863944

SMOKED FOODS
Fjordling use traditional west coast Norwegian family smoking and curing methods to 'retain the natural flavour of the food and to achieve a moist succulent result'. Their range includes quality cuts of Scottish beef and Welsh lamb, trout, salmon and prawns all of which can be delivered to your door – what a tempting thought!

Prices are per pound weight with Oak Smoked Chicken from £3.65; Smoked Eel £8.45 and Smoked Duck Breasts from £8.95. Also on offer is a Bumper Selection Box containing smoked salmon, beef fillet, mature cheddar, Fjordling pâté and hot smoked duck breast for £33.95 – a mini version is available at £18.95.

Catalogue: *A4, Leaflets, 6 pages, B/W, Free* Postal charges: *Free* Delivery: *Royal Mail* Methods of Payment: *COD, Cheque, Visa, Access / Mastercard*

Food & Drink

FORTNUM & MASON
181 Piccadilly
London
W1A 1ER

Telephone:
071 734 8040
Fax:
071 437 3278

FOOD AND WINE
From the prestigious London-based emporium of the same name – purveyors of groceries to twelve generations of the Royal Family – comes this tantalising catalogue of food and wine. Discreetly printed with elegant pen and ink illustrations, it features many varieties of teas and coffees as well as preserves, mustards and dressings. There is a good selection of biscuits, chocolates and fresh foods such as smoked salmon and foie gras.

There are also some marvellous Stiltons, an interesting range of wines and spirits and of course the hampers for which Fortnum's is so justly famous. Prices are on the high side, but what you'd expect for the very best.

Catalogue: *A5, Catalogue, 16 pages, B/W, Free* Postal charges: *Varies with item* Delivery: *Royal Mail* Methods of Payment: *Cheque, Postal Order, Visa, Access / Mastercard, American Express, Diners Club*

FOX'S SPICES LTD
Units J & K
Mason's Road
Industrial Estate
Stratford-Upon-Avon
Warwickshire
CV37 9NF

Telephone:
0789 266420
Fax:
0789 267737

SPICES, HERBS, SEASONINGS AND CONDIMENTS
Fox's Spices is a 25-year-old company specialising in the blending of fine quality herbs, spices and seasonings. They offer exclusive products in 'no frills' economy packaging direct to the consumer by speedy mail order service.

Their range offers over 300 varieties of fine quality everyday herbs, spices and peppers including exciting Indonesian and Oriental blends, Bumbus (£1.25 per 4oz sachet plus postage), sambals and chilli sauces, Indian curry powders and Balti mixtures, wholegrain 'mix-it-yourself' mustard mixtures (8oz bags, £1.30 each plus postage), and a host of pepper and salt mills, gift selections and 'starter packs'.

Catalogue: *Annually, A5, Catalogue, 24 pages, Colour and B/W, Free* Postal charges: *Varies with item* Delivery: *Royal Mail, Parcelforce, United Carriers* Methods of Payment: *Cheque, Postal Order, Visa, Access / Mastercard*

Food & Drink

FREE RANGE
Gees Farmhouse
Chase Park Road
Yardley hastings
Northamptonshire

Telephone:
0604 696509

FREE-RANGE AND ORGANIC FOODS

Free Range produce a list of free-range, organic and speciality farmhouse foods, ready frozen for convenience. They also sell their own home-cured bacon and a selection of freshly frozen fish from Devon.

Poultry starts at £1.80 per lb for free-range chicken; chicken breasts cost £4.25. There are also free-range legs for £1.80 and poussin at £2.25 each.

There's a varied selection of game, including venison haunch at £3.10 per lb, venison saddle for £4.80 and diced rabbit for £3.15 per lb.

Catalogue: *A5, Leaflets, 2 pages, B/W, Free* Postal charges: *Varies with item* Methods of Payment: *Cheque*

GARVIN HONEY CO
158 Twickenham Road
Isleworth
Middlesex
TW7 7BL

Telephone:
081 560 7171
Fax:
081 569 8036

HONEY

Winnie the Pooh would love this catalogue, which boasts fourteen different varieties of honey imported from all over the world. You can order it clear or set, in 1lb jars or resaleable plastic tubs and even in buckets up to 56lb! Just as well that honey keeps almost indefinitely.

An enthusiastically written catalogue, it is plain that honey produces serious devotees, many of whom write in and are quoted along with their recipes. Attractively boxed gift packs of twelve jars are available at £15.99 while three sample jars are just £2.00.

Catalogue: *A5, Leaflets, Colour and B/W, Free* Postal charges: *Free* Delivery: *Royal Mail* Methods of Payment: *Cheque, COD, Visa, Access / Mastercard*

GLENDEVON SMOKED SALMON
Crook of Devon
Kinross
KY13 7UL

Telephone:
0577 840297
Fax:
0577 840626

SMOKED SALMON

Glendevon Smoked Salmon is a well-established, family-run business selling finest quality, oak-smoked Scottish salmon. Smoked Salmon in distinctive scarlet gift boxes can be mailed to most parts of the world. It makes an ideal gift for those of all ages on all occasions, birthdays, Christmas or as a thank-you present.

The prices for delivery in the UK are 8oz £10.50, 1lb £17.00 and 2lbs £28.00 for sliced packs off the skin. The 2lb unsliced pack on the skin costs £25.00. Prices for the rest of the world are included in the brochure.

Catalogue: *Bi-annually, Third A4, Brochure, 1 page, B/W, Free* Postal charges: *Free* Delivery: *Royal Mail* Methods of Payment: *Cheque, Visa, Access / Mastercard, Postal Order*

Food & Drink

GOODMAN'S GEESE
Goodmans Brothers
Walsgrove Farm
Great Witley
Worcester
WR6 6JJ

Telephone:
0299 896 272
Fax:
0299 896 889

FREE-RANGE GEESE

Goodman's catalogue features a range of free-range geese from a company which has won many of the country's most impressive titles including the BOCM Farmer's Weekly Competition and the Miller's Best of British Women's Food Section.

Each goose comes with a recipe leaflet to help you to make the most of this versatile bird, with stuffings and sauces and ideas for leftovers. The geese, all reared out of doors and fed on grass and corn, are free-range and are available from September until Christmas.

Catalogue: *Bi-annually, Third A4, Brochure, 6 pages, B/W, Free* Postal charges: *Varies with item* Delivery: *Royal Mail* Methods of Payment: *Cheque, Postal Order*

GOURMET BY POST
13 Hawthorn Road
Sutton
Surrey
SM1 4PF

Telephone:
081 395 2391

MUSHROOMS

Gourmet by Post offer a range of dried wild mushrooms prepared in France by Sabarot Wassner.

Gourmet by Post stress that wild mushrooms need careful preparation. They should be soaked in hot, but not boiling, water for at least 45 minutes, but not more than twelve hours, then drained, rinsed and patted dry. The mushrooms can be fried but they must be cooked very gently as placing them in hot fat may well lead to 'spitting'.

The catalogue gives each variety's Latin name as well as a brief description of the mushroom. The last two pages of the catalogue offer some recipe suggestions.

Catalogue: *A5, Catalogue, 8 pages, B/W, Free* Postal charges: *Free* Delivery: *Royal Mail* Methods of Payment: *Cheque, Access / Mastercard, Visa*

GRAIG FARM
Dolau
Llandrindod Wells
Powys
LD1 5TL

Telephone:
0597 851655
Fax:
0597 851655

CONSERVATION GRADE AND ORGANIC MEAT

This farm was winner of the 1993 National Organic Food Award and also the ADAS/Sunday Telegraph Food Marketing Award. They are accredited by the Soil Association and produce Conservation Grade pork, lamb, mutton and beef as well as chicken and turkey. Their informative brochure explains how the animals are raised and explains just what conservation grade means.

They also have a selection of wild game which includes venison, rabbit, wild boar.

Catalogue: *A5, Leaflets, 4 pages, B/W, Free* Postal charges: *£4.50* Delivery: *Courier* Methods of Payment: *Cheque*

Food & Drink

GRANTS OF DALVEY
Freepost 1032
Alness
Rossshire
IV17 0BR

Telephone:
0349 884111
Fax:
0349 884100

SCOTTISH GIFTS, WHISKY

'Lasting Impressions' is a brand new catalogue launched by the old Scottish family, Grant of Alness, whose firm manufactures unusual gifts of quality. Aimed at the corporate market as well as the individual, it produces business accessories such as credit-card holders £24.95, briefcase tags £13.95, pocket flasks £34.95 and travel alarm clocks for £49.95.

Each item is crafted from stainless steel with a solid brass badge, which can be personalised. In addition the company makes ten-year-old malt whisky, which is available at a discount if another purchase is made from the catalogue.

Catalogue: *Annually, Third A4, Leaflet, 12 pages, Colour, Free* Postal charges: *£2.95* Delivery: *Royal Mail* Methods of Payment: *Cheque, Postal Order, Visa, Access / Mastercard, American Express, Diners Club*

GREAT GLEN FINE FOODS LTD
Old Ferry Road
North Ballachulish
Fort William
PH33 6RZ

Telephone:
08553 277
Fax:
08553 577

SCOTTISH SPECIALITY FOODS

Great Glen Foods has a speciality food shop on the west coast of Scotland stocking the best of Scottish produce. They now also offer a selection of the best and most popular items by mail order. This includes jams, marmalades, honey, sauces, mustards, jellies, chutneys, biscuits, shortbread, cakes, puddings, haggis, game, soups, smoked fish and meat, wines, spirits, teas, coffee, cheese and oatcakes.

They also produce their own homemade confectionery, such as Islay Tablet (Scottish fudge), coconut ice, chocolate truffles and Scottish country tablet.

Islay tablet flavoured with ten-year-old malt whisky is £1.35 for a 100g pack and £4.99 for a 450g gift box. Chocolate truffles with rum are £3.99 for a 150g gift box.

Catalogue: *Annually, A5, Catalogue, 4 pages, Colour, Free* Postal charges: *Varies with item* Delivery: *Parcelforce* Methods of Payment: *Cheque, Postal Order, Visa, Access / Mastercard, American Express*

Food & Drink

HAMPERS OF BROADWAY
Cotswold Court
The Green
Broadway
Worcs
WR12 7AA

Telephone:
0386 853040

HAMPERS
Hampers offers a complete range of gifts, from baskets to large and small hampers full of the delicacies stocked in their shop. The hampers can be tailor-made to customers' requirements.

The business is run alongside their delicatessen shop which offers a selection of fine foods, from cheese to parma ham, from smoked Scottish salmon to delicious homemade pâtés, quiches and puddings. In addition the company carries a wide variety of savoury and cocktail biscuits and pastries.

Hamper prices range from £41.45 through to £410.00 for the Connoisseur's selection.

Catalogue: *A5, Catalogue, 10 pages, B/W, Free* Postal charges: *Varies with item* Delivery: *Royal Mail* Methods of Payment: *Cheque, Visa, Access / Mastercard*

HAY HAMPERS
The Barn
Corby Glen
Grantham
Lincs
NG33 4NJ

Telephone:
0476 550420/476/548
Fax:
0476 550 777

FOOD, WINE AND HAMPERS
Hay Hampers are a friendly family-owned business who provide a wide range of gift packs and picnic hampers suitable for every occasion.

The range includes Stilton Packs (from £13.62), Chocolate Packs (bottle of wine plus truffles), Smoked Salmon Packs, and Wine Gift Packs all the way to the medium and large picnic hampers from £55.00 to £211.00.

Hays will also make up hampers on request and the gifts and hampers are always beautifully presented in wooden boxes, wicker baskets or colourful cartons.

Catalogue: *A4, Catalogue, 8 pages, Colour, Free* Postal charges: *Varies with item* Delivery: *Courier* Methods of Payment: *Cheque, Postal Order, Visa, Access / Mastercard*

HEAL FARM
Kings Nympton
Umberleigh
Devon
EX37 9TB

Telephone:
0769 572077
Fax:
0767 572839

TRADITIONAL MEATS
This farm produces meats naturally and is certified by the Rare Breeds Survival Trust. They specialise in traditional breeds of pigs and also produce their own beef and lamb. Other local specialist producers provide them with butter, clotted cream, honey and chocolates.

The produce is available in seasonal hampers, starter packs, prepared recipe dishes or meat packs. The starter pack costs £31.50, while a saddle of venison is £6.05. A leg of mutton is £6.58 per lb; marinaded in wine and port, 6–8 servings costs £16.00. Chickens and ducks are £2.95 per lb.

Food & Drink

HOLME HOUSE FARM
Raisbeck
Penrith
Cumbria
CA10 3SG

Telephone:
05396 24618
Fax:
05396 24551

Catalogue: *A4, Brochure & leaflets, single sheets, B/W, Free* Postal charges: *Varies with item* Delivery: *Courier* Methods of Payment: *Cheque*

VENISON

This farm only produces naturally reared venison which is supplied vacuum packed and sent either by overnight courier or first class post. It can then either be eaten immediately or frozen. The small brochure also outlines the reasons why you should choose venison for health, and, as an added incentive, provides appetisingly illustrated recipes.

The meat comes in various cuts including shoulder joint, haunch joint, diced and smoked. It can also be provided as sausages, burgers, pâtés, pies and in a ready cooked casserole. Two 6oz haunch steaks sell for £4.95 and a 2lb boneless shoulder joint for £7.90.

Catalogue: *Third A4, Brochure, 6 pages, Colour, Free* Postal charges: *Varies with item* Delivery: *Royal Mail* Methods of Payment: *Cheque, Postal Order, Visa, Access / Mastercard*

HOMEBREW MAIL ORDER
Freepost
67/69 Park Lane
Hornchurch
Essex
RM11 1BR

Telephone:
0708 745943
Fax:
0708 743699

BEER AND WINE KITS

For those who prefer to make their own wine or beer, Homebrew is just the catalogue. It offers a good range of kits, ingredients and equipment for beginners and experts alike.

The catalogue is straightforward and easy to use, each section and individual prices being clearly marked. For beginners there is an inclusive beginners kit and the company will also happily offer advice over the phone.

A gallon Muscadet kit sells for £5.99 and a 40-pint John Bull bitter kit for £5.15. There are even kits for spirits and liqueurs.

Catalogue: *A5, Catalogue, 12 pages, B/W, Free* Postal charges: *£3.50* Delivery: *Royal Mail* Methods of Payment: *Cheque, Postal Order, Visa, Access / Mastercard*

Food & Drink

HOUSE OF HAMILTON LTD
Westfield House
By Harburn
West Lothian
Scotland
EH55 8RB

Telephone:
0506 418434
Fax:
0506 418413

OAK-SMOKED SCOTTISH SALMON AND GRAVADLAX
House of Hamilton oak-smoked Scottish salmon and gravadlax (fresh Scottish salmon marinated in dill) are enjoyed by some of the finest and most prestigious hotels and premium retail outlets in the country. They are now also available direct from the 'house', by mail order from £10.10 per lb for whole trimmed sides.

The company recently won the *Daily Mail Weekend* magazine taste test and all their smoked Scottish salmon has 'quality approved' status, a scheme run and enforced by independent inspectors. The fish have the benefit of clean, clear, tidal waters and their flesh is pink, translucent, with the minimum of fat. No artificial colouring or preservatives are used at any time.

All the products are prepared fresh to order then vacuum packed and dispatched 'on ice'. They are ideal for home freezing for up to 3 months with no loss of flavour or texture.

Catalogue: *Annually, A5, Brochure, 5 pages, Colour, Free* Postal charges: *Varies with item* Delivery: *Courier* Methods of Payment: *Cheque, Visa, Access / Mastercard, American Express*

HUMPHREYS
16 Leeds Road
Ilkley
West Yorkshire
LS29 8DJ

Telephone:
0943 609477

HANDMADE CHOCOLATES
A miniature catalogue this, featuring a delightful range of chocolates. These include Belgian chocolates such as pralines, and Gianduja, as well as traditional English varieties such as Ginger, Apricot Parfait and Rose Creams. There also Swiss style truffles filled with Rum, Kirsch and Cointreau, amongst other delights.

They will make personalised moulds and boxes for hotels, restaurants and corporate presentations and also supply celebration cakes and gifts. Their Gold box, containing 15 chocs, is £5.10, while a medium sized presentation box is £10.60.

Catalogue: *Loose-leaf, Leaflet, Colour, Free* Postal charges: *Varies with item* Delivery: *Royal Mail* Methods of Payment: *Cheque*

Food & Drink

HURLINGHAM HAMPERS & CATERING COMPANY
361 New Kings Road
London
SW6 4RJ

Telephone:
071 384 2521
Fax:
071 384 2521

HAMPERS AND SPECIALIST CATERING
Hurlingham supply specialist food for business lunches, weddings, birthday parties and many other social or business occasions.

The company prepares and delivers dishes for dinner parties with prices between £10.00 and £15.00 per person. The shop also supplies fresh salads, genuine French baguettes, and individual dishes for customers' freezers are available on request from £3.00.

Hurlingham's Christmas hamper service starts from £25.00 for a Port and Stilton basket to £225.00 for the De Luxe Celebration Hamper.

Catalogue: *A4, Leaflet, 2 pages, Colour, Free* Postal charges: *Free* Delivery: *Courier* Methods of Payment: *Cheque, Visa, Access / Mastercard*

INTERNATIONAL WINE COMPANY LTD
6 The Cross
Enderby
Leics
LE9 5PF

Telephone:
0800 777911
Fax:
0533 753700

QUALITY WINES, CHAMPAGNE, PORT
The International Wine Company Ltd is Britain's fastest growing wine by mail order business. They offer excellent wines at competitive prices, e.g. 1993 Petit-Chablis 'Armorial' at just £4.99 per bottle or Piper Heidsieck Champagne for only £11.99.

The minimum order is only twelve bottles; customers are encouraged to mix their own cases; there are no membership fees or ongoing commitments, no risk in purchasing (if the wines are not to the customers taste they will refund in full), and all prices include VAT. Free delivery for orders over 24 bottles.

Catalogue: *Monthly, A4, Brochure, 6 pages, Colour, Free* Postal charges: *Varies with item* Delivery: *Business Express* Methods of Payment: *Cheque, Postal Order, Visa, Access / Mastercard, American Express, Diners Club*

INVERAWE SMOKEHOUSES
Taynuilt
Argyll
Scotland
PA35 1HU

Telephone:
08662 446
Fax:
08662 274

RANGE OF OAK-SMOKED SEAFOOD AND GAME.
Inverawe Smokehouses produce a range of oak-smoked seafood and game from smoked salmon to oysters, from pâté to kippers, smoked venison to Argyll ham. Started fifteen years ago on the shores of Loch Etive, this family-run business uses only the old Highland style of smoking.

With their new Inter-Fish express delivery service, they can have orders on your table, ready to eat, in 24 hours. They also specialise in worldwide mail order.

Customers range from single people to young couples and habitual party throwers. The ideal present for friends and family at Christmas or at any

Food & Drink

time of year – sent direct. You can often see their stand at food shows and exhibitions. Prices start at £7.95.

Catalogue: *A5, Catalogue, 8–10 pages, Colour, Free* Postal charges: *Varies with item* Delivery: *Royal Mail, Parcelforce* Methods of Payment: *Cheque, Postal Order, COD, Visa, Access / Mastercard, American Express*

ITALIAN COOKERY WEEKS
PO Box 2482
London
NW10 1HW

Telephone:
081 208 0112
Fax:
071 401 8763

ITALIAN COOKERY HOLIDAYS

Learn how to cook traditional Italian dishes and enjoy a very special holiday at the same time. In an ancient farmhouse in the glorious olive country of Umbria or in a whitewashed masseria in Puglia on the Mediterranean coast, you will be able to spend a week learning the secrets of Italian cuisine from some of the best Italian chefs.

The all-in price of £895.00 plus £12.00 travel insurance per person covers return flights with coach transfer to the farmhouse, seven night's accommodation, full board with excellent food and wine, daily tuition in cookery, various trips to local markets and a one-day excursion to the nearby historic cities. Each day finishes with dinner in a typical trattoria.

Only twenty places are offered each week. Courses start on 15th May and run until 25th September.

Catalogue: *Annually, Brochure, 16 pages, Colour, Free* Postal charges: *Varies with item* Delivery: *Royal Mail* Methods of Payment: *Cheque, Visa, Access / Mastercard, American Express*

JAMES WHITE APPLE JUICES
Whites Fruit Farm
Helmingham Road
Ashbocking Suffolk
IP6 9JS

Telephone:
0473 890111
Fax:
0473 890001

APPLE JUICES

James White is an interesting small company which sells freshly pressed fruit juices. These are a million miles away from the stuff you buy in supermarkets and are bottled like fine wines. The range includes apple, pear and grape juices. They also produce a selection of Suffolk cider, made from a number of different apples. The only disadvantage is you have to buy by the case.

Bramley juice is £22.00 per case, Cox and pear £23.00 and grape £25.00. Special edition cider is a little more, at £26.50.

Catalogue: *A4, Leaflet, 1 page, B/W, Free* Postal charges: *Free* Delivery: *Royal Mail* Methods of Payment: *Cheque*

Food & Drink

L ROBSON & SONS
Craster
Alnwick
Northumberland

Telephone:
0665 576223

SMOKED KIPPERS AND SALMON
L Robson & Sons of Northumberland produce a small range of oak-smoked kippers and oak-smoked salmon. Kippers cost £3.90 for a ¼ box (approx 1 lb), £6.75 for a ½ box (approx 2 lbs), £10.45 for a large box (approx 4 lbs 8oz) and £18.50 for an extra large box (approx 10lbs).

Salmon is priced at £6.50 for 8oz sliced vacuum packed, £10.80 for 1lb sliced vacuum packed and £6.40 per lb for sides of unsliced salmon vacuum packed. Prices are subject to change during the season.

Catalogue: *A5, Leaflet, 1 page, B/W, Free* Postal charges: *Varies with item* Delivery: *Royal Mail* Methods of Payment: *Cheque, Postal Order*

LEWIS AND COOPER
92 High Street
Northallerton
N Yorks
DL7 8PP

Telephone:
0609 772880
Fax:
0609 777933

FOOD HAMPERS
Lewis and Cooper have been established well over a hundred years, and they are known to lovers of good food throughout Britain. In their market place shop and local premises in the busy market town of Northallerton, they have been making up gift packs and food hampers for business and personal customers for well over half a century. As a result, they are experienced in carefully and professionally packing food hampers and gifts for distribution nationwide. Over the years they have despatched literally thousands of food hampers to grateful recipients.

Special hampers can be made for any occasions – weddings, anniversaries, prizes. Business requirements are a speciality.

Catalogue: *Biannually, A5, Brochure, 8 pages, Colour, Free* Postal charges: *Varies with item* Delivery: *Parcelforce* Methods of Payment: *Cheque, Postal Order, Visa, Access / Mastercard*

LIZ SEEBER
Antiquarian Cookery
Books
10 The Plantation
Blackheath
London
SE3 0AB

Telephone:
081 852 7807
Fax:
081 318 4675

ANTIQUARIAN FOOD AND DRINK ITEMS
Liz Seeber stocks more than 400 antiquarian cookery books and also sells other items such as collectable menus, leaflets, cookery magazines and original manuscripts. Also stocked are antiquarian books on wine, beer, cocktails and other drinks.

Liz's stocklist provides very detailed descriptions of each book, down to minute details of the condition of the pages and binding. The list contains books from the 17th century to the present day, ranging in price from £2.00 to several hundred pounds, and covers many aspects of cookery both English and foreign.

Food & Drink

Liz Seeber herself is a cookery enthusiast with lots of practical experience and is both knowledgeable and willing to help others find what they are looking for.

Catalogue: *Updated daily, A4, Stocklist, 32 pages, B/W, Free* Postal charges: *Varies with item. With valuable items also includes a charge for insurance in transit.* Delivery: *Royal Mail, Parcelforce* Methods of Payment: *Cheque, Visa, Access / Mastercard*

LOCH FYNE WHISKIES
Inveraray
Argyll
PA32 8UD

Telephone:
0499 2219
Fax:
0499 2238

WHISKY

Loch Fyne Whiskies stock a diverse range of single and vatted malts as well as grain and blended whiskies. They are one of only two known retail businesses wholly dependent on the sale of whisky and whisky goods. Their price list is very user-friendly, with helpful tips for the novice buyer, including a taste score to help you sort out the softer varieties from those with a more acquired taste. They recommend a number of whiskies, including Dalwhinnie single malt (43%) at £23.99.

They also sell a number of books on the subject, including D Cooper's *A Taste of Scotch* (£9.95) and the *Malt Whisky Companion*, along with a couple of videos.

Catalogue: *A4, Catalogue, 8 pages, B/W, Free* Postal charges: *Varies with item* Delivery: *Royal Mail* Methods of Payment: *Cheque, Visa, Access / Mastercard*

MAJESTIC MAIL ORDER
Albion Wharf
Hester Road
London
SW11

Telephone:
0727 847912
Fax:
0727 810884

BEERS, WINES AND SPIRITS

A comprehensive list of the best of the wines, beers and spirits on offer at Majestic's 44 warehouses and available via mail order. Divided into 27 sections, giving the best wines from the finest grape growing areas in the world, as well as beers, spirits and something for the 'softies', it is an excellent place to start if planning a party.

Prices are very reasonable with French reds from as little as £2.29 a bottle and English white wines at £6.99. Lager prices are competitive with 24 bottles of Becks for only £18.00.

Majestic have many practical ways to help customers, from tasting before you buy to free glass loan on orders.

Catalogue: *Monthly, Third A4, Brochure, 12 pages, Colour and B/W, Free* Postal charges: *Varies with item* Delivery: *Royal Mail* Methods of Payment: *Cheque, Postal Order, Visa, Access / Mastercard*

Food & Drink

MEAT MATTERS
67 Woodland Rise
London
N10 3UN

Telephone:
081 442 0658

ORGANIC MEAT, POULTRY AND GAME

Meat Matters sells a very wide range of organic meat, poultry and game as well as organic eggs. All cuts are available in lamb, pork and beef, as well as organic chickens and chicken pieces. In addition, they sell a variety of home recipe organic sausages, children's sausages and beefburgers, including gluten-free products.

They offer dinner party marinaded dishes, barbecue products for the summer and Christmas organic turkeys. There is no minimum order, which seems excellent given the free delivery service within London (£8.00 elsewhere).

Organic stewing steak is £2.99 per lb. Gluten-free organic pork sausages £2.79 per lb, organic leg of lamb marinaded in rosemary and juniper £5.99 per lb and chicken breasts £4.99 per lb.

Catalogue: *Biannually, A5, Catalogue, 4 pages, B/W, Free* Postal charges: *Varies with item* Delivery: *Courier* Methods of Payment: *Cheque, COD*

MEG RIVERS CAKES
Middle Tysoe
Warickshire
CV35 0SE

Telephone:
0295 688101
Fax:
0295 680799

CAKES

Meg Rivers runs a bakery in Middle Tysoe, Warwickshire which will also send its cakes out by mail order. Each cake is made from the finest ingredients and baked in small batches to ensure high quality. They also run a Cake Club, which costs £83.50 for a year; you then receive a different cake every other month.

As well as an interesting range of cakes (apricot and almond, cherry, madeira, summer fruit cake), they also sell some cups and saucers and decorative cake tins.

A Cricket cake costs £12.50, dundee and Festival cakes £13.50, iced birthday cakes £19.50 and a two-tier wedding cake £150.00.

Catalogue: *Annually, A4, Leaflet, 1 page, B/W, Free* Postal charges: *Varies with item* Delivery: *Royal Mail* Methods of Payment: *Cheque, Postal Order, Visa, Access / Mastercard*

MELCHIOR CHOCOLATES
Chittlehampton
Umberleigh, Devon
EX37 9QL

Telephone:
0769 540643

CHOCOLATES

This company produces a simple leaflet with brief details of its handmade chocolates. There are three different boxes available, all of which come in milk or dark chocolate or a combination of both. Apparently they won the 'best chocolates' award in foodie *Henrietta Green's Food Lovers Guide to Britain* – quite a recommendation.

Food & Drink

Oval opera box truffles, which are 230gm net weight, cost £14.95 while 400gm are £20.95. Clear bag truffles and pralines are £16.95 for 500gm.

Catalogue: *Quarterly, A4, Leaflet, 1 page, B/W, Free* Postal charges: *Free* Delivery: *Royal Mail* Methods of Payment: *Cheque, Visa, Access / Mastercard*

MOREL BROS, COBBETT & SON
Unit 1
50 Sulivan Rd
London
SW6 3DX

Telephone:
071 384 3345
Fax:
071 384 3123

FINE FOODS AND GROCERIES
Established since the late 18th century, Morel Bros, Cobbett & Son, have just launched their first mail order catalogue for over 60 years.

The catalogue itself is a work of art and one can only marvel at the variety and quality of foods it contains. These foods, syrups, sauces and spices are sourced from all over the world – there are vinegars from Modena, pâtés from Perigord, anchovies from Sardinia and wild white pepper from Cameroon.

All the foods are specially selected from companies that Morel Bros, Cobbett & Son believe provide the highest possible quality product. Their teas are from Betjeman & Barton of Paris (125gm of unscented Afternoon Dream is £3.65) and their coffees are from the Savoy Group (227gm of Regular is £2.35).

Catalogue: *28.5 × 17.5cm, Catalogue, 30 pages, Colour, Free* Postal charges: *£3.95* Delivery: *Courier* Methods of Payment: *Cheque, Visa, Access / Mastercard*

MRS GILL'S COUNTRY CAKES
5 Link House
Leat Street
Tiverton
Devon
EX16 5LG

Telephone:
0884 242744
Fax:
0884 257440

FOOD AND DRINK
A cake maker from Devon, winner of Best Cakes Rosette in 'Henrietta Green's Food Lovers Guide to Britain', Mrs Gill bakes fruit and Christmas cakes, as well as those for special occasions: weddings, birthdays and Simnel cakes. The Gourmet fruit cake recipe sounds mouthwatering, and shows great attention to detail. The cakes come in different sizes, three for the fruit cake, four for the Christmas variety, with the latter also offering two styles of icing, top iced or iced all over. However, a Christmas cake iced all over cannot be sent in the special gift boxes.

Catalogue: *Third A4, Brochure, 1 page, B/W, Free* Postal charges: *Varies with item* Delivery: *Royal Mail* Methods of Payment: *Cheque*

Food & Drink

NORMAN HOLLAND
159 Gordon Road
Ilford
Essex
1GL 2XS

Telephone:
081 478 0192

TEAS

A one-man business, Norman Holland combines quality with prompt, personal service. He stocks a small range of some of the best known teas, tins, infusers and tea-cloths. Finest Assam is priced at £2.20 per 500gm, Finest Ceylon at £2.30 per 500gm, Finest Earl Grey (scented with real oil of Bergamot) £3.70 per 500gm and Finest China Jasmine at £3.50 per 500gm.

Infusers are one-cup size and cost £1.80 each. Tea-cloths made from linen and cotton, printed in blue and white with a design of teas and teapots, are £2.50.

Catalogue: *A4, Leaflet, 1 page, B/W, Free* Postal charges: *Free* Delivery: *Royal Mail* Methods of Payment: *Cheque, Postal Order*

ORIENTALIS TRADING CO LTD
145–151 Lavenham Road
London
SW18 5EP

Telephone:
081 877 9377
Fax:
081 877 3373

INNOVATIVE AND UNUSUAL RANGE OF FOOD AND SNACKS

Orientalis provide a wide range of exciting oriental foodstuffs by post. Among those available are satay broad beans, garlic and chili flavoured peanuts, oriental mix (200gm for 95p) and spicy prawn rolls.

Singaporean satay marinade and satay peanut sauce are available, as is Kara brand coconut cream (200ml for 60p) – the freshest purest and handiest way to buy this essential curry ingredient.

Also obtainable are a range of totally different fruit juices and beverages sporting chunks of real fruit in each can and, of course, various Chinese sauce mixes (59p) and Indian curry spices, including Szechuan Sizzling Beef, Lemon Chicken, Stir Fry Vegetable and other mixes for perfect vegetarian meals.

Catalogue: *Quarterly, A4, Catalogue, 4 pages, B/W, Free* Postal charges: *Varies with item* Delivery: *Royal Mail, Parcelforce, own van in local area* Methods of Payment: *Cheque, Postal Order, Visa, Access / Mastercard, American Express*

PAXTON & WHITFIELD
93 Jermyn Street
London
SW1Y 6JE

Telephone:
071 358 1398

QUALITY CHEESES

Paxton & Whitfield have been cheesemongers since 1797. The mail order list is a selection from their stock of 'postable' cheeses and quality foods and wines. They have also been chosen for their suitability as gifts and business thank-yous.

Stiltons and cheddars are available separately, along with hams, ports and wines, but the emphasis is on selections and hampers. Gift vouchers are also available.

Food & Drink

The 'Triumphant British' selection, featuring 12oz wedges of Blue Stilton, Wensleydale, Tornegus and Extra Mature Farmhouse Cheddar, sells at £22.50. A must for any serious cheesie.

Catalogue: *298 × 104mm, Catalogue, 16 pages plus inserts, B/W, Cheese guide, describing all cheeses in stock, costs £1; mail order list alone is free.* Postal charges: *Varies with item* Delivery: *Royal Mail* Methods of Payment: *Diners Club, American Express, Access / Mastercard, Visa Cheque*

PEMBERTON'S VICTORIAN CHOCOLATE
Bronyscawen Farm
Llanboidy
Carmarthenshire
SA34 0EX

HANDMADE CHOCOLATES
This chocaholic's paradise is based on a farm near Carmarthan, West Wales. Elizabeth Jones, who trained as a chocolatier in Belgium and Switzerland, uses her skills to make exclusive chocolates in the traditional way from the finest ingredients.

More than 150 items are produced by her team, from chocolate lovespoons and masks to traditional Welsh biscuits, cakes and Bara Brith. Among the mail order goods are handmade chocolates and truffles in basketwork decorated with ribbons from £14.95.

The farm is open to the public during the summer, and visitors are able to see how these chocolates are made and to enjoy some of the quality products in their Garden Cafe.

Catalogue: *Third A4, Brochure, 4 pages, Colour, Free* Postal charges: *Varies with item* Delivery: *Royal Mail* Methods of Payment: *Cheque, Postal Order*

REID WINES (1992) LTD
The Mill
Marsh Lane
Hallatrow
Bristol
Avon
BS18 5EB

Telephone:
0761 452645
Fax:
0761 453642

FINE WINES AND SPIRITS
Reid pride themselves on their extensive lists of fine wines, especially their Burgundy and Bordeaux, although this catalogue extends beyond this range.

The helpful, and honest, commentaries on their stock are invaluable aids to the expert and clear enough to guide even the novice drinker. Their own favourites, the 'Selection', seem to be value for money, with Chardonnay at £5.85 a bottle and House champagne at £11.50 a bottle.

The range of wine vinegars, olive oils and spirits complete what is an impressive array of liquids.

Catalogue: *Biannually, A5, Catalogue, 36 pages, B/W, Free* Postal charges: *Varies with item* Delivery: *Royal Mail, In-house delivery Courier* Methods of Payment: *Cheque, Postal Order*

Food & Drink

RICHARD KIHL
164 Regents Park Road
London
NW1 8XN

Telephone:
071 586 3838
Fax:
071 586 2960

FINE AND RARE WINES
Richard Kihl are no ordinary wine merchants, they specialise in the high end of the market, selling quality wines at good but nevertheless hefty prices. Their simple price list gives only the year, name and price and is clearly for people who already know their wines well.

There are some wonderful bottles here for the connoisseur: for example, a case of 1959 Chateau Latour – but it will set you back some £2880. However, there are cases for a good deal less and you can even get some for around £70.00. A good source of excellent wines.

Catalogue: *A4, Price list, 12 pages, B/W, Free* Postal charges: *Varies with item* Delivery: *By arrangement* Methods of Payment: *Cheque*

RICHARD WOODALL
Lane End
Waberthwaite
Nr Millom
Cumbria
LA19 5YJ

Telephone:
0229 717237
Fax:
0229 717007

CUMBERLAND HAMS
The Woodalls have been producing fine quality hams since 1828 on their farm in Cumbria. The 'Cumberland Hams', approximately 11–17lb in weight, spend one month in a dry cure then hang for a further two months for maturing. 'Cumbria Air Dried Hams' (Parma Style) has herbs added during the curing process before air drying for at least 12 months. It is available either as a whole ham or sliced in 4 and 8oz vacuum packs.

Also available are 'Mature Royal Hams' cured in molasses and vinegar, 'Home Cured Bacon' and 'Dry Cured Beef'. Prices vary between £2.85 and £7.15 per lb, while bacon is between £2.10 and £2.76 per lb. Dry cured beef is £4.20 per 8oz.

Catalogue: *A5, Brochure, 6 pages, Colour, Free* Postal charges: *Varies with item* Delivery: *Royal Mail* Methods of Payment: *Cheque, Postal Order*

SANDRIDGE FARMHOUSE BACON
Sandridge Farm
Bromham
Chippenham
Wiltshire
SN15 2JN

Telephone:
0380 850304

SLICED BACON, JOINTS AND COOKED HAMS
This Wiltshire farm sells 'cured bacon that sizzles in the pan and traditional hams with texture and flavour'. Old local recipes have been revived to produce the range of 'Village Hams', which are exclusive to Sandridge. Each ham is individually selected and prepared, some taking eight months to mature. All the pigs are reared on home-grown grain and personal callers are welcome not only at the shop, but can also look round the farm and walk the farmtrail.

Traditional Wiltshire cured bacon sells for £2.47

Food & Drink

per lb, Golden Rind (which is smoked over oak and beech) is £2.57 per lb, while Apple Cure is £3.10 per lb. Hams are from £35.00.

Catalogue: *Brochure, Colour, Free* Postal charges: *Varies with item* Delivery: *Interlink, Royal Mail* Methods of Payment: *Cheque*

SARAH MEADE'S SPECIAL OCCASION CAKES
P.O. Box 323
Chislehurst
Kent
BR7 5SS

Telephone:
081 295 2002
Fax:
081 295 0259

HANDMADE FRUIT CAKES
Sarah Meade's luxury fruit cakes are all handmade and decorated using fine ingredients, and they are baked in the traditional way to the company's own family recipes. Ingredients are listed to help the customer choose their ideal fruit cake and there are no restrictions on the use of alcohol or time taken to mature the cakes.

The fruit cakes are packaged in either one of the range of five boxes (£19.50 gift size) or they can be gift-wrapped in coloured Sarah Meade paper. The cakes can be sent as a gift or for a special occasion (happy birthday, get well, good luck, congratulations, etc), and messages will be iced on to the cake at no extra charge.

Catalogue: *A4, By Advertising, 3 pages, Colour and B/W, Free* Postal charges: *Free* Delivery: *Royal Mail* Methods of Payment: *Cheque, Postal Order, Visa, Access / Mastercard*

SCOTTISH TEA SELECTORS
Wine Port Warehouse
Brodick
Isle of Arran
KA27 8DD

Telephone:
0770 302595
Fax:
0770 302599

QUALITY TEAS
Scottish Tea Selectors supply a large range of first quality India teas and fruit teas in either packs or their own range of chests and chestlets. 1 × 100gm pack of Earl Grey costs £1.95, while 6 cost £11.70. A 250gm chest of English Afternoon Tea is £2.50 and 6 cost £15.00. Fruit teas include Apple, Lemon, Blackcurrant and Orange, and chests start at £1.60.

Also available are a selection of muslin spice sachets, including Whisky Toddies and Mulled Wine at £1.75 for eight.

Catalogue: *A4, Leaflet, 8 pages, Colour and B/W, Free* Postal charges: *Varies with item* Delivery: *Royal Mail* Methods of Payment: *Cheque, Postal Order*

Food & Drink

SEDLESCOMBE VINEYARD
Robertsbridge
East Sussex
TN32 5SA

Telephone:
0580 830715
Fax:
0580 830122

ORGANIC WINE
This English vineyard produces organic wines which are approved by the vegetarian society and suitable for vegans. A 1991 Late Harvest dry (11% vol) comes from the Bacchus grape and costs £6.75 a bottle.

They also produce an interesting range of fruit wines, such as the medium dry apple. At £3.25 a bottle, this seems well worth investigating.

Catalogue: *A4, Leaflet, 1 page, B/W, Free* Postal charges: *Free* Delivery: *In-house delivery* Methods of Payment: *Visa, Access / Mastercard, American Express, Diners Club Cheque*

SEVERN & WYE SMOKERY
Walmore Hill
Minsterworth
Glos
GL2 8LA

Telephone:
0452 750777
Fax:
0452 750776

SMOKED FISH AND POULTRY
The Severn & Wye Smokery is situated on the edge of the Forest of Dean, between two of England's most celebrated salmon rivers. Here, the art of smoking fish and meats is still carried out by hand. The whole operation, from filleting and slicing through to producing the final product, uses traditional skills. The speciality is locally caught salmon, both fresh when in season and smoked all year round.

A 2lb pack of pre-sliced smoked salmon sells for £19.00. Other smoked products include prawns, kippers, fillets of mackerel, trout, and eel, as well as chicken and duck breasts.

Catalogue: *Third A4, Leaflet, 8 pages, B/W, Free* Postal charges: *Varies with item* Delivery: *Royal Mail* Methods of Payment: *Cheque*

SIMPLY SALMON
Severals Farm
Arkesden
Saffron Walden
Essex
CB11 4EY

Telephone:
0799 550143
Fax:
0799 550039

SALMON
Simply Salmon produces a range of the finest smoked salmon from selected lochs on the Isle of Skye and the north-west coast of Scotland. Each side of salmon is specially smoked in kilns over oak chippings.

Salmon is available in a huge variety of packs, starting with 2 × 8oz trimmings at £8.75 to 6 × 1lb packs of Scottish Eagle Smoked Salmon at £77.95. The company also runs a Simply Salmon Club with yearly membership. Various amounts of salmon can be sent every month or every 2 months at prices from £39.95–£169.90. Also available are speciality hampers, individual delicacies: e.g. 2 × 8oz smoked duck breasts (£13.95) and a selection of fine wines.

Catalogue: *A4, Catalogue, 6 pages, B/W, Free* Postal charges: *Free* Delivery: *Royal Mail* Methods of Payment: *Cheque, Postal Order, Visa, Access / Mastercard*

Food & Drink

ST JAMES'S TEAS LTD
Sir John Lyon House
Upper Thames Street
London
EC4V 3PA

Telephone:
071 248 4117
Fax:
071 454 0006

QUALITY TEAS
St James's Teas specialise in high quality teas chosen to drink as they are or to blend at home. Each tea is described to help you understand and appreciate their different qualities and to guide you towards exciting blending possibilities.

Teas on offer include Assam, Darjeeling, Ceylon and China Keemun. They also sell St James's Decaffeinated Tea, which is exclusive to the company's mail order service and health food shops. Prices start at £1.55 per 125gm packet. Alternatively, teas can be bought in the St James's range of caddies from either the historical or classical collections.

Catalogue: *Third A4, Leaflet, 6 pages, B/W, Free* Postal charges: *Varies with item* Delivery: *Royal Mail* Methods of Payment: *Visa, Access / Mastercard, American Express Cheque*

STEAMBOAT ORIENTAL FOODS
P O Box 452
Bradford
West Yorkshire
BD4 7TF

Telephone:
0274 742936

ORIENTAL FOODS
Steamboat Oriental sell foods from exotic places all around the world. You can choose from an enormous range of herbs and spices, including black onion seed at 59p for 50gm, bouquet garni at 45p for 10 sachets, basil at 49p for 50gm and alfalfa seeds at 45p for 50gm.

From China and Taiwan come bean flavour noodles at £1.39 for 150gm, carrot noodles at 69p for 250gm and glutinous rice at £1.50 for 400gm. Mushroom and funghi include dried Chinese mushrooms at £1.29 for 30gm and straw mushrooms at £1.59 for 420gm. A wonderful resource for the adventurous cook.

Catalogue: *A4, Catalogue, 20 pages, B/W, Free* Postal charges: *Varies with item* Delivery: *Royal Mail* Methods of Payment: *Cheque, Postal Order, Visa, Access / Mastercard*

SUMMERBEE PRODUCTS
Organic Food Service
Freepost
Windsor House
Lime Avenue
Torquay, Devon
TQ1 3BR

Telephone:
0803 212965

ORGANIC BEAUTY PRODUCTS
Summerbee Products can provide a range of high quality organic food supplements and organic health and beauty products by mail order.

Their beauty products include royal jelly day & night creams (50ml of each £13.95), gardenia handcream, avocado cleansing milk (125gm £4.80) and pollen deep cleansing lotion. They also sell a wide range of aromatherapy oils and their royal jelly is available in pure acacia honey, capsules, pure form and in blended form with pollen in a set clover honey.

They sell a range of minerals and food supplements

Food & Drink

which include green-lipped mussel extract (120 tablets £8.95), evening primrose oil and garlic oil.

Catalogue: *A5 & A4, Leaflets, 8 pages, B/W, Free* Postal charges: *Free* Delivery: *Royal Mail, ANC Carriers* Methods of Payment: *Visa, Access / Mastercard, Cheque, Postal Order*

SWADDLES GREEN FARM
Hare Lane
Buckland St Mary
Chard
Somerset
TS20 3JR

Telephone:
0460 234387
Fax:
0460 234591

ORGANIC MEAT
Swaddles Green Farm is a traditional holding run organically. They specialise in delivering direct to your door the finest quality meat that is accredited organic by UKROFS and is full of old fashioned succulence and flavour. Meat is farmed the old way and is from traditional English breeds ideally suited to the slower, gentler rearing methods. It is butchered at the farm in their refrigerated cutting rooms and delivered vacuum packed and ready to cook.

They have a large selection of poultry, pork, beef and lamb, sausages, bacon and ham, charcuterie and pies and pâtés. Free-range chicken costs £2.45 per lb and rack of lamb £4.05 per lb. There are also a range of specials stuffed and marinated on the farm.

Catalogue: *A5, Catalogue, 8 pages plus inserts, B/W, Free* Postal charges: *Free* Delivery: *In-house delivery, Courier* Methods of Payment: *Cheque, Postal Order, COD, Visa, Access / Mastercard*

TANNERS WINES LTD
26 Wyle Cop
Shrewsbury
Salop
SY1 1XD

Telephone:
0743 232007
Fax:
0743 344401

WINES AND SPIRITS.
Tanners Wines have been trading in Shropshire and the Welsh Marches since 1872 and are now firmly established as one of the leading mail order wine merchants in the country. Excellent wines at all price levels are available from throughout the world with a particularly fine selection from France, Australia, New Zealand and Chile.

Orders over £75 in volume are delivered free of charge in mainland UK and smaller orders attach a £6 delivery charge. Knowledgeable advice is always available.

Tanners Claret is £4.45 a bottle, Tanners Champagne £10.99, Tanners Chardonnay £4.95 and Tanners Sauvignon £4.75.

Catalogue: *Biannually, A5, Catalogue, 112 pages, B/W, Free* Postal charges: *Varies with item* Delivery: *Courier* Methods of Payment: *Cheque, Postal Order, Visa, Access / Mastercard, American Express*

Food & Drink

TAVERNORS TRADITIONAL HAMPERS
Yew Tree House
Lucton
Nr Leominster
Herefordshire
HR6 9PJ

Telephone:
0586 780384
Fax:
0586 780384

FOOD HAMPERS
Incorporating a carefully chosen selection of some of the finest traditional British fare, Tavernors high quality hampers form the ideal gift at Christmas and Easter or any special occasion.

There are 19 different hampers to choose from, available either in a box or a traditional willow hamper. Hampers include the 'Kingsland' which contains a bottle of Cockburn's Fine Ruby Port, a ceramic pot of Cropwell Bishop English blue Stilton and Walkers fine oatcakes for £20.40 boxed or £33.12 in a hamper. The 'Croft' contains 1 bottle each of Glenfiddich single malt whisky, Taylor's late bottled vintage port, Bodenham vintage white wine, cider liqueur, Herefordshire perry, St Emilion red wine, elderflower cordial and Herefordshire apple juice for £68.08 boxed or £84.77 in a hamper.

Three different Christmas hampers are also available, priced between £20.69 and £49.52.

Catalogue: *A5, Catalogue, 8 pages, B/W, Free* Postal charges: *Varies with item* Delivery: *Royal Mail, Courier* Methods of Payment: *Cheque, Postal Order, Visa, Access / Mastercard*

TAYLORS OF HARROGATE
1 Parliament Street
Harrogate
North Yorkshire
York
HG1 2QU

Telephone:
0423 531211
Fax:
0423 565191

TEA AND COFFEE
Unfortunately Bettys & Taylors' catalogue was being amended as we went to press so we were unable to see a copy. However, they did send us a price list featuring their enormous range of teas and coffees. Teas are sold loose, in caddies and as tea-bags, and the selection literally comes from all over the world. As well as standard blends such as Earl Grey and English breakfast, there are more exotic teas for the adventurous. How about Zulu tea, or choicest fancy Formosa Oolong?

There is an equally good range of coffee, both loose and pre-ground. They also sell accessories, including cafètieres and the various parts for them, such as new gauzes and glass beakers.

Catalogue: *A4, Catalogue, Colour, Free* Postal charges: *£5.60* Delivery: *Royal Mail* Methods of Payment: *Cheque, Visa, Access / Mastercard*

Food & Drink

TAYLORS OF OXFORD
31 St Giles
Oxford
OX1 3LD

Telephone:
0865 58853
Fax:
0865 511700

HAMPERS, GIFT BASKETS AND BOXES
Taylors produce delightful traditional hampers and gift boxes which they will deliver worldwide. They make the perfect prize or memorable present and come either in standard versions or made up to your own specifications.

Each selection is beautifully presented, with gift baskets starting at £19.95 and hampers from £25.95. The Christmas box offers good value with simpler presentation at £49.50. Wine boxes are available from around £20.00.

Catalogue: *Annually, A5, Brochure, 16 pages, Colour, Free* Postal charges: *Varies with item* Delivery: *Parcelforce, Home Express (U.K)* Methods of Payment: *Cheque, Postal Order, Visa, Access / Mastercard, American Express, Diners Club*

THE BEER CELLAR & CO LTD
Forge Court
Reading Road
Yateley
Surrey
GU17 7RX

Telephone:
0252 861875
Fax:
0252 861200

PREMIUM BOTTLED BEER
The Beer Cellar is Britain's leading specialist beer supplier. They have a huge range of over 150 of the world's finest bottled beers from more than 30 countries. Their full colour catalogue comes complete with tasting notes by Roger Protz, a world authority on beer.

You can select your own case or choose from a range of pre-selected cases. These come in twelve- or twenty-four-bottle versions and start from £17.45 for twelve different beers from as many countries. You can also choose a case of the best of British for £18.95, the World's Strongest Brews for £21.95, or Roger Protz's own introductory case featuring twelve different beer styles for £19.75.

Catalogue: *3 a year, A5, Catalogue, 32 pages, Colour, Free* Postal charges: *Varies with item* Delivery: *Courier, Parcelforce* Methods of Payment: *Cheque, Postal Order, Visa, Access / Mastercard*

THE CLARK TRADING COMPANY
17 Southbrook Road
Lee
London
SE12 8LH

Telephone:
081 297 9937
Fax:
081 297 9993

EXOTIC FOODS
The Clark Trading Company specialises in the most exotic food items to come out of France and Italy, such as truffles, foie gras, extra virgin olive oils and wild porcini mushrooms.

The French products come from Auguste Cyprien, a company based in a restored Augustinian abbey in the Perigord region, while the red wine vinegar comes from south of Modena, Italy, and is produced in the traditional method, using heated oak chippings. Vinegars aged twelve, sixteen and twenty years are also available.

Food & Drink

THE FRESH FOOD CO
100 Bayswater Rd
London
W2 3HJ

Telephone:
081 969 0351
Fax:
081 969 0351

Catalogue: *A5, Catalogue, 12 pages, B/W, Free* Postal charges: *Varies with item* Delivery: *Royal Mail* Methods of Payment: *Cheque*

VARIETY OF FRESH FOODS FROM UK AND ABROAD

The Fresh Food Co and its sister company, The Fresh Fish Co, have been sending the very best and hardest-to-find fresh fish and other foods direct to the general public for nearly five years.

Most of their suppliers are well known in the kitchens of Britain's top hotels and restaurants. The fish is sent to you direct from the quay in Cornwall where their best fish are landed from clean waters by small boats. Mojama, wind-dried tuna from Spain (250gm for £12.50), is a product unchanged since the manufacturing technique was perfected by the Phoenicians 3000 years ago. Innes sourdough loaf (2kg for £12.50) is a delicious, and unusual, organic brown bread.

Many other original and mouthwatering foods are available for dispatch, such as Brogdale apples, O'Hagan's sausages, Rabelais de luxe French pork and poultry and Green & Black's chocolate.

Catalogue: *Biannually, A4, Catalogue, 8 pages, B/W, Free* Postal charges: *Free* Delivery: *Royal Mail, Courier, Parcelforce* Methods of Payment: *Cheque, Postal Order, Visa, Access / Mastercard, American Express*

THE MASTER OF MALT
The Corn Exchange
The Pantiles
Tunbridge Wells
Kent
TN2 5TE

Telephone:
0892 513295
Fax:
0892 890567

MALT WHISKIES

For the connoisseur who wants the best without leaving the comfort of the armchair – membership of the Malt Whisky Association is the answer. With a comprehensive range of almost 200 whiskies from the Highlands and Islands of Scotland, America and Ireland, there is a wide selection to suit everyone's taste. If you are unable to make your mind up, their sets of miniatures enable you to drink your way around Scotland for as little as £25.95.

Annual membership is £12.50 for one year and gives access to special savings, with a 10-year-old Laphroaig at £20.95 and a 28-year-old Clynelish at £62.85.

Catalogue: *Third A4, Brochure, 8 pages, B/W, Free* Postal charges: *Varies with item* Delivery: *Royal Mail* Methods of Payment: *Cheque, Postal Order, Visa, Access / Mastercard*

Food & Drink

THE MOFFATT FISHERY
Hammerlands
Moffat
Dumfriesshire
DG10 9QL

Telephone:
0683 21068
Fax:
0683 21068

SUPERIOR SMOKED SALMON
Glenmoffat superior smoked salmon is handcrafted using traditional recipes in a non-automated process. All their fresh salmon is selected from the best available from their Scottish waters and because they use a small-batch technique they believe they are able to impart flavour and texture unachievable by larger processors supplying the supermarkets. Their low overheads mean they are able to pass on cost savings to their customers.

The leaflet comprises a 'letter' to customers and a product and price list/order form. 2lb side of hand-sliced smoked salmon, £22.95; 4oz pack long sliced smoked salmon, £5.80; 1lb smoked trout fillets, £7.50; 1lb pack of sliced smoked salmon delivered by post once a month for 12 months, £12.50 a month.

There is a second leaflet offering game and salmon by post, including red deer diced at £2.25 per lb; venison steaks, 4oz-8oz rump, £4.50 per lb; 100% venison mince, £1.50 per lb; pigeon, £1.00 each; rabbit, 95p per lb; game sausage, £2.20 per lb; smoked salmon burgers, 60p each; salmon fishcakes, 60p each and fresh trout (gutted), £1.85 per lb.

Catalogue: *A4, Leaflet, 2 pages, B/W, Free* Postal charges: *Varies with item* Delivery: *Royal Mail or Datapost for larger orders* Methods of Payment: *Cheque, Postal Order, Visa, Access / Mastercard*

THE MOUSETRAP
2 St Gregory's Alley
Norwich
NR2 1ER

Telephone:
0603 614083

FINE CHEESES
The Mousetrap is a cheese emporium providing a long and impressive list of international products that reads like part of the cheese shop sketch. There are at least six varieties of cheddar, including Chewton Mature Farmhouse at £3.32 and Rutland cheddar with beer, garlic and parsley for £3.36. From Ireland, you can sample Coolleeney Camembert at £4.76; from Scotland, Lanark Blue Ewes at £7.12. Then there is Celtic Promise from Wales at £6.56 each, or Leiden with cumin from Holland for £3.44. There are also cheeses from Spain, Germany, Switzerland and of course France.

Other products include meats and pâtés, mostly salamis and ham; olives, fish and homemade items such as pesto alla Genovese and smoked salmon pâté with fresh cream and brandy. All in all, irresistible!

Catalogue: *A4, Brochure, 7 pages, B/W, Free* Postal charges: *Varies with item* Delivery: *Royal Mail* Methods of Payment: *Cheque*

Food & Drink

THE NADDER CATERING SHOP
4 North Street
Wilton
Salisbury
Wilts
SP2 0HE

Telephone:
0722 744707

DELICATESSEN FOODS
Nadder do not issue a catalogue, but rather a simple A4 price list. This gives very brief details of a good range of herbs and spices as well as a smaller selection of food. This includes mixed forest mushrooms for £1.50, sundried tomatoes at a £2.00 for a 4oz packet and Nadder wholegrain mustard for £3.80.

Catalogue: *A4, Leaflet, 1 page, B/W, Free* Postal charges: *Varies with item* Delivery: *Royal Mail* Methods of Payment: *Cheque*

THE OIL MERCHANT
47 Ashchurch Grove
London
W12 9BU

Telephone:
081 740 1335
Fax:
081 740 1319

A RANGE OF OILS FOR COOKING
The Oil Merchant stocks a wide variety of oils from the Mediterranean countries and also the USA. Extra virgin olive oils, nut and seed oils, herbed oils and flavoured oils, plus mustards, sun-dried tomatoes, vinegars, pastes and sauces and other Mediterranean delicacies are all available by post. Some items that are not suitable for posting may be collected, with a 20% collection discount.

Catalogue: *A4, Leaflet, 8 pages, B/W, Free* Postal charges: *Varies with item* Delivery: *Royal Mail* Methods of Payment: *Cheque, Postal Order*

THE OLD SMOKEHOUSE
Brougham Hall
Brougham
Penrith
Cumbria
CA10 2DE

Telephone:
0768 67772

SMOKED FOODS
The Old Smokehouse is based at Brougham Hall in Cumbria and produces a range of Cumbrian foods prepared in the traditional manner. It offers a variety of game, meats, cheeses, sausages and chutneys. A brace of smoked pheasant costs £18.40; 8oz sliced smoked salmon £8.50.

Also available are a range of gift selections such as the 'Country House Selection Pack' (four smoked trout, one smoked guinea fowl, 8oz sliced venison, 1lb mature smoked cheddar, Cumberland sausage, apricot chutney and chocolate truffles: £47.00). Truffles are a recent introduction to the range. Made from the finest continental chocolate flavours they include cherry and Kirsch and Black Russian. All truffles come boxed and gift-wrapped. Prices start at £8.00 for 200gm.

Catalogue: *Annually, Third A4, Catalogue, 10 pages, B/W, Free* Postal charges: *Free* Delivery: *Royal Mail* Methods of Payment: *Cheque, Postal Order*

Food & Drink

THE ORGANIC WINE COMPANY
P.O. Box 81
High Wycombe
Bucks
HP13 5QN

Telephone:
0494 446557

ORGANIC WINE
The Organic Wine company pride themselves, as all 'organic' retailers do, on the fact that their product has been produced using the most natural ingredients available. The reasons they present seem convincing – but there's always a feeling with this type of organisation that they're preaching to the converted. Now's your chance to prove this assumption wrong.

Their champagnes cost from £16.50 for a bottle of 'Cuvée des Trois Cépages' to £16.99 for a bottle of 'L'Oeil de Perdix'. Sparkling wine is, of course, cheaper at £7.50 for a bottle of Bacchus Brut. Naturally, they also have a good range of red and white wines and rosés.

Catalogue: *Quarterly, A5, Catalogue, 20 pages, B/W, Free* Postal charges: *Varies with item* Delivery: *In-house delivery* Methods of Payment: *Cheque, Postal Order, Visa, Access / Mastercard*

THE REAL MEAT COMPANY LTD
East Hill Farm
Heytesbury
Warminster
Wilts
BA12 0HR

Telephone:
0985 840501
0985 40436
Fax:
0985 840243

HIGH WELFARE ADDITIVE-FREE MEAT
Real Meat Express offers a true alternative to factory farming. Beef, lamb, pork, chicken, bacon, ham, duck, turkeys and geese are all produced free-range. No growth promoters or routine drug regimes are used. They insist on the highest of standards and all the farms are independently inspected by Bristol University.

A special isothermic capsule keeps the meat chilled in transit, to arrive fresh and ready to eat or freeze as required. The delivery service is very rapid, with orders placed before midday arriving anywhere in Britain the next morning (Tuesday to Saturday).

Catalogue: *Quarterly, A4, Catalogue, 1 page, Colour, Free* Postal charges: *Varies with item* Delivery: *Courier* Methods of Payment: *Cheque, Postal Order, Visa, Access / Mastercard, American Express, Diners Club*

THE SALMON POOL
Unit 11
Crofthead Farm Centre
Livingston
West Lothian
EH54 6DG

Telephone:
0506 415252
Fax:
0506 418328

SCOTTISH SALMON
This small brochure describes an enticing range of Scottish salmon. All the products are smoked in Scotland and packed in special boxes to ensure the fish arrives in good condition.

Oak-smoked salmon is £25.45 for sliced sides (1.75lb), while whisky-smoked salmon is a little more, at £22.07. Finally there is peat-smoked salmon at £26.10. The fish comes in trimmed sides, sliced sides and fully sliced.

Catalogue: *Quarterly, A6, Brochure, 4 pages, B/W, Free* Postal charges: *Free* Delivery: *Royal Mail* Methods of Payment: *Cheque, Postal Order, Visa, Access / Mastercard, American Express*

Food & Drink

THE SCOTTISH GOURMET
Thistle Mill
Biggar
Scotland
ML12 6LP

Telephone:
0899 21001
Fax:
0899 20456

FRESH SCOTTISH PRODUCE

The Scottish Gourmet is Britain's leading home dining club. They send out a seasonal monthly menu to members, featuring the best and freshest Scottish produce bought in from the country's small producers. Products include cheese, smoked fish and meat, game, Aberdeen Angus beef, rare breed lamb and mutton.

Orders are packed in ice and delivered to the door within 24 hours of dispatch. The annual subscription is £9.95. Four portions of mushrooms with Lanark blue are £6.97; tarragon rabbit, £9.85; Blairgowrie pheasant, £10.88 and a Caledonian cheeseboard, £6.93.

Catalogue: *Monthly, A5, Brochure, 16 pages, Colour, Free* Postal charges: *Varies with item* Delivery: *Parcelforce* Methods of Payment: *Cheque, Postal Order, Stage Payments, Visa, Access / Mastercard, American Express, Diners Club*

THE TEA CLUB
PO Box 221
Guildford
Surrey
GU1 3YT

TEAS

As a nation of almost obsessive tea-drinkers, this publication must be of interest to virtually everyone in the UK. The Tea Club publishes its magazine three time a year, often with free samples of new and classic teas. Full of interesting articles on all kinds of teas, it makes fascinating reading. You'll never be able to have a simple tea-bag again!

There are competitions every month, opportunities for tea tasting and discounts on teas for members.

Catalogue: *Quarterly, A4, Brochure, B/W, £10.00 annually* Postal charges: *Varies with item* Delivery: *Royal Mail* Methods of Payment: *Cheque, Postal Order*

THE TEA HOUSE
15 Neal Street
Covent Garden
London
WC2H 9PU

Telephone:
071 240 7539
Fax:
071 836 4769

QUALITY TEAS

The Tea House specialises in fine teas, infusions, loose-leaf teas and tea-bags. It sells nearly 100 varieties of pure and blended tea from around the world, and tea-time accessories like infusers and novelty teapots.

Favourite classics include Assam, Earl Grey and Darjeeling. 30 fruit flavoured and spice flavoured teas are also popular; so too are Chinese and Japanese green teas like Jasmine. Caffeine-free herbals, camomile and hibiscus and whole fruit teas are refreshing and healthy.

Teas cost from £1.30–£3.50 for 125gm, according to each variety. Also on sale are fortune-telling

Food & Drink

teacups at £10.50; tea-chests with fine tea at £3.95 and £7.65 and teabricks for £8.75.

Catalogue: *Annually, A4, Brochure, 8 pages, B/W, Free* Postal charges: *Varies with item* Delivery: *Royal Mail* Methods of Payment: *Cheque, Postal Order, COD, Visa, Access / Mastercard, American Express*

THE TOFFEE SHOP
7 Brunswick Road
Penrith
Cumbria
CA11 7LU

Telephone:
0768 62008

TOFFEE AND FUDGE

The Toffee Shop is based in Cumbria and supplies a small range of handmade toffees and fudges by mail order. Assortments can be made up from the following flavours: Butter Fudge, Chocolate Fudge, Butter Toffee and Treacle Toffee. Mint Fudge is also available but is not mixed with anything else.

A variety of box sizes are available: 8oz at £2.95, 1lb at £5.80, 1lb 8oz at £8.80, 2 lb at £10.90 and 3lb at £14.90. Messages can be enclosed with your order, which you can supply if desired.

Catalogue: *A5, Leaflet, 1 page, B/W, Free* Postal charges: *Free* Delivery: *Royal Mail* Methods of Payment: *Cheque, Postal Order*

THE VILLAGE BAKERY
Melmerby
Penrith
Cumbria
CA10 1HE

Telephone:
0768 881515
Fax:
0768 881848

ORGANIC BAKERY GOODS

This traditional bakery produces organic bread and cakes from wood-fired brick ovens. They are leading a rediscovery of retained-heat baking using the renewable fuel resource of wood and organically grown ingredients. The result is food you can trust, combining traditional craftsmanship with a modern concern for the environment. And what's more, it all tastes terrific!

Specialities include vegan 'Celebration Fruit Cake' for £9.95, oatcakes at £5.95 for four packets, flapjacks made without sugar at £6.75 for 3 packets and a whole range of Christmas goods from £4.25.

Catalogue: *Annually, A5, Brochure, 4 pages, Colour, Free* Postal charges: *Varies with item* Delivery: *Royal Mail, Parcelforce* Methods of Payment: *Cheque, Postal Order, Visa, Access / Mastercard, Diners Club*

THE WATERMILL
Little Salkeld
Penrith
Cumbria
CA10 1NN

Telephone:
0768 881523

TRADITIONAL FLOURS

The Watermill at Little Salkeld produces stoneground flour in the traditional manner and is one of the country's few millers of organic grains. The company also offers a range of organic dried fruits and nuts, pulses, teas and coffees, herbs and books.

Most types of flour are available, including 100% wholewheat (72p per 500gm), 85% wheatmeal (72p

Food & Drink

per 500gm), rye flour, maslin flour and unbleached white flour. Also available are oatmeal, porridge oats, wheaten bran, barley, muesli base (95p per kilo) and instant yeast (40p per 2oz).

Books on offer include 'The Watermill Baking Book', which is full of delicious recipes tried and tested in the Watermill tea room.

Catalogue: *A5, Catalogue, 8 pages, B/W, Free* Postal charges: *£6.20* Delivery: *Royal Mail* Methods of Payment: *Cheque, Postal Order, Visa, Access / Mastercard*

THE WEALD SMOKERY
Mount Farm
Flimwell
East Sussex
TN5 7QL

Telephone:
0580 87601

SMOKED FOOD

The Weald Smokery offers a wide range of smoked foods, most of which can be served straight from the pack without the need for cooking. The brochure does, however, offer some recipe examples which further enhance the smoked flavour of some of their produce.

On offer are smoked Scottish salmon sliced at £13.50 per lb, smoked chicken breast at £3.95 per pack (boneless approx. 12oz), smoked Scottish rainbow trout, smoked duck breast, smoked mussels at £3.50 per 8oz, smoked freshwater eel at £9.65 per lb, smoked Toulouse sausage, smoked haddock, smoked venison and gravadlax at £25.00 for a whole side (approx. 2lb 8oz).

Catalogue: *Third A4, Leaflet, 6 pages, B/W, Free* Postal charges: *Varies with item* Delivery: *Royal Mail, Courier* Methods of Payment: *Cheque, Postal Order, Visa, Access / Mastercard*

THE WHISKY CONNOISSEUR
Thistle Mill
Biggar
Scotland
ML12 6LP

Telephone:
0899 21001
Fax:
0899 20456

WHISKY

This Scottish based club sends out regular lists of specialist whiskies for the connoisseur. Many of the blends are old and rare and unavailable in the shops. They include outstanding cask-strength single malts from the Highlands, Islands, Lowlands and Speyside. The club also have their own bottlings and new presentations from the leading independent bottlers.

Membership is £10 per year, £30 for five years, £50 for lifetime. Whiskies change with each programme but currently Lagavulin is £42.93, Talisker £42.68, Rosebank £39.79 and Immortal Memory £17.93.

Catalogue: *Monthly, A5, Brochure, 12 pages, Colour, Free* Postal charges: *Varies with item* Delivery: *Parcelforce* Methods of Payment: *Cheque, Postal Order, Stage Payments, Visa, Access / Mastercard, American Express, Diners Club*

Food & Drink

THE WHITE HOUSE COFFEE ROASTERS
104 Parliament Terrace
Upper Parliament Street
Nottingham
NG1 5FX

Telephone:
0602 419033

COFFEE AND TEA
The White House has a delightful shop in Nottingham selling all kinds of speciality teas, coffees and accessories. Recently they have expanded to offer a mail order service, producing an attractive catalogue with informative background on coffee and tea, and an extensive price list. They also include a sample bag of coffee – at least they did with ours, which was much enjoyed!

To keep postage down, the minimum order is 5lb, and there is an excellent range to choose from. Coffee is from 95p to £1.10 for 4oz while tea is £1.20 for 125gm.

Catalogue: *A5, Catalogue, 12 pages, Colour and B/W, Free* Postal charges: *Varies with item* Delivery: *Royal Mail* Methods of Payment: *Cheque, Postal Order, Visa, Access / Mastercard*

TICKLEMORE CHEESE SHOP
1 Ticklemore Street
Totnes
Devon
TQ9 5EJ

Telephone:
0803 865926

CHEESES
Based in Totnes, Ticklemore supply a well balanced list of fine British cheeses.

Cheeses are marked in terms of seasonal availability, suitability for vegetarians and if they use unpasteurised milk. The range includes 'Beenleigh Blue' – a rich, mature, blue-veined ewes' milk cheese made by Ticklemore. Available from July to March only, it costs £4.85 per lb. Somerset Camembert costs £1.60 for 8oz, Devon blue £3.35 per lb, Devon Rustic £3.35 per lb and Harbourne blue, a creamy piquant, semi-hard goats' milk cheese is £4.55 per lb.

Catalogue: *A4, Leaflet, 1 page, B/W, Free* Postal charges: *£2.00* Delivery: *Royal Mail* Methods of Payment: *Cheque, Postal Order*

TRAIDCRAFT
Traidcraft plc
Kingsway
Gateshead
Tyne and Wear
NE11 0NE

Telephone:
091 491 0855
Fax:
091 487 0133

TEAS, COFFEES, SWEETS AND SNACKS FROM AROUND THE WORLD
Traidcraft plc is an alternative trading organisation challenging the economic exploitation of the poor by demonstrating that trade with the 'Third World' can and should be based on justice, concern for people and care for the environment. As well as foods, teas and coffees, Traidcraft has a range of other products available in the following catalogues: Interiors, Alternatives and Paper and Cards.

This catalogue, Foods, offers a wide range of teas, coffees and snacks from places such as India, Arabia and Tanzania, giving you a taste of the world at large.

Catalogue: *A4, Leaflet, 5 pages, Colour, Free* Postal charges: *Varies with item* Delivery: *Royal Mail* Methods of Payment: *Cheque, Access / Mastercard*

Food & Drink

VINCEREMOS
65 Raglan Road
Leeds
Yorkshire
LS2 9DZ

Telephone:
0532 431691

ORGANIC AND SPECIALITY WINES, BEERS AND SPIRITS

Vinceremos are distributors of fine, organic and speciality wines. Organic wines are made from grapes grown without synthetic chemical fertilisers and sprays. Better for you and the environment, these wines come from high quality producers in the major regions of France, Italy, Germany, Hungary and New Zealand.

They also sell organic beers from Germany and the UK, organic ciders from Herefordshire, Russian vodkas, Cuban rums and wines from Lebanon, Morocco, India and Zimbabwe.

An organic taster case of twelve different wines is £49.95, while a bargain selection of two bottles each of six organic wines is just £43.50. A German organic lager case of twenty 50cl bottles is £26.00. A fine wine case with twelve different bottles is £63.00.

Catalogue: *A5, Catalogue, 12-16 pages, B/W, Free* Postal charges: *Varies with item* Delivery: *Home Express* Methods of Payment: *Cheque, Postal Order, Visa, Access / Mastercard*

W T WARREN & SON
Bosweddeon Road
St Just
Penzance
Cornwall
TR19 7JU

Telephone:
0736 788538

CAKES

W T Warren make the traditional Cornish saffron cake. It is said to date back to the time when Phoenician traders exchanged spices for Cornish tin. Saffron was used to give food flavour and a warm, buttery appearance. Saffron itself is the dried stigmas from the flower Crocus Sativus.

The cake is a rich, highly fruited dough cake, usually eaten cold or with butter, sometimes heated or lightly toasted. At only £4.00, you might want to consider tasting this unique historical concoction.

Catalogue: *Third A4, Leaflet, 1 page, Colour, Free* Postal charges: *Varies with item* Delivery: *Royal Mail* Methods of Payment: *Visa, Access / Mastercard Cheque, Postal Order*

WHITTARD OF CHELSEA
73 Northcote Road
London
SW11 6PJ

Telephone:
071 924 1888
Fax:
071 924 3085

FINE TEAS AND COFFEES

Whittard provide some of the finest teas and coffees to homes throughout the country, and this helpful catalogue explains the history of tea and how to make a good cup.

The teas are divided into Darjeeling, Ceylon, Assam, China, Scented and House Specialities. The House Specialities, at £2.50 for a 125gm tin, are carefully selected by Whittard's expert team of tasters for consistent quality.

Food & Drink

The coffee range is listed in order of strength. The Whittard coffee range of thirteen coffees is available at £4.80 per lb, but there are many more exotic beans, such as the Hawaiian Kona at £24.00 per lb.

Catalogue: *Third A4, Leaflet, 8 pages, B/W, Free* Postal charges: *Varies with item* Delivery: *Royal Mail* Methods of Payment: *Cheque, Postal Order, Visa, Access / Mastercard*

WICKER & BOX
St Leonards House
141 Moore Road
Mapperley
NOTTINGHAM
NG3 6EL

Telephone:
0602 603485

CHAMPAGNE HAMPERS

Wicker & Box will deliver champagne gifts nationwide to celebrate special occasions. These include single boxes of champagnes or a variety of wicker hampers. These can contain just champagne or also port, Belgian chocolates, smoked salmon and Stilton cheese.

A bottle of champagne costs £30.00, a magnum £40.00; two bottles of champagne and chocolates are £49.50; a bottle of port and a jar of Stilton is £33.50.

Catalogue: *Third A4, Brochure, Colour, Free* Postal charges: *Free* Delivery: *Courier* Methods of Payment: *Cheque, Postal Order*

WILLIAM GRANT & SONS INTERNATIONAL LTD
The Glenfiddich
Distillery
Dufftown
Banffshire
AB55 4DH

Telephone:
0340 820373
Fax:
0340 820805

WHISKY AND ASSOCIATED PRODUCTS

William Grant is a whisky distillery selling Glenfiddich malt whisky and drinking accessories.

Accessories include waiter trays for £2.95, ancient reserve water jugs in green or blue for £12.95 and crystal whisky tumblers (six) for £129.00.

The whisky starts at £2.45 for 5cl of BV Founder's Reserve through to £40.00 for 70cl of Classic Glenfiddich pure malt scotch whisky. A special gift presentation is also available for the Excellence, an eighteen-year-old Glenfiddich pure malt.

Catalogue: *A4, Leaflet, 6 pages, B/W, Free* Postal charges: *Varies with item* Delivery: *Royal Mail* Methods of Payment: *Cheque, Visa, Access / Mastercard, American Express*

WOOTTON VINEYARDS
Wootton
North Town House
North Wootton
Shepton Mallet
Somerset
BA4 4AG

Telephone:
0749 890359

ENGLISH WINES

Wootton Vineyard of Somerset produces a small range of British wines and a brandy.

Their five wines available for drinking now are: 'Special Selection' (medium), blended from grapes grown in the south-west, 'Seyval Blanc' (dry), 'Müller Thurgau' (dry), 'Shönburger' (medium dry) and 'Auxerrois' (oak-fermented dry). Prices range from £3.99 per bottle to £6.00.

Unique to the Vineyard is 'Wootton Eau de Vie', a white brandy made from their own wines which is the

Footwear

first Eau de Vie distilled from English wine and costs £14.75 per bottle. Also available is 'Somerset Punch', a fortified drink, based on a 200-year-old recipe at £4.35 per bottle.

Catalogue: *A5, Leaflet, 1 page, B/W, Free* Postal charges: *Varies with item* Delivery: *Courier* Methods of Payment: *Cheque*

CARTMELLS OF KESWICK
16 Lake Road
Keswick
Cumbria
CA12 5BX

Telephone:
07687 72740

SHOES

Cartmells offers a range of AA shoes and sandals that fit and look good. Each shoe is marked with the fitting it is available in, otherwise it comes in an accommodating average-plus fitting.

The brochure gives line illustrations of many of the shoes on offer, along with a brief description. One of their ranges, Rieker anti-stress shoes, has been designed for lightness, flexibility and extreme comfort. The shoes are built with special anti-stress soles which really work. There are a number of styles and colours, in comfortable fittings, for ladies and gentlemen. Prices for this brand start at £34.50 and go up to £49.50.

Catalogue: *A4, Leaflet, 4 pages, B/W, Free* Postal charges: *Varies with item* Delivery: *Royal Mail* Methods of Payment: *Cheque, Visa, Access / Mastercard*

COSYFEET
The Foot Comfort Centre
5 The Tanyard
Leigh Road
STREET
Somerset
BA16 0HR

Telephone:
0458 47275
Fax:
0458 45988

FOOTWEAR

Cosyfeet produce an interesting range of products for people who suffer from foot problems. This could be because of swollen feet, arthritis, odema, diabetes and so on. Their slippers are soft and washable, while the shoes are lightweight with leather uppers. Some come with 'easy entry' velcro fastenings which make getting them on and off painful feet much less of a business.

Ladies bootee washable slippers are £15.95, while the men's are £17.95. The lightweight leather shoes are £40.00 and £43.00 respectively.

Catalogue: *Biannually, A5, Catalogue, 20 pages, Colour, Free* Postal charges: *Varies with item* Delivery: *Royal Mail* Methods of Payment: *Cheque, Postal Order, Visa, Access / Mastercard*

FASHION WORLD
P O Box 123
China Lane
Manchester
M1 8BH

Telephone:
061 236 5511

WOMEN'S SHOES AND CLOTHES

Fashion World are a fashion mail order company specialising in women's wear and shoes, with some children's wear as well.

Everything is available in sizes 12 to 26 and they give a guarantee of a full refund or replacement for any item if you are not happy with your purchase.

Footwear

The full range of clothing is covered, from separates, dresses and swimwear to lingerie, footwear and nightwear.

Catalogue: *Biannually, A4, Catalogue, 186 pages, Colour, Free* Postal charges: *Free* Delivery: *Royal Mail* Methods of Payment: *Cheque, Visa, Access / Mastercard*

G T HAWKINS
Overstone Road
Northampton
NN1 3JJ

Telephone:
0604 32293
Fax:
0604 231413

WALKING SHOES AND BOOTS

Hawkins have been manufacturing walking shoes and boots for over a century. There are classic boots for the long-distance walker who might want to do some light climbing and heavy shoes for the person who leads an outdoor life but wants to wear a comfortable shoe in town too. There are many styles for walkers who come between these two requirements.

Every part of the foot is cared for in the top of the range Cairngorm boot, with stiffeners to protect toe and heel sections and hard rubber soles to cushion the feet, even on the most difficult terrain.

Catalogue: *Third A4, Brochure, 8 pages, Colour, Free* Postal charges: *Varies with item* Delivery: *Royal Mail* Methods of Payment: *Cheque*

MADE TO LAST
8 The Crescent
Hyde Park
Leeds
Yorkshire
LS6 2NW

Telephone:
0532 304983

HANDMADE SHOES AND BOOTS

Made to Last is a workers' co-operative, making boots and shoes for women, men and children. Over the last ten years they have built up a fine reputation for stylish, well fitting, casual footwear, as well as for their friendly, professional service.

They use top quality leathers in a stunning range of colours and textures with hard-wearing, micro-cellular soles. 1994 sees the launch of their new 'vegetarian' collection. Their children's shoes took first prize in the 1993 shoe and sock awards, beating industry giants Startrite into second place.

Children's boots are £36.95, strap shoes £42.00, 8-hole Derby boots £59.00 and Classic men's lace-ups £59.00.

Catalogue: *A4, Catalogue, 1 page, Colour, Free* Postal charges: *£3.50* Delivery: *Royal Mail* Methods of Payment: *Cheque, Postal Order, Visa, Access / Mastercard*

Footwear

MARIO BERTULLI
Shirlina Ltd
PO Box 498
London
W10 5QH

Telephone:
071 289 1145

HEIGHT INCREASING SHOES

Mario Bertulli produces a range of height increasing shoes for men. A special manufacturing process is used so the elevation inside the shoe can be worked in natural cork, which is so strong it will last for years. Glovesoft leather covers the natural cork, guaranteeing comfort and easy wear. The shoe itself looks like any other ordinary shoe without particularly high or clumsy looking heavy heels.

Each shoe is pictured with details of the height increase afforded – usually between 5 and 7cm. There are many styles to suit most activities and fashions with prices ranging from £41.00 to £136.00 for the luxury collection.

Catalogue: *A5, Catalogue, 42 pages, Colour, Free* Postal charges: *£3.00 per pair* Delivery: *Royal Mail* Methods of Payment: *Cheque, Postal Order, Visa, Access / Mastercard*

MORLANDS
Northover
Glastonbury
Somerset
BA6 9YA

Telephone:
0458 835007
Fax:
0458 834646

LADIES AND MEN'S LINED SHEEPSKIN SLIPPERS

Morlands of Glastonbury was established in 1870. They offer a wide range of lined sheepskin slippers for both ladies and men. The slippers come in a variety of colours (red, black, brown, navy, green) and in sizes 3 to 9 for women and sizes 6 to 12 for men.

Each slipper has a different style and name; for example, the ladies Fife slipper at £37.99 a pair. Some items have a limited availability and therefore it is advisable to phone to check what is in stock. If you order up to three pairs, there is a postage and packaging fee of £3.50. When ordering a pair of slippers you are advised to state a second colour choice in case the colour you have chosen is not available.

Catalogue: *2 × A4, Leaflet, 2 pages, B/W, Free* Postal charges: *Varies with item* Delivery: *Royal Mail* Methods of Payment: *Cheque, Postal Order*

RICHER
Royal Mills
Station Road
Steeton
Keighley
West Yorkshire
BD20 6RA

Telephone:
0274 56 47 47

CLOTHES FOR 5' 2" AND UNDER

A variety of outerwear, lingerie and shoes for men and women of 5' 2" and under, and for sizes 8 to 34 for women and sizes 32 to 56 for men. Order phoneline available between 8.30 am and 4.30 pm Monday to Friday. Recommend a friend and save £5.00 on your first order. Good quality clothing and clear illustrated catalogue.

Catalogue: *A4, Catalogue, 126 pages, Colour, Free* Postal charges: *Varies with item* Delivery: *In-house delivery* Methods of Payment: *Cheque, Postal Order, Visa, Access / Mastercard*

Footwear

SALLY SMALL SHOES LTD
71 York Street
London
WIH 2BJ

Telephone:
071 723 5321
Fax:
071 723 5321

SMALL WOMEN'S SHOES
Sally Small produces quality ladies shoes in the smallest sizes. Most shoes are all leather (uppers, linings and soles) but some are available with resin or rubber soles.

There are styles for all occasions, from weddings and other smart events to everyday wear and walking. Most shoes are available in two or three different colours including white, black, navy, brown and red. Shoe sizes range from Continental 31 to 34 with half sizes. Prices start at £39.95 and go up to £75.00.

Catalogue: *Third A4, Leaflet, 6 pages, Colour, Free* Postal charges: *£1.75 per pair* Delivery: *Royal Mail* Methods of Payment: *Cheque, Postal Order, Visa, Access / Mastercard*

SHELLYS INTERNATIONAL
1–3 Edgware Road
London
NW2 6JZ

Telephone:
081 450 0066
Fax:
081 208 4340

SHOES
Shellys have several well-known and fashionable shops in London selling trendy footwear, but they also run a sophisticated mail order operation which spans the world.

Their colourful catalogue comes in an impressive folder, along with various money-off offers adding up to £18.00. It features a good range of men's and women's shoes, including many with Dr. Martens soles. These are mostly for the fashion-conscious youth market. Prices are reasonable, at around £42.00 for a pair of Docs. An excellent source.

Catalogue: *A4, Catalogue, 32 pages, Colour, £2.00* Postal charges: *Varies with item* Delivery: *Royal Mail* Methods of Payment: *Cheque, Postal Order, Visa, Access / Mastercard, American Express, Diners Club*

SUNDAES
Station Street
Holbeach
Spalding
Lincolnshire
PE12 7LF

Telephone:
0406 424124
Fax:
0406 426129

SANDALS
Handmade in masses of bright summer colours and natural shades, there's something different for sandal wearers from Sundaes. Hard-wearing and comfortable, Sundaes are created using the best quality materials with leather uppers and linings.

There are 35 styles for all the family (some women's styles up to size 10), including a selection of award winning ECCO shoes and Hogl courts, plus the unique Sundaes sandals and belts.

Smart thong flip-flops on a low wedge are £29.95; soft peep-toe sandals from £42.95; children's multi-colour sandals at £24.95 and belts from £10.95.

Catalogue: *Biannually, A5, Catalogue, 20 pages, Colour, Free* Postal charges: *Varies with item* Delivery: *Royal Mail, Parcelforce* Methods of Payment: *Cheque, Postal Order, Visa, Access / Mastercard*

Furniture

AK QUALITY FURNITURE
Shop 2
No 4, The Chippings
Tetbury
Gloucestershire
GL8 8ET

REPRODUCTION FURNITURE

AK Quality Furniture manufacture English reproduction furniture for the home and office. Situated in the heart of the Cotswolds, their small company employs only local craftsmen to recreate fine pieces of furniture.

The 'Amberley Office' collection includes details like drawers with curl mahogany and inlaid feather banding. They also use walnut burr and fine yew. Desks start at £390.00 in mahogany and go up to £1265.00 in walnut. Cabinets for the home include a television cabinet at £611.00 in mahogany and a bureau top box for £317.00, again in mahogany.

Catalogue: *A5, Catalogue, 9, Colour, Free* Postal charges: *Varies with item* Delivery: *By arrangement* Methods of Payment: *Cheque*

BRITANNIC TEAK
28 Ravenswood Road
Clapham South
London
SW12 9PJ

Telephone:
081 675 4808
Fax:
081 675 4652

GARDEN FURNITURE

The Britannic range is the widest selection of outdoor and conservatory teak furniture to be manufactured in Europe. Each piece is crafted in England with timbers only sourced from plantations listed in the Friends of the Earth Good Wood Guide.

Their range of eleven styles of seats is classified into three weights: light (from £153.00), middle (from £225.00) and heavy (from £378.00). Tables can accommodate from two to twelve people in rectangular or circular configurations. Rectangular versions start at £259.00 (seats four); round tables at £441.00 (seats four to six) while folding tables start at £369.00. Overall, an excellent source for high quality garden furniture which will last a lifetime.

Catalogue: *A4, Catalogue, 30 pages, Colour, Free* Postal charges: *Varies with item* Delivery: *Royal Mail* Methods of Payment: *Cheque, Visa, Access / Mastercard*

CHURCHWOOD DESIGN
Fern Lea
Over Haddon
nr Bakewell
Derbyshire
DE4 1JE

Telephone:
0298 872422

KITCHEN FURNITURE

Churchwood Design make a wide range of kitchen furniture using traditional designs, especially for free-standing items such as dressers, larder cupboards, tables, etc.

They will also design whole fitted kitchens to order. Only top quality timber is used, which goes through a lengthy process of grading, de-nailing and cleaning before being put into use. Sourced from mills, schools and railway stations, the wood has slowly seasoned into a state where it is ideal for furniture-making.

Furniture

They have a plan and design service which is completely free and without obligation.

Catalogue: *A4, Catalogue, 4 pages, Colour, Free* Postal charges: *Varies with item* Delivery: *Royal Mail* Methods of Payment: *Cheque*

CLASSIC CHOICE
Unit 1
Brynmenyn Industrial
Estate
Bridgend
Glamorgan
CF32 9TD

Telephone:
0656 725111
Fax:
0656 725404

QUALITY UPHOLSTERED FURNITURE
Classic Choice has been making quality upholstered furniture for over ten years. Besides the attractive prices, which are kept down by coming direct from the manufacturer, the main advantage is the ease of ordering. There is a wide choice of fabrics – over 40 – and these can be interchanged between the models. In addition, there are matching fabrics for curtains and cushions so you can have a completely coordinated look.

For those anxious about ordering furniture by mail, there is a reassuring 21-day money-back and two year construction guarantee.

Catalogue: *Biannually, A4, Catalogue, 28 pages, Colour, Free* Postal charges: *Varies with item* Delivery: *In-house delivery* Methods of Payment: *Cheque, Postal Order, COD, Visa, Access / Mastercard*

CLOAKROOMS
Dodbroke House
Kingsbridge
Devon
TQ7 1NW

Telephone:
0548 853583

HANDCRAFTED FURNISHINGS FOR CLOAKROOMS, ETC
This small company produces traditional wooden furnishings such as clothes airers, racquet holders, boot and shoe racks and hat and coat racks. The designs are all simple and made by hand. They can be ordered in a number of different finishes.

The coat stand costs £34.50, while hat, shoe and boot racks are between £9.00 and £15.95. A clothes airer is £34.50, a boot jack £3.95 and coat hooks £6.95. There is also a shoe cleaning box for £34.50.

Catalogue: *Third A4, Brochure, B/W, Free* Postal charges: *Varies with item* Delivery: *Royal Mail* Methods of Payment: *Cheque, Visa, Access / Mastercard*

COLOUR YOUR WORLD
Sun Cottages
Higher Tremar
Cornwall
PL14 5HB

Telephone:
0579 343099

CHILDREN'S FURNITURE
Colour Your World handmake children's bedroom furniture from American ash with ash veneer side and back panels. For instance, the cupboard comprises three drawers, a toy cupboard and a wardrobe. All the furniture items are hand-painted using only water-based paints and varnishes which are also solvent free.

Furniture

Although there are eight base colours, the company offers a colour matching service to find the shade to suit the customer's requirements. Colour Your World personalises the furniture with a solid brass plaque with the child's name engraved on it. Colourful teddy bears and clowns in different poses adorn the furniture.

Catalogue: *A5, Brochure, 4 pages, Colour, Free* Postal charges: *Varies with item* Delivery: *Royal Mail* Methods of Payment: *Cheque, COD*

CUBESTORE
58 Pembroke Road
London
W8

Telephone:
081 994 6016

MODULAR FURNITURE

Cubestore have specialised in shelving and storage systems for home and work for over 25 years. They produce cubes, oblongs, drawers, record units, cupboards and wardrobes, as well as special units, trestles and tops to make desks and so on.

The super-slim aluminium wall shelving comes with neat brackets and made-to-measure shelves. There are also free-standing, stacking shelf units in a range of sizes, all of which have adjustable shelves.

Finishes include white, black, grey and real beech veneer. White cubes start from £14.00, beech cubes from £26.00. Wall shelving is about £40.00, while free-standing shelf units are from under £20.00

Catalogue: *Annually, A5, Catalogue, 32 pages, Colour, Free* Postal charges: *Varies with item* Delivery: *Courier* Methods of Payment: *Cheque, Postal Order, Visa, Access / Mastercard*

DAVID ARBUS RATTAN FURNITURE
The Granary
Railway Hill
Barham
Canterbury
Kent

Telephone:
0227 831540

HANDMADE FURNITURE

All of David Arbus's furniture is made to order. The catalogue shows just a selection of pieces, most of which are line drawings. His workshop can be visited by appointment, or you can arrange for him to visit you with his portfolio.

Dining chairs cost between £80.00 and £140.00; dining tables are priced from between £150 and £400.00; bedheads cost from £60.00 to £100.00. If you have a penchant for rattan furniture, David Arbus's work looks skilful and is completed with great care.

Catalogue: *A4, Leaflet, 6 pages, Colour and B/W, Free* Postal charges: *Varies with item* Delivery: *By arrangement* Methods of Payment: *Cheque*

Furniture

EMPEROR CLOCKS CO
Emperor House
Lyndhurst Road
Ascot
Berkshire
SL5 9DW

Telephone:
0800 252026
Fax:
0344 26115

CLOCKS
Emperor make an impressive range of reproduction clocks which can either be order fully-assembled or as kits. These are said to be easy to put together and not require any particular skills.

Their brochure features everything from small carriage clocks through wall-mounted clocks to large grandfather clocks. There is a great deal of choice of faces, dials and brass fittings, so you really can get what you want. In case you think that building a clock is beyond you, there is even a free video to reassure customers as to just how easy it is!

They also sell reproduction tables, bureaus and cabinets. Prices range from a few hundred up to several thousand pounds.

Catalogue: *A4/A5, Brochures, Colour, Free* Postal charges: *Varies with item* Delivery: *Royal Mail* Methods of Payment: *Cheque, Visa, Access / Mastercard, American Express, Diners Club*

ESSENTIAL ITEMS
Church House
Plungar
Notts
NG13 0JA

Telephone:
0949 61172/0602
456252
Fax:
0602 843254

STOOLS AND OTTOMANS
Essential Items is one of the country's most established companies manufacturing and designing 'made to order' stools and ottomans. These come in many different styles and sizes, suitable for every room in the home. They have built up an enviable reputation for personal attention to customer's needs and can help with advice on fabric and tapestries.

A 115cm × 41cm × 33cm stool covered in calico is £170.50, with the slightly larger model of 138cm × 48cm × 33cm coming in at £185.00. There is a charge of £10.00 for using customers' own material. A Filing Ottoman 56cm × 48cm × 53cm, retails for £195.00.

Catalogue: *Annually, A4, Brochure, Colour and B/W, Free* Postal charges: *Varies with item* Delivery: *Parcelforce* Methods of Payment: *Cheque, Postal Order, COD, Visa, Access / Mastercard*

FOAMPLAN RUBBER & PLASTICS LTD
164 Holloway Road
London
N7 8DD

Telephone:
071 609 8569
Fax:
071 700 0275

FOAM FOR MATTRESSES/CUSHIONS
Foamplan have a wide range of quality latex and foam products in assorted sizes. These are suitable for most cushions, mattresses and upholstery. Their informative catalogue lists many different sizes and shapes of their product, but if you can't find what you're looking for they're happy to custom-cut to measurements you supply.

Their Profile Deluxe Super Soft Overlay looks likely to give you a sound night's sleep. While they are

Furniture

willing to cut the material to any size you wish, the standard range goes from £39.95 for a 36" mattress size to £59.95 for 60".

Catalogue: *A4, Leaflet, 12 pages, Colour, Free* Postal charges: *Varies with item* Delivery: *Royal Mail* Methods of Payment: *Cheque, Visa, Access / Mastercard*

GOLDPINE OF SUSSEX LTD
Hackhurst Lane
Lower Dicker
E Sussex
BN27 4BW

Telephone:
0323 845353
Fax:
0323 844053

SOLID PINE BEDROOM AND DINING ROOM FURNITURE

Goldpine offers a large range of handcrafted solid pine dining and bedroom furniture. Every piece is individually made with dovetailed drawers and hand-carving as standard features. They also offer a number of options, so any decor can be matched.

All the furniture is fully guaranteed and you can even enjoy your new furniture for 21 days before deciding to keep it. Goldpine offers you very low prices all the year round, such as a 4'5" bed for £299, a twelve drawer chest for £499, a rug chest for £199 and a triple wardrobe for only £795.

Catalogue: *Annually, A4, Brochure, 16 pages, Colour, Free* Postal charges: *Varies with item* Delivery: *In-house delivery* Methods of Payment: *Cheque, Postal Order, COD, Stage Payments, Visa, Access / Mastercard*

HADDONCRAFT LTD
The Forge House
East Haddon
Northampton
NN6 8DB

Telephone:
0604 770711
Fax:
0604 770027

BESPOKE JOINERY

Haddoncraft has been formed by Haddonstone Ltd to make full use of the skills possessed by their craftsmen at Brixworth, Northamptonshire. Haddonstone themselves are world-renowned for high quality stonework, true in detail and spirit to classical designs and principles. This same knowledge and understanding has been developed by Haddoncraft to provide a range of complementary services for both private and professional clients.

An example of their collection is the Acanthus Table Lamp for £245.00 and the Elizabethan Smoker's Stand for £325.00. Practically any item from the collection can be finished in reproduction bronze and all enquiries are subject to an individual quotation.

Catalogue: *A4, Catalogue, 8 pages, Colour, Free* Postal charges: *Varies with item* Delivery: *Royal Mail* Methods of Payment: *Cheque*

Furniture

HAMLET FURNITURE LTD
McMullen Rd
Darlington
DL1 1XY

Telephone:
0325 381811

SOLID WOOD FURNITURE

Every item of furniture in the Hamlet range is made from solid oak or pine, from carcasses to backs of units and all drawer components. Every item except beds is supplied rigidly constructed, ready for immediate use.

The range includes chairs, tables, dressers, corner units, wardrobes, bookcases and beds. Fitted kitchens are also made to order, and chairs and stools can be upholstered in your own choice of fabric.

The Hamlet craftsmen take tremendous pride in their work and fit each drawer, handle and hinge by hand to ensure that everything looks right and works perfectly.

Catalogue: *A4, Catalogue, 24 pages, Colour, Free* Postal charges: *Varies with item* Delivery: *Royal Mail* Methods of Payment: *Cheque, Postal Order, Visa, Access / Mastercard*

HOLLOWAYS
Lower Court
Suckley
Worcestershire
WR6 5DE

Telephone:
0886 884754

CONSERVATORY FURNITURE AND GARDEN ORNAMENTS

Holloways are a family-run business located in rural Worcestershire and one of the UK leaders in conservatory furnishings and garden ornaments.

They have many different styles of seating and dining furniture for conservatories, many of which are available in customised colours, sizes and fabrics. They can also help with blinds, flooring, heating, fans and other practical aspects of owning a conservatory. Much of the furniture is English willow and rattan (Jakarta chaise longue in rattan, £310.00), and fabrics to cover them are available from designers such as Monkwell, Romo, Sanderson and Designers Guild.

There is also a wide range of garden ornamentation from wall fountains to wirework jardinieres and earthenware wall plaques.

Catalogue: *Annually, A5, Catalogue, 24 pages, Colour, Free* Postal charges: *£2.95* Delivery: *Royal Mail* Methods of Payment: *Cheque, Postal Order, Visa, Access / Mastercard*

Furniture

JARABOSKY ORIGINAL RAILWAY SLEEPER FURNITURE
Old Station Yard
Exley Lane
Elland
West Yorkshire
HX5 0SW

Telephone:
0422 311922
Fax:
0422 885655

HARDWOOD FURNITURE MADE FROM OBSOLETE SOUTH AFRICAN RAILWAY SLEEPERS

Jarabosky have been marketing their exclusive range of original furniture for six years and it is probably one of the most exciting and original in the UK today: it is all made out of old railway sleepers.

Beautifully handcrafted, the wood is from 300- to 600-year-old exotic hardwood timbers which have been retrieved from Colonial African railroads. This recycling is a conscious effort to help preserve the environment, but also produces wonderful furniture. There is an extensive standard range for the bedroom, dining room and garden, but the company also offers a bespoke option. Each piece is completely heat, water and alcohol proof. All glass is 6mm and toughened.

A 48"-long linen chest in Jarrah timber costs £525.00, a 25" square wafer coffee table in Rhodesian Teak, £295.00, an 8-seater Chateau dining table with six high-back dining chairs and two carvers £3990.00, and a hat rack a more modest £30.00.

Catalogue: *A4, Brochure, 12 pages, Colour, Free* Postal charges: *Varies with item* Delivery: *In-house delivery* Methods of Payment: *Cheque, COD, Stage Payments, Visa, Access / Mastercard*

K RESTORATIONS
2A Ferdinand Place
London
NW1 8EE

Telephone:
071 482 4021

FURNITURE RESTORATION

K Restorations carry out a re-leathering service. All you have to do is measure the leather that needs replacing and choose the new colour.

Prices start at £27.00 for a 12" × 12" section, and increase to £52.00 for a 36" × 18" piece. Their leaflets include copies of many satisfied customers' letters, along with the odd favourable review from magazines and newspapers. So, if you think your desk needs resurfacing, never fear – these are the people to go to.

Catalogue: *A4, Leaflets, 7 pages, B/W, Free* Postal charges: *Varies with item* Delivery: *Royal Mail* Methods of Payment: *Cheque, Visa, Access / Mastercard*

Furniture

LAURA ASHLEY BY POST
PO Box 5
Newtown Powys
SY16 1WW

Telephone:
0800 868 100

HOME FURNISHINGS
Laura Ashley have shops all round the world but also offer a mail order service. This concentrates on items for the home rather than clothes, but the style is still the same. There are covers, cushions, furniture, curtains, blinds, wallpapers, tiles, table linen, bathroom fittings and bedlinen. In short, all you need for the home.

A lampshade sells for £17.00, cushion covers for £4.95 and a Denbigh chair for £575.00. A single Pinehurst bedframe is £345.00, while wallpaper is £8.95 per roll.

The fashion catalogue features T-shirts, dresses, trousers, leggings, wrap-over skirts, shorts and jumpers, as well as shoes, belts and socks, all shot in exotic locations and shown clearly on models.

Woven espradilles cost £19.95; cotton jersey T-shirt, £12.95; printed dungarees, £44.95; printed swimsuit, £24.95; cotton jersey skirt, £19.95.

Catalogue: *Biannually, A4, Catalogue, 43 pages, Colour, Laura Ashley by post catalogue is free, but 176 page home furnishings book is available at only £3.50; please phone.* Postal charges: *Varies with item* Delivery: *Royal Mail* Methods of Payment: *Cheque, Postal Order, Visa, Access / Mastercard*

LLOYD LOOM DIRECT
PO Box 4
Holbeach
Spalding
Lincs.
PE12 ODS

Telephone:
0406 365288

BRITISH-MADE WOVEN FIBRE FURNITURE
Made in the UK in a way which is faithful to the originals of American inventor, Marshall B. Lloyd, Lloyd Loom is neither cane, nor wicker, nor rattan. Unlike these, it is immune to splitting, cracking or woodworm.

The company weaves its own fibre and steam bends its own solid beechwood frames. The woven fibre used is spun brown Kraft paper woven with paper wrapped round wire. It is this wire which gives the furniture its prodigious strength and durability. The process is completed by sizing with glue and then spraying with three coats of lacquer, which seals both frame and weave for long life.

The leaflet features the Cambridge Skirted Chair, £160.00; the Cambridge Table, £80.00; Linen Basket, £85.00; Popular Armchair, £140.00; Amy Armchair, £145.00; and the Stamford Dining Chair, £115.00. All are available in four colours: natural, milk white, holly green or Ontario blue.

Catalogue: *A5, Leaflet, 4 pages, Colour, Free* Postal charges: *£10.00* Delivery: *Royal Mail* Methods of Payment: *Cheque, Postal Order, Visa, Access / Mastercard*

Furniture

LYNPLAN
43 Imperial Way
Croydon Airport
Croydon
CR9 4LP

Telephone:
081 681 1831
Fax:
081 680 5727

FURNITURE COVERS AND FABRICS

Lynplan offer a comprehensive range of well-priced soft furnishings as well as a couple of useful furniture repair services. If, for instance, you want to give your furniture a new look, you can use their Tailored cover service which is available by mail.

If you feel your favourite sofa or armchair needs something more radical, you may want to consider their Re-Upholstery and Renovation Service. This is available throughout mainland Britain for any make of furniture.

Lynplan have one price list for Parker Knoll, Clintique, Ercol, G-Plan and Minty furniture, and another for all other makes, so the chances are they will cover your pieces, as it were.

Catalogue: *A4, Catalogue, 8 pages, Colour, Free* Postal charges: *Varies with item* Delivery: *Royal Mail* Methods of Payment: *Cheque*

M C REPRODUCTIONS
16 Queens Road
Petersfield
Hants
GU32 3BD

Telephone:
0730 823278
Fax:
042860 7005

OAK FURNITURE

M C Reproductions produce a range of solid English oak tables. All tables use traditional pegged mortise and tenon joints, and arrive fully assembled. The finish is a hand-rubbed, antiqued and distressed medium oak tone, but golden light oak or dark oak are also available.

Coffee tables measure 101cm × 61cm × 46cm and end tables 61cm × 61cm × 46cm. Coffee tables cost £245.00; with a shelf £345.00. End tables cost £155.00; with a shelf £195.00. Kitchen tables are also available at £295.00.

Catalogue: *A4, Leaflet, 8 pages, Colour, Free* Postal charges: *Varies with item* Delivery: *Royal Mail* Methods of Payment: *Cheque, Postal Order, Visa, Access / Mastercard*

MANOR BARN
34 Main Street
Addingham
Ilkley
W. Yorks
LS29 0PJ

Telephone:
0943 830176
Fax:
0943 830991

HANDCRAFTED FURNITURE

Manor Barn, based near Ilkley in West Yorkshire, specialise in making copies of classical 17th and 18th century solid oak furniture in their Jacobus Collection. They actively invite customers to visit their showroom, not only to discuss particular requirements, but also to spend time sightseeing in the area.

Many of the items are offered in pine as well as oak, which reduces the price to about half. Manor Barn will also supply the furniture at bare wood stage for the customer to finish at home and they will supply a Jacobus finishing pack, containing exactly the same materials as their craftsmen use.

Furniture

MARKS & SPENCER HOME SHOPPING
P O Box 288
Warrington
Cheshire
WA1 4SS

Telephone:
0925 851100

Fax:
0925 812485

Catalogue: *A5, Catalogue, 8 pages, Colour, Free* Postal charges: *Varies with item* Delivery: *In-house delivery, Courier* Methods of Payment: *Cheque, Visa, Access / Mastercard*

HOME FURNISHINGS

Marks & Spencer are synonymous with high quality and excellent service. They now offer a home shopping service which carries this through to mail order, although the range is strictly for the home – no clothes or food.

The lavishly illustrated guide has wonderful ideas for every room in the house and covers everything from the overall design, with wall coverings and upholstery, to the fine detail such as candlesticks and napkins.

Many of the items reflect the value that often accompanies Marks & Spencer goods, with an 18 piece tea-service at only £40.00. However, it is a catalogue for all tastes and pockets and also includes a dining table in yew for £1,500.00.

Catalogue: *Biannually, A3, Catalogue, 146 pages, Colour, Free to Marks & Spencer card holders . In other cases £1.00* Postal charges: *Varies with item* Delivery: *In-house delivery* Methods of Payment: *Cheque, Postal Order*

NEW CONCEPT
Cox Hall Lane
Tattingstone
Ipswich
IP9 2NS

Telephone:
0473 328006

TREATMENT COUCHES

New Concept is a company of designer craftsmen who specialise in the production of portable treatment couches and accessories for therapists and chiropractors. The timber used for the couches comes from renewable sources and all upholstery is fire resistant.

The range includes the 'Professional', which has an adjustable leg height system and is available with multi-position lifting back rest, face hole and insert (from £259.35). The 'Companion', a fully portable massage chair, weighs just 12.5kg and costs £285.00.

Catalogue: *Annually, A4, Catalogue, 9 pages, Colour, Free* Postal charges: *Varies with item* Delivery: *In-house delivery* Methods of Payment: *Cheque, Postal Order, Visa, Access / Mastercard*

Furniture

NORFOLK FENDER SEATS
Elder Farm
Grimston
King's Lynn
Norfolk
PE32 1BJ

Telephone:
0485 600203

FENDER SEATS

Norfolk Fender Seats offer to drop by and measure up your fireplace free of charge. You can also take the opportunity to study samples of the leather they use in their seats. Each seat is unique, being made to order by local craftsmen.

If you fancy a warm seat by the fire, you can choose from brushed or burnished steel with an assortment of ornamentation – brass studs, for instance. Your seat really will be designed to fit in with your room and existing decor, so there are no hard and fast rules. Prices start at just below £500.00

Catalogue: *A4, Leaflet, 4, Colour and B/W,* Postal charges: *Varies with item* Delivery: *In-house delivery* Methods of Payment: *Cheque*

OAK DESIGN
The Croft
48 Winkfield Road
Windsor
Berks
SL4 4AF

Telephone:
0753 830210
Fax:
0753 830210

OAK FURNITURE

A member of the Guild of Master Craftsmen, Oak Design produce a range of high-quality furniture. The ever-widening range now includes Welsh dressers and reproduction coffee tables, as well as tables and chairs.

Many of these elegant pieces, with their pleasing simplicity, can be supplied in a choice of woods, from American red and white oak to European oak, ash and beech, and in a variety of finishes. A unique custom finishing service even enables the furniture to be matched to existing kitchen fittings.

The price range reflects the variety of styles and sizes, from a 4-seater trestle table at £210.00 to a 12-seater traditional farmhouse table at £950.00. Chairs are from £69.00 to £210.00.

Catalogue: *A4, Brochure, 4 pages plus inserts, Colour, Free* Postal charges: *Varies with item* Delivery: *Courier* Methods of Payment: *Cheque*

OPTIONS BEDROOMS LIMITED
Unit B
Roan Industrial Estate
Mortimer Road
Mitcham
Surrey
CR4 3HS

Telephone:
081 685 1525

FITTED FURNITURE

The catalogue features fitted furniture for every room in the house, direct from the Options factory, designed for the customer's individual needs by their team of experts.

By selling direct from the factory and cutting out the middle-man, Options can keep prices down and get your new furniture to you as quickly as possible.

Catalogue: *A4, Catalogue, 24 pages, Colour, Free* Postal charges: *Varies with item* Delivery: *In-house delivery* Methods of Payment: *Cheque, Visa, Access / Mastercard*

Furniture

ORIGINALS FROM THE LANE
73 North Lane
Rustington
West Sussex
BN16 3PP

Telephone:
0903 783598

HAND-PAINTED FURNITURE
A small company, Originals From The Lane design and make individual pieces of furniture. These are available hand-painted, waxed or in a primer finish for you to paint yourself.

They have a special collection for nurseries and children's rooms as well as a standard range which includes a 12" square table in primer for £47.00. A bedside cabinet with a hand-painted finish costs £141.00. They will also make pieces to order, such as a wardrobe in painted pine with hand-decorated panels for £899.00. Or there is a tall pine bookcase, painted and distressed with gilded details for £450.00. You can even commission your own special piece, but whichever way you choose, you can be sure that Originals furniture is unique.

Catalogue: *A4, Brochure, Variable number of pages, Colour, Free* Postal charges: *Varies with item* Delivery: *Parcelforce, Courier* Methods of Payment: *Cheque, Postal Order, Visa, Access / Mastercard*

ORYX TRADING
33 Cornwall Gardens
London
SW7 4AP

Telephone:
071 938 2045
Fax:
071 937 9087

GARDEN FURNITURE AND UMBRELLAS
This company operates as an import export broker, specialising in garden furniture. Taking its inspiration from the days of the British Empire, there is a limited range of sturdy hardwood furniture and canvas canopy umbrellas.

The fashionable umbrellas come in two sizes, 9' 10" and 12' 4", and include both a concrete base and metal spike for soft or hard surface fixing. The smaller model is £295 and the larger £595. Expensive but delightful!

Catalogue: *A4, Catalogue, 9 pages, Colour, Free* Postal charges: *Varies with item* Delivery: *By arrangement* Methods of Payment: *Cheque, Postal Order, Visa, Access / Mastercard*

PERKINS
105 Ack Lane East
Bramhall
Cheshire
SK7 2AB

Telephone:
061 440 9860

RADIATOR COVERS
This catalogue specialises in decorative radiator grilles and surrounds. There are three basic styles to suit modern or traditional interiors. The covers are made from wood or MDF and painted, although there is an option to have a solid wood cover and metallic grille. Covers are delivered with fittings or can be fitted by the company.

There are clear instructions for measuring your radiators and a 3' cover starts at £162.00. If you are really good at DIY, they can be bought in kit form for

Furniture

self-assembly for around £100.00. Radiator shelves are also available, with or without a built-in towel rail.

Catalogue: *A4, Catalogue, 4 pages plus inserts, Colour, Free* Postal charges: *£20.00 per cover* Delivery: *By arrangement* Methods of Payment: *Cheque, Postal Order, Visa, Access / Mastercard*

PLUMBS
Brookhouse Mill
Old Lancaster Lane
Preston
PR1 7PZ

Telephone:
0772 50811
Fax:
0772 561328

LOOSE FURNITURE COVERS

25 years of experience have helped Plumbs develop their easy care, drip-dry fabric: Qualitex. They use it in their own, mostly floral, printed designs.

Plumbs have everything you need to give your three-piece suite a new lease of life; they claim they can provide covers for any shape or size of furniture. A Queen Anne 2-seater sofa cover in 'Tiger Lily' or 'Diana' design will set you back £73.14 – a further £12.19 if you want a frilled valance.

In addition to covers, Plumbs offer coordinating made-to-measure 'high-fashion' curtains, pelmets, tie-backs and scatter cushions.

Catalogue: *A4, Catalogue, 32 pages, Colour, Free* Postal charges: *£2.25* Delivery: *Royal Mail* Methods of Payment: *Cheque, Postal Order, Visa, Access / Mastercard*

PRETTY CRAFTY
10 The Seekings
Whitnash
Leamington Spa
Warwickshire
CV31 2SH

Telephone:
0926 332208

HANDMADE FURNITURE

Pretty Crafty items are made from solid hardwoods, mainly beech and mahogany, and are all hand-crafted. The small range includes stylish footstools with antique-effect metal studs. A rectangular stool with Queen Anne-style or turned legs, a 13" × 18" pad and 9" legs is £68.00. Self-assembly stools are also available for slightly less. A firescreen with 'Picture-to-view' space of 16" × 18" is £85.00, while a turned hatstand costs £31.00.

An unusual gift idea is Pretty Crafty's Pine Hatstand Kit. This comes in pine and is complete with instructions and tips on how to create artistic finishing touches – it can also be gift-wrapped on request and costs £16.99.

Catalogue: *A4, Brochure, 6 pages, B/W, Free* Postal charges: *Varies with item* Delivery: *By arrangement* Methods of Payment: *Cheque, Postal Order*

Furniture

RAINFORD
Rainford House Of Elegance Ltd.
Wentworth Street
Birdwell
Barnsley
S70 5UN

Telephone:
0226 350360
Fax:
0226 350279

INTERIOR DESIGN

Rainford Interiors offer high quality period products at remarkably inexpensive prices. All of the products are manufactured by the company, who keep a close eye on the quality, and the pieces include both modern and antique styles.

The brochure advertises furniture to suit a particular room or style and examples are shown from pictures of previously decorated rooms. They offer full room interior decorating or just a few pieces to decorate an already furnished room (marble hearths £105, ceiling domes, dado rails and niches). All of the products are plaster-cast by Rainford Interiors.

Catalogue: *A4, Brochure, 3 pages, Colour and B/W, Free* Postal charges: *Free* Delivery: *Royal Mail* Methods of Payment: *Cheque, Visa, Access / Mastercard*

ROCKINGHAM FENDER SEATS
Grange Farm
Thorney
Peterborough
PE6 OPJ

Telephone:
0563 770308
Fax:
0563 270512

FENDER SEATS

Rockingham make a variety of fender seats for the fireplace. These include traditional club fenders, custom-made to your requirements; standard size 'Manor House' club fenders and low-level fenders, as well as fire curtains and fireside accessories.

Fire Guards and screens are 'child-proof', with an opening top to allow easy access to your fire. At 32" wide × 16" deep × 30" high, they cost £109.00 each. The company's blacksmiths are able to make other designs of fire-guards, including three-sided or totally enclosed in burnished/black steel or brass.

Catalogue: *A3, Leaflet, 8 pages, Colour and B/W, Free* Postal charges: *Varies with item* Delivery: *In-house delivery* Methods of Payment: *Cheque, Visa, Access / Mastercard*

SAXON LEATHER UPHOLSTERY LTD
Eldon Street
Bolton
Lancs
BL2 2HX

Telephone:
0204-365377
Fax:
0204-387554

TRADITIONAL LEATHER FURNITURE

Using only the finest British materials, Saxon Leather Upholstery have developed a range of elegant handcrafted furniture in more than 20 distinctive styles. Quality is high and each piece beatifully finished.

Colour match is guaranteed, as each order is cut from the same batch of leather. A range of over 50 colours is available, including plains, pastels and antique effects. All pieces come with a 2-year guarantee. Orders over £500.00 are available on 24 months interest-free credit, which you may need with these prices. A 'Tudor' stool costs £75.00, an art deco-style 'Cotswold' chair £622.00, and a classic 'Chesterfield' 3-seater bed-settee £1,100.00.

Furniture

**SIMON HORN
FURNITURE LIMITED**
117–121 Wandsworth
Bridge Road
London
SW6 2TP

Telephone:
071 731 1279
Fax:
071 736 3522

Catalogue: *A4, Catalogue, 20 pages, Colour, Free* Postal charges: *Varies with item* Delivery: *In-house delivery* Methods of Payment: *Cheque*

CLASSICAL AND ANTIQUE FURNITURE

Simon Horn Furniture Limited was founded in 1982 and offers a unique collection of furniture recreated from a variety of designs from museums, libraries, antique pieces and contemporary prints. The catalogue offers a wide range of furniture from four poster beds (£2,485 for the smallest), wardrobes and chairs to commodes, curtains and bedside tables.

The furniture specialists and makers are French and English in nationality and therefore Simon Horn offers continental furniture as well. The furniture is made from beechwood, cherrywood, chestnut, mahogany, oak, rosewood or walnut, and once a bed has been purchased, Simon Horn offers made-to-measure mattresses and divans to go with them.

Catalogue: *A4, Brochure, 7 pages plus leaflet, Colour, Free* Postal charges: *Varies with item* Delivery: *Royal Mail* Methods of Payment: *Cheque*

SMALLCOMBE CLOCKS
Towers Road Industrial
Estate
Rectory Road
Grays
Essex
RM17 6ST

Telephone:
0375 377181
Fax:
0375390286

VARIOUS TYPES OF CLOCKS

Smallcombe Clocks are renowned for their superior handmade timepieces. Their brochure offers floor-standing longcase clocks (£595.00–£2,350.00) available in mahogany or oak finish. Your clock will be delivered by the company for no extra charge. All of the clocks are fully guaranteed with a money-back guarantee.

The insides of the clocks are made by a leading German manufacturer, Hermle, and the outside casework is finished by Smallcombe Clocks. Every case is based on a classic design with the finish showing great detail and precision.

Catalogue: *A4, Brochure, 5 pages, Colour and B/W, Free* Postal charges: *Free* Delivery: *Royal Mail* Methods of Payment: *Cheque, Visa, Access / Mastercard*

Furniture

SOFAS AND SOFABEDS
Branches include
219 Tottenham Court
Road
London
W1P 9AF

Telephone:
071 636 6001

SOFAS, CHAIRS AND SOFABEDS

This well-known high street chain offers a wonderful range of sofas and sofabeds of all sizes. The catalogue shows over 50 different styles of sofas as well as armchairs. These start at just over £300, with sofabeds from under £700. The covering service allows customers to choose from a wide range of over 10,000 fabrics or to provide their own.

Delivery can be within six to eight weeks and is free within ten miles of any of their shops (a full list of these is given in the catalogue).

Catalogue: *Third A4, Catalogue, 34 pages, Colour, Free* Postal charges: *Varies with item* Delivery: *In-house delivery* Methods of Payment: *Cheque, Visa, Access / Mastercard*

THE ANTIQUE BEDSTEAD COMPANY LTD
Baddow Antique Centre
The Bringy
Great Baddow
Chelmsford
Essex
CM2 7JW

Telephone:
0245 471317

RESTORED BEDSTEADS

The Antique Bedstead Company has around 300 restored Victorian brass and iron bedsteads of every conceivable style and size. These wonderfully crafted beds are not only beautiful pieces of period furniture but also genuine investments for the future.

From rare brass bedsteads with cast fittings and brass scroll work, to stove enamelled white and black iron bedsteads, the range is truly amazing. The company also supplies quality mattresses.

A typical 4' 6" cottage bedstead from 1865 costs £565.00. If customers cannot visit the showroom at Great Baddow, the company will deliver anywhere in the country, and payment will only be requested upon the customer's approval.

Catalogue: *A4, Brochure, 24 pages, B/W, Free* Postal charges: *Varies with item* Delivery: *In-house delivery* Methods of Payment: *Cheque*

THE HEATED MIRROR CO LTD
Sherston
Wilts
SN16 0LW

Telephone:
0666 840003
Fax:
0666 840001

MIRRORS

Heated mirrors have the advantage of not steaming up. The company's mirrors work off the lighting circuit, the same way as a strip-light over a washbasin, and have been tested to a European standard which includes subjecting the mirror to water-spray for ten minutes to ensure it is safe if splashed.

The mirrors are quick and easy to install and are available in a range of frames including antique gold and pine. Prices start at £146.88.

Catalogue: *A4, Leaflet, 4 pages, Colour, Free* Postal charges: *Free* Delivery: *Parcelforce* Methods of Payment: *Cheque, Visa, Access / Mastercard*

Furniture

THE HEVENINGHAM COLLECTION
Peacock Cottage
Church Hill
Nether Wallop
Stockbridge
Hampshire
SO20 8EY

Telephone:
0264 781124
Fax:
0264 781124

IRON FURNITURE
The Heveningham Collection by Annie Eadie is a range of very elegant wrought-iron furniture for both interior and exterior use. The collection is based on old Italian designs and would suit the most stately of homes.

All items are supplied in black or dark green metal paint finish with cream natural canvas or, for external use, showerproof fabric cushions. Alternative fabrics are available at extra cost.

The range includes a chaise longue, dining tables, chairs, Versailles tubs and candlesticks. Dining chairs are available without arms for £330.00 or £370.00 with arms. Stools start at £385.00 and armchairs at £545.00.

Catalogue: *A4, Catalogue, 8 pages, Colour, Free* Postal charges: *Free* Delivery: *By arrangement* Methods of Payment: *Cheque, Postal Order, Visa, Access / Mastercard*

THE IRON DESIGN COMPANY
Summer Carr Farm
Thornton Le Moor
Northallerton
North Yorkshire
DL6 3SG

Telephone:
0609 778143
Fax:
0609 778846

IRON FURNITURE
This attractive glossy brochure features a selection of unusual yet classically designed metal furniture and accessories. Handcrafted in a variety of paint finishes, such as smithy black and verdigris, the products are designed for both indoor and outdoor use. All are very attractive and fashionable. The company will also undertake bespoke commissions and adaptations to its standard range.

Prices are reasonable, ranging from £16.00–£18.00 for a single candlestick to £395.00 for a reclining sofa. The range also includes weather vanes, gates, fencing, lamps, firegrates, curtain rails and finials, as well as tables and mirrors.

Catalogue: *Third A4, Catalogue, 26 pages, Colour, Free* Postal charges: *Varies with item* Delivery: *Parcelforce* Methods of Payment: *Cheque, Postal Order*

THE MANCHESTER FUTON COMPANY
33 Blossom Street
Ancoats
Manchester
M4 6AJ

Telephone:
061 236 8196
Fax:
061 773 6029

FUTONS AND BASES
From a workshop in the heart of Manchester comes a little bit of the East. The Futon Company can provide everything you need for a good night's sleep and turn it into an attractive piece of furniture by day.

The futons come in a stunning range of covers, complemented by a variety of bases in a range of finishes. And if you still can't find what you want, the company will make bases, futons and covers to order.

Prices seem very reasonable, with futons starting at £70.00 and bases at £40.00.

Furniture

Catalogue: *A5, Brochure, 12 pages, B/W, Free* Postal charges: *Varies with item* Delivery: *In-house delivery* Methods of Payment: *Cheque, Postal Order, Visa, Access / Mastercard, American Express, Diners Club*

THE ODD CHAIR COMPANY
66 Derby Road
Longridge
Lancs
PR3 3FE

Telephone:
0772 786262
Fax:
0772 784290

CHAIRS AND SOFAS

The Odd Chair Company offer a large selection of late 19th century and early 20th century upholstered furniture. They guarantee always to have over 400 pieces of comfortable furniture in stock, including fireside chairs, sofas and chesterfields.

At the same address, is the Knole Sofa Company, dealers in old and new Knole sofas – all made with springs and feather cushions. The Hever Castle Knole Sofa (38" high × 36" wide × 72" long) costs £1,250.00, and comes complete in the fabric of your choice. The Schoolbred Chesterfield Sofa (28" high × 38" wide × 80" long), originally designed for the Schoolbred Furniture Company in 1874 and now copied by the Knole Sofa Company, costs £1,400.

Catalogue: *Third A4, Leaflet, Colour, Free* Postal charges: *Free* Delivery: *In-house delivery* Methods of Payment: *Cheque, Visa, Access / Mastercard*

THE RADIATOR COVER COMPANY
167 Lower Richmond Road
Mortlake
London
SW14 7HX

Telephone:
081 392 2058

RADIATOR COVERS

The Radiator Cover Company produce 'Flexiform', a range of covers that can be cut to measure for your requirements. Prices are based on overall length and grille choice; the cover can be up to 36" high and 15" deep, with the base matched to your skirting height, all at no extra cost.

The woven mesh design cover comes in 14 different styles, in either polished brass or painted metal. The Regency collection offers covers handmade from solid brass, with rosettes at alternating joints. Prices for the covers start at £156.00 for 3ft and increase according to length and style.

Catalogue: *A4, Leaflet, 6 pages, Colour, Free* Postal charges: *Varies with item* Delivery: *Royal Mail* Methods of Payment: *Cheque, Visa, Access / Mastercard*

Furniture

THE SUMMERFIELD COLLECTION
Pixley House
Pixley
Ledbury
Herts
HR8 2QB

Telephone:
0531 670345

FURNITURE
The Summerfield Collection features handcrafted English furniture, especially stools. Any size of stool can be supplied, with a choice of Queen Anne or ball and claw legs. Legs can be finished to match existing furniture. Heights of stools range from 12" to 20". No varnishes or polyurethane sprays are used, and the filling for cushions is normally foam. Fire resistant horsehair is, however, now available.

Prices range from £90.00 for a stool 12" wide by 36" long to £183.00 for a stool 24" wide and 46" long. All legs are the same price, regardless of height.

Catalogue: *A4, Leaflet, 2, Colour, Free* Postal charges: *Varies with item* Delivery: *In-house delivery* Methods of Payment: *Cheque, Postal Order, Visa, Access / Mastercard*

TREEHUGGER DESIGN
The Sawmills
Upper Froyle
Alton
Hampshire
GU34 4JJ

Telephone:
0420 22615
Fax:
0420 22615

SOLID OAK TABLES
Bespoke cabinetmakers, Treehugger Design, will adapt their furniture to suit your needs. They provide a useful Design Pack from which you can select the style of furniture you want. It shows basic designs of solid oak tables, dressers, bureaus and chairs. These then come with options for features like legs, drawers and rails, so you end up with something both unique and useful to you. Prices range from £50.00 for the top area of a table plus £40.00 for each leg, to £280.00 for a rocking chair.

Their complete brochure is not yet available, but if you would like photographs or drawings of specific styles or pieces, give them a call.

Catalogue: *A4, Brochure, 12 pages, B/W, Free* Postal charges: *Varies with item* Delivery: *By arrangement* Methods of Payment: *Cheque*

TRESKE
Station Works
Thirsk
North Yorkshire
YO7 4NY

Telephone:
0845 522770
Fax:
0845 522692

SOLID WOOD FURNITURE
Treske make the widest range of furniture offered by any UK manufacturer. Personal callers can inspect it at their outlets in North Yorkshire and London. They pride themselves in retaining complete control over the woods used in their products, buying, sawing and curing everything they use.

Individual items of furniture range from upholstered chairs (Bowback Carver, £199.00) and wooden chairs (Folding chair, £45.00) to shelving starting at £129.00. They also sell corner cabinets starting at £392.00.

Fitted kitchens come in two styles, an attractive

Furniture

Sycamore version and a more traditional Painted Kitchen. Installation is only made after you've been visited by one of their designers.

Catalogue: *A4, Catalogue, 40 pages, Colour, £1.00* Postal charges: *Varies with item* Delivery: *In-house delivery* Methods of Payment: *Cheque, Postal Order, Visa, Access / Mastercard*

TRICIA CLARK DESIGNS
2 Broomes Barn
Pilsley
Bakewell
Derbys
DE45 1PF

Telephone:
0246 583386
Fax:
0246 583386

CHILDREN'S FURNITURE
Tricia Clark Designs produce a range of wooden products for the home. All items are handmade using non-toxic paints and inks screen-painted on wood from managed forests.

The TCD Range, ideal for the nursery or child's room, includes coat pegs (£8.50), mirrors, bookshelves (£19.90), toy boxes and treasure boxes. Designs include a teddy bear and dancing frog. The Beatrix Potter Range is similar, but decorated with favourite characters such as Peter Rabbit and Jemima Puddleduck.

The Greengage Range, suitable for use throughout the home, has hanging shelves, mirrors and a linen box (£118.25). One-off commissions and other items of occasional furniture are also available, all of which can be stencilled and painted.

Catalogue: *A4, Leaflet, 1 page, Colour, Free* Postal charges: *Free* Delivery: *Royal Mail* Methods of Payment: *Cheque, Postal Order*

TRUMPS
9 Hersham Centre
Hersham
Surrey
KT12 4HL

Telephone:
0932 246951
Fax:
0932 254334

RATTAN FURNITURE
The 'Medway Rattan Collection' is a new edition to the Trumps range of rattan furniture. It comprises two living collections, 'Milan' and 'Valencia', the 'Seville' lounge collection and the 'Classic' and 'Palm Court' dining collections. The 'Milan' range comes in green only and has a distinctive open-lattice panelling. The living collection comprises armchair, loveseat, coffee table, side table and footstool.

Prices start at £175 for the footstools, while dining tables are available with glass or wooden tops from £254.00.

Catalogue: *A4, Catalogue, 9 pages, Colour, Free* Postal charges: *Varies with item* Delivery: *In-house delivery* Methods of Payment: *Cheque*

Furniture

TULLEYS OF CHELSEA
289 Fulham Road
London
SW10 9TZ

Telephone:
071 352 1078

Fax:
071 352 5677

FURNITURE
This smart colour brochure clearly displays a comprehensive range of sofas and armchairs. Quality materials are guaranteed, including hardwood frames and natural curled feather cushion fillings.

A 2-seater uncovered sofa starts at around the £700.00 mark; the covered version will add a couple of hundred pounds to the price, plus fabric. Tulleys currently have over 8,000 fabric designs to choose from.

They also have a collection of reproduction furniture. You can complete your living room with a mahogany veneer television and video cabinet for £730.00 – if you so desire.

Catalogue: *A4, Catalogue, 24 pages, Colour, Free* Postal charges: *Free* Delivery: *In-house delivery* Methods of Payment: *Cheque, Visa, Access / Mastercard, American Express*

WATKIN ROBERTS
Felin Isaf
Llwyngwril
Gwynedd
LL37 2JA

Telephone:
0341 250567

HANDCRAFTED FURNITURE
Watkin Roberts feature just three items of furniture in their simple leaflet. These are a Pine Candlebox, which stands 13" high and costs £24.00; a Pine Stool, 10" high with a seat 14" by 9" and a Pine Cabinet with Shelf of 17" × 15" × 5", suitable for a bathroom or as a spice rack, which costs £35.00. All are illustrated with simple line drawings.

Catalogue: *Third A4, Leaflet, 1 page, B/W, Free* Postal charges: *£3.00* Delivery: *By arrangement* Methods of Payment: *Cheque*

WOOD'N IT?
Unit 8a
Whinfield Way
Rowlands Gill
Gateshead
NE39 1EH

Telephone:
0207 545546

PAINTED FURNITURE
Wood'n It? make solid pine furniture in all known paint effects: marbling, rag-rolling, dragging and so on. They can also paint any picture that you want on pine or reproduce any pattern to suit your existing decor. They pride themselves in being a 'green' company and so take pleasure in painting natural themes, but they're willing to paint any topical or personal event you wish.

Of their dining room furniture, a 4-seater table in their Whinfield design (29" × 42" × 30") costs £380.00. A larger 6-seater table (29" × 63" × 33") costs £460.00. Chairs cost £107.00.

Catalogue: *A4, Leaflet, 2 pages, Colour, Free* Postal charges: *Varies with item* Delivery: *Parcelforce* Methods of Payment: *Cheque*

Gadgets

WOODEN TOPS
4 Holbien Gardens
Northampton
NN4 9XT

Telephone:
0604 705056

DRESSING TABLES AND COORDINATES
Wooden Tops sell either covered or uncovered highly decorative furniture: dressing tables (starting at £39.50), occasional tables (starting at £12.00) and cabinet tables (starting at £21.50). You choose your fabric from their wide range, including traditionally named designs like English Garden and Garland of Roses, which extends to three possible colourways for each design. They also provide a full range of coordinates for the rest of your room.

You can also buy a mirror (starting at £45.00) from Wooden Tops. Built in period designs, you can choose from a hand-painted oval mirror or a cheval mirror for the bedroom.

Catalogue: *Third A4, Brochure, 20 pages, Colour, Free* Postal charges: *Varies with item* Delivery: *Royal Mail* Methods of Payment: *Cheque, Postal Order, Visa, Access / Mastercard*

WOOLPIT INTERIORS
The Street
Woolpit
Bury St Edmunds
Suffolk
IP30 9SA

Telephone:
0359 240895
Fax:
0359 242282

FURNITURE ACCESSORIES
Woolpit are one of the leading designers and manufacturers of decorative lighting and accessories in the country. They export to Europe, Australia and the USA. Their products include lamps, furniture and accessories in several styles to complement either traditional or modern interiors.

There are over 200 variations within the range of lamp bases alone. A limed oak square base from the 'Classic Column' collection costs £72.00. Exclusive candle- and lampshades include: the Woolpit Country Collection, the Empire Collection, Traditional Tartans and the Toile de Jouy collection.

Among the decorative accessories are a bedside table for £250.00 and a jardiniere for £310.00.

Catalogue: *A4, Leaflets, Colour, Free* Postal charges: *Varies with item* Delivery: *Royal Mail* Methods of Payment: *Cheque, Visa, Access / Mastercard*

BETTERWARE UK LTD
Stanley House
Park Lane
Castle Vale
Birmingham
B35 6LJ

Telephone:
021 693 1111

HOUSEHOLD GOODS
Betterware is a home shopping system whereby goods are ordered from a locally appointed coordinator. The catalogue contains every household gadget you can imagine: cleaning materials for the home, containers and clothes and linen storage bags.

Betterware cares about the environment and works towards improvements in the conservation of energy and natural resources and the minimisation of waste.

Gadgets

DAMART
Bingley X
West Yorkshire
BD17 1AD

Telephone:
0274 568234

MODERN ORIGINALS
8 Forge Court
Reading Road
Yateley
Camberley
Surrey
GU17 7RX

Telephone:
0252 878785

MULTI SHARP TOOLS
Hyde House
The Hyde
London
NW9 6LH

Telephone:
081 200 7551
Fax:
081 200 3420

Catalogue: *A4, Catalogue, 131 pages, Colour, £1.50* Postal charges: *Varies with item* Delivery: *In-house delivery* Methods of Payment: *Cheque, Postal Order*

ASSORTED HOUSEHOLD GADGETS
Contained within Damart Collections catalogue is a selection of general household gadgets from bathroom items to a folding shopping trolley. There are lots of useful everyday items and a few car accessories, as well. Prices range from £3.50 to £28.99.

Catalogue: *A4, Catalogue, 39 pages, Colour, Free* Postal charges: *Varies with item* Delivery: *In-house delivery* Methods of Payment: *Cheque, Postal Order*

'NEW IDEAS FROM AROUND THE WORLD'
Modern Originals offer a range of innovative and entertaining items, some traditional, others hightech. Of the former, there is the 'Traditional Handmade Cotton Quilt' (£119.95) and a 'smart leather briefcase' (£59.95). The latter, which some might call gadgets, range from a 'Slendertone Facial Toner' (£79.95) through a 'cervical pillow' (£29.95), scientifically designed to give you unrivalled bedtime comfort, to an 'antenna dish' (£34.95), said to give excellent indoor TV and radio reception.

Scattered through the catalogue are various items of clothing and footwear. These include a 100% Aran wool hand-knitted pullover (£69.95), a reproduction US Air Force leather pilot's jacket (£169.95) and thermal socks (two pairs: £14.95). An attractive, interesting read.

Catalogue: *Quarterly, 180 × 210 mm, Catalogue, 44 pages, Colour, Free* Postal charges: *£3.95* Delivery: *Royal Mail* Methods of Payment: *Cheque, Postal Order, Visa, Access / Mastercard*

LABOUR SAVING GADGETS
The brochure describes pictorially as well as verbally a range of labour-saving household and gardening items. The items range from 'The Silver Solution' at £16.95 to a 'High Reach Pruner and Saw Outfit', an ingenious device for cutting high branches without a step-ladder (£34.95).

Some items are available from recognised outlets such as Homebase and Texas. However, the greatest range is provided by Multi Sharp's mail order service – The Buyer's Choice.

The company offer a no quibble, no questions

Gardening

asked guarantee that if the product does not meet with the customer's approval, then it can be returned and money refunded.

Catalogue: *A5, Catalogue, 8 pages, B/W, Free* Postal charges: *Varies with item* Delivery: *Royal Mail* Methods of Payment: *Cheque, Postal Order, Visa, Access / Mastercard*

SCIENCE MUSEUM
Freepost SU361
Dept 5317
Hendon Road
Sunderland
SR9 9AD

Telephone:
091 514 4666
Fax:
091 514 4574

SCIENCE-BASED GOODS
The Science Museum's catalogue is aimed at the younger generation, with many of the products science-based, some useful, and others just great fun. The gifts on offer range from clothes (£16.95 for a T-shirt) and games (£8.99) to food processors (£49.95 for an ice-cream maker) and household gadgets. The catalogue is brought out once a year, including new and fun ideas for the developing scientist.

Catalogue: *Annually, A3, Catalogue, 32 pages, Colour, Free* Postal charges: *Varies with item* Delivery: *Royal Mail* Methods of Payment: *Cheque, Visa, Access / Mastercard*

AGRIFRAMES LTD
Charlwoods Road
East Grinstead
West Sussex
RH19 2HG

Telephone:
0342 328644
Fax:
0342 327233

GARDENING PRODUCTS
Agriframes is one of the biggest and best of the gardening catalogues. It offers a very large range of specialist gardening products and equipment.

Customers can order direct from the company's factories and personal callers are welcome at their East Grinstead offices. The owners of the company even offer their own private garden to visitors in order for them to see how they have used the Agriframes structures.

Catalogue: *Quarterly, 210mm × 195mm, Catalogue, 48 pages, Colour, Free* Postal charges: *Varies with item* Delivery: *Royal Mail* Methods of Payment: *Cheque, Visa, Access / Mastercard*

ALLWOOD BROTHERS
Mill Nursery
Hassocks
West Sussex
BN6 9NB

Telephone:
0273 844229

PLANT AND FLOWER SUPPLIERS
Allwood's catalogue gives a great range of gardening aids, plants and flowers to purchase by mail order. The company exhibits at all the leading flower shows: Chelsea, Harrogate Spring Show, Malvern, The Royal, South of England, Southport, etc. The catalogue also provides the customer with useful snippets of advice on the products advertised.

The Ariel Collection of ten modern Allwoodii pinks is £11.00, and the perennial South African sunshine flower costs £5.50 for five large plants.

Catalogue: *A5, Catalogue, 24 pages, B/W, Free* Postal charges: *Varies with item* Delivery: *Royal Mail* Methods of Payment: *Cheque, Visa, Access / Mastercard*

Gardening

ARCADIA NURSERIES
Brass Castle Lane
Nunthorpe
Middlesborough
Cleveland
TS8 9EB

Telephone:
0642 310782
Fax:
0642 300817

FUCHSIA
Arcadia specialise in fuchsias, and their colourful catalogue features just about every variety imaginable. There are plants not only for gardens but also for hanging baskets and harsh climates. They also offer a number of other flowers, including geraniums, primroses, roses, begonias and polyanthus.

But the selection doesn't stop at plants; there is also a good range of accessories such as baskets and patio plant holders, and even T-shirts and books. Prices are competitive and on certain selections postage is free.

Catalogue: *A5, Catalogue, 32 pages, Colour, 50p* Postal charges: *Varies with item* Delivery: *Royal Mail* Methods of Payment: *Cheque, Postal Order, Visa, Access / Mastercard*

BAKKER HOLLAND
PO Box 111
Spalding
Lincolnshire
PE12 6EL

Telephone:
0775 711411
Fax:
0775 711381

PLANTS AND GARDEN EQUIPMENT
The Bakker catalogue offers an enormous quantity of plants for both the house and garden. Balcony and patio plants include a pack of three scabiosa 'Butterfly Blue' at £5.25 and bougainvillaea at £6.95 each. Hydrangeas cost £5.95 each and a pack of three lavatera, £7.95. Standard trees include hibiscus at £13.95 each and dwarf lilacs at £11.25. Gladiolas start at £9.95 for a pack of 25 and climbing roses start at £5.95 for a pack of two golden showers.

Also available are bonsai trees from £14.95 to £29.50 and packs of 36 mixed perennials for £24.95.

Catalogue: *200 mm × 260 mm, Catalogue, 84 pages, Colour, Free* Postal charges: *£1.95* Delivery: *Royal Mail* Methods of Payment: *Cheque, Postal Order, Visa, Access / Mastercard*

BRADLEY GARDENS NURSERY
Sled Lane
Wylam
Northumberland
NE41 8JL

Telephone:
0661 852176

NURSERY SPECIALISING IN HERBS
This nursery is featured in the 'Good Gardens Guide' and welcomes disabled visitors and guided tours. It is set in a restored walled garden and specialises in herbs, both pot-grown and fresh-cut. Bedding plants, container and patio plants are also available in season.

Bradley Gardens is open from mid-March to 31st October and all plants can be seen growing in the display borders. A shop selling herb related products, gifts, books, seeds and terracotta is on site.

Catalogue: *Third A4, Leaflet, 3 pages, B/W, Free* Postal charges: *Customer collects* Delivery: *Visitor collects* Methods of Payment: *Cheque*

Gardening

CLASSIC GARDEN
Lower Puncheston
Pembrokeshire
SA62 5TG

Telephone:
0348 881451

PLANT CONTAINERS AND SUPPORTS

Classic Garden produce wooden plant boxes which are both practical and elegant. They have supplied the Queen's House at Greenwich and also government establishments and international hotels throughout Europe.

The planters are made from solid British hardwoods, with panels of exterior grade ply, and liners of rigid polypropylene. They can either be supplied as flatpacks or made specially to order.

A Hartford tub 14" × 14" × 14" is £52.50, while a large window box of 50" × 10" × 12" is £77.50. The pyramid plant support is £79.95.

Catalogue: *Brochure, 8 pages, Free* Postal charges: *Varies with item* Delivery: *Parcelforce* Methods of Payment: *Cheque, Visa, Access / Mastercard*

DAMART
Bingley X,
West Yorkshire
BD17 1AD

Telephone:
0274 568234

GARDENING SUPPLIES

Damart, the thermal clothing specialists, have diversified into gardening equipment which is available from any of their shops and also by mail order, or order and collect and save postage. A variety of small items are available from bird feeders to wellingtons. Prices from £2.99 to £21.99.

Catalogue: *A4, Catalogue, 39 pages, Colour, Free* Postal charges: *Varies with item* Delivery: *In-house delivery* Methods of Payment: *Cheque, Postal Order*

DAVIES & CLIFFORD LTD
Beta Works
Oxford Road
Tatling End
Gerrards Cross
Bucks
SL9 7BB

Telephone:
0753 886254
Fax:
0753 887319

PORTABLE BUILDINGS

Davies & Clifford specialise in individually constructed portable buildings. Although their catalogue features all types and sizes, they can also custom-make buildings. Each one is made by a skilled carpenter so the quality is high with considerable attention to detail.

The black and white illustrations show everything from small garden sheds up to large pavilions. Each is given a full description and lists the different dimensions. There is a good range of garages and stables as well as site offices, aviaries and workshops.

Catalogue: *A5, Catalogue, 24 pages, B/W, Free* Postal charges: *Varies with item* Delivery: *In-house delivery* Methods of Payment: *Cheque, Visa, Access / Mastercard*

Gardening

DE JAGERS & SONS LTD
The Nurseries
Marden
Kent
TN12 9BP

Telephone:
0622 831235
Fax:
0622 832416

PLANTS AND BULBS

De Jagers offers more than 500 varieties of bulbs and plants, including the largest selection of lilies in Europe. The bulbs and plants are all top quality and satisfaction is guaranteed. The company has been catering to both amateur and professional gardeners since 1870, and now has two 98-page full-colour brochures each year.

Catalogue: *Biannually, 207mm × 145mm, Catalogue, 98 pages, Colour, 2 × 1st class stamps, refundable* Postal charges: *£3.35* Delivery: *Parcelforce* Methods of Payment: *Cheque, Postal Order, Visa, Access / Mastercard*

DEACONS NURSERY
Moor View
Godshill
Isle of Wight
PO38 3HW

Telephone:
0983 840750/522283

FRUIT TREES AND SOFT FRUIT BUSHES

Deacons Nursery specialise in the production of over 200 varieties of apple trees; also peach, plum, pear, melon, raspberry, strawberry, redcurrant and kiwi fruit. They have a wide range of family trees (trees with more than one variety of fruit grafted on). Trees like Bramleys sell at £16.25; simple apple trees go for £10.50.

Catalogue: *Annually, A5, Catalogue, 50 pages, B/W, Free* Postal charges: *Varies with item* Delivery: *Securicor, Parcelforce* Methods of Payment: *Cheque, Postal Order, Visa, Access / Mastercard*

DIG AND DELVE ORGANICS
Fen Road
Blo' Norton
Diss
Norfolk
IP22 2BR

Telephone:
0379 898377

ORGANIC GARDENING MATERIALS

Dig and Delve Organics exist to help you garden organically. Their motto being 'Good for You and the Earth', they take pains to ensure that all their goods live up to such high standards. Everything they stock is safe and won't harm the environment.

Cabbage lettuces include buttercrunch (72p a packet), resilient in hot weather; saladin (92p) which has large, solid iceberg heads and Windermere (72p), which produces pale, crisp hearts. Also available are herbs and wild flower seeds, manures, mulches and some household and veterinary products.

Catalogue: *Annually, A5, Catalogue, 36 pages, B/W, £1.00* Postal charges: *Varies with item* Delivery: *Royal Mail* Methods of Payment: *Cheque, Postal Order, Visa, Access / Mastercard*

Gardening

EXMOUTH GARDEN PRODUCTS
Units 7–8 Salterton Workshops
Budleigh Salterton
Devon
EX9 6RJ
Telephone:
0395 442796
Fax:
0395 442851

GREENHOUSE ACCESSORIES
This catalogue focuses on products for the greenhouse and will be of interest to any serious gardener. The range includes glazing clips, clips for fitting bubble film and shading, nuts and bolts, shelving and shelving brackets and staging. They also sell bubble insulation film and shade netting in packs or by the metre.

A new and unique product is the Ex-Fit Support System which makes the best use of space in your greenhouse. It will hold seed and drip trays, troughs, shelves, plant pots and tools and is a cinch to fit.

A pack of 50 glazing clips is £2.40, a pack of 10 1" cropped head nuts and bolts, £2.10, bubble film 1.5m × 20m, £17.00, and vent openers, £15.50.

Catalogue: *Annually, A5, Brochure, 10 pages, Colour, Free* Postal charges: *Varies with item* Delivery: *Royal Mail, Parcelforce* Methods of Payment: *Cheque, Postal Order, Visa, Access / Mastercard*

FOUNTAINS & STATUES LTD
Unit 2
Coomb Farm Buildings
Balchins Lane
Westcott
Surrey
RH4 3LE
Telephone:
0306 742227
Fax:
0306 742227

FOUNTAINS AND STATUES
Fountains & Statues produce classical garden sculptures ranging from the basic 15" 'Head Planter' at £35.00 to the ornate 84" 'Merboy Fountain' at a giddy £16,905. The more expensive pieces wouldn't look that out of place in the gardens of a Tuscan Villa; the cheaper pieces will probably be consigned to roof-terraces in Fulham.

Each piece is created from the best materials and, with an eye towards conservation, the fountains are designed to recirculate their water. Such pricey items are hardly the kind of thing you buy on impulse. As Fountains & Statues suggest, one of their pieces might make an ideal gift to mark a special occasion – a wedding, retirement or birthday.

Catalogue: *A4, Catalogue, 20 pages, Colour, Free* Postal charges: *Free* Delivery: *Royal Mail* Methods of Payment: *Cheque, Postal Order*

GROOM'S
Pecks Drove Nurseries
Spalding
Lincs
PE12 6BR
Telephone:
0775 722421

BULBS FOR THE GARDEN
Groom's catalogue features large and small photographs of many of the bulbs which it offers with a description, denoting when to plant, when it flowers, colour and price. As well as bulbs, there are fresh daffodils which can be sent by post for £8.90 as a gift; garden packs which consist of a mixture of 110 bulbs for £19.36; and a woodland mixture of daffodils and

Gardening

narcissi, 50 for £7.40 or 1,000 for £111.99. The catalogue includes a stamped, self-addressed envelope, second class post, for you to return your order.

Catalogue: *Annually, A5, Catalogue, 48 pages, Colour, Free* Postal charges: *Varies with item* Delivery: *Royal Mail* Methods of Payment: *Cheque, Postal Order, Visa, Access / Mastercard*

HADDONSTONE LTD
The Forge House
East Haddon
Northampton
NN6 8DB

Telephone:
0604 770711
Fax:
0604 770027

STONE GARDEN ORNAMENTS
Haddonstone is a leading manufacturer of ornamental and architectural stonework. Divided into two books, their delightful, high quality catalogue deals first with Garden Ornaments and secondly with Architectural and Interior Stonework.

Garden Ornaments covers a vast and wonderful range, from a simple, classic 'Regency Urn' for £50.11, to a collection of fountains costing four figures. Among their Architectural and Interior pieces, Haddonstone offer columns, half-columns, pilasters, plaques and an assortment of plinths. All are of very high quality and the catalogue itself is a work of art with terrific photographs.

Catalogue: *A4, Catalogue, 108 pages, Colour, Free* Postal charges: *Varies with item* Delivery: *Courier* Methods of Payment: *Cheque, Visa, Access / Mastercard*

HAMPTONS LEISURE
The Pin Mill
New Street
Charlfield
Wotton under Edge
Glos
GL12 8ES

Telephone:
0453 842889
Fax:
0453 843938

TEAK SHOREA AND CAST ALUMINIUM GARDEN FURITURE
Hamptons Leisure produce fine, quality garden furniture. Each piece is manufactured to their own designs in teak, cast aluminium and hardwood, making it suitable for gardens, patios and conservatories. They also stock a selection of hammocks in various designs, including chair hammocks and children's sizes.

Steamer chairs in various hardwoods start at £145.00, a 4' Windermere bench is £135.00 and a wonderful Lutyens 8' bench costs £593.00.

Catalogue: *Annually, A4, Catalogue, 16 pages, Colour, Free* Postal charges: *Varies with item* Delivery: *Parcelforce, TNT* Methods of Payment: *Cheque, Postal Order, Visa, Access / Mastercard*

Gardening

HEATHER VALLEY (WOOLLENS) LTD
16 Comely Bank Avenue
Edinburgh
EH4 1EL

Telephone:
031 236 9911

GARDEN, HOME, CLOTHES AND HOUSEHOLD GOODS
Based in Edinburgh, this catalogue combines elegant soft suits and dresses and coordinating separates and outdoor wear. Towards the back of the brochure, there's plenty to inspire you for the home and garden, as well. There are fourteen sections in this brochure, with a stop press sale page at the back.

Catalogue: *A4, Catalogue, 136 pages, Colour, Free* Postal charges: *Varies with item* Delivery: *Parcelforce* Methods of Payment: *Cheque, Postal Order, Stage Payments, Visa, Access / Mastercard*

HILL FARM HERBS
Park Walk
Brigstock
Northants
NN14 3HH

Telephone:
0536 373694
Fax:
0536 373246

PLANTS, SEEDS, AROMOTHERAPY PRODUCTS
Hill Farm is run from an old stone farmhouse in the village of Brigstock in Northamptonshire. For the last six years they have been offering their wide selection of plants and seeds by mail.

As well as individual plants listed alphabetically, there are Special Collections to get you going. These include a 'Beginner's Herb Garden', 'Herbs for Cooking' and 'Fragrant Herbs'. The same company has a leaflet on aromatherapy products, both the oils themselves and books and accessories.

Catalogue: *8" × 4", Catalogue, 30 pages, B/W, 25p* Postal charges: *Varies with item* Delivery: *Royal Mail* Methods of Payment: *Cheque, Postal Order, Visa, Access / Mastercard*

HOLLOWAYS
Lower Court
Suckley
Worcestershire
WR6 5DE

Telephone:
0886 884754

CONSERVATORY FURNITURE AND GARDEN ORNAMENTS
Holloways are a family-run business located in rural Worcestershire and are one of the UK leaders in conservatory furnishings and garden ornaments.

They have many different styles of seating and dining furniture for conservatories, many of which are available in customised colours, sizes and fabrics. They can also help with blinds, flooring, heating, fans and other practical aspects of owning a conservatory. Much of the furniture is English willow and rattan (Jakarta chaise longue in rattan, £310.00) and fabrics to cover them are available from designers such as Monkwell, Romo, Sanderson and Designers Guild.

There is also a wide range of garden ornamentation from wall fountains to wirework jardinieres and earthenware wall plaques.

Catalogue: *Annually, A5, Catalogue, 24 pages, Colour, Free* Postal charges: *£2.95* Delivery: *Royal Mail* Methods of Payment: *Cheque, Postal Order, Visa, Access / Mastercard*

Gardening

JACQUES AMAND LTD
The Nurseries
Clamp Hill
Stanmore
Middlesex
HA7 3JS

Telephone:
081 954 8138
Fax:
081 954 6784

BULBS
Gardening specialists Jacques Amand stock a wide range of seasonal flowering bulbs, including all the usual plants, from begonias starting at £2.75 for three to geraniums starting at £1.95 each. But in their spring catalogue, they also introduce a number of new, unusual plants.

Orchid growers may like to investigate the striking outdoor orchid Cypripedium reginae (£11.95 each; three for £34.95). Laboratory grown, it takes two years to flower – but the wait looks worth it. For indoor planting, they present eucrosia (telephone for prices), a bulbous plant originally from Ecuador and Peru. You can also visit the Jacques Amand nurseries in March and April when the spring flowering bulbs for their autumn collection are in full bloom.

Catalogue: *A4, Catalogue, 32 pages, Colour, 75p* Postal charges: *£2.95* Delivery: *Royal Mail* Methods of Payment: *Cheque, Postal Order, Visa, Access / Mastercard*

**JOHN CHAMBERS'
WILD FLOWER SEEDS**
15 Westleigh Road
Barton Seagrave
Kettering
Northants
NN15 5AJ

Telephone:
0933 652562

ORGANIC GARDENING SEEDS
Enliven your garden with John Chambers' Wild Flower Seeds. This is the most comprehensive range of seeds for native British flowers in the country; there are also ornamental and cultivated grass species and mixtures, everlasting flowers and agricultural crops.

For 90p you can choose wild angelica, wild basil or colt's foot. Recreate a meadow on your own back lawn. Wonderful flowers like Scottish primrose, Michaelmas daisy and parsley are all here. You can even order nettles – common, small or stinging.

Catalogue: *Annually, A5, Catalogue, 54 pages, Colour and B/W, Free* Postal charges: *Varies with item* Delivery: *Royal Mail* Methods of Payment: *Cheque, Postal Order*

JOHNSON'S
London Road
Boston
Lincs
PE21 8AD

Telephone:
0205 365051

FLOWERS, VEGETABLES, HERBS AND GRASS SEEDS
The catalogue is divided into various sections beginning with flower seeds, all detailed alphabetically and coded to denote their variety, as well as vegetables, beans and peas, and lawns. Prices are given beside each entry and there are six colour photographs of the grown items on each double page spread. Descriptions include where they should be planted, colour, height and planting times. The catalogue does not make it clear whether it accepts telephone orders by credit card.

Gardening

LINK STAKES
30 Warwick Road
Upper Boddington
Daventry
Northants
NN11 6DH

Telephone:
0327 60329
Fax:
0327 62428

Catalogue: *Annually, A5, Catalogue, 88 pages, Colour, Free* Postal charges: *Varies with item* Delivery: *Royal Mail* Methods of Payment: *Cheque, Postal Order*

PLANT SUPPORTS
This company sells ingenious plant supports. Their Link-Stakes and Loop-Stakes are very effective means of supporting most plants in flower borders, pots and window boxes, as well as in the vegetable garden. Made of strong galvanised wire coated with dark green plastic, they are very durable (20 years +), unobtrusive and safe.

Link-Stakes, suitable for clumps, are available in five sizes ranging from 12" high at a price of £3.45 per dozen to 40" high for £15.90 per dozen. Loop-Stakes are for specimen plant stems and come in three sizes from 24" to 48". They also carry a range of other useful gardening aids.

Catalogue: *Annually, A5, Catalogue, 6 pages, Colour, Free* Postal charges: *Varies with item* Delivery: *Parcelforce* Methods of Payment: *Cheque, Postal Order, Visa, Access / Mastercard*

NEWBROOK PRODUCTS LTD
Hillside Mill
Swaffham Bulbeck
Cambridge
CB5 0LU

Telephone:
0223 812729
Fax:
0223 813199

GARDENING
This company sells a number of interesting products. 'Portapath' is an award-winning lightweight but extremely strong system of interlocking treads and connectors which simply clip together to form instant pathways, patios or floors.

Another neat idea is 'Bugchasers', wristbands incorporating a slow release insecticide-free mosquito repellent. 'Envirotape' is a teflon coated adhesive tape used as a barrier against crawling insects, while 'Bugcharm' is an insecticide-free aphid control system which attracts aphids' natural predators to infected areas.

A 'Portapath' kit (10' × 1') is £19.95, 'Bugchasers' are £2.50 each, 'Envirotape' is £8.95 per 30' roll and 'Bugcharm' costs £5.00 for a pack of three.

Catalogue: *Annually, A4 or A5, Brochure, 1–4 pages, Colour, Free* Postal charges: *Varies with item* Delivery: *Royal Mail, Parcelforce* Methods of Payment: *Cheque, Postal Order, Visa, Access / Mastercard*

Gardening

NORFOLK GREENHOUSES
P.O. Box 22
Watton
Norfolk
IP25 6PA

Telephone:
0638 510568

GARDEN STRUCTURES
Norfolk Greenhouses produce structures in a number of different styles, including carports, garden rooms, conservatories and sheds. All products have a galvanised steel frame, glass-clear, shatterproof pvc sheeting and need no foundations.

'Chiswick' sheds cost from £89.00 to £199.00. The most expensive model has a centre roof-light. The 'Rotunda' greenhouse has eight sides and a hinged door. Approximately 5'3" in diameter by 7'2" high, the standard model costs £89.00 and the deluxe model £119.00.

Catalogue: *A4, Leaflet, 2 pages, Colour, Free* Postal charges: *Varies with item* Delivery: *Royal Mail* Methods of Payment: *Cheque, Postal Order, Visa, Access / Mastercard*

ORCHARD NURSERIES
Orchard Place
Flint House Road
Three Holes
Wisbech
Cambs
PE14 9JN

Telephone:
0345 8613

PLANTS, SHRUBS, FLOWERS
Orchard Nurseries provide a range of popular flowers, shrubs and plants. They make a point of stating that they are the main supplier of snowdrops and aconites which are cultivated and grown at a nursery – natural stocks of these plants have become depleted since retailers began digging them up and reselling them.

Petunias come in several different varieties. Mirage Multiflora is particularly suited to the changeable UK climate, and costs from £5.00 for 25. Pansies are sold in two sizes, all mixed colours: 25 mini pansies cost £4.00 and 25 plus pansies cost £6.50.

Catalogue: *Annually, A5, Catalogue, 4 pages, B/W, Free* Postal charges: *Varies with item* Delivery: *Royal Mail* Methods of Payment: *Cheque, Postal Order, Visa, Access / Mastercard*

ORYX TRADING
33 Cornwall Gardens
London
SW7 4AP

Telephone:
071 938 2045
Fax:
071 937 9087

GARDEN FURNITURE AND UMBRELLAS
This company operates as an import export broker, specialising in garden furniture. Taking its inspiration from the days of the British Empire, there is a limited range of sturdy hardwood furniture and canvas canopy umbrellas.

The fashionable umbrellas come in two sizes, 9' 10" and 12' 4", and include both a concrete base and metal spike for soft or hard surface fixing. The smaller model is £295 and the larger £595. Expensive but delightful.

Catalogue: *A4, Catalogue, 9 pages, Colour, Free* Postal charges: *Varies with item* Delivery: *By arrangement* Methods of Payment: *Cheque, Postal Order, Visa, Access / Mastercard*

Gardening

PELCO FERTILIZERS
251 London Road East
Batheaston
Bath
BA1 7RL

Telephone:
0225 859962
Fax:
0225 859006

FERTILIZER

Pelco Fertilizers produce Super-dug, a concentrated organic dung which contains the millions of living organisms essential in the creation of humus. Super-dug enriches all soil types, improving texture by breaking down clay and adding body to light soils. At the same time it slowly releases vital plant foods and trace elements. It is weed-free and environmentally friendly with no peat or added chemicals. It is economical (you use handfuls, not barrow-loads) and can be used all year round.

Super-dug is available in Giant Economy 25kg sacks at £13.25 for one sack, £11.75 each for two, £10.00 each for three to five sacks and £9.50 each for six or more sacks.

Catalogue: *A4, Leaflet, 5 pages, B/W, Free* Postal charges: *Free* Delivery: *Courier* Methods of Payment: *Cheque, Postal Order, Visa, Access / Mastercard*

R HARKNESS & CO
The Rose Gardens
Hitchin
Herts
SG4 0JT

Telephone:
0462 4027

PLANTS AND FLOWERS

If it's roses you want, Harkness are the people to help. Their catalogue comes complete with full descriptions of the various varieties they offer. They also suggest collections for edging paths and borders, ground cover, or to train as climbers (from £11.50), and gift bouquets for special occasions (£15.75).

Prices are reasonable. Hybrid tea bush roses start just below the £4.00 mark; bush roses cost roughly the same. Miniatures are from around £3.00 and standard roses are priced from about £14.00.

Catalogue: *Biannually, A4, Catalogue, 38 pages, Colour, Free* Postal charges: *Varies with item* Delivery: *Royal Mail* Methods of Payment: *Cheque, Postal Order, Visa, Access / Mastercard*

ROSENEY FARM DESIGNS
Lanlivery
Bodmin
Cornwall
PL30 5DL

Telephone:
0208 872664

DOVECOTES

Roseney Farm Designs produce a range of dovecotes based on traditional wooden designs which have graced gardens for many years. They are made in WBP ply which will withstand wind and weather and are finished in microporous paint or varnish. Dovecotes can be supplied finished or in kit form and are suitable for wall or pole mounting or, in some cases, both. Prices range from £54.28 to £305.97 for kits and £106.10 to £611.94 for assembled units.

Roseney can also supply poles, bird tables and, most importantly, the doves or pigeons themselves.

Gardening

Catalogue: *A5, Catalogue, 8 pages, B/W, Free* Postal charges: *Varies with item* Delivery: *Royal Mail* Methods of Payment: *Cheque, Postal Order, Visa, Access / Mastercard*

S E MARSHALL & CO
23–24 Regal Road
Wisbech
Cambs
PE13 2RF

Telephone:
0945 583407

Fax:
0945 588235

SEEDS

Marshall's is Britain's foremost vegetable seeds specialists, said to be the first choice for quality, value and service. Their catalogue offers a superb selection of the healthiest, tastiest, most reliable varieties, together with an extensive range of onion sets and seed potatoes, as well as soft fruit and colourful flowers.

All the seeds are thoroughly tested for quality and germination, and should any product fail in any way, they will provide a replacement or refund the purchase price. Beetroot Boltardy is 59p per packet; onion giant fen globe £1.99 for 100 sets, busy Lizzie starbright, 100 seedlings for £11.95 and ten strawberry Cambridge favourite for £3.85.

Catalogue: *Annually, A5, Catalogue, 48 pages, Colour, Free* Postal charges: *Varies with item* Delivery: *Royal Mail, Parcelforce* Methods of Payment: *Cheque, Postal Order, Visa, Access / Mastercard*

SAMUEL DOBIE & SONS LTD
Broomhill Way
Torquay
Devon
TQ2 7QW

Telephone:
0803 616888

SEEDS, BULBS, YOUNG PLANTS, GARDEN EQUIPMENT

Dobie's are a long established supplier of over 1000 varieties of flower and vegetable seeds. They also stock bulbs and a selection of garden equipment. None of the products is sold through retail outlets and can only be ordered by mail. In recent years, Dobie's have developed an extensive range of young bedding and patio plant packs which offer excellent value.

Flower and vegetable seeds start at 47p a packet, while a pack of 100 petunia mini plants is £9.75. Thirty-five impatiens (busy Lizzie) easiplants are £7.85 and a pair of self-watering hanging baskets cost £15.95.

Catalogue: *Annually, 230 × 210mm, Catalogue, 128 pages, Colour, Free* Postal charges: *Varies with item* Delivery: *Royal Mail, Parcelforce* Methods of Payment: *Cheque, Postal Order, Visa, Access / Mastercard*

Gardening

SEEDS BY POST
Monks Farm
Pantlings Lane
Kelvedon
Essex
CO5 9PG

Telephone:
0376 572456
Fax:
0376 571189

SEEDS
Described as 'Europe's No 1 Organic Seed Catalogue', this publication could not differ more from conventional seed catalogues if it tried (which presumably it has). No garish pictures here, nor indeed the sort of bedding plants needed to produce so much colour.

Printed on recycled paper, it simply lists its marvellous collection of herbs, wildflowers, vegetables and organic gardening products. There is even a range of herbal drinks, organic wines and essential oils. Plenty of organic growing advice is given and poisonous plants are clearly marked. Seed prices vary from about 85p to £2.00 for rarer species.

Catalogue: *Annually, 190mm × 240mm, Catalogue, 72 pages, B/W, £1.00* Postal charges: *Free* Delivery: *Royal Mail* Methods of Payment: *Cheque, Postal Order, Visa, Access / Mastercard*

SUTTONS SEEDS LTD
Hele Road
Torquay
Devon
TQ2 7QJ

Telephone:
0803 614455
Fax:
0803 615747

SEEDS
Suttons are one of the major UK seedsmen and, as one would expect, produce a comprehensive catalogue covering flowers, shrubs, fruit and vegetables. Most entries are coupled with inspirational colour photographs of flourishing blooms and perfect garden produce. A brief description of each plant plus its growing habit is also given.

The main catalogue lists seeds only, with prices ranging from as little as 75p a packet to £2.29 for some hybrids. In the ancillary catalogue, 'Suttons Plus', seedlings, plantlets, bulbs and garden equipment are listed, again accompanied by photographs and a brief description.

Catalogue: *Annually, A5, Catalogue, 128 pages, Colour, Free* Postal charges: *Free* Delivery: *Royal Mail* Methods of Payment: *Cheque, Postal Order, Visa, Access / Mastercard*

THE EASTERN CONNECTION
Hoods
Town Lane
Brockford
Stowmarket
Suffolk
IP14 5NF

Telephone:
0449 766783

GARDEN ORNAMENTS
As the name implies, this brochure relates to goods imported from the Far East. In this case they are heavy cast-bronze statuary of a pair of cranes, birds regarded as symbols of prosperity and happiness in Eastern culture.

Mainly designed with garden displays in mind, the cranes are available in two finishes, black bronze and verdigris. There are several sizes available, from 60" and 48" high (one pair), to a table-sized version at 19" and 16" high. Prices start at £49.00, rising to £499.00.

Gardening

THE FLOWER LOFT
E4 Mourabout
Dorchester
Dorset
DT1 1YA

Telephone:
0305 251853
Fax:
0305 251853

Catalogue: *A4, Leaflet, 4 pages, Colour and B/W, Free* Postal charges: *Varies with item* Delivery: *Royal Mail* Methods of Payment: *Cheque, Postal Order*

DRIED FLOWERS AND PLANTS, CRAFT DECORATIONS

This catalogue is divided into several sections, the first showing plants which can be used for all kinds of arrangements, along with ideas of how to get the best from them.

Then there are a variety of displays for flower arrangements, including baskets and bowls made from willow and fern, a rattan tricycle 15" long for £4.99 and a set of two wishing well buckets, 7" and 8" in diameter, for £6.99.

The Flower Loft also provides a range of children's toys from wooden trains and alphabet frames to furniture for dolls houses and cuddly toys. There are also gifts for adults, including Christmas decorations in holly and berries, wooden candlesticks and trinket boxes.

Catalogue: *A5, Catalogue, 20 pages, B/W, Free* Postal charges: *Varies with item* Delivery: *Royal Mail* Methods of Payment: *Cheque, Postal Order, Visa, Access / Mastercard*

THE ORGANIC GARDENING CATALOGUE
Coombelands House
Addlestone
Surrey
KT15 1HY

Telephone:
0932 820958

ORGANIC GARDENING STOCK

Produced by the Henry Doubleday Research Association, sales from this catalogue help to fulfil the aims of promoting organic growing in the UK and abroad.

A useful chart on crop rotation is included, while the lists of untreated seeds seems endless. Prices per packet include: chicory at 63p, cress at 60p, strawberries at 99p and spinach at 58p. Also on offer are many beautiful environmentally friendly flower seeds (digitalis 'foxy' costs 90p a packet), as well as books, plants, fertilisers and the 'nature's own' compost range. This includes 15 litres of potting for £5.25, a 40-litre module for £8.90, and 40-litre tomato potting at £9.05.

Catalogue: *Annually, A5, Catalogue, 48 pages, Colour, Free* Postal charges: *Varies with item* Delivery: *Royal Mail* Methods of Payment: *Cheque, Postal Order, Visa, Access / Mastercard*

Gardening

THE ROMANTIC GARDEN NURSERY
Swannington
Norwich
NR9 5NW

Telephone:
0603 261488

GARDEN PRODUCTS
Situated in the heart of Norfolk, The Romantic Garden Nursery are specialist suppliers of box topiary. This includes animals and spirals, ornamental standards and many unusual hardy and half-hardy plants. In addition to flowers, they sell a range of gifts from all over Europe. These include Italian china, ornaments, unusual tableware, silk flowers and gift cards.

The range of plants includes viburnum tinus 'Eve Price', a dense, bushy evergreen shrub with glossy leaves and white flowers. There is also a wide range of wisteria, including wisteria chinensis (from £85.00) and wisteria floribunda (£24.99).

Catalogue: *A5, Catalogue, 28 pages, B/W, Free* Postal charges: *Varies with item* Delivery: *Courier* Methods of Payment: *Cheque, Postal Order, Visa, Access / Mastercard*

THE THAI HOUSE CO
11 The Paddock
Maidenhead
Berkshire
SL6 6SD

Telephone:
0628 75091
Fax:
0628 770892

THAI GARDEN HOUSES
The Thai House Co manufacture Thai-style garden houses in a range of sizes. An attractive and unusual garden feature, the Thai-style house is ideal as a playhouse for children.

They are made of softwood and stand on eight circular posts. Five steps lead up to the door and on both sides there are three windows, each with a shutter. The houses come in 12', 9' or 6' heights with floor areas of 8' × 5', 6' × 4' or 4' × 3'. Prices are £1195.00, £995.00 and £895.00. Delivery to most of southern and central England, plus assembly, is free. The houses can also be self assembled.

Catalogue: *A4, Leaflet, 3 pages, Colour and B/W, Free* Postal charges: *Free to Southern England* Delivery: *In-house delivery* Methods of Payment: *Cheque*

THE TRADITIONAL GARDEN SUPPLY CO
Unit 12
Hewitts Industrial Estate
Elmbridge road
Cranleigh
Surrey
GU6 8LW

Telephone:
0483 273366
Fax:
0483 273388

GARDENING EQUIPMENT
The Traditional Garden Supply Company offer everything you'll ever need to complete your English country garden. There's also a retail showroom, so you can even inspect the products before you buy. Some of their furniture is inspired by the American Shaker ideal of simplicity and functionality.

A New England-style bench includes a water-resistant box and sports closed-in boards reminiscent of traditional Shaker wash-stands and church pews. Prices start at £149.99.

The 'Cedar Tool Store' (from £129.99) can be

Gardening

used in your potting shed or greenhouse, or it looks good enough to keep by your back door.

Catalogue: *Annually, A5, Catalogue, 32 pages, Colour, Free* Postal charges: *£2.75* Delivery: *Royal Mail* Methods of Payment: *Cheque, Postal Order, Visa, Access / Mastercard*

THE VALLEY CLEMATIS NURSERY
Willingham Road
Hainton
Lincoln
LN3 6LN

Telephone:
0507 313398
Fax:
0507 313705

NURSERY PLANTS
The Valley Clematis Nursery has over 350 varieties in stock, most of which are available through the catalogue. Each plant is described in terms of colour, height, planting aspect and flowering months. The majority of plants are priced at £5.00, although some go up to £8.00 (e.g. armandii var, apple blossom).

Plants are sold aged 18–24 months and sent in 1-litre pots. Ordering early is recommended as particular varieties often sell out. For autumn delivery you are advised to order in March or April. No orders are despatched during May to September.

Catalogue: *Annually, A5, Catalogue, 39 pages, Colour, Free* Postal charges: *Varies with item* Delivery: *Royal Mail, Courier* Methods of Payment: *Cheque, Postal Order, Visa, Access / Mastercard*

THE VERNON GERANIUM NURSERY
Cuddington Way
Cheam
Sutton
Surrey
SM2 7JB

Telephone:
081 393 7616
Fax:
081 786 7437

CUTTINGS OF OVER 1,100 VARIETIES OF GERANIUM
Vernon's grow over 1,100 different types of geranium and their catalogue will appeal to all – from the beginner to the expert. In full colour, it shows many of the different types, colours and uses and gives full care instructions for these easily maintained plants – with lots of tips and advice, it's almost a reference book. Prices for cuttings range from less than £1.00 to a few pounds, plus postage and packing, which varies according to the size of order.

Catalogue: *Annually, A4, Catalogue, 48 pages, Colour, £1.50 refundable* Postal charges: *Varies with item* Delivery: *Royal Mail* Methods of Payment: *Cheque, Postal Order, Visa, Access / Mastercard*

Gardening

TWO WESTS & ELLIOTT LIMITED
Unit 4
Carwood Road
Sheepbridge Industrial Estate
Chesterfield
Derbys
S41 9RH

Telephone:
0246 451077

GARDENING
Two Wests & Elliott deal in quality greenhouse and conservatory equipment which will be of use to any keen gardener. Their range includes all manner of items for indoor gardening, such as shelving, soil warming cables, seed trays, watering systems, extractor fans and automatic vent openers.

Commercial benching costs from £52.30; a potting bench is priced at £49.95; adjustable shelving starts at £19.35. Max/min thermometers are £7.95 and an air circulation fan £36.65.

Catalogue: *Annually, A5, Catalogue, 52 pages, Colour, £1.00*
Postal charges: *Varies with item* Delivery: *Royal Mail* Methods of Payment: *Cheque, Postal Order, Visa, Access / Mastercard*

UNWINS SEEDS LTD
Mail Order Department
Histon
Cambs
CB4 4ZZ

Telephone:
0945 588522

GARDEN SEED, BULBS AND YOUNG PLANTS
Unwins offer hundreds of high quality seed varieties of flowers and vegetables that have all been tried and tested to make sure that they will thrive in typical British conditions.

Sweet peas are Unwins' speciality and their catalogue lists over 50 premium quality varieties, giving customers the opportunity to grow superior plants and blooms. They also sell bulbs for all seasons, young plants and soft fruit. All products are backed by a no-quibble guarantee.

Prices per packet of seeds, until 30.6.94, are: sweet pea royal wedding 99p, marigold royal king £1.25, tomato moneymaker 89p and brussels sprout Peer Gynt £1.85.

Catalogue: *3 per year, A5, Catalogue, 100, 24 & 16 pages, Colour, Free* Postal charges: *Varies with item* Delivery: *Royal Mail, Parcelforce* Methods of Payment: *Cheque, Postal Order, Visa, Access / Mastercard*

VIGO
Bollhayes
Clayhidon
Devon
EX15 3PN

Telephone:
0823 680230

FRUIT PRESSES AND CRUSHERS
This is a wonderful catalogue for anyone with one or more fruit trees in their garden and too much fruit for their family and friends to eat. Vigo supplies fruit crushers and presses so you can put all those apples or whatever to good use. They also supply various accessories such as straining bags, funnels, yeast and so on.

There is plenty of advice and information on how to use the presses or crushers and also how to store the juice once made. There is a section on cider making and further details are sent with each

Gardening

machine. Crushers sell from £125.00 and presses from £75.00.

Catalogue: *A5, Catalogue, 6 pages plus inserts, B/W, Free* Postal charges: *Varies with item* Delivery: *Parcelforce* Methods of Payment: *Cheque, Visa, Access / Mastercard*

WHICHFORD POTTERY
Whichford
Nr Shipston-on-Stour
Warwickshire
CV36 5PG

Telephone:
0608 484416
Fax:
0608 684833

GARDEN POTTERY AND TILES

Whichford produce a wonderful folder-cum-catalogue featuring their top quality terracotta. It is all produced by traditional means and they even blend and prepare their own local clays. The entire range carries a 10-year guarantee against lamination in the frost.

There really is just about every type of pot on show here. Some of the larger urns, for instance, a pedestal urn (16" × 15"), seem relatively cheap at £31.50. If you want something large, try one of the Ali Baba jars: 27" × 18" at £128.00. Waterproofed saucers are also available, starting at £2.95 for a $5^{1}/_{2}''$ saucer. Well worth a look for any terracotta fan.

Catalogue: *A4, Catalogue, 16 pages, Colour, Free* Postal charges: *£13.50* Delivery: *Courier* Methods of Payment: *Cheque*

WINDSOR DESIGNS
The Pin Mill
New St
Charfield
Wootton-Under-Edge
Gloucestershire
GL12 8ES

Telephone:
0453 842889
Fax:
0453 843938

GARDEN FURNITURE AND ACCESSORIES

Windsor Designs offers a wide range of outdoor furniture in solid teak, natural shorea and cast aluminium. The range includes chairs and benches, pool and deck loungers, planters, tables and drinks trolleys.

All Windsor products are sourced from the finest materials. The wood comes from sustainable, properly harvested sources and the wooden products are all manufactured using traditional mortise and jtenon joinery. Cushions are offered for all products in a range of weather and mildew-resistant finishes. Prices vary according to material, style and size.

Catalogue: *A4, Catalogue, 16 pages, Colour, Free* Postal charges: *Varies with item* Delivery: *Royal Mail* Methods of Payment: *Cheque, Visa, Access / Mastercard*

General Catalogues

ABBOTT'S PACKAGING LIMITED
Gordon House
Oakleigh Road South
New Southgate
London
N11 1HL

Telephone:
081 368 1266
Fax:
081 368 0886

PACKAGING MATERIALS
Packaging of all sorts and sizes, from corrugated case products to cushioning materials. Offers 24–48 hour delivery of all products stocked at local branches, which are nationwide. Postal packets, bottle packs and computer packaging are just a few of the packagings on offer from this company.

Catalogue: *A4, Brochure, 57 pages, Colour, Free* Postal charges: *Varies with item* Delivery: *Royal Mail* Methods of Payment: *Cheque, Postal Order*

ACCELERATED LEARNING
Accelerated Learning Systems Ltd
50 Aylesbury Road
Aston Clinton
Aylesbury
Bucks.
HP22 5AH

Telephone:
0296 631177
Fax:
0296 631074

LEARNING EQUIPMENT, TAPES AND KITS
Accelerated Learning System 2000 is founded on extensive research into how people learn best which was conducted by a number of leading universities. These programmes use a combination of audio, video and course books to ensure that a person can learn in the most suitable way for them. There are a number of different courses: for example, languages, drawing, music and diet control. Each language course costs £99.00, with a choice of French, Spanish, German and Italian. Other courses vary in price and they each contain a physical learning video and booklet, twelve audio cassettes, a text book with memory maps, the name game book and word cards and games.

Catalogue: *A4, Leaflet, 4 pages plus other leaflets, Colour, Free* Postal charges: *Varies with item* Delivery: *Royal Mail* Methods of Payment: *Cheque, Postal Order, Visa, Access / Mastercard*

ARGOS DISTRIBUTORS LTD
Unit 1 Lyne Hill
Industrial Estate
Penkeridge
Staffordshire
ST19 5NT

Telephone:
0800 555899

HUGE RANGE
Argos is the innovative High Street store where you order by catalogue within the shop itself. But to make shopping even easier, Argos have set up a free home delivery service called Argos Direct. This is available on selected items such as 3-piece suites from £349.99, multi-gyms from £199.00, mountain bikes from £129.99 and outdoor toys from £69.99.

To order is easy: look through the Argos catalogue and if the Argos Direct red lorry symbol appears, call 0800 555899, quoting your order and credit card details. (For other queries call 0800 252747). They will then deliver to your door within fourteen days of order. NOTE: catalogues themselves are only available through Argos stores.

General Catalogues

Catalogue: *Biannually, A4, Catalogue, 380 pages, Colour, Free but only available from Argos stores* Postal charges: *Varies with item* Delivery: *Own delivery fleet* Methods of Payment: *Visa, Access / Mastercard, American Express, Diners Club Cheque*

CATAWARE
Victoria Mill
Bakewell
Derbyshire
DE45 1DA

Telephone:
0629 813993

Fax:
0629 814419

CAT THEME ITEMS
This catalogue is a collection of 1000+ cat-themed items for you, your cats and the cat lovers in your life. There are many useful and unusual items, including cat care, homewares, jewellery, stickers and stamps, gifts and games, toys and books.
  Ladies briefs with various cat motifs are £2.50, a cat pendulum clock is £16.90 and a cat ice cube tray £4.50. A comfortable cat radiator bed sells for £14.90 and a Cosibin cat home for £29.99. Cat and butterflies window stickers are £1.90, while a selection of cat stickers is 99p. Finally there is a rather attractive pewter cat climbing brooch and porcelain ginger cat earring for just £7.90. Cat lovers order one now!

Catalogue: *Annually plus newsletters, A5, Catalogue, 96 pages, Colour, £1.00 refundable* Postal charges: *Varies with item* Delivery: *Royal Mail, Parcelforce* Methods of Payment: *Cheque, Postal Order, Visa, Access / Mastercard*

CHESTER-CARE
Sidings Road
Low Moor Est.
Kirkby in Ashfield
Notts
NG17 7JZ

Telephone:
0623 757955

Fax:
0623 757955

ACCESSORIES TO HELP THE ELDERLY OR DISABLED
This catalogue has been designed to make daily living easier for the elderly and the disabled. Inside are more than 750 items and there is a 10% discount to anyone ordering at least six products. The items range from lap desks (£17.25), easi-pegs (£3.29 for ten) and Strong Boy jar openers (£6.59) to stay-warm plates (£4.39), Arran riser chairs (£417) and neck support pillows (£16.49). Every item helps someone with a physical disability or problem.

Catalogue: *Quarterly, A4, Brochure, 40 pages, Colour, 50p* Postal charges: *Varies with item* Delivery: *Royal Mail* Methods of Payment: *Cheque, Postal Order, Visa, Access / Mastercard*

DTS
20 Stafford Street
Market Drayton
Shropshire
TF9 1HY

Telephone:
0630 655875

Fax:
0630 655015

TATTOO EQUIPMENT AND SUPPLIES
For 85 years this family business has been supplying tattooists with all their needs. Their products include machines, materials, hygiene, designs, design resources and specialist books.
  They also stock office and stationery supplies and daylight simulation lighting for all arts and crafts (the bulbs cost £4.30). In addition, there is a line of para-medical supplies and hygiene/sterilisation hardware

General Catalogues

and consumables. Their camouflage cosmetic preparations come in a sixteen colour trial palette for £8.95, while temporary body art transfers start at just 76p. They also have an extensive range of books and magazines.

Catalogue: *Annually, A4, Catalogue, 40 pages, B/W, Free* Postal charges: *Varies with item* Delivery: *Royal Mail, Parcelforce* Methods of Payment: *Cheque, Postal Order, COD, Visa, Access / Mastercard*

FREEMANS
139 Clapham Road
London
SW99 0YX

Telephone:
0345 900 100
Fax:
071 587 1059

GENERAL GOODS
Virtually synonymous with mail order, Freemans offer everything from lingerie to motor insurance. In fact, it's hard to think of anything they don't stock. From computer games to garden ponds, their range is as thorough as it is diverse.

A great deal of the gigantic catalogue is devoted to clothes, although you won't find exclusive designer labels here. One trick worth knowing is that along with other giant catalogues they offer large discounts on your first order. If you request a catalogue and do nothing this seems to go up, with ever more persistent letters urging you to order. The top discount is around 25% – well worth it on a large purchase.

Catalogue: *A4, Catalogue, 1064 pages, Colour, Free* Postal charges: *Free* Delivery: *In-house delivery* Methods of Payment: *Cheque, Postal Order, Stage Payments, Visa, Access / Mastercard*

GRAHAM & GREEN
4, 7 and 10 Elgin
Crescent
London
W11 2JA

Telephone:
071 727 4594
Fax:
071 229 9717

LADIES CLOTHES AND HOME ACCESSORIES
Graham & Green offers the customer unique and original accessories for the home, chosen from around the world. There are a number of different styles to suit varied tastes (Indie, Mexican and Floral) and a range of different items from patchwork quilts (£345), twig baskets (£10.95) and painted candlesticks (£25.75) to tartan rugs (£12.50), Mexican dolls (£8.25) and candelabras (£275). The clothes are dressy and they come in four different styles for women (Stella, Anita, Ramona and Jessica (red lycra top, £110).

Catalogue: *Large, folding leaflet, Leaflet, 16 pages, Colour, Free* Postal charges: *Varies with item* Delivery: *Royal Mail* Methods of Payment: *Cheque, Visa, Access / Mastercard*

General Catalogues

GRATTAN
Anchor House
Ingleby Road
Bradford
BD99 2XG

Telephone:
0274 575511
Fax:
0274 574499

EVERYTHING!
Providing one of the widest range of goods through mail order in the country, Grattan's giant catalogues are classics. Each of the seventeen sections is easy to follow and filled with great value items as well as some luxury goods.

Everything is here, from a new bedroom for £400.00 or new shoes from £20.00. There are plenty of brand names in electronics, appliances and clothes, although you will not find exclusive designer labels. Like other similar operations, they offer discounts on your first order as well as the option to pay in instalments.

Catalogue: *Biannually, A4, Catalogue, 1087 pages, Colour, Free* Postal charges: *Varies with item* Delivery: *Royal Mail, Courier* Methods of Payment: *Cheque, Postal Order, Stage Payments*

GREAT UNIVERSAL STORES
Universal House
Devonshire Street
Manchester
M60 1SS

Telephone:
061 272 8282

GENERAL
Great Universal stock a broad range of products, from mens' and women's clothing to soft furniture and bathroom fittings. Catering for the mass market, here's where you'll find an astonishing variety of floral furniture covers, extensively veneered reproduction furniture and assorted keep-fit equipment.

Of the clothing, a woman's 'Essential Nightdress', available in a choice of two lengths and three colours, costs just £9.99. You can pick up a pack of two nightdresses for £16.99. Children's hooded tops in two colours cost only £6.99 and men's twill shirts start at £14.99.

Catalogue: *Biannually, A4, Catalogue, 1042 pages, Colour, Free* Postal charges: *Free* Delivery: *Royal Mail* Methods of Payment: *Cheque, Postal Order, Visa, Access / Mastercard*

GREENPEACE, THE CATALOGUE
PO Box 10
Gateshead Tyne & Wear
NE8 1LL

Telephone:
091 491 0034
Fax:
091 487 0133

GIFTS
Profits from this catalogue go to help Greenpeace fund its campaigning activities. As one might expect, it is full of environmentally friendly products. These includes clothes, mugs, brooches, bowls, cards, keyrings and even a hammock. The quality seems high and the designs surprisingly attractive.

A Greenpeace sweatshirt sells for £18 and a T-shirt for £7.95. A knit-your-own sweater is £49.95, while cycle shorts are £16.50 and a Bangladeshi jute mat £8.95. The hammock is £26.95.

Catalogue: *Biannually, Catalogue, 19 pages, Free* Postal charges: *Varies with item* Delivery: *Royal Mail* Methods of Payment: *Cheque, Visa, Access / Mastercard*

General Catalogues

GUS HOME SHOPPING
Northwick Avenue
Barbourne
Worcester
WR3 7AX

GENERAL
GUS Home Shopping's 'Family Album' catalogue is probably not much different from any other multi-purpose general catalogue. It includes an extensive range of men, women and children's clothes plus the usual furniture items. Much of the stock also appears in GUS's 'Great Universal' catalogue.

Bargains of particular note include a three-piece 'holiday' set of women's clothing: a T-shirt, a dress and a pair of shorts for £29.99. Men's trousers are available from just £12.99.

If you want something for the home, you could choose a five-door wardrobe for £299.99, an antique finish bed for £109.99 or a Parkinson Cowan gas cooker for £369.99.

Catalogue: *Biannually, A4, Catalogue, 1042 pages, Colour, Free* Postal charges: *Free* Delivery: *Royal Mail* Methods of Payment: *Cheque, Postal Order, Visa, Access / Mastercard*

IDEAL HOME MAIL ORDER
9 Flag Business Exchange
Peterborough
PE1 5TX

Telephone:
0733 890155
Fax:
0733 344977

GENERAL HOUSEHOLD
Ideal Home Mail Order publishes its Home Shopping catalogue three times a year. Each one offers a range of goods, suitable for all ages from children through to the elderly. There is something useful for everyone here, whether it's for the kitchen, gardening or car. There are also personal aids, DIY equipment and gifts. Prices range from under £5.00 to over £100.00

Catalogue: *A5, Catalogue, 32-48 pages, Colour, Free* Postal charges: *Varies with item* Delivery: *Royal Mail, Parcelforce* Methods of Payment: *Cheque, Postal Order, Visa, Access / Mastercard*

KAY & COMPANY
The Tything
St Oswalds Road
Worcester
WR99 2BR

Telephone:
071 707 1077

DEPARTMENT STORE
Kays, currently celebrating its 200th year in business, is one of the largest mail order companies in the country. Their gigantic catalogue, the size and weight of a London telephone directory, is crammed with thousands of goods. There is literally something for everybody here, from clothes and shoes through kitchen and bathroom to hi-fi, photographic and automotive.

Most items are well-known brands and prices are competitive, escpecially if you use the credit-free payment schemes. There are also substantial discounts on the first order (especially if you wait until they send you a reminder, when the discount seems

General Catalogues

to go up!). It can therefore be worth ordering a large item first. They have local phone numbers all over the country, too many to list, but call the London one for a number in your area.

Catalogue: *A4, Catalogue, 1044 pages, Colour, Free* Postal charges: *Varies with item* Delivery: *White Arrow* Methods of Payment: *Cheque, Postal Order, Stage Payments, Visa, Access / Mastercard*

LANGLEY HOUSE LTD
P O Box 239
36 Hilton Street
Manchester
M99 1LH

Telephone:
061 236 4488

CLOTHING, HOUSEHOLD GOODS AND GIFTS
Langley House have brought together something for everyone in this catalogue. Clearly illustrated sections show a wide range of clothing for women and men, home accessories, handy gadgets and gifts for friends and family.

Langley House tries to secure goods at reasonable prices and pass these savings on to the customer. For example, a valet stand costs £9.99 and a garden seat, with black cast-iron arms and legs and wooden slats, is just £34.99.

Catalogue: *A5, Catalogue, 64 pages, Colour, Free* Postal charges: *Varies with item* Delivery: *Royal Mail* Methods of Payment: *Cheque, Postal Order, Visa, Access / Mastercard*

LITTLEWOODS HOME SHOPPING GROUP
Kershaw Avenue
Crosby
Merseyside
L72 0LG

Telephone:
0800 616611
Fax:
051 920 1515

WIDE RANGE OF CLOTHES, ACCESSORIES AND HOUSEHOLD PRODUCTS
Littlewoods Home Shopping Group is one of the most established general home shopping companies, with over 60 years' experience in the sector. The Littlewoods Home Shopping Catalogue is published twice a year and comprises 1,000 pages featuring fashion clothing, childrenswear, top sportswear brands, a full range of household goods, furniture, electrical equipment, and toys.

The Littlewoods catalogue is also noted for its production of exclusive top name designer ranges by Workers for Freedom and Vivienne Westwood.

Catalogues published by Littlewoods Home Shopping Group also include Littlewoods, John Moores, Peter Craig, Janet Frazer, Burlington and Brian Mills.

Catalogue: *Biannually, 23cm × 27cm, Catalogue, Colour, 1,000 pages, Free* Postal charges: *Free; small charge for 48-hour delivery* Delivery: *Parcelforce; Home Express carrier company which is owned by Littlewoods Home Shopping* Methods of Payment: *Cheque, Postal Order, COD, Stage Payments*

General Catalogues

MUJI
26 Great Marlborough Street
London
W1V 1HL

Telephone:
071 494 1197

GENERAL
The Japanese store MUJI has shops in London and Glasgow, and now offers a mail order service as well. The goods are never branded and have no logo on them, the philosophy being that the value is in the product itself, not in its designer or manufacturer. The principles holding together the quirky range goods are sound natural materials, simple functional design, no excessive decoration and no-nonsense packaging at a reasonable price.

The stylish catalogue concentrates on clothes (vests, boxer shorts, socks, pyjamas, camisoles), stationery and storage devices (metal and cardboard containers).

No prices are printed and the company requests customers telephone before ordering to check availability and price.

Catalogue: *200 × 210mm, Catalogue, 16 pages, Colour, Free* Postal charges: *Varies with item* Delivery: *Royal Mail* Methods of Payment: *Cheque, Postal Order, Visa, Access / Mastercard, American Express, Diners Club*

QVC
Marco Polo Building
Chelsea Bridge
Queenstown Road
London
SW8 4NQ

Telephone:
0800 50 40 30

TV SHOPPING
Forget queues and crowded streets, QVC offers you an easy and enjoyable way to shop, right from the comfort of your own home. Hour after hour, 24 hours a day, seven days a week, they broadcast demonstrations of a wide range of goods on television.

The range covers most household items, including clothes, sports goods, jewellery, leisure goods and entertainment memorabilia. There are many designer names and famous brands too, all with full money-back guarantees. Ordering is simplicity itself. If you see something you like, just dial 0800 50 40 30 and they'll have it packaged and delivered to your front door within five working days.

Catalogue: *On TV* Postal charges: *Varies with item* Delivery: *Parcelforce* Methods of Payment: *Cheque, Postal Order, Visa, Access / Mastercard, American Express, Diners Club*

STUDIO CARDS AND GIFTS
Birley Bank
Preston X
PR1 4AE

Telephone:
0772 259351

CARDS, GIFTS AND GENERAL GOODS
Studio pack their catalogue with all manner of traditional cards and novelty gifts. First off are the cards for special occasions, the only proviso being, you have to like cute pictures of cats, dogs and teddy bears or animated woodland scenes of animals fishing. A 'Classic Occasion' set of ten cards costs £3.99. Novelty gifts include a musical ceramic figure of a

General Catalogues

mother and child for £15.99 or a lovely 'Twinkling Musical Rose Light' for £10.99.

You'll also find such gems as the 'Tool Tidy Wall Rack' (£5.99), silver cleaning solution (£4.99) and an exclusive range of 'Chef' teapots (£14.99), cheese dishes (£9.99), cruet sets (£7.99) and egg cups (£2.99). Each item is modelled on a cheerful chef with a red scarf.

Catalogue: *Annually, A4, Catalogue, 196 pages, Colour, Free* Postal charges: *£1.95* Delivery: *Royal Mail* Methods of Payment: *Cheque, Postal Order, Visa, Access / Mastercard*

TEDDY BEARS OF WITNEY
99 High Street
Witney
Oxford
OX8 6LY
Telephone:
0993 702616
Fax:
0993 702344

TEDDY BEARS FOR COLLECTORS
Established as a shop in 1985, Witneys have always aimed to offer collectors the best possible choice of old and new teddy bears. They now offer the same service by mail, and their catalogue contains nearly 200 traditional bears from over 1000 available in the shop.

Favourites include 'Barnaby' (no.1) by Merrythought, which sells for £58.00, 'Little Bertie' (no.19) by Deans at £38.00, 'Bentley' (no.29) by Big Softies and Max (no.123) by Hermann for £55.00.

Catalogue: *Annually, Catalogue, 24 pages, Colour, £3.00* Postal charges: *Varies with item* Delivery: *Parcelforce* Methods of Payment: *Cheque, Postal Order, COD, Stage Payments, Visa, Access / Mastercard*

THE EBERSBACH COLLECTION LTD
Ingrams Well
Ingrams Well Road
Sudbury
Suffolk
CO10 6XJ

GENERAL EXOTIC ITEMS
The Ebersbach Collection covers a range of exotic as well as more commonplace items. Among the exotic are polyester satin kimonos starting at £39.95. They are specially made for the Ebersbach Collection in Kyoto, Japan. Each one is fully lined in warm red.

There's also a bentwood rocking chair (£59.95), based on an original design from 1860. The cane back and seat of the original have been updated with patchwork leather or tapestry upholstery.

Along more practical lines, there's a selection of sturdy suitcases. Prices range from the 'Flight Case' at £69.00 to a large case on wheels for £99.00.

Catalogue: *A5, Leaflet, 5 pages, Colour, Free* Postal charges: *Varies with item* Delivery: *Royal Mail* Methods of Payment: *Cheque, Visa, Access / Mastercard*

Gifts

A PACK OF CARDS
Hollins Hill House
Utkinton
Tarporley
Cheshire
CW6 OJP

Telephone:
0892 760549

PLAYING CARDS AND BRIDGE ACCESSORIES

A Pack of Cards aims to offer one of the largest selections of playing cards in the country. It carries over 50 designs, 36 of which are shown in the brochure, along with personalised cards. Bridge cloths, scorers, pens and pencils are all shown in the brochure. All enquiries for other items connected with cards are always welcome.

Cards cost from £8.75 to £12.50; plain velvet bridge cloths cost £16.50; white enamel bridge pens cost £21.50; and a pack of four scorepads costs £6.95.

Catalogue: *Annually, A5, Brochure, 6 pages, Colour, Free* Postal charges: *Varies with item* Delivery: *Royal Mail* Methods of Payment: *Cheque*

A T CROSS UK LTD
Business Gifts Division
Concorde House
Concorde Street
Luton
Beds
LU2 0JD

Telephone:
0582 422793
Fax:
0582 456097

QUALITY PENS AND PENCILS

Alonzo T Cross established his business in 1846 and since then the company's craftsmen have established an enviable reputation for excellence in materials, quality and style. Many of the designs are unique, with more than 20 patents on Cross pens and pencils.

This catalogue illustrates clearly the range of writing instruments, desk sets and accessories that are outstanding gifts for a lifetime of use.

The fountain pens in the 'Signature' range start at £190.00, and those in the 'Classic Black' range are only £55.00. Desk sets start at £74.00 and go up to £215.00.

Catalogue: *A4, Catalogue, 24 pages, Colour, Free* Postal charges: *Varies with item* Delivery: *Royal Mail* Methods of Payment: *Cheque, Postal Order, Visa, Access / Mastercard*

ACORNE AIR SPORTS
Wycombe Air Centre
Booker
Marlow
Bucks
SL7 3DR

Telephone:
0494 451703
Fax:
0494 465456

GIFT VOUCHERS

Acorne provide gift vouchers for nationwide introductory sessions in flying, gliding, helicopters, tandem skydiving, parachuting, ballooning and karting. The vouchers are wonderful gifts for birthdays, Christmas, retirement and anniversaries.

The vouchers are personalised for the recipient and supplied in a colourful folder together with a certificate, address list of all clubs accepting Acorne vouchers and full redemption instructions.

For an extra charge of £14, a presentation pack consisting of clipboard, log book, pen, sticker, introductory audio-cassette and booklet, magazine subscription and BGA/BPA/AOPA Student Pilot

Gifts

Membership is available for all courses, except Karting.

An Explorer voucher for Tandem Skydiving is £279.00, which entitles the bearer to two jumps.

Catalogue: *A4, Brochure, 6 pages, Colour, Free* Postal charges: *Varies with item* Delivery: *Royal Mail* Methods of Payment: *Cheque, Visa, Access / Mastercard*

APPALACHIA – THE FOLK ART SHOP
14a George Street
St Albans
Herts
AL3 4ER

Telephone:
0727 836796
Fax:
0992 467560

TRADITIONAL AMERICAN-MADE ARTS, CRAFTS AND SOFT FURNISHINGS

A spin-off from the successful shop of the same name in St Albans, this small brochure features the most popular items from the retail outlet. There is one large photograph with many items featured, plus about eight other smaller photographs depicting two or three items.

The range includes Tillie freestanding doll with dried herbs and flowers, £39.99; handmade distressed Kentucky clocks, from £24.99; vertical heart cookie-cutter garland, £17.99; dried cinnamon apple slices hanging garland, £9.99; US-made cotton throws, £59.99; and the Naturelovers Watercolour, £110.00.

Catalogue: *A5, Brochure, 6 pages, Colour, Free* Postal charges: *Orders up to £10.00, £1.00; between £10.00 and £25.00, £2.00; between £25.00 and £40.00, £3.50; more than £40.00, £4.50. Varies with item* Delivery: *Royal Mail* Methods of Payment: *Cheque, Postal Order, Visa, Access / Mastercard*

BALLOON CLUB OF GREAT BRITAIN LIMITED
Montgolfier House
Fairoaks Airport
Chobham
Woking
Surrey
GU24 8HU

Telephone:
0276 855111
Fax:
0276 858868

BALLOON TRIPS

Taking flight in a balloon is a great way of seeing the local countryside and it makes an unusual present for someone with a sense of adventure. Balloon flying is now very safe and if the qualified pilot has any qualms about bad weather then the flight will be postponed.

First-time fliers are given a special certificate to mark the occasion as well as a celebratory, complimentary glass or two of champagne (or soft drink). Take-off times are normally in the morning or early evening when the conditions are usually most favourable.

Catalogue: *A5, Brochure, 4 pages, Colour, Free* Methods of Payment: *Cheque, Visa, Access / Mastercard*

Gifts

BIJOU CHILDREN'S MAGICAL THEATRE
Brook House
Dranllwyn Lane
Machen
nr Newport
Gwent
NP1 8QS

Telephone:
0633 440466

PERSONALISED CHILDREN'S BOOKS

Bijou was first established in 1959 and has brought the highest standards of magical entertainment to children both here and abroad. These same high standards are now being applied to the production of these lovely children's books.

In these books, your child becomes the STAR and appears on almost every full-coloured page. A Personalised Baby Book costs only £8.50; *Dinosaur Adventure*; *Robin Hood*; *Tom and Jerry*; *Beauty and the Beast*; *The Space Adventure*; *A Christmas Story*, all at £6.50. There are more than twenty books available. Send for a leaflet and samples of these books which will make a gift to treasure.

Catalogue: *A4, Brochure, 4 pages, Colour, Free* Postal charges: *Varies with item* Delivery: *Royal Mail, Parceline* Methods of Payment: *Cheque, Postal Order, COD*

BLOOMS OF GUERNSEY
Portinfer Coast Road
Vale
Guernsey
Channel Islands

Telephone:
0481 53085
Fax:
0481 53840

FLOWERS AND DOLLS

Blooms of Guernsey have won several awards for their exhibits and they offer a mail service sending pinks, gypsy, chincherinchees, lilies, carnations, Miss Dianas and freesias.

To the United Kingdom, there is no charge for postage and packing, and complimentary fern is added. For the rest of Europe, there is a £5.00 charge, and flowers sent to Europe are done so at the purchaser's risk.

Blooms also sell teddy bears and rabbits which can include a personal message on a red or blue sweater and a Guernsey lily doll with a porcelain face and soft body, but which cannot have a message.

Catalogue: *Loose-leaf, Leaflet, 5 pages, Colour and B/W, Free* Postal charges: *Varies with item* Delivery: *Royal Mail* Methods of Payment: *Cheque, Postal Order, Visa, Access / Mastercard, American Express*

BUNCHES
PO Box 20
Kirkby in Ashfield
Nottingham
NG17 8ES

Telephone:
0623 750343
Fax:
0623 758704

FLOWERS

This brochure comes quite literally through the post. As part of the Post Office's diversification plans, a flowers by post service is now offered through their branches or by telephone. There are seven bouquets to choose from, one of which is exclusively of roses and two of which are a combination of flowers and chocolates.

The flowers are predominantly carnations, and the simplest bouquet sells for £9.99, with a luxury selec-

Gifts

tion for £24.99. Orders should be placed at least three days in advance, five for special occasions like Mother's Day.

Catalogue: *Third A4, Leaflet, 12 pages, Colour, Free* Postal charges: *Free* Delivery: *Royal Mail* Methods of Payment: *Cheque, Postal Order, Visa, Access / Mastercard*

BURBERRYS
MBNA International Bank Ltd
P.O. Box 1003
Chester Business Park
Wrexham Road
Chester
CH4 9YZ

Telephone:
071 930 7803
Fax:
071 839 2418

AN EXTENSIVE RANGE OF GIFTS, FOODS, CLOTHES AND ACCESSORIES
As well as providing a wide range of tailored clothes for both adults and children, Burberrys of London offer toys (£25.00 for a teddy bear), knitwear, raincoats (£405.00), umbrellas, luggage, fragrances and watches (£325.00). There are also food hampers containing jams, whisky, biscuits, chocolate, etc.

All the merchandise in the catalogue is available from their stores in the United Kingdom or direct through mail order. All gifts are gift-wrapped on request with no extra charge, and you can even have your raincoat monogrammed with your own initials.

Catalogue: *A4, Catalogue, 20 pages, Colour and B/W, Free* Postal charges: *Varies with item* Delivery: *Royal Mail* Methods of Payment: *Cheque, Visa, Access / Mastercard*

CALENDAR MEMORIES
Bravequest
PO Box 7
Brentford
Middlesex
TW8 9BU

Telephone:
081 958 7194
Fax:
081 958 2962

PERSONALISED CALENDARS
This innovative company will take any photographs and make them into a calendar. So you could have different photos of your family and pets each month – an ideal gift for someone living abroad.

A twelve month calendar, requiring a dozen photographs, costs £16.95 inclusive, while a quarterly version, needing just four photos, is £9.95. Originals can be in colour or black and white, but must be prints not slides or negatives.

Catalogue: *A5, Leaflet, 1 page, Colour, Free* Postal charges: *Free* Delivery: *Royal Mail* Methods of Payment: *Cheque, Postal Order, Visa, Access / Mastercard*

CHINACRAFT
1 Beauchamp Place
London
SW3 1NG

Telephone:
071 225 1696
Fax:
071 225 2283

GIFTS, TABLEWARE AND CRYSTAL
An independent family business, Chinacraft was established nearly 50 years ago and it is the largest British privately-owned tableware, gift and crystal specialist.

They stock such major brand names as Wedgwood, Royal Doulton, Royal Crown Derby, Aynsley, Spode, Royal Worcester, Swarowski, Border Fine Arts, Country Artists and others too numerous to mention.

Gifts

There is an enormous range from which to choose, with small items (gold plated golfer's penknife/keyring, £17.99) to the larger (antique English wooden chests, £895).

Catalogue: *Annually, 20cm × 20cm, Catalogue, 25 pages, Colour, Free* Postal charges: *Varies with item* Delivery: *Royal Mail* Methods of Payment: *Cheque, Postal Order, Visa, Access / Mastercard, American Express, Diners Club*

CHOC EXPRESS BY THORNTONS
Mint House
Newark Close
Royston
Herts
SG8 5HL

Telephone:
0763 241444
Fax:
0763 244666

LUXURY CHOCOLATES BY POST

With Choc Express you can send a Chocogram direct to any UK address (overseas service also available). Each Chocogram contains a selection of luxury Thorntons milk, dark and white chocolates contained in a unique crush-proof outer box. A full-size greetings card is included with your personal message of up to twenty words.

Chocogram 18 (225gm) costs £12.95 inclusive of post and packaging. Chocogram 32 (400gm) costs £19.95 inclusive of post and packaging.

Order by telephone hotline or by post, quoting product choice, your address, destination address, message and latest delivery date, making cheques payable to Choc Express Ltd.

Catalogue: *Annually, A5, Catalogue, 6 pages, Colour, Free* Postal charges: *Free* Delivery: *Royal Mail, Parcelforce* Methods of Payment: *Cheque, Postal Order, Visa, Access / Mastercard, American Express, Diners Club*

CHUNKYDORY
55 Cuckoo Hill Road
Pinner
Middlesex
HA5 1AU

Telephone:
081 866 7263

COSTUME JEWELLERY

Costume jewellery at affordable prices, covering the spectrum from fun to elegance. Each item is uniquely gift-wrapped. Chunkydory trades at charity functions, craft fairs and party plans and advertises in women's magazines. A wide range of costume jewellery is available in silver, glass, gold, pearls and wood. Prices range from £2.50 to £25.00, with postage and packing extra.

Papier mâché gift boxes are also available from £2.50 to £2.95. The brochure is on stapled paper with line drawings showing the different designs.

Catalogue: *A3, Brochure, 29 pages, B/W, £1.00* Postal charges: *Varies with item* Delivery: *Royal Mail* Methods of Payment: *Cheque, Postal Order*

Gifts

DIAMOND FLOWERS
Les Arbres
Les Gigands
St. Sampsons
Guernsey
Channel Islands
GY2 4YX

Telephone:
0481 46375
Fax:
0481 43462

FLOWERS

Diamond Flowers will post flowers from Guernsey to the UK by the first post Mondays to Thursdays. They will send carnations, spray carnations and freesias or a mixed bouquet in various sizes. The company grow their own blooms and they then pick, pack and post them.

Each selection contains the customer's selection, plus fern and a gift card containing the message from the sender. Diamond Flowers also include in the box a complimentary sachet of plant food together with hints on flower care. These helpful tips should ensure that the flowers remain fresh and in bloom for longer.

Catalogue: *Third A4, Brochure, 8 pages, Colour, Free* Postal charges: *Varies with item* Delivery: *Royal Mail* Methods of Payment: *Cheque, Postal Order, Visa, Access / Mastercard*

EDRADOUR DISTILLERY
Pitlochry
Perthshire
PH16 5JP

Telephone:
0796 472095
Fax:
0796 472002

DISTILLERY GIFTS

Edradour, founded in 1825, is the smallest whisky distillery in Scotland. Set in the hills above Pitlochry, amidst magnificent Perthshire countryside, it is probably the finest example of traditional Scottish whisky distilling.

The colour leaflet provides a clear presentation of the distillery's labelled gifts, with easy to understand descriptions and full colour pictures.

An example of the type of gifts on offer are the Presentation Flagon with Edradour Single Malt Whisky for £29.00, the sweatshirt with distillery logo for £15.50 and the Pewter Quaich for £10.50. All highly original.

Catalogue: *A5, Leaflet, 8 pages, Colour, Free* Postal charges: *Varies with item* Delivery: *Royal Mail* Methods of Payment: *Cheque, Visa, Access / Mastercard, American Express*

FIRST IMPRESSIONS
Lewes Road
Forest Row
East Sussex
RH18 5LM

Telephone:
0342 824246
Fax:
0342 822289

CHEAP JEWELLERY AND GIFTS

With a name like 'First Impressions', it's surprising to find their catalogues so impenetrable. There's a small note, 'Catalogue Guide', at the bottom of their price list which tells you they've got six different catalogues: 'where an item is illustrated, the page number is listed in the column on this order form marked "Page"'.

Admittedly, each of their six catalogues is sumptuously produced. Their collection of brooches ranges from very large (£3.60) to medium (£3.00) and

Gifts

covers a wide variety of subjects. Among other things, there are also buckles, dinner table decorations and photoframes.

Catalogue: *A6, Brochure, Colour, Free* Postal charges: *Varies with item* Delivery: *Royal Mail* Methods of Payment: *Cheque, Postal Order*

FLYING FLOWERS
PO Box 5555
St Helier
Jersey
Channel Islands
JE4 8XJ

Telephone:
0534 865665
Fax:
0534 865554

FRESH FLOWER BOUQUETS

Whether it's a birthday, anniversary, Christmas or a thank you, sorry or get well soon message, it can be said with flowers. This company will send beautiful nursery-fresh bouquets direct from Jersey to any UK address. They have been in business for the last thirteen years, establishing themselves as the UK's largest carnation grower and fresh flower postal company.

Bouquets are made with fresh flowers and greenery and include wrap, flower food, care leaflet and a message card. Prices include sturdy, 'gift-wrapped' packaging and delivery. Twelve mixed carnations are just £9.99, 15 assorted carnations cost £13.99, 20 are £16.99 and 30 assorted carnations and freesias are £19.99.

Catalogue: *None* Postal charges: *Free* Delivery: *Royal Mail* Methods of Payment: *Cheque, Postal Order, Visa, Access / Mastercard, American Express*

FOREVER FLOWERING
Orchard House
Mortlake Road
Kew Gardens
Surrey
TW9 4AS

Telephone:
081 392 9929
Fax:
081 392 9929

FLOWER DELIVERY SERVICE

Forever Flowering offers fresh flowers personally selected, exquisitely arranged and delivered by post the very next day. When the customer rings, his or her personal preferences will be discussed and the company will recommend the freshest blooms available that morning.

Prices start from £20.00 and items range from baskets to hand-tied bouquets. The gift arrives in perfect condition, handsomely wrapped and with a hand-written card, all in a sturdy presentation box.

Catalogue: *Third A4, Leaflet, 6 pages, Colour, Free* Postal charges: *Varies with item* Delivery: *Courier* Methods of Payment: *Cheque, Visa, Access / Mastercard*

Gifts

FRIENDS OF THE EARTH
Helston
Cornwall
TR13 0TE

Telephone:
0209 831999

GIFTS AND CLOTHES
Not surprisingly, everything in this catalogue is eco-friendly but also stylish and attractive. All cotton clothing items are 'green', in that no harmful sprays have been used on the plants or chemicals in the manufacturing process. In addition to its small range of clothes, this catalogue offers soaps, stationery (recycled, of course), unbleached towels, mugs, glasses, a birdfeeder and an umbrella with a rainforest design.

Mugs are £2.99 each, 100 envelope re-use labels £2.25 and a rugby shirt £18.00. Profits go to furthering the cause.

Catalogue: *A5, Catalogue, 8 pages, Colour, Free* Postal charges: *Varies with item* Delivery: *Royal Mail* Methods of Payment: *Cheque, Postal Order, Visa, Access / Mastercard*

GLENDEVON SMOKED SALMON
Crook of Devon
Kinross
KY13 7UL

Telephone:
0577 840297
Fax:
0577 840626

SMOKED SALMON
Glendevon Smoked Salmon is a well-established, family-run business selling finest quality, oak-smoked Scottish salmon. Smoked salmon in distinctive scarlet gift boxes can be mailed to most parts of the world. It makes an ideal gift for those of all ages on all occasions: birthdays, Christmas or as a thank-you present.

The prices for delivery in the UK are 8oz: £10.50, 1lb: £17.00 and 2lbs: £28.00 for sliced packs off the skin. The 2lb unsliced pack on the skin costs £25.00. Prices for the rest of the world are included in the brochure.

Catalogue: *Biannually, 3rd A4, Brochure, 1 page, B/W, Free* Postal charges: *Free* Delivery: *Royal Mail* Methods of Payment: *Cheque, Postal Order, Visa, Access / Mastercard*

GRANTS OF DALVEY
Freepost 1032
Alness
Rossshire
IV17 0BR

Telephone:
0349 884111
Fax:
0349 884100

SCOTTISH GIFTS, WHISKY
'Lasting Impressions' is a brand new catalogue launched by the old Scottish family, Grants of Dalvey, whose firm manufactures unusual gifts of quality. Aimed at the corporate market as well as the individual, it produces business accessories such as credit card holders, £24.95; briefcase tags, £13.95; pocket flasks £34.95; and travel alarm clocks for £49.95.

Each item is crafted from stainless steel with a solid brass badge, which can be personalised. In addition, the company makes 10-year-old malt whisky, which is available at a discount if another purchase is made from the catalogue.

Gifts

GUERNSEY FRESH FLOWERS
La Couture Road
St Peter Port
Guernsey
Channel Islands
GY1 2EA

Telephone:
0481 722280
0481 716599
Fax:
0481 714656

Catalogue: *Annually, Third A4, Leaflet, 12 pages, Colour, Free* Postal charges: £2.95 Delivery: *Royal Mail* Methods of Payment: *Cheque, Postal Order, Visa, Access / Mastercard, American Express, Diners Club*

FLOWERS
Guernsey send freshly picked bouquets of carnations, roses and freesias anywhere in the UK or Europe. The process does, however, require a little forethought. Orders need to be placed well in advance – up to a fortnight for national festivals like Mothers' Day.

If you're prepared to take the trouble, Guernsey guarantee well-presented quality flowers treated with a special preservative to ensure long-life. Prices range from twelve carnations at £9.75 to twenty red, pink or yellow roses for £20.25. Orders to Europe are £4.00 more. They also send out fluffy teddy bears!

Catalogue: *3rd A4, Leaflet, 12 pages, Colour, Free* Postal charges: *Free* Delivery: *Royal Mail* Methods of Payment: *Cheque, Postal Order, Visa, Access / Mastercard*

HALCYON DAYS
14 Brook Street
London
W1Y 8AA

Telephone:
071 629 8811

ANTIQUE POTTERY
Halcyon Days specialise in antique pottery, including Treen, Tôle and Staffordshire, as well as Georgian enamels. Their range of contemporary enamels are inspired by things as diverse as museum artifacts and the lyrics of pop songs.

In association with the Great Ormond Street Children's Hospital Fund, they have produced a range of Peter Pan enamels. A small spiral vase costs £59.50; a photograph frame costs £63.00; an oval box costs £75.00; and a round box costs £41.50.

Catalogue: *A5, Catalogue, 32 pages, Colour, Free* Postal charges: *Varies with item* Delivery: *Royal Mail* Methods of Payment: *Cheque, Postal Order, American Express, Diners Club, Visa, Access / Mastercard*

HELP THE AGED
Helpage Ltd.
PO box 28
London
N18 3HG

Telephone:
081 803 6861
Fax:
071 895 1407

GIFTS AND CARDS
Help the Aged's catalogue is quite eclectic in its choice of goods and should appeal to most people. There are the usual cards and gifts, but also useful devices specifically designed for older people. For example, the pill organiser is a neat box which ensures you take the right pill at the right time. There's an ingenious fold-away shopping bag which has wheels in the base and a thermal pad which can be put on any seat to take away the chill.

Gifts

There is also a 'handyman corner' with a a selection of tools, devices to help one get in and out of the bath and a good range of gardening equipment. Overall, a nicely produced, interesting catalogue.

Catalogue: *A4, Catalogue, 40 pages, Colour, Free* Postal charges: *Varies with item* Delivery: *Royal Mail* Methods of Payment: *Cheque, Visa, Access / Mastercard*

HOUSE OF HAMILTON LTD
Westfield House
By Harburn
West Lothian
Scotland
EH55 8RB

Telephone:
0506 418434
Fax:
0506 418413

OAK-SMOKED SCOTTISH SALMON AND GRAVADLAX
Treat your friends at any time of the year to this quality approved Scottish salmon. Winners of the *Daily Mail Weekend* magazine taste test, House of Hamilton's oak-smoked Scottish salmon is guaranteed to delight.

All fish is packed in polystyrene boxes with our ice-keeper bags to ensure optimum temperature control in transit which is in itself only a matter of hours. Ideal for Christmas, New Year, birthdays, Easter, Ascot, Wimbledon, Henley . . . in fact, at any time of year! Whole fully trimmed sides of smoked salmon start at £10.10 per lb, prime slice packs £13.60 for 1lb, £6.80 for 8oz. Gravadlax starts at £11.88 per lb.

Catalogue: *Annually, A5, Brochure, 5 pages, Colour, Free* Postal charges: *£4.30 including ice pack* Delivery: *Overnight courier* Methods of Payment: *Cheque, Visa, Access / Mastercard, American Express*

INTERFLORA
Interflora House
Watergate
Sleaford
Lincolnshire
NG34 7TB

Telephone:
0500 434343
0529 304545
Fax:
0529 414340

VARIETY OF DIFFERENT FLORAL ARRANGEMENTS AND OTHER GIFTS
Interflora offers a guaranteed personal flower delivery service which operates in over 150 countries world-wide.

It has been in operation for over 70 years and the wealth of experience and skill accumulated over this time is used to provide the customer with an unrivalled service and an extensive range of beautiful floral gifts suitable for every occasion.

The product range has recently been added to with the 'Gift Collection', which includes flowers and helium balloons, handmade chocolates and soft toys.

Using the very latest technology, orders placed for UK delivery before 1pm will arrive the same day and sometimes this applies to overseas orders, depending on time difference. Flower prices start from £7.50 for a single bloom in an attractive presentation box, £15.00 for a seasonal bouquet, £17.50 for a dainty hand-tied bouquet and £13.95 for handmade chocolates and flowers.

Catalogue: *Quarterly, Brochure, 4 pages, Colour, Free* Postal charges: *£2.95* Delivery: *In-house delivery* Methods of Payment: *Cheque, Visa, Access / Mastercard*

Gifts

INTERFLORA
Interflora House
Sleaford
Lincolnshire
NG34 7TB

Telephone:
0529 304545

FLOWER TRANSMISSION
Interflora is of course extremely well known and this leaflet describes its services in full, while giving illustrations of the company's range of products and services, i.e. flowering plants from £12.50 each up to £27.50 for a hand-tied bouquet. These prices include delivery.

The brochure and accompanying letter primarily promote the company's Flowerline, which is a 24 hour Free Call service on 0500 434343. A useful order form on the back of the leaflet assists customers in placing their order.

Catalogue: *A5, Leaflet, 4 pages, Colour, Free* Postal charges: *Varies with item* Delivery: *Courier* Methods of Payment: *Cheque, Visa, Access / Mastercard*

JANE MOORE
44 Leam Terrace
Leamington Spa
CV31 1BQ

Telephone:
0926 420833

JEWELLERY
Jane Moore makes enamelled silver jewellery. Brooches cost from £38.00 to £90.00, tie-clips £65.00, and triangular ear-hooks cost £80.00.

Her artist's statement says: 'The inspiration for my jewellery often derives from the figures and creatures, both real and imaginary, which are depicted in the art of ancient cultures. I develop my ideas in my sketchbook and eventually produce a finished design which I have photo-etched on to silver sheet. Then, using enamels, I colour the image.'

Catalogue: *A6, Leaflet, 3 pages, Colour, Free* Postal charges: *Varies with item* Delivery: *Royal Mail* Methods of Payment: *Cheque*

KEELEY DESIGNS
Keeley Designs
Leighton Buzzard
Beds
LU7 8YZ

LULLABYE TAPES
Keeley Designs produce just one product: a book-and-cassette pack of twelve traditional lullabies. Just the thing to indulge your children as the evenings draw in and the shadows grow longer. Each lullaby is presented as a beautiful picture with melody-line music and words, so you can hum, whistle or sing along too.

The pack costs £9.50. You can listen to the tapes, follow each lullaby in the appropriate book and then stick the picture somewhere memorable.

Catalogue: *A6, Leaflets, 3, Colour, Free* Postal charges: *Varies with item* Delivery: *Royal Mail* Methods of Payment: *Cheque, Postal Order*

Gifts

LAXEY COTTAGE CRAFTS
Beechwood
Fairy Cottage
Laxey
Isle of Man

Telephone:
0624 861191

ORNAMENTS

Laxey Cottage Crafts produce a range of small statues of the kind that many people enjoy collecting. They look antiquated, very English and ideal for the traditionally minded.

Subjects include a pair of cats on cushions, 100 mm tall and available in red, black or copper fleck decoration, for £14.00; and a pair of small rabbits, 130 mm tall, costing £15.10.

There's also a collection of miniature figures, including a lion and lamb (90 mm); Princess Victoria (110 mm) and WG Grace (125 mm); all for £11.10.

Catalogue: *A4, Leaflets, 4, Colour, Free* Postal charges: *Varies with item* Delivery: *Royal Mail* Methods of Payment: *Cheque*

LEWIS AND COOPER
92 High Street
Northallerton
N Yorks
DL7 8PP

Telephone:
0609 772880
Fax:
0609 777933

FOOD HAMPERS

Lewis and Cooper have been established well over a hundred years, and they are known to lovers of good food throughout Britain. In their Market Place shop and local premises in the busy market town of Northallerton, they have been making up gift packs and food hampers for business and personal customers for well over half a century. As a result, they are experienced in carefully and professionally packing food hampers and gifts for distribution nationwide. Over the years they have despatched literally thousands of food hampers to grateful recipients.

Special hampers can be made for any occasions – weddings, anniversaries, prizes. Business requirements are a speciality.

Catalogue: *Bi-annually, A5, Brochure, 8 pages, Colour, Free* Postal charges: *Varies with item* Delivery: *Parcelforce* Methods of Payment: *Cheque, Postal Order, Visa, Access / Mastercard*

MAGNIFICENT MOUCHOIRS
140 Battersea Park Road
London
SW11

Telephone:
071 720 5667
Fax:
071 371 7115

HANDKERCHIEFS

Magnificent Mouchoirs don't just make handkerchiefs. In addition to a range that includes handkerchiefs (all at £6.95) decorated with chess boards, balloons, a Monopoly board or even a section of the Bayeux tapestry, they produce ties, braces and boxer shorts.

Ties (all £19.95) are covered in various designs, including classic cars, a chess set and a musical score. There are also ready-tied silk bow ties (£14.95) in the same designs. Boxer shorts (£12.95) are made from these patterns and a selection of tartans.

There is also a range of Monopoly T-shirts

Gifts

(£14.95), featuring the traditional designs including 'Mayfair', 'Go To Jail' and 'Pay £10 fine or take a chance'.

Catalogue: *A5, Catalogue, 5, Colour, Free* Postal charges: *Free* Delivery: *Royal Mail* Methods of Payment: *Visa, Access / Mastercard Cheque, Postal Order*

MEMENTOS
16 Connaught Street
London
W2 2AG

Telephone:
071 262 3226
Fax:
071 262 1363

SILVER GIFTS

Mementos produce a varied collection of silver gifts. For women there are scent bottles (£51.75), make-up brushes (£31.00) and nail buffers (£46.50). Ideas for men include silver golf tees (£37.00), letter openers (£30.50), tie slides (£25.50) and cuff-links (43.50). The range also extends to christening presents, hallmarked photograph frames and wedding gifts.

Mementos also offer a marvellous silver and gold-plating service. Send them a champagne cork from your wedding day or a baby's first pair of shoes and they will plate them in silver or gold to give a lasting reminder of life's happiest moments. Champagne corks can be silver-plated and engraved for £24.50 and a baby shoe gold-plated for £49.50.

Catalogue: *A5, Leaflets, 6 pages plus inserts, Colour, Free* Postal charges: *Varies with item* Delivery: *Royal Mail* Methods of Payment: *Visa, Access / Mastercard, American Express, Diners Club Cheque, Postal Order*

MIKE FITZ DESIGNS
37 Meadway
Harpenden
Herts
AL5 1JN

Telephone:
0582 762231

WATCH STANDS

Watch stands were first used in the 18th century when a man's watch was placed on a stand near to a candle at night so that it could be seen. Later styles were adapted for use on a mantelpiece, making more of a feature of the watch, so the more ornate the watch, the more fancy its stand.

Mike Fitz continues this tradition utilising the same porcelain, brass, silver, bronze and woods as his predecessors. However, the woods he uses are all from sustainable sources. Swiss Bernex pocket watches can be obtained from the same company together with a variety of chains.

Catalogue: *Loose leaf, Leaflets, 5 pages, Colour and B/W, Free* Postal charges: *Free* Delivery: *Royal Mail* Methods of Payment: *Cheque, Postal Order*

Gifts

ONE PLANET ONE PEOPLE
PO Box 922
London
SW17 8BR

Telephone:
081 672 9547

PERSONALISED T-SHIRTS AND SWEATSHIRTS
Personalised bar coded T-shirts and sweatshirts make an ideal gift for birthdays, Christmas, Valentines, anniversaries and leaving presents.

A giant bar code, printed on premium 100% cotton T-shirts, discreetly identifies personal details such as: country of birth, date of birth or star sign, sex, colour of eyes, colour of hair, height and birth weight.

T-shirts and sweatshirts are priced at £12.99 and £16.99 respectively (which includes VAT, Freepost and P&P). Delivery is fourteen days from receipt of order. All personal data will remain strictly private and confidential.

Catalogue: *A4, Leaflets, 2 pages, B/W, Free* Postal charges: *Free* Delivery: *Royal Mail* Methods of Payment: *Cheque, Postal Order*

PANDA POSTERS
83 Fortess Road
Kentish Town
London
NW6 1AG

POSTERS
Panda produce a range of posters of the kind that usually get hung on the back of the lavatory door. There's the usual 'witty' fare, including 'Politics For Beginners' with a variety of rather blunt insights into the world of politics, and one of those peculiar slogan posters, saying: 'If you can't dazzle them with brilliance, baffle them with bull shit!'.

There are inspirational posters, for instance 'Don't Quit' ('Success is failure turned inside out, the silver tint of the clouds of doubt . . .') and 'A Smile' ('A smile costs nothing but gives much . . .'). They cost £1.95 each.

Catalogue: *A4, Leaflets, 3, B/W, Free* Postal charges: *Varies with item* Delivery: *Royal Mail* Methods of Payment: *Cheque, Postal Order*

PERSONAL PRESENTS
The Coach House
38 Knoll Road
Dorking
Surrey
RH4 3EP

PERSONALISED GIFTS
Personal Presents offers a diverse range of gifts, primarily for men both young and old. The range includes Duchamps ceramic tap emblem cufflinks at £25.95, a 'Stressbuster Kit' which includes Ken Powell's 'Burnout' book, aromatherapy stress essence, a set of Chakra healing gems, a pair of Baoding Iron Balls and a candle scented with pure essential oils for £24.95.

A two tie and handkerchief set in either Monopoly or Le Mans design is £24.95 and an Art Gift Set which includes 24 watercolour pencils, a pad, paintbrush and techniques leaflet is £22.95.

Gifts

PINKS BY POST
The Plant House
10 Exeter Road
Exmouth
Devon
EX8 1RS

Telephone:
0395 267737
Fax:
0395 267737

Catalogue: *Third A4, Leaflets, 20 pages, Colour, Free* Postal charges: £3.50 Delivery: *Royal Mail* Methods of Payment: *Cheque, Postal Order*

FRESH FLOWERS AND DRIED FLOWERS BY FIRST CLASS POST
Fresh cut flowers, harvested twice a week, and posted before midday for first class mail delivery the following day. Standard box of twenty blooms, £9.00; 30 blooms, £12.00; and a Special box of twenty pinks and ten freesias, £15.00. Flowers are wrapped in soft paper, their stems soaked and covered in clingfilm and posted in special boxes. Order by telephone or via their black and white order forms.

Catalogue: *By Advertising, Free* Postal charges: *Free* Delivery: *Royal Mail* Methods of Payment: *Cheque, Visa, Access / Mastercard, Postal Order*

POMANDER
New Rowney Farm
Shefford
Beds
SG17 5QG

Telephone:
0462 851117

GIFT IDEAS – POT POURRI, SCENTED CANDLES
Pomander's extensive range of bath foams and massage oils, back scrubbers and loofahs banish bathtime boredom. Their range of products also includes: 24-hour scented candles from £8.20 and embroidered tapestry cushions from £55.00, as well as a superb range of herbs, spices, oils and vinegars.

Catalogue: *A4, Catalogue, 8 pages, Colour, Free* Postal charges: *Varies with item* Delivery: *Royal Mail* Methods of Payment: *Cheque*

REMEMBER WHEN
368 Brighton Road
South Croydon
Surrey

Telephone:
081 688 6323

NEWSPAPERS FROM THE DAY YOU'RE BORN
Remember When provide original issues of historical newspapers. They cannot supply a catalogue, since they have up to two million newspapers in stock.

Each newspaper usually costs £17.00. It's folded in four and sent in a card wrap. You can, however, pay £19.00 to have it rolled and sent in a presentation tube, or £32.50 to have it sent in a personalised portfolio. Papers date from 1642 to 1992, and include titles such as The Times, the Daily Telegraph and the Daily Express.

Catalogue: *A5, Leaflets, 1, Colour, Free* Postal charges: *Varies with item* Delivery: *Royal Mail* Methods of Payment: *Visa, Access / Mastercard Cheque, Postal Order*

Gifts

ROBIN AND NELL DALE
Bank House Farm
Holme Mills
Holme, Carnforth
Lancs
LA6 1RE

Telephone:
0524 781646

HANDMADE STUMP DOLLS AND CHESS FIGURES

Having worked together for twenty years, Robin and Nell Dale have had plenty of time to develop their range of limited edition chess sets. They started off making stump dolls, which became collector's items. Some of their chess sets are now in national collections.

Chess sets cost from £380.00 to £5000.00. The 'Battle of Waterloo' set costs £470.00. Individual pieces cost from pawns for £38.00 to knights for £50.00.

A stump doll nativity set contains pieces from £25.00 to £40.00. Among the other alternatives are model sportsmen: a cricketer (£25.00), a huntsman (£20.50) or mad golfers (£26.50).

Catalogue: *A5, Leaflets, 2, Colour and B/W, Free* Postal charges: *Varies with item* Delivery: *Royal Mail* Methods of Payment: *Cheque, Postal Order*

SCROLL NAMES LTD
The Towers
Village Way
Bispham
Nr Blackpool
FY2 0AB

Telephone:
0253 595454

HISTORY SURNAME SCROLLS AND GIFTS

These scrolls from the 'Hall of Names' contain the histories of more than 90,000 British and some continental names. Each history outlines the profile of a family name often from about 1100 A.D. starting in early tribal times and tracing the family as it grew.

Each personal scroll is beautifully printed with a colourful heraldic border and contains many interesting details including ancestors' coats of arms and mottos. Scrolls make an ideal gift for birthdays or any other special occasion and cost £7.99 unframed, or £19.99 in a wooden frame.

Also available are coats of arms on an embossed copper and hardwood shield from £39.99, and laser prints from £6.99.

Catalogue: *Annually, A4, Brochure, 2 pages, B/W, Free* Postal charges: *Varies with item* Delivery: *Royal Mail* Methods of Payment: *Cheque, Postal Order, Visa, Access / Mastercard*

SEND-A-SHRUB
Broome Lodge
Bungay Suffolk
NR35 2HX

Telephone:
050 845 432

SHRUBS

This a rather clever variation on the flower sending idea, you get the whole shrub! This will last for years and go on reminding the recipient of your immense generosity.

There are fifteen varieties in stock which are specially packed along with a message card. Buddleias are £12.00, camellias £13.00, forsythia £1200, hon-

Gifts

eysuckle £13.00, hibiscus £15.00, magnolias £15.00 and shrub roses £12.00.

Catalogue: *A5, Brochure, 4 pages, Colour, Free* Postal charges: *£3 per shrub* Delivery: *Royal Mail* Methods of Payment: *Visa, Access / Mastercard Cheque*

SILVER DIRECT
PO Box 925
Shaftesbury
Dorset
SP7 9RA

Telephone:
0747 828977
Fax:
0747 828961

SILVER AND SILVER PLATED GOODS
Silver Direct say they can deliver Bond Street silver at affordable prices. Their top quality, solid, hallmarked silver and silver plated items include everything from photograph frames to cutlery and from clocks to candle snuffers. Many of the designs are classic and traditional in style, making ideal presents for anniversaries, christenings, weddings and birthdays.

Prices start at a very reasonable £10.00 rising to £500.00 for the more elaborate items.

Catalogue: *Annually, A5, Brochure, 8 pages, Colour, Free* Postal charges: *Varies with item* Delivery: *Royal Mail, Parcelforce, Securicor* Methods of Payment: *Cheque, Visa, Access / Mastercard*

SPENCER THORN JEWELLERS
Belle Vue,
Bude,
Cornwall,
EX23 8JY

Telephone:
0288-353905
Fax:
0288-353905

NAPKIN HOOKS
Described as 'the essential dress accessory', the Diner's Napkin Hook is as practical as it is unusual. Designed to hang from a shirt button, or between the shirt overlap, or even from the collar, these stylish jewellery items are bound to be the subject of conversation at the dinner table.

The napkin hooks are crafted in hallmarked sterling silver and available in a variety of designs: Original, Crown, Concorde, Jaguar, Bentley and Hinged.

Prices, which include VAT and postage and packing, vary from £29.50 (Original) to £39.50 (Hinged). Both versions can be hand-engraved with up to three initials at £3.25 per letter.

Catalogue: *A4, Leaflets, 1 page, B/W, Free* Postal charges: *Varies with item* Delivery: *Royal Mail* Methods of Payment: *Cheque, Visa, Access / Mastercard, American Express*

STUBBS HUNK DESIGNS
Home Farm
Swinfen
Lichfield
Staffs
WS14 9QR

Telephone:
0543 481211

PAINTED CERAMICS
Stubbs Hunk Designs produce hand painted pots, bins and jars. Their hand painted bread bins sell at £90.00 each, with orders taking between four and six weeks to process. Designs include pig, cockerels, sheep, Friesian cows and geese. Each bin is 19 cm high and 28 cm in diameter.

You can also order storage jars, including a set of three (tea, coffee and sugar) for £80.00. A small oval

Gifts

tray costs £55.00, a trinket box will set you back £60.00 and a utensil holder is priced at £29.95.

Catalogue: *A4, Leaflets, 3, Colour and B/W, Free* Postal charges: *Free* Delivery: *Royal Mail* Methods of Payment: *Cheque, Visa, Access / Mastercard*

TELEFLORIST
British Teleflower Service Ltd
Teleflower House
Unit 35
Romsey Industrial Estate
Greatbridge Road,
Romsey
SO51 OHR

Telephone:
0794 511128
Fax:
0794 511199

FLOWERS DELIVERED TO YOUR DOOR
Unlike Interflora, there is no central telephone number through which you place orders. Instead, you find a florist displaying the Teleflorist "dove" sign and order through them. They then phone the order through to the nearest Teleflorist to the recipient. The florist will have a design book from which you can choose certain arrangements. Orders can be placed before midday and delivered on the same day.

Catalogue: *None* Postal charges: *£2.10* Delivery: *In-house delivery* Methods of Payment: *Cheque, Postal Order, Visa, Access / Mastercard*

THE ANIMAL WELFARE TRUST
Tylers Way
Watford by-Pass (A4)
Watford
Herts
WD2 8HQ

Telephone:
081 950 8215/0177

GIFTS
The Animal Welfare Trust is a registered charity founded in 1971 to care for and re-home dogs, cats and other animals which would otherwise be abandoned, left to stray or put to sleep. The Trust prides itself on its policy that no healthy animal is ever put to sleep, however long its stay.

The catalogue offers a wide range of gift products, the proceeds of which are used to assist in the upkeep of the Trust's Animal Rescue Centre. An illustration of the range are the Peg Bags with pig design at £3.25 to golfing style umbrellas for £21.50.

Catalogue: *A4, Catalogue, 12 pages, Colour, Free* Postal charges: *Varies with item* Delivery: *Royal Mail* Methods of Payment: *Cheque, Postal Order, Access / Mastercard, Visa*

THE BUTTON BADGE COMPANY LTD
30/31 Coppice Trading Estate
Kidderminster
Worcs
DY11 7QY

Telephone:
0562 823375
Fax:
0562 824860

SPECIALIST BADGES
The Button Badge Company, founded in London in 1961, is probably the oldest specialist badge maker of its type in the country. They have built up an international clientele which includes famous names throughout the world. Whilst many clients order in very large quantities, the company also regularly produces small orders in numbers from 1,000.

Button Badge personalised badges are for all occasions, whatever it may be: for a conference, sales exhibition or business function. The badges help break

Gifts

down barriers and identify individuals at a glance.

The badges are available in four base colours: white, black, silver and gold. Easy pop-out panels are provided to insert new names. Sample prices range from £2.80 per item for a quantity of 25 oval silver badges through to £1.40 for 500.

Catalogue: *A4, Catalogue, 9 pages, Colour, Free* Postal charges: *Varies with item* Delivery: *Royal Mail* Methods of Payment: *Cheque, Postal Order*

THE CAMEO COLLECTION
PO Box 35
Loughton
Essex
IG10 2PE

JET JEWELLERY
The Cameo Collection offers a range of authentic replicas of the Whitby jet brooches worn by fashionable ladies in Victorian times (and which feature in A.S.Byatt's excellent novel 'Possession').

Original Whitby cameos are very difficult to obtain and even when found are usually prohibitively expensive. These beautiful replicas are hand-made in England and – like the originals – have brooch fittings of brass. Five different cameos are currently available.

Orders for 1–10 cameos cost £19.95 per cameo; for orders of 11 or more, the price is £15.95.

Catalogue: *A4, Leaflets, 2 pages, B/W, Free* Postal charges: *Varies with item* Delivery: *Royal Mail* Methods of Payment: *Cheque*

THE EGYPTIAN HOUSE
56 Kendal Street
London
W2 2BP

Telephone:
071 402 5317
Fax:
071 706 3922

EGYPTIAN HAND CRAFTED MERCHANDISE
The Egyptian House is sponsored by the Egyptian government with all profits going towards helping to improve the living standards, education and training of 'the productive families' of Egypt.

The catalogue offers a superb collection of the very best of Egyptian craftsmanship. This includes heat blown perfume bottles, hand decorated in gold from £7.95 and inlaid hand crafted mother of pearl marquetry boxes from £9.95. They also sell Egyptian artifacts hand carved in alabaster, such as the attractive scarab from £7.95 which makes an ideal paperweight. The range of Pharaonic design jewellery includes a charm bracelet in silver from £13.50.

Catalogue: *Annually, A4, Catalogue, 24 pages, Colour, £3.00* Postal charges: *Varies with item* Delivery: *Courier, Royal Mail* Methods of Payment: *Cheque, Postal Order, Visa, Access / Mastercard, American Express*

Gifts

THE EMPTY BOX CO
Coomb Farm Buildings
Balchins Lane
Westcott
Nr Dorking
Surrey
RH4 3LE

Telephone:
0306 740193

BOXES
This enterprising catalogue offers a range of hat boxes. Available in three sizes and two shapes (circular and octagonal), they can be stacked or fitted inside one another. If used for hats, they will store two to three. There are twenty-one colours and patterns to choose from, although the company will also make a box up in your own fabric. A 20" round hat box costs £42.00.

The company also make wedding dress boxes, to store not only the nuptial gown, but also any mementos of the big day. A standard box, complete with tissue paper for wrapping the dress, is £39.90. Just the sort of unusual catalogue that makes mail order such fun.

Catalogue: *A5, Leaflets, 5 pages, Colour, Free* Postal charges: *Varies with item* Delivery: *Royal Mail* Methods of Payment: *Cheque, Postal Order, Visa, Access / Mastercard*

THE FURNISHING TOUCH
45 High Street
Reigate
Surrey
RH2 9AE

Telephone:
0737 249688

HAMPERS AND BASKETS
The Furnishing Touch produce handmade Madeiran Willow Trunks and baskets. Toy trunks range from the larger model (30" × 18" × 18") at £59.50 to the smaller version (24" × 13" × 12") at £32.50. Never again will your living room floor resemble Hamleys at six o'clock on the first day of the winter sales. Picnic baskets start at £ 39.95 for a lidded basket, containing a bottle divider and a leather strap (18" × 13" × 11") and increase in price to £42.50 for a large party hamper (27" × 16" × 15") – ideal for summer outings.

Catalogue: *A4, Leaflets, 1, Colour, Free* Postal charges: *Free* Delivery: *Royal Mail* Methods of Payment: *Cheque, Visa, Access / Mastercard*

THE INDIA SHOP
5 Hilliers Yard
Marlborough
Wilts
SN8 1NB

Telephone:
0672 515585

HANDICRAFTS MADE IN INDIA
The India Shop imports and sells the best of the many handicrafts made in India. They buy only from India by travelling there personally two or three times a year, mainly from co-operatives.

As well as jewellery and home accessories, they sell a wide range of block printed and woven textiles including quilts, bedspreads, table linen and cushions. They also sell an increasing range of furniture, old and new. They have shops in Edinburgh, St Andrews and Marlborough as well as an expanding mail order service. Madras tablecloths (60" × 60"), £12.50; Kutch double bedspread (90" × 108"),

Gifts

£39.95; hoop earrings, from £9.50; printing block set, £7.50; and animal quilt set, £35.00.

Catalogue: *A5, Leaflets, 10 pages, Colour, Free* Postal charges: *£1.50* Delivery: *Royal Mail* Methods of Payment: *Cheque, Postal Order*

THE MUSEUMS & GALLERIES COLLECTION
Nancegollan
Helston
Cornwall
TR13 0TT

Telephone:
0209 831 831

CHRISTMAS CARDS, REPLICAS AND GIFTS

The Museums & Galleries Collection offers a selection of quality Christmas cards and gifts produced from important collections around the world. You can order by post or by telephone and on receiving your order you receive a free gift worth £5.95.

You can choose to buy Christmas cards (The Three Kings £2.99 for ten), biscuits (£9.95), jewellery (£5.75 for a brooch), writing paper (£3.99) and much more. If you spend over £20.00 you may also order the 'Mystery Parcel' for only £5.99.

When you order your Christmas cards the company will provide a personalised printing service which includes your name, greeting and address to be printed on your cards. This, however, does cost extra (£18.50 for twenty to eighty cards).

Catalogue: *Annually, A3, Catalogue, 20 pages, Colour, Free* Postal charges: *Varies with item* Delivery: *Royal Mail* Methods of Payment: *Cheque, Postal Order, Visa, Access / Mastercard, American Express*

THE NATIONAL TRUST FOR SCOTLAND
5 Charlotte Square
Edinburgh
EH2 0DF

Telephone:
031 243 9399
Fax:
031 243 9302

GENERAL GIFTS

The National Trust for Scotland has a range of nearly 120 items in their 12-page mail-order catalogue, all of which are pictured and succinctly described and priced. Most of the items are also available in the various NTS shops around Scotland.

The catalogue contains everything from the Scottish delicacy Clootie dumplings to Christmas cards and cufflinks to crackers, as well as books, videos, and artifacts with a Scottish theme.

Catalogue: *8.5 × 7.8 in , Catalogue, 12 pages, Colour, Free* Postal charges: *£3.25* Delivery: *Royal Mail* Methods of Payment: *Cheque, Postal Order, Visa, Access / Mastercard, American Express*

Gifts

THE NATURAL HISTORY MUSEUM
Freepost SU361
Dept 5315
Hendon Road
Sunderland
SR9 9AD

Telephone:
091 514 2777
Fax:
091 514 4574

A VARIETY OF PRODUCTS FROM AROUND THE WORLD

The Natural History Museum offers a wide range of products following the theme of animals and their environment. Shopping is made easy through postal order with a small contribution being made to the museum through every purchase made.

Gifts on offer are kitchenware, clothes (£14.95 for a sweatshirt), toys, games and bed clothes (£64.95 for a duvet set). All products are printed with a different species of animal, with a donation from the mail order service to help preserve wildlife and the environment.

Catalogue: *Annually, A3, Catalogue, 32 pages, Colour, Free* Postal charges: *Varies with item* Delivery: *Royal Mail* Methods of Payment: *Cheque, Access / Mastercard, Visa*

THE OLD PHOTOGRAPH COMPANY
The Old Smithy
Sandy Lane
Preesall
Poulton Le Fylde
Lancs
FY6 0PA

Telephone:
0253 810133

PHOTOGRAPHIC REPRODUCTION

The Old Photograph Company provide a reproduction service for, as you might guess, old photographs. Family portraits or scenes from the past – for instance old postcards – can be copied, enlarged and enhanced. Even if your original picture is damaged in some way, it can sometimes still be reproduced. They will mount the finished picture in a period frame.

To have your picture reproduced in black and white or sepia tone and framed will cost from £25.00 for the Solid Yew Embossed finish or the Solid Yew Gilt Insert.

Catalogue: *A5, Leaflets, Colour, Free* Postal charges: *£2.50* Delivery: *Royal Mail* Methods of Payment: *Cheque*

THE PEN SHOP
14 Portland Terrace
Newcastle upon Tyne
NE2 1QQ

Telephone:
091 281 3358
Fax:
091 281 6260

PENS AND PENCIL SETS

With their distinctive and exclusive inlaid nib, Sheaffer's pen and pencil sets are prestige writing instruments. Each fountain pen is crafted by hand to emphasise the detailed craftsmanship of these quality products. The catalogue illustrates over 30 different designs, including the sleek Targa and the prestige Connoisseur. All designs have the choice of fountain pen, ballpoint and pencil, and some are available in a range of colours.

The range of accessories reflects classic values. The Edwardian set is crafted in solid oak and hallmarked in silver and an exclusive limited edition commissioned from Royal Doulton is available with a laque fountain pen.

Gifts

Catalogue: *19cm × 25cm, Catalogue, 46 pages, Colour, Free* Postal charges: *Varies with item* Delivery: *Royal Mail* Methods of Payment: *Cheque, Postal Order, Visa, Access / Mastercard*

THE SCIENCE MUSEUM
Exhibition Road
London
SW7 2DD

Telephone:
0793 480200

GIFTS

The Science Museum sells a range of gadgets and gifts. You can buy T-shirts featuring the wild-haired Albert Einstein or a pensive Sigmund Freud. Both designs cost £12.95. Alternatively, if you want to flaunt an interest in astronomy, you can invest in one of their pure silk ties. 56" long and 4" at its widest point, each tie costs £24.95.

More frivolously, you could endulge your puerile streak with 'The Watch that Roars' (£14.95). At the touch of a button, your miniature tyrannosaurus rex head emits a 'blood-curdling' (little) roar.

Catalogue: *A4, Catalogue, 32 pages, Colour, Free* Postal charges: *Varies with item* Delivery: *Royal Mail* Methods of Payment: *Cheque*

VINTAGE GOLF
PO Box 733
London
SW18 3LZ

GOLFING GIFTS

As their name suggests, Vintage Golf offer a selection of golf related gifts from times gone by.

They have a miniature golf bag and set of clubs for £25.00. The detail is impressive: the 7" golf bag has a zip open pouch for that extra, hidden gift, and a set of wooden shafted clubs; two woods, two irons and a polished brass putter.

On a lighter note, there's a character owl golfer (£25.00). Hand made and free-standing, this 13" figure has a real feather face and a fur fabric body. It's immaculately dressed in a tweed cap, a red jumper and plus fours.

Catalogue: *A5, Leaflets, 2, Colour, Free* Postal charges: *Varies with item* Delivery: *Royal Mail* Methods of Payment: *Cheque, Postal Order*

Health & Beauty

AMPLIVOX ULTRATONE
Amplivox House
Stanneylands Road
Wilmslow
Cheshire
SK9 4HH

Telephone:
0625 530959
Fax:
0625 530693

HEARING DEVICES
This range of devices, which are designed to help when sight and hearing begin to fail, will be a great relief to the many people in this country who find day-to-day tasks more difficult as they get older. There are practical gadgets to let you watch television, carry on normal conversations in crowds and read small print more easily.

Many of the quality products provide simple solutions to the problems of getting older, such as the alarm clock with a vibrating plate which can be placed under a pillow to wake you, £11.95, and the portable door chime which can be carried around the house to ensure that you don't miss any important visitors.

Catalogue: *A5, Catalogue, 12 pages, Colour, Free* Postal charges: *Varies with item* Delivery: *Royal Mail* Methods of Payment: *Cheque, Postal Order, Visa, Access / Mastercard*

AROMATHERAPY ASSOCIATES LTD
68 Maltings Place
Bagley Lane
London
SW6 2BY

Telephone:
071 371 9878
Fax:
071 371 9894

AROMATHERAPY PRODUCTS
A unique range of genuine aromatherapy products carefully created by professional therapists. Tried and tested within the tranquility of their London Treatment Centre, the Aromatherapy Associates range is known and loved by their many discerning clients. Previously available only through selected clinics, spas and health clubs, these blends – renowned for their quality – offer an opportunity for experiencing the pleasures of aromatherapy within the home.

Aromatherapy Associates' brochure features the complete range, grouped for Body, Mind, Spirit or Skin with fragrance notes to help selection. Choose from Bath, Body or Facial Oils, Body Creams or Essences.

Catalogue: *Quarter A4, Catalogue, Colour, 8 pages, Free* Postal charges: *£2.00 for one to two items; £3.00 for three* Delivery: *Royal Mail, Parcelforce* Methods of Payment: *Cheque, Postal Order, Visa, Access / Mastercard*

ARRAN AROMATICS LTD
Isle of Arran
Scotland
KA27 8DD

Telephone:
0770 302595
Fax:
0770 302599

SOAPS
Arran Aromatics Ltd produce a range of environmentally friendly handmade soaps from Scotland that are made without cruelty to animals.

The 'Scottish Country Range' includes pure vegetable soaps hand wrapped in recycled paper at 65p each, massage soaps starting at 90p each, soap gift sets starting at £2.40 and bath oils in 200ml bottles at £2.60.

Health & Beauty

The 'Natural Fruit Range' has glycerine soaps made from pure fruit juices such as apple, lemon, strawberry and peach at 68p each and 100ml bottles of fruit bath foams at £1.95. There are also honey soaps, shampoos and body lotions and 'Fleurs de Provence' soaps and bath foams at similar prices.

Catalogue: *A4, Brochure, 7 pages, Colour, Free* Postal charges: *Varies with item* Delivery: *Royal Mail* Methods of Payment: *Cheque, Postal Order*

AVON DIRECT MAIL SERVICES
Earlstrees Road
Industrial Estate
Corby
Northants
NN17 4AZ

Telephone:
0800 663664

COSMETIC AND GIFTS
Established in the UK in 1959, Avon is probably best known for its direct selling methods and distinctive dingdong trademark. Now available through mail order, it has also considerably expanded its range. You can now buy jewellery, hair care products, CDs and videos, giftware, lingerie and handbags in addition to its original cosmetics and skincare products.

Although all products exclusively carry the Avon label, much of the packaging is reminiscent of High Street competitors. Prices remain reasonable with lipstick from £2.99 and there are often added incentives to purchase with free extras or reduced price jewellery.

Catalogue: *140mm × 165mm, Catalogue, 128 pages, Colour, Free* Postal charges: *£1.95* Delivery: *Royal Mail* Methods of Payment: *Cheque, Postal Order, Visa, Access / Mastercard*

BAY HOUSE AROMATICS
296a Ditchling Road
Brighton
BN1 6JG

Telephone:
0273 559444
Fax:
0273 559444

AROMATHERAPY PRODUCTS
The motto of Bay House Aromatics is 'pure oils in plain bottles'. And they seem to live up to this, with no fancy packaging or fancy prices, just the purest quality oils by return. As well as essential oils, they sell massage blends, vegan skin creams and lotions, aromatic oil vaporisers, gift baskets and aromatherapy starter kits.

In short they stock everything for aromatherapy, whether you're a complete beginner or qualified practitioner. Typical prices include 9ml lavender oil for £1.95, vaporisers from £3.95, 100ml sweet almond oil for £2.30, and 100ml lemon and rose hand and body lotion for £3.00.

Catalogue: *3 times a year, A4, Brochure, 9 pages, Colour, Free* Postal charges: *Varies with item* Delivery: *Royal Mail, Parcelforce* Methods of Payment: *Cheque, Postal Order, Visa, Access / Mastercard*

Health & Beauty

BIOCEUTICALS LTD
Biobees
Nutri House
26 Zennor Rd
London
SW12 0P5

Telephone:
081 675 5664
Fax:
081 675 2257

NATURAL VITAMINS, MINERALS AND HERBAL FOOD SUPPLEMENTS

Bioceuticals Ltd is the first British research based manufacturing company to offer complete natural high potency supplements, hypo allergenic formulas, additive free base, digestive aids, sustained release vegetarian vegan products, a successful Biopathy colon cleansing programme and Ayurvedic natural supplements.

Biobees Brand fresh royal jelly is obtainable at £185.00 for 100 grams and sportsmen and women can obtain the Muscelbolic nutritional boost at £29.75 for a month's supply. These are just two of a large range of health and beauty products.

Catalogue: *A4, Catalogue, 6 pages, Colour, Free* Postal charges: *10%* Delivery: *Royal Mail, Parcelforce, Parceline* Methods of Payment: *Cheque, Postal Order, COD*

BIORESEARCH LTD
Alan Robinson Chemist
19 The Downs
Altrincham
Cheshire
WA14 2QD

Telephone:
061 929 7575/929 9298
Fax:
061 929 9632

COSMETICS

Dr Alan Robinson has been developing Retinol Anti-Ageing products in his Cheshire Pharmacy for over 6 years. During that time he has supplied many thousands of satisfied customers. His company BioResearch was set up alongside his existing Pharmacy Direct range to bring people the latest in skin care technology without the high costs large cosmetic companies charge. It was also a way to guarantee customers received only his genuine formulas.

The products use only tried and tested ingredients and no animal testing is carried out. Retinol anti-wrinkle formula is £9.95 for 50gms, almond oil & collagen moisturiser £4.95, AHA treatment cream £11.95 and eye repair cream £9.95 for 30gms. There is a full money back guarantee if anything fails to satisfy.

Catalogue: *Bi-monthly, Various, Newsletter, Various, B/W, Free* Postal charges: *£1.00* Delivery: *Royal Mail* Methods of Payment: *Cheque, Postal Order, Visa, Access / Mastercard, American Express*

Health & Beauty

BODY SHOP BY MAIL
Hawthorn Road
Wick
Littlehampton
West Sussex
BN17 7LR

Telephone:
0903 733888
Fax:
0903 734949

NATURALLY-BASED HEALTH AND BEAUTY PRODUCTS
Founded by Anita Roddick in 1976 The Body Shop use the finest natural ingredients and the knowledge and experience of other cultures to make exclusive products to their own original recipes.

In their catalogue is a selection of their products and clear information on how to choose what is best for you. This selection covers hair products such as Brazil Nut Conditioner (60ml for £1.10) direct from the Kayapo Indians in the Amazonian rainforest which is ideal for dry hair and hair that has been chemically treated. There are face products such as Aloe Vera Moisture Cream (50ml for £2.90), naturally-based make ups which involve no animal testing and a range of perfumes, body bath and shower products.

Catalogue: *A4, Catalogue, 22 pages, Colour, Free* Postal charges: *Varies with item* Delivery: *Royal Mail* Methods of Payment: *Cheque, Postal Order, American Express, Visa, Access / Mastercard*

BUTTERBUR AND SAGE LTD
101 Highgrove Street
Reading
Berkshire
RG1 5EJ

Telephone:
0734 314484
Fax:
0734 314504

ESSENTIAL OILS
Butterbur and Sage provide a range of beauty products, including essential oils, which are made from organic compounds found in plants. Normally present in small quantities, large amounts of plant material are used to extract the precious oil which then has a wide range of uses. They are volatile, extremely fragrant and highly concentrated.

Among the exotically-described oils are amyris oil from the Caribbean at £3.10 for 10ml and clove stem oil from Madagascar at £25.75 for 1 litre.

Catalogue: *A4, Catalogue, 6 pages, B/W, Free* Postal charges: *Varies with item* Delivery: *Royal Mail* Methods of Payment: *Cheque, Postal Order, Visa, Access / Mastercard*

CAMEO CARDS
Linken House
48 Spa Road
Melksham
Wiltshire
SN12 7NY

Telephone:
0225 709795
Fax:
0225 791341

FOOT MASSAGES
The name of this company belies its single product, a foot massager. The brochure gives plenty of technical information about the history of feet massage and reflexology, as well as its applications today. There are also detailed diagrams of the areas of the feet which respond to reflexology and their corresponding body zones.

The massage device itself resembles a flattened abacus and seems easy to use. It retails at £19.90.

Catalogue: *A4, Leaflets, 2 pages, B/W, Free* Postal charges: *Free* Delivery: *Royal Mail* Methods of Payment: *Cheque, Postal Order*

Health & Beauty

CARADOC LTD
Goethean House
Woodman Lane
Clent
Stourbridge
West Midlands
DY9 9PX

Telephone:
0562 886858
Fax:
0562 886219

ANTHROPOSOPHICAL TOILETRIES & DEMETER QUALITY FOOD PRODUCTS
All Caradoc's products are produced by Bio-Dynamic farming methods which are sustainable, holistic and harmonious and involve no use of artificial or chemical biocides. Bio-Dynamic farming is based on the teachings of Rudolf Steiner who first developed the concept of Bio-Dynamics in the 1920's. Bio-Dynamics takes into account the whole environment around us. Any profit made by the company goes straight back into supporting Bio Dynamic agriculture in this country. The company sells a large range of products, from food (sage pastilles £2.75, oat flakes £2.30), compost bins and books to face cleansers (lip cream £6.60, face mask £14.25). Orders should always be despatched within a week.

Catalogue: *A5, Catalogue, 52 pages, B/W, 50p* Postal charges: *Free* Delivery: *Royal Mail* Methods of Payment: *Cheque*

CEDAR HEALTH LTD
Hazel Grove
Cheshire
SK7 5BW

Telephone:
061 483 1235

NATURAL HEALTH PRODUCTS
Cedar Health provide products that new agers will be overjoyed to get their hands on. There are solutions to a number of conditions offered here, including osteoporosis. This is a condition in which the density of bone is diminished, and usually occurs in women after they have been through their menopause. They suggest using a calcium citrate formula in combination with half as much magnesium citrate, some boron and vitamin D.

Aromatherapy products also feature largely. Their 'Tegarome' costs £8.49 for a 30 ml bottle; 'Babibad' costs £6.49 for a 125 ml bottle and 'Flexarome' costs £9.49 for the same amount.

Catalogue: *Third A4, Leaflets, 8, Colour and B/W, £1.50* Postal charges: *Varies with item* Delivery: *Royal Mail* Methods of Payment: *Cheque, Postal Order, Visa, Access / Mastercard*

D R HARRIS & CO LTD
29 St James St
London
SW1A 1HB

Telephone:
071 930 3915
Fax:
071 925 2691

TOILETRIES – SOAPS, SHAVING PREPARATIONS, SKINCARE
D R Harris, Royal Warrant Holders, have been making the finest quality perfumes, toiletries and soaps in England for over 200 years.

Shaving preparations are a speciality, whether you choose their luxurious shave cream (£5.65 per tube) or opt for the even more pleasurable experience of using a best badger brush (from £35.80) together with shave soap from a refillable wooden bowl.

Health & Beauty

Their skincare preparations have natural ingredients such as cucumber, rose and almond oil and are not tested on animals.

For Mondays (or the morning after the night before) you could try Harris's world famous Crystal Eye Drops (£5.65) and Pick-Me-Up (£5.10).

Catalogue: *Annually, A4, Brochure, 2 pages, B/W, Free* Postal charges: *Varies with item* Delivery: *Royal Mail* Methods of Payment: *Cheque, Visa, Access / Mastercard, American Express, Postal Order*

DOLMA
19 Royce Avenue
Hucknall
Notts
NG15 6FU

Telephone:
0602 634237

VEGAN PERFUMES, TOILETRIES AND AQUEOUS AROMATICS

This tiny but neat catalogue features a range of beauty products which contain no animal substances or anything that has been tested on animals. These include vegan perfumes, aromatic body shampoos, hair care, soap, men's shaving products, skin care, facial oils and foot care.

Perfumes are £7.00 for 9ml with a 1.8ml trial size for £1.75. Body shampoo is £3.00 for 200ml while hair treatment oil is £2.30. There is a free 1.8ml perfume to new customers who spend £12.00 on their first order.

Catalogue: *, Leaflets, B/W, Free* Postal charges: *Varies with item* Delivery: *Royal Mail* Methods of Payment: *Cheque, Postal Order*

EVENING PRIMROSE HEALTH CLUB LTD
Unit 37
Blenheim Close
Pysons Road Ind Estate
Broadstairs
Kent
CT10 1UD

Telephone:
0843 602717
Fax:
0843 864198

NATURAL HEALTH PRODUCTS

EPHC has been established since 1989, selling a comprehensive range of health products and supplements through mail order. Their prices undercut normal shops by some margin. For example, 90 500mg Evening Primrose Oil Capsules high in GLA are just £4.95 as are 90 'One a Day' Ginseng tablets and Odourless Garlic tables and 180 'One a Day' Fish Oil capsules.

Their latest product is Slimrite, a new natural slimming concept that detoxifies the system, alleviating hunger whilst still allowing three nourishing meals a day.

Catalogue: *Annually, Tabloid, By Advertising, 8 pages, Colour, Free* Postal charges: *Varies with item* Delivery: *Royal Mail* Methods of Payment: *Cheque, Postal Order, Visa, Access / Mastercard*

Health & Beauty

FAMILY PLANNING SALES LTD
28 Kelburne Road
Cowley
Oxford
OX4 3SZ

Telephone:
0865 749333
Fax:
0865 748746

CONTRACEPTIVES AND DIAGNOSTICS

F P Sales Ltd is the trading arm of the Family Planning Association and has been handling personal mail orders for the FPA for over twenty years. It deals with all non-prescription family planning supplies, especially a full range of Kitemarked condoms, at prices well below RRSP. The range includes related items such as pregnancy tests and ovulation kits. FPS also has access to the advice services and book centre of the FPA. As a separate service, it covers the needs of diabetics for a range of diagnostics and other products not available on prescription.

Typical postpaid prices for Kitemarked condoms (January 1994, money-saving 4-dozen packs): Durex Extra Safe £17.40, Mates Superstrong £13.57, Jiffi Rainbow £11.25, Durex Allergy £18.63. There are further savings on orders of 12 dozen.

Catalogue: *A4, Leaflets, 1 page, B/W, Free* Postal charges: *Varies with item* Delivery: *Royal Mail, Parcelforce White Arrow TNT* Methods of Payment: *Cheque, Visa, Access / Mastercard, Postal Order*

FLEUR AROMATHERAPY
Pembroke Studios
Pembroke Road
London
N10 2JE

Telephone:
081 444 7424
Fax:
081 444 0704

AROMATHERAPY AND ESSENTIAL OILS

Fleur Aromatherapy is a leading supplier of top quality, pure essential oils and aromatherapy products. They only use the finest and purest ingredients and the organic range is fully certified. In addition, Fleur offers bath and massage oils, gift packs, skincare, floral waters, books, tapes, storage boxes and vaporisers.

Full information is given on how to use these products and there is a useful telephone advice line during office hours. Lavender is £3.99, Relaxing Massage Oil £3.65, an Aromatherapy Start Kit £18.45 and a Vaporising Ring £2.95.

Catalogue: *Bi-annually, A4, Brochure, 4 pages, Colour and B/W, Free* Postal charges: *Varies with item* Delivery: *Royal Mail, Parcelforce* Methods of Payment: *Cheque, Postal Order, COD, Visa, Access / Mastercard*

G BALDWIN & CO
173 Walworth Road
London
SE17 1RW

Telephone:
071 703 5550
Fax:
071 252 6264

AROMATHERAPY OILS, HERBS AND HERBAL REMEDIES

G. Baldwin & Co are medical herbalists who have been established for 150 years. They supply a mind-boggling range of oils, herbal powders, culinary herbs, roots and barks along with books, bottles and jars, incense sticks, oil burners and charcoal.

Their essential oils contain no additional additives

Health & Beauty

and are 100% pure. 50ml of Cedarwood oil costs £5.90 while 50ml of Frankincense Olibanum is £37.79. Aromatherapy boxed sets come in large and small sizes. The small set (£24.99) contains twelve 10ml bottles of different oils and the large set (£95.49) 24 bottles.

Catalogue: *Bi-annually, A5, Brochure, B/W, Free* Postal charges: *Varies with item* Delivery: *Royal Mail, Parcelforce 48 and 24 Hour Trackback Amtrak 24 hour* Methods of Payment: *Cheque, Postal Order, Visa, Access / Mastercard, American Express*

GEO F TRUMPER LTD
166 Fairbridge road
London
N19 3HT

Telephone:
071 272 1765
Fax:
071 281 9337

GENTS TOILETERIES
Geo F. Trumper's full-colour brochure reeks of quality and tradition. Trumper's has been an exclusive barber and perfumer since 1875, and the history of Trumper and his products is given both here and in a small poetic booklet, 'The Art of Shaving'.

The delightful range of luxury and everyday cosmetics are beautifully packaged. The multitude of shaving brushes, manicure sets and mirrors surely offer the last word in gentlemen's grooming. But luxury comes at a price: a six-piece manicure set in a grey leather case costs £99.00, while the Silver Scroll Military Hairbrush and Comb set is a hefty £434.00.

Catalogue: *A5, Catalogue, 32 pages, Colour, Free* Postal charges: *Varies with item* Delivery: *Royal Mail* Methods of Payment: *Cheque, Visa, Access / Mastercard, American Express, Diners Club*

GERARD HOUSE
475 Capability Green
Luton
Beds
LU1 3LU

Telephone:
0582 487331
Fax:
0582 484941

ESSENTIAL OILS
Gerard House provide a comprehensive range of aromatherapy essential oils. Essential oils are the whole organic substances which give plants their scent. The brochure includes full descriptions of the various products, with ideas for their use and facts about aromatherapy. Basil costs £4.20 for 10 ml; the same quantity of Cypress costs £3.60.

Also available are number of Cathay and Gerard herbal remedies. These include Angus Castus tablets at £3.95 for a hundred; garlic capsules at £2.75 for a hundred; and ginseng tablets at £5.25 for 100.

Catalogue: *Third A4, Leaflets, Colour and B/W, Free* Postal charges: *Varies with item* Delivery: *Royal Mail* Methods of Payment: *Cheque, Visa, Access / Mastercard*

Health & Beauty

GOLDSHIELD NATURAL CARE
Bensham House
324 Bensham Lane
Thornton Heath
Surrey
CR7 3EQ

Telephone:
081 6659670
Fax:
081 665 6433

HEALTHCARE
Goldshield Natural Care is one of the premier vitamin, mineral and food supplement companies in the UK. Specialising in mail order they provide consumers with a range of high quality products. By cutting down on distribution costs they can supply over 150 different lines at prices substantially lower than those found in the high street.

All the products have been carefully selected by their team of professionals which include doctors, pharmacists and dietitians. Their aim is 'to help you take your health care into your own hands'.

'Super Rich Evening Primrose Oil' is £7.95 for 180 capsules, 'One-a-day Cod Liver Oil with Multivitamins' £6.95 for 180 capsules, 'Garlic Pearls one-a-day' £4.95 for 200 capsules and 'Super Cod Liver Oil one-a-day' £3.95 for 180 capsules.

Catalogue: *Quarterly, A5, Catalogue, 40 pages, Colour, Free* Postal charges: *Varies with item* Delivery: *Royal Mail* Methods of Payment: *Cheque, Postal Order, Visa, Access / Mastercard*

GREEN THINGS
PO Box 59
Tunbridge Wells
Kent
TN3 9PT 0

Telephone:
0892 864668
Fax:
0892 863558

NATURAL HERBAL BEAUTY CARE
A comprehensive range of natural toiletries and beauty care range with special introductory offers for new customers. The products are made from blends of plant oils, natural herbal extractors and essential oils. Ingredients are biodegradable and packaging kept to a minimum. The range is free from mineral oils, petrochemicals and artificial colourants and have not been tested on animals. Postage paid on orders over £10.00, under £10.00 add 25p per item. Some special offers postage free.

Catalogue: *21mm × 10mm, Natural Herbal Beauty Care, 11 pages, Colour and B/W, Free* Postal charges: *Varies with item* Delivery: *Royal Mail* Methods of Payment: *Cheque, Postal Order*

HARTWOOD AROMATICS
Coronet House
Upper Well st.
Coventry
CV1 4AG

Telephone:
0203 64931
Fax:
0203 555422

AROMATHERAPY PRODUCTS
Hartwood Aromatics is a friendly, long established family business specialising in high quality, pure essential oils and aromatherapy products. All the products are natural and vegan-safe with no animal testing. There are health enhancing aromatherapy goods for the whole family, from babycare teething creams right through to adult's luxurious facial care and exotic perfumes.

They also sell quality vitamins, minerals, herbal tablets, aromatherapy and health books, burners and

Health & Beauty

massage couches. They offer free customer advice along with worldwide speedy delivery. 'French Lavender Essential Oil' is £3.50 for 10ml, 'Special Massage Balm' £3.85 for 35ml, 'White Dove Baby Nappy Rash Cream' £5.90 and 'Lotus Facial Lotion, Normal Skin' £9.50 for 100ml.

Catalogue: *Annually, A5, Catalogue, Colour, Free* Postal charges: *Varies with item* Delivery: *Royal Mail, Parcelforce Courier* Methods of Payment: *Cheque, Postal Order, Visa, Access / Mastercard*

HEALTH DIRECT
Bourne Mill
Guildford Road
Farnham
Surrey
GU9 9PS

Telephone:
0252 737898
Fax:

HEALTH AIDS
There's something in this catalogue for just about any infirmity making it a veritable hypochondriac's bible. A 'Posture Trainer' is £12.99; Retinol: 'The skin treatment that older people are talking about' is £29.99 and some 'StayKups' to give yourself a 'firmer feminine figure – no more sagging' for £6.49 per pair.

'The Diet of the Decade' claims that with a 30 day course costing £14.95 you can lose up to a stone. 'Every Woman's Self-Help Guide to Total Fulfilment' seems to be a G-Spot massager and which comes (sic) complete with a guidebook for £17.99. Fascinating reading.

Catalogue: *Annually, A5, Catalogue, 46 pages, Colour, Free* Postal charges: *£2.25* Delivery: *Royal Mail* Methods of Payment: *Cheque, Postal Order, Visa, Access / Mastercard*

HOLISTIC RESEARCH COMPANY
Bight Haven
Robin's Lane
Lolworth
Cambridge
CB3 8HH

Telephone:
0954 781074

NEW AGE PRODUCTS AND DEVICES
This interesting company sells a range of devices for 'healthy living in a modern world'. These include water purifiers, ionisers, natural light light bulbs and juicers.

What's unusual about them is that they take the trouble to test every model on the market and then give an unbiased view of which they have found to be the best and most efficient. The catalogue goes to considerable lengths, for example, to discuss the merits of various water purification systems, finally coming down in favour of an American distillation machine which removes virtually all impurities.

The best juicer comes out at some $348.00 but there are cheaper models. A water distiller is £339.00 and ionisers are from around £20.00. There is also a range of other, often more bizarre products.

Catalogue: *A5, Catalogue, 20 pages plus inserts, B/W, Free* Postal charges: *Varies with item* Delivery: *Royal Mail* Methods of Payment: *Cheque, Postal Order*

Health & Beauty

HOUSE OF HEARING
Amplivox and Ultratone
Stanneylands Road
Wilmslow
Cheshire
SK9 4YB

Telephone:
0625 536051

HEARING AIDS

From their manufacturing base in Oxford, Amplivox and Ultratone can provide miniaturised electronic components for anyone with hearing problems. The commitment to research and development has brought many achievements in the past such as 'Poppit', 'Micra', Secrette' and 'Gemini', some hearing aids so discreet that they can be concealed in spectacle frames. Both adults and children can be helped by this specialist facility.

Catalogue: *A5, Brochure, 8 pages, Colour, Free* Postal charges: *Varies with item* Delivery: *Royal Mail* Methods of Payment: *Cheque, Visa, Access / Mastercard*

ID AROMATICS LTD
12 New Station Street
Leeds
Yorkshire
LS1 5DL

Telephone:
0532 424983
Fax:
0532 424983

AROMATHERAPY PRODUCTS

Established in 1983 to supply high class aromatherapy products, Id Aromatics stock over 100 of the finest quality essential oils and 150 perfume oils. Their Lavender from France sells for £2.75 per 10 mls, while Italian Bergamot is £3.25 . Clarysage, also from France, is £5.25 per 10 mls and the Orange, from Guinea £1.40 per 10 mls.

Catalogue: *Annually, A4, Catalogue, Colour, Free* Postal charges: *Varies with item* Delivery: *Parcelforce, Royal Mail Courier* Methods of Payment: *Cheque, Postal Order, Visa, Access / Mastercard*

J. FLORIS
89 Jermyn Street
London
SW1Y 6JH

Telephone:
071 930 2885
Fax:
071 930 1402

ENGLISH PERFUMES AND TOILETRIES

Floris have been making and selling perfumes and toiletries since 1730 and can boast 2 Royal Warrants. They have a delightful shop in London but also operate a world wide mail order service.

Their products are very English – understated, beautifully packaged and subtle. Toilet waters sell for £14.50 for 50ml, perfumes from £20.50 for 7.5ml. They have a wonderful range of bathroom luxuries and shaving products for men. Cologne is £23.25 and aftershave £18.75 for 100ml.

Catalogue: *A5, Catalogue, 16 pages, Colour, Free* Postal charges: *Varies with item* Delivery: *Royal Mail* Methods of Payment: *Cheque, Visa, Access / Mastercard, American Express, Diners Club*

Health & Beauty

JERSEY LAVENDER LTD
Rue du Pont Marquet
St Brelade
Jersey
Channel Islands
JE3 8DS

Telephone:
0534 42933
Fax:
0534 45613

LAVENDER BEAUTY PRODUCTS

This small but attractive brochure features toiletries, fragrances, pot-pourri items and tasteful gifts. They all come from the family run lavender farm of David and Elizabeth Christie in Jersey. First planted in 1983 the lavender now extends to seven acres and is open to the public during the summer.

There are essential oils at £4.15, soaps at £1.95 and bath foams at £3.50. Gifts include a die cast model of the Jersey Lavender Van, cards, books and pens. Styling of the toiletries is a cross between Woods of Windsor and the National Trust.

Catalogue: *A5, Leaflets, 6 pages, Colour, Free* Postal charges: *Varies with item* Delivery: *Royal Mail* Methods of Payment: *Cheque*

KINGFISHER PUBLISHING
Woodford
Kettering
Northants
NN14 4BR

COSMETICS

Kingfisher Publishing's 'International' collection of cosmetics by Pia St Luce includes something for every part of your body. Their range of eye makeup products include mascaras from £2.50 and kohl pencils for £1.19 each. If you've over-plucked or just never had much there anyway, you can buy a brow definer pencil for £1.99.

Their skin care products include cleansers for £2.79, eye makeup remover gel for £2.29 and a range of foaming face washes at £2.29 each.

Catalogue: *A5, Brochure, 16 pages, Colour, Free* Postal charges: *Varies with item* Delivery: *Royal Mail* Methods of Payment: *Cheque*

KIWI INTERGALACTIC
74 Dartmouth Road
London
NW2 4HA

Telephone:
0459 106747
Fax:
081 8305811

THERAPY TABLES

Kiwi Intergalactic produce therapy tables for every occasion. The catalogue features all the tables photographed either in the sea or in a river, rather like something that's been washed up from a curious wreck. But don't let that put you off. If it's therapy tables you're after this is the company.

The Genesis II model (£450.00) enables you to work on two people at once. It also features a clever removeable section so that pregnant women can lie on their fronts without feeling like a see-saw.

Catalogue: *A5, Leaflet, 4 pages, Colour, Free* Postal charges: *Varies with item* Methods of Payment: *Cheque*

Health & Beauty

LARKHALL NATURAL HEALTH
225 Putney Bridge Road
London
SW15 2PY

Telephone:
081 874 1130
Fax:

NATURAL HEALTH PRODUCTS
Larkhall offer a full range of health products, from low potency general supplements providing nutrients in government daily allowances, to medium potency supplements for those looking for slightly stronger products. At the top end of this spectrum are supplements for the 'knowledgeable nutritional connoisseur or health practitioner'. Most products are made by Larkhall themselves, enabling them to maintain stringent standards.

Larkhall's 'Super One-a-day Antioxidant Formula' containing vitamins A, C and E costs £4.20 for 28 tablets or £10.00 for 3 × 28 tablets. Their 'Micro Multi' vitamin tablet, two of which yield the accepted daily requirement of all essential vitamins costs £4.00 for 200 or £10.00 for 3 × 200.

Catalogue: *A4, Brochure, 20 pages, Colour, Free* Postal charges: *Varies with item* Delivery: *Royal Mail* Methods of Payment: *Cheque, Visa, Access / Mastercard*

MARTHA HILL LTD
Freepost MH3533
Corby
Northants
NN17 3BR

Telephone:
0780 450259
Fax:
0780 450398

SKIN CARE PRODUCTS
Manufacturers of natural, cruelty free skin care products, Martha Hill believe in the honest approach towards beauty. From hair care to foot care you can pamper your body, safe in the knowledge that all Martha Hill Products use neither expensive or environmentally damaging packaging, nor do they ever test their wares on animals.

Buy a special 'Skin Treatment' set containing herbal cleanser, seaweed peeling mask and face pack at £7.75 to give your skin a special treat. There's also banana body lotion at £7.75 for 150 ml or gardeners' cream at £6.95 for 50 ml, for those tired green fingers.

Catalogue: *A5, Brochure, 12, B/W, Free* Postal charges: *Varies with item* Delivery: *Royal Mail* Methods of Payment: *Cheque, Postal Order, Visa, Access / Mastercard, American Express*

MASON PEARSON
37 Old Bond Street
London W1X 3AE

HAIR BRUSHES
Mason Pearson haircare offer a variety of solutions to brushing your hair. Admittedly, this doesn't automatically strike one as a tremendously complicated task, but it probably pays to know such nuggets of information as a nylon brush is good for penetrating even the most difficult hair. Furthermore, a bristle and nylon tuft brush is especially good for thick or long hair.

Health & Beauty

Women's hairbrushes come in four sizes: large (£25.50-£40.00), medium (£13.00-£40.00), handy (£12.75-£28.50) and pocket (£2.00 – £14.50). They are available in boar bristle, bristle and nylon mixture and straightforward nylon. Men's military style brushes are available in the same combinations.

Catalogue: *A4, Leaflets, 2, Colour, Free* Postal charges: *Varies with item* Delivery: *Royal Mail* Methods of Payment: *Cheque, Postal Order*

MEADOWS
Forest Farm House
Pope Street
Godmersham
Canterbury Kent
CT4 7DN

Telephone:
0227 731489
Fax:
0227 731489

NATURAL CREAMS AND OILS
Meadows sell a very large range of essential oils for aromatherapy and other uses. Everything is made from totally natural ingredients and not tested on animals. They also stock 14 different types of 'natural creams' for skincare. These include 'Tea Tree and Lavender', 'Rose and Geranium' and 'Peppermint and Honey Foot Cream'. Each one is given a helpful description saying what is for and how to use it.

They also sell toners, pot pourri, containers, vaporisers, candles and incense sticks. Lavender essential oil is £1.30 for 5g and 10g is just £1.80, Elderflower water is £2.20 for 100ml, pot pourri/ vaporising oils £1.20. The creams are between £1.30 and £2.20 for 30ml.

Catalogue: *A4, Leaflets, 5, B/W, Free* Postal charges: *Varies with item* Delivery: *Royal Mail* Methods of Payment: *Cheque*

MEGAFOOD
4 Langthwaite Road
Langthwaite Industrial
Estate
South Kirkby
Pontefract
West Yorkshire
WF9 3AP

Telephone:
0977 646797
Fax:
0977 646797

VITAMINS AND MINERALS
Megafood was introduced in 1991, following a scientific breakthrough which enabled vitamins and minerals to be constituted from a food base. This means that the body does not have to work to recognise Megafood products in order to absorb them, unlike most other vitamins and minerals. Digestion is simple and problem free, which makes them an ideal supplement for all the family.

Megafood are so confident that their customers will be satisfied with their products that they offer a money-back guarantee. They also offer a mystery gift with every first order.

Prices range from £2.99 for a 30-day supply of zinc tablets to £31.65 for 'Alpha', the full spectrum super potency vitamin and mineral formula.

Catalogue: *Annually, Brochure, 6 pages, B/W, Free* Postal charges: *Varies with item* Delivery: *Royal Mail Interlink* Methods of Payment: *Visa*

Health & Beauty

MICHELINE ARCIER AROMATHERAPY
7 William Street
London
SW1X 9HL

Telephone:
071 235 3545

AROMATHERAPY PRODUCTS
Madame Micheline Arcier has been practising aromatherapy for 34 years. Her products are formulated and hand blended by herself and her daughter Marie-Christine. They are made from top quality essential oils and vegetable oils, free from chemicals, preservatives and colouring, and are not tested on animals. Face oils are prepared for different skin conditions. Body and bath oils are helpful for stress, aches and pains, colds, circulatory and lymphatic problems etc. Burning essences, either calming, uplifting, antiseptic or exotic, are used on a ceramic electric burner.

All Micheline Arcier products are also available in trial sizes: Rose face oil for dry skins, £9.50 for 10ml; Geranium body oil for circulation, £4.00 for 15ml; Anti-stress bath oil, £4.50for 15ml; Lavender bath oil, £4.50 for 15ml.

Catalogue: *Annually, A4, Brochure, 4 pages, Free* Postal charges: *Varies with item* Delivery: *Parcelforce, Royal Mail* Methods of Payment: *Cheque, Postal Order, Visa, Access / Mastercard*

MOLTON BROWN
Molton Brown By Mail
PO Box 2514
London
NW6 3AR

Telephone:
071 625 6550
Fax:
071 493 2356

HEALTHCARE AND BEAUTY PRODUCTS
Molton Brown beauty products are created with herbal extracts and pure essential oils and for over 20 years these preparations have been made without animal testing. There are beauty products for both men and women and all of them are packaged colourfully but simply.

For men, there is a sea moss body range (bath salts £16.00, firming lotion £18.00, soap and shower gel) and for women, the skin sense range (cleansers £3.15, washing gel £3.15 and toners £3.15). They also offer make-up products with a shade chart allowing you to choose from a variety of colours (fawn, red gold, mango, ink).

Catalogue: *A5, Catalogue, 23 pages, Colour, Free* Postal charges: *Varies with item* Delivery: *Royal Mail* Methods of Payment: *Cheque, Postal Order, Visa, Access / Mastercard*

MOUNTAIN BREEZE
6 Priorswood Place
East Pimbo
Skelmersdale
WN8 9QB

Telephone:
0695 21155
Fax:
0695 50286

IONISERS AND AIR PURIFIERS
Mountain Breeze are one of the most well-known manufacturers of ionisers and their products sell in a wide range of stores. However, they also have a mail order arm and will supply goods direct.

They send out a number of brochures featuring various different types of ionisers. Some are suitable for personal use, others for the workplace. They also sell humidifiers and combination machines which not

Health & Beauty

only ionise the air but also filter it. These might be of particular interest to asthma and hay-fever sufferers. Prices start at around £15 and rise to £300 for an 'industrial' Air System.

Catalogue: *A4, Brochure, Colour, Free* Postal charges: *Varies with item* Delivery: *Royal Mail* Methods of Payment: *Cheque, Visa, Access / Mastercard*

NATURAL HEALING CENTRE
72 Pasture Road
Goole
North Humberside
DN14 6HE

Telephone:
0405 769119

NEW AGE BOOKS AND ACCESSORIES
Set up by a healer, teacher and mystic in 1970, the Spiritual Venturer Association is a healing and teaching organisation offering conferences, courses and workshops. 1994 courses include a fun-sounding day out, 'Healing with Dolphins' at Kirkby Fleetham Hall – 'a day full of healing and laughter which will include film of personal encounters with dolphins and "live" commentary' from Dr. Horace Dobbs. Cost includes buffet lunch, tea and coffee, £25.

As well as courses they offer a mail order service for complimentary goods. These include books, crystals, gems and minerals. They also sell an impressive range of essential oils for aromatherapy.

Catalogue: *A4, Catalogue, 16 pages, Colour and B/W, Free* Postal charges: *10%* Delivery: *Royal Mail* Methods of Payment: *Cheque, Postal Order, Visa, Access / Mastercard*

NATURAL HEALTH PRODUCTS
Dept X
The Croft
Hipswell
Richmond
N. Yorks
DL9 4AY

Telephone:
0748 834417
Fax:
0748 833648

NATURAL PRODUCTS FOR HEALTH
A range of products which are guaranteed not to have been tested on animals, including a selection of herbal remedies with explanations of the common complaints for which they have been traditionally used.

There are also many other unique products to help you look good, stay in shape and in good health, from slimming aids to hormone replacement tablets. The catalogue contains recommendations from satisfied customers.

As the company buy in bulk they can pass on their savings to the customers: evening primrose oil is only £4.95 for three months supply and Renew, an anti-wrinkle cream, is only £9.95 for a jar.

Catalogue: *A5, Catalogue, 38 pages, Colour, Free* Postal charges: *Varies with item* Delivery: *Royal Mail* Methods of Payment: *Cheque, Postal Order, Visa, Access / Mastercard*

Health & Beauty

NATURAL HERBAL RESEARCH
34 Upton Lane
Forest Gate
London
E7 9LN

VITAMINS AND OTHER HEALTH PRODUCTS
An interesting mixture of products in this brochure – alongside cod liver oil capsules (£11.90 for 540) and oriental ginseng (£9.90 for 180 tablets) you'll find a collection of John Wayne western classics (£3.25 per video) and a 24-piece model Japanese Bullet trainset for £19.95.

There's also a 'French Style' body stocking for £11.95 and temporary tattoos at £7.95 for 31. Back to health, they are able to offer Prostabrit tablets at £19.95 for 60 capsules.

Catalogue: *A5, Brochure, 16 pages, Colour, Free* Postal charges: *Varies with item* Delivery: *Royal Mail* Methods of Payment: *Access / Mastercard, Visa Cheque, Postal Order*

NECTAR BEAUTY SHOPS
95a Belfast Road
Carrickfergus
Northern Ireland
BT38 8XX

Telephone:
0960 351580
Fax:
0960 351740

BEAUTY AND SKINCARE PRODUCTS
This is a comprehensive range of cruelty free beauty products available by mail order and also through retail outlets where each shop also offers a complete range of gift baskets made to order.

The range includes face cleansers, men's toiletries, lotions for body and hand and a full range of skin and hair care products for use both in and out of the sun. Also offers a fragrance free range. Prices for all products vary from £1.30 for men's shaving cream to £6.95 for Factor 20 sun cream.

Catalogue: *Third A4, Leaflets, 18 pages, Colour, Free* Postal charges: *Varies with item* Delivery: *Royal Mail* Methods of Payment: *Cheque, Postal Order, Visa, Access / Mastercard*

NEWTONS TRADITIONAL REMEDIES
5 High Street
Solihull Lodge
Shirley
Solihull
West Midlands
B90 1HA

Telephone:
021 430 7847

UNUSUAL REMEDIES
This catalogue comes from a small, but long established family firm of medical herbalists. Based in the West Midlands they market alternative medicines and health supplements.

Peppered with plenty of written thanks from satisfied customers, the catalogue features slimming pills, hypertension remedies, internal cleansing systems, anti-rheumatics, laxatives, muscle-builders, energy givers, beauty products, sleeping pills, aphrodisiacs and most intriguing of all something called 'Vigoboost', the 'intimate fun supplement' for middle-aged men only (what happens if you are not middle-aged or even a man?!)

Slimming pills are £11.95 for a one month course and 100 catarrh tablets sell for £6.50.

Health & Beauty

NORFOLK LAVENDER
England's Lavender Farm
Freepost 196
King's Lynn
Norfolk
PE31 7BR

Telephone:
0485 70384
Fax:
0485 71176

Catalogue: *A5, Catalogue, 28 pages, Colour, Free* Postal charges: £1.50 Delivery: *Royal Mail* Methods of Payment: *Cheque, Postal Order, Visa, Access / Mastercard*

LAVENDER

This lavender farm extends to 100 acres at Heacham, and is open to the public during the summer months. As well as predictable ranges of lavender-based toiletries, fragrances, soaps, sachets and gifts, the company also supplies the plants themselves. As some of the lavender varieties are unusual ones, this is an attractive option. There is a minimum order for plants – six at £15.00.

Additional toiletries include a new rose and lavender fragrance, with a cologne spray at £5.45 , and aromatherapy oils. The catalogue helpfully contains samples of its fragrances as well as beautiful photographs of lavender fields in bloom. No product is tested on animals.

Catalogue: *A5, Catalogue, 24 pages plus inserts, Colour, Free* Postal charges: £3.00 Delivery: *Royal Mail* Methods of Payment: *Cheque, Postal Order, Visa, Access / Mastercard*

PEERS ESSENTIAL OILS
9a The Mead
Cirencester
Glos
GL7 2BB

Telephone:
0285 653399

ESSENTIAL OILS

Peers Essential Oils offer a full range of oils, absolutes and oil carriers. They make a point of supplying oils strictly from known sources. Each new batch of oils is independently tested using chromatographic techniques and aroma evaluation. All Peers products are free from additives, chemicals, colouring and artificial preservatives. None have been tested on animals.

Patchouli oil costs from £1.50 for 10 ml to £9.70 for 100 ml. Spanish sage is priced from £1.75 for 10 ml to £11.55 for 100 ml.

Catalogue: *A4, Leaflets, 4, B/W, Free* Postal charges: *Varies with item* Delivery: *Royal Mail* Methods of Payment: *Cheque, Postal Order, Visa, Access / Mastercard*

PETWORTH HOUSE
Polesdon Lane
Ripley
Woking
Surrey
GU23 6LR

Telephone:
0483 225222

KEEP-FIT EQUIPMENT

Petworth House provide a broad and exclusive range of sporting, leisure and fitness equipment. It is now the largest retailer in Great Britain, serving over half a million customers.

Their new exercise bike costs £299.00. Going the whole hog, a home gym is available for only 249.99. It includes a possible 150 lb liftweight.

Health & Beauty

Requiring much less effort is their range of snooker tables. A 6' × 3'6" costs £199.99; a 7' × 3'6" costs £299.99. All models fold neatly away, are mahogany finished and have pro cushions.

Catalogue: *A4, Leaflets, Colour and B/W, Free* Postal charges: *Varies with item* Delivery: *Royal Mail In-house delivery* Methods of Payment: *Cheque, Postal Order, Visa, Access / Mastercard*

PURPLE FLAME AROMATICS
61 Clinton Lane
Kenilworth
Warwickshire
CV8 1AS

Telephone:
0926 55980
Fax:
0926 513117

AROMATHERAPY SUPPLIES
Purple Flame claim to have produced the first individual computerised aromatherapy treatment profile. Designed by professional aromatherapists, the programme will give a personal health and treatment profile for any one of numerous clients – it's ideal for colleges, clinics, hospitals and health spas. The programme is IBM compatible and menu driven. It costs £35.00.

They also sell an aromatherapy massage sequence video (£23.00) which introduces the various techniques involved in aromatherapy massage. You can also enrol in one of their courses, which require a £60.00 deposit.

Catalogue: *A4, Leaflets, 10 pages, B/W, Free* Postal charges: *Varies with item* Delivery: *Royal Mail* Methods of Payment: *Cheque, Visa, Access / Mastercard*

QUINESSENCE
3a Birch Avenue
Whitwick
Leicestershire
LE67 5GB

Telephone:
0530 838358
Fax:
As above

AROMATHERAPY PRODUCTS
The Quinessence aromatherapy collection includes information on the extraction of essential oils and the various uses of aromatherapy. Essential oils, they remind us, have been used for healing since Egyptian times.

Aromatherapy massage oils cost £3.50 for 50 ml or £5.99 for 100 ml. Arranged according to use, they can be applied to everything from cellulite to stretch marks. Aromatherapy lotions vary in price, from £3.40 for 100 ml of rose toner to £6.99 for rose facial.

You can also buy what are called 'oil synergies' to act against anything from pollen to viruses. The anti-pollen oil synergy costs £5.50 for 100 ml, the anti-virus synergy costs £5.25 for the same amount.

Catalogue: *A5, Leaflets, 5 pages, Colour and B/W, Free* Postal charges: *Varies with item* Delivery: *Royal Mail* Methods of Payment: *Visa, Access / Mastercard Cheque, Postal Order*

Health & Beauty

RENAHALL LTD
61 Lime Tree Avenue
Rugby
Warks
CV22 7QT

Telephone:
0788 811454

VITAMINS AND OILS
Renahall offer a basic range of vitamins and oils with regular new introductions. They have been in business for 12 years and avoid glossy advertising and coloured brochures. Many of their customers are elderly and appreciate the basic range and prices.

Vitamin C ascorbic acid cots £6.25 for 240 grams; 150 vitamin E capsules cost £4.95.

Catalogue: *Leaflets, Colour and B/W, Free* Postal charges: *Varies with item* Delivery: *Royal Mail, Parcelforce* Methods of Payment: *Cheque, Postal Order*

SAMUEL PAR
PO Box 15
Havant
Hants
PO9 1RQ

Telephone:
0272 767616

BEAUTY PRODUCTS
Samuel Par skin care products are available by mail order or exclusively from Fenwicks in Bond Street, London. Treatments are designed for 'Balancing', 'Purifying', 'Regenerating' and 'Contouring and Firming'. None of their products are tested on animals.

Treatments for 'Balancing', for instance, consist of 5 products designed to stabilise the pH of your skin while maintaining the right level of acidity. These include: 'Moisturising Base Cream' (£17.75 for 30 ml) and 'Astringent Skin Tonic' (£11.50 for 200ml).

Catalogue: *A5, Brochure, 8 pages, Colour, Free* Postal charges: *Varies with item* Delivery: *Royal Mail* Methods of Payment: *Visa, Access / Mastercard Cheque, Postal Order*

SCENT TO YOU
Trading House
Penn Street
Nr Amersham
Buckinghamshire
HP7 0PX

Telephone:
0494 712855
Fax:
0494 718489

PERFUME
Although printed on glossy paper with colour photographs, the emphasis in this catalogue is definitely on price. The products are mainly discounted perfumes, the sort which are usually so expensive in department stores. All the top names are here including YSL, Dior, Chanel and Givenchy. There is also a small range of cosmetics and skincare goods by Clarins.

Savings vary. On Chanel No. 19 at £37.95 for example, you are only saving £1.05, whereas a Miss Dior spray at £25.00 saves you a hefty £20.00. But it is certainly worth looking at this catalogue before you march off to a store or chemist.

Catalogue: *A4, Catalogue, 12 pages, Colour, Free* Postal charges: *£1.95* Delivery: *Parcelforce* Methods of Payment: *Cheque, Postal Order, Visa, Access / Mastercard, American Express, Diners Club*

Health & Beauty

SHIRLEY PRICE
Essentia House
Upper Bond Street
Hinckley
Leics
LE10 1RS

Telephone:
0455 615466
Fax:
0455 615054

AROMATHERAPY PRODUCTS
This is an aromatherapy catalogue and the full range of products is offered, from essential oils to skin, body and haircare. There is a helpful leaflet explaining what aromatherapy is and another outlining the essential oils and how to use them. In addition to body care products, there are also vaporisers, oil burners and a large selection of books on aromatherapy and related subjects.

Shirley Price also runs training courses for anyone interested in becoming a professional aromatherapist. Prices for essential oils range between £2.60 for 12ml of cedarwood to £42.25 for 3ml of the much rarer Jasmin Absolute.

Catalogue: *A5, Leaflets, Colour, Free* Postal charges: *Varies with item* Delivery: *Royal Mail* Methods of Payment: *Cheque, Postal Order, Visa, Access / Mastercard*

SUMMERBEE PRODUCTS
Windsor House
Lime Avenue
Torquay
Devon
TQ2 5JL

Telephone:
0803 212965

NATURAL HEALTH PRODUCTS
Summerbee specialise in natural health products, taking care not to use any synthetic chemicals, and few preservatives. As their name suggests, many of the products are made with honey; cover yourself from top to toe with Honey Pollen Body Lotion, at £4.80 for 125g; treat yourself to some finest quality Golden Pollen Capsules (£6.95 for two bottles), or maybe some organic honeycomb: £11.95 for four combs.

Royal Jelly, for feeling vital and healthy, is next on the list – whether you need a 'Mega strength' course, in Acacia honey (£23.00), or neat – 20g at £13.95. Essential oils, moisturisers, cleansers and tonics add to the vast range on offer – also a good selection of minerals and food suppplements to help you feel on top of the world.

Catalogue: *A5, Leaflets, B/W, Free* Postal charges: *Free* Delivery: *Royal Mail* Methods of Payment: *Cheque, Visa, Access / Mastercard, Postal Order*

Health & Beauty

THE CLAY COMPANY
Clay House
Penny Lane
Liverpool
L18 1DG

Telephone:
051 733 6900

BODY AND SKINCARE PRODUCTS
The Clay Company produce a range of products using only natural French clays which are non-animal tested, contain no added colouring and are suitable for all skin types.

The high mineral content of the clays enrich the body system, improve circulation and stimulate cellular rejuvenation improving both the skin and muscle tissue, breaking down and drawing off toxins and impurities. All products are specially designed for easy home use: 'The Body Contour Wrap' from £14.95; 'Anti-cellulite Mask' £9.95; 'Foot Soothing Mask' £4.95; 'Tissue Firming Face Mask £3.95; Nail Improving Mask £1.95.

Catalogue: *Bi-annually, A5, Brochure, 6 pages, Colour, Free* Postal charges: *Varies with item* Delivery: *Royal Mail, Parcelforce* Methods of Payment: *Cheque, Postal Order, Visa, Access / Mastercard*

THE HOMOEOPATHIC SUPPLY CO.
Fairview
4 Nelson Road
Sheringham Norfolk
NR26 8BU

Telephone:
0263 824683
Fax:
0263 821507

HOMOEOPATHIC PUBLICATIONS AND ACCESSORIES
This company publishes a cross between a newsletter and a catalogue. Full of information, it has generous descriptions of all its products. These cover everything homoeopathic, from posters through books and guides to bottles, containers, labels, dispensing aids, grids, cases and remedy storage boxes. However, they do not sell remedies themselves.

For this there is a separate insert from another company, Helios. Helios 97 Camden Road Tunbridge Wells Kent TN1 2QR Tel: 0892 536393

Catalogue: *Monthly, A4, Catalogue, 12, Colour and B/W, Free* Postal charges: *Varies with item* Delivery: *Royal Mail* Methods of Payment: *Cheque, Postal Order, Visa, Access / Mastercard, American Express*

ULTRATONE
36 George Street
London
W1E 1QZ

Telephone:
071 935 8393/0631

BODYSHAPER PRODUCTS
Ultratone simulates the natural impulses causing muscles to contract and relax at a controlled and comfortable rate in a regular pattern. The brochure contains detailed illustrations and comprehensive information. For those who just want to concentrate on toning up their face, there's also the Ultratone Facial. You can order over the telephone and keep the equipment for a fourteen day trial and there are also home demonstrations on offer. Or you can visit the London showroom for a free demonstration.

Health & Beauty

Prices range from £115.00 for Ultratone Facial to £642.00 for Salon 10 Plus & Facial Accessory.

Catalogue: *Monthly, A4, Brochure, 10 pages, Colour, Free* Postal charges: *Varies with item* Delivery: *Royal Mail* Methods of Payment: *Cheque, Postal Order, Visa, Access / Mastercard, American Express, Diners Club, Stage Payments*

VITAL FOODS LTD
Freepost B.D. 257
PO Box 13
Bingley
West Yorkshire
BD16 1BR

Telephone:
0274 589026

HEALTH FOOD AND SUPPLEMENTS

This catalogue is like a small health food shop. On one side you have a range of vitamin and mineral supplements and on the other skin care and beauty products made from herbs and plants. There is plenty of dietary information to help you choose and discounts up to £12.00 are available for orders over £100.00.

The beauty and body care products are made by Creighton's and there are also aromatherapy oils, healthcare books, water filters and ionisers.

A pack of 30 Ginseng tablets is £4.25 and 30 evening primrose oil capsules £5.25.

Catalogue: *A5, Catalogue, 8 pages, Colour, Free* Postal charges: *Varies with item* Delivery: *Royal Mail* Methods of Payment: *Cheque, Postal Order, Visa, Access / Mastercard*

VIVIENNE LEE-SMITH DANCING
184 Mount Road
High Barnes
Sunderland
Tyne & Wear
SR4 7BQ

Telephone:
091 528 4028

EXERCISE/DANCE VIDEO

This company produces just one video, 'Belly Dance to a Better Body'. The routine is a beautiful, gentle yet thorough body workout. The tape includes a good warm-up, to prepare the body for the basic movements of Arabic dance, as well as costumed displays of the finger cymbals and ethnic stick dances.

The authentic ethnic and cabaret dance techniques are carefully taught by a TV personality and qualified fitness teacher. Each tape costs £20.00.

Catalogue: *None* Postal charges: *Free* Delivery: *Royal Mail* Methods of Payment: *Cheque, Postal Order*

WELEDA
Weleda (UK) LTD
Freepost 200
Ilkeston
Derbyshire
DE7 8DR

Telephone:
0602 309319
Fax:
0602 440349

HOMEOPATHIC MEDICINES, OILS AND REMEDIES

Weleda have maintained their principles concerning the balance of the body and health with nature since 1923. Founded in Switzerland, this company is now a worldwide name and offers a homoeopathic remedy for most ailments of the human body.

Included with the leaflet is a brochure offering remedies for a large number of different illnesses. It also includes a leaflet selling essential oils which offers

Health & Beauty

you a starter pack of sixteen essential oils plus one bottle of sweet almond oil for the offer price of £40.25 (retail price £60.25). Separate bottles of oil are on offer for £3.25 each. They come packed in simple brown glass dropper bottles and no product is tested on animals.

Catalogue: *A4, By Advertising, 10 pages, Colour and B/W, Free* Postal charges: *Varies with item* Delivery: *Royal Mail* Methods of Payment: *Cheque, Postal Order*

WOODS OF WINDSOR
Queen Charlotte Street
Windsor
Berks
SL4 1LZ

Telephone:
0753-855777
Fax:
0753 868125

TRADITIONAL ENGLISH PERFUMERY PRODUCTS

Woods of Windsor produce a beautiful range of traditional English toiletries in seven floral fragrances along with a classic collection of products for gentlemen in a spicy citrus fragrance. All the fragrances were derived from recipes found in the archives of their shop, established in 1770.

There is also a delightful selection of home fragrance products including scented sachets, room sprays, drawer liners and pot pourris. These come in all the floral scents as well as cinnamon and orange and traditional fragrance. Eau de toilette sells for £7.95, luxury toilet soap for £6.30 (box of 3 × 100gms), scented drawer liners £6.75 and gentlemen's aftershave £10.50.

Catalogue: *Annually, A4, Brochure, 26 pages, Colour, Free* Postal charges: *Varies with item* Delivery: *Royal Mail* Methods of Payment: *Cheque, Postal Order, Visa, Access / Mastercard, American Express, Diners Club*

YOGA DHAM PRODUCTIONS
67 Pinner Park Avenue
North Harrow
Middx
HA2 6JY

Telephone:
081 428 6691
Fax:
081 421 4868

YOGA TAPES AND VIDEOS

Tara Patel is a qualified teacher with the British Wheel of Yoga, and uses her experience to show the benefits of Yoga through this range of video and audio cassettes. The range of materials is divided into those suitable for beginners, intermediate and advanced.

The reviews which Tara has received from various publications concerned with Yoga are included in the catalogue to help those wanting to chose a suitable exercise plan. The range is reasonably priced with audio cassettes at £5.95 and videos at £14.95. Other accessories, such as exercise mats are also available from Yoga Dham.

Catalogue: *A5, Leaflets, 6 pages, B/W, Free* Postal charges: *Varies with item* Delivery: *Royal Mail* Methods of Payment: *Cheque, Postal Order, Visa, Access / Mastercard, American Express*

Health & Beauty

ZENA COSMETICS
5 Harrington Road
London
SW7 3BR

SKIN CARE PRODUCTS

If you have a burning desire to improve your skin, you can try following Zena's 'Ella Baché' method. This could include using elastine and collagen emulsion in the morning at £21.50 for a 100 ml; lurocreame at night at £26.95 for 60 ml; and scented bath oil (for the body every day) at £17.95 for 100 ml. Naturally, this is for those of us with dry and dehydrated skin. Other programmes are also available.

If you really need a 'shock treatment' for your tired skin, then 'Superactive Ampoules' at £36.00 for a box of eight are for you. Although Madame Baché doesn't test her products on animals, she does admit to testing them on her own skin.

Catalogue: *A5, Brochure, 16 pages, Colour, £1.95* Postal charges: *Varies with item* Delivery: *Royal Mail* Methods of Payment: *Cheque, Postal Order, Visa, Access / Mastercard, American Express*

A BUCKINGHAM LTD
Benham House
The Bayle
Folkestone
Kent
CT20 1SD

Telephone:
0303 850041

FIRST DAY COVERS

Advertising as 'The First in First Day Covers' Buckingham publish luxurious first day covers. One of their most prestigious products is their range of silk covers – a technique imported from America.

Among their range of covers are 'Railway Covers', a regular series since 1980; 'Royalty Covers', to cover all major royal events (though probably not infidelity, separation or divorce); 'Cricket Covers', all of them illustrating great players of today, some of them signed by the players, themselves; and 'Signed Covers', which have been personally autographed by a person directly involved with the stamp issue.

Catalogue: *A4, Leaflets, 1 page, B/W, Free* Postal charges: *50p* Delivery: *Royal Mail* Methods of Payment: *Cheque, Postal Order, Visa, Access / Mastercard, American Express, Diners Club*

ANDREW BOTTOMLEY
The Coach House
Huddersfield Road
Thongsbridge
Holmfirth
West Yorkshire
HD7 2TT

Telephone:
0484 685234
Fax:
0484 681551

ANTIQUE ARMS AND ARMOUR

A mail order catalogue of antique arms and armour ranging from a Bulgarian Officer's dagger to a complete suit of armour. A comprehensive selection of pistols, daggers, swords and even helmets. All items post free within the United Kingdom. Mail order service operates world wide.

Catalogue: *A4, Catalogue, 56 pages, B/W, Free* Postal charges: *Varies with item* Delivery: *Royal Mail* Methods of Payment: *Cheque, Postal Order, Visa, American Express, Access / Mastercard, Stage Payments*

Hobbies & Crafts

ANNE ROWENA
4 Trinity Street
Cambridge
CB2 1SU

Telephone:
0223 66841

KNITTING YARN
This company offers the full range of Rowan and Annabel Fox, 100% natural knitting yarns. Using designers like Kaffe Fassett and Kim Hargreaves, they maintain a high fashion profile, providing hand knitters the opportunity to knit anything from the simplest styles to complicated masterpieces. Annabel brings her own innovative style to her designs, keeping fashion, practicality and cost-effectiveness in mind. The patterns range from babies to men and the yarns from silk to chunky tweed – something for all the family.

Rowan DK 50g £2.25; Annabel Fox Aran 100g £3.99; knitting kits from £50; plain ladies waistcoat £20 to knit.

Catalogue: *Bi-annually, Poster, folded, Brochure, 4 pages, Colour, Free* Postal charges: *Varies with item* Delivery: *Parcelforce* Methods of Payment: *Visa, American Express, Diners Club, Other*

BAINES ORR (LONDON) LTD
1–5 Garlands Road
Redhill
Surrey
RH1 6NX

Telephone:
0737 767363
Fax:
0737 768627

GEMSTONES
This company sells a huge range of professionally polished gemstones. They source these from one of the world's largest suppliers, based in South Africa. Their catalogue features both finished jewellery and just the gems themselves.

They also sell fittings for earrings, cufflinks and rings as well as 'Gemsai' tree kits, which are miniature trees laden with gems. There is a range of tools and some picture frames too. Most of the catalogue consists of price lists which assume you know what you are after.

Catalogue: *A4, Catalogue, 22 pages, Colour, Free* Postal charges: *Varies with item* Delivery: *Courier, Parcelforce* Methods of Payment: *Cheque*

BECKFOOT MILL
Clock Mill
Denholme
Bradford
W Yorks
BD13 4DN

Telephone:
0274 830063

CUDDLY TOY PATTERNS
Beckfoot Mill are specialist suppliers of cuddly toy kits, quilting and embroidery supplies. Their wonderful range of soft toys should make a dent in even the hardest of hearts. All you have to do is stitch the toys together – filling is included. With their characteristically frazzled expressions, these are the kind of furry beasts that end up on university bookshelves as much as nestled in cribs. Rowena Rabbit (£6.55) looks addled but irresistible in her smock while Mini-Monkey (£2.15) appears to have had his fingers in a plug socket.

Hobbies & Crafts

They also offer a range of 'Patch N Quilt' kits which allow the novice to have a go at quilt making without having to attempt a full size one.

Catalogue: *A5, Leaflets, 8 pages, Colour, Free* Postal charges: *Varies with item* Delivery: *Royal Mail* Methods of Payment: *Cheque, Postal Order, Visa, Access / Mastercard*

CLIVEDON COLLECTION
Witham Friary
Frome
Somerset
BA11 5HH

Telephone:
0749 850728
Fax:
0749 850729

BADGES, KEYRINGS AND MODELS
Clivedon claim to be the manufacturers of the world's finest aviation giftwear. This means things like tie pins and badges in the shape of famous planes. They supply promotional giftwear to the world's aviation and defence industries, taking pains to ensure that all their models are accurate reproductions. Badges are £3.95 with minimum order: £10.00, tie bars £8.50, cufflinks £15.00 and key rings £4.00.

Looking through their price list is like surveying a roll call of great flying machines. It really is quite remarkable how much detail goes into even the simplest tie pin. Other ranges, including animals and cars are also available.

Catalogue: *A4, Catalogue, 24 pages, Colour, Free* Postal charges: *Varies with item* Delivery: *Royal Mail* Methods of Payment: *Cheque, Visa, Access / Mastercard*

CONNOISSEUR COLLECTORS' CLUBS
Express Buildings
Howsell Road
Malvern Link
Worcs
WR14 1TF

Telephone:
0684 567770
Fax:
0684 892865

EXCLUSIVE COLLECTABLES
This company, staffed by a small team of enthusiasts, runs four Clubs for Collectors. These are The Connoisseur Thimble Collectors' Club, The Connoisseur Spoon Collectors' Club, The Connoisseur Bell Collectors' Club and The Connoisseur Plate Collectors' Club.

Membership, which is free, brings a quarterly newsletter featuring articles on collecting, collectors' correspondence and Club news. Members also have the opportunity to acquire a wide variety of thimbles, spoons, bells or plates, many designed and crafted exclusively at the company's studios in Worcestershire.

Thimbles range from £7.45 to £9.85. while spoons are from £8.75 and bells from £16.75.

Catalogue: *Quarterly, A5, Newsletter, 4 pages, Colour, Free* Postal charges: *Varies with item* Delivery: *Royal Mail* Methods of Payment: *Cheque, Postal Order, Visa, Access / Mastercard, American Express*

Hobbies & Crafts

CORGI SALES
Meridian West
Leicester
LE3 2WJ

Telephone:
0533 826666

MODEL CARS
Corgi Classics feature model historic cars, vans, buses and trucks from all over the country. This might be your only opportunity to buy a 1959 Jaguar MK2 for £9.99, a shame it's only a few inches long.

The range of classic coaches includes an AEC Regal – Wallace Arnold (£16.50), a model of one from the 24 such coaches Wallace Arnold operated in the 50s. Plenty of fun for both the casual car enthusiast and serious collector.

Catalogue: *A4, Leaflets, 4, Colour, Free* Postal charges: *Varies with item* Delivery: *Royal Mail* Methods of Payment: *Cheque, Postal Order, Visa, Access / Mastercard*

CRAFTS AT HOME
7 Palace Place
Paignton
Devon
TQ3 3EQ

Telephone:
0803 550888
Fax:
0803 550888

CRAFT MATERIALS
A catalogue of best sellers by Lavender and Lace, Lanarte Anchor, DMC, Heritage, Kinectic and others. They specialise in cross-stitch, tapestry and toy making but are happy to supply special orders and can supply virtually any other craft materials. They also sell an exclusive cross-stitch kit of Cockington Forge, Devon.

Catalogue: *Annually, Catalogue, 32 pages, Colour, Free* Postal charges: *95p* Delivery: *Royal Mail* Methods of Payment: *Cheque, Postal Order, COD*

ELIZABETH BRADLEY DESIGNS LTD
1 West End
Beaumaris
Anglesey
N. Wales
LL58 8BD

Telephone:
0248 811055
Fax:
0248 811118

NEEDLEWORK KITS AND DESIGNS
Elizabeth Bradley's catalogue features a collection of classic and traditional designs, many of which are based on Victorian patterns and pieces. They may be made into cushions or framed as pictures. Joined together and edged with a border they make a classic and attractive needlework carpet.

The kits and designs range between £46.00 and £54.00. The kits are beautifully presented and packaged and would make a welcome present or an exciting project. The needlework designs can be bought as ready-made pieces, cushions or carpets and the company also provides a cushion making and framing service for their customers.

Catalogue: *A3, Catalogue, 4 pages, Colour, Free* Postal charges: *Varies with item* Delivery: *Royal Mail* Methods of Payment: *Cheque, Visa, Access / Mastercard*

Hobbies & Crafts

GMC PUBLICATIONS LTD
Castle Place
166 High Street
Lewes
East Sussex
BN7 1XU

Telephone:
0273 477374
Fax:
0273 478606

BOOKS AND VIDEOS ON WOODWORKING

The Guild of Master Craftsmen have brought together some of the most useful and impressive titles for anyone with an interest in wood. There are books, videos and magazines for the novice and the expert alike.

The materials are divided into ten sections, covering furniture making, dolls houses and specialist handicrafts. Books range from £4.95 to £16.95 and videos from £9.95. The range is constantly updated so that you can master a new skill with every new catalogue.

Catalogue: *A5, Catalogue, 16 pages, Colour, Free* Postal charges: *Varies with item* Delivery: *Royal Mail* Methods of Payment: *Cheque, Postal Order, Visa, Access / Mastercard, American Express, Diners Club*

GREENWICH ZERO
Catalogue Centre
Ferry Lane
Shepperton on Thames
Middx
TW17 9LQ

Telephone:
0932 253333
Fax:
0932 241679

MARITIME NOVELTIES AND CLOTHES

The catalogue of the Maritime Trust, Greenwich Zero has the support of HRH Prince Philip. Whether or not he's a regular customer is another matter. The Trust was founded with the intention of preserving Britain's historical ships and to display them for the public.

Their catalogue features all kinds of interesting gifts and clothes. For example, a kit to build a model of the legendary Cutty Sark which, like most items here, is pricey at £125.00. A pair of elegant polished brass theatre glasses are £69.00 while a tough-looking compass is a more affordable £19.95.

The clothing also has a nautical flavour with a Breton fisherman's cap for £9.95 and a traditional naval duffel coat for £149.00.

Catalogue: *11 x 7.5, Catalogue, 24 pages, Colour, Free* Postal charges: *£2.99* Delivery: *Royal Mail Courier* Methods of Payment: *Cheque, Postal Order, Access / Mastercard, Visa*

HEIRLOOM PATCHWORK
Rose Hall
Sydenham Damerel
Tavistock
Devon
PL19 8PU

Telephone:
0822-87256

PATCHWORK QUILTS

Christine Pattison makes her beautiful quilts from quality cottons and polycotton backing. They come with either 2oz or 4oz wadding. Machine and hand quilting are combined to make extremely durable, machine-washable quilts to a number of simple, elegant designs.

Names and dates can be added to the quilts which can also be made from the customer's own materials. The range is augmented by pillows and cushions.

Hobbies & Crafts

A single costs £140.00, a double £190.00 and a Kingsize £240. Cot-sized baby quilts are £49.95. Kits are available from £35.00.

Catalogue: *Third A4, Leaflets, 6 pages, B/W, Free* Postal charges: *Varies with item* Delivery: *Royal Mail* Methods of Payment: *Cheque*

JACKSONS OF HEBDEN BRIDGE
Croft Mill
Hebden Bridge
West Yorks.
HX7 8AP

Telephone:
0422 842964
Fax:
0422 842385

NEEDLEWORK AND TAPESTRY KITS
Jacksons of Hebden Bridge is a fourth generation family business established over 70 years. Their general collection of complete kits for needlework and tapestry contains a wide range of items both decorative and practical, from pictures to cushions, door stops, bell pulls, rugs and much, much more. There is a wide range of prices and skill levels for beginner or expert.

Their specialist products include complete tapestry kits for items of church furnishings in which they are world leaders. The range includes kneelers, communion rail kneelers, pew cushions, etc, which can be seen in more than 7,000 locations worldwide. Their special studio design facilities are available to customers.

Catalogue: *Annually, A5, Catalogue, 24 pages, Colour, Free* Postal charges: *Varies with item* Delivery: *Royal Mail, Parcelforce Panic Link* Methods of Payment: *Cheque, Postal Order, Visa, Access / Mastercard*

JANET COLES BEADS LTD
Perdiswell Cottage
Bilford Road
Worcester
WR3 8QA

Telephone:
0905 755888
Fax:
0905 756641

LOOSE BEADS, NECKLACES, EARRINGS, JEWELLERY KITS
Rich-looking colour catalogue which introduces you to the world of beads. The catalogue is divided into sections according to materials and is suitable for newcomers, who are looking for kits to make up their own necklaces and earrings, to practised beaders. All the jewellery is supplied in both kit and made-up form. Each kit contains everything you will need to make it up (except a needle) and includes ear-fittings for pierced ears. If you want clip-on ear-fittings, these have to be ordered separately as an extra. All the beads are pictured 'same size' so you can see exactly what they will look like. They are also used in many of the made-up necklaces so you can get a clear idea of what they will look like strung up. The business is run by the Coles family and the catalogue is written in a very personal and at the same time, educational, way. Prices range from jewel colour beads, ten for

Hobbies & Crafts

18p and desert earrings, £1.50 for a kit, £3.00 made up, to Meteorite two-strand necklace, £27.95 made up, £23.95 in kit form.

Catalogue: *Annually, A4, Catalogue, 112 pages, Colour, £2.50*
Postal charges: *Varies with item* Delivery: *Royal Mail* Methods of Payment: *Visa, Access / Mastercard Cheque, Postal Order*

MADEIRA THREADS (UK) LTD
PO Box 6
Thirsk
North Yorkshire
YO7 3YX

Telephone:
0845 524344
Fax:
0845 525046

EMBROIDERY KITS AND SAMPLERS
Madeira Threads are part of Europe's leading manufacturing group of high quality embroidery threads. They produce a wide range of embroidery kits in cross-stitch, both charted and printed. The Oriental Collection OR1-OR6 costs £9.95 each. They also produce samplers (Scottish 17th Century sampler, £18.25); surface stitchery (Keepsakes, £9.75); raised (Floral Fantasy, £16.00); ribbon which costs between £6.95 and £7.50; crewel embroidery (Cushion HCEC 07, £23.30); Jacobean designs; plus seasonal, greeting and anniversary card embroidery designs.

Madeira manufactures wooden embroidery hand frames and offers various ranges of their threads suitably packed in gift boxes for the embroiderer, lacemaker, quilter or fisherman. A handling charge of £1.00 per order, plus postage at cost, is made.

Catalogue: *Annually, A4, Catalogue, 40 pages, Colour, £2.50*
Postal charges: *Varies with item* Delivery: *Royal Mail, Parcelforce Parceline* Methods of Payment: *Cheque, Postal Order, Visa, Access / Mastercard*

MICHAEL EVANS & CO
Unit 1
Little Saxbys Farm
Cowden
Kent
TN8 7DX

Telephone:
0342 850755
Fax:
0342 850926

RODS AND FLY-LINES
Michael Evans has obviously made his passion into his business, sharing his love of game angling and fly fishing with an expanding band of customers. With a collection of rods, lines, weights and videos all designed to improve your angling skills the present collection of products is not large, but it is well considered.

Mr Evans provides an honest and helpful explanation with each range, which illustrates his experience and knowledge, and a wider commentary to lead the novice through the bewildering range of materials. Prices start at £14.99 for a video to £395.00 for a 15 foot Speycatcher rod.

Catalogue: *A4, Leaflets, 10 pages, B/W, Free* Postal charges: *Varies with item* Delivery: *Royal Mail* Methods of Payment: *Cheque, Postal Order, Visa, Access / Mastercard*

Hobbies & Crafts

MICHAEL LAZARUS ASSOCIATES
242/244 St John Street
London
EC1V 4PH

Telephone:
071 250 3988
Fax:
071 608 0370

KITES
The beauty of the Ferrari Sky Ram Kite is not only that it looks good and is great fun to fly, but that you can fly it – first time – even if you have never flown a kite before. The Ferrari has no sticks or spars so it is safe to fly, even in crowded places; it can be folded into your pocket and being made from Ripstop nylon it is practical indestructible.

The Ferrari Sky Blade Stunt Kite is a new revolutionary 'swinging' kite designed to fly in any wind, from the lightest breeze to gale force strength. Experts will delight in its fingertip control for the most complicated aerobatics and beginners with the ease in which they can learn to fly a stunt kite.

Catalogue: *A4 & A5, Brochure, 1 page, Colour, Free* Postal charges: *Varies with item* Delivery: *Royal Mail* Methods of Payment: *Cheque, Postal Order, Visa, Access / Mastercard*

MULBERRY SILKS
2 Old Rectory Cottage
Easton Grey
Malmesbury
Wiltshire
SN16 0PE

Telephone:
0666 840881

EMBROIDERY SILKS
Mulberry Silks offers a wide range of hand-wound embroidery silks in medium or fine thickness.

An extensive range of colours is available and shades can be matched to magazine cuttings, photographs etc. No shade card available. Large amounts of one colour available. Prices range from £2.75 to £12.00. Individual callers welcome – but telephone first.

Catalogue: *A5, Leaflet, 6 pages, B/W, Free* Postal charges: *Varies with item* Delivery: *Royal Mail* Methods of Payment: *Cheque, Postal Order*

OAKLEY FABRICS LTD
8 May Street
Luton
LU1 3QY

Telephone:
0582 34733

MATERIALS AND ACCESSORIES FOR STUFFED TOYS
Oakley's brochure is aimed at toymakers, and includes a clear explanation of the latest safety standards and the effect they will have on professional toymakers. They have also reviewed all of their materials to speed up your choice. The materials include everything from fillers at 64p per pound to £1.48 per pound, to complete kits from the simple to the advanced for around £20.00.

Catalogue: *A4, Leaflets, 14 pages, B/W, Free* Postal charges: *Varies with item* Delivery: *Royal Mail* Methods of Payment: *Cheque, Postal Order, Visa, Access / Mastercard*

Hobbies & Crafts

PEDOMETERS INTERNATIONAL LTD
1 Whittle Close
Drayton Fields
Daventry
Northants
NN11 5RQ

Telephone:
0327 706030
Fax:
0327 71633

PEDOMETERS, MAP MEASURERS AND COMPASSES

Pedometers International have an extensive range of instruments for walkers, ramblers, runners, and joggers. Pedometers are, as the name implies, the company's speciality, but compasses (for both walkers and drivers) and map measurers are also available.

The pedometers are precision instruments which count the number of paces you take and translate the information into a dial reading of miles, kilometres or paces. All pedometers have an audible tick during use and weigh from 1-2 ounces; the largest have a diameter of 2".

Pedometers vary from around £20.00 to £115.00.

Catalogue: *A4, Catalogue, 6 pages plus inserts, Colour and B/W, Free* Postal charges: *£1.95* Delivery: *Royal Mail* Methods of Payment: *Visa, Access / Mastercard Cheque, Postal Order*

PORTSMOUTH GOLF CENTRE
Great Salterns Golf Course
Burrfields Road
Portsmouth
PO3 5HH

Telephone:
0705 699519

GOLFING ACCESSORIES

Golf is one of the most popular hobbies in this country and this catalogue can help anyone who wants to update their equipment or get the right ranges to help them on the fairways. The Golf Centre stocks all major brands of clubs, bags, balls and bags to improve your game and the smartest shirts and shoes to improve your look for example, Hi-Tec golf shoes at £55.00.

Many of the prices found here are competitive, with a Macgregor Wentworth golf bag at £34.99 and a dozen Dunlop balls for £7.99.

Catalogue: *Quarterly, A3, Brochure, 4 pages, Colour, Free* Postal charges: *Varies with item* Delivery: *Royal Mail* Methods of Payment: *Cheque, Access / Mastercard, Visa*

PRIMAVERA
FREEPOST
PO Box 141
Cardiff
CF4 1ZZ

Telephone:
0800 243 400

NEEDLEPOINT KITS AND ACCESSORIES

Primavera offer needlepoint kits featuring beautiful floral and fruit designs for DIY cushion-covers. Their fine 26-page brochure has clear photographs of each design, including their 'Best Sellers' range and new designs. These can be purchased as complete kits, including canvas, wool, instructions and needle for between £35.00–£45.00 or as canvas only for between £21.00–£26.00.

A few accessories are also on offer, including a 24" hardwood frame for £16.75 and anglepoise magnifying lamp for £42.00.

Hobbies & Crafts

PRINCESS PLEATERS
Fenny Compton
Warks
CV33 0YD

Telephone:
0608 737926

Fax:
0608 737926

Catalogue: *A5, Catalogue, 32 pages, Colour, Free* Postal charges: *Free* Delivery: *Royal Mail* Methods of Payment: *Cheque, Postal Order, Visa, Access / Mastercard*

PLEATING MACHINES
The pleating machine takes the tedium out of smocking and gathering. Dressmakers, both amateur and professional, can easily increase their output with this solidly constructed machine.

Made in Britain with a solid timber base, brass rollers and 24 fine steel needles, the Princess pleater is hand-operated, so that the user retains complete control over the operation. It comes complete with clear instructions for use. The pleater is available for only £89.95 and extra needles cost £6.50 per set.

Catalogue: *A5, Brochure, 4 pages, Colour, Free* Postal charges: *Varies with item* Delivery: *Royal Mail* Methods of Payment: *Cheque, Postal Order, Visa, Access / Mastercard*

PUSH POSTERS
P O Box 327
Clydebank
Dunbartonshire
G81 3HE

Telephone:
041 9514460

Fax:
041 9514464

MUSIC POSTERS AND MEMORABILIA
A real cornucopia for music lovers, Push brings together posters, programmes, photographs and backstage passes from some of the worlds best-known bands.

There are almost 4,000 posters of bands across the musical spectrum – from Anthrax to Soft Cell – ranging in price from £2.50 to £5.99 depending on size (from 20" × 12" to a massive 60" × 40"). Along with over 700 tour programmes all for less than £10.00 each, 1,000 backstage passes and original roadie IDs – some of them extremely rare – and over 1,000 sets of concert photographs of some of the biggest concerts of the last fifteen years, these are prime collector's items. There is also a comprehensive range of film and personality posters, many of them film promotion stock.

Catalogue: *Quarterly, A5, Catalogue, 60 pages, B/W, Free* Postal charges: *Varies with item* Delivery: *Royal Mail* Methods of Payment: *Cheque, Postal Order, Visa, Access / Mastercard*

Hobbies & Crafts

READICUT WOOL CO LTD
PO Box No 1
Ossett
West Yorkshire
WF5 9SA

Telephone:
0924 810810

NEEDLECRAFT AND RUG KITS

Readicut provide embroidery kits in a variety of designs. These range from the tasteful to the unashamedly sentimental. The Paddington Bear kit, (£21.99) is one of the former; the 'My Child' poem (£14.99) perhaps one of the latter, with its poem beginning: 'My child / you are the poem I dreamed of writing / the masterpiece I longed to paint . . .'

All kits contain embroidery thread, chart, fabric, needle and instructions. There are numerous ideas for religious verses and commemorative bon mots.

In addition, Readicut offer a wide range of rug kits. Styles include Chantelle (80" × 120" from £367.00) and Shensian (27" × 54" from £66.00). There's even a rather florid 'Welcome' mat (14" × 28" from £27.00).

Catalogue: *210 × 200 mm, Catalogue, 75 pages, Colour, Free*
Postal charges: *Varies with item* Delivery: *Royal Mail*
Methods of Payment: *Cheque, Postal Order, Visa, Access / Mastercard*

RIDINGS CRAFT LTD
Newton House
Grey Street
Leeds Road
Wakefield
WF1 3HQ

Telephone:
0924 822666
Fax:
0924 822766

DOLLS

Doll-makers up and down the country are probably already familiar with the excellent Ridings Craft. They sell dolls, accessories and patterns to suit every requirement. There may even be some truth in their claim that the finished product will become a family heirloom.

Most of the stock adheres to traditional lines, with more than the occasional dip into the past. Sandringham doll kits start at £26.50 for the basic 'Heidi' kit (£30.45 for the complete kit). As the name suggests, this range is more contemporary in feel with miniature versions of the Chelsea set. Amanda, a blue-eyed blonde costs £37.50 for her basic kit and £40.90 for the complete works.

Catalogue: *Bi-annually, A4, Catalogue, 16 pages, Colour, Free*
Postal charges: *£2.25* Delivery: *Royal Mail, Parcelforce* Methods of Payment: *Cheque, Postal Order, Visa, Access / Mastercard, American Express*

Hobbies & Crafts

SCOTLAND DIRECT
Thistle Mill
Biggar
Scotland
ML12 6LP

Telephone:
0899 21001
Fax:
0899 20456

COLLECTIBLES
Scotland Direct specialises in high quality collectible items. It incorporates The Thimble Guild which sends out monthly programmes with selections of thimbles to members.

Aside from thimbles, which start at £3.95, they supply small decorative items such as china boxes and attractive architectural models of country cottages, churches and post boxes. They also stock items for lovers of animals, birds and butterflies and a range of novelty items, such as the charming Hush-a-Bye Babies.

Catalogue: *Monthly, A5, Brochure, 12 pages, Colour, Free* Postal charges: *Varies with item* Delivery: *Parcelforce* Methods of Payment: *Cheque, Postal Order, Stage Payments, Visa, Access / Mastercard, American Express, Diners Club*

SILK SHADES (H&G)
12 Market Place
Lavenham
Suffolk
CO10 9QZ

Telephone:
0787 247029
Fax:
0787 247029

SILK MATERIAL FOR INTERIORS
An extensive range of silks for dressmaking, upholstery and curtains. There are more than twenty different silks including classics such as dupion, organza and taffeta and variations such as basket weave, tartan and gold printed varieties. The range of colours and patterns available is wide.

As part of their service to ease the difficulties of interior re-decoration, they can provide swatches of materials to match curtains and carpets and provide large swatches on request.

Catalogue: *A4, Leaflets, 5 pages, B/W, Free* Postal charges: *Varies with item* Delivery: *Royal Mail* Methods of Payment: *Cheque, Postal Order, Visa, Access / Mastercard*

SORCERER'S APPRENTICE
4–8 Burley Lodge Road
Leeds
LS6 1QP

Telephone:
0532 451309

OCCULT AND NEW AGE GOODS
The Sorcerer's Apprentice stocks a range of supernatural substances that 'you'd never thought you'd see' with over 500 rare herbs, gems, oils, perfumes, roots, fossils, botanics, resins, sacraments, seeds, aromatics, dyes, waxes, crystals, barks, minerals, philtres, compounds, brews and essences.

Gemstones and minerals include pieces of green agate for £1.86, 10ct moonstones for £55.19, 1 oz of Selenite for £1.65, and small chips of natural lapis for £2.62. The range of magical equipment includes an Alexandrian Sanctuary Lamp (genuinely 2000 years old) in decorated terracotta for £39.10 and a seance kit containing 16 items for £49.65. The Sorcerer's Apprentice also has a vast selection of books on the Occult, Magic and Herbalism.

Hobbies & Crafts

STANLEY GIBBONS
5 Parkside
Christchurch Road
Ringwood
Hants
BH24 3SH

Telephone:
0425 472363

STAMP COLLECTING PRODUCTS

Stanley Gibbons are one of the most established suppliers of stamps. Their range of catalogues is almost as wide as their stock of stamps – you can pick a catalogue on just about any subject, from 'Railways on Stamps' (£9.50) to 'Chess on Stamps' (£5.00).

Luxury, hingeless, one-country, blank and thematic albums manufactured by DAVO of Holland start at £66.95 and extend up to £224.95. More down to earth examples, such as lighthouse mounts start at 75p for 21 mm × 24mm.

They also provide a number of accessories, like the Uvitec Micro Short Wave Ultra Violet Lamp for £41.50 or a watermark detector for £14.75.

Catalogue: *Annually, A5, Catalogue, 32 pages, Colour, Free* Postal charges: *Varies with item* Delivery: *Royal Mail* Methods of Payment: *Cheque, Postal Order, Visa, Access / Mastercard*

THE BRIGHTON BEAD SHOP
21 Sydney Street
Brighton
Sussex
BN1 4EN

Telephone:
0273 675077
Fax:
0273 692803

BEADS AND THREADS

The Brighton Bead shop can supply over 400 designs of beads in a wide range of colours. These fashion accessories come in a wide range of materials, including Cloisonne, bone, Indian silver, rosewood and pewter. The designs take their inspiration from all areas of the world with Celtic art, Indian religious motifs and traditional African markings making some of the more striking examples.

They also supply everything needed to make your own original jewellery. Whether you are a novice or an expert you can now afford to own unique jewellery as beads start at only one pence each, and even the most luxurious items are only £1.50.

Catalogue: *A5, Catalogue, 46 pages, Colour, Free* Postal charges: *Varies with item* Delivery: *Royal Mail* Methods of Payment: *Cheque, Postal Order, Visa, Access / Mastercard*

Catalogue: *A4, Catalogue, 36 pages, B/W, 50p* Postal charges: *Varies with item* Delivery: *Royal Mail* Methods of Payment: *Cheque, Postal Order, Visa, Access / Mastercard*

Hobbies & Crafts

THE DOLLS HOUSE EMPORIUM
Dept VG1
Victoria Road
Ripley
Derbyshire
DE5 3YD

Telephone:
0773 513773
Fax:
0773 513772

DOLLS HOUSES AND FURNITURE
Founded in 1979 The Dolls House Emporium has a long established and excellent reputation for quality and service to customers. They produce two catalogues split between children's and collector's ranges. Each contains selections of high quality wooden dolls' houses which come both as kits or ready made.

They also feature furniture, fittings and accessories for both young and mature dolls' house enthusiasts. In fact the Emporium supplies everything for the doll's house, from the cellar and garden up to the attic and roof. All items are made one-twelfth scale.

Dolls' house kits start from £49.90, with built houses from £149.90. Accessories start at just 50p and furniture from £2.95.

Catalogue: *Bi-annually, A4, Catalogue, 48 pages, Colour, Free* Postal charges: *Varies with item* Delivery: *Royal Mail Courier* Methods of Payment: *Cheque, Visa, Access / Mastercard, Postal Order*

THE ART VENEERS COMPANY
Industrial Estate
Mildenhall
Suffolk
IP28 7AY

Telephone:
0638 712550
Fax:
0638 712330

VENEERS AND MARQUETRY SUPPLIES
The Art Veneers Company publish a fully illustrated combined manual/catalogue with a price list. The catalogue comprises a series of informative articles on various aspects of veneering and the techniques used in marquetry. It contains full details of the company's selections of veneers, tools, polishes, and has colour pages illustrating a range of veneers, motifs and bandings. The company also produce a range of collectors' sets which comprise veneer samples which can be used for restoration.

For sizes 18" x 6", cabinet veneers such as elm cost 90p, plum £1.80 and rosewood, santos £2.00.

Catalogue: *A4, Leaflets, 10 pages, B/W, £2.70* Postal charges: *Varies with item* Delivery: *Royal Mail* Methods of Payment: *Cheque, Postal Order, Visa, Access / Mastercard*

THE ODDBALL JUGGLING COMPANY
323 Upper Street
Islington
London
N1 2XQ

Telephone:
071 354 5660
Fax:
071 704 2577

JUGGLING SUPPLIES
Susi and Max, the owners of Oddball, were the first people in the UK to open retail juggling shops. They now also run a mail order service selling just about anything a juggler could want.

Beanbags start at £3.25 a set. These are ideal for beginners since they're easier to catch than balls and won't roll away if you drop them. For the accomplished juggler, there are juggling torches from £13.75, clubs from £9.25 and fire devilsticks from £25.00.

Hobbies & Crafts

The catalogue also includes heaps of advice on what to buy for your level of skill, the history of the art and how to go about performing. Various books on the subject are also available, including 'Circus Techniques' by Hovey Burgess (£14.00).

Catalogue: *A4, Catalogue, 22 pages, B/W, Free* Postal charges: *10%* Delivery: *Royal Mail* Methods of Payment: *Cheque, Postal Order, Visa, Access / Mastercard*

THE ROCKING HORSE SHOP
Fangfoss
York
YO4 5QH

Telephone:
0759 368737
Fax:
0759 368194

BOOKS, PLANS, TIMBER AND ACCESSORIES FOR ROCKING HORSES

A genuine wooden rocking horse is one of the most delightful and timeless of playthings and this rural company specialises in everything to make or restore them. This includes books, plans, videos, timber packs, tools and an extensive range of specialist accessories.

All leather and woodwork is made on the premises so tailor made saddles and bridles for old horses present no problems. There is a fascinating range of projects from very simple to truly challenging. Complete rocking horses are made to commission and restorations are also undertaken.

Plans for a medium, fully carved horse are £8.99, £11.99 for a carousel style. Glass eyes start from 90p a pair and stirrups come in at £6.50.

Catalogue: *A5, Catalogue, 24 pages, Colour, 2 × 1st class stamps* Postal charges: *Varies with item* Delivery: *Royal Mail, Parcelforce* Methods of Payment: *Postal Order Cheque, Visa, Access / Mastercard, Other*

TITLES DIRECT
Unit 8
First Avenue
Globe Park
Marlow
Buckinghamshire
SL7 1YA

Telephone:
0800 14 14 14
Fax:
0628 483104

COMPACT DISCS AND CASSETTES OF POPULAR MUSIC

Titles Direct is designed to help music lovers to keep in touch with the latest sounds whether their taste is rock, jazz, rave or dance. The brochure offers a wide choice of titles by various artists such as Def Leppard, Prince, Garth Brooks and Mariah Carey. The albums can be ordered on cassette (£5.49–£24.99) or compact disc (£8.99–£15.99) with no limits on the amount ordered. It's advisable to phone before placing an order to check availability.

Catalogue: *A4, Brochure, 6 pages, Colour and B/W, Free* Postal charges: *Varies with item* Delivery: *Royal Mail* Methods of Payment: *Visa, Access / Mastercard Cheque*

Hobbies & Crafts

UTTINGS GUN COMPANY
54 Bethel Street
Norwich
Norfolk
NR2 1NR

Telephone:
0603 632226

Fax:
0603 619849

AIR RIFLES AND HANDGUNS

Uttings' guns – from an AK47 at £229.00 and Colts from £69.00 – are available for sale or hire and illustrated with a clear account of their capabilities.

Uttings also provide an impressive section of knives from Whitby Fox to Swiss Army and a comprehensive range of accessories from catapults to reproduction grenades.

Catalogue: *Annually, A4, Catalogue, 16 pages, Colour, £1.00*
Postal charges: *Varies with item* Delivery: *Royal Mail* Methods of Payment: *Cheque, Postal Order, Visa, Access / Mastercard, American Express*

WANSBECK DOLLS' HOUSES
Cherry Lodge
Outwood Lane
Bletchingley
Surrey
RH1 4LR

Telephone:
0883 744728

DOLLS' HOUSES

Wansbeck sell quality wooden dolls' houses and kits manufactured both by themselves and other high class suppliers. The range of furniture includes handmade items by British craftsmen, for serious collectors, as well as more sturdy designs for children. They also stock porcelain dolls and kits, rugs and rug kits, shop furniture and fittings and 12 volt light fittings and kits. In addition they have all kinds of DIY materials, including wallpapers, mouldings, sheet and stripwood, doors and windows.

A three-storey townhouse with six rooms is £220.00, a quality dresser £40.00, a bunk bed with ladder £11.20 and wallpapers £1.20 per sheet.

Catalogue: *Annually, A4, Catalogue, 36 pages, Colour and B/W, £2.50* Postal charges: *Varies with item* Delivery: *Royal Mail, Parcelforce* Methods of Payment: *Cheque, Postal Order, Access / Mastercard, Visa*

WASHI (UK)
6 Chapel Lane
Barrow on Trent
Derby
DE73 1HE

Telephone:
0332 703807

Fax:
0332 703807

JAPANESE HANDICRAFT PRODUCTS

Washi is the Japanese term for hand made paper, a tradition which dates back to the 8th century. It is made from a pulp containing Mulberry tree bark and is extremely flexible as well as durable.

This interesting catalogue offers you the opportunity to make boxes and containers covered with Washi paper. Kits include everything needed along with clear instructions. You only have to choose the Washi paper and style of container to be covered. There are tissue boxes, pencil holders, miniature chests of drawers, spectacle holders and photograph frames. A tissue box is £11.95 and an octagonal box £11.99.

Catalogue: *A4, Catalogue, 14 pages, Colour and B/W, Free* Postal charges: *Free* Delivery: *Royal Mail* Methods of Payment: *Cheque, Postal Order, Visa, Access / Mastercard*

Hobbies & Crafts

WEDMORE NEEDLECRAFT
5 the Borough Mall
Wedmore Somerset
BS28 4EB

Telephone:
0934 713462

NEEDLECRAFT SUPPLIES
Wedmore sells all sorts of supplies for needlecraft. These include threads, wools, zweigart fabrics and canvasses as well as needles, accessories, organisers, hoops, rotating bars, frames, magnetic boards and damasks.

A standing frame with footrest is priced at £32.50, an anglepoise frame is £24.95, velour guest towels are £3.00 and a single thread canvas deluxe 39" £15.00.

Catalogue: *A5, Leaflets, 10 pages, B/W, Free* Postal charges: *Varies with item* Delivery: *Royal Mail Courier* Methods of Payment: *Cheque, Visa, Access / Mastercard, Postal Order*

WILLOW FABRICS
27 Willow Green
Knutsford
Cheshire
WA16 6AX

Telephone:
0565 621098
Fax:
0565 653233

EMBROIDERY FABRICS
Willow Fabrics is a mail order house specialising in embroidery fabrics. They stock over 250 Zweigart fabrics and colours for immediate dispatch. These include many different Aida Cloths, Damask, Cotton and Linen Evenweaves, Afghans, Aida and Evenweave ribbons. There are also lace edgings, tapestry canvas, threads and sundries.

Very popular with their customers for the friendly and personal service, Willows has many repeat orders. Aida 14 is from £11.50 per metre, Bantry linen from £16.90, Londa 27 tpi from £7.80 and Aida ribbons from £1.50 per metre.

Catalogue: *Bi-annually, A4, Catalogue, 19 pages, B/W, 3 first class stamps.* Postal charges: *Varies with item* Delivery: *Parcelforce, Royal Mail* Methods of Payment: *Cheque, Postal Order, Visa, Access / Mastercard*

YATELEY INDUSTRIES
Mill Lane
Yateley
Camberley
Surrey
GU17 7TF

Telephone:
0252 872337
Fax:
0252 860620

FABRICS PRINTED IN HAND BLOCKS
This sheltered workshop, providing employment for people with disabilities, produces good quality fabrics and craft items. Using block and screen printing they can produce several thousand designs in over 30 different colours to fulfil orders for any occasion.

After designing and carving the pattern blocks in their workshops, the Yateley team use high quality natural fabric to produce products for every room in the house. With a range that includes cushions, cravats and oven gloves from £2.99 to £70.44, there is a wide choice to suit many tastes.

Catalogue: *A5, Brochure, 30 pages, Colour, Free* Postal charges: *Varies with item* Delivery: *Royal Mail* Methods of Payment: *Cheque, Postal Order, Visa, Access / Mastercard*

Home

4 WOOD FLOORS
Unit B
Wellington Trading Estate
Wellington
Somerset
TA21 8ST

Telephone:
0823 660912
Fax:
0823 660913

HARDWOOD FLOORING
A comprehensive brochure featuring a wood flooring collection. Flooring woods are selected only from areas of re-forestation and concern is such that the company have joined forces with The World Wildlife Fund for Nature and funds are donated for every square metre of flooring sold. Guide to daily maintenance is given and information on how to lay the floors is given. Samples are available on request.

Catalogue: *A4, Brochure, Colour and B/W, Free* Postal charges: *Varies with item* Delivery: *Royal Mail* Methods of Payment: *Cheque, Visa, Access / Mastercard*

ABBEY QUILTING LTD
Selinas Lane
Dagenham
Essex
RM8 1ES

Telephone:
081 592 2233
Fax:
081 593 3787

MATTRESS PROTECTORS
This brochure is aimed at the corporate market as well as personal customers who are unable to reach the company's principal stockists in department stores. There is one product: a synthetic, non-allergic mattress protector, available in both flame retardant and waterproof versions.

Machine washable and easy to fit, the Cumulus protector retails at £15.99 for a standard single bed and £22.99 for a standard double. The company will also make special sizes to order. Samples of the material are included in the brochure.

Catalogue: *A5, Brochure, 4 pages plus inserts, Colour, Free* Postal charges: *Free* Delivery: *Royal Mail* Methods of Payment: *Cheque*

ARISTOCAST ORIGINALS
Bold Street
Sheffield
S Yorks
S9 2LR

Telephone:
0742 561156
Fax:
0742 431835

REPRODUCTION PLASTER
Aristocast do not so much sell reproduction plasterwork as recreations of the originals. Their glossy catalogue features ornate Georgian and Victorian centre pieces, panel mouldings, cornices and niches. All are manufactured in much the same way as the originals with the same eye for detail.

There are also larger structures such as archways, arch corners, corbels and even porticoes and canopies for use on the outside of the house. The range of fire surrounds are particularly attractive and come in a number of different styles. Aristocasts have been involved in many major renovation projects including Brocket Hall, the British Embassy in Washington and the Grosvenor House Hotel, London. Prices, though, remain reasonable, with centrepieces from just £23.00 and niches from around £100.00.

Catalogue: *A4, Catalogue, 18 pages, Colour, Free* Postal charges: *£15.00* Delivery: *Royal Mail* Methods of Payment: *Access / Mastercard, Visa Cheque*

Home

ART HISTORY DESIGN
The Stables Studios
Nethercott Barton
Iddesleigh
Nr. Winkleigh
Devon
EX19 8SN

Telephone:
0837 810610
Fax:
0392 413538

HAND FINISHED PRODUCTS

Devonshire land and seascapes have inspired Art History to design a collection of hand-finished decorative products for those seeking originality and style. Art History will produce to either the customer's verbal description or to an example of colour swatch to meet individual requirements. Catalogue contains hand painted terracotta pots and hand painted fire screens, flower shelves and brackets, as well as jewellery hand crafted in silver wire; and many other items. Prices range from £2.50 to £360.00 plus postage and packing. Catalogue £2.00 extra.

Catalogue: *A4, Catalogue, 14 pages, Colour, £2.00* Postal charges: *Varies with item* Delivery: *Royal Mail* Methods of Payment: *Cheque, Postal Order*

BIRCHALL'S
The Pipe Shop
14 Talbot Road
Blackpool
Lancs
FY1 1LF

Telephone:
0253 24218
Fax:
0253 291659

PIPES AND TOBACCO

Birchall's was founded in 1834 and is one of the country's oldest tobacconists. Their attractive, sepia catalogue features specialist loose tobaccos along with their own blends. There are mixtures from Britain, America, Denmark and Germany, each with a brief description of aroma and smoking qualities. There is also a selection of chewing and wrapped tobaccos.

The centre of the catalogue is devoted to Ferndown briar pipes, made by the traditional British manufacturer K & J.S. Briars. There is also a good selection of Havana cigars as well as cigars from elsewhere. Finally there is a video called *At Peace with your Pipe*, which is said to be of interest to anyone who enjoys a puff.

Catalogue: *A5, Catalogue, 16 pages, B/W, 25p* Postal charges: *10% of total* Delivery: *Royal Mail* Methods of Payment: *Visa, Access / Mastercard Cheque, Postal Order*

BLACK DOG OF WELLS
18 Tor Street
Wells Somerset
BA5 2US

Telephone:
0749 672548

DECORATIVE TERRACOTTA

This small family business has been making decorative terracotta for over twenty years. Their small brochure illustrates a large range of miniature relief plaques designed by Philippa Threlfall. Each piece is hand finished and fired at 1100 degrees which means it can safely be left outside.

The terracottas are mounted on 5" square dark blue card and come in special plastic bags. A 4.5" version is £10.50, 3.5" £8.50.

Catalogue: *Third A4, Leaflets, B/W, Free* Postal charges: *Free* Delivery: *Royal Mail* Methods of Payment: *Cheque*

Home

BRITISH TELECOM
In Touch
BT Freepost GW 7520
Glasgow
G2 6BR

Telephone:
0800 800 150

TELEPHONES AND ACCESSORIES

In Touch Magazine brings you the latest and best ideas from British Telecom. There is a vast range of telephones, answering machines and mobile phones, with helpful and flexible options on renting or buying ... but there is also much more.

The latest in video technology is now available for only a few pounds a month. For only £38.97, Videophones can bring you face to face with family and friends, and for only £19.99 the Sky multi-channel package, including Sky Movies Gold, can be delivered straight to your living room. The rental options also have the benefit of full maintenance protection by BT's trained staff.

Catalogue: *Bi-annually, A5, Catalogue, 60 pages, Colour, Free* Postal charges: *£2.99* Delivery: *Royal Mail* Methods of Payment: *Cheque, Postal Order, Visa, Access / Mastercard*

BRUFORD & HEMING LIMITED
28 Conduit Street
New Bond Street
London
W1R 9TA

Telephone:
071 629 4289
Fax:
071 493 5879

SILVERWARE

This London-based Silversmith and jewellers are known for their fine antique silver and jewellery. Their catalogue, however, displays only newly produced silver items, all fully hallmarked.

Assorted gift items include a wide range of photograph frames from around £20.00 to over £100.00, and other more unusual items for special occasions. Of the latter, small perfume bottles are £39.00; a silver and leather desk address book £66.00 and a pair of silver-plated candlesticks £300.00.

Ladies jewellery is pleasantly displayed in an additional colour leaflet, with sections on 'under £300.00', 'under £500.00' and 'Antique and Estate Jewellery' for pricier items.

Catalogue: *A5, Catalogue, 40 pages, Colour, Free* Postal charges: *Varies with item* Delivery: *Royal Mail* Methods of Payment: *Cheque, Visa, Access / Mastercard, American Express*

Home

BUTTERFLIES GALORE
21 Westall Centre
Holberrow Green
Nr Redditch
Worcestershire
B96 6JY

Telephone:
0386 793240
Fax:
0386 793253

DECORATIVE BUTTERFLIES
This is an unusual catalogue, specialising in ornamental butterflies. They come in two sizes – 15" and 7½" across the wingspan. Photographs illustrate how you can display them on walls, fences or even plants. Special fixings are supplied and presentation gift boxes of three butterflies are available.

The six most popular British butterflies are represented here, and cost £12.80 each for the small version and £23.50 for the large. If you order six large butterflies there is a reduction in price, effectively giving you one free.

Catalogue: *A4, Leaflet, 2 pages, Colour, Free* Postal charges: *£2.40* Delivery: *Royal Mail* Methods of Payment: *Cheque, Postal Order*

BYRON & BYRON LTD
4 Hanover Yard
Off Noel Road
London
N1 8BE

Telephone:
071 704 9290
Fax:
071 226 7351

CURTAIN RAILS
Reflecting current trends in furnishing fashion, this catalogue features a range of distinctive decorative curtain poles, finials, and holdbacks. Beautifully designed in a range of patterned, painted and wood finishes, they will complement virtually any room.

There are some rather theatrical examples for bathrooms in the 'Animantia' range, which include starfish, clams and scallops. Then there are highly decorated poles in the 'Decoupage' collection, which as its name implies, are covered in fabric or paper. A gilt-finished round ball finial sells for £24.50, while a hardwood holdback is £30.25.

Catalogue: *A4, Leaflets, 8 pages, Colour, Free* Postal charges: *£10.00* Delivery: *Royal Mail* Methods of Payment: *Cheque*

CANNOCK GATES
Martindale
Hawks Green
Cannock
Staffs
WS11 2XT

Telephone:
0543 462500
Fax:
0543 506237

STEEL AND TIMBER GATES
Cannock Gates manufactures and sells both steel and timber gates in a huge variety of sizes and styles, as well as accessories such as window grilles, railings, letter boxes and garden products. They will also build a gate not available in the catalogue from photographs or drawings.

They advise on measuring, fittings and fixings, hinges, locks, delivery times and prices. As they are the manufacturers and do not have a chain of shops, you are dealing directly and will get instant answers and prices matched pound for pound, like for like, with any competitor.

Delivery usually takes three days. Prices depend on the size and design. They also sell timber arbours, gazebos, obelisks and letter boxes.

Home

CC PRODUCTS
152 Markham Road
Charminster
Bournemouth
BH9 1JE

Telephone:
0202 522260

PORTABLE URINALS
The Hygienic Portable Loo (urinal only) is a great aid to motorists caught short on journeys. It is also invaluable for the disabled, the infirm who live alone and the whole family when conventional toilets are unavailable.

Two separate hand held applicators in polythene, one male and one female, are connected by a short tube to a two litre vacuum packed reservoir with a built-in non-return valve which ensures no leaks or odours. The unit also includes a tap so it can be re-used and has been medically approved.

Each unit cost £17.00 and is sent under plain cover.

Catalogue: *Annually, A4, Catalogue, 20 pages, Colour, Free* Postal charges: *Varies with item* Delivery: *United Carriers* Methods of Payment: *Cheque, Postal Order, Visa, Access / Mastercard, American Express*

Catalogue: *Annually, 8" × 4", Brochure, 4 pages, Colour, Free* Postal charges: *Varies with item* Delivery: *Royal Mail* Methods of Payment: *Cheque, Postal Order*

CELEBRATION CRYSTAL CO LTD
Freepost
Montford Bridge
Shrewsbury
Shropshire
SY4 1BR

Telephone:
0743 850851
Fax:
0743 850146

CUT GLASS CRYSTAL
A family run business, Celebration Crystal has been established for over fifteen years producing decorated glassware. There are three ranges, one of which is machine-made, the other two hand-cut from lead crystal. The products can be etched, giving a frosted effect, coloured, with up to three enamel colours or silvered (or a combination of all three).

Examples in the catalogue reflect commissions as diverse as Ruddles Brewery and Ford's Amateur Golf Tournament. A full range of glassware is available from tankards to decanters, jugs, glasses, trophy cups, rose bowls and plaques. Prices are individually determined according to requirements.

Catalogue: *A4, Leaflets, 4 pages plus inserts, Colour, Free* Postal charges: *Varies with item* Delivery: *Royal Mail* Methods of Payment: *Cheque, Postal Order*

Home

CHURCHTOWN FARM
St Martin's
Isles of Scilly
TR25 OQL

Telephone:
0720 422169

FLOWER GIFTS BY POST

The Isles of Scilly have long been famous for growing flowers. Churchtown Farm now offers you the opportunity to share some of the beauty of the Islands with your friends and family by sending a gift of flowers by post.

The Farm specialises in scented narcissi and show pinks. Flowers are sent all year round although the varieties depend on the time of year. All flower gifts are sleeved and ribbon-wrapped with a card for a personal message.

There are three sizes of gift packs: 12 flowers cost £5.00 30 flowers are £8.00 (3 bunches) and 40 flowers (4 bunches) £10.00.

Catalogue: *Third A4, Leaflets, 6 pages, Colour, Free* Postal charges: *Varies with item* Delivery: *Royal Mail* Methods of Payment: *Cheque, Visa, Access / Mastercard*

CLASSIC SILKS
140 Watlington Road
Runcton Holme
Kings Lynn
Norfolk
PE33 0EJ

Telephone:
0553 810604

SILK FABRIC

As their name suggests, Classic Silks deal exclusively in fine silks. All items need to be dry-cleaned. Some fabric, like 'Indian Dupion', are hand woven and hand dyed, and any irregularities in the fabric are part of its character, rather than faults or flaws.

Pure silk taffeta starts at £16.75 per metre of plain fabric (width: 112 cm) or £18.50 for the same width of 'Jacquard'. More expensive is 'Heavy Moire Jacquard' at £29.95 or 'Twin Pearl Embroidered' silk at £28.25. 'Duchess' satin starts at £22.00 per metre and increases to £45.50 per metre.

Catalogue: *A4, Leaflets, 1, B/W, Free* Postal charges: *Varies with item* Delivery: *Royal Mail* Methods of Payment: *Cheque, Postal Order, Visa, Access / Mastercard*

COLOGNE AND COTTON
74 Regent Street
Leamington Spa
Warks
CV32 4NS

Telephone:
0926 332573
Fax:
0926 332575

COTTON SHEETS, DUVET, PILLOW AND CUSHION, COVERS AND COLOGNES

Cologne and Cotton was established in 1989 in Royal Leamington Spa to reintroduce the pleasures of these two completely natural products: 100% pure cotton bed and table linen, and a range of eaux de cologne based on original 18th century formulas. No synthetics, no animal products, only the purest of essential oils from France.

A wide range of products includes white damask napkins (£4.95 each) and Immortelle Cologne (£12.95) to larger objects such as king-sized cutwork duvet covers (£59.95).

Home

COMFORT CARE
Unit 8A
Abbey Estates
Mount Pleasant,
Alperton
Wembley
Middx
HA0 1QU

Telephone:
081 248 1743
Fax:
081 903 7162

Catalogue: *A5, Catalogue, 12 pages, Colour, Free* Postal charges: *Varies with item* Delivery: *Royal Mail* Methods of Payment: *Cheque, Visa, Access / Mastercard*

SPECIAL NEEDS

Comfort Care supplies special aids to those suffering from backaches, bunions, claw and hammer toes and incontinence problems. They specialise in boots and slippers with accommodating fittings. For example, sufferers from swollen feet, raised or curled toes will find relief in the specially designed slippers which sell for £12.45, with a boot version for £14.95. These have been recommended or used by hospitals, nursing homes, chiropodists, social services and physiotherapists.

They also offer a well-balanced range of health supplements including 'colon clean plus', for clean healthy bowels (£10.00), 'Feverfew' and 'valerian' capsules and balm for painful backs and joints. Their Medi-patch seems a good idea too. Designed for external relief from aches and pains, it gets direct to the pain with no pills or side effects and costs £10.99 per pack. They also supply a number of personal security products from £12.50.

Catalogue: *4 to 6 a year, A5, Brochure, 20 pages, Colour and B/W, Free* Postal charges: *Varies with item* Delivery: *Royal Mail, Parcelforce* Methods of Payment: *Cheque, Postal Order, Access / Mastercard, Visa, Other*

CROFT MILL
Lowther lane
Foulridge
Colne
Lancashire
BB8 7NE

Telephone:
0282 869625
Fax:
0282 870038

BEDDING, FURNISHING FABRICS AND CLOTHES

Home of the best in clothing and bedding/furnishing fabrics from the world's leading producers, Croft Mill is situated in a very pretty part of N.E. Lancashire and is open to visitors all year.

For those who can't visit they have a catalogue which details all offers and is issued seven or eight times per year.

Catalogue: *7 issues per year, A4, Catalogue, 16 pages, Colour, Free* Postal charges: *Varies with item* Delivery: *Parcelforce Datapost* Methods of Payment: *Cheque, Postal Order, Visa, Access / Mastercard*

Home

CRUCIAL TRADING LTD
The Market Hall
Craven Arms
Shropshire
SY7 9NY

Telephone:
0588 673666

Fax:
0588 673623

NATURAL FIBRE FLOOR COVERING

Crucial Trading provide a range of natural floor coverings. Their brochure includes samples of six different fabrics, including Jute and Seagrass – ideal for traditional living; perhaps that holiday cottage endlessly plagued by the sandy feet of excited children or the heavy boots of enthusiastic walkers. As the catalogue shows, the materials look just as at home in a sumptuous drawing room.

It looks sensible to send for their sample index box, which includes examples of all 114 of their natural floorcoverings. You need to send a deposit cheque for £10.00, but after that you need only pay the return postage of £4.10. This is refunded if you make a purchase within twelve months.

To give you some idea of their prices, Aran or Fair Isle floorcoverings normally sell for £29.30 per square metre.

Catalogue: *A4, Brochure, 24 pages, Colour, Free* Postal charges: *Varies with item* Delivery: *Royal Mail* Methods of Payment: *Cheque, Visa, Access / Mastercard*

CUSHIONS
Unit 6
98 Victoria Road
London
NW10 6NB

Telephone:
081 963 0994

Fax:
081 961 0430

CUSHIONS

Cushions are *the* cushion specialists. Their off-the-peg range features classic fabrics with a contemporary feel. These include raw silks, denim, chambray, gingham, ticking and towelling. They also offer a cushion couture service, where they will design, make-up and trim to any specification.

An example of their product is the 'Beach Buddy' a small and convenient towelling cushion with a waterproof inner liner. Ideal for travelling, on the beach or by the pool they come in 9 colours and cost £13.50 (including pad). Their cotton ticking, gingham, denim and chambray cushions start from from £12.95 while silk tartans are from £18.50. The couture service starts at £9.50, excluding fabric.

Catalogue: *Annually, A4, Brochure, 4 pages, Colour, Free* Postal charges: *Varies with item* Delivery: *Parcelforce* Methods of Payment: *Cheque, Postal Order*

Home

CYNOSURE LTD
Ipsden
Oxon
OX10 6AJ

Telephone:
0491 680231
Fax:
0491 680438

SILVER AND SILVER PLATE
Cynosure sell silver and silver plate gifts, presentation items and cutlery all at realistic prices. They supply interesting items from major manufacturers but also make some themselves as well as supporting various individual craftsmen. Most of the stock is English made and they also offer a repair, replating, engraving and valuation service.

A silver plate coaster of 3½" costs £15.50, an oval silver dish of the same size £17.00, and a 7-piece place setting in 25 year silver plate £44.20 (there is a free canteen with six or more place settings). Slightly more expensive is a wonderful silver woodcock for some £480.00.

Catalogue: *Annually, A4, Catalogue, 8 pages, B/W, Free* Postal charges: *Varies with item* Delivery: *Royal Mail Courier, Parcelforce* Methods of Payment: *Cheque, Postal Order, Visa, Access / Mastercard, Diners Club*

DAMART
Bingley X
West Yorkshire
BD17 1AD

Telephone:
0274 568234

ASSORTED HOUSEHOLD GADGETS
Contained within Damart Collections catalogue is a selection of general household gadgets from bathroom items to a folding shopping trolley. There are lots of useful everyday items and a few car accessories as well. Prices are within the range £3.50 to £28.99.

Catalogue: *A4, Catalogue, 39 pages, Colour, Free* Postal charges: *Varies with item* Delivery: *In-house delivery* Methods of Payment: *Cheque, Postal Order*

DECORATIVE STAINED GLASS LIMITED

Annan
Scotland
DG12 5BL

Telephone:
0461 204051
Fax:
0461 203718

DECORATIVE STAINED GLASS
The Decorative Stained Glass range includes roundels, mirror boxes and photoframes for trade or retail. You can choose from a variety of co-ordinated designs – for instance 'Harvest Mice and Poppies'.

Boxes start at £4.75 (small Standard or Beatrix Potter design) and increase to £8.35 for the larger version. A Beatrix Potter photoframe will cost you from £6.30 (small) to £8.35 (medium).

They also stock accessories such as window suckers at 13p (small) or 16p (large) each, and transparent stands for 38p (small) to 55p (large).

Catalogue: *Annually, A4, Leaflets, 10 pages, Colour and B/W, Free* Postal charges: *Varies with item* Delivery: *Royal Mail* Methods of Payment: *Cheque, Stage Payments*

Home

DIY PLASTICS UK LTD
Regal Way
Farringdon
Oxon
SN7 7XD

Telephone:
0367-242932
Fax:
0367 242200

BUILDING MATERIALS

DIY plastics provide 'plastics for every project'. This includes a wide variety of 'plastic glass' which comes in all different shapes and sizes and can be used for greenhouses, conservatories or extensions. The clearly designed catalogue contains not only price lists and measurement tables but also artwork illustrating how to go about a number of typical DIY tasks – a useful addition.

Secondary double glazing is a popular use for clear sheets, which are £19.90 for sheets 5 m by 1270 mm wide. There are also some DIY tools and accessories along with draught excluders, Mastic, sealants and security equipment.

Catalogue: *A4, Catalogue, 24 pages, Colour, Free* Postal charges: *Varies with item* Delivery: *Royal Mail* Methods of Payment: *Cheque, Visa, Postal Order, Access / Mastercard*

FILANTE PRODUCTS
2 Watership Drive
Hightown
Ringwood
Hants
BH24 1QY

Telephone:
0425 479409

DOOR NUMBERS AND NAMES

If you have ever wondered what you could give to somebody moving house, but were running out of ideas, how about giving them their house number or name to affix to the front door?

Filante Products offer a wide range of styles of numbers, from the ornate Art Deco to the simple English Classical. Many colours are also available for the metal plaques, including white with the script being in colour. As with numbers, house names can appear in many ways, on one line or two, in full capitals, or just the initial letter capitalised. Simple decorations can be added to the plaque too.

Catalogue: *Loose leaf, Leaflets, 4 pages, Colour and B/W, Free* Postal charges: *Varies with item* Delivery: *Royal Mail* Methods of Payment: *Cheque*

FINISHING TOUCHES BY JENNIFER HAYNES
234 Main Road
Hawkwell Hockley,
Essex
SS5 4EG

Telephone:
0702 207442

HAT BOXES

These delightful hat boxes don't only have to be for hats, but can be used for all sorts of other purposes. Handmade, they come in all sizes and are covered in all sorts of material. This can include fabric from Sanderson, Laura Ashley or Ann French Wallpaper.

Boxes can be fully made up to your own design or provided in kit form. The company also sells continental dried flower arrangements and window dressing.

Prices start at £24.95 for a kit and rise to around £42.00.

Catalogue: *A5, Leaflets, Colour, Free* Postal charges: *£4.50* Delivery: *Royal Mail* Methods of Payment: *Cheque, Postal Order*

Home

FUTON EXPRESS
23/27 Pancras Road
London
NW1 2QB

Telephone:
071 833 3945
Fax:
071 833 8199

FUTONS

The futon is a firm, healthy bed which can quickly and simply be turned into extra seating. The base units are robust, while the firm cotton mattress (futon) is comfortable and helpful to allergy sufferers.

Futon Express sell a wide range of bases and futons in different thicknesses. A 6-layer is recommended for regular sleeping use, although two 3-layer mattresses will suffice and are more manageable in larger sizes.

To preserve the futon it should be rolled and turned, never shaken, at least once a week, while a slatted wooden base is important to avoid the futon becoming damp.

Catalogue: *Loose leaf, Leaflets, 8 pages, Colour and B/W, Free* Postal charges: *Varies with item* Delivery: *Courier* Methods of Payment: *Cheque, Postal Order, Visa, Access / Mastercard*

GIGI TRADING HOUSE
128 The High Street
Hungerford
Berks
RG17 ODL

Telephone:
0488 681211

HOUSEHOLD GOODS

In addition to their range of linen goods, Gigi stock an affordable range of lighting, china, ironware, basketware and household gifts. The accent is squarely on keeping prices as low as possible.

'Country Check' tablecloths start at £8.50 (54" sq) and rise to £21.00 (54" × 144"). There are also napkins for £1.50 each. All are 100% cotton and manufactured in Scotland.

Classic Egyptian cotton articles include flat sheets from £6.50 each, duvet covers from £24.00 and pillowcases from £3.00 a pair.

Catalogue: *A5, Brochure, 8, Colour, Free* Postal charges: *Varies with item* Delivery: *Royal Mail* Methods of Payment: *Cheque, Postal Order, Visa, Access / Mastercard*

GLAZEBROOK & CO
PO Box 1563
London
SW6 3XD

Telephone:
071 731 7135
Fax:
071 371 5434

STERLING SILVER AND SILVER PLATE CUTLERY

Outstanding British cutlery in terms of quality and craftsmanship at prices that are very competitive, with storage cloths, boxes and delivery all free of charge.

There are a number of time-honoured and classic patterns available in either sterling silver or silver plate ranging from 44-piece to 124-piece services for those who like entertaining in the grand manner. Pieces can, of course, be purchased individually as well.

A 44-piece time-honoured pattern in silver plate is

Home

£415.00 approximately and in sterling silver £1,130.00, but prices can change with the fluctuating price of silver.

Catalogue: *A4, Catalogue, 6 pages, Colour and B/W, Free* Postal charges: *Free* Delivery: *Parcelforce* Methods of Payment: *Cheque*

GRAHAM & GREEN
4, 7 and 10 Elgin
Crescent
London
W11 2JA

Telephone:
071 727 4594
Fax:
071 229 9717

LADIES CLOTHES AND HOME ACCESSORIES
Graham & Green offers the customer unique and original accessories for the home, chosen from around the world. There are a number of different styles to suit varied tastes (Indie, Mexican and Floral) and a range of different items from patchwork quilts (£345), twig baskets (£10.95) and painted candlesticks (£25.75) to Tartan rugs (£12.50), Mexican dolls (£8.25) and candelabras (£275). The clothes are dressy and they come in four different styles for women (Stella, Anita, Ramona and Jessica (red lycra top, £110)).

Catalogue: *Large, folding leaflet, Leaflets, 16 pages, Colour, Free* Postal charges: *Varies with item* Delivery: *Royal Mail* Methods of Payment: *Cheque, Visa, Access / Mastercard*

H. L. BAZAARS LTD
Dept MS85
Churchbridge
Oldbury
Warley
West Midlands
B69 1BR

Telephone:
021 541 1918

HOUSEHOLD LINEN
A comprehensive catalogue featuring all types of bed-linen, towels, table linen, tea towels and rugs plus other items. A good variety is contained within the catalogue and substantial discounts are available on bulk orders to the hotel trade. 24-hour telephone order service available. Catalogue clearance centres in Liverpool, Lancashire and Cheshire. Personal callers are welcome to the mail order warehouse close to junction 2 on the M5 motorway.

Catalogue: *A4, Catalogue, 31 pages, Colour, Free* Postal charges: *£2.65* Delivery: *Royal Mail* Methods of Payment: *Cheque, Visa, Access / Mastercard, Postal Order*

HEATHER VALLEY (WOOLLENS) LTD
16 Comely Bank
Avenue
Edinburgh
EH4 1EL

Telephone:
061 236 9911

HOME, GARDEN, CLOTHES AND HOUSEHOLD GOODS
Based in Edinburgh, Heather Valley offer elegant soft suits and dresses and co-ordinating separates and outdoor wear. Towards the back of the brochure, there's plenty to inspire you for the home and garden as well. There are fourteen sections in this brochure, with a stop press sale page at the back.

Catalogue: *A4, Catalogue, 136 pages, Colour, Free* Postal charges: *Varies with item* Delivery: *Parcelforce* Methods of Payment: *Cheque, Stage Payments, Visa, Access / Mastercard, Postal Order*

Home

HINES OF OXFORD
Tapestry Importers
Weavers Barn
Windmill Road
Headington
Oxford
OX3 7BR

Telephone:
0865 741144

WALL HANGING TAPESTRIES
A family owned business importing fine quality Woven Art Tapestries. The reproductions cover the period from Medieval times to the 18th century and are woven in various attractive textures, such as wool, cotton and artificial silk. The tapestries are lined and ready for hanging. Information can be supplied relating to the historical background of the tapestries, if available. The tapestries can be viewed at Weavers Barn, preferably by prior appointment. Open Monday to Friday 9 am to 5 pm.

Catalogue: *A4, Brochure, 99 pages, Colour, Free* Postal charges: *Free* Delivery: *In-house delivery* Methods of Payment: *Cheque, Postal Order*

HOMEPRIDE FOODS
Compass House
80 Newmarket Road
Cambridge
CB5 8DZ

Telephone:
071 231 9923

KITCHEN AND COOKING AIDS
Fred, the Homepride man, comes into his own with a kitchen-full of ideas to brighten up any home. There is everything that is needed to ease cooking tasks, many of them sporting a smiling 'Fred'. The goods are surprisingly attractive and good quality and the catalogue goes beyond the kitchen, with a unique range of superb quality clothing and books.

Prices range from the reasonably priced such as a Fred salt and pepper set at £12.95 to the more luxurious, including a set of traditional cast-iron cook's scales with Bronze weights at £59.94 and the Fred Rugby shirt at £24.95.

Catalogue: *A5, Catalogue, 16 pages, Colour, Free* Postal charges: *Varies with item* Delivery: *Royal Mail* Methods of Payment: *Cheque, Postal Order, Visa, Access / Mastercard*

HOUSE OF BRASS
122 North Sherwood Street
Nottingham
NG1 4EF

Telephone:
0602 475430

BRASS FITTINGS FOR THE HOME IN A VARIETY OF PERIOD STYLES.
A large selection of quality classical period reproduction brassware hand finished to high standards.

The range includes door knockers, letter boxes, light and bathroom fittings, locks and bedsteads, window and cabinet furniture.

Brass headboards from £85.00 each upwards to £510 each. Different character knockers include the Medusa, the Dolphin, the Lion and the Fox. 160 mm Medusa is £14.00. Some black painted as well as brass finishes.

Catalogue: *A4, Catalogue, 14 pages, Colour, Free* Postal charges: *Varies with item* Delivery: *Royal Mail* Methods of Payment: *Cheque, Access / Mastercard, Visa*

Home

HOUSEHOLD ARTICLES
Sanderstead Station
Approach
South Croydon
Surrey
CR2 0YY

Telephone:
081 651 6321

CAFETIÈRES

Household Articles' collection of products include a broad range of ideas for serving coffee. Their range of cafetières starts with the 'Café Royale', available in 3 cup (£15.15), 6 cup (£17.55) and 8 cup (£18.40) sizes in either cream, black, green, red, white or smoke. There are slight variations in price for each colour.

Next up in the range is 'La Cafetière Enamel', available in similar colours to the 'Café Royale' and in either 4 cup (£23.00), 8 cup (£26.00) or 12 cup (£32.00) sizes.

Top of the range is either a chrome finish or gold finish 'La Cafetière'. It comes in 3, 4, 6, 8 and 12 cup sizes, from £28.50 to £40.75 for chrome and from £37.20 to £53.20 for gold.

Catalogue: *A4, Leaflets, 4, Colour, Free* Postal charges: *Free* Delivery: *Royal Mail* Methods of Payment: *Cheque, Postal Order*

HYBURY CHINA
P O Box 358
Kingston upon Thames
Surrey
KT1 2YE

Telephone:
081 974 5518
Fax:
081 549 2040

CHINA

Hybury China supplies white bone china seconds from famous English manufacturers. They have two suites of china: 'Classic', with its plain, contemporary style, and 'Elegance', which has a delicate wave in the rim of the china, giving a more traditional look. Hybury offer continuity of supply of these ranges.

'Classic' collection prices range from £3.25 for a $10\frac{1}{2}''$ plate and £1.80 for a $6\frac{1}{4}''$ plate to £3.25 for a teacup and saucer. The 'Elegance' collection includes a $10\frac{1}{4}''$ plate for £4.50; a $6\frac{1}{2}''$ plate for £1.95 and a teacup and saucer for £3.25.

Catalogue: *Annually, A4, Brochure, 5 pages, B/W, Free* Postal charges: *Varies with item* Delivery: *TNT White Arrow* Methods of Payment: *Cheque, Postal Order, Visa, Access / Mastercard*

ISHTAR
25 Upper Oldfield Park
Bath
BA2 3JX

Telephone:
0225 311948
Fax:
0225 442133

RUGS

This is a sample catalogue of a much larger range of rugs, cushions and ceramics made by Bedouin women based in Jebel Bani Hamida, Jordan. Richly coloured and based on traditional Bedouin designs, each rug is made from 100% wool. They are truly delightful to look at.

Because they are handmade, each rug takes three and a half months for delivery. A small rug, 1.1m × 0.5m sells for £107.00 and a large one, 2.08m × 1.23m for £499.00. The ceramics are more modern in design and can be specially commissioned to suit your own designs. There is a showroom in Bath for a greater selection or they will send you more details.

Catalogue: *A4, Catalogue, 6 pages, Colour, Free* Postal charges: *Varies with item* Delivery: *By arrangement* Methods of Payment: *Cheque, Postal Order*

J & J CASH LTD
Torrington Avenue
Coventry
CV4 9UZ

Telephone:
0203 466466
Fax:
0203 462525

LABELS
Based in Coventry and established since 1846, Cash's is synonymous with woven labels for school uniforms and the like. This catalogue, however, shows that its range is much wider. There are designer tapes, for professionals as well as doting grannies who knit, as well as woven greetings cards and pictures.

They also do a line in executive stationery and golf ball boxes, both with inset woven pictures, as well as bookmarks and limited edition woven silk pictures.

Prices for Cash's original nametapes start at £5.99 for 20 and designer labels £6.99 for 36.

Catalogue: *A4, Leaflets, 42 pages, Colour, Free* Postal charges: *Free* Delivery: *Royal Mail* Methods of Payment: *Cheque, Postal Order*

JALI LTD
Apsley House
Chartham
Canterbury
Kent
CT4 7HT

Telephone:
0227 831710
Fax:
0227 831950

DECORATIVE PELMETS, BRACKETS, RADIATOR COVERS AND CORNER UNITS
Reasonably priced and well designed self-assembly kits for pelmets, brackets, radiator covers, corner units and edge trims which can be easily fitted by the average handyman.

All brackets and kit pieces are precision-made and will push together without cutting -just a screwdriver and a little wood glue are required. Screws and plugs are provided where necessary. For shelves, edge trims and pelmets that require cutting to size, a fine-toothed tenon saw is ideal.

All designs are made from MDF which is easily painted. Simple instructions as well as installation ideas and suggestions are included with each order.

Catalogue: *A5, Catalogue, 19 pages, Colour, Free* Postal charges: *£4.00* Delivery: *Parcelforce Courier* Methods of Payment: *Access / Mastercard, Visa Cheque, Postal Order*

Home

JOHN DRON LTD
Unit 5
Blundells Road
Bradville
Milton Keynes
MK13 7HA

Telephone:
0908 311388
Fax:
0908 222200

HOUSEHOLD SUPPLIES

This is a basic catalogue of products commonly used by the hotel and catering trade, but also available to personal customers. However, it is probably only of interest to those who wish to bulk buy.

The range of goods includes cleaning products, paper products, hot water bottles, sheets, towels and personalised stationery. Savings are good, but storage problems could arise. Two cases of toilet rolls at £23.90 for example would leave you with fourteen rolls to store! Better value perhaps, are the towels, available in a choice of colours. A hand towel is £3.20 and bath sheet £10.20 – these compare well with department store prices.

Catalogue: *A4, Brochure, 8 pages, B/W, Free* Postal charges: *Varies with item* Delivery: *Royal Mail* Methods of Payment: *Cheque, Postal Order*

JUST FABRICS
PO Box 88
Carterton
Oxon
OX18 3YP

Telephone:
0993 823391

PATCHWORK QUILTS

Just Fabrics stock a variety of designs of patchwork quilts. You can buy 'Justine', a checkerboard quilt in pink, green and blue on a white background from £79.00 for a single quilt (193 mm × 264 mm) to £105.00 for the king sized version (264 mm × 279 mm). Equally colourful is the delightful 'Heather', just the thing to add some colour to your bedroom. Prices range from £155.00 for a single quilt (180 mm × 250 mm) to £215.00 for a king sized quilt (270 mm × 270 mm).

Catalogue: *A4, Leaflets, 2, Colour, Free* Postal charges: *£4.50* Delivery: *Royal Mail* Methods of Payment: *Cheque, Postal Order, Visa, Access / Mastercard*

KENNETH CLARK CERAMICS
The North Wing
Southover Grange
Southover Road
Lewes
East Sussex
BN7 1TP

Telephone:
0273 476761
Fax:
0273 479565

TILES

This ceramic tile company based in Lewes, Sussex, has been in operation for over 30 years. They produce beautiful and unique ceramic tile patterns and murals. The catalogue covers a good selection of the range, including some examples of murals.

Mainly traditional in style and colour, they often use Victorian decorative techniques. The tiles are distinctive but expensive, costing up to as much as £16.00 each. However, the company points out that most tiles or borders can be teamed with cheaper commercial, plain tiles, if the overall cost becomes prohibitive.

Home

Catalogue: *Third A4, Catalogue, 52 pages, Colour, Free* Postal charges: *Varies with item* Delivery: *By arrangement* Methods of Payment: *Cheque*

KNIGHTINGALES CATALOGUE LTD
P O Box 555
Bamber Bridge
Preston
PR5 8AZ

Telephone:
0772 627227

HOME FURNISHINGS

This catalogue offers a variety of bedroom and bathroom accessories. The duvets range extends from children's (Disney, Postman Pat, etc.) to adults', while the bathroom wear is almost all towelling, bathrobes, none of which seem to be aimed at the younger end of the market. Most items are illustrated.

As well as offering mail order service there are over 30 shops around Great Britain, although predominantly in the North of England a few in Scotland and a handful in and around Greater London. There is a warning that pricing in the shops may vary from mail order.

Catalogue: *A4, Catalogue, 8 pages, Colour, Free* Postal charges: £2.95 Delivery: *Royal Mail* Methods of Payment: *Cheque, Postal Order, Access / Mastercard, Visa*

LEEDS FUTONS
13 Hyde Park Corner
Leeds
LS6 1AF

Telephone:
0532 743753

FUTONS

Futons are Japanese-style floor mattresses that provide a firm, healthy, natural sleeping surface. When combined with a base, they make easily convertible bed sofas. This company produces 3 types of futon and 5 styles of pine base as well as covers, cushions and bolsters. They also make tables, chests, screens, shelves, massage tables and mats.

The futons contain either 100% cotton, a cotton and polyester/wool mix, or a cotton/foam mix. Bases are available in plain sanded pine, with clear varnish or in black lacquer.

Double futons range from £114.00 to £128.00 (covers £27.00 to £45.00) and the accompanying bases vary from £96.00 to £287.00.

Catalogue: *A4, Catalogue, 8 pages plus inserts, Colour, Free* Postal charges: *Varies with item* Delivery: *By arrangement* Methods of Payment: *Cheque*

Home

LETTERBOX COMPANY
Wingfield Road
Tebworth
Leighton Buzzard
Beds
LU7 9QG

Telephone:
0525 874599
Fax:
0525 875746

EXTERIOR LETTERBOXES
You can add a touch of distinction to your home with these elegant, practical post boxes – ideal if your dog eats the post or for those with double-glazed front doors. All models are made from high quality zinc-plated steel, specially chosen for extra protection from all weather conditions.

Each box is supplied with a cylinder locks for added security along with two keys. They can easily be mounted on posts or walls. The boxes come in a range of colours and sizes with prices from £22.00 to £65.00.

Catalogue: *Annually, A4, Leaflet, 4 pages, Colour, Free* Postal charges: *Varies with item* Delivery: *Home Express delivery* Methods of Payment: *Cheque, Visa, Access / Mastercard, Postal Order*

LIBERTY MAIL ORDER
210–220 Regent Street
London
W1R 6AH

Telephone:
071 734 1234
Fax:
071 734 8323

FABRICS
Liberty has been producing textile collections since 1878. The classic Liberty collections are made either in Tana Lawn (100% cotton) or Varuna wool (100% wool). The catalogue reproduces a wide range of Liberty's patterns in their true colours and actual sizes to aid reference.

The Tana Lawn collection includes the famous paisley pattern 'Peacock Feather' and the equally well known range of flower prints inspired by Japanese art. Tana Lawn is generally available in 90cm widths and Varuna wool in 140cm widths at £11.00 per metre. All Varuna wool fabrics cost £19.50 per metre.

Catalogue: *A4, Catalogue, 12 pages, Colour, Free* Postal charges: *Varies with item* Delivery: *Royal Mail* Methods of Payment: *Cheque, Postal Order, Visa, Access / Mastercard, American Express, Diners Club*

LIMERICKS LINENS
PO Box 20
Tanners Lane
Barkingside
Ilford
Essex
IG6 1QQ

Telephone:
0268 520224

LINENS
This traditional household linen company sells not only bedding, but also table linen, cushions, rugs and a few traditional 'country furniture' items. They also stock a beautiful range of Chinese patchwork quilts. The Zoe quilt, in pure cotton, costs £97.95 for a single.

They have a comprehensive range of blankets and towels, including tartan towel sets with a large bath towel (70 cm × 120 cm) for £10.75. The prices seem very reasonable for this quality of merchandise and the company is small enough to care about individual customers.

Home

Catalogue: *A5, Catalogue, 36 pages, Colour, Free* Postal charges: *Varies with item* Delivery: *Royal Mail* Methods of Payment: *Visa, Access / Mastercard Cheque, Postal Order*

LORD ROBERTS WORKSHOPS
6 Western Corner
Edinburgh
EH12 5PY

Telephone:
031 337 6951

BRUSHES
Lord Roberts Workshops produce an astonishing variety of brushes. Their brochure, entitled 'The Brush Factory' features a range of handcrafted boot scrapers (£35.50) and a special set of brushes for a golfer (£9.40).

There are also novelty brushes like 'Bobby Badger', hand made to keep boots and shoes from soiling your best carpets. Naturally, there's a complete range of brushes to cover most household requirements. A vegetable brush, for instance, costs £2.50 and a lavatory brush costs £2.96.

Catalogue: *A5, Leaflets, 4, Colour, Free* Postal charges: *Free* Delivery: *Royal Mail* Methods of Payment: *Visa, Access / Mastercard Cheque, Postal Order*

MARION
(Ceramic House Plaques)
39 St Matthews Road
Cosham
Portsmouth
Hants
PO6 2DL

Telephone:
0705 384856

CERAMIC HOUSE PLAQUES
Marion have been producing their delightful hand painted ceramic house plaques for the last twelve years. Each plaque is fired in a kiln several times and as a result will not crack in frost or fade in the sun.

Each one is unique, custom painted and can feature any design you wish. Customers in the past have used house names, pets, the house itself, wildlife and flowers. Prices start from £22 for 6"x 8" oval and rise to £41.25 for 11" × 13" oval.

Catalogue: *Annually, 150 × 200 mm, Brochure, 4 pages, Colour, Free* Postal charges: *Varies with item* Delivery: *Royal Mail, Parcelforce* Methods of Payment: *Cheque, Postal Order*

MELIN TREGWYNT
Tregwynt Mill
Castle Morris
Haverfordwest
Dyfed
SA62 5UX

Telephone:
03485 644
Fax:
03485 694

BLANKETS AND SPREADS
Based in Wales, Melin Tregwynt produce high quality woollen blankets in sizes to suit every bed. They also sell large fringed 'throws', ideal for picnics, children's beds and sofas. The designs are simple checks with strong, attractive colours and the whole effect is strikingly beautiful.

They also produce the new Designers' Guild range of blankets, which come in large scale multicheck, classic cobalt and indigo tartan as well as chrome yellow and lime plaid. A single (72" × 96") costs £115.00 with a king-sized version (108" × 96") £165.00.

Home

MULBERRY HALL
17 Stonegate
York
N Yorks
YO1 2AW

Telephone:
0904 620736

Catalogue: *A5, Catalogue, 14 pages, Colour, Free* Postal charges: *Varies with item* Delivery: *Royal Mail* Methods of Payment: *Cheque, Postal Order, Visa, Access / Mastercard, American Express*

FINE CHINA AND CRYSTAL SPECIALISTS

Based in one of the finest medieval buildings in York, Mulberry Hall enjoys a reputation as one of the best sources in Europe for fine china and crystal.

The beautiful catalogue illustrates a selection of pieces from some of the continent's finest manufacturers, including: Lalique; Herend; Baccarat; Royal Copenhagen; Wedgwood; Stuart; Spode; Masons; Waterford; Coalport; Lladro; Royal Crown Derby; Royal Doulton; Royal Worcester; Georg Jensen ; Halcyon Days Enamels; and Mulberry Hall's own fine Sheffield Cutlery.

Prices vary enormously, from a Waterford crystal fruit bowl at £595.00, to a pair of Sheffield-silver fish servers at £99.50. Royal Copenhagen figurines are a hefty £1,545.00 while Royal Doulton dinner plates are more affordable at between £18.25. and £27.75.

Catalogue: *A4, Catalogue, 30 pages, Colour, Free* Postal charges: *Varies with item* Delivery: *Royal Mail* Methods of Payment: *Cheque, Visa, Access / Mastercard*

NORTHERN FLAGS LTD
125 Water Lane
Leeds
LS11 9UD

Telephone:
0532 420490
Fax:
0532 420357

FLAGS

Northern Flags manufacture corporate, advertising or national flags in a variety of sizes from ½ yard (18" × 9") to 6 yard (18' × 9'). The range of flags of the United Kingdom include the St George's Cross, St Andrew's Cross and St David's Cross. Most national flags are available including those of Micronesia, Slovakia and Tajikistan. Prices for standard sizes range from £9.75 to £187.20.

Due to the use of advanced printing techniques Northern Flags can reproduce any design or picture which can provide great promotional opportunities for business. Also available are a variety of banners, windsocks, pennants and flagstaffs.

Catalogue: *A4, Catalogue, 8 pages, Colour, Free* Postal charges: *Varies with item* Delivery: *Royal Mail* Methods of Payment: *Cheque*

Home

OLIVERS LIGHTING COMPANY
6 The Broadway
Crockenhill
Swanley
Kent
BR8 8JH

Telephone:
0322 614224

REPRODUCTION LIGHT SWITCHES
Olivers classic reproduction light switches offer quality, authenticity, and craftsmanship. Traditionally styled they still adhere to the most stringent modern safety standards. The switches are made from lacquered brass and set into wooden backplates of mahogany or oak.

Olivers also produce a range of matching sockets. All switches and accessories fit directly into standard wall boxes, enabling simple and safe assembly without having to employ an electrician (though remember to turn off the electricity first!).

Single switches start at £24.00 while a quadruple costs from £60.00 upwards. Accessories vary from £15.00 to £45.00.

Catalogue: *A5, Brochure, 6 pages, Colour, Free* Postal charges: *Varies with item* Delivery: *Royal Mail* Methods of Payment: *Visa, Access / Mastercard Cheque, Postal Order*

ORIEL INTERNATIONAL
The Priory
Newport
Saffrron Walden
Essex
CB11 3TH

Telephone:
0799 540995
Fax:
0799 541966

HARVEST BOXES
This small company produces imaginative 'pictures'. These are made from collections of dried flowers, beans, seeds and seashells set behind glass in wooden frames. The result is a very attractive wall decoration that will compliment any style of interior.

They are available in eight sizes and three frame colours. Each picture is hand made in England and signed by the maker. Prices are between £10.00 and £50.00.

Catalogue: *Annually, A4, Catalogue, 4 pages, Colour, Free* Postal charges: *Varies with item* Delivery: *Royal Mail* Methods of Payment: *Cheque, Postal Order, Visa, Access / Mastercard*

PATRICIA LUKE
Chapel Cottage
Lutener Road
Midhurst
West Sussex
GU29 9AT

Telephone:
0730 812728

CARDS AND MUGS
This small mail order company sells limited edition prints which come in a number of different forms. For example there are cards, mounted prints, coasters, table mats, trays, chopping boards, even Post-it pads!

Most feature farm animals and are also available on fine china mugs, T-shirts and sweatshirts. Prices are very reasonable with a cards 70p, coasters £1.50, T-shirts £8.50 and mugs £4.50.

Catalogue: *A5, Leaflet, 1 page, Colour, Free* Postal charges: *Varies with item* Delivery: *Royal Mail* Methods of Payment: *Cheque*

Home

PERKINS
105 Ack Lane East
Bramhall
Cheshire
SK7 2AB

Telephone:
061 440 9860

RADIATOR COVERS
This catalogue specialises in decorative radiator grilles and surrounds. There are three basic styles to suit modern or traditional interiors. The covers are made from wood or MDF and painted, although there is an option to have a solid wood cover and metallic grille. Covers are delivered with fittings or can be fitted by the company.

There are clear instructions for measuring your radiators and a 3-foot cover starts at £162.00. If you are really good at DIY, they can be bought in kit form for self-assembly for around £100.00. Radiator shelves are also available, with or without a built in towel rail.

Catalogue: *A4, Catalogue, 4 pages plus inserts, Colour, Free* Postal charges: *£20.00 per cover* Delivery: *By arrangement* Methods of Payment: *Cheque, Postal Order, Visa, Access / Mastercard*

PHILIP BRADBURY GLASS
83 Blackstock Road
London
N4 2JW

Telephone:
071 226 2919
Fax:
071 359 6303

REPLACEMENT GLASS
Philip Bradbury produce patterned glass on their own premises using traditional methods. These can be used in door frames, above front doors, as part of windows and so on. They have a number of standard patterns but can also match pieces from existing houses. This is particularly useful if you have, say, a Victorian door with inset panes of patterned glass one of which gets broken.

They will also custom make glass to any design and frequently do this for house numbers and names. Panels start from £65.00 while transoms are £55–£75. Their leaflet includes some sample paper patterns and a small square of glass.

Catalogue: *A4, Leaflets, 4 pages, B/W, Free* Postal charges: *Varies with item* Delivery: *By arrangement* Methods of Payment: *Cheque, Visa, Access / Mastercard*

PLANTATION SHUTTERS
93 Antrobus Road
London
W4 5NQ

Telephone:
081 994 2886

SHUTTERS
Slatted wooden shutters have been popular in America since the time of the Civil War. Now available in Britain, these Plantation Shutters are imported from one of America's largest manufacturers and are made from clear Oregon pine to resist warping. They are available in a large range of sizes that can be installed anywhere in the home. They come in sets of four shutter panels, hinged together in pairs with each pair hinged to a 2" wide vertical mounting batten. Each set also comes with a pair of knobs and a fastening hook.

Home

There are three shutter arrangements: full window, café style (bottom half only) or tier upon tier. Prices start at £33.26 for sets 16" high and 28" wide and go up to £249.71 for 48" high and 76" wide.

Catalogue: *A4, Catalogue, 2 pages, Colour, Free* Postal charges: *£5.00* Delivery: *Royal Mail* Methods of Payment: *Cheque, Postal Order, Visa, Access / Mastercard*

POZZANI
Phoenix House
Newmarket
Louth
Lincs
LN11 9EJ

Telephone:
0507 608100
Fax:
0507-608090

DOMESTIC WATER PURIFIERS
Tap water can frequently be unappetising, with unpleasant tastes, colours, and smells from chemical treatment processes or other sources. The Pozzani IX230 system removes impurities and restores drinking water to its natural, refreshing taste.

Pozzani's 3-stage, ceramic-based filtration system greatly reduces water pollutants, while leaving useful minerals intact. This safe and economical system fits neatly under a sink unit. It connects easily to the cold water supply via a simple screw-in piercing device, thus avoiding any need to cut the pipe.

The system, priced £78.95, comes complete with a choice of taps, and is guaranteed for three years. Filter cartridges, priced £12.95, have a life-span of six months.

Catalogue: *A5, Leaflets, 4 pages, Colour, Free* Postal charges: *Varies with item* Delivery: *Royal Mail* Methods of Payment: *Cheque, Visa, Access / Mastercard*

PRETTY FRILLS BLIND CO
2 Roberts Mews
High Street
Orpington
Kent
BR6 0JP

Telephone:
0689 897183
Fax:
0689 897182

CURTAIN AND BLIND FABRICS AND ACCESSORIES
As wholesale trade suppliers, Pretty Frills have been selling everything for curtains and blinds for many years. As well as making soft shade blinds for department stores and interior designers, they have many smaller customers.

Their range includes linings, fabrics, rails, several styles of blind kits, tie-back kits, roller kits and beautiful brass accessories. They also have many exclusive products designed and made by themselves.

Roller kits start from £3.30, linings from £1.12 per metre, brass tie-backs 29p and corded curtain rails from £3.95.

Catalogue: *Annually, Catalogue, Colour and B/W, Free* Postal charges: *Varies with item* Delivery: *Royal Mail, Parcelforce* Methods of Payment: *Cheque, Visa, Access / Mastercard*

Home

PROFILE INTERIORS
P O Box 25
Market Harborough
Leics
LE16 9DH

Telephone:
0858 465558

SWAGS
Profile Interiors offer a unique swag design service with original patterns which are very different from those that can be bought over the counter. They can also reproduce designs from pictures. The company's patterns are supplied with full instructions for making and fitting and an estimate of the quantity of fabric that will be required.

Prices start at £24.50 for one size of swag + standard tail. The company also supplies fabrics and wallpapers at discount prices as well as linings and accessories.

Catalogue: *A4, Leaflets, 3 pages, B/W, Free* Postal charges: *Free* Delivery: *Royal Mail* Methods of Payment: *Cheque, Postal Order*

RAINBOW FAIRWEATHER DECORATIVE FURNITURE
555 King's Road,
London
SW6 2EB

Telephone:
071 736 1258/8693
Fax:
071 384 2040

DOMESTIC RADIATOR CABINETS
Rainbow's Cover Charm radiator cabinets do not simply 'disguise' the presence of a domestic radiator they actually transform it into an elegant piece of furniture.

Designed with ease of assembly and installation in mind, the cabinets come with a choice of brass or wooden grilles and in an impressive 130 sizes. Cleverly, the fronts are easily removable for valve adjustments. The hard-wearing finish is available in white or magnolia. Cabinets can also be custom made on request.

Prices range from £91.00 for a 24" cabinet to £290.00 for a 38" cabinet with solid brass grille.

Catalogue: *A4, Brochure, 4 pages, Colour and B/W, Free* Postal charges: *Varies with item* Delivery: *Courier* Methods of Payment: *Cheque, Postal Order, Visa, Access / Mastercard*

RAINFORD HOUSE OF ELEGANCE

Wentworth Street
Birdwell
S70 5UN

Telephone:
0226 350360
Fax:
0226 350279

DECORATIVE MOULDINGS
Rainford Interiors specialise in the manufacture of period plasterwork and fittings which are recreated using traditional techniques and craft skills. It boasts an impressive range of fire surrounds in plaster, cultured marble, cast iron or wood. Prices start at £99.00 and go up to £1400.00. Also available are back panels and hearths in marble or cast iron.

The company also produces a large range of cornices, niches, domes, dado rails, wall friezes, plaques, overdoors, and more. Panel moulding is available in 5-foot lengths and starts at £2.50. Corbels range from £22.50 to £29.50 per pair while centre pieces start from £9.95.

Home

READY-MADE CENTRE LIMITED
54 Seamford New Road
Altrincham
Cheshire
WA14 1EE

Telephone:
061 941 1714
Fax:
061 926 8408

Catalogue: *Annually, A4, Catalogue, 17 pages, Colour, Free* Postal charges: *Varies with item* Delivery: *In-house delivery* Methods of Payment: *Cheque, Postal Order, Visa, Access / Mastercard*

BEDLINENS, NIGHTWEAR, HOME FURNISHINGS
Established now for over 25 years, Ready-Made Centre is a specialist company supplying top quality traditional bedlinen and nightwear. Perhaps their most striking feature is the great value for money. Many of the items are exclusive to Ready-Made Centre and all are manufactured in the UK.

Some best sellers in the range include cotton chenille robes from just £29.99 and satin wraps from £29.95. Bedspreads are from £19.99 and easy-care cotton sheets from just £9.99, which seems particularly good value. All goods are supplied with a full money-back guarantee.

Catalogue: *Bi-annually, A5, Catalogue, 40 pages, Colour, Free* Postal charges: *Varies with item* Delivery: *Royal Mail, Parcelforce* Methods of Payment: *Cheque, Postal Order, Visa, Access / Mastercard*

ROGER PEARSON
Springwood House
Hockley Lane
Wingerworth
Chesterfield
SW42 SQ9

Telephone:
0246 276393

CARVED MARBLE FIREPLACES
Although not strictly speaking a mail order company we thought we would include Roger Pearson simply because he produces such beautiful work! The lavishly produced colour brochure shows a wonderful range of hand carved marble fireplaces in many different styles.

All are designed and carved by Roger himself and can be custom made to fit virtually any fireplace. There are 22 basic designs which range in price from just under £1000 to nearly £4000. They can be viewed by appointment in the Chesterfield showroom where specifics can be discussed. If you want a really stunning centrepiece for a room this is the place to go.

Catalogue: *A4, Brochure, 24 pages, Colour, Free* Postal charges: *Varies with item* Delivery: *By arrangement* Methods of Payment: *Cheque*

Home

RUSSELL HOUSE TAPESTRIES
P O Box 12 (v)
Wiveliscombe
Taunton
Somerset
TA4 2YZ

Telephone:
0984 624135

NEEDLEPOINT KITS & RELATED KITS
Russell House Tapestries produce kits for the needle-worker who is looking for quality designs. The kits are inspired by the patterns and rich colour combinations found in oriental rugs and are available in both printed or charted versions. Prices range from £33.99 to £43.95.

The finishing kits for cushions help to make completed needlework into luxurious velvet cushions. Components come ready cut out and marked for easy assembly. The zip is inserted and piping cord covered. Kits are available in 31 colours and cost £12.99.

Catalogue: *Bi-annually, A5, Brochure, 13 pages, Colour, £2.50 refundable* Postal charges: *Varies with item* Delivery: *Royal Mail* Methods of Payment: *Cheque, Postal Order, Visa, Access / Mastercard*

SAFE PRODUCTS GROUP
2A Ferdinand Place
London
NW1 8EE

Telephone:
071 267 5688/482 4021

PROTECTIVE COVERS FOR FURNITURE
The Safe Products Group produces protective covers for household objects. Chief among these is 'Tablesafe', a durable covering for tables that resists heat and water damage. Its in-built padding also prevents delicate surfaces from being scratched or dented. 'Tablesafe' can be custom-made and costs £1.75 per square foot.

The company also produces 'Bedsafe', a machine-washable and dry-cleanable mattress covering that prevents soiling and helps to prolong the life of your mattress. It also protects against allergic reactions to dust mites. Flame-retardant and crumple-free it is also comfortable to sleep on.

Single-bed covers start at £16.99, double-bed covers at £21.99 and Kingsize covers at £25.99.

Catalogue: *A4, Leaflets, 6 pages, loose-leaf, Colour and B/W, Free* Postal charges: *Varies with item* Delivery: *Royal Mail* Methods of Payment: *Cheque, Visa, Access / Mastercard*

SARABAND FURNITURE LTD
Rooksmoor Mills
Bath Road
Nr Stroud
Glos
GL5 5ND

Telephone:
0453 872577

NATURAL FLOORINGS
Saraband don't send out a catalogue but rather a fat little envelope stuffed with small squares of sample floor coverings. All are variations on natural matting but the eleven different designs are both attractive and striking. Some are suitable for simple mats, others for a sophisticated and different floor covering.

A one page price list gives the cost per metre, which

Home

starts at around £10.00 for a saguaros and rises to £19.95 for a 100% wool on a jute back.

Catalogue: *A4, Leaflet, 1 page, B/W, Free* Postal charges: *Varies with item* Delivery: *By arrangement* Methods of Payment: *Cheque*

SEVENTH HEAVEN
Chirk Mill
Chirk
Clwyd
LL14 5BU

Telephone:
0691 777622/773563
Fax:
0691 777313

ANTIQUE BEDSTEADS AND QUALITY BEDDING

Seventh Heaven aim to recapture the 'romance of the bed' with the most varied and extensive collection of antique beds in the UK, most dating from between 1800 and 1920. These splendidly restored bedsteads make a graceful and stylish addition to any bedroom.

Specialising in Victorian cast iron and brass bedsteads, the company also restore and sell antique wooden beds, and produce quality mattresses in virtually any size. These are said to simultaneously provide luxurious comfort and firm support. There is also a range of fine, lace-trimmed bed linen, samples of which are provided with the catalogue.

Prices for bedsteads range from £250.00 to about £3,000.00, while mattresses vary from £135.00 to £1,530.00.

Catalogue: *A4, Catalogue, 16 pages plus inserts, B/W, Free* Postal charges: *Varies with item* Delivery: *Courier* Methods of Payment: *Cheque*

SIGNS OF THE TIMES
Tebworth
Leighton Buzzard
Bedfordshire
LU7 9QG

Telephone:
0525 874185
Fax:
0525 875746

HOUSE SIGNS

This company makes hand painted cast house signs, although it should be mentioned that they cast out of a polymer rather than iron or metal. There is a large choice of both shapes and styles which include various motifs such as squirrels, horseheads, wild flowers and a hay wagon.

Alternatively you can have your own motif made up, either from a picture or photograph, for an extra £21.00. Signs start at £21.00 and go up to £109.00.

Catalogue: *A5, Brochure, 8 pages, Colour, Free* Postal charges: *Varies with item* Delivery: *Royal Mail* Methods of Payment: *Cheque, Visa, Access / Mastercard*

Home

SILVER DIRECT
PO Box 925
Shaftesbury
Dorset
SP7 9RA

Telephone:
0747 828977
Fax:
0747 828961

SILVER AND SILVER PLATED GOODS
Silver Direct say they can deliver Bond Street silver at affordable prices. Their top quality, solid, hallmarked silver and silver plated items include everything from photograph frames to cutlery and from clocks to candle snuffers. Many of the designs are classic and traditional in style, making ideal presents for anniversaries, christenings, weddings and birthdays.

Prices start at a very reasonable £10.00 rising to £500.00 for the more elaborate items.

Catalogue: *Annually, A5, Brochure, 8 pages, Colour, Free* Postal charges: *Varies with item* Delivery: *Royal Mail, Parcelforce Securicor* Methods of Payment: *Cheque, Visa, Access / Mastercard*

STENCIL ESSENTIALS
Ash Farm House
Poole Keynes
Cirencester
Glos
GL7 6EG

Telephone:
0285 770535

STENCIL EQUIPMENT
Stencil Essentials produce a stencil pen that is supposed to take the effort out of stencil cutting. It comes with a standard tip or fine tip suitable for use on thick acetates or very fine designs. You need to specify which you prefer. It costs £19.95 or £21.95 with both tips.

There are a number of different stencil designs. 'Galleons' cost £10.00 cut or £5.00 uncut; 'Fleur de Lys' cost the same. Other items include five acetate sheet 16" × 12" for £4.75 and five acetate sheets 24" × 18" for £8.50.

Catalogue: *A4, Leaflets, Colour, Free* Postal charges: *Free* Delivery: *Royal Mail* Methods of Payment: *Cheque, Postal Order*

STEVENSONS OF NORWICH
Roundtree Way
Norwich
NR7 8SQ

Telephone:
0603 400824
Fax:
0603 405113

PLASTER AND GRP MOULDINGS
Fine institutions from all over the world use Stevensons for new and refurbishment work on fibrous plaster and GRP mouldings. These include the Japanese embassy in London and the Metropolitan Museum of Art in New York. From panel mouldings and corbels to classic columns and ceiling roses, Stevensons can produce virtually anything right up to complete ceilings.

Supplied in lengths of 10', basic cornices start at £16.45 for a 'Large Egg and Dart' pattern, and go up to £16.95 for 'Large Acanthus'. The 'Adam Collection' of cornices occupies the top end of the range, at £32.45. Exterior decorations include door pediments at £449.00 and Portico from £995.00 to £1,250.00.

Catalogue: *Annually, A4, Catalogue, 32 pages, Colour, Free* Postal charges: *Varies with item* Delivery: *In-house delivery* Methods of Payment: *Cheque, Access / Mastercard*

Home

SUE FOSTER FABRICS
57 High Street
Ernsworth
Hampshire
PO10 7YA

Telephone:
0243 378831

FURNISHING FABRICS
Sue Foster offer quality furnishing fabrics at a reasonable price. They can supply for curtains, loose covers and upholstery by most major manufacturers. They also sell furniture in calico, or loose covered or upholstered in the material of your choice.

Although the material is discounted, none of it is seconds, and they guarantee to exchange any fabric with a flaw, as long as it hasn't been cut. They can only make an exact colour match if you write requesting a stock cutting.

Catalogue: *A4, Leaflets, 1, B/W, Free* Postal charges: *Free* Delivery: *Courier* Methods of Payment: *Visa, Access / Mastercard, American Express Cheque, Postal Order*

TÉMÉRAIRE
20 Church Street
Brixham
Devon
TQ5 8HG

Telephone:
0803 851523
Fax:
0803 858494

PHILOSOPHICAL AND SCIENTIFIC INSTRUMENTS
Téméraire recreate unique precision instruments from the past, wherever possible using original blueprints and dies and often the original manufacturing companies.

One of their finest models is the 'Edinburgh Display Barograph', a superb weather forecasting and recording instrument. The mechanism is English-made in solid brass, set on a dark mahogany base French-polished in the traditional manner. A drawer in the base keeps a year's supply of recording papers. It costs £499.50 and has the option of a personalised engraving at £9.75.

Also available are World War II marching compasses, re-commissioned from the original makers, a pocket barometer and desk-top weather forecaster.

Catalogue: *A5, Leaflets, Many inserts, Colour, Free* Postal charges: *Varies with item* Delivery: *Royal Mail* Methods of Payment: *Cheque, Postal Order, Visa, Access / Mastercard*

TERESA BELL
Top House Farm
Burn
Selby
North Yorkshire
YO8 8LR

Telephone:
0757 270343

PATCHWORK QUILTS
Teresa Bell produces three designs of quilt all of which use anything from twenty to forty different fabrics. Only 100% cotton is used from textile designers such as Osborne & Little, Colefax & Fowler and Jane Churchill.

The 'Victoria Quilt' uses 6" squares, the 'Charlotte' 4" and the 'Sophie-Louise' a combination of 4" squares, strips and block patchwork of up to 500 pieces. All items are quilted using wadding and backed with co-ordinating fabric. Also available are

Home

cot quilts, cushions, pillowcases and tapestry kits for both cushions and teddies.

Cushions cost £10.00 and quilts start at £70.00 (single size) and go up to £185 (Kingsize).

Catalogue: *Third A4, Leaflets, 4 pages, Colour, Free* Postal charges: *£5.00* Delivery: *Royal Mail* Methods of Payment: *Cheque, Postal Order, Visa, Access / Mastercard*

TERRY LEISURE PRODUCTS
15 Aston Road
Billingham
Cleveland
TS22 5DF

BIRD FEEDER
Terry Leisure's 'Brainy Birdfeeder' is advertised with a comprehensive description of how the feeder works. Suitable bird food is placed in each of the feeder's 36 pockets. Birds can't get straight to the pockets because of a clip-on plastic screen with a hole in it. Food can only be obtained through the hole. Brainy birds, notably tits, learn to manipulate the mechanism of the birdfeeder so that there's always a pocket of food available to them.

At £23.00, the 'Brainy Birdfeeder' is a must for tit fanatics everywhere. If you want tits galore, you need the 'Brainy Birdfeeder'.

Catalogue: *A4, Leaflets, 1, Colour, Free* Postal charges: *Free* Delivery: *Royal Mail* Methods of Payment: *Cheque, Postal Order*

THE AMERICAN STRETCH LIMOUSINE COMPANY
57 Coburg Road
Wood Green
London
N22 6UB

Telephone:
081 889 4848
Fax:
081 889 7500

LIMOUSINE SERVICE
The American Stretch Limousine Company is not strictly a mail order business but they do send out a brochure detailing their interesting service. Their modern fleet of stretch limousines offer sumptuous upholstery, with seating for six in a cocoon of electronic sophistication. Absolute discretion is guaranteed with dual electric dividers and privacy glass.

Vehicles are fitted with television, video and stereo, as well as intercom and mood lighting. They also offer bar facilities incorporating crystal cut decanters and glasses and an ice chest. To keep in touch, a telephone and facsimile are also available. Sheer luxury!

Prices start at £35.00 per hour and include a selection of free drinks.

Catalogue: *Annually, D2, Brochure, 6 pages, B/W, Free* Postal charges: Delivery: Methods of Payment: *Cheque, Postal Order, Visa, Access / Mastercard, American Express, Diners Club, Other*

Home

THE CANVAS & NYLON CO
'Our Way'
North Street
Winkfield
Berkshire
SL4 4TF

Telephone:
0344 882539

PORTABLE GARAGES
The Canvas & Nylon Co, as the name suggests, manufacture and repair all canvas and nylon goods. This catalogue specifically promotes one of their main lines, portable garages. A strong galvanised frame, which is pre-assembled, operates on a perambulator system so it can be raised or lowered easily. It is covered with a nylon or canvas. The nylon coverings come in two densities, medium and heavy, the former being only recommended for short term use.

The catalogue gives helpful information on the pros and cons of the different styles as well as advice on measuring your garage. Prices start at £120.00.

Catalogue: *A4, Leaflets, 2 pages, Colour and B/W, Free* Postal charges: *£20.00* Delivery: *Parcelforce* Methods of Payment: *Cheque*

THE CHELSEA TRADING CO
3 Astwood Mews
London
SW7 4DE

Telephone:
071 373 8188
Fax:
071 373 8193

TRADITIONAL HOUSEHOLD EQUIPMENT
A basic leaflet with simple drawings illustrates the Chelsea Trading Company's traditional and practical items for the home. These include a wooden towel rail (over 30" high by 27" wide) in either a natural or mahogany finish for £25; and a classic mahogany finished coat-stand with Bentwood frame for £19.99.

The Traditional Clothes Airer (basic model: £35.00) looks particularly useful for those who have trouble swinging their cat. It comes complete with detailed assembly instructions and a variety of helpful hints on what else you can hang from it.

Catalogue: *3rd A4, Leaflets, 6 pages, B/W, Free* Postal charges: *Free* Delivery: *Royal Mail* Methods of Payment: *Cheque, Visa, Access / Mastercard*

THE EMPTY BOX CO
Coomb Farm Buildings
Balchins Lane
Westcott
Nr Dorking
Surrey
RH4 3LE

Telephone:
0306 740193

BOXES
This enterprising catalogue offers a range of hat boxes. Available in three sizes and two shapes (circular and octagonal), they can be stacked or fitted inside one another. If used for hats, they will store two to three. There are 21 colours and patterns to choose from, although the company will also make a box up in your own fabric. A 20" round hat box costs £42.00.

The company also make wedding dress boxes, to store not only the nuptial gown, but also any mementos of the big day. A standard box, complete with

Home

tissue paper for wrapping the dress, is £39.90. Just the sort of unusual catalogue that makes mail order such fun.

Catalogue: *A5, Leaflets, 5 pages, Colour, Free* Postal charges: *Varies with item* Delivery: *Royal Mail* Methods of Payment: *Cheque, Postal Order, Visa, Access / Mastercard*

THE END OF DAY LIGHTING COMPANY
44–45 Parkway
London
NW1

Telephone:
071 485 6846

LIGHTING

With The End of Day Lighting Company, you should be able to satisfy all your lighting requirements. There are a variety of styles, from Art Deco to more traditional ceiling pendants and side lights. There are even fake Victorian street lamps, complete with their own lampposts. Unfortunately, the catalogue contains no price list.

Still, if you want a wrought iron Kensington chandelier type light or some Art Deco uplighters, this is the right place to look.

Catalogue: *A4, Leaflets, 7, Colour, Free* Postal charges: *Varies with item* Delivery: *Royal Mail* Methods of Payment: *Cheque*

THE ENGLISH STAMP COMPANY
Sunnydown
Worth Matravers
Dorset
BH19 3JP

Telephone:
0929 439117

DECORATING WITH STAMPS

Another unusual and interesting catalogue. This one only sells devices to 'decorate with stamps'. This does not mean covering your wall with 25p stamps, but rather using specially made devices to make impressions on any surface.

The stamps come in all kinds of patterns and are said to be easy to apply. You can scatter a wall with little stars, cherubs or roses for example. The catalogue will supply everything you need, which is simply a stamp, an applicator and stamp paint.

A stamp of a moon is £5.95, Fleur de lys £11.95. Paint is £2.95 and a roller £2.95. Complete kits are £22.95.

Catalogue: *A5, Catalogue, 12 pages, B/W, Free* Postal charges: *£1.95* Delivery: *Royal Mail* Methods of Payment: *Cheque, Postal Order*

THE GARDEN ROOM
Marindin House
Chesterton
Nr Bridgenorth
Shropshire
WV15 5NX

Telephone:
07465 575

DECORATIVE IRON CURTAIN RAILS

The Garden Room use the traditional skills of the blacksmith and ironfounder to create a range of exquisite handcrafted curtain poles. These are available in three sizes 12mm, 16mm and 20mm diameter. All rails come in a choice of finishes including gunmetal, matt black and matt black with gold embellishments. Tie backs are also available in the same finishes. Curtain rings and

Home

brackets are included in the price of the rails.

Special requirements (e.g. bay windows) can be accommodated by sending templates of the dimensions. Rails start from £8.50 per foot for 12mm diameter and go up to £10.00 per foot for 20mm. Rail ends in a selection of designs start at £11.50.

Catalogue: *A4, Leaflets, 5 pages, Colour and B/W, Free* Postal charges: *£10.00* Delivery: *Royal Mail* Methods of Payment: *Cheque, Postal Order*

THE GENERAL TRADING COMPANY LTD
The Catalogue Department
144 Sloane Street
London
SW1X 9BL

Telephone:
071 730 0411
Fax:
071 823 4624

FURNITURE, KITCHENWARE, ACCESSORIES, GIFTS

The General Trading Company has been selling superior household goods for the last 120 years. Their shop, in Sloane Square, London, boasts no less than four Royal Warrants and includes a floor of antiques.

The catalogue, while just scraping the surface of the vast range in the shop, nevertheless has an excellent selection of items for all parts of the house. There are chairs, lamps, picture frames, candle sticks, garden furniture, cutlery, plates, glassware and some toys.

All the goods are beautifully made and the sort of the thing you might not find elsewhere. Naturally the prices reflect this but are by no means outrageous. A pair of pentagon candlesticks sell for £67.00, an ice bucket for £23.00 and a button-back armchair is £530.00.

Catalogue: *9" × 9", Catalogue, 24 pages, Colour, £1.00* Postal charges: *Varies with item* Delivery: *Royal Mail* Methods of Payment: *Cheque, Visa, Access / Mastercard, American Express, Diners Club*

THE HOME & MOTORING SERVICE
1 Eton Court
Eton
Windsor
Berkshire
SL4 6BY

Telephone:
0753 621162

HOUSEHOLD & LEISURE GOODS OVER THE VALUE OF £50 AND NEW CARS

Membership of the Home and Motoring Service entitles those who have signed up to preferential prices on more than 25,000 top brand name household and leisure goods and new cars.

Before making a major purchase, members simply call the Service, where they are provided with unbiased information and very competitive prices.

Membership of the Service is available for three months at the nominal fee of just £1. The annual membership fee is £39. However, this will be refunded on request to those who have not saved at least £50 in their first year's membership.

Home

Catalogue: *None* Postal charges: *Varies with item* Delivery: *Royal Mail Courier, Parcelforce* Methods of Payment: *Cheque, Visa, Access / Mastercard*

THE INDIA SHOP
5 Hilliers Yard
Marlborough
Wiltshire
SN8 1NB

Telephone:
0672 515585

CUSHIONS, COVERINGS, FURNITURE
The India Shop imports and sells the best of the many handicrafts made in India. Where possible goods are bought from co-operatives on the company's thrice yearly visits to the sub-continent. As well as jewellery and home accessories the company sells a wide range of block printed and woven textiles including quilts, bedspreads, table linen and cushions. There is also an increasing range of old and new furniture.

Bedspreads in a variety of styles and colours start at £21.50 for singles and £27.50 for doubles. Candlesticks start at £9.95 and treasure chests made from Shesham wood also start at £9.95.

Catalogue: *A5, Catalogue, 10 pages, Colour, Free* Postal charges: *£1.50* Delivery: *Royal Mail* Methods of Payment: *Cheque, Postal Order, Visa, Access / Mastercard*

THE LIGHT BRIGADE
20 Rodney Road
Cheltenham
Gloucestershire
GL50 1JJ

Telephone:
0242 226777
Fax:
0242 226777

LIGHTS
The Light Brigade produces a range of hand-made wall lights, candle sconces and shades in a wide variety of colour finishes. The lights and shades can also be colour-matched to suit your decor or left unpainted for you to do yourself.

Double wall lights start at £42.50 unpainted and go up to £75.00 in antiqued gold, florentine gold, pewter or colour-matched. Single wall lights range from £29.50 to £89.50, while candle wall sconces start at £19.50. Packs of beeswax candles in various colours cost £3.95. Shades range in price from £3.95 to £14.95.

Catalogue: *A4, Brochure, 11 pages, Colour, Free* Postal charges: *Varies with item* Delivery: *Parcelforce* Methods of Payment: *Cheque, Postal Order, Visa, Access / Mastercard, American Express*

THE LONDON SHUTTER COMPANY
St Martin's Stables,
Windsor Road,
Ascot
Berkshire
S15 7AF

Telephone:
0344 28385
Fax:
0344 27575

HIGH-QUALITY WOODEN SHUTTERS
The London Shutter Company supplies crafted window and door shutters from Ohline, one of the largest shutter manufacturers in the USA. Made of incense cedar from California and Oregon, these beautiful shutters will suit most rooms.

The company's finishing service offers an endless range of colours and stains, together with a facility for hand-painted designs. All shutters come with a five-year guarantee and are installed by specialist fitters. Samples are available, along with a free

Home

advice and measuring service prior to ordering.

Prices are naturally governed by size: a 18" × 6" Brentwood shutter can cost as little as £25.32, while a 108" × 36" Bel Air is £432.32.

Catalogue: *A4, Brochure, 24 pages plus inserts, Colour, Free* Postal charges: *Varies with item* Delivery: *In-house delivery* Methods of Payment: *Cheque*

THE MERCHANT TILER
Twyford Mill
Oxford Road
Adderbury
Oxfordshire
OX17 3HP

Telephone:
0295 812179
Fax:
0295 812189

WALL AND FLOOR TILES

The Merchant Tiler offers the most comprehensive range of distinctly individual tiles in one catalogue. All of the tiles are carefully chosen to give you a wide choice at a low price. The Fired Earth Collection of tiles are all handmade. After selecting your tiles from many samples, The Merchant Tiler will install them for free.

The tiles come in a wide range of colours and designs for nearly every room in your house. For example, if you are an animal lover you can purchase tiles with hand painted mice, badgers, squirrels, rabbits or hedgehogs (£0.33 each) and anyone with exotic taste can choose from the old Mexico range (£1.67 each).

Catalogue: *A4, Catalogue, 28 pages, Colour, Free* Postal charges: *Varies with item* Delivery: *Royal Mail* Methods of Payment: *Visa, Access / Mastercard Cheque*

THE ORIGINAL BUTTERFLY MAN
Craft Workshop
Berwyn Lodge
Glyndyfrdwy Village
Corwen
Clwyd
LL21 9BH

Telephone:
049083 300

DECORATIVE METAL BUTTERFLIES FOR HOME DECORATION

The Original Butterfly Man produces beautiful replicas of some of Britain's best-loved butterflies. With rust-resistant aluminium wings and durable nylon bodies, these hand-painted, eye-catching models look simply stunning when attached to external walls and surfaces of any home.

All butterflies have legs, proboscis and antenna and are fitted with a sprung-steel fixing bracket so that they actually "flutter" in the breeze. All types are available with open wings, some with closed. Sizes range from 16" × 10" to 12" × 6". A selection of 15 butterfly species are available, from the dazzling Adonis blue at £42.50 to the striking red admiral at £25.50.

Catalogue: *A4, Leaflets, 2 pages, Colour and B/W, Free* Postal charges: *Varies with item* Delivery: *Royal Mail* Methods of Payment: *Postal Order Cheque*

Home

THE RADIATOR COVER COMPANY
167 Lower Richmond Road
Mortlake
London
SW14 7HX

Telephone:
081 392 2058

RADIATOR COVERS
A radiator cover consists of a casing faced with a decorative front panel which is easily removed for maintenance and cleaning. Apart from turning an eyesore into a feature, covers draw in cold air through the vents at the bottom and force it past the radiator while the insulation at the back stops heat being lost to the wall. For radiators positioned under windows a replacement sill can be incorporated.

Fronts can be made from brass, metal lattice or screenlite (a top quality hardboard). Tops come in wood or marble. Prices start at £212.00 in screenlite for sizes up to 35" wide.

Catalogue: *Third A4, Brochure, 6 pages plus inserts, Colour, Free*
Postal charges: *Varies with item* Delivery: *In-house delivery*
Methods of Payment: *Cheque, Postal Order*

THE STENCIL FACTORY
105 Upgate
Louth
Lincolnshire
LN11 9HF

Telephone:
0507 600948

STENCILS
The brochure contains a range of hand-cut stencils for decorating walls and furniture throughout the home. All the stencils are cut from semi-transparent film which can be used over and over again and are helpfully labelled according to difficulty of use.

There are stencils for borders e.g. 'Three Swallows' (25 × 13 cm, £4.00) and 'Eight Pointed Stars' (23 × 7 cm, £3.50). There are corner stencils, 'fishy' stencils ideal for bathrooms, giant stencils e.g. Palm Tree (124 × 135 cm, £15.00) and a large range of children's stencils.

Catalogue: *A5, Catalogue, 44 pages, Colour and B/W, Free* Postal charges: *Free* Delivery: *Royal Mail* Methods of Payment: *Cheque, Postal Order*

TRUPRINT
Stafford Park 18
Telford
TL1 1TP

Telephone:
0952 292162

MAIL ORDER PHOTOPROCESSING
Truprint is Europe's largest mail order photoprocessor. They return a free film with every order and guarantee that all orders are returned within seven days or they'll give you your money back. They also sell a full range of photo-related products, from reprints and enlargements through to photo transfer items such as photo-shirts.

Their competitive pricing includes 24 compact prints for £2.99, photo-shirts from £8.99 and Truprint single-use cameras from £3.49.

Catalogue: *2, A5, Catalogue, 12 pages, Colour, Free* Postal charges: *Varies with item* Delivery: *Royal Mail* Methods of Payment: *Cheque, Visa, Access / Mastercard, Postal Order*

Home

UNITED CUTLERS
Petre Street
Sheffield
S4 8LL

Telephone:
0742 433984
Fax:
0742 437128

CUTLERY
United Cutlers specialise in hallmarked sterling silver and silver plated cutlery, and boast an impressive pedigree of awards to back-up their successful sales history. All cutlery sets come with a guarantee and are mostly dishwasher proof.

The range includes up to eighteen different styles. Separate items of either silver plated or stainless steel cutlery will set you back from around £9.00 or £6.50 for a coffee spoon, and £16.50 or £9.00 for a serving spoon. As you can imagine, sterling silver is considerably more expensive: the serving spoon costs a handsome £65.00.

An 88 piece set comprising 12 × 7 piece place settings in stainless steel costs £780.00, compared to a lofty £3,650.00 for the equivalent in sterling silver. But these prices remain competitive for such quality.

Catalogue: *A5, Catalogue, 8 pages, Colour, Free* Postal charges: *Free* Delivery: *Courier* Methods of Payment: *Cheque, Postal Order, Visa, Access / Mastercard, Diners Club, American Express*

UNWINS SEEDS LTD
Mail Order Department
Histon
Cambs
CB4 4ZZ

Telephone:
0945 588522

GARDEN SEED, BULBS AND YOUNG PLANTS
Unwins offer hundreds of high quality seed varieties of flowers and vegetables that have all been tried and tested to make sure that they will thrive in typical British conditions. Sweet Peas are Unwins' speciality and their catalogue lists over 50 premium quality varieties, giving customers the opportunity to grow superior plants and blooms. They also sell bulbs for all seasons, young plants and soft fruit. All products are backed by a no-quibble guarantee. Prices per packet of seeds, until 30.6.94, are: sweet pea royal wedding 99p, marigold royal king £1.25, tomato moneymaker 89p and brussels sprout Peer Gynt £1.85.

Catalogue: *3 per year, A5, Catalogue, 100, 24 & 16 pages, Colour, Free* Postal charges: *Varies with item* Delivery: *Royal Mail, Parcelforce* Methods of Payment: *Cheque, Postal Order, Visa, Access / Mastercard*

VIGO
Bollhayes
Clayhidon
Devon
EX15 3PN

Telephone:
0823 680230

FRUIT PRESSES AND CRUSHERS
This is a wonderful catalogue for anyone with one or more fruit trees in their garden and too much fruit for their family and friends to eat. Vigo supplies fruit crushers and presses so you can put all those apples or whatever to good use. They also supply various accessories such as straining bags, funnels, yeast and so on.

Home

There is plenty of advice and information on how to use the presses or crushers and also how to store the juice once made. There is a section on cider making and further details are sent with each machine. Crushers sell from £125.00 and presses from £75.00.

Catalogue: *A5, Catalogue, 6 pages plus inserts, B/W, Free* Postal charges: *Varies with item* Delivery: *Parcelforce* Methods of Payment: *Cheque, Visa, Access / Mastercard*

WEATHER SIGNS
Cherington
Court Street
Winsham
Chard
Somerset
TA20 4JE

Telephone:
0460 30601

WEATHER VANES

Weather Signs offer a range of silhouette weather vanes in aluminium and steel. Individually made, the standard steel parts are zinc plated and the whole assembly is protected in a special matt black weather resistant finish.

The standard range of designs include animals, birds, boats, cars, dragons and sportsmen. Special commissions are possible, subject to suitability.

Small weather vanes start at £85.00 and large ones at £139.00. A variety of plinths and brackets are available to suit most locations and roof types.

Catalogue: *A4, Leaflets, 2 pages, Colour and B/W, Free* Postal charges: *Varies with item* Delivery: *Royal Mail* Methods of Payment: *Cheque, Postal Order*

WOOLPIT INTERIORS
The Street
Woolpit
Bury St Edmunds
Suffolk
IP30 9SA

Telephone:
0359 240895
Fax:
0359 242282

FURNITURE ACCESSORIES

Woolpit are one of the leading designers and manufacturers of decorative lighting and accessories in the country. They export to Europe, Australia and the USA. Their products include lamps, furniture and accessories in several styles to complement either traditional or modern interiors.

There are over 200 variations within the range of lamp bases alone. A limed oak square base from the 'Classic Column' collection costs £72.00. Exclusive candle and lamp shades include: the Woolpit Country Collection, the Empire Collection, Traditional Tartans and the Toile de Jouy collection.

Among the decorative accessories are a bedside table for £250.00 and a jardiniere for £310.00.

Catalogue: *A4, Leaflets, Colour, Free* Postal charges: *Varies with item* Delivery: *Royal Mail* Methods of Payment: *Cheque, Visa, Access / Mastercard*

Jewellery

YATELEY INDUSTRIES
Mill Lane
Yateley
Camberley
Surrey
GU17 7TF

Telephone:
0252 872337
Fax:
0252 860620

FABRICS PRINTED IN HAND BLOCKS

This sheltered workshop, providing employment for people with disabilities, produces good quality fabrics and craft items. Using block and screen printing they can produce several thousand designs in over 30 different colours to fulfil orders for any occasion.

After designing and carving the pattern blocks in their workshops, the Yateley team use high quality natural fabric to produce products for every room in the house. With a range that includes cushions, cravats and oven gloves from £2.99 to £70.44, there is a wide choice to suit many tastes.

Catalogue: *A5, Brochure, 30 pages, Colour, Free* Postal charges: *Varies with item* Delivery: *Royal Mail* Methods of Payment: *Cheque, Postal Order, Visa, Access / Mastercard*

CHUNKYDORY
55 Cuckoo Hill Road
Pinner
Middlesex
HA5 1AU

Telephone:
081 866 7263

COSTUME JEWELLERY

Costume jewellery at affordable prices, covering the spectrum from fun to elegance. Each item is uniquely gift-wrapped. Chunkydory trades at charity functions, craft fairs and party plans and advertises in women's magazines. A wide range of costume jewellery is available in silver, glass, gold, pearls, and wood. Prices range from £2.50 to £25.00 with postage and packing extra.

Papier maché gift boxes are also available from £2.50 to £2.95. The brochure is on stapled paper with line drawings showing the different designs.

Catalogue: *A3, Brochure, 29 pages, B/W, £1.00* Postal charges: *Varies with item* Delivery: *Royal Mail* Methods of Payment: *Cheque, Postal Order*

FALCON ROBINSON BOOKS & STONES
4 Rushbrook House
Union Road Corner
Union Grove
London
SW8 2QY

Telephone:
071 627 1463
Fax:
071 627 1463

REAL STONE JEWELLERY AND STONE ORNAMENTS

Falcon sell real stone pendants in many different shapes. They come side drilled and supplied with 32" of black cord ready to wear. Their Heart in rose quartz measures 1.25" and costs £4.00. For the same price you can get a five point star either in rose quartz or yellow calcite, a pyramid in fluorite or rose quartz and a donut, again in rose quartz or green inclusion.

For one pound more there is a dinosaur in brown or green with black inclusion jasper, or a dolphin in hematite. Cut point rock crystals with silver plated mountings come undrilled for just £6.00.

Catalogue: *Other 3, A4, Other Price List, 1 page, B/W, Free* Postal charges: *Varies with item* Delivery: *Royal Mail* Methods of Payment: *Cheque, Postal Order*

Jewellery

ST JUSTIN
The Emporium
17 Bohella Rd
St Mawes
Cornwall
TR2 5DL

Telephone:
0326 270983

CELTIC PEWTER JEWELLERY
All St Justin jewellery is crafted by hand and eye in Cornwall and many of their designs are truly ancient, going back more than 1,200 years to monasteries in remote corners of Britain. Some go back even beyond that to the ancient Britons.

The oldest St Justin design is the Triskele brooch (£11.99) based on an original from the 1st century AD. Along with a wide range of brooches there are crosses, ear rings, necklaces, hair slides, bangles and rings as well as intricately crafted buckles, spirit flasks, tie pins and pewter boxes (£17.99).

Catalogue: *Annually, A5, Catalogue, 28 pages, Colour, Free* Postal charges: *Free* Delivery: *Royal Mail* Methods of Payment: *Cheque, Postal Order*

CHURCHILL TABLEWARE LTD
Crane Street
Hanley
Stoke On Trent
ST1 5RB

Telephone:
0782 268870
Fax:
0782 260061

CHINA TABLEWARE
Churchill Tableware are long established family potters with a history in the business dating back over two centuries.

They offer the widest possible range of tea, lunch and dinner services along with first class gift and transit packaging.

There is a mixture of traditional and new patterns from the briar rose traditional floral design (20 cm plates, £1.45 each) to the gingham (20 cm plate, £1.11). All their products are crafted from the finest English earthenware in the heart of Stoke-On-Trent.

Catalogue: *A5, Catalogue, 24 pages, Colour, Free* Postal charges: £6.50 Delivery: *Royal Mail* Methods of Payment: *Cheque, Visa, Access / Mastercard*

DIVERTIMENTI (MAIL ORDER) LIMITED
PO Box 323
Yateley
Camberley
Surrey
GU17 7ZA

Telephone:
0252 861212
Fax:
0252 876770

KITCHENWARE
Divertimenti offer a wide range of marvellous kitchenware, from the high-tech Magimix to the simple pestle and mortar. The catalogue unashamedly boasts that the quality required by professional cooks takes priority over domestic needs, but these utensils are more likely to be long-lasting if they are manufactured to a higher specification.

Mail order customers can also order a 24-page booklet giving a guide to the care of cooking utensils. Divertimenti has two shops in central London which carry a far greater range of cookery and kitchenware than is available by mail order.

Catalogue: *Quarterly, A4, Catalogue, 24 pages, Colour, Free* Postal charges: £3.50 Delivery: *Royal Mail* Methods of Payment: *Cheque, Postal Order, Visa, Access / Mastercard*

Kitchenware

HOMEPRIDE FOODS
Compass House
80 Newmarket Road
Cambridge
CB5 8DZ

Telephone:
071 231 9923

KITCHEN AND COOKING AIDS

Fred, the Homepride man, comes into his own with a kitchen-full of ideas to brighten up any home. There is everything that is needed to ease cooking tasks, many of them sporting a smiling 'Fred'. The goods are surprisingly attractive and good quality and the catalogue goes beyond the kitchen, with a unique range of superb quality clothing and books.

Prices range from the reasonably priced such as a Fred salt and pepper set at £12.95 to the more luxurious, including a set of traditional cast-iron cook's scales with bronze weights at £59.94 and the Fred rugby shirt at £24.95.

Catalogue: *A5, Catalogue, 16 pages, Colour, Free* Postal charges: *Varies with item* Delivery: *Royal Mail* Methods of Payment: *Cheque, Postal Order, Visa, Access / Mastercard*

HYBURY CHINA
P O Box 358
Kingston upon Thames
Surrey
KT1 2YE

Telephone:
081 974 5518
Fax:
081 549 2040

CHINA

Hybury China supplies white bone china seconds from famous English manufacturers. They have two suites of china: 'Classic', with its plain, contemporary style, and 'Elegance', which has a delicate wave in the rim of the china, giving a more traditional look. Hybury offer continuity of supply of these ranges.

'Classic' collection prices range from £3.25 for a 10½" plate and £1.80 for a 6¼" plate to £3.25 for a teacup and saucer. The 'Elegance' collection includes a 10¼" plate for £4.50; a 6½" plate for £1.95 and a teacup and saucer for £3.25.

Catalogue: *Annually, A4, Brochure, 5 pages, B/W, Free* Postal charges: *Varies with item* Delivery: *TNT White Arrow* Methods of Payment: *Cheque, Postal Order, Visa, Access / Mastercard*

KITCHEN STORE
Freepost SU361
Dept 5318
Hendon Road
Sutherland
SR9 9AD

Telephone:
091 514 5144
Fax:
091 514 4574

KITCHEN EQUIPMENT

Kitchen Store provides the complete home cook's catalogue: a fascinating selection of kitchen equipment, gifts and clever gadgets.

The catalogue is imaginatively produced with clear illustrations of the items on sale. You can choose from a range of Ancient Inspiration earthenware ornaments such as an Aegean urn for £19.95 and Candleholders (pair) for £26.95. The more traditional mincer for £13.99 is an attraction along with what the Kitchen Store describes as 'Probably the World's Best Pressure Cooker' for £54.95!

Catalogue: *200mm × 200mm, Catalogue, 32 pages, Colour, Free* Postal charges: *£3.25* Delivery: *Royal Mail* Methods of Payment: *Cheque, Visa, Access / Mastercard*

Kitchenware

LAKELAND PLASTICS LTD
Alexandra Buildings
Windermere
Cumbria
LA23 1BQ

Telephone:
05394 88100
Fax:
05394 88300

CREATIVE KITCHENWARE

Lakeland has been a family run business for the last 30 years, supplying all you'll ever need for the kitchen and home. There are over 800 intriguing ideas to save time and money from foil, clingfilm and baking parchment through preserving, microwave and freezer accessories, to specialist food items.

The bright, interesting catalogue, coupled with a genuinely friendly service makes this an ideal source for kitchen products. There are 50 cake tin liners for £3.20, a lattice pastry cutter for £5.95, pure vanilla extract for £5.95 and lemon tap for just 99p.

Catalogue: *Bi-annually, A5, Catalogue, 80 pages, Colour, Free* Postal charges: *Varies with item* Delivery: *Parcelforce* Methods of Payment: *Cheque, Postal Order, Visa, Access / Mastercard*

MERCHANTMEN
664 Garratt Lane
London
SW17 0NP

Telephone:
081 947 9733

CHINA

Merchantmen present a fine porcelain dinner service from the Seltmann factory in Bavaria. 'Wild Pastures', in subtle shades of green, blue and yellow, features golden poppies, now rarely seen in nature. The extensive range is dishwasher proof and microwave safe. It comes with a number of ovenproof pieces such as flan and pie dishes, Provençale soup bowls and tureens.

Prices begin at £7.43 for a milk or cream jug. You can also buy six dinner plates (24 cm) for £43.71; a covered vegetable dish for £49.90; and a large oval meat platter £39.50.

Catalogue: *A4, Leaflets, 2 pages, Colour, Free* Postal charges: *£3.95* Delivery: *Royal Mail* Methods of Payment: *Visa, Access / Mastercard, Cheque, Postal Order*

SCOTTS OF STOW
The Square
Stow on the Wold
Gloucestershire
GL54 1AF

Telephone:
0249 449111

KITCHENWARE AND TABLEWARE FROM AROUND THE WORLD

Scotts sell up-market kitchen equipment from a well-designed, tasteful catalogue. There are plenty of cast iron products, from saucepans through to trivets. They have a nice range of traditional appliances, such as iron and brass scales and a hand-operated coffee grinder. They also stock modern gadgets and appliances, such as the industrial-size toasters by Dualit and the comprehensive food processor by Magimix. There is a good selection of china, trays, pans, griddles and so on as well as a smaller range of household items.

A solid brass ship's clock is £29.95, a cast iron pepper mill £17.95 and a Dualit toaster £99.99.

Kitchenware

Catalogue: *Quarterly, 190 × 210, Catalogue, 36 pages, Colour, Free* Postal charges: *Varies with item* Delivery: *Royal Mail* Methods of Payment: *Cheque, Postal Order, Visa, Access / Mastercard*

THE DOMESTIC PARAPHERNALIA CO
Unit 15
Marine Business Centre
Dock Road
Lytham
Lancs
FY8 5AJ

Telephone:
0253 736334
Fax:
0253 795191

CLOTHES AIRER
The Domestic Paraphernalia Co offer a curiously named 'Sheila Maid' clothes airer which turns out to be one of those clothes racks which are suspended above a bath or stove. Constructed from traditional pine and cast iron, this increasingly popular piece of revivalism means you won't have to spread your laundry over every radiator in the house on those wet winter afternoons. With the cast iron components available in red, blue, green, black or white, you can now suspend your sheets in style.

The order form gives a choice of four basic sizes, ranging from 58" at £34.00 to 8' at £40.00. There's also an option for additional pulley power (£5.50 for a double pulley) and an extraordinarily long 32' cord (£3.25).

Catalogue: *A5, Leaflets, 2 pages, Colour, Free* Postal charges: *£3.00* Delivery: *Royal Mail* Methods of Payment: *Cheque, Postal Order, Visa, Access / Mastercard*

THE HANGING KITCHEN CO
Wyndham Farm
Station Road
Ningwood
Isle of Wight
PO30 4NJ

Telephone:
0983 760842
Fax:
0983 760842

CAST IRON, PINE AND OAK KITCHENWARE
The Hanging Kitchen Company designs and produces practical, high quality, traditional, kitchenware. All the items are handmade in cast iron and pine and are available in a variety of colours and finishes to fit every style of kitchen.

Best selling designs include the 'Original Kitchen Maid', a traditional clothes airer, a free standing vegetable rack, a ceiling rack (Batterie de Cuisine), a plate rack, a herb and spice rack and garden herb planters. Prices range from 65p to £45.00. A bespoke design and manufacturing service is also available

Catalogue: *Annually, A4, Brochure, 1 page, Colour, Free* Postal charges: *£1.90* Delivery: *Parcelforce* Methods of Payment: *Cheque, Postal Order, Visa, Access / Mastercard*

Luggage

COACH
The Coach Store
8 Sloane Street
London
SW1X 9LE

Telephone:
071 235 1507
Fax:
071 235 3556

FINE LEATHER HANDBAGS AND ACCESSORIES
Coach offers simple but attractive gift ideas for both men and women from leather handbags (£62–£210)and wallets (£65–£150) to waist pouches (£90) and cosmetic cases (£45). Every item is made from fine leather with gold plated clutches, buttons and poppers, and comes in a wide variety of colours (blue, green, white, black, red), and for an extra £20 there is a Coach leather cleaning kit to keep them in perfect condition.

Catalogue: *Quarterly, A5, Catalogue, 65 pages, Colour, Free* Postal charges: *£3.50* Delivery: *Royal Mail* Methods of Payment: *Cheque, Postal Order, Visa, Access / Mastercard, American Express*

THE STOCKBAG COMPANY
140 Battersea Park Road
London
SW11 4NB

Telephone:
071 498 8811
Fax:
071 498 0990

TRAVEL BAGS
The Stockbag Company supply canvas and leather luggage exclusively by mail. Made from double-layered pure cotton canvas and leather they come in many shapes and sizes for both men and women. All items are available in either olive green or desert tan.
   The range includes shoulder bags (starting at £34.95), rucksacks (£46.95), traveller and overnight bags, suit carriers and briefcases (£64.50). They also sell sports bags and a wash bag as well as Panama hats from a separate catalogue (£29.95 to £59.95).

Catalogue: *Annually, A5, Brochure, 7 pages, Colour, Free* Postal charges: *Free* Delivery: *Royal Mail* Methods of Payment: *Cheque, Access / Mastercard, Visa, American Express*

COCHRANES OF OXFORD LTD
Leafield
Witney
Oxon
OX8 5NY

Telephone:
0993 878641
Fax:
0993 878416

SCIENTIFIC EQUIPMENT FOR SCHOOLS
Educational equipment and some toys for children of pre-school age to 18 years and also University students. Interesting equipment from construct-o-straws to crystals. Molecular models or a base with planets orbiting the sun or a star dome are just some of the wonderful models on offer. Kites and stunt kites are also available for you to erect yourself. The whole spectrum of science subjects are covered from astronomy to physics and chemistry.

Catalogue: *A4, Leaflets, 10 pages, Colour and B/W, Free* Postal charges: *Varies with item* Delivery: *In-house delivery* Methods of Payment: *Cheque, Postal Order*

Museums

MARSHCOUCH
36 Glebe Close
Hemel Hempstead
Herts
HP3 9PA

Telephone:
0442 63199 or 257832
Fax:
0442 866 786

PORTABLE COUCHES FOR PHYSICAL THERAPY
Designed to meet the demands of the physical therapist, Marshcouch's portable treatment couches are custom built to the highest specifications using sustainable materials.

Couches are specially constructed to the customer's specifications of height, width and upholstery. Durable, strong, fully guaranteed, Marshcouches are used by educational establishments, health authorities, blood transfusion centres, health centres, sports clubs, and health clinics throughout the country.

The 'Standard Hardwood Leg Folding Couch' costs £137 while the 'Multiheight Lifting Backrest Couch' is £275. A refurbishment facility is also available.

Catalogue: *A4, Brochure, 4 pages, Colour, Free* Postal charges: *£14.04* Delivery: *Courier* Methods of Payment: *Cheque, Visa, Access / Mastercard*

BRITISH MUSEUM PUBLICATIONS
British Museum Connection
46 Bloomsbury Street
London
WC1B 3QQ

Telephone:
071 343 1234
Fax:
071 436 7315

BOOKS AND GIFTS
Each new title from the British Museum press is listed and reviewed in detail in this thick catalogue. Topics range from Nigel Barley's *Smashing Pots* (£14.95), an account of ritual pot production and destruction in African society, to Lionel Casson's *Ships and Seafaring in Ancient Times* (£14.95).

The second half of the catalogue covers the entire British Museum backlist, with black and white photographs of many book jackets. The order form also has details of exhibition guides, slide sets with commentary (£7.95) and postcard packs (£3.50).

Catalogue: *A5, Catalogue, 60 pages, Colour and B/W, Free* Postal charges: *Varies with item* Delivery: *Royal Mail* Methods of Payment: *Cheque, Visa, Access / Mastercard, American Express, Diners Club*

PAST TIMES
Witney
Oxfordshire
OX8 6BH

Telephone:
0993 779444
Fax:
0993 700749

HISTORICAL GIFTS AND DECORATIVE ACCESSORIES
Past Times is Britain's leading historic gifts retailer with a worldwide mail order service and 35 shops throughout the country. The catalogue offers a unique range of fine and unusual gifts and decorative accessories, all with an authentic feel of the past. Set by historical period in chronological order from Roman to twentieth century, the catalogue includes fine silk scarves, jewellery, games, toys, stationery and books, household and garden items, food and toiletries.

Museums

Tabula, a Roman game played by the Emperor Claudius, is £9.95; a stunning 34" mediaeval rose window silk scarf with rolled hems £29.95; a romantic Elizabethan gimmal ring in sterling silver £9.95; and a beautifully finished pure cotton Victorian nightdress £23.95.

Catalogue: *Several, 255 × 200mm, Catalogue, 64 pages, Colour, Free* Postal charges: *Varies with item* Delivery: *Parcelforce* Methods of Payment: *Cheque, Postal Order, Visa, Access / Mastercard, American Express*

SCIENCE MUSEUM
Freepost SU361
Dept 5317
Hendon Road
Sunderland
SR9 9AD

Telephone:
091 514 4666
Fax:
091 514 4574

SCIENCE-BASED GOODS
The Science Museum's catalogue is aimed at the younger generation with many of the products science-based, some useful, and others just great fun. The gifts on offer range from clothes (£16.95 for a T shirt) and games (£8.99) to food processors (£49.95 for an ice cream maker) and household gadgets. The catalogue is brought out once a year, including new and fun ideas for the developing scientist.

Catalogue: *Annually, A3, Catalogue, 32 pages, Colour, Free* Postal charges: *Varies with item* Delivery: *Royal Mail* Methods of Payment: *Cheque, Access / Mastercard, Visa*

THE NATURAL HISTORY MUSEUM
Freepost SU361
Dept 5315
Hendon Road
Sunderland
SR9 9AD

Telephone:
091 514 2777
Fax:
091 514 4574

A VARIETY OF PRODUCTS FROM AROUND THE WORLD
The Natural History Museum offers a wide range of products following the theme of animals and their environment. Shopping is made easy through postal order with a small contribution being made to the museum through every purchase made.

Gifts on offer are kitchenware, clothes (£14.95 for a sweatshirt), toys, games and bed clothes (£64.95 for a duvet set). All products are printed with a different species of animal, with a donation from the mail order service to help preserve wildlife and the environment.

Catalogue: *Annually, A3, Catalogue, 32 pages, Colour, Free* Postal charges: *Varies with item* Delivery: *Royal Mail* Methods of Payment: *Cheque, Access / Mastercard, Visa*

Musical Instruments

THE VICTORIA AND ALBERT MUSEUM
Freepost SU361
Dept 5316
Hendon Road
Sunderland
SR9 9AD

Telephone:
091 514 2999
Fax:
091 514 4574

A WIDE RANGE OF GIFTS FROM THE V&A MUSEUM
Produced by the Victoria and Albert Museum, this catalogue offers a range of beautiful gifts inspired by the museum's collection: from jewellery and textiles (£24.95 for a pair of pearl earrings) to glass, ceramics and furniture (£115.00 for a table).

This catalogue is ideal for collectors because most of the products are centred on a theme, for example, cats, flowers and teddy bears. Gifts are delivered within 48 hours. Most of the products are handmade (for example, the Celtic pewter brooch) and each gift is unique.

Catalogue: *Annually, A3, Catalogue, 36 pages, Colour, Free* Postal charges: *Varies with item* Delivery: *Royal Mail* Methods of Payment: *Cheque, Visa, Access / Mastercard*

BOOSEY & HAWKES MUSICAL INSTRUMENTS LIMITED
Deansbrook Road
Edgware
Middlesex
HA8 9BB

Telephone:
081 952 7711
Fax:
081 951 3556

MUSICAL INSTRUMENTS AND ACCESSORIES
The well-known Boosey & Hawkes have brought together the finest manufacturers of musical instruments in one catalogue. There are almost 100 full colour photographs together with full and helpful descriptions of each instrument making it a joy to browse through.

The range of brass, woodwind and stringed instruments is impressive. There is an equally good selection of accessories for both the beginner and the experienced performer. Altogether a very professional and useful catalogue.

Prices range from £2.95 for tutor books to £8270.00 for a Keilworth bass saxophone.

Catalogue: *Annually, A4, Catalogue, 52 pages (two volumes), Colour, Free* Postal charges: *Varies with item* Delivery: *Royal Mail* Methods of Payment: *Cheque, Postal Order, Visa, Access / Mastercard, American Express*

KEYBOARDS DIRECT
PO Box 222
Plymouth
Devon
PL1 1BG

Telephone:
0345 626051
Fax:
0752 347598

KEYBOARD INSTRUMENTS AND SOFTWARE
Keyboards Direct specialises in musical instruments from Yamaha, Roland, Casio and Technics. Models include portable keyboards, organs, clavinova and digital pianos, synths and hi-tech. They also stock a full range of software and accessories.

All equipment is supported by expert before and after sales assistance and user advice from the exclusive KD 'HelpLine Studio'. Prices are very keen and include free delivery, which seems a bargain.

Portable keyboards range in price from just £65.00

Musical Instruments

for the Yamaha PSS21 to £1399.00 for the PSR5700. The top selling Yamaha Clavinova digital piano CLP123 is just £1699.00, some £300 off the retail price.

Catalogue: *3 a year, A4, Catalogue, 16 pages, Colour, Free* Postal charges: *Varies with item* Delivery: *Parcelforce* Methods of Payment: *Cheque, Postal Order, Visa, Access / Mastercard, American Express*

THE PIANO WORKSHOP
30A Highgate Road
Kentish Town
London
NW5 1NS

Telephone:
071 267 7671
Fax:
071 284 0083

PIANOS

The Piano Workshop is based in London's Kentish Town. It offers a very comprehensive range of new and second hand pianos plus restoration and tuning facilities. They also offer a 'hire with option to purchase' on any of their new or nearly new upright pianos and some selected new grand pianos from as little as £8.00 per week.

The makes of instrument carried include the full range of Young Chang pianos starting at £1499 (RRP £1665) for the EC100 (Walnut open-pore). Also carried are pianos by Weber, Schimmel, Rippen, Knight, Bluthner and Fuchs & Mohr.

Catalogue: *A4, Catalogue, 12 pages, B/W, Free* Postal charges: *Varies with item* Delivery: *In-house delivery* Methods of Payment: *Cheque*

AA COMPUTER PRINT
42 Priestlands
Romsey
Hampshire
SO51 8FL

Telephone:
0794 512953
Fax:
0794 830805

COMPUTER STATIONERY

This is a mail order computer stationery catalogue for use in the home or office. It sells continuous word processing paper, letterheads, cheques, listing paper and labels. They also have a range of fax rolls, invoice forms and envelopes. The catalogue even states which software is most compatible with what range and there is also a service for bespoke forms, where printing is in black on white or tinted NCR paper.

Prices are highly competitive, especially if you buy in bulk. Continuous stationery in A4 is £8.99 for 500 sheets and £13.50 for 1000 (100gms Bond). Fax rolls are from £2.03 if bought in boxes of twelve.

Catalogue: *A4, Catalogue, 6 pages, B/W, Free* Postal charges: *Varies with item* Delivery: *By arrangement* Methods of Payment: *Cheque*

Office Equipment

ADVANCED COMPUTER FURNITURE LTD
3 Sambourne Park
Sambourne
Nr. Redditch
Worcs
B96 6PE

Telephone:
0527 893036
Fax:
0527 893046

OFFICE FURNITURE
ACF offers a range of personal office equipment at an affordable price. Items supplied include a workstation for £99.00, a PC workstation for £159.00 and a personal office for £247.00. The personal office is both user friendly and flexible in configuration, offering left and right handed users the perfect working environment. It has a sliding printer shelf with two height settings and a shelving unit to keep busy desks tidy.

The company offers a 30 day money back guarantee, a twelve month guarantee on all products and three colour options of computer grey, chocolate brown or light oak.

Catalogue: *A4, Leaflets, 4 pages, Colour, Free* Postal charges: *Varies with item* Delivery: *Parcelforce* Methods of Payment: *Cheque, Postal Order*

BEST BUYS OFFICE EQUIPMENT DIRECT
533 High Road
Ilford
Essex
IG1 1TZ

Telephone:
081 514 7887
Fax:
081 553 3343

OFFICE EQUIPMENT AND COMPUTERS
Best Buys catalogue offers an extensive range of the latest colour notebook machines, such as the Toshiba 486 for £2529.00. They also stock conventional PCs by all the major manufacturers, including Hewlett Packard, IBM and Olivetti. As for printers, they have laser and bubblejet versions by Cannon, Hewlett Packard, Epson, Olivetti and Brother. The Hewlett Packard DeskJet 310 seems particularly well-priced at £179.00.

Best Buys also sell fax machines, copiers and an assortment of office equipment, including budget desks from £79.95. Prices are competitive and they advise calling to check since they are constantly changing in this very volatile market.

Catalogue: *A4, Catalogue, 8 pages, Colour, Free* Postal charges: *Varies with item* Delivery: *Courier* Methods of Payment: *Visa, Access / Mastercard, Cheque, American Express*

Office Equipment

BUDGET WORKSTATIONS
Unit 14
Glenville Mews
Kimber Road
London
SW18 4NJ

Telephone:
081 871 4322
Fax:
081 870 7986

COMPUTER DESKS/STANDS
Purpose designed computer workstations are Budget's speciality. Their reasonable prices look particularly attractive in the light of recent moves to legislate against inadequate working conditions for computer users.

Not overly attractive items, their range nevertheless seems well thought out for most users' needs. The 'PC Compact' (£89.00) is fairly typical, comprising a 24" × 18½" worktop, pull-out keyboard shelf, ample knee room and separate printer and stationery shelves.

All workstations come in four colours from soft grey to dark mahogany and are produced with protected metalwork, easy-glide runners for sliding shelves and braked castors as standard.

Catalogue: *A4, Catalogue, 12 pages, Colour, Free* Postal charges: *Varies with item* Delivery: *Courier* Methods of Payment: *Access / Mastercard, Visa, Cheque*

CHARLES WHITE LTD
Unit C4–C18
Poplar Business Park
10 Prestons Road
London
E14 9RL

Telephone:
071 515 2500
Fax:
071 515 3575

OFFICE SUPPLIES
By gathering together everything that the business needs to run smoothly, Charles White takes the strain out of setting up or sorting out your business or office. After years of experience they have been able to choose both the vital elements for business success and more specialised options to suit the vast range of businesses in the country.

In seventeen sections, the catalogue offers a range of quality products at affordable prices. From VDU workstations from £185.00 to memo pads at only one pence. One of Charles White's specialities is conference planning, with complete presentation systems, conference furniture and stationery – everything except the refreshments, in fact.

Catalogue: *Annually, A4, Catalogue, 368 pages, Colour, Free* Postal charges: *Varies with item* Delivery: *Royal Mail* Methods of Payment: *Cheque, Postal Order, Visa, Access / Mastercard*

Office Equipment

COLVIN DIRECT
Hammond House
Croydon Road
Caterham
Surrey
CR3 6PB

Telephone:
0883 340511
Fax:
0883 340327

OFFICE SUPPLIES
To keep the wheels of industry turning smoothly requires effort and organisation. The Colvin range of office supplies can make that task a great deal easier.

The catalogue has an easy to use and comprehensive index and the products are arranged alphabetically within the catalogue – a very helpful, common-sense touch. The full range contains over 12,000 items, and so only a fraction of those can be shown in this catalogue, but Colvin have chosen those which are most popular. From Treasury tags to Post-it notes, goods are available singly or in bulk at prices that will certainly please the accountants. Lever arch files start at £20.88 for 10 and laser copier paper from £19.95 for 2,500 sheets.

Catalogue: *Annually, A4, Catalogue, 66 pages, Colour, Free* Postal charges: *Varies with item* Delivery: *Royal Mail* Methods of Payment: *Cheque, Postal Order, Visa, Access / Mastercard*

EM RICHFORD LIMITED
Curzon Road
Chilton Industrial Estate
Sudbury
Suffolk
CO10 6XD

Telephone:
0787 375241
Fax:
0787 310179

RUBBER STAMPS AND MARKING DEVICES
Since 1878, EM Richford have been meeting the needs of businesses across the country with a range of stamps to make onerous tasks less repetitive and more efficient. They stock a wide array of gadgets to date, number, stencil and mark anything coming into your business.

The teams are willing to use their vast experience to help you get the best from their products and have a flexible production system which means that many common designs are in stock and can be delivered without delay. From advanced electronic Date/Time stamps at £83.95 to traditional self-inking pads at £11.64 (all prices are exclusive of VAT) there will be something to make the worst administrative task more bearable.

Catalogue: *Annually, A4, Catalogue, 50 pages, Colour, Free* Postal charges: *Varies with item* Delivery: *Royal Mail* Methods of Payment: *Cheque, Visa, Access / Mastercard*

Office Equipment

F PARR LTD
Merse Road
North Moons Moat
Redditch
Worcs
B98 9PL

Telephone:
0527 585777
Fax:
0527 66430

FACTORY, WAREHOUSE, SHOP AND OFFICE EQUIPMENT
Parrs catalogue is mainly for factories, shops and offices but there is a good deal of interest to the general public as well. There's a marvellous range of porters' trolleys, which they call sack trucks for some reason, suitable for anything from an ordinary suitcase up to large industrial boxes. There are even ingenious ones which will climb stairs.

Then there's shelving, plastic storage containers, water pumps, staple guns, wrapping materials, computer tables, filing cabinets, office equipment and furniture, fire extinguishers and so on. It makes for fascinating reading and you can get many useful products for around the house and garage.

Catalogue: *A4, Catalogue, 308 pages, Colour, Free* Postal charges: *Varies with item* Delivery: *In-house delivery* Methods of Payment: *Cheque, Visa, Access / Mastercard, American Express*

FILOFAX
JUST FAX
43 Broadwick Street
London
W1V 1FT

Telephone:
071 734 5034
Fax:
071 734 5034

FILOFAX AND ACCESSORIES
Filofax, that icon of the eighties, have in fact been in business long before the rise (and fall) of the yuppie. Established in 1921 they have gone on selling the same basic idea ever since. However, the range has expanded considerably as this neat catalogue, which is itself punched to fit into a Filofax, shows.

There are sections of Filofax binders, pocket organisers, Deskfax, accessories and a huge range of leaves covering everything from diaries to expense sheets. Prices start at £25.00 for an empty pocket edition up to £125.00 for a deluxe leather version.

Catalogue: *4 x 7, Catalogue, 24 pages, Colour, Free* Postal charges: *Varies with item* Delivery: *Royal Mail* Methods of Payment: *Cheque, Postal Order, Access / Mastercard, American Express, Visa*

MANAGEMENT GAMES
Methwold House
Methwold
Thetford
Norfolk
IP26 4PF

Telephone:
0366 728215
Fax:
0366 728604

MANAGEMENT TRAINING SOFTWARE AND COURSES
One of the world's most experienced simulation specialists, this company publishes a complete range of ready-to-use materials and resources for management, supervisory and sales training. These include simulations, case studies, training packages and computer-aided learning software.

Subject areas covered include: administration, chairing a meeting, customer care, learning to learn, negotiating and transactional analysis.

Business simulations include 'Tycoon' which

Office Equipment

represents 'a typical company manufacturing a hypothetical consumer-durable product in the year 2021'. The exercise is run over four to ten rounds, each representing one year's trading. The cost is £495.00.

Catalogue: *A5, Catalogue, 10 pages, B/W, Free* Postal charges: *Free* Delivery: *Royal Mail* Methods of Payment: *Cheque*

MINILABEL
Oak Hall Manor
Sheffield Park Gardens
Sussex
Sheffield Park Gardens
Sheffield Park
Sussex
TN22 3QY

Telephone:
0825 790889
Fax:
0825 790461

LABELS

As you might guess from their name, this company produces every type of label you can imagine. They also supply business cards and luggage tags all of which can be personalised in a wide range of colours and typefaces.

In addition to personalised labels, there are many pre-printed labels, both humorous and useful, which can be attached to cards, diaries and noticeboards. A good selection is included in the catalogue.

Catalogue: *A5, By Advertising, 18 pages, B/W, Free* Postal charges: *Varies with item* Delivery: *Royal Mail* Methods of Payment: *Cheque, Postal Order, Visa, Access / Mastercard*

NEAT IDEAS
Sandall Stones Road
Kirk Sandall Industrial
Estate
Doncaster
S Yorks
DN3 1QU

Telephone:
0800 500 192
Fax:
0800 600 192

OFFICE EQUIPMENT

As their name suggests, Neat Ideas stock a vast range of storage devices that should keep any home or office free from clutter. Their well designed catalogue features just about everything for the office, including computers and fax machines.

The Office Workcentre, an all-in-one office furniture system, costs £229.00. It includes a 2 door cupboard and an eye level over-desk storage unit, with handy compartments for books and directories. A miniature version costs £139.95.

Catalogue: *A4, Catalogue, 236 pages, Colour, Free* Postal charges: *Varies with item* Delivery: *Courier* Methods of Payment: *Cheque, Access / Mastercard, Visa, American Express*

NOBO DRAKE
St Fagans Road
Fairwater
Cardiff
CF5 3AE

Telephone:
0222 560333
Fax:
0222 554909

DISPLAY AND TRAINING AIDS

Nobo Drake's large catalogue is mainly for offices and features a wide range of items for the workplace. These include conference equipment, notice boards and flip charts. There are also writing boards, display systems and projecting equipment.

Some of the devices are very ingenious, such as the electronic 'Noboboard' which is like a conventional white board but everything you write on it can be printed out on a sheet of paper. Clever but pricey at nearly £1500.

Office Equipment

There is also a separate 32 page catalogue for primary and middle schools. This features multimedia resources for teachers including photocopy masters, language tapes, wallcharts, posters and so on.

Catalogue: *Annually, A4, Catalogue, 160 pages, Colour, Free* Postal charges: *Varies with item* Delivery: *Royal Mail* Methods of Payment: *Cheque*

PAPER DIRECT BY DELUXE
FREEPOST (LE6296)
Hinkley
LE10 0BR

Telephone:
0800 616244
Fax:
0455 631929

PAPER AND OFFICE STATIONERY
This company sells an ingenious idea from America – pre-printed paper which you can then use in your laser printer or copier. This means you can produce full colour brochures, letterheads, mailers and forms from a standard printer.

There is a large selection of paper to choose from both in different formats and with different designs. They even provide envelopes and a clever sheet which enables you to produce your own business cards. They can also supply software for most word processing programs and DTP packages which will help with templates.

Obviously this does cost more than long print runs but if you want to run off just a few copies it seems a wonderful idea.

Catalogue: *A5, Catalogue, 48 pages, Colour, Free* Postal charges: *Varies with item* Delivery: *Parcelforce, Royal Mail* Methods of Payment: *Cheque, Visa, Access / Mastercard, American Express, Postal Order*

RAYDEK
Raydek House
118 Saltley Trading Estate
Birmingham
B8 1BL

Telephone:
021 326 8800
Fax:
021 327 6281

INDUSTRIAL SAFETY EQUIPMENT
Raydek signs and safety products leave no stone unturned in their attempt to provide a comprehensive system of warning notices and preventative devices. If Raydek can't issue the warning you want, it's hard to think who can.

Aluminium signs start at £9.65 for 300 mm × 450 mm; all you have to do is describe the type of sign you want and they'll do the rest. Raydek can provide any artwork necessary. Luminous signs in rigid plastic begin at £4.95 for 150 mm × 150 mm. If you want to make your own sign, they offer a prespaced vinyl lettering service in a variety of type faces. Prices begin at 30p per letter for a 15 mm high character – reflective and fluorescent characters are 30% more expensive.

Catalogue: *A4, Catalogue, 84 pages, Colour, £1.50* Postal charges: *Varies with item* Delivery: *Royal Mail* Methods of Payment: *Visa, Access / Mastercard, Cheque*

Optical

THANET GLOBE EMPORIUM
Orange Street
Canterbury
CT1 2JA

Telephone:
0227 450055
Fax:
0227 760548

GLOBES

The Thanet Globe Emporium offer a full range of antique-looking globes to compliment any director's office suite. Who would have thought the world could be packaged in such a variety of ways?

If you want something simple, the 'Granada' (12" diameter × 17" high) costs £110.00. A substantial base looking vaguely like emerald marble supports a raised relief globe displayed on a brass-plated inclination mounting. Alternatively, you might prefer the 'President', at £2900.00. As you can guess from the price, this is a serious item: a solid wood floor mounting and solid brass meridian support a 20" globe. It features a 'touch-on' light and an antique style map.

Catalogue: *Annually, A4, Catalogue, 15 pages, Colour, Free* Postal charges: *Varies with item* Delivery: *Royal Mail* Methods of Payment: *Cheque, Visa, Access / Mastercard*

VERTAGO
3 Vickers Business Centre
Priestley Road
Basingstoke
Hants
RG24 9NP

Telephone:
0256 24755
Fax:
0256 25033

FILING SYSTEMS

Vertago's 'Snapfile' series of products is sold as the world's first 'go anywhere truly portable document managing and filing system'. The files can be suspended from a hook or fixing point, both of which are supplied, and the clear wallets snap on and off the suspension unit, enabling easy access. The system is intended for a busy executive or salesman 'on the road'.

The system can also be used in the home where papers that would otherwise have just sat in drawers can be hung on the back of your kitchen or study door.

The Snapfile system starts at £29.74, with a variety of extensions being priced separately.

Catalogue: *Annually, A4, Leaflets, Colour, Free* Postal charges: *Varies with item* Delivery: *Royal Mail* Methods of Payment: *Cheque, Visa, Access / Mastercard*

C&T EYEWEAR LTD
PO Box 41
Teddington
Middlesex
TW11 05X

Telephone:
081 943 4815

RAY-BAN SUNGLASSES

C&T offer 40% off the retail price for genuine Bausch & Lomb Ray-Ban sunglasses. Recently these have once again become fashion items, usually with prices to match.

The leaflet pictorially displays their extensive range of glasses, ranging from the Wayfarer Black G-15 at £44.00 to The General II Gold RB-50 at £111.00.

Every pair of Ray-Ban glasses sold have a one year

Optical

guarantee and prices include a soft or hard case, depending on model. All frames are adjustable.

Catalogue: *A4, Leaflets, 4 pages, Colour, Free* Postal charges: *£1.00* Delivery: *Royal Mail* Methods of Payment: *Cheque, Postal Order, Visa, Access / Mastercard*

LEISURETEC
815 London Road
Westcliff-on-Sea
Essex
SS0 9SY

Telephone:
0702 470056

BINOCULARS

A mail order catalogue within a catalogue, Leisuretec specialises in binoculars and theatre glasses. The main supplier in its range is the German company Bresser, whose binoculars are grouped into 3 sections. The first, the 'Professional' range embodies state of the art technology and carries a twenty year guarantee. The second, the 'Exclusive' range, while still being above average quality, only carries a ten year guarantee while the last group, the 'Classic', carries a still impressive five year guarantee.

No prices are given in the German brochure, but other makes vary from around £62.00 to £300.00.

Catalogue: *Annually, 210mm × 200mm, Catalogue, 56 pages, Colour, Free* Postal charges: *£3.95* Delivery: *Royal Mail* Methods of Payment: *Cheque, Postal Order, Visa, Access / Mastercard, American Express*

BIKE CITY LTD
Tranquility House
1 Tranquility
Crossgates
Leeds
W Yorks
LS15 8QU

Telephone:
0532 326600

CYCLES & ACCESSORIES

Bike City sell a good selection of bicycles for gents, ladies and children. Adult cycles, such as the gents Topeka with a 12 speed Shimano gearset, cantilever brakes and alloy rims start at £99.99. A ladies model, the Masquerade with 5 speed Shimano indexed gear set and again alloy wheel rims is around the same price. Boy's and girl's cycles start at £69.99.

The company also sells a range of accessories including racks. Their intro pack consists of a helmet, lights and lock and sells for £34.99.

Catalogue: *2, A5, Brochure, 10 pages, Colour, Free* Postal charges: *Varies with item* Delivery: *Data Express, Parcelforce* Methods of Payment: *Cheque, Postal Order, Stage Payments, Visa, Access / Mastercard*

Outdoor (inc. Camping)

CANNOCK GATES
Martindale
Hawks Green Est
Cannock
Staffs
WS11 2XT

Telephone:
0543 462500
Fax:
0543 506237

GATES
Cannock Gates offer a range of stock gates manufactured both from steel and timber in a huge variety of sizes and styles. In addition, they will happily piece together the gate of your dreams from sketches or photos.

Prices seem competitive. A simple, classic wrought iron single gate 2'6" wide and 6' high will cost £36.25; a top-of-the-range double gate design, such as 'Royal Split Arch', 12' wide and 6' high comes to just over £900.00.

The smaller selection of timber models are crafted from top quality Swedish redwood. Their best-selling model is the 'Derbyshire', from around £100 for the single version.

Catalogue: *A4, Catalogue, 20 pages, Colour, Free* Postal charges: *Varies with item* Delivery: *Courier* Methods of Payment: *Cheque, Postal Order, Visa, Access / Mastercard, American Express*

FARLOW'S OF PALL MALL
5 Pall Mall
London
SW1

Telephone:
071 839 2423
Fax:
0285 652446

FISHING TACKLE, SHOOTING ACCESSORIES AND COUNTRY CLOTHING
With a business that has been in operation since 1840 and a Royal Warrant holder since 1982, this mail order side of the central London retail operation brings together products from the company's two shops.

All the items are clearly shown with lengthy descriptions where necessary. These range from salmon and sea trout, as well as chalk stream and still-water trout fishing tackle to fishing accessories – fly boxes, hooks, canvas bags, pouches, wading staffs, suspenders – and the correct fishing clothes: boots or waders, waterproof jackets, fishing waistcoats and gloves. There is also a selection of clothes for shooting – felt hats, tweed caps, deerstalkers, shooting suits, quilted jackets, ankle boots, Barbours – and country clothing from silk underwear to tweeds and woollens.

Prices range from £99.99 for a daiwa salmon fly rod, to £329.50 for a 100% cotton shooting jacket.

Catalogue: *A4, Catalogue, 24 pages, Colour, £2.50* Postal charges: *Varies with item* Delivery: *Royal Mail* Methods of Payment: *Cheque, Postal Order, Visa, Access / Mastercard, American Express, Diners Club*

Outdoor (inc. Camping)

HOUSE OF HARDY
Willowburn
Alnwick
Northumberland
NE66 2PG

Telephone:
0665 602771
Fax:
0665 602389

FISHING TACKLE

House of Hardy was founded in 1872 to specialise in making the world's finest fishing tackle. They use only the best materials available as they build their tackle up to a standard, never down to a price.

They make a variety of rods including custom-made split bamboo rods, reels, fly lines, leaders, fly selections and boxes, keepnets, fishing bags, vests and jackets. Prices range from £85.00 for a fibalite spinning rod to £777.00 for a custom made split bamboo fly rod.

Catalogue: *A4, Catalogue, 36 pages, Colour, Free* Postal charges: *Varies with item* Delivery: *Royal Mail* Methods of Payment: *Cheque, Visa, Access / Mastercard*

PLEASURE AND LEISURE INFLATABLES LTD
Earls Way,
Church Hill Road
Industrial Estate,
Thurmaston, Leicester
LE4 8DL

Telephone:
0533-695065/696333
Fax:
0533-609219

INFLATABLE CASTLES

P&L were the creators of the original 'bouncy castle' concept in 1976 and they continue to produce them today. All P&L products meet UK safety regulations, have low maintenance costs and are easy to deflate.

The castles include the king-size 'Konkord' and the smaller 'Birthday Kastle', suitable for the average back-garden. P&L's other products range from small inflatable boats, trains and animals suitable for play groups and schools, to huge adventure worlds that can bring a 'total environment experience' to leisure centres or shopping complexes.

Inflatables can be designed and built to any specification but sample prices are £8215.00 for 'Jungle World', £2730.00 for 'Konkord Castle' and £360.00 for a soft 'Play Train'.

Catalogue: *242 mm × 244 mm, Catalogue, 20 pages, Colour, Free* Postal charges: *Varies with item* Delivery: *By arrangement* Methods of Payment: *Cheque*

RAINBOW HORSE SUPPLIES
Bromley Mill,
Bromlet Road
Congleton,
Cheshire
CW12 1PT

Telephone:
0260 273771
Fax:
0260 278436

HORSE RUGS AND OUTDOOR WEAR

Designed to traditionally high standards by people who really understand horses and ponies, Rainbow's products combine good performance and long-lasting quality. The range covers exercise sheets (£28.00), rugs (£44.00–£63.00), and machine-washable quilts (£35.00–£60.00). All rugs, sheets and quilts can be supplied initialled with felt capitals $3\frac{1}{2}''$ high.

Rainbow also produce a distinctive collection of hard-wearing, light weight outdoor clothes for country pursuits such as fishing, riding and shooting.

All clothing has a Cyclone fabric outer lining,

Pets

making them warm and waterproof and a fleece inner lining. The Yorkshire fishing jacket and overtrousers sell for £110.00 and £35.00 respectively.

Catalogue: *A5, Catalogue, 8 pages plus inserts, Colour, Free* Postal charges: *Varies with item* Delivery: *Royal Mail* Methods of Payment: *Cheque*

CAT CLAWS
Cat Claws (BASCO)
PO Box 71
Croydon
CR0 2ZZ

Telephone:
081 656 8888
Fax:
081 656 8776

CAT CARE PRODUCTS
Cat Claws offers a range of gifts for cat owners. The catalogue offers products such as flea collars (£2.50), dental care products (£8.95), toys and scratching pads (£6.95). Packaging and postage are extra only if you order goods worth £15.00 or over. With these products on offer you can keep your cat clean, healthy and happy.

Catalogue: *21.5 × 14mm, Leaflets, 12 pages, B/W, Free* Postal charges: *Varies with item* Delivery: *Royal Mail* Methods of Payment: *Cheque, Visa, Access / Mastercard*

CATAWARE
Victoria Mill
Bakewell
Derbyshire
DE45 1DA

Telephone:
0629 813993
Fax:
0629 814419

CAT THEME ITEMS
This catalogue is a collection of 1000+ cat-themed items for you, your cats and the cat lovers in your life. There are many useful and unusual items including cat care, homewares, jewellery, stickers and stamps, gifts and games, toys and books.

Ladies briefs with various cat motifs are £2.50, a cat pendulum clock is £16.90 and cat ice cube tray £4.50. A comfortable cat radiator bed sells for £14.90 and a cosibin cat home for £29.99. Cat and butterflies window stickers are £1.90 while a selection of cat stickers is 99p. Finally there is a rather attractive pewter climbing cat brooch and porcelain ginger cat earrings, for just £7.90. Cat lovers order one now!

Catalogue: *Annual plus newsletters, A5, Catalogue, 96 pages, Colour, £1.00 refundable* Postal charges: *Varies with item* Delivery: *Parcelforce, Royal Mail* Methods of Payment: *Cheque, Postal Order, Access / Mastercard, Visa*

Photographic

ERIC FISHWICK LTD
Grange Valley
Haydock
St Helens
Merseyside
WA11 0XE

Telephone:
0744 611611
Fax:
0744 26592

EVERYTHING PHOTOGRAPHIC

'Everything photographic' is how one might sum up the range of this catalogue. Fishwick's have been major suppliers of photographic materials and equipment for over 25 years and are famous for their 'by return' mail order service. They specialise in stocking all those unusual (and often unheard of!) accessories that normally cannot be found on the high street.

But that does not mean they don't have all the famous names such as Canon, Nikon, Minolta, Olympus, Pentax etc. – by all means they do – and most at discount prices. Part-exchange is welcome and all their used equipment is sold with a money-back guarantee if not completely satisfied.

Catalogue: *Bi-monthly, A1, Catalogue, 2 pages, B/W, Free* Postal charges: *Varies with item* Delivery: *Parcelforce* Methods of Payment: *Cheque, Postal Order, Visa, American Express, Access / Mastercard, Diners Club*

FLASH FOTO LTD
4 Parkmead
London
NW7 2JW

Telephone:
081 959 4513
Fax:
081 959 1388

PHOTOGRAPH ALBUMS AND OTHER ACCESSORIES

Flash Foto specialise in photographic albums. Their 50 page version for slides, prints, or negative storage is just £11.50 while a plastic dustproof archival storage box is £5.95. A useful logbook for photographic records is £5.95.

They also produce an ingenious device for storing slides which can be suspended in a filing cabinet. This takes 50 slides and retails for £15.00.

Catalogue: *2, ⅔rds A4, Catalogue, 12 pages, Colour, Free* Postal charges: *Varies with item* Delivery: *Royal Mail, Parcelforce* Methods of Payment: *Cheque, Postal Order, Visa, Access / Mastercard*

JESSOPS OF LEICESTER LTD
Jessop House
98 Sudamore Road
Leicester
LE3 1TZ

Telephone:
0533 320033
Fax:
0533 320060

PHOTOGRAPHIC ACCESSORIES, DARKROOM EQUIPMENT

Jessops have a great number of photographic shops up and down the country but also operate a mail order arm. Their catalogue features just about every accessory you could need. Along with films, batteries, bags, filters and tripods are darkroom chemicals, equipment, paper as well as frames, mounts and storage systems.

They also sell a good range of binoculars and telescopes and projectors and screens.

Catalogue: *A4, Catalogue, 12 pages, Colour, Free* Postal charges: *Varies with item* Delivery: *Royal Mail* Methods of Payment: *Cheque, Visa, Access / Mastercard*

Photographic

MEMORIES ON VIDEO
24 York Gardens
Winterbourne
Bristol
BS17 1QT

Telephone:
0454 772857

COPYING CINE FILM/SLIDES/PHOTOS AUDIO TAPES
Memories on Video is a small family business established in 1984 but has become Britain's leading house for the transfer of cine film onto video tape. They can cope with any format of film and can also transfer slides, photographs and negatives on to video.

In addition they can convert any foreign video to play in Britain and vice versa. Other services include video tape duplication, video and audio tape repair and copying old reel to reel sound recordings on to modern cassettes. They also produce corporate and training videos. Over the years they have established a reputation both for personal service and for often accomplishing the impossible!

Catalogue: *A4, Brochure, 6 pages, Colour, Free* Postal charges: *Varies with item* Delivery: *Royal Mail, Parcelforce* Methods of Payment: *Cheque, Postal Order, COD, Visa, Access / Mastercard*

TECNO RETAIL
Unit 9
Hampton Farm Est
Hampton Road West
Feltham
Middx
TW13 6DB

Telephone:
081 898 9934
081 898 2772
Fax:
081 894 4652

PHOTOGRAPHIC, VIDEO AND PERSONAL ELECTRONICS
Tecno is a leading specialist retailer of imaging equipment, from conventional still cameras starting at £15.00 right up to £2000. They also sell camcorders, video accessories, editing equipment and video recorders.

Prices are always very competitive, with frequent exclusive offers. For example, currently they are offering a Canon A2HI camcorder for just £999.00, saving some £400.00 on the RRP. They also sell films and tapes at low prices, with a 10% discount for batches of ten, which can be mixed.

Catalogue: *Bi-annually, A4, Catalogue, 64–72 pages, Colour, Free* Postal charges: *Varies with item* Delivery: *Royal Mail Courier* Methods of Payment: *Cheque, Postal Order, Visa, Access / Mastercard, American Express, Diners Club*

THE CPL GROUP
Duchess House
18–19 Warren Street
London
W1P 5DB

Telephone:
071 388 7836
Fax:
071 383 4629

PHOTOGRAPHIC LABORATORY SERVICES
The CPL Group offers a wide range of services for the development of photographs ranging from film processing, black and white printing, computer graphics and machine printing to print mounting, illuminated display boxes and reversal printing. Prices depend on the size of the photographs and the service needed (film processing: £4.05 for one 35mm × 36 roll). All of the handmade colour prints are of a high quality and the photographic services are carried out by trained, professional technicians.

Photographic

THE TIME MACHINE
RTM House
139 Back High Street
Newcastle upon Tyne
NE3 4ET

Telephone:
091 213 0477
Fax:
091 213 0595

Catalogue: *29.8 × 16 mm, Catalogue, 39 pages, Colour, Free* Postal charges: *Varies with item* Delivery: *Royal Mail* Methods of Payment: *Cheque*

PHOTOGRAPHIC RESTORATIONS
The Time Machine specialise in restoring and recreating photographs from old prints. Prints can be produced to most sizes in black & white, full colour, sepia, silhouette or hand tinted.

Using digital processing, scratches and missing parts can be rebuilt, dirt removed and details from other photographs, e.g. open eyes, added. As each restoration involves different degrees of work quotations are sent out beforehand. A gift service is also available which includes high-quality gift wrapping and a personal message card. Prices for enhancement to postcard size start at around £25.00.

Catalogue: *Third A4, Leaflet, 6 pages, B/W, Free* Postal charges: *Free* Delivery: *Royal Mail* Methods of Payment: *Cheque, Postal Order*

TRUPRINT
Stafford Park 18
Telford
TL1 1TP

Telephone:
0952 292162

MAIL ORDER PHOTOPROCESSING
Truprint is Europe's largest mail order photoprocessor. They return a free film with every order and guarantee that all orders are returned within 7 days or they'll give you your money back. They also sell a full range of photo-related products, from reprints and enlargements through to photo transfer items such as photo-shirts.

Their competitive pricing includes 24 compact prints for £2.99, photo-shirts from £8.99 and Truprint single-use cameras from £3.49.

Catalogue: *2, A5, Catalogue, 12 pages, Colour, Free* Postal charges: *Varies with item* Delivery: *Royal Mail* Methods of Payment: *Cheque, Visa, Access / Mastercard, Postal Order*

WRIGHT & LOGAN
20 Queen Street
Portsea
Portsmouth
Hampshire
PO1 3HL

Telephone:
0705 829555

PHOTOGRAPHS OF WARSHIPS
The Wright & Logan collection consists of over 50,000 different negatives of warships and support vessels of different nationalities and types from the 1920s onwards. They come framed and with a two line, type set caption. The top line will consist of the ship's name and any dates supplied by the customer while the bottom line will include class and type of vessel along with the name of a loved one who served on the ship.

All the photographs are hand printed from original

Recordings

large format negatives on fibre based photographic paper. They are all carefully mounted and sealed into a quality bevelled cut matt overlay and hand finished before framing. The recommended size is 12" by 7". Prices range from £37.95 to £39.95.

Catalogue: *A5, Catalogue, 6 pages, B/W, Free* Postal charges: *Free* Delivery: *Royal Mail* Methods of Payment: *Cheque, Postal Order*

YORK PHOTO
Brunel Road
Newton Abbot
Devon
TQ12 4XL

Telephone:
0626 67373
Fax:
0626 62749

MAIL ORDER PHOTOPROCESSING

York Photo is the world's largest mail order photoprocessing laboratory. Its no frills, value for money approach means York supplies its customers with a high quality product at the best price. Along with this basic service, York Photo offers reprints, enlargements, posters, photo-shirts, jigsaws, canvas texture prints and coasters, all made from customer photographs.

Up to 27 compact prints cost just £1.90 while York film is 99p.

Catalogue: *Bi-annually, A5, Catalogue, 12 pages, Colour, Free* Postal charges: *Varies with item* Delivery: *Royal Mail* Methods of Payment: *Cheque, Postal Order, Visa, Access / Mastercard*

ACCELERATED LEARNING SYSTEMS LTD
50 Aylesbury Road
Aston Clinton
Aylesbury
Bucks
HP22 5AH

Telephone:
0296 631177
Fax:
0296 631074

AUDIO LANGUAGE COURSES

Accelerated Learning Systems are based on extensive research into how we learn best. The courses present the information needed in new ways that make it easier and faster to learn.

The programmes use a combination of audio, video and course books to learn in the combination that suits the customer best. They are written by acknowledged leaders in their fields and designed to make learning a pleasure.

The home study language courses are offered in French, Spanish, German and Italian and are priced at £99.00 each. The pack consists of twelve full cassettes, 200 page text book, physical learning video with booklet, name game and word cards. Other courses are available on request.

Catalogue: *A5, Leaflets, 6 pages, Colour, Free* Postal charges: *Varies with item* Delivery: *Royal Mail* Methods of Payment: *Cheque, Postal Order, Visa, Access / Mastercard*

Recordings

ACORN MUSIC
PO Box 17
Sidmouth
Devon
EX10 9EH

Telephone:
0395 578145
Fax:
0395 578145

MUSIC
A wide variety of music on LP, CD and cassette to cater for every taste from jazz, nostalgia and vocalists to books and videos by mail order. A vast amount to choose from mailed direct to the customer.

Catalogue: *A4, Leaflets, 12 pages, B/W, Free* Postal charges: *Varies with item* Delivery: *In-house delivery* Methods of Payment: *Cheque, Postal Order*

BAGS OF BOOKS
1 South Street
Lewes
Sussex
BN7 2BT

Telephone:
0273 479320

SPOKEN WORD TAPES
Bags of Books specialise in books on tape for children in the 2–16 year old range. Some of these recordings are unabridged and can be used with a book for reading along. The catalogue helpfully lists tapes both under authors and categories, such as poetry, plays and short stories.

Matilda is £7.49 for the tape plus £3.99 for the accompanying book. The now famous *Queen & I* tape is £7.99.

Catalogue: *Annually, A4, Catalogue, 20 pages, B/W, Free* Postal charges: *Varies with item* Delivery: *Royal Mail, Parcelforce* Methods of Payment: *Cheque, Visa, Access / Mastercard*

BBC VIDEO
Video Plus Direct
PO Box 190
Peterborough
PE2 6UW

Telephone:
0733 232800
Fax:
0733 238966

VIDEOS AND CASSETTES
BBC Video is not surprisingly one of the country's largest distributors of tapes with a vast number of well known titles. Its largest selections are in comedy, children's and sport.

Recent releases in comedy include *French and Saunders 4* (£10.99) and *Smashie and Nicie: Radio Fab FM* (£10.99). The children's collection includes old favourites such as *Watch With Mother* (£8.99) and *Andy Pandy* (£8.99) along with more recent hits like *The Animals of Farthing Wood 1–3* (£9.99).

The Young Classic Collection includes *The Borrowers* (£14.99) and *The Secret Garden* (£10.99). Sport has highlights from Wimbledon, FA Cup Finals and Rugby League. Drama features the whole *BBC Shakespeare Series* and every episode of *Doctor Who*.

Catalogue: *A4, Catalogue, 8 pages, Colour, Free* Postal charges: *£2.50* Delivery: *Royal Mail* Methods of Payment: *Cheque, Postal Order, Visa, Access / Mastercard, American Express, Diners Club*

Recordings

BRITANNIA MUSIC CO LTD
PO Box 31
Ilford
Essex
IGI 2AE

CD AND CASSETTE RECORDINGS BY MAIL

Britannia Music offers customers a mail order music club and allows them to choose from the best in Pop, Rock, Easy Listening and Classical.

The leaflet offers a saving of over £75 on introduction to the club, along with further savings on club discounts. There is a monthly magazine from which customers can shop at leisure and choose their favourite music on either cassette or CD format.

Britannia has been providing a quality service for 25 years and all recordings are supplied by the world's leading record companies and come with Britannia's guarantee of quality.

Catalogue: *Monthly, 190mm × 210mm, Leaflets, 6 pages, Colour, Free* Postal charges: *Varies with item* Delivery: *Royal Mail* Methods of Payment: *Cheque, Visa, Access / Mastercard*

CAP & GOWN SERIES
PO Box 14
Penkridge
Stafford
Staffs
ST19 5SQ

Telephone:
0785 713560

MATHS VIDEOS

Cap & Gown Series have specialised in the making of Maths Videos for the last 7 years and are the U.K. market leaders in this field. Situated in rural Staffordshire, they are able to keep costs down to a minimum and yet provide a fast delivery service to all parts of the UK.

The Maths Videos prove extremely useful for students to catch up on work lost at school and means they can study in the privacy of their own home, saving the expense of a private tutor. The tapes are prepared by a chartered mathematician, Dr A.K. Hannaby.

Prices range from £52.50 for *National Curriculum Mathematics – Key stage 3* (a set of three tapes) to *A-Level Maths – The Agreed Common Core* (seven tapes) for £135.00.

Catalogue: *A5, Brochure, 8 pages, Colour, Free* Postal charges: *Varies with item* Delivery: *Royal Mail* Methods of Payment: *Cheque, Visa, Access / Mastercard*

Recordings

CD SELECTIONS
PO Box 1011
Southover
Tolpuddle
Dorchester
Dorset
DT2 7YG

Telephone:
0305 848725
Fax:
0305 848516

CDs, VIDEOS
This excellent catalogue is crammed full of CDs at bargain prices. Divided into classical, jazz, country and popular, it offers a good selection of releases from many different artists on a variety of labels.

Each CD is only given the briefest of descriptions and a price, which can be spectacularly low: there are Beethoven symphonies for £1.99! You therefore have to know what you want since there is no advice on which recording to buy. It might also be a good idea to buy several at a time since p+p is a fixed £2.35. There is also a smaller selection of videos.

Catalogue: *A4, Catalogue, 48 pages, Colour, £2.95* Postal charges: *£2.35* Delivery: *Royal Mail* Methods of Payment: *Cheque, Postal Order, Visa, Access / Mastercard*

GEMA RECORDS
PO Box 54
Reading
Berks
RG5 3SD

Telephone:
0635 867140
Fax:
0635 873019

CDs, TAPES, RECORDS AND VIDEOS
Built up over the last 20 years, the Gema Records catalogue offers an extensive range of CDs, LPs and cassettes. This includes thousands of deletions and hard to find titles so it can be an ideal place to track down that elusive album.

There is also a comprehensive range of back catalogues and inputs. Prices are good too, with budget CDs from £4.00, mid price from £7.00 and full price from £10.00. As for vinyl, back catalogue LPs start at £3.00 while full price albums are from £6.50.

Catalogue: *Quarterly, A4, Catalogue, 40 pages, B/W, Free* Postal charges: *Varies with item* Delivery: *Royal Mail, Parcelforce* Methods of Payment: *Cheque, Postal Order, Visa, Access / Mastercard*

INTEGRITY MUSIC
PO Box 101
Eastbourne
Sussex
BN21 3UX

Telephone:
0323 430033
Fax:
0323 411981

CHRISTIAN CASSETTES, CDs, VIDEOS AND SONGBOOKS
Integrity Music is one of the leading suppliers of high quality Christian music in the UK. They cover all tastes, from classical music to aerobics videos, from children's tapes to black gospel – and everything in-between!

The company has earned a reputation for its excellent range of family orientated products and friendly customer service department. Each item is backed by a 100% satisfaction guarantee. Cassettes are £7.99, videos £9.99, compact discs £10.99 and kid's videos £7.99.

Catalogue: *Bi-annually, A4, Brochure, 8 pages, Colour, Free* Postal charges: *Varies with item* Delivery: *Royal Mail Courier* Methods of Payment: *Cheque, Postal Order, Visa, Access / Mastercard*

Recordings

INTERNATIONAL VIDEO NETWORK LTD
107 Power Road
Chiswick
London
W4 5BR

Telephone:
081-742-2002
Fax:
081-995-7871

TRAVEL VIDEOS

Now you can not only shop from your armchair but also travel! The Video Travel Library includes several different series of films showing locations from around the world. 'Video Visits' concentrates on exotic, romantic, and interesting destinations, while 'Fodor's Travel Videos' are indispensable preparation for your own travel, with useful hints on language, currency, accommodation, transport and customs.

'Video Expeditions' combine stunning scenery from some of the world's most remote spots with adventure and action, while 'The Endangered World' series charts the progress of animal conservation in Africa. The catalogue also includes films on the underground railways of the world's great cities along with the Reader's Digest collection of travel and natural history videos. Tapes range from £9.99 to £12.99.

Catalogue: *Quarterly, 190 × 190 mm, Catalogue, 20 pages, Colour, Free* Postal charges: *Varies with item* Delivery: *Royal Mail* Methods of Payment: *Cheque, Visa, Access / Mastercard, Diners Club, American Express*

KEY MAIL ORDER
2 Cheam Road
Sutton
Surrey
SM1 1SR

Telephone:
081 676 0708
Fax:
081 659 3446

CDs AND LPs

Key Mail Order ship records and CDs from all parts of the world for those who are serious about their love of music. Many materials are distributed exclusively through Key Mail, including music by Tom Robinson. Many limited editions and promotional materials have also been acquired at very reasonable prices, from £4.99 to £44.99. There are also extensive sections covering the work of classic groups ranging from Abba to The Beatles.

The company also sells books covering some of the biggest groups the world has seen.

Catalogue: *A4, Leaflets, 2 pages, B/W, Free* Postal charges: *Varies with item* Delivery: *Royal Mail* Methods of Payment: *Cheque, Postal Order, Visa, Access / Mastercard*

Recordings

MAGPIE DIRECT
PO Box 25
Ashford
Middx
TW15 1XL

Telephone:
0784 251262
Fax:
0784 241168

ALL MUSIC FROM 50s, 60s AND 70s
Magpie has over ten years' experience of selling music by post. They cover ALL the British labels, both major and minor, who have released music from the 50s, 60s and 70s by the original artists.

They also offer a full search facility to customers for those hard to find CDs, LPs and cassettes. Finally, they publish an informative monthly magazine about music of the three above decades. CDs range in price from £3.99 to £90.00 for complete sets.

Catalogue: *Monthly, A4, Catalogue, 36 pages, B/W, Free* Postal charges: *Varies with item* Delivery: *Royal Mail* Methods of Payment: *Cheque, Postal Order, Visa, Access / Mastercard*

MR BENSON'S VIDEO COLLECTION
375 Harrow Road
London
W9 3BR

Telephone:
081 960 4868
Fax:
081 969 7291

VIDEO SALES
Mr Benson's portfolio contains many discounted video titles, as well as special offers involving the latest titles. Refreshingly, the list of titles doesn't seem polarised around mass-market fodder; there's a selection of World Cinema titles including four Czech classics from the mid-sixties: Milos Forman's *A Blonde in Love* (£15.99); Jiri Menzel's *Closely Observed Trains* (£15.99); Jan Kadar's *The Shop on the High Street* (£15.99) and Vera Chytilova's *Daisies* (£15.99).

If you're looking for something more down to earth, you can choose between *Heathers* (£8.99) with Winona Rider, or one of Jack Nicholson's best: *Five Easy Pieces* (£12.99). Then, of course, there's *Lethal Weapon* (£12.99) with Mel Gibson.

Catalogue: *Monthly, A4, Leaflets, Colour, Free* Postal charges: *£2.25* Delivery: *Royal Mail* Methods of Payment: *Cheque, Visa, Access / Mastercard, Postal Order*

MS EXPRESS RECORDS
7 Dahomey Road
Streatham
London
SW16 6NB

VINYL, CASSETTES AND CDs
MS Express Records grade their stock from 'mint condition' to only 'fair' and 'no picture cover'. Rarities include The Associates *Wild and Lonely* at £12.00; *Top Studio Demos* (£25.00) and the legendary *I'm a Cult Hero* (£35.00) by the Cure; and *Night Club Recording* (£35.00) by Prince.

If you're just looking for ordinary 7" singles, this is also the place. Everything by Carmel from £1.00 or slightly more; the complete works of Goodbye Mr Mackenzie for roughly the same.

Catalogue: *A5, Catalogue, 52 pages, B/W, Free* Postal charges: *Varies with item* Delivery: *Royal Mail* Methods of Payment: *Cheque, Postal Order*

Recordings

NATURAL HERBAL RESEARCH
34 Upton Lane
Forest Gate
London
E7 9LN

VIDEOS AND HEALTH PRODUCTS
An interesting mixture of products in this brochure – alongside John Wayne western classics (£3.25 per video) and a 24-piece model Japanese bullet trainset for £19.95, you'll find cod liver oil capsules (£11.90 for 540) and oriental ginseng (£9.90 for 180 tablets).

There's also a 'French style' body stocking for £11.95, temporary tattoos at £7.95 for 31 and Prostabrit tablets at £19.95 for 60 capsules.

Catalogue: *no info, A5, Brochure, 16 pages, Colour, Free* Postal charges: *Varies with item* Delivery: *Royal Mail* Methods of Payment: *Access / Mastercard, Visa, Cheque, Postal Order*

NEW WORLD CASSETTES
Paradise Farm
Westhall
Halesworth
Suffolk
IP19 8RH

Telephone:
0986 781682
Fax:
0986 781645

NEW AGE RECORDINGS
Produced by New World, the world's largest producer of 'Music for Relaxation', this exclusive collection of recordings aims to promote 'New Age' music. Many titles are available on both chrome cassette and CD. Popular titles include *Keeper of Dreams* by Philip Chapman in which 'pianos and strings combine to produce a calm inner stillness that refreshes the mind'. Featured musicians include Terry Oldfield (brother of Mike) whose titles include *Spirit of the Rainforest, Cascade* and *Reverence*; Medwyn Goodall and David Sun.

One series of recordings combines natural sounds and soothing subliminal suggestions with 3-D sound effects. All cassettes are priced at £6.95 and CDs at £10.95.

Catalogue: *A5, Catalogue, 32 pages, Colour, Free* Postal charges: *£1.95* Delivery: *Royal Mail* Methods of Payment: *Visa, Access / Mastercard, Cheque*

RECORD CORNER
27 Bedford Hill
Balham
London
SW12 9EX

Telephone:
081 673 1066
Fax:
081 675 6665

COUNTRY MUSIC
Record Corner offers a choice of almost 400 country hits, from the all-time greats to the current best sellers. CDs and singles of some of the best names are available at competitive prices, with Steve Goodman's *USA One Way* at £12.90, and Randy Travis's *Greatest Hits* for £10.00. There is a complete list of songs accompanying every album and single included.

The catalogue provides access to both imports and the best British music, and gives details of other magazines for country music lovers in this country so that you can catch your favourite singer live.

Catalogue: *A4, Brochure, 16 pages, B/W, Free* Postal charges: *Varies with item* Delivery: *Royal Mail* Methods of Payment: *Cheque, Postal Order, Visa, Access / Mastercard*

Recordings

SOUND IDEAS
117 Athelstan Road
Southampton
SO2 4DG

Telephone:
0703 333405

AUDIO TAPES FOR EDUCATION AND IMPROVEMENT
Whether you want to stop smoking or biting your nails or to take control of a stressful life, there are audio tapes to help you.

The self-hypnosis tapes are put together by British therapists and available for £8.99. Subliminal versions of the tapes are also available for £14.99. Sound Ideas also produce a range of relaxation tapes for your favourite pets at £5.99 each.

There are also ten tapes to help your children learn everything from multiplication tables to French, all following the National Curriculum. Each tape costs £4.99 but the set is available for £29.99.

Catalogue: *A4 and A5, Leaflets, 5 pages, B/W, Free* Postal charges: *Varies with item* Delivery: *Royal Mail* Methods of Payment: *Cheque, Postal Order, Visa, Access / Mastercard*

STORYLINE
20 Carrbrook Crescent
Stalybridge
Cheshire
SK15 3LP

Telephone:
0457 834406

CASSETTE LENDING LIBRARY
Storyline are a books on tape lending library – a brilliant idea for anyone who travels a lot by car. Stories are read by stars like Charles Dance, David Attenborough and Edward Woodward. You can listen to Ben Kingsley read *A Passage to India* or Sir John Geilgud reading from *Brideshead Revisited*. Membership costs £8.00 for a year or £22.00 for life. After that, tapes cost just 75p with an average hire charge of £3.00.

The stock isn't limited to fiction. There's *In Search of The Trojan War* by Michael Wood: an account of his search for the lost city of Troy; or *The White Nile*, by Alan Moorehead: the story of Burton and Spekes journey to discover the source of the Nile.

Catalogue: *A5, Catalogue, 50, B/W, Free* Postal charges: *Varies with item* Delivery: *Royal Mail* Methods of Payment: *Cheque, Postal Order*

TADPOLE LANE PRODUCTIONS LTD
19 St Thomas Street
Winchester
Hants
SO23 9HJ

Telephone:
0962 865454
Fax:
0962 856752

VIDEOS
Over the last few years, Tadpole has earned a unique reputation for producing high quality video programmes featuring the best of British Heritage: great properties of the National Trust; the houses and gardens of great stately homes like Chatsworth, Castle Howard and Woburn Abbey; and famous gardens like Kew, Wisley and Blenheim Palace. Other places featured include Warwick Castle, Beaulieu, Stourhead, St Michael's Mount,

Recordings

Chartwell, Powys Castle, Ness Gardens and Fountains Abbey. They also produce a range of unusual and often amusing travel videos, featuring places as far apart a Malawi and the West Indies.

Treasures of the Trust costs £13.95; *Treasure Gardens* with Alan Titchmarsh costs £12.95 and *The Perfect English Village* costs £9.95.

Catalogue: *Annually, Third A4, Catalogue, 5 pages, Colour, Free* Postal charges: *£1.95* Delivery: *Royal Mail* Methods of Payment: *Cheque, Visa, Access / Mastercard, Postal Order, COD*

TAPEWORM
10 Barley Mow Passage
London
W4 4PH

Telephone:
081 994 6477

CASSETTES FOR CHILDREN

Tapeworm is the brainchild of two sisters-in-law: a company specialising in children's stories on cassette. There are over 160 titles to choose from, a boon for long car journeys, the sick room or any parent who finally tires of retelling little Johnnie's favourite story!

The selection includes fairy stories, stories for the very young, short stories for the four to seven group and classics of children's literature along with some music and Christmas specials. They also stock a smaller selection of videos. Prices range from £3.50 to £11.00.

Catalogue: *A5, Catalogue, 16, B/W, Free* Postal charges: *Free* Delivery: *Royal Mail* Methods of Payment: *Cheque*

THE CLASSIC PICTURES COLLECTION
Studio 50
Shepperton Film Studios
Studios Road
Shepperton
Middlesex
TW17 0QD

Telephone:
0932 572017

CLASSIC FILMS

This is a small, well-produced catalogue which features classic and more modern films. It is divided into various sections: War in the Air (*Colditz*, £9.99; *On A Wing and A Prayer*); A Year to Remember (*60 Pathe News Films from 1930–1993* at £10.99 each); Classic Comedy (*The Golden Years of British Comedy 1940s*, £10.99; *Peter Sellers – Very Best Of*, £10.99); War File (*Vietnam, The Chopper War*, £10.99; *Fighter Aces*, £10.99); Children (*Paul McCartney's Rupert and the Frog Song*, £4.99); Modern Music (*Genesis Videos*, £9.99; *James Brown – Live in London*, £9.99); Ballet and Opera (*Death in Venice*, £14.99); and Stand Up Comedy (*Victoria Wood – Sold Out Live*, £12.99; *Billy Connolly – An Audience With*, £10.99); Special Interest (*Kama Sutra*, £12.99); and Sport and Fitness (*Cindy Crawford – The Next Challenge Workout*, £12.99; *The World's Greatest Goals*, £9.99).

Catalogue: *Quarterly, A5, Catalogue, 20 pages, Colour and B/W, Free* Postal charges: *£1.00* Delivery: *Royal Mail* Methods of Payment: *Cheque, Postal Order, Visa, Access / Mastercard*

Recordings

THE FRENCH VIDEO COMPANY
26 Addison Place
London
W11 4RJ

Telephone:
071 603 4690
Fax:
071 602 1922

FRENCH VIDEOS
The French Video Company distributes a small range of cartoons, films and games on VHS which are ideal for parents whose children are learning French.

Bleu, l'enfant de la Terre (*Bleu, Child of the Earth*) for over four year olds are animated films of a sensitive and charming science fiction story. There are two cassettes which can be bought individually. *Le Gummi* is a Walt Disney cartoon featuring the Gummi bears and their escapades. *Le secret du lac* (*The Secret of the Lake*) for eight and over is an adventure film starring Andy Thomas, the hero of *ET*.

They also sell 'Language Lotto', a game to play with your children which allows them to learn French while having fun. Prices start at £14.75.

Catalogue: *A4, Leaflets, 2 pages, B/W, Free* Postal charges: *£2.00* Delivery: *Royal Mail* Methods of Payment: *Cheque, Postal Order*

TRAVELLERS TALES
Great Weddington Ash
Canterbury
Kent
CT3 2AR

Telephone:
0304 812531

SPOKEN WORD CASSETTES
Travellers Tales produce spoken word versions of more than 2,000 book titles. Among their distinguished narrators are Timothy West, Prunella Scales and Nigel Havers. The service is, in fact, that of a library. In order to join, you have to pay either £20.00 for a year or £100.00 for life. Anyone over eighteen with a bank account is eligible to join; those under eighteen can join with the permission and guarantee of their parent or guardian.

Once a member, you can select a title from their autobiography/biography/memoirs section. There's Jilly Cooper's *The Common Years* read by Norma West and Dirk Bogarde's *A Particular Friendship* read by Bogarde, himself. General fiction includes Paul Theroux's *The Consul's File* read by Ed Bishop and Evelyn Waugh's *Brideshead Revisited* read by Jeremy Irons.

Catalogue: *A5, Catalogue, 94 pages, B/W, Free* Postal charges: *Varies with item* Delivery: *Royal Mail* Methods of Payment: *Cheque, Visa, Access / Mastercard*

Recordings

WILDSOUNDS
PO Box 9
Holt
Norfolk
NR25 7AW

Telephone:
0263 741100
Fax:
0263 741100

RECORDINGS OF WILDLIFE
With over 60 titles to choose from Wildsounds is a leading supplier of wildlife sound recordings, the perfect gift for birdwatchers, naturalists and gardeners.

The four volume pack *All the Bird Songs of Britain and Europe* features over 415 species on cassette, all of which are announced beforehand in English for £29.95. The CD set has 396 species, unannounced but indexed by track number for £49.95.

Other titles include *Sound through the Seasons*, a sound guide to the insects, amphibians, birds and large mammals of Western Europe; *Frogs and Toads*, the calls of twenty European species, each announced; and *Lifesong*, the amazing sounds of threatened birds from around the world.

Catalogue: *Annually, A4, Catalogue, 6 pages, B/W, Free* Postal charges: *Varies with item* Delivery: *Royal Mail* Methods of Payment: *Cheque, Postal Order, Visa, Access / Mastercard*

WILLIAM CLERK PRODUCTIONS
2 Manor House
Bringhurst
Market Harborough
Leics
LE16 8RJ

Telephone:
0536 771786

INSTRUCTIONAL VIDEOS
No catalogue – just a piece of paper detailing the six educational videos which this small company produces. These are on a variety of interesting subjects and cost from £10.99 to £19.99. The titles are: *Understanding Falconry*, *Understanding Stencilling*, *Breeding Birds of Prey*, *Owls*, *Living with Flowers* and *Flowers for Christmas*. Not the sort of thing available at your local video store!

Catalogue: *Third A4, Leaflet, 1 page, B/W, Free* Postal charges: *£2.00* Delivery: *Royal Mail* Methods of Payment: *Cheque*

WINDOWS MAIL ORDER
1–7 Central Arcade
Newcastle upon Tyne
NE1 5BP

Telephone:
091 232 8765

CLASSICAL RECORDS, TAPES, CDs AND SHEET MUSIC
With one of the most extensive collections of classical recordings and sheet music in the country, Windows can provide any recording for musicians or enthusiasts and offer a 'four for the price of three' special.

CDs, records and tapes from names such as Decca, Philips and Deutsche Grammophon are available from £12.99. Windows also provide a selection of folk music, including traditional Northumbrian music and a range of musical instruments, sheet music and video tapes dealing with all aspects of music.

Catalogue: *Quarterly, A4, Brochure, 7 pages, B/W, Free* Postal charges: *Varies with item* Delivery: *Royal Mail* Methods of Payment: *Postal Order, Visa, Access / Mastercard Cheque*

Software

ADDISON WESLEY PUBLISHERS LTD
Finchampstead Road
Wokingham
Berks
RG11 2NZ

Telephone:
0734 794000
Fax:
0734 794035

SOFTWARE AND BOOKS
The Complete Computing Catalogue is a comprehensive source for Addison-Wesley's computer books and software. Most are available from bookshops but you can also order direct. The books cover all levels of ability as well as many different platforms such as IBM, DOS, Windows and Mac.

As well as introductory books there are titles for the advanced user and computer science enthusiast. Each publication is given a full description and as a result the catalogue is fun to browse through. There are special sections of the cutting edge technologies of CD-ROM, virtual reality and hypermedia. Prices vary but as with all computer books are quite high.

Catalogue: *A4, Catalogue, 112 pages, B/W, Free* Postal charges: *Free* Delivery: *Royal Mail* Methods of Payment: *Cheque, Visa, Access / Mastercard, American Express, Diners Club*

ALDUS EUROPE LTD
Aldus House
West One Business Park
5 Mid New Cutlins
Edinburgh
EH11 4DU

Telephone:
031 453 2211
Fax:
031 453 4422

SOFTWARE
One of the foremost producers of desktop publishing software, Aldus have dressed their brochure up as an informative magazine. However cosmetic the exercise, many of the articles are well-written, informative and cleverly illustrated. In between they feature the software they'd like you to buy!

Aldus produce a variety of highly regarded programmes such as PageMaker (£695.00), Freehand, (£450.00), Persuasion (£350.00) and Fetch (£195.00). Together these would come to some £1690.00 but if ordered as a package from this catalogue they are just £995.00. Quite a saving though it might also be worth checking computer magazines.

Catalogue: *A4, Catalogue, 36 pages, Colour, Free* Postal charges: *Free* Delivery: *Royal Mail* Methods of Payment: *Cheque, Postal Order, Visa, Access / Mastercard*

AVP SOFTWARE
School Hill Centre
Chepstow
Gwent
NP6 5PH

Telephone:
0291 625439
Fax:
0291 629671

EDUCATIONAL SOFTWARE
AVP has been publishing educational resources since 1969 and is now the leading supplier of software for UK schools. They produce an extensive range of catalogues for primary and secondary schools both on specific subjects and computers.

AVP also produces catalogues designed for the home user who is looking for genuine educational software. This doesn't mean just games, but programs that will take a child right through the National Curriculum to GCSE. There are also programs for

Software

teaching yourself a language and learning about diet and health, computer art or graphics, music and desktop publishing along with reference works.

Noddy's Playtime for Early Learning on IBM format is £25.99, *ADI Junior Reading 4/5 Years* £19.99, *Micro French* £28.20, *Mavis Beacon Teaches Typing* £35.99 and *Encarta* 1994 a CD-ROM encyclopaedia £99.00.

Catalogue: *5 a year, A4, Catalogue & Brochure, 204 pages, Colour, Free* Postal charges: *Varies with item* Delivery: *Royal Mail, Parcelforce* Methods of Payment: *Cheque, Postal Order, Visa, Access / Mastercard*

COMPUTERMATE SUPPLIES
The Wheel
Robin Way
Cuffley
Hertfordshire
EN6 4QB

Telephone:
0707 875757
Fax:
0707 875513

PC SOFTWARE

Computermate sell software for IBM PCs and compatibles. This is available on both floppies and CD-ROM. Their simple catalogue is nevertheless well laid out and each product is given a useful description.

There are sections on leisure (mostly games), classroom, office, CD player and bookshelf. They also sell some hardware, such as discs, joysticks and soundcards. However, they do not stock computers themselves. They also offer a useful up-date service which keeps you abreast of the latest developments and releases.

Catalogue: *A5, Catalogue, 56 pages, B/W, Free* Postal charges: *Varies with item* Delivery: *Royal Mail* Methods of Payment: *Visa, Access / Mastercard, Cheque, Postal Order*

CONNECT SOFTWARE
3 Flanchford Road
London
W12 9ND

Telephone:
081 743 9792
Fax:
081 743 8073

ACCOUNTING SOFTWARE

Connect Software give detailed information on their Office Manager (£58.89) package. They claim this clever piece of accounting software will 'help you deal quickly and efficiently with all your everyday office paperwork' and this seems soundly based, given the wealth of features mentioned. The database comprises 1000 separate lists, each of which can hold up to 500 records, with 20 fields for each record.

The Money Manager feature can be used on its own to handle VAT, budgets, multiple currencies and reports. As accounting programs go, it looks easy to use and quick to set up.

Catalogue: *A4, Leaflets, 8 pages, Colour and B/W, Free* Postal charges: *Free* Delivery: *Royal Mail* Methods of Payment: *Visa, Access / Mastercard, Cheque, American Express*

Software

EASTERN SOFTWARE PUBLISHING LTD
Suite 2
Cowdra Centre House
Cowdray Avenue
Colchester
C01 1GF

Telephone:
0206 44456
Fax:
0206 763313

BUSINESS SOFTWARE
Eastern Software offer a solid range of business software for a broad range of applications. They guarantee delivery within 24 hours and offer a full technical support service.

Their 'Success' program (£99.00) will help you write a business plan or you can try to forecast the future with 'Forecast Pro' (£495.00). A series of tutorial programs from £69.00 tackle the mysteries of Microsoft Excel, the intricacies of Lotus 1-2-3 and the vagaries of Microsoft Windows.

For the practically minded, architectural drawing and space planning can be achieved using 'Floorplan Plus' at £79.00 for the DOS version and £99.00 for Windows.

Catalogue: *A4, Catalogue, 24 pages, Colour, Free* Postal charges: £10.50 Delivery: *Courier* Methods of Payment: *Cheque*

GUILDSOFT LTD
The Computer Complex
City Business Park
Stoke
Plymouth
Devon
PL3 4BB

Telephone:
0752-606200
Fax:
0752 606174

COMPUTER SOFTWARE
Guildsoft deal in a variety of specialist, relatively unusual software for the home and business markets. Their Windows/Graphics selection also offers a selection of design and illustration programs. Unlike some of the larger distributors, they seem keen to invite enquiries regarding the suitability of a product.

Their 'Learn to Speak' program (£69.00) is a complete language course of 36 lessons, including grammar, pronunciation and interaction with 5 native speakers. Or you can let off steam with their 3-D Dinosaur adventure (CD-Rom: £59.95; 3.5" disk: £49.95). Venture into a virtual reality dinosaur theme park; create your own dinosaur or pit your wits against a mad scientist to race through a time-tunnel maze and save the dinosaurs before a comet hits the earth.

Catalogue: *A5, Catalogue, 36 pages, B/W, Free* Postal charges: £5.00 Delivery: *Courier* Methods of Payment: *Visa, Access / Mastercard, American Express, Cheque*

KEYBOARDS DIRECT
PO Box 222
Plymouth
Devon
PL1 1BG

Telephone:
0345 626051
Fax:
0752 347598

KEYBOARD INSTRUMENTS AND SOFTWARE
Keyboards Direct specialises in musical instruments from Yamaha, Roland, Casio and Technics. Models include portable keyboards, organs, clavinova and digital pianos, synths and hi-tech. They also stock a full range of software and accessories.

All equipment is supported by expert before and after sales assistance and user advice from the exclusive KD 'HelpLine Studio'. Prices are very keen

Sports

and include free delivery, which seems a bargain.

Portable keyboards range in price from just £65.00 for the Yamaha PSS21 to £1399.00 for the PSR5700. The top selling Yamaha Clavinova digital piano CLP123 is just £1699.00, some £300 off the retail price.

Catalogue: *3 a year, A4, Catalogue, 16 pages, Colour, Free* Postal charges: *Varies with item* Delivery: *Parcelforce* Methods of Payment: *Cheque, Postal Order, Visa, Access / Mastercard, American Express*

RICKITT EDUCATIONAL MEDIA
Ilton
Ilminster
Somerset
TA19 9HS

Telephone:
0460 57152
Fax:
0460 53176

EDUCATIONAL SOFTWARE.
Rickitt's catalogue features the best educational programs from all the leading software houses. They support all the important platforms, including Archimedes A3000 and A5000, IBM PC, Nimbus BBC, Amiga, Amstrad, Atari and Apple.

The catalogue is well arranged with programs listed by subject (such as English language, history or music) and within that by age group. Each program is given a full, unbiased description so you really can make an informed choice. They also sell unusual satellite maps of the UK, Europe and the world as well as some computer accessories.

Catalogue: *A4, Catalogue, 56 pages, Colour, Free* Postal charges: *Varies with item* Delivery: *Royal Mail* Methods of Payment: *Cheque, Access / Mastercard, Visa*

PARKES WESTON SUPPLIES LTD
Unit 2A Parkway Estate
St Modwen Road
Plymouth
Devon
PL6 8LH

Telephone:
0752 672226
Fax:
0752 667070

SPORTS
Parkes Weston Supplies distribute Snowbee commercial and sport fishing equipment. As well as accessories ranging from chest waders to polarised fishing sunglasses, there is also a selection of Snowbee fishing equipment, lure kits, nets and so on.

The catalogue comes in two styles: a full colour set of six A4 leaflets stapled together with a four page price list, or a 12-page black and white A5 version, but the illustrations in the latter are poor black and white reproductions of the individual leaflets. The A5 catalogue contains some rods (absent from the leaflets), but there is no order form although the prices are included.

Catalogue: *A4, Catalogue, 16 pages, Colour, Free* Postal charges: *Free* Delivery: *Royal Mail* Methods of Payment: *Cheque, Postal Order, COD*

Sports Equipment

MICHAEL EVANS & CO
Unit 1
Little Saxbys Farm
Cowden
Kent
TN8 7DX

Telephone:
0342 850755
Fax:
0342 850926

RODS AND FLY LINES

Michael Evans has obviously made his passion into his business, sharing his love of game angling and fly fishing with an expanding band of customers. With a collection of rods, lines, weights and videos all designed to improve your angling skills the present collection of products is not large, but it is well considered.

Mr Evans provides an honest and helpful explanation with each range, which illustrates his experience and knowledge, and a wider commentary to lead the novice through the bewildering range of materials. Prices start at £14.99 for a video to £395.00 for a 15' Speycatcher rod.

Catalogue: *A4, Leaflets, 10 pages, B/W, Free* Postal charges: *Varies with item* Delivery: *Royal Mail* Methods of Payment: *Cheque, Postal Order, Visa, Access / Mastercard*

PETWORTH HOUSE
Polesdon Lane
Ripley
Woking
Surrey
GU23 6LR

Telephone:
0483 225222

KEEP-FIT EQUIPMENT

Petworth House provide a broad and exclusive range of sporting, leisure and fitness equipment. It is now the largest retailer in Great Britain, serving over half a million customers.

Their new exercise bike costs £299.00. Going the whole hog, a home gym is available for only £249.99. It includes a possible 150lb liftweight.

Requiring much less effort is their range of snooker tables. A 6' × 3'6" costs £199.99; a 7' × 3'6" costs £299.99. All models fold neatly away, are mahogany finished and have pro cushions.

Catalogue: *A4, Leaflets, Colour and B/W, Free* Postal charges: *Varies with item* Delivery: *Royal Mail In-house delivery* Methods of Payment: *Cheque, Postal Order, Visa, Access / Mastercard*

PORTSMOUTH GOLF CENTRE
Great Salterns Golf Course
Burrfields Road
Portsmouth
PO3 5HH

Telephone:
0705 699519

GOLFING ACCESSORIES

Golf is one of the most popular hobbies in this country and this catalogue can help anyone who wants to update their equipment or get the right ranges to help them on the fairways. The Golf Centre stocks all major brands of clubs, balls and bags to improve your game, and the smartest shirts and shoes to improve your look – for example, Hi-Tec golf shoes at £55.00.

Many of the prices found here are competitive, with a Macgregor Wentworth golf bag at £34.99 and a dozen Dunlop balls for £7.99.

Catalogue: *Quarterly, A3, Brochure, 4 pages, Colour, Free* Postal charges: *Varies with item* Delivery: *Royal Mail* Methods of Payment: *Cheque, Access / Mastercard, Visa*

Sports Equipment (inc. Cycles)

3-D CRICKET
PO Box 300
The Runnings
Kingsditch Trading Estate
Cheltenham
Glos
GL51 9NJ

Telephone:
0242 241819
Fax:
0242 222994

CRICKET CLOTHES AND EQUIPMENT
Competitively-priced specialist mail order company supplying cricket clubs and private individuals in the UK and over 40 countries worldwide.

They have a vast stocklist that includes all the major manufacturers of cricket equipment from bats, balls, whites and sweaters (all sizes) to outdoor nets and matting.

Nearly everything is sold at significantly less than the RRP and when a bat can cost up to £170.00 there are serious savings to be made.

Catalogue: *A4, Catalogue, 44 pages, Colour, Free* Postal charges: *£4.00* Delivery: *Parcelforce, Royal Mail* Methods of Payment: *Cheque, Visa, Access / Mastercard*

ALLEGRO BAGS LTD
19 Triangle
Sowerby Bridge
HaliFax:
HX6 3NE

Telephone:
0422 834668
Fax:
0422 834669

CUSTOMISED SPORTS BAGS
Allegro Bags manufacture promotional merchandise – bags – for awareness marketing. Their range is considerable and includes a large capacity holdall with handles lifted on to the shoulder of the bag in order for an advertising slogan to be uninterrupted. It also features a detachable shoulder strap, two end pockets and baseboard all from £6.85 per item for a quantity of 100.

Other bags in Allegro's range, and fully illustrated in their brochure, include a nylon or polyurethane wrist bag which is ideal for people on the move, and see-through bags using clear PVC to allow the customer's product clear visibility from the outside.

Catalogue: *A4, Leaflets, 4 pages, Colour, Free* Postal charges: *Varies with item* Delivery: *Royal Mail* Methods of Payment: *Cheque*

BIKE CITY LTD
Tranquility House
1 Tranquility
Crossgates
Leeds
W Yorks
LS15 8QU

Telephone:
0532 326600

CYCLES & ACCESSORIES
Bike City sell a good selection of bicycles for gents, ladies and children. Adult cycles, such as the gents Topeka with a 12 speed Shimano gearset, cantilever brakes and alloy rims start at £99.99. A ladies model, the Masquerade with 5 speed Shimano indexed gear set and again alloy wheel rims is around the same price. Boy's and girl's cycles start at £69.99.

The company also sells a range of accessories including racks. Their intro pack consists of a helmet, lights and lock and sells for £34.99.

Catalogue: *2, A5, Brochure, 10 pages, Colour, Free* Postal charges: *Varies with item* Delivery: *Data Express, Parcelforce* Methods of Payment: *Cheque, Postal Order, Stage Payments, Visa, Access / Mastercard*

Sports Equipment (inc. Cycles)

BURGESS VIDEO GROUP
Unit 18
Industrial Estate
Brecon
Powys
Wales
LD3 8LA

Telephone:
0874 624448
Fax:
0874 625889

FISHING VIDEOS AND FISHING EQUIPMENT
This interesting company sells fishing videos for all different levels. Their colourful brochure gives full details of over 70 different titles. All are in VHS PAL format (i.e. for the British market) but they can also be ordered in any European format (SECAM etc.)

The videos are divided into sections on trout fishing, salmon and steelhead fly fishing, saltwater fly fishing, basic fly fishing, fly tying and fly casting. Each is given a brief description and all feature experts in the field.

Prices vary but start at around £6.99 rising to £14.99.

Catalogue: *A5, Brochure, 8 pages, Colour, Free* Postal charges: *Varies with item* Delivery: *Royal Mail Courier* Methods of Payment: *Cheque, Visa, Access / Mastercard*

CAPTAIN O M WATTS
49 Albemarle Street
Piccadilly
London
W1X 3FE

Telephone:
071 493 4633
Fax:
071 495 0755

YACHTING GOODS
This unusual catalogue caters for yachtsmen. Illustrated in colour, it provides specialist equipment and accessories for the serious yachting enthusiast. At one end of the spectrum there are electronic navigational instruments, such as the map and chart plotter at £1100.00, and at the other flashlights at £25.95.

Other items include protective sailing wear, videos, books, maps, binoculars, compasses and a small range of reproduction and antique collectable items and gifts. Captain Watts also has a shop in Piccadilly, which sells similar goods.

Catalogue: *Quarterly, 150mm × 245mm, Leaflet, 8 pages, Colour, Free* Postal charges: *Varies with item* Delivery: *Royal Mail* Methods of Payment: *Cheque, Postal Order, Visa, Access / Mastercard*

GEOFFREY BUTLER CYCLES
15 South End
Croydon
Surrey
CR0 1BE

Telephone:
081 688 5094
Fax:
081 680 2068

BIKES AND ACCESSORIES
Geoffrey Butler is of course one of the great names in bicycles. They specialise in racing bikes and have a world-wide reputation. Their pamphlet is geared towards the knowledgeable cyclist; few pictures and extensive listings mean you really have to know what you want. Makes and measurements are, however, listed under easy-to-spot headings: 'Race Frames'; 'Shoe Plates'; 'Thermal Jackets' to name but a few.

There are several special offers and the machines themselves are often marked at a discount, for example the Rockhopper FS is just £489.99 – a £210.00 saving on the RRP.

Sports Equipment (inc. Cycles)

HAMILTON & TUCKER BILLIARD CO
Park Lane
Knebworth
Herts
SG3 6PG

Telephone:
0438 811995
Fax:
0438 814939

Catalogue: *A4, Catalogue, 8 pages, Colour, Free* Postal charges: *Varies with item* Delivery: *Courier, Royal Mail* Methods of Payment: *Cheque, Visa, Access / Mastercard, Postal Order*

BILLIARD TABLES
This interesting company sells reproduction billiard tables. Following Victorian and Edwardian designs, the tables are beautifully hand crafted from oak, mahogany and walnut. There are a great many models to choose from, including 'convertibles' which can double up as dining tables, and of course they come in various sizes up to full size.

There is an excellent range of complementary accessories such as marker boards, cues and cue racks. Prices are not cheap but you wouldn't expect them to be for this quality. Full sized tables can be anything from £3000 to £12,000, although you can get a smaller one from just £1450.

Catalogue: *A4, Catalogue, 12 pages, Colour, Free* Postal charges: *Varies with item* Delivery: *In-house delivery* Methods of Payment: *Cheque*

MAYBURY SPORTS
139 Northwood Road
Thornton Heath
Surrey
CR7 8HX

Telephone:
081 653 5440
Fax:
081 771 3497

NETBALL EQUIPMENT
This is a refreshingly different sports catalogue, in that it focuses on a sport traditionally played by women only – netball. Maybury supplies everything that is needed for the sport from clothes through nets to balls.

Netball skirts are available in a variety of styles, including tartan kilts, and in different lengths. Colour choice is vast and sizing flexible enough to kit out the thinnest to the stoutest of players. Skirts sell for between £7.95 and £19.00.

Other products include sweatshirts, polo shirts and blouses, knickers and shorts, socks, waterproof jackets, windsuits, netball shoes and a referee's whistle.

Catalogue: *A4, Catalogue, 4 pages, Colour, Free* Postal charges: *£2.60* Delivery: *Royal Mail* Methods of Payment: *Cheque, Postal Order, Visa, Access / Mastercard*

Sports Equipment (inc. Cycles)

MICHAEL LAZARUS ASSOCIATES
242/244 St John Street
London
EC1V 4PH

Telephone:
071 250 3988
Fax:
071 608 0370

KITES

The beauty of the Ferrari Sky Ram Kite is not only that it looks good and is great fun to fly, but that you can fly it – first time – even if you have never flown a kite before. The Ferrari has no sticks or spars so it is safe to fly, even in crowded places; it can be folded into your pocket and being made from Ripstop nylon it is practically indestructible.

The Ferrari Sky Blade Stunt Kite is a new revolutionary 'swinging' kite designed to fly in any wind, from the lightest breeze to gale force strength. Experts will delight in its fingertip control for the most complicated aerobatics and beginners with the ease in which they can learn to fly a stunt kite.

Catalogue: *A4 & A5, Brochure, 1 page, Colour, Free* Postal charges: *Varies with item* Delivery: *Royal Mail* Methods of Payment: *Cheque, Postal Order, Visa, Access / Mastercard*

MULLARKEY & SONS
184–185 Waterloo Street
Burton-on-Trent
Staffordshire
DE14 2NH

Telephone:
0283 38375

FISHING EQUIPMENT

Mullarkey & Sons produce a vast range of fishing tackle and accessories for the angler. Their tackle guide runs to over 160 pages crammed full of the latest in equipment. It carries poles, whips, match rods, coarse rods, carp rods, specimen rods, feeder rods, fly rods and more, plus reels, multipliers, fly lines, spinners, nets and tackle boxes.

The Shakespeare luggage collection includes holdalls, carryalls, net bags and reel cases. Recently introduced is the 'Bankshack Bivvy' which makes umbrellas with overwraps seem like hard work to erect. The most portable bivvy on the market it weighs less than 5kg and costs £150.00.

Catalogue: *A5, Catalogue, 163 pages, Colour, £1.00 refundable* Postal charges: *Varies with item* Delivery: *Royal Mail Courier, Parcelforce* Methods of Payment: *Cheque, Postal Order, Visa, Access / Mastercard, American Express*

PELICAN FISHING TACKLE
Bridge House Mills
Haworth
Nr Keighley
West Yorkshire
BD22 8PA

Telephone:
0535 43899

FISHING TACKLE

Pelican Fishing Tackle produce a range of equipment and accessories for the angling enthusiast. The catalogue contains everything from 'Newprene socks' – ideal for wear in gumboots or waders for £9.90, through 'Trout cufflinks' in pewter at £7.00 per pair to camera gadget bags at £16.50 and an ingenious thermometer which can be used to measure the rise or fall in water levels at £7.95.

For the home there are a range of framed salmon

Sports Equipment (inc. Cycles)

flies starting at £6.95 and rod-holders for the car to avoid breakage during closing or opening doors at £12.50.

Catalogue: *A5, Catalogue, 12 pages, B/W, Free* Postal charges: *Free* Delivery: *Royal Mail* Methods of Payment: *Cheque, Postal Order*

PENDLE ENGINEERING
Unit 6
Pendle Industrial Estate
Southfield Street
Nelson
Lancs
BB9 0LD

Telephone:
0282 699555
Fax:
0282 612904

COMPREHENSIVE RANGE OF CYCLE CARRIERS
Pendle Engineering offers a comprehensive range of cycle carriers. The range accommodates most vehicles from a typical small hatchback to off-the-road four wheel drives.

Their range of tow bar mounted racks provide an extremely simple yet strong method of transporting cycles, with the added advantage of being able to tow at the same time. Prices range from £69.00 to £97.00.

The strap-on-rack is designed for vehicles without a tow bar, it will safely carry three cycles, and fits most cars. Price £59.99.

As an added safety feature Pendle recommend the use of an auxiliary lighting unit if the cycles being carried obscure the rear lights or number plate. Price £30.00.

Catalogue: *Annually, A4, Brochure, 4 pages, Colour, Free* Postal charges: *£7.50* Delivery: *Parcelforce Greenline* Methods of Payment: *Cheque, Visa, Access / Mastercard*

ROBIN HOOD GOLF CENTRE
200–202 Robin Hood Lane
Hall Green
Birmingham

Telephone:
021 778 4161

GOLF TROPHIES
Robin Hood provide one of the most extensive ranges of golf trophies in the country. You can buy shields, plaques, cups, tankards, bowls or any number of small novelty trophies.

Pewter figurines include a caddy, a gentleman and a lady each at £33.50. There are also hand painted model golf sets: 'Golf Bag Against a Fence' costs £29.95; 'Free Standing Golf Bag' costs £28.25; and a 'Golf Bag with Trolley' costs £27.15.

Catalogue: *A4, Catalogue, 12, Colour, Free* Postal charges: *Varies with item* Delivery: *Royal Mail* Methods of Payment: *Cheque, Postal Order, Visa, Access / Mastercard, American Express, Diners Club*

Sports Equipment (inc. Cycles)

SCOTTS OF NORTHWICH
185–187 Witton Street
Northwich
Cheshire
CW9 5LP

Telephone:
0606 46543
Fax:
0606 330551

FISHING TACKLE
Scotts of Northwich is a supplier of angling equipment and accessories. Their catalogue features an impressive range of fishing poles and rods including designs by Daiwa and Shimano. At the top end of the range are Shakespeare poles available in their new modulus carbon Put-Over, starting at £450.00. Leger rods in all brands start at under £50.00 while reels start at under £20.00.

Accessories include the essential brolley (starting at £23.95), boxes, bank sticks, tackle items, nets, feeders and floats. There are of course a large range of hooks by such makers as Tubertin and Kamasan.

Catalogue: *A4, Catalogue, 56 pages, B/W, Free* Postal charges: *Varies with item* Delivery: *Royal Mail* Methods of Payment: *Cheque, Postal Order, Visa, Access / Mastercard*

SIMPSON'S OF TURNFORD
Nunsbury Drive
Turnford
Broxbourne
Herts
EN10 6AQ

Telephone:
0992 468799
Fax:
0992 466227

ANGLING PRODUCTS
The aim of the Simpson's guide is to pre-select a range of quality angling equipment from among the plethora of items available today. It certainly seems useful to flick through a limited range of products than to meet the myriad options head on. Substantial discounts are offered in proportion to the extent previous purchases from Simpson's 'Angling Guidelines' have been made.

The Eclipse T400-IMX rod is featured preferentially. Prices range from £184.20 for the 'Multi-range' model to £193.00 for the 'Extreme Range' version.

Catalogue: *Annually, A4, Brochure, 10 pages, Colour and B/W, Free* Postal charges: *Varies with item* Delivery: *Securicor delivery available, Royal Mail* Methods of Payment: *Cheque, Visa, Access / Mastercard*

SMART TART CYCLES
4 Foulds Terrace
Bingley W Yorks
BD16 4LZ

Telephone:
0274 511570
Fax:
0274 510736

SPECIALISED CLOTHING AND GOODS FOR CYCLE ENTHUSIASTS
This unique company supplies the cycling needs of the shorter person, mostly female. They produce the 'only mountain bike for small folks', which has a 13" frame. Specially made by a UK frame builder, it is constructed from Reynolds 7 tubing and is a high quality machine. It comes in several models ranging in weight and therefore price. They start at £400.00 and go up to £510.00.

Smart Tarts also sell cycling clothes in small sizes, made by Precision and Cannondale. A six panel pair

Sports Equipment (inc. Cycles)

of shorts is £39.95, Trek jerseys and shorts £35 to £40 and cycling shoes between £60 and £110.

Catalogue: *A4, Leaflets, 8, B/W, Free* Postal charges: *Varies with item* Delivery: *Royal Mail* Methods of Payment: *Postal Order, Cheque*

SUPERNOVA CYCLES LIMITED
Yarm Road
Industrial Estate
Darlington
County Durham
DL1 4XX

Telephone:
0325 469 181
Fax:
0325 381 386

BICYCLES
Supernova Cycles have bicycles for all the family at hugely reduced prices. All the bicycles carry an extensive 25-year guarantee and are delivered semi-assembled so that within 15 minutes you should be able to watch heads turn as you cruise through the streets.

By buying in bulk the company have secured massive discounts which they have passed on to customers. There is a bicycle to suit every pocket from the 10 speed 'Matrix' at £119.99 to the 21 speed 'Revolution' at £229.00. With helmets at £19.99 discount prices extend to accessories too.

Catalogue: *A4, Catalogue, 16 pages, Colour, Free* Postal charges: *Varies with item* Delivery: *Courier* Methods of Payment: *Cheque, Postal Order, Visa, Access / Mastercard*

SWIMSHOP
52/58 Albert Rd
Luton
Beds
LU1 3PR

Telephone:
0582 416545
Fax:
0582 20001

SWIMWEAR AND SWIMMING ACCESSORIES
Swimshop sells a large range of swimwear in all sorts of styles for men, women and children including such names as Speedo, Maru, Arena and Kiefer.

They also sell lots of pool and beach equipment. There is a vast range of floats and inflatables from dolphins to alligators. There are paddles, kickboards, fins and snorkels, stopwatches and life-saving equipment – in short anything and everything you could want at beach or poolside. Their ranges are sourced from all over the world – their swim fins are in four different types from the UK and the USA and range from £8/9 to £72.00 a pair.

Catalogue: *Annually, A5, Catalogue, 72 pages, Colour, Free* Postal charges: *Varies with item* Delivery: *Royal Mail* Methods of Payment: *Cheque, Postal Order, Visa, Access / Mastercard*

THE FRIENDLY FISHERMAN
25 Camden Road
Tunbridge Wells
Kent
TN1 2PS

Telephone:
0892 528677

ANGLING EQUIPMENT
The Friendly Fisherman's 'Predator' catalogue for specialist lure fishing and pike tackle, includes boat equipment. The catalogue helps you select lures and describes various fishing methods from boats. Apparently the last two record British pike were both caught on lures.

Nilmaster of Finland offer a colourful range of plugs and lures costing from £5.20 to £14.95. Once

Sports Equipment (inc. Cycles)

you've worked out the relevant 'depth', 'colour', 'action', and 'size' for the type of fishing you want to attempt (and the catalogue helps you out here) you can make an informed choice.

Catalogue: *A4, Catalogue, 24 pages, Colour, Free* Postal charges: *£1.50* Delivery: *Royal Mail* Methods of Payment: *Cheque, Postal Order, Visa, Access / Mastercard*

VALE TACKLE CENTRE
100 Pershore Road
Hampton
Evesham
Worcestershire
WR11 6PK

Telephone:
0386 765885

FISHING TACKLE

Vale Tackle Centre provide angling equipment and accessories and through their mail order service are promoting a range of products this year at discounted prices. Their three main promotions this year are on Mitchell, Browning and Silstar products.

Mitchell Reels such as the Prince 40 (with two spools) is reduced from £32.95 to £25.99, and the Challenge 40 (with two spools) from £41.95 to £34.99. There is 10% off all Browning Quiver Tips and Leger Rods, Match Rods, Carp Rods and Reels and large reductions on a range of Silstar Poles. The Mondiale PO Pole 11m, for example, is down from £300.00 to £220.00.

Catalogue: *A4, Leaflets, 6 pages, B/W, Free* Postal charges: *Varies with item* Delivery: *Royal Mail* Methods of Payment: *Cheque, Postal Order, Visa, Access / Mastercard*

FREETIME SPORTS
33 Abbey Road
Grimsby
S Humberside
DN32 0HQ

Telephone:
0472 357357

TRAINING SHOES

Freetime specialise in mail order sports footwear. Their colourful price leaflet, packed with cut-price trainers and boots, is laced with a number of incentives that might confuse those new to home buying. When you see 'special offer' stamped liberally on each page, you occasionally think twice before ordering.

Having said that, there are genuine bargains here. Hi-Tec Pioneer hiking or walking boots are £24.99, a reduction of £20.00, and Adidas Torsion Response trainers sell for £34.99 instead of the normal price of £59.99.

Catalogue: *A5, Leaflets, 8 pages, Colour, Free* Postal charges: *£3.49* Delivery: *Courier* Methods of Payment: *Cheque, Postal Order, Access / Mastercard, Visa, American Express*

Sportswear

INITIALS INTERNATIONAL LTD
Park House
34 Bridge Street
Walton-on-Thames
Surrey
KT12 1AJ

Telephone:
0932 841901
Fax:
0932 841901

PERSONALISED CHILDREN'S T AND SWEATSHIRTS AND GOLF TOWELS

You can delight your children with these unique clothes which come personalised with brightly coloured animal alphabet letters. The durable 100% cotton T-shirts and extra rugged 50% cotton/50% poly sweatshirts, are both colourfast and machine washable. They are available in ages 3/4, 5/6, 7/8 and 9/10 in white, navy, red and royal blue. T-shirts are £7.99 while sweatshirts cost £12.95. They also sell the perfect gift for the golfer – a personalised golf towel. This measures 40 × 60 cms and comes in royal blue or emerald green with a male or female 3" motif and up to three 1" embroidered initials, all for £5.99. There is also a matching shoe bag for £5.99, or you can buy the set for £10.99.

Catalogue: *8"× 8", Brochure, 2 pages, Colour, Free* Postal charges: *£2.00* Delivery: *Royal Mail* Methods of Payment: *Cheque, Postal Order, Visa, Access / Mastercard*

M AND M
45 High Street
Stourbridge
West Midlands
DY8 1DE

Telephone:
0384 443344
Fax:
0384 443217

SPORTS GOODS

M and M sell discounted, brand name sportswear and equipment. Their colourful catalogue certainly seems full of bargains. A pair of AD Adidas Seattle trainers cost £14.99, some £35.00 off the retail price. There's a good range of other shoes too, from Reebok, Nike and Puma to mention just a few.

They also sell shirts, shorts, jackets and cricket gear, along with football boots and golf shoes. The last couple of pages are devoted to an end of line sale, with even better bargains. There's £24.00 off a Nike track suit and £35.00 off a pair of Nike shoes. A useful catalogue for anyone interested in sport.

Catalogue: *Bi-annually, A4, Catalogue, 24 pages, Colour, 30p* Postal charges: *£2.99* Delivery: *Royal Mail* Methods of Payment: *Cheque, Postal Order, Visa, Access / Mastercard*

SWIMSHOP
52/58 Albert Rd
Luton
Beds
LU1 3PR

Telephone:
0582 416545
Fax:
0582 20001

SWIMWEAR AND SWIMMING ACCESSORIES

Swimshop sells a large range of swimwear in all sorts of styles for men, women and children including such names as Speedo, Maru, Arena and Kiefer.

They also sell lots of pool and beach equipment. There is a vast range of floats and inflatables from dolphins to alligators. There are paddles, kickboards, fins and snorkels, stopwatches and life-saving equipment – in short anything and everything you could want at beach or poolside. Their ranges are sourced

Stationery

from all over the world – their swim fins are in four different types from the UK and the USA and range from £8/£9 to £72.00 a pair.

Catalogue: *Annually, A5, Catalogue, 72 pages, Colour, Free* Postal charges: *Varies with item* Delivery: *Royal Mail* Methods of Payment: *Cheque, Postal Order, Visa, Access / Mastercard*

AA COMPUTER PRINT
42 Priestlands
Romsey
Hampshire
SO51 8FL

Telephone:
0794 512953
Fax:
0794 830805

COMPUTER STATIONERY

This is a mail order computer stationery catalogue for use in the home or office. It sells continuous word processing paper, letterheads, cheques, listing paper and labels. They also have a range of fax rolls, invoice forms and envelopes. The catalogue even states which software is most compatible with what range and there is also a service for bespoke forms, where printing is in black on white or tinted NCR paper.

Prices are highly competitive, especially if you buy in bulk. Continuous stationery in A4 is £8.99 for 500 sheets and £13.50 for 1000 (100gms Bond). Fax rolls are from £2.03 if bought in boxes of twelve.

Catalogue: *A4, Catalogue, 6 pages, B/W, Free* Postal charges: *Varies with item* Delivery: *By arrangement* Methods of Payment: *Cheque*

BUSINESS STATIONERY DIRECT
Open House
3 Watling Drive
Sketchley Meadows
Business Park
Hinckley, Leicestershire
LE10 3EY

BUSINESS STATIONERY PLAIN AND PERSONALISED

Create full colour professional stationery and presentations yourself – instantly – with Paper Direct.

Paper Direct sell an exclusive range of pre-printed colour designs including brochures, letterheads, business cards, postcards, certificates and fun papers. These are all ready for you to personalise by simply running them through your laserprinter or photocopier. And there's no waste – just print the amount you require. Great for small businesses – stationery, reports, leaflets, presentations, menus etc or for home use for parties, messages and invitations.

A box of 100 letterheads is £14.95 and 50 matching envelopes is £10.95. Plain copier paper is from £2.99 per ream and colour laser papers are £12.95 per 100 sheets.

Catalogue: *Bi-annually, A5, Brochure, 16 pages, Colour, Free* Postal charges: *Varies with item* Delivery: *Translink* Methods of Payment: *Cheque, Visa, Access / Mastercard, American Express*

Stationery

FILOFAX

JUST FAX
43 Broadwick Street
London
W1V 1FT

Telephone:
071 734 5034
Fax:
071 734 5034

FILOFAX AND ACCESSORIES

Filofax, that icon of the eighties, have in fact been in business long before the rise (and fall) of the yuppie. Established in 1921 they have gone on selling the same basic idea ever since. However, the range has expanded considerably as this neat catalogue, which is itself punched to fit into a Filofax, shows.

There are sections of Filofax binders, pocket organisers, Deskfax, accessories and a huge range of leaves covering everything from diaries to expense sheets. Prices start at £25 for an empty pocket edition up to £125 for a deluxe leather version.

Catalogue: *4 × 7, Catalogue, 24 pages, Colour, Free* Postal charges: *Varies with item* Delivery: *Royal Mail* Methods of Payment: *Cheque, Postal Order, Access / Mastercard, American Express, Visa*

LUCY ADAM CARDS
11 Freelands Road
Cobham
Surrey
KT11 2NA

Telephone:
0932 863145

GIFT CARDS

Lucy Adam produce a range of blank greeting cards that are suitable for almost any occasion. There are nine different packs, including thirty different cards of Turkish carpets and twenty different cards featuring ancient and modern embroidery, all embossed with gold highlighting, each available at £15.00 per pack.

In addition to the prepacked cards, you can select your own at a variety of prices, ranging from 75p each to 50p each for a number of Eastern looking cards.

Catalogue: *A5, Leaflets, Colour, Free* Postal charges: *Varies with item* Delivery: *Royal Mail* Methods of Payment: *Cheque*

NEAT IDEAS
Sandall Stones Road
Kirk Sandall Industrial Estate
Doncaster
S Yorks
DN3 1QU

Telephone:
0800 500 192
Fax:
0800 600 192

OFFICE EQUIPMENT

As their name suggests, Neat Ideas stock a vast range of storage devices that should keep any home or office free from clutter. Their well designed catalogue features just about everything for the office, including computers and fax machines.

The Office Workcentre, an all-in-one office furniture system, costs £229.00. It includes a 2 door cupboard and an eye level over-desk storage unit, with handy compartments for books and directories. A miniature version costs £139.95.

Catalogue: *A4, Catalogue, 236 pages, Colour, Free* Postal charges: *Varies with item* Delivery: *Courier* Methods of Payment: *Cheque, Access / Mastercard, Visa, American Express*

Stationery

PAPER DIRECT BY DELUXE
FREEPOST (LE6296)
Hinkley
LE10 0BR

Telephone:
0800 616244
Fax:
0455 631929

PAPER AND OFFICE STATIONERY
This company sells an ingenious idea from America – pre-printed paper which you can then use in your laser printer or copier. This means you can produce full colour brochures, letterheads, mailers and forms from a standard printer.

There is a large selection of paper to choose from both in different formats and with different designs. They even provide envelopes and a clever sheet which enables you to produce your own business cards. They can also supply software for most word processing programs and DTP packages which will help with templates.

Obviously this does cost more than long print runs but if you want to run off just a few copies it seems a wonderful idea.

Catalogue: *A5, Catalogue, 48 pages, Colour, Free* Postal charges: *Varies with item* Delivery: *Parcelforce, Royal Mail* Methods of Payment: *Cheque, Visa, Access / Mastercard, American Express, Postal Order*

PAPYRUS
25 Broad Street
Bath
BA1 5LW

Telephone:
0225 463418
Fax:
0225 447070

HIGH CLASS STATIONERY
Papyrus Stationers have established an excellent reputation for their handmade desk accessories and books. A highly skilled team of craftsmen create marbled paper and practice the ancient craft of bookbinding to create these classic items.

A large A4 journal, half-bound in buckram or leather, with a silk marker will set you back £29.50; a large folding blotter with pockets £47.50. All stationery products are made with their durable marbled paper.

Papyrus also produce photo albums and frames, and a number of leather, pewter and brass items, such as a giant brass paperclip at £7.50, and an English pewter letter knife at £22.50. A great source of unusual gifts.

Catalogue: *A5, Catalogue, 16 pages, Colour, Free* Postal charges: *Varies with item* Delivery: *Royal Mail* Methods of Payment: *Cheque*

PARKER PEN
Estate Road
Newhaven
East Sussex
BN9 0AU

Telephone:
0273 513233
Fax:
0273 514773

PENS, PENCILS AND ACCESSORIES
From the name synonymous with writing instruments comes a range of luxury products. There are seventeen different designs in a range of finishes and with a choice of nibs to ensure the smoothness that is part of the Parker standard.

Parker have produced a range of pen and pencil sets which make ideal gifts, and which start from £9.98. At the top end of the range are pens such as

Stationery

the 18ct gold Duofold Presidential at £5,500.00 or the sterling silver Premier at £195.00, all of which are delivered in gift boxes.

Catalogue: *A5, Catalogue, 32 pages, Colour, Free* Postal charges: *Varies with item* Delivery: *Royal Mail* Methods of Payment: *Cheque, Postal Order*

SAVE THE CHILDREN
S.C.F. Trading Dept.
P.O. Box 40
Burton upon Trent
Staffs.
DE14 3LQ

Telephone:
0283 510111

CHRISTMAS CARDS, GIFTS AND FAYRE
This catalogue has been released to help raise money for the Save The Children Fund. Any profit made goes towards helping all kinds of children in over fifty countries, who are either ill, homeless, orphaned or uneducated.

The catalogue offers a wide range of Christmas goods: for example, Christmas cards (£2.55 for ten), crackers (£19.99 for six), stationery kits, toys, kitchenware and jewellery (£2.99 for a pair of earrings). If you place an order costing £65.00 or over then postage and packaging is free.

Catalogue: *Annually, A4, Catalogue, 36 pages, Colour, Free* Postal charges: *Varies with item* Delivery: *Royal Mail* Methods of Payment: *Cheque, Postal Order, Visa, Access / Mastercard, American Express*

THE PEN SHOP
14 Portland Terrace
Newcastle upon Tyne
NE2 1QQ

Telephone:
091 281 3358
Fax:
091 281 6260

PENS AND PENCIL SETS
With their distinctive and exclusive inlaid nib, Sheaffer's pen and pencil sets are prestige writing instruments. Each fountain pen is crafted by hand to emphasise the detailed craftsmanship of these quality products. The catalogue illustrates over 30 different designs, including the sleek Targa and the prestige Connoisseur. All designs have the choice of fountain pen, ballpoint and pencil, and some are available in a range of colours.

The range of accessories reflects classic values. The Edwardian set is crafted in solid oak and hallmarked in silver and an exclusive limited edition commissioned from Royal Doulton is available with a lacquer fountain pen.

Catalogue: *19cm × 25cm, Catalogue, 46 pages, Colour, Free* Postal charges: *Varies with item* Delivery: *Royal Mail* Methods of Payment: *Cheque, Postal Order, Visa, Access / Mastercard*

Stationery

THE PRINTING WORKS
287 Finchley Road
London
NW3 6ND

Telephone:
071 431 5423

Fax:
071 431 5420

HIGH QUALITY STATIONERY IN SMALL QUANTITIES
Products from the personal, home and gift catalogue include: 100 personal cards, £19.00; 15 engraved, monogram notelets and envelopes, £14.99; 100 correspondence cards, £39.00; 50 Toon cards, £11.50 (all prices inclusive of artwork).

From the business catalogue, there are 10 business cards, £19.00; 100 letterheads, £39.00; 100 compliment slips, £20.00. When phoning for a catalogue, quote the agent number 100226 and name: Ben Norton.

Catalogue: *Quarterly, 35x25cm, Catalogue, 15 pages, Colour, Free* Postal charges: *Varies with item* Delivery: *Parcelforce* Methods of Payment: *Cheque, Postal Order, Visa, Access / Mastercard, American Express*

THE STROKE ASSOCIATION
CHSA Cards Ltd
20 Halcyon Court
St Margarets Way
Huntingdon
Cambs

Telephone:
0480 413280

GIFTS AND CARDS
The Stroke Association deals with research, advice, prevention, welfare and rehabilitation for stroke sufferers and their families. For over 21 years the charity has produced card and gift catalogues, and 100% of the profit is covenanted towards their work.

The catalogue is full to the brim with Christmas cards, both traditional and modern, complemented by novelty gifts, as well as good ideas for a healthier lifestyle and useful gadgets to use around the home.

Christmas cards start at £1.99 and go up to £2.75 for 10; wrapping paper at 99p; lap trays are £9.99; three ladies handkerchiefs cost £2.99.

Catalogue: *Annually, A5, Catalogue, 16 pages, Colour, Free* Postal charges: *Varies with item* Delivery: *Parcelforce, Royal Mail* Methods of Payment: *Cheque, Postal Order, Visa, Access / Mastercard*

TRAIDCRAFT
Kingsway
Gateshead
Tyne & Wear
NE11 0NE

Telephone:
091 491 0591

STATIONERY
This paper and cards catalogue has a bright selection of floral designs on cards and giftwraps. There's also a range of stationery for children and a section which includes a handmade paper collection from Third World sources. Lots or original and environmentally responsible ideas for gifts, for personal use and for around the office and home.

Catalogue: *A4, Brochure, 12 pages, Colour, Free* Postal charges: *Varies with item* Delivery: *In-house delivery* Methods of Payment: *Cheque, Postal Order*

Toys

TRISHA KERR CROSS AT PAPIER MARCHE
8 Gabriel's Wharf
56 Upper Ground
London
SE1 9PP

Telephone:
071 401 2310

DESIGNER STATIONERY
Trisha has worked as a designer in New York and London. Her range of attractive stationery printed on recycled paper and card is available only from her shop in London or by mail order.

Choose from sixteen designs of greetings cards (at 60p each) with matching giftwraps. Select writing papers with borders of bright poppies and anemones or trailing pastel convolvulus. All supplied with toning colours of envelopes and matching notepads. (Sets from £1.50 to £12.00).

Handpainted cards are £2.00 each; clip photo frames with hand painted mounts are £5.00 each; and mirrors with hand painted frames are from £15.00 to £19.50.

Catalogue: *A4, Brochure, Colour and B/W, Free* Postal charges: *£3 per order Varies with item* Delivery: *Royal Mail* Methods of Payment: *Cheque, Postal Order, Visa, Access / Mastercard*

AIR CIRCUS
20 Wansdyke Business Centre
Oldfield Lane
Bath
Avon
BA1 5AR

Telephone:
0225 466333
Fax:
0225 464188

KITES
Kite flying was invented by the Chinese thousands of years ago and is now a fast growing, popular outdoor sport. This colourful catalogue carries a full range of kites for beginners and experts alike. Starting at £4.99 for a traditional, one-line, cutter kite, prices go up to £200.00–£300.00 for an advanced sports kite.

The catalogue gives helpful technical information, such as the wind power needed for various models, making it easy to choose the right kite for your needs. Line accessories are also supplied and an assortment of games such as juggling balls and frisbees.

Catalogue: *A5, Catalogue, 16 pages, Colour, 40p* Postal charges: *£3.00* Delivery: *Royal Mail* Methods of Payment: *Cheque, Postal Order, Visa, Access / Mastercard*

APES ROCKING HORSES
Ty Isaf
Pont-y-GwyddelLlanfair
T.H.
Abergele
Clwyd
LL22 9RA

Telephone:
074579 365

ROCKING HORSES
Pam and Stuart MacPherson produce magnificent and exceedingly lifelike 'British Pony' rocking horses made specially for individual clients. 'Megan', 'George', 'Comet' and 'Orien' are limited editions based on real ponies and cost around £1500.00. The horses, produced in fibre-glass, are strong enough to take adult weight and mounted onto wooden rockers. They are given finishing touches of a horsehair mane and tail and an authentic removable leather harness.

'The Gipsy Bridge' series is based on the traditional wooden horse and comprises of four different

Toys

models; from 'Daisy' – for children up to eight years old at £850.00, to 'Albert' for any size rider, at £1850.00.

A miniature version of 'Arian' for your bookshelf will cost £350.00, and as with all the other horses, this one is also finely hand-painted.

Catalogue: *A5, Brochure, 6 pages, Colour, Free* Postal charges: *Varies with item* Delivery: *Courier* Methods of Payment: *Cheque*

COLLECTORS' TOYS
Fisher's Mill,
Bridge Hill,
Topsham,
Exeter
Devon
EX3 0QQ

Telephone:
0392-877600
Fax:
0392-877600

WOODEN DOLLS

Since 1976 Eric Horne has been making modern collectors' versions of the classic 'Dutch' (peg) dolls so popular at the turn of the century. Produced both in 'contemporary' and 'traditional' styles, these beechwood dolls are turned by hand and painted with high-gloss enamel.

The dolls range in height from a minuscule ¼" up to 18". Most are jointed at the elbows, knees, shoulders and hips, the joints held together by wooden pins. Male and female versions are available, with a choice of hair and shoe colour. Doll prices start at £10.20 and climb to £83.25.

A range of 1/12 scale miniature furniture is also available. Spring 1994 sees the launch of a new range of hand-painted 6" dolls, and a limited edition of Eric Horne's Pedlar Man.

Catalogue: *A5, Brochure, 8 pages, B/W, Free* Postal charges: *Varies with item* Delivery: *Royal Mail* Methods of Payment: *Visa, Access / Mastercard, Cheque, American Express*

CURIOUS CATERPILLAR
Ravensden Farm
Bedford Road
Rushden
Northants
NN10 0SQ

Telephone:
0933 410650
Fax:
0933 410108

TOYS AND GIFTS

Curious Caterpillar supplies party presents, toys and gifts suitable for any time of year. However, they have a particularly good range of small toys for Christmas stocking fillers. A bulk price list is available for schools and fund raisers who are able to buy in larger quantities.

Impressively, most orders are dispatched within two days and prices are very reasonable. 'Thousand faces' are just 50p each, gliding birds 20p, fun braids £2.95 and animal mugs 50p.

Catalogue: *Annually, A5, Catalogue, 32 pages, Colour, Free* Postal charges: *Varies with item* Delivery: *Royal Mail, Parcelforce Blue Band motors* Methods of Payment: *Cheque, Postal Order, Visa, Access / Mastercard*

Toys

EARLY LEARNING CENTRE
South Marston
Swindon
Wilts
SN3 4TJ

Telephone:
0793 832832
Fax:
0793 823491

TOYS FOR YOUNG CHILDREN

Early Learning Centres provide a wide range of durable and very reasonably priced toys for young children. 70% of their products are under £5.00 and their toys are rigorously tested and observe all the appropriate regulations as a matter of course.

Everything they sell reflects a philosophy that children learn more, and learn more quickly, when they enjoy what they're doing. They only sell toys that make learning more fun – they don't sell toy guns or weapons and avoid items that rely on fashion and TV fads.

Parents may well know their high street shops, while not realising that they also offer a mail order service.

Catalogue: *Bi-annually, 210 × 250mm, Catalogue, 84 pages, Colour, Free* Postal charges: £3.75 Delivery: *Royal Mail* Methods of Payment: *Access / Mastercard, Visa, Cheque, Postal Order*

FROG HOLLOW
21 High Street
Pewsey
Wiltshire
SN9 5Af

Telephone:
0672 64222
Fax:
0672 62462

GIFTS AND TOYS

As well as the shop in Kensington, London, Frog Hollow have a mail order division in Wiltshire. The company offers a range of personalised gifts for children (some of which can be for adults too) of all ages as well the more usual toys, games and books.

The frog motif is strong throughout the catalogue and each item is pictured with a brief explanation together with the price. The 6-page order form is very detailed with each item listed in page order and its price listed next to it.

Membership details of the Frog Hollow Birthday Club forms the last page of the order form.

Catalogue: *A5, Catalogue, 24 pages, Colour, Free* Postal charges: *Varies with item* Delivery: *Royal Mail* Methods of Payment: *Cheque, Postal Order, Visa, Access / Mastercard*

HAMLEYS LTD
188/196 Regent Street
London
W1R 6BT

Telephone:
071 734 3161
Fax:
071 434 2655

TOYS

Hamleys are of course one of the most famous toy shops in the world and their huge Regent Street store stocks just about every toy available. They used to issue a catalogue but stopped doing so some years ago. However, they still have a mail order department and will dispatch goods anywhere in the country.

The problem is you have to know what you want in the first place, but in these days of endless TV ads for toys children are usually amazingly well informed on just what they do want, in which case all is needed is a call to Hamleys – and a bullet proof credit card!

Catalogue: *None* Postal charges: £5.00 Delivery: *Royal Mail* Methods of Payment: *Cheque, Visa, Access / Mastercard*

Toys

IT'S CHILD'S PLAY
Treworthal Barn
Treworthal
Newquay Cornwall
TR8 5PJ

Telephone:
0637 830896

TRADITIONAL WOODEN TOYS AND FURNITURE

This company manufactures traditional wooden toys. Their simple catalogue has line drawings of the range, which includes tops, pull-alongs, carts and bricks. They also stock cars, letters, a counting frame, a rocking horse and skittles. There's a small selection of furniture such as chairs, tables and stools.

All are chunky in design and painted with non-toxic paints. A whip and top is £2.85, jigsaws £3.15, a bus £12.70, a cart with bricks £31.10, a chair £19.95. At the more expensive end are the rocking horse at £325.00, a dolls' house for £104.00 and a climbing frame for £300.00.

Catalogue: *A5, Leaflets, 9, Free* Postal charges: *Varies with item* Delivery: *Royal Mail* Methods of Payment: *Cheque, Postal Order*

JAMES GALT & CO
Brookfield Road
Cheadle
Cheshire
SK8 2PN

Telephone:
061 428 1211
Fax:
061 428 4320

TOYS & EDUCATIONAL PRODUCTS

Galt sell a huge range of educational toys and teaching materials, mostly to schools themselves but they will also supply individuals. Their well-produced, colour catalogue is about the size of a telephone directory and includes just about everything for the nursery and junior school.

Sections cover sand & water, furniture & storage, imaginative play (puppets, dolls, models etc), art, teacher resources (books, pencils, templates etc), jigsaws & games, energetic play (climbing frames, PE equipment), nursery, infant & toddler, language, maths, construction, technology, science, music, electronic learning and geography & history. In short, a comprehensive catalogue.

Catalogue: *A4, Catalogue, 354 pages, Colour, Free* Postal charges: *£3.95* Delivery: *Royal Mail* Methods of Payment: *Access / Mastercard, Visa, American Express, Diners Club, Cheque*

JIGSAW TOYS
Hendre Fawr
Llanfairynghornwy
Anglesey
Gwynedd
LL65 4LW

Telephone:
0407 730620
Fax:
0407 730620

CHILDREN'S TOYS

Jigsaw manufacture panelled toy chests using traditional joinery methods incorporating solid brass lifting handles. The finish to the timber is achieved by applying several hand polished layers of beeswax polish and the boxes are made to order with the child's name carved in the front panel and the word 'Toys' carved on the lid.

The chests are beautifully hand-painted in distinctive old style colours to compliment the decorative themes. Alternative background colours can be

Toys

provided at the customer's request at an additional premium. The chests measure 32" × 18" × 16" and the lids have an adjustable friction stay fitted to safeguard little fingers.

Prices start at £130.00 per chest, including postage and packing, and go up to £190.00, depending on colour and design.

Catalogue: *Third A4, Leaflets, 6 pages, Colour, Free* Postal charges: *Free* Delivery: *Royal Mail* Methods of Payment: *Cheque*

LEAF PUBLICATIONS
12 Summerdown Road
Eastbourne
BN20 8DT

CHILDREN'S BOOKS
Not exactly a toy but a means of getting them! Leaf Publications produce just one book, 'The Xtra Pocket Handbook'. Written by an enterprising 14-year-old, it tells children of a similar age how to supplement their pocket money by doing various odd jobs.

The book gives a full guide to the legal position, advice on how to best invest money and a large section on how get part time jobs. An ideal birthday or Christmas present for a very reasonable £2.95.

Catalogue: *None* Postal charges: *Free* Delivery: *Royal Mail* Methods of Payment: *Cheque, Postal Order*

LETTERBOX
PO Box 114
Truro
Cornwall
TR1 1FZ

Telephone:
0872 580885
Fax:
0872 580866

ORIGINAL PRESENTS BY POST FOR CHILDREN OF ALL AGES
A cornucopia of gift ideas for children from letterbox moneyboxes, £12.99, and personalised Mason Pearson hairbrushes, £19.99, to personalised wall-clocks, £29.99, and Noah's Ark hooks, £7.99. Each item is clearly photographed with the catalogue number, description and price underneath. There are 326 different present ideas in the 1993/4 catalogue, perfect for stocking up your bottom drawer for christenings, birthdays and Christmas.

The company also runs occasional ends of lines sales through the catalogue. This is denoted by a separate sheet telling you which items in the catalogue are being discontinued and what the new sale price is.

Catalogue: *Annually, A4, Catalogue, 20 pages, Colour, Free* Postal charges: *Varies with item* Delivery: *Royal Mail* Methods of Payment: *Cheque, Postal Order, Visa, Access / Mastercard*

Toys

MATCHRITE
167 Winchester Road
Bristol
BS4 3NJ

Telephone:
0272 716256

JOKES
Ever wondered where you can buy a 'whoopee cushion', 'volcanic sugar' or 'Dracula blood'? The answer is in every schoolboy's dream publication, Matchrite's 'Joke Shop By Post'. Produced like an old fashioned comic, it is crammed with wizard wheezes. A 'Large Dog's Turd' costs just 99p; the 'Stink Spray' to accompany it is £1.50. There is just about every joke and novelty you've ever heard of and quite a few you might wish you hadn't – all great fun.

Those with the stamina for a truly gruesome spectacle can buy a 45-minute VHS video featuring Jeremy Beadle reading from the Matchrite catalogue and then trying out the jokes. An horrific prospect if ever there was one.

Catalogue: *A4, Catalogue, 16 pages, B/W, Free* Postal charges: *Varies with item* Delivery: *Royal Mail* Methods of Payment: *Cheque, Visa, Access / Mastercard, Postal Order*

MICHAEL STOKES
The Old Rectory
Kelston
Bath
BA1 9AG

Telephone:
0225 317318

CLIMBING FRAMES
Michael Stokes's 'Campaign Climbing Frame' has been sold by mail order for over ten years. With its tactile wooden construction and unique design it stimulates the child's imagination and encourages physical confidence. The climbing frame caters for ages two to twelve and is an attractive addition to any garden. The frames are delivered direct to the customer's home, and if required assembled free of charge.

The frame includes a 6' slide wide enough for two children, and overhang ladder, lookout ladder and roll bar. Each part is rust resistant or weatherproofed and will give years of use. Adaptations or alterations on the original design are possible. The price for the frame is £435.00 and a three ladder extension is £110.00.

Catalogue: *Third A4, Brochure, 6 pages, B/W, Free* Postal charges: *Free* Delivery: *By arrangement* Methods of Payment: *Cheque, Postal Order*

PADDINGTON & FRIENDS
1 Abbey Street
Bath
BA1 1NN

PADDINGTON BEAR PRODUCTS
If you're a devotee of the small brown bear, Paddington, who turned up from Peru with a label and no fixed address, this is the catalogue for you. Dolls start at £38.00 for a 'Junior Paddington', standing 14" high with a choice of colours for his hat, coat and boots, and rise to £99.50 for a special limited edition 14" model with jointed legs, made of

Toys

quality mohair. He comes with a real leather suitcase containing 'Peruvian' coins.

There are numerous other products, including books at £4.99 each; stationery from £2.40 for an A4 document wallet; and jigsaws at £3.99. Towelling bibs (from £3.50); unbreakable tableware from £3.99; and rattles from £2.50 are available for babies and toddlers.

Catalogue: *A5, Catalogue, 16 pages, B/W, Free* Postal charges: *£3.00* Delivery: *Royal Mail* Methods of Payment: *Cheque, Postal Order, Access / Mastercard, Visa, American Express*

PARTY PIECES
Freepost (RG910)
Childs Court Farm
Ashampstead
Berkshire
RG8 7BR

Telephone:
0635 201844
Fax:
0635 201911

TOYS FOR PARTIES
A godsend for parents having to deal in today's competitive market for children's birthday parties, this brilliant catalogue has everything you could possibly need bar an entertainer and infinite patience. There is a good selection of the obligatory party bags, plus items with which to fill them, along with food boxes, party tableware, balloons, hats, games, books and themed partyware.

Reasonably priced, the ranges include old favourites as well as current fads such as Aladdin and Captain Scarlet. A circus plate setting, which includes plate, napkin, cup/lid/straw is 40p while jungle and dinosaur masks are just 25p each. A must for any hard pressed parent.

Catalogue: *200mm × 200mm, Catalogue, 12 pages, Colour, Free* Postal charges: *£2.95* Delivery: *Royal Mail* Methods of Payment: *Cheque, Postal Order, Visa, Access / Mastercard*

REAL LIFE TOYS
Holbrook Industrial
Estate
Halfway
Sheffield
S Yorks
S19 5GH

Telephone:
0742 510300
Fax:
0742 510810

ELECTRICAL CARS AND LIFE SIZE TOYS
This interesting loose-leaf catalogue features a number of electric cars for children. They come as self-assembly packs which any average DIYer can manage. The cars themselves look and perform like the real thing and have all the features you'd expect of a full size car. There are three models, the Jeep, the Mayfair (which looks like a Model T Ford), and the Scout, a more modern design. All are powered by 12-volt motors.

Real life also sell a self-assembly rocking horse which is about the size of a small pony. All the toys can be bought either just as patterns, partial or complete kits. The cars cost a total of around £450-£500 while the horse is about £210.00.

Catalogue: *Annually, A4, Catalogue, 24 pages, Colour, Free* Postal charges: *Varies with item* Delivery: *Royal Mail Courier* Methods of Payment: *Cheque, Visa, Access / Mastercard*

Toys

ROBERT MULLIS
55 Berkeley Road
Wroughton
Swindon
Wilts
SN4 9BN

Telephone:
0793 813583

ROCKING HORSES
Rocking horse makers Robert Mullis make their product to order. Each horse takes six to eight weeks to complete, although some orders may be drawn from stock. Prices are not cheap, from around £715.00, but you'd expect that for something of this quality. There is also a series of rocking animals, 'The Moonraker Collection' which are a little less at around £325.00. Orders can be secured with a 10% deposit.

Of course, while many people buy a rocking horse to ride, some are ordered for purely decorative reasons. The 'Special Presentation' rocking horse (price on application) is ideal for the latter.

Catalogue: *A4, Leaflets, 4, Colour, Free* Postal charges: *Varies with item* Delivery: *In-house delivery* Methods of Payment: *Cheque, Postal Order*

SKIPPER YACHTS
Granary Yacht Harbour
Dock Lane
Melton
Suffolk
IP12 1PE

Telephone:
0394 380703
Fax:
0394 380936

TOY YACHTS
Skipper produce the sort of wooden toy yacht that everyone imagines they had in their childhood. The loose leaf brochure has colour photographs of 10 different models, from a simple 6" Thames Barge up to a 32" Ocean Racer.

All are hand made in Britain out of wood and use genuine sail cloth. They look splendid and are priced very reasonably. The little barges start at just £3.62, a large 20" yacht is £40.00 while the magnificent 32" Ocean Racer is £154.80 and comes in its own special box. There are also kits to make your own.

Catalogue: *A4, Brochure, 2 pages, Colour, Free* Postal charges: *Varies with item* Delivery: *Royal Mail* Methods of Payment: *Cheque*

SPORTS & PLAYBASE
Skelmanthorpe
Business Park
Skelmanthorpe
Huddersfield
HD8 9DZ

Telephone:
0484 864948

EDUCATIONAL TOYS AND PLAY MATERIALS
This catalogue sells a wide range of play materials, games and learning tools for children aged between three and eleven years. SPB provide everything that a school, playscheme or creche could need and will also be a useful source for the parent.

There is a good selection of number and colour games as well as early learning devices. There is also a full range of ingenious maps, cones and Belisha beacons to teach children the rules of the road. Their bean bags are colourful and practical and the PVC table covers and aprons a godsend.

Catalogue: *A4, Catalogue, 20 pages, Colour, Free* Postal charges: *Varies with item* Delivery: *Royal Mail* Methods of Payment: *Cheque*

Toys

THE DOLLS HOUSE EMPORIUM
Dept VG1
Victoria Road
Ripley
Derbyshire
DE5 3YD

Telephone:
0773 513773
Fax:
0773 513772

DOLLS' HOUSES AND FURNITURE

Founded in 1979 The Dolls House Emporium has a long established and excellent reputation for quality and service to customers. They produce two catalogues split between children's and collectors' ranges. Each contains selections of high quality wooden dolls' houses which come both as kits or ready made.

They also feature furniture, fittings and accessories for both young and mature dolls' house enthusiasts. In fact the Emporium supplies everything for the doll's house, from the cellar and garden up to the attic and roof. All items are made one twelfth scale.

Dolls' house kits start from £49.90, with built houses from £149.90. Accessories start at just 50p and furniture from £2.95.

Catalogue: *Bi-annually, A4, Catalogue, 48 pages, Colour, Free*
Postal charges: *Varies with item* Delivery: *Royal Mail Courier*
Methods of Payment: *Cheque, Visa, Access / Mastercard, Postal Order*

THE JUMPING BEAN CO.
Leon Gate
Lenton
Nottingham
Notts
NG7 2LX

Telephone:
0602 792838
Fax:
0602 780963

COMPUTER GAMES

'Noddy's Playtime' is a graded creativity and entertainment package for home computers based on solid entertainment principles for 3–7 year olds. 'Noddy's Big Adventure' is the sequel. There is a choice of three carefully defined learning levels which have been designed in consultation with teachers.

In 'Noddy's Playtime' children can drive with Noddy and explore the magic world of Toytown where there are eight special learning locations including Market Place (a game of letter recognition), Post Office (counting) and Chimney House (musical fun). Also included is a junior Art Package which develops your child's creative ability.

'Playtime' is available on PC, Amiga, ST and Acorn Archimedes and 'Big Adventure' on Acorn Archimedes, Amiga, PC and PC Windows. Prices range from £24.99–£34.99.

Catalogue: *A4, Leaflets, 4 pages, Colour, Free* Postal charges: *£1.95* Delivery: *Royal Mail* Methods of Payment: *Cheque, Postal Order*

Toys

THE WORLD OF DOLLS
Willersley
Isle Abbotts
Taunton
Somerset
TA3 6RW

Telephone:
0460 281407

DOLLS, DOLLS' FURNITURE AND CLOTHING
The World of Dolls produces four charming dolls in two different sizes: Jessica is 46 cm, while Samantha, Nicole, and Monique stand slightly taller at 50 cm. The exquisite, if limited, range of furniture, nightwear, and bed linen will delight any doll enthusiast.

The clothes are available to suit either size of doll. Prices vary from £2.75 for a nightshirt to £6.50 for a dressing gown. Bed linen prices range from about £1.00 to £10.00. Furniture prices are, not surprisingly, rather higher – the pine wardrobe, for example, costs £77.00.

The catalogue comes complete with sample fabrics. A mailing list service for news of future products is also available.

Catalogue: *A5, Catalogue, 8 pages, Colour, Free* Postal charges: *Free* Delivery: *Royal Mail* Methods of Payment: *Cheque*

TODDLER TOYS
4 Harriet Street
London
SW1X 9QT

Telephone:
071 245 6316
Fax:
071 245 6310

CHILDREN'S TOYS
Wide ranging catalogue containing toys for children as young as new born to twelve years. Toys of interest such as a Crystal Radio Kit and Map Maker Kit in the Science and Learning section to books for all ages. A price list is included which also states which toys need batteries. Airmail deliveries overseas if required. Customers are advised to take out insurance on large orders at a cost of £0.65 up to £150.00 or £1.20 up to £500.00 max. (for the U K only).

Catalogue: *A4, Catalogue, 35 pages, Colour, Free* Postal charges: *Varies with item* Delivery: *Royal Mail* Methods of Payment: *Cheque, Postal Order, Visa, Access / Mastercard, American Express*

TP ACTIVITY TOYS
Severn Road
Stourport-on-Severn
Worcs
DY13 9EX

Telephone:
0299 827728
Fax:
0299 827163

OUTDOOR PLAY EQUIPMENT AND INDOOR TOYS AND GAMES
A wide range of exciting play equipment and toys for children from trampolines and slides, climbing frames and swings, tree houses and roller coasters to sandpits and pogo sticks, farms and dolls' houses, garden games and tandem rockers. Many of the items are suitable for nurseries and play schemes, but they are also excellent buys for individuals.

Items are photographed outdoors with children actually using them and have a detailed description. In the centre of the catalogue is a list of all the items with prices. Makes a welcome change from the plastic children's garden equipment.

Toys

TREASURES & HEIRLOOMS
Glasant Fawr
Llangadog
Dyfed
SA19 9AS

Telephone:
0550 777137/777809
Fax:
0550 777354

Catalogue: *Annually, A4, Catalogue, 44 pages, Colour, Free* Postal charges: *Varies with item* Delivery: *Royal Mail* Methods of Payment: *Cheque, Postal Order, Visa, Access / Mastercard*

HANDCRAFTED WOODEN TOYS AND GIFTS
Woodpecker Gifts, shown in catalogue form as Treasures and Heirlooms, have been making toys and gifts for over 30 years, using 24 different species of British timber with non-toxic finishes.

The range of boats offer bath time play as well as fishing fun on the carpet and start from £9.95 for the Dinghy, up to £27.25 for the Trawler. Every boat comes with a play element of either a mast/fishing rod and fish set or cargo and tackle, as appropriate. The vehicles form a sturdy play range, suitable for the garden as well as indoors, and are priced from £9.75 for the 'Vintage Racing Car' to a full 'Puffa Train Set' for £87.50.

Catalogue: *Annually, A5, Brochure, 8 pages, Colour, Free* Postal charges: *Varies with item* Delivery: *Parcelforce, Royal Mail* Methods of Payment: *Cheque, Postal Order, Visa, Access / Mastercard*

TRIDIAS
124 Walcot St
Bath
BA1 5BG

Telephone:
0225 469455
Fax:
0225 448592

TOYS
Tridias, with five shops as well as a mail order department, is one of the largest independent toy retailers in the UK. With 28 years' experience, it is still family owned and run.

Their selection is based on the strict criteria of quality, value for money and design. It ranges from cheap pocket-money/stocking-fillers (from 20p) through exclusive wooden toys (Puppet Theatre £19.95, Fort £34.95) to Rocking Horses (£545.00).

They avoid heavily advertised 'character' merchandise, preferring toys with an interesting or educational element that will occupy children of all ages.

Catalogue: *Quarterly, A5, Catalogue, 48 pages, Colour, Free* Postal charges: £2.95 Delivery: *Parcelforce* Methods of Payment: *Cheque, Postal Order, Visa, Access / Mastercard*

Toys

UNIQUE TEDDY BEARS OF BROADWAY
76 High Street
Broadway
Worcestershire
WR12 7AJ

Telephone:
0386 858323
Fax:
0386 858112

TEDDY BEARS
Bears on Broadway is THE place for bears. Their stock includes antique and modern collectors' bears and children's traditional bears along with books, cards and many bear related items. They sell Steiff bears, including limited editions; Hermann; British Manufacturers' and Artists' bears and many shop exclusive limited editions. They also have a teddy hospital for all bear repairs.

'Star Teddies', lucky zodiac bears for each sign, are £15.00; a 'Cotswold Teddy Bear Museum' bear £10.99; a 'Merrythought Titanic Bear' £48.00 and a 'Steiff 1907 UK Limited Edition Bear' £250.00.

Catalogue: *2–6 times a year, A4, Catalogue, 4+ pages, Colour and B/W,* Free Postal charges: *Varies with item* Delivery: *Royal Mail, Parcelforce* Methods of Payment: *Cheque, Postal Order, Visa, Access / Mastercard, American Express*

WENDLEY LIMITED
Pontypool
Gwent
NP4 6YY

Telephone:
0495 764881

TOY BEARS
Wendley Ltd. produce the Dean's catalogue of traditional toys. Dean's have made bears since 1925 and continue to make replicas of bears from times past. They do this in two ways: by using new material to make a bear look just as it did when it came off the production line may years ago; and by trying to copy the signs of wear and tear that characterise an old bear. Their 'Nigel' bear is modelled on one of the most appealing in their museum and costs a hefty £87.00.

Catalogue: *A4, Brochure, 16, Colour, Free* Postal charges: *Varies with item* Delivery: *Royal Mail* Methods of Payment: *Cheque, Postal Order, Visa, Access / Mastercard*

WOODEN HORSE STABLES
Llandeilo Lodge
Dryslwyn
Carmarthen
Dyfed
SA32 7BY

Telephone:
0558 668232

ROCKING HORSES
Wooden Horse Stables produce rocking horses from the broad-leaved trees of native Welsh woodlands. All their timber is felled by one Wyn Davies in the heart of winter, when the sap is down. Before it is eventually honed to make a rocking horse, each plank will have been air dried, then passed through a kiln to reduce the moisture content to the correct levels for crafting.

The Court Henry collection is available in elm, ash, oak, sweet chestnut, sycamore and cherry. Top quality leather saddles and tack, along with flowing natural horsehair manes and tails give each rocking horse the perfect finish. A small Court Henry Elm will set you back £692.00.

Travel

Catalogue: *A5, Brochure, 6, Colour and B/W, Free* Postal charges: *Varies with item* Delivery: *Courier* Methods of Payment: *Cheque, Visa, Access / Mastercard, Postal Order*

AIRLINE TICKET NETWORK
Network House
Navigation Village
Riversway
Preston
PR2 1EY

Telephone:
0772 727272
Fax:
0772 760287

DISCOUNTED AIRLINE TICKETS

Airline Ticket Network offers up to 60% off long-distance fares. As the national sales centre for more than 100 leading scheduled airlines, it has a range of 250,000 discount fares to 600 destinations, from Thailand to Bali, from the Middle East to South Africa and everywhere in between.

A fully bonded member of ABTA, it can also offer a range of accommodation from budget to luxury hotels at just about every destination served. The company's booklet discusses some of the 'tricks' of the travel trade and claims never knowingly to advertise a fare unless seats are available. You can check availability free on 0800 727 747 or on Teletext page 275.

Catalogue: *Bi-annually, Catalogue, 2 pages, B/W, Free* Postal charges: *Varies with item* Delivery: *Royal Mail* Methods of Payment: *Cheque, Postal Order, Visa, Access / Mastercard*

EDWARD STANFORD
12–14 Long Acre
Covent Garden
London
WC2E 9LP

Telephone:
071 836 1321
Fax:
071 836 0189

MAPS AND TRAVEL BOOKS

Established in 1852 Stanford's remains the first stop for adventurers and armchair travellers alike. It is the world's largest map and travel bookseller, offering over 30,000 titles for travel or reference. Their unique selection includes touring or wall maps for every part of the world, including the complete range of Ordinance Survey maps of Britain.

Their travel guidebooks cover everywhere from Alaska to Zimbabwe and they also have an outstanding collection of travel literature. There are specialist sections on climbing, sailing, navigational charts, world atlases and even globes.

A *National Geographic* political wall map of the world is £9.95, the *Michelin Motoring Atlas of France* £11.95, *The Good Pub Guide* £12.99 and *India – A Travel Survival Kit* £14.95.

Catalogue: *Annually, A5, Catalogue, 32 pages, Colour, Free* Postal charges: *Varies with item* Delivery: *Parcelforce, Royal Mail* Methods of Payment: *Cheque, Visa, Access / Mastercard*

Travel

ITALIAN COOKERY WEEKS
PO Box 2482
London
NW10 1HW

Telephone:
081 208 0112
Fax:
071 401 8763

ITALIAN COOKERY HOLIDAYS

Learn how to cook traditional Italian dishes and enjoy a very special holiday at the same time. In an ancient farmhouse in the glorious olive country of Umbria or in a whitewashed villa in Puglia on the Mediterranean coast you will be able to spend a week learning the secrets of Italian cuisine from some of the best Italian chefs.

The all-in price of £895.00 plus £12.00 travel insurance per person covers return flights with coach transfer to the farmhouse, seven night's accommodation, full board with excellent food and wine, daily tuition in cookery, various trips to local markets and a one-day excursion to the nearby historic cities. Each day finishes with dinner in a typical trattoria.

Only twenty places are offered each week. Courses start on 15th May and run until 25th September.

Catalogue: *Annually*, Brochure, 16 pages, Colour, Free Postal charges: *Varies with item* Delivery: *Royal Mail* Methods of Payment: *Cheque, Visa, Access / Mastercard, American Express*

JACK ROGERS & CO. LTD
Unit 1 Mill Hill Industrial Estate
Flower Lane
Mill Hill
London
NW7 2HU

Telephone:
081 906 8505
Fax:
081 906 2245

TRAVEL PRODUCTS

Jack Rogers & Co. Ltd provide useful items for travel that are reasonably priced and value for money. The catalogue provides everything imaginable for the discerning traveller, from 'Earbuster' personal protectors to a range of 'Valiant Traveller' products in leather. Prices range from as low as 72p for a brass suitcase padlock to £8.50 plus VAT for a leather multi-pocket belt pouch.

Catalogue: *A4*, Brochure, 57 pages, Colour, Free Postal charges: *Free* Delivery: *Royal Mail* Methods of Payment: *Cheque, Postal Order*

THE AIRFARES GUIDE
PO Box 290
Southampton
SO9 7LX

Telephone:
0703 787880
Fax:
0703 788397

THE DEFINITIVE GUIDE TO AIRFARES

The *Independent* calls this 'The best source of fares' and certainly it is a way to ensure you get the very best deal the next time you fly. The company produces a comprehensive listing of the cheapest airfares out of Britain on all airlines in all classes, to all destinations, from all UK airports.

The secret is that airlines only appoint certain agents as wholesalers and this company publishes their net 'wholesale' rates along with all validity and seasonal regulations and information on how to buy at these special prices.

Watches & Clocks

Catalogue: *Quarterly, A5, Catalogue, 98 pages, £15.00 per issue* Postal charges: *Varies with item* Delivery: *Royal Mail* Methods of Payment: *Cheque, Postal Order, Visa, Access / Mastercard*

THE AMERICAN STRETCH LIMOUSINE COMPANY
57 Coburg Road
Wood Green
London
N22 6UB

Telephone:
081 889 4848
Fax:
081 889 7500

LIMOUSINE SERVICE

The American Stretch Limousine Company is not strictly a mail order business but they do send out a brochure detailing their interesting service. Their modern fleet of stretch limousines offer sumptuous upholstery, with seating for six in a cocoon of electronic sophistication. Absolute discretion is guaranteed with dual electric dividers and privacy glass.

Vehicles are fitted with television, video and stereo, as well as intercom and mood lighting. They also offer bar facilities incorporating crystal cut decanters and glasses and an ice chest. To keep in touch, a telephone and facsimile are also available. Sheer luxury!

Prices start from £35 per hour and include a selection of free drinks.

Catalogue: *Annually, D2, Brochure, 6 pages, B/W, Free* Postal charges: Delivery: Methods of Payment: *Cheque, Postal Order, Visa, Access / Mastercard, American Express, Diners Club*

ALEXANDERS
3 Castle Street
FARNHAM
Surrey
GU9 7HR

Telephone:
0252 737373
Fax:
0252 733721

WATCHES

Alexanders are one of the country's leading Tag Heuer stockists. For the uninitiated, Tag Heuer produce high quality sports watches. Their brochure presents what they regard as the twelve finest examples of the range, but they're willing to answer queries on any model.

At £470.00 for the cheapest on show, you may want to take advantage of Alexanders' one year's interest free credit scheme. After paying a 10% deposit, you can make 12 monthly payments by direct debit. Alexanders also guarantee to buy back your watch at the price you paid for it if you decide to purchase a more expensive model at a later date. This looks like a sound investment if you're into expensive sports watches.

Catalogue: *8.5 x 4, Leaflets, 8 pages, Colour, Free* Postal charges: *£5.00* Delivery: *Royal Mail* Methods of Payment: *Cheque, American Express, Access / Mastercard, Diners Club, Visa, Stage Payments*

Watches & Clocks

CLOCKWORK & STEAM
The Old Marmalade Factory
PO Box 4472
Long Hanborough
Oxon
OX8 8LR

Telephone:
0993 883883
Fax:
0993 882660

MECHANICAL WATCHES

Clockwork and Steam specialise in the direct sale of interesting and collectable mechanical clocks and watches. They have an expanding range of quality watches from all around the world which will appeal to anyone who loves timepieces made with traditional engineering skills.

One striking (though not literally!) example is the 'Russian State Railways' pocket watch which sells for a reasonable £29.95. The 'Red October' pocket watch, issued to commemorate the Russian Revolution is £37.95 while a lady's pendant watch with enamel cover is a little more at £79.95. At the top of the range is a superb quality 'Russian Chronograph' wrist watch at £159.95.

Catalogue: *A5, Catalogue, 8 pages, Colour, Free* Postal charges: *Varies with item* Delivery: *Royal Mail* Methods of Payment: *Cheque, Postal Order, Access / Mastercard, Visa*

Subject Index

adult products 16, 49–50, 98
air purifiers 268–9
air sports 231–2
airbrushing 18
airers 325, 337
airline tickets, discounted 399–400
antiquarian books 27, 30, 33
apple juices 154
arms and armour 101, 278
aromatherapy products 41–2, 254–5, 257–8, 260–63, 267–9, 272, 274, 276
art books 26
art exhibitions 19, 106
artists' materials 17
audio visual equipment 132

baby clothes 21–2, 52–3, 67, 99
baby food 22
baby products 21–2, 39, 67
badges 248–9, 280
bags, sports 373
balloon trips 232
banknotes 102–3, 107
bargains, directory of 39
baskets 250
bath accessories 245
bathrobes 82
beauty advice books 41–2
beauty products 254–78
bedding 46, 50–51, 57, 68–9, 84, 95, 300, 304, 306, 309, 312–13, 321, 328
bedroom furniture 68–9, 184, 186–7, 196–8, 203, 305, 311, 321
bedsteads, restored 197, 321
beer kits 125
beers 135, 156, 167
bicycles 223, 350, 373–4, 377–9
billiard tables 375
binoculars 350
birdcare products 47, 60, 215, 324
blinds 317
blouses 50, 58, 61, 86, 89
bodyshaper products 275–6
book clubs 24–7, 29, 35–41
books 18, 23–42, 110–11, 233, 269, 282, 368, 391
 discount 24, 28, 35

boots 77, 179
boxes 250, 304, 315
brassware 307
bridal wear 73
bridge accessories 231
building materials, traditional 124–5
building supplies 124, 304
buildings, portable 124, 207, 214, 325
burglar alarms 126
butterflies, decorative 102, 329

cafétières 308
cakes 137, 139, 141, 145, 157–8, 162, 173, 176
calendars, personalised 234
camcorders 355
cameos 17
candles 245
car accessories 20, 26, 303
cars
 American 19
 model 280–81, 393
 new 20, 327
cashmere wear 54, 61–2, 75–6, 87, 91, 93
cassettes
 pre-recorded 30–31, 41, 241, 292, 358–60, 362–7
 spoken word 41, 358, 364, 366
casual clothes 56, 58, 71, 82, 83
cat care products 353
cat theme items 224
catalogues on sale
 bargains 39
 clothes 39, 54
 fine art 106
 furniture 106
caterers, specialist 153
catering supplies 139
ceramics 247–8, 308–9
champagne 153, 177
charity cards and gifts 42–8, 60, 238–40, 248, 385–6
cheeses 142–3, 146, 150, 159–60, 169, 175
chess sets 105
children's book clubs 25–7, 29, 32, 35–9

Subject Index

children's books 24–8, 31–2, 34, 36, 40, 233, 391
children's cassettes 358, 365
children's clothes 51, 56–7, 62, 72, 74, 76, 78–9, 94
   infants 21, 52–3, 61–2, 69, 84, 88, 99
children's footwear 81, 179, 181, 380–81
children's furniture 183–4, 193, 201, 390–91
children's videos 30–31, 358, 366
china tableware 308, 314, 334–6
chocolates 134, 136–7, 139–40, 146, 150, 152, 157–8, 160, 170, 235
christening gowns 93
Christian music 360
Christmas cards 18, 42–3, 46, 48, 251, 385–6
climbing frames 390, 392, 396
cloakrooms, furnishings 183
clocks 48, 185, 196
clothes 39, 49–101, 189, 225–9, 301, 306
   hot weather 95
   made to measure 52, 61, 87, 100
   patterns 87
   traditional 59–60, 64–5, 67–8, 99
clothes airers 325, 337
coats of arms 106, 246
coffees 135, 137, 146, 158, 166, 175, 176–7
coins 102–3, 107
collectibles 101–7, 280, 289
collectors' clubs 280
comfort products 74, 84, 96, 224, 301
comics 27, 103
commercial equipment 127–8
compact discs 292, 358–63
compasses 286
computers
   accessories 108–23, 131–2, 342–3
   books 28, 110–11, 368
   games 113–14, 121, 131, 395
   hardware 108–23, 131–2, 343
   portables 108, 110, 112–14, 116, 119, 343
   shareware 113, 116, 119–20, 122
   software 108, 111–13, 116, 119–22, 368–71
   training 118
   workstations 344
conference equipment 347–8
conservatories 214
conservatory furniture 187, 210–11
consumer guides 37

contraceptives 260
cookery books 26, 33
cosmetics 255–6, 265, 268
couches, treatment 191, 339
country clothes 53, 55–6, 63, 69–70, 84–5, 96–8, 351–3
crafts 278–94
cricket equipment 373
crystal glassware 102, 104–5, 234–5, 314
cuddly toy patterns 279–80
curtain fittings 298, 309, 317, 326–7
cushions 302, 308–9, 328
cutlery 327, 331

dance videos 276
decorating stamps 326
decorative products 296
design services 18
designer clothes 39, 70, 80
diagnostic kits 260
dining room furniture 184, 186–9, 191–2, 198, 202
disabled people, accessories for 96, 224
DIY supplies 44, 124–9, 304, 309
dolls 103, 105, 233, 288, 388, 396
dolls' houses 291, 293, 390, 395–6
dress fabrics 50, 312
dressing tables 203

Easter gifts 137, 139
educational cassettes 364
educational software 368–9, 371
educational toys 390, 394
educational videos 359, 367
Egyptian artifacts 249
elderly people, accessories for 44, 96, 224
electrical appliances 39, 130–33, 225–9
electrical DIY supplies 126
electronic parts 133
embroidery supplies 284–5, 288, 294
environmentally friendly products 226, 238
ethnic artefacts 46, 49
ethnic clothes 46, 49, 58–9, 82, 95–7
exercise videos 276

fabrics 50, 57, 285, 294, 301, 312, 323
factory equipment 346
fender seats 192, 195
fertilizers 215
film scripts and books 18
fireplaces 319
first day covers 278

Subject Index

fish 141, 144–7, 150, 152–5, 163, 169–71, 174, 238, 240
fishing tackle 284, 351–2, 371–2, 374, 376–80
flags 314
flooring 129, 295, 302, 320–21
flours 173–4
flower delivery services 134, 233–4, 236–7, 239–41, 245–6, 248, 300
flowers 205–6, 208–12, 214–16, 218–20, 331
foam products 185–6
folk art 232
food and drink 134–78
food supplements 256, 262, 276, 363
foot massagers 257
footwear 59, 77–8, 81, 86, 178–81, 301, 380–81
fragrances 52, 259, 264, 273–4, 277
fruit presses 221–2
fruit trees 208
furnishing fabrics 57, 294, 301, 323
furnishings, home 189, 191, 225–9, 311, 319
furniture 43, 106, 182–203, 223, 225–9, 327
   accessories 203, 225
   covers 190, 194, 320
   fitted 182–3, 187, 192, 200–201
   made to order 184
   modular 184
   painted 192, 202
   reproduction 182, 196, 202
   restoration 188
   solid wood 186–8, 190, 192, 194, 200, 202
   woven fibre 189
futons 198, 305, 311

gadgets 203–5
garages, portable 207, 325
garden buildings 207, 214, 219
garden equipment 44, 84, 205–7, 209, 211–12, 216, 219–22, 306
garden furniture 68–9, 182, 193, 210, 214, 222, 327
garden ornaments 187, 209–11, 215, 217, 219
gates 298, 351
gemstones 16, 279, 289
general catalogues 223–30
gifts 231–53
glass, replacement 316
glassware 102, 104–5, 234–5, 314

globes 349
golf accessories 253, 286, 309, 372, 377, 381
golf clothes 80–81
greetings cards 18, 42–8, 229–30, 238–40, 251, 383, 385–7
guns 293

hair brushes 266–7
hair care books 41–2
hampers 52, 139–40, 146, 149–50, 153, 166–7, 177, 242, 250
hams 142–3, 153–4, 161–2
handbags 338
handkerchiefs 89, 242–3
harvest boxes 315
hat boxes 250, 304
headstones 128–9
health aids 224, 263, 301
health and beauty 254–78
health and science books 31
hearing devices 254, 263
heraldic scrolls and shields 106, 246
herbal remedies 260–61, 270–71
herbs 146, 170
hi-fi 131–2
hobbies and crafts 278–94
holidays 154, 399–400
home accessories 203, 225
home furnishings 189, 191, 225–9, 311, 319
home goods 225–9, 295–332
homoeopathic supplies 263, 275
honey 147
horse rugs 352
house signs 304, 313, 321
household appliances 39, 130–31
household goods 46–7, 203–4, 225–9, 303, 306, 310, 327
   traditional 325

incontinence products 74, 301
Indian handicrafts 250–51, 328
industrial equipment 127–8
inflatable castles 352
interior design 195
ionisers 268–9, 276

jams 136–7, 146
Japanese handicrafts 293
jewellery 15–16, 45–8, 68, 70, 235–6, 241, 247, 249, 333–4
kits 283–4
joinery, bespoke 186

405

Subject Index

jokes 392
juggling supplies 291–2

keep-fit equipment 223, 271–2, 372
keyrings 280
kitchens, fitted 182–3, 187, 192, 200–201
kitchenware 47, 84, 307, 327, 334–7
kites 285, 387
knitting yarns 279
knitwear 54, 59–62, 68, 73, 75–6, 80–81, 86–91, 93, 95, 101

labels 309, 347
labour saving gadgets 204–5
ladies' wear 49–93, 95–7, 99–101, 189, 225–9, 306
  differently sized 57, 59, 72, 83
language courses 42, 223, 357, 366
lavender products 271
leather furniture 195
leather goods 91
legal books 38
leisure goods 327
leisurewear 56, 58, 71, 82, 83
letterboxes 312
lighting 203, 315, 326, 328
limousine service 20–21
lingerie 49–50, 55, 58, 66, 71, 73–5, 77, 85, 99
LP records 358, 360, 362
luggage 52, 338
lullaby cassettes 241

management courses 346–7
maps 23, 29, 33, 399
maritime goods 23, 45, 282, 374
marquetry supplies 291
Masonic regalia 64
maternity wear 51, 67
mattress covers 295, 320
meats, traditional 150
men's toiletries 258–9, 261, 268, 270, 277
menswear 49–71, 73, 75–6, 78–84, 86–98, 100–101, 225–9, 351–3
  differently sized 57, 63, 78, 83, 98
mirrors 197, 203
models 280–81, 393–4
modems 109, 114–15, 118
motoring accessories 20, 26, 303
mouldings, decorative 295, 318, 322
museum gifts 18, 205, 251–3, 339–41
mushrooms 148, 170

music, sheet 33–4, 367
music memorabilia 17, 287
musical instruments 341–2

napkin hooks 247
natural health products 258–9, 266, 269–70, 274–6
nautical goods 23, 45, 282, 374
needlework supplies 281, 283–4, 286, 290, 294, 320
netball equipment 375
New Age products 35, 269, 289, 363
newspapers, historical 245
nightwear 51, 55, 66, 100, 319
nurseries, garden 205–6, 208, 211–12, 214–15, 219–20
nursery equipment 39, 67

oak furniture 190, 192, 200
office equipment and supplies 342–8
  furniture 182, 342–4, 346–7
oils, cooking 170
oils, essential 255, 257, 261, 265, 267, 269, 271, 274–5
optical equipment 349–50
organic supplies
  bakery goods 173
  beauty products 164–5
  books 40–41
  gardening materials 208, 212, 218
  meat 143, 147–8, 157, 165, 171
  wines 163, 171, 176
oriental foods 159, 164
ornaments 104–5, 242
outdoor clothes 49, 79, 83, 92, 97, 351–3
outdoor goods 350–53
outdoor play equipment 390, 392, 396
oysters 138, 153–4

packaging materials 223
Paddington bear products 392–3
paintings 16–17
paints, DIY 126–7
party toys 393
patchwork quilts 279–80, 282–3, 310, 312, 323–4
pedometers 286
pens 231, 252, 384–5
perfumes 52, 259, 264, 273–4, 277
personal goods 74, 84, 96, 224, 301
personal organisers 346, 349
personalised gifts 34, 233–4, 244, 381–2
pet accessories 352–3, 364

Subject Index

photographic equipment 354–5
photographic reproductions 252
photographic restorations 356
photoprocessing 330, 355–7
pine furniture 186–7, 190, 194, 202
pipes 296
plants 205–6, 208–12, 214–16, 218–20, 331
plaster, reproduction 295, 318, 322
playing cards 231
pleating machines 287
porcelain 104–5
portraits 18
posters 18, 244, 287
pottery, antique 239
pregnancy test kits 260
prints, limited edition 16–17, 315

radiator covers 193–4, 199, 309, 316, 318, 330
rattan furniture 184, 201
rocking horses 387–8, 390, 393–4, 398
rug kits 288
rugs 308–9

safety products 348
sailing equipment 23, 45, 282, 374
salmon 141, 144–7, 150, 152–5, 163, 169–71, 174, 238, 240
sandals 181
science-based goods 205
scientific equipment 106–7, 338
Scottish clothes 68, 70, 75, 78, 86, 89, 90, 93
Scottish foods 68, 149, 172
Scottish gifts 68, 251
sculptures 16–17
security products 128, 301
seeds 211–2, 216–17, 221, 331
self-improvement books 38
semi-precious stones 16, 279, 289
shirts 54–5, 60–61, 65, 80, 86–9, 91–4
shoes 59, 77–8, 81, 86, 178–81, 301, 380–81
shooting accessories 351
shutters 316–17, 328–9
signs 304, 313, 321, 348
silk clothes 80, 88
silk fabrics 285, 289, 300
silverware 243, 247, 297, 303, 305–6, 322
skincare products 257–9, 265–6, 268, 270, 273, 275, 278
slippers 178, 180, 301

smoked foods 141, 144–7, 150, 152–5, 163, 169–71, 174, 238, 240
soaps 254–5, 258–9, 265
sofas and sofabeds 197, 199, 202
software 108, 111–13, 116, 119–22, 368–71
special needs, goods for 44, 74, 84, 96, 224, 301
spices 146, 170
spirits and liqueurs 144–6, 149, 156, 160, 165
sports equipment 371–80
stained glass 127, 303
stamps 107, 278, 290
stationery 43, 45, 47–8, 60, 309, 342–8, 382–6
stencil equipment 126–8, 322, 330
stereo equipment 131–2
stonework 186, 333
stools 185, 194, 200
stuffed toy materials 285
sunglasses 349–50
surveillance equipment 132–3
swags 318
swimwear 52, 86, 379, 381–2

T-shirts 18, 31, 42, 45, 47–8, 64, 84, 244, 315, 381
table linen 43–4, 300, 304, 306, 312, 328
tableware 45, 47–8, 95, 234–5, 308, 314, 334–6
tailors 52, 87, 100
talking books 41, 358, 364, 366
tapestries 307
tapestry kits 283
tattooing supplies 29, 224–5
teas 137, 146, 158–9, 162, 164, 166, 172–3, 175–7
teddy bears 230, 233, 398
telephones 130, 297
television scripts 18
television shopping 229
televisions 131
theatrical books 23, 34
therapy tables 265
thermal clothing 78
tiles 129, 310, 329
tobacco 296
toffee and fudge 173
toiletries 254–5, 257–9, 262, 264–6, 277
  natural 257–9, 262, 266
toilets, portable 19
tools 44, 125–6

Subject Index

towels 82, 306, 310
toys 28, 45, 47, 52, 223, 387–98
   traditional 390
training shoes 380–81
travel books 29, 399
travel products 399–401
travel videos 361, 364–5
trenchcoats 72
trophies 377
tweeds 73

umbrellas 52, 60, 248

vacuum cleaners 130–31
vegan toiletries 259
veneers 291
venison 142, 147, 151, 153–4, 169
video, copying to 355
video equipment 133, 355
video games 131
videos, pre-recorded 26, 30–31, 276–7, 282, 358–67

vinyl records 358, 360, 362
vitamins and minerals 256, 262, 266–7, 270, 273

warehouse equipment 346
warship photographs 356–7
watch stands 243
watches 52, 401–2
water purifiers 317
weather vanes 332
whisky 149, 156, 168, 174, 177, 236, 238
wildlife recordings 367
wine kits 125
wines 134–8, 141–2, 144–6, 153, 156, 160–61, 163, 165, 171, 176–8
woodworking publications 282
work clothes 49, 62, 96
wrist bands 94

yachting goods 23, 45, 282, 374
yachts, toy 394
yoga tapes and videos 277